Register Now for Onli[ne]
to Your Book[.]

Your print purchase of *Applied Social Research, 10th Edition,* **includes online access to the contents of your book**—increasing accessibility, portability, and searchability!

Access today at:

http://connect.springerpub.com/content/book/978-0-8261-7284-6 or scan the QR code at the right with your smartphone and enter the access code below.

> XCW6P6Y1

Scan here for quick access.

Timothy P. Hilton, PhD, MSW, is Professor of Social Work at Eastern Washington University. He received his master's degree and PhD from the University of Chicago. His main areas of research are housing and homelessness, low-wage work, and welfare. Prior to his academic career, he served as a social worker and administrator for homeless services and welfare-to-work programs. He was then hired by the Mayor's Office of Workforce Development in Chicago to evaluate employment and training programs for lower skilled and otherwise disadvantaged job seekers and later served as a policy analyst for the City of Chicago.

Hilton's research has been both qualitative and quantitative; however, his recent work has been primarily qualitative. He has published research articles on employment and training programs serving low-skilled job seekers, substance abuse services, rural homelessness, and parenting while homeless. In addition to academic research, Hilton has extensive experience in program evaluation, primarily in the areas of employment services (for adults and youth) and homeless services programs. He recently completed an evaluation of services (and service gaps) for homeless students and their families in Spokane County, Washington. This research led to the creation of new programs within area schools to connect families with housing services and address students' academic, social, and mental health needs.

Peter R. Fawson, PhD, MSW, received his MSW and his PhD from the University of Utah, College of Social Work. He is an Associate Professor of Social Work at Appalachian State University and previously was a faculty member at Eastern Washington University. Dr. Fawson has conducted program evaluations for the juvenile and criminal justice system in Utah and Washington State. He has trained, developed, implemented, and evaluated a violence prevention program targeting teen dating violence. He has developed a series of workshops at the university and community level to raise men's awareness of their male privilege, discuss men's violence against women, and explore different ways men can help prevent and decrease all forms of violence. Fawson's research interests consist of partner violence, healthy masculinities, prevention and intervention programs, and forensic social work.

Thomas J. Sullivan, PhD, MA, is Professor Emeritus of Sociology and Social Work at Northern Michigan University, after more than three decades as a faculty member at the university. He specializes in social psychology, research methods, applied sociology, and medical sociology. He earned his undergraduate degree in sociology from San Francisco State University and his MA and PhD in sociology from the University of California at Santa Barbara. He is the author of *Sociology: Concepts and Applications in a Diverse World,* 8th edition (2009); *Introduction to Social Problems,* 10th edition (2015); *Methods of Social Research* (2001); and *Applied Sociology: Research and Critical Thinking* (1992). He has published articles in *Social Science & Medicine* and the *Humboldt Journal of Social Relations.* His applied work has focused on evaluation research of social service delivery in elementary schools and of teen pregnancy prevention and intervention services. He has served in various elected and appointed positions for the American Sociological Association, the Society for Applied Sociology, and the Midwest Sociological Society.

Cornell R. DeJong, MSW, is Professor Emeritus of Sociology and Social Work at Northern Michigan University, after four decades as a faculty member at the university. He specializes in intimate partner violence, research methods, and social work field education. He earned an undergraduate degree in psychology from Calvin College and an MSW from the University of Michigan. He completed additional advanced work in research methodology and social welfare at the University of Wisconsin–Madison. As a program evaluation consultant, he has conducted studies of Head Start, community mental health, schools, and substance abuse prevention. He has held social work practice positions in both corrections and mental health. He has over 10 years' experience conducting and evaluating domestic violence group services for men who batter. Professional memberships include the National Association of Social Workers and the Council on Social Work Education.

APPLIED SOCIAL RESEARCH

A Tool for the Human Services

10th Edition

Timothy P. Hilton, PhD, MSW

Peter R. Fawson, PhD, MSW

Thomas J. Sullivan, PhD, MA

Cornell R. DeJong, MSW

SPRINGER PUBLISHING COMPANY

Springer Publishing Company, LLC
11 West 42nd Street
New York, NY 10036
www.springerpub.com
http://connect.springerpub.com

Acquisitions Editor: Kate Dimock
Compositor: Exeter Premedia Services Private Ltd.

ISBN: 978-0-8261-7283-9
ebook ISBN: 978-0-8261-7284-6
Instructor's PowerPoints: 978-0-8261-7286-0
Instructor's Test Bank: 978-0-8261-7287-7
DOI: 10.1891/9780826172846

Instructor's Materials: Qualified instructors may request supplements by emailing textbook@springerpub.com.

19 20 21 22 23 / 5 4 3 2 1

Library of Congress Cataloging-in-Publication Data

Names: Hilton, Timothy, 1973- author. | Fawson, Peter R. | Sullivan, Thomas
   J., 1944- author.
Title: Applied social research: a tool for the human services / Timothy P.
   Hilton, PhD, MSW, Peter R. Fawson, PhD, MSW, Thomas J. Sullivan, PhD, MA,
   Cornell R. DeJong, MSW.
Description: Tenth Edition. | New York: Springer Publishing Company, LLC,
   [2019] | Revised edition of Applied social research, 2014. | Includes
   index.
Identifiers: LCCN 2019000257 | ISBN 9780826172839
Subjects: LCSH: Social service—Research—Methodology. | Human
   services—Research—Methodology. | Social service—United States.
Classification: LCC HV11 .M59 2019 | DDC 361.0072—dc23
LC record available at https://lccn.loc.gov/2019000257

Contact us to receive discount rates on bulk purchases.
We can also customize our books to meet your needs.
For more information please contact: sales@springerpub.com

Timothy Hilton: https://orcid.org/0000-0003-2367-8474

To Samantha, Annabel and Natalie,
For putting up with my summer in the library
—TPH

To Rachel,
who has endless passion for justice and is my idea of wonder
—PRF

To Nancy,
Who accepted my fleeting presence
—TJS

To Susan,
From where the sun now stands, we shall commute no more forever
—CRD

CONTENTS

PREFACE

Human services professionals face tremendous challenges today. Clients, government agencies, and other funders increasingly expect professionals to produce measurable and verifiable outcomes. Agencies and independent professionals are also called on to work efficiently and select interventions, general practices, and policies based on available evidence. At the same time, competition for funding and other important resources (including clients) has become fiercer and the problems human services professionals are called on to address more complex.

Many students in social work and other human services programs are less than enthusiastic about research. We often hear new students ask the following question: "Why do I need to study research methods when I just want a career helping people?" We respond by arguing that being a competent researcher is critically important to human services professionals, perhaps more now than ever before. Research can help professionals determine which interventions will help clients the most. Understanding research is also necessary in evaluating our work—to determine whether our programs, policies, and practices are effective and efficient. We also argue that understanding research methods can help professionals in every stage of the practice—from engaging clients or communities, to assessing problems and resources, to selecting interventions and monitoring progress, to evaluating outcomes and integrating findings in enhancing our programs, services, and policies.

Our main goal with this textbook is to help students better understand the utility of research to human services. That is to say, we present research as a tool for practice, something that can be used to help professionals in their work with clients, designing programs and services, and advocating for policy changes. In addition to presenting research as a tool for practice, we also emphasize connections between human service research and practice, stressing that each plays important and complementary roles in addressing social and personal problems.

As researchers and teachers, we find it personally rewarding to see students' ambivalence toward research dissipate as they see its importance to their careers and as they develop new skills and confidence. For many students, understanding the logic of research and the scientific method is empowering and allows them to develop and apply critical thinking skills within the context of their chosen professions and in other aspects of life as well.

Since the previous edition of the textbook we have added a new coauthor, Peter Fawson. Dr. Fawson is an associate professor at Appalachian State University where he frequently teaches research methods. He is also an active researcher, primarily publishing on the subject of domestic violence and related services. Timothy Hilton, who was one of the authors on the last edition, is now the lead author on the textbook. He and the other coauthors have worked hard to incorporate their own research into this edition while stressing relationships between their work and human services practice.

This textbook is primarily an introduction to social research as it relates to the human services. As such, we have presented all the topics of scientific research that are important for such an introduction; but we have offered a challenge as well—we hope students will learn that social research has many parallels with human services practice and that understanding these parallels will make them better practitioners as well as social scientists. The challenge also is to recognize the ways in which the two can be linked—by incorporating research activities into practice, and by shaping practice settings into research opportunities.

FEATURES

There are two new main features to this edition. Each chapter opens with a **Vignette** describing a situation in which a human services professional is faced with a task or dilemma that can be addressed through research or by employing a research technique in practice. These vignettes are designed to help students understand the utility of research methods to everyday practice situations and, in some cases, get an intimate look at applied social research. Some of these vignettes are based on interviews with human services professionals. Others are based on our own experiences and those of human services professionals with whom we have spoken over the past several years, including many of our former students. We refer back to these vignettes throughout each chapter while stressing the applicability of various research methods and concepts.

The second new major feature is the **Practitioner Profile**, included in each most chapter. These Practitioner Profiles present actual human services professionals who are not professional researchers but nonetheless incorporate research methods into their practice. In the first chapter, the vignette and the Practitioner Profile are linked. In the remaining chapters, the Practitioner Profiles are not directly linked to the main text, but the themes discussed reflect the concepts raised in each chapter. The main purpose of the Practitioner Profiles is to help reinforce the ideas that research methods are used to address dilemmas commonly faced in practice and that research is a core element of human services practice and not restricted to academics and other professional researchers.

Similar to the Practitioner Profiles, several chapters also include one or more **Research in Practice** features designed to help students better understand applications of research methods and concepts and the overall research process. Several of the Research in Practice features are based on interviews with researchers and practitioners while others are based on published research.

At the end of each chapter, there is a list and brief description of the **Main Points** of the chapter, which serves as a review of the major concepts covered. Following the Main Points is a list of **Important Terms for Review**. This list serves as a vocabulary review for students and may be helpful for students studying for quizzes or tests.

Following the Important Terms for Review are three sets of questions, **Critical Thinking**, **Evaluating Competency**, and **Self-Assessment**. The Critical Thinking questions pertain to the general themes raised in each chapter. They are designed to help students see research within a larger context while challenging them to critically evaluate what they know and how they know it. Some Critical Thinking questions force students to apply research concepts to their practice interests. (We provide some answers to Critical Thinking questions in Chapter 1, but in the remaining chapters the questions are posed without answers.) The Critical Thinking questions may be used by instructors as prompts for in-class discussions.

Evaluating Competency questions are based on core social work competencies within the Council of Social Work Education's 2015 Educational Policy and Accreditation Standards (EPAS). Each chapter addresses two or more core competencies. Several of the Evaluating Competency questions pertain to Competency 4, focusing on social workers' engagement in practice-informed research and research-informed practice, and Competency 9, focusing on evaluation of practice. We also address several other competencies including Competency 2 (Ethics and Professional Behavior), Competency 3 (Difference and Diversity in Practice), Competency 5 (Policy Practice), and Competency 7 (Assessment). Many of these questions ask students to reflect on potential applications of research concepts and methods in social work practice.

Each chapter contains **10 Self-Assessment** questions. These are multiple choice questions covering several of the main points within the chapter. Answers to these questions can be found at the very end of the chapter. These questions are designed as practice test questions and to help students assess their knowledge of the major concepts and terms within each chapter.

To supplement the book materials, qualified instructors can request a Test Bank and PowerPoints by sending an email to textbook@springerpub.com.

APPLIED SOCIAL RESEARCH

1

RESEARCH IN THE HUMAN SERVICES

INTRODUCTION

Spokane, Washington, is a medium-sized city of about 200,000. Many residents and community activists have expressed concern in recent years by what some refer to as a "driving while Black" problem. That is to say, some are concerned by their impression that police officers disproportionately stop African Americans in the city. This issue has been raised at several community meetings in recent years and has received some media attention. One police captain, Brad Arleth, was particularly interested in this issue but was concerned about a lack of verifiable information or data on the extent of the problem. As he explains,

We didn't know the real number, the real picture. . . . And then it occurred to me, a law enforcement agency should be able to answer a question from the community about something they want to know if it is within our ability to answer the question. (Quotes are from a personal communication/interview with Edward Byrnes and Brad Arleth on May 16, 2018.)

Captain Arleth soon connected with Ed Byrnes, a social worker and researcher at the nearby Eastern Washington University. As Byrnes explained,

I got involved in the activist community when I moved here. There are lots [of] people in our community trying to do something but they're kind of in the dark. So what drew me to that meeting was that it is a topic I actually knew something about, disproportionality. There were no local data about this,

and I wanted to make it clear to the activist community and the police that this was a conversation in the absence of facts.

Throughout this chapter, we discuss the work of Byrnes and Arleth (2015) and the issue of community policing and racial disproportionality as we highlight the value of research in the human services. As you read the chapter and learn more about their work, please consider the following questions: (a) How does research impact human services? (b) What are the goals of social research and how do they relate to the goals of human services? (c) What lessons can you learn while studying research methods that can be applied to the planning and delivery of human services? (d) How can research be used to help reduce bias in human services?

This book is about the use of research in the human services. The term **human services** refers to activities with the primary goal of enhancing the relationship between people and societal institutions so that people may maximize their potential and alleviate distress. At the broadest level, the human services include formal systems such as government welfare programs, mental health services, child development and family support programs, addiction prevention and intervention programs, and correctional services of the justice system.

Research is increasingly essential to the delivery of human services and to the professionals who are mandated with the responsibility of making the delivery of these services effective, efficient, and responsive to human needs. The aforementioned policing example helps to illustrate this. To remain effective, police departments must have the confidence of the communities they serve. To promote justice, they must assess their work while examining and addressing potential biases that interfere with equal treatment of people within communities they serve. Research can help in accomplishing both of these goals. It can help people see issues through new lenses while revealing what is true and what is not. It can also help professionals and others to reconsider their perceptions. While perceptions are important in research processes, they must also be checked to avoid biases that create false impressions.

Arleth and Byrnes created a research design based on similar designs from other cities to examine whether there was disproportionality in police stops of drivers and pedestrians by race. As Byrnes stated, "I'm not a favorite with the activist community because I've said, 'It's complicated.' It's complicated because that's where the data points to." As he explained, "When we looked at instances where police officers exercised some discretion in deciding whether or not to pull someone over or to stop a pedestrian, there wasn't any significant difference between racial groups." According to Arleth, "Where we did see a real difference were the number of arrests that resulted after someone was stopped, with minorities being significantly more likely to be arrested." Arleth explained that this was not necessarily a result of police officer bias because a majority of these arrests were the result of an outstanding warrant. "When an officer pulls someone over and sees they have an outstanding warrant they don't have any choice. That person is going to be arrested," he explained. As Byrnes described,

Our challenge is to help the community see that this is a complex issue. Is there bias in the city? Of course. But it isn't as simple as saying that our cops are racist. In fact when stops were made by designated traffic unit officers, typically using radar speed detection from hundreds of feet away, then the data show officers don't stop minority motorists at a higher rate than Whites.

"One thing we need to do is help people clear up old warrants," Arleth argued. Arleth, Byrnes, and others in the city are now working on initiatives to do just that. They are also researching police training curricula to identify programs to better address potential officer biases and create better relationships with communities they serve.

While the research shows that our officers are not disproportionately targeting minorities, I can never say there are not biases within the department. We all have biases and we must work to minimize them. In the end we need to keep the confidence of the communities we serve and we'll do whatever it takes to earn it.

For the human service professionals like Arleth and Byrnes charged with taking action to address social issues, the challenge is to access, organize, and evaluate knowledge that research has generated and then use this scientific evidence as the basis for making practice decisions.

Numerous linkages exist between research and human service practice. By linkages, we mean that research can contribute to the goals of practice, just as properly conducted practice can contribute to the goals of research. Because research provides the means for understanding the problems with which professionals work and the means for evaluating change, practitioners in human services are certain to encounter the need to understand, apply, and, in some cases, even conduct research in carrying out the goals of their professions. Some would go further and argue that the link between research and practice is even more intimate—namely, that there can be (and should be) a fruitful merger of the two. In fact, the notion that scientific research and human service practice are totally distinct enterprises is gradually disappearing (Okpych & Yu, 2014). Two reasons explain this.

First, strong parallels are now recognized between the conduct of research and the conduct of practice. By parallels, we mean that the two endeavors have some similar structures, follow some similar processes, and use some similar techniques. Practitioners can benefit by incorporating into practice some of the techniques that are used in research. Both research and practice, for example, are based on observation, but the observations of practitioners often are characterized as being unstructured and intuitive. Some of the more precise and structured observational techniques (discussed in Chapters 7 and 9) that researchers use can be adapted for practice purposes.

Second, properly conducted practice intervention can provide scientifically valid knowledge about human behavior and the effectiveness of intervention. For example, practitioners can scientifically assess the effectiveness of their interventions if those interventions are organized in a manner that researchers call *single-system design* (discussed in Chapter 11), which parallels the scientific experiment.

The purpose of this book is to introduce students in the human services to social research logic, methods, and design. We do this by emphasizing the parallels and linkages between research and practice. Because research and practice are intertwined, human service professionals need training in the techniques of social research as much as they need to know about group processes or theories of personality. In some situations, human service providers will *consume* social research as they apply the findings of research to practice intervention. Therefore, they need to understand the logic of research and be able to assess critically the procedures of research to decide whether, and if so in what fashion, research findings can be introduced into practice. Human service workers are also called on to *collaborate* with researchers who are conducting studies involving agency services, data, or clients. In some cases, human service professionals also are expected to *conduct* social research as part of their overall intervention strategy so that they know how to design and carry out scientifically valid research projects.

HUMAN SERVICES RESEARCH

Goals of Research

The word *research* is applied to many activities: the student who browses in the library for a few hours; the social worker who, while visiting clients about other issues, makes a mental note of some of their social characteristics; the parole officer who routinely inquires about a parolee's family life as part of an intake interview. All these people might claim to be doing research. Yet the term, as it is commonly used in the social and behavioral sciences, has a considerably more precise meaning, according to which none of these activities would be considered as scientific research. This is not to say that these activities are unimportant. They may have a variety of uses. Social research, however,

has specific goals that can be achieved only by using proper procedures.

Social research is the systematic examination (or reexamination) of empirical data, collected by someone firsthand, concerning the social or psychological forces operating in a situation. Three major elements characterize this definition. First, social research is *systematic*—that is, all aspects of the research process are carefully planned in advance, and nothing is done in a casual or haphazard fashion. The systematic nature of research is at the core of the scientific method, which is discussed in detail in Chapter 2. Second, social research involves the collection of *empirical data*—that is, information or facts about the world that are based on sensory experiences. As such, it should not be confused with philosophizing or speculating, which lacks the empirical base of research. Third, social research studies *social and psychological factors* that affect human behavior. Biological, physiological, nutritional, or other such factors would be a part of social research only to the extent that they affect, or are affected by, social and psychological factors.

Consider the work of Arleth and Byrnes on disproportionality. They approached their research systematically, following the scientific method to design an answerable research question. They relied on empirical data, namely police records of traffic and pedestrian stops. Their study involved a look at some aspect of human behavior, specifically police officers' propensity to stop drivers and pedestrians of certain racial groups. This was clearly an example of social research.

Research in the human services generally focuses on one or more of the following goals: description, prediction, explanation, or evaluation. **Descriptive research** has as its goal description, or the attempt to discover facts or describe reality. Descriptive research, for example, might deal with questions such as these: What are people's attitudes toward welfare? How widespread is child abuse? How many people avail themselves of the services of home healthcare workers? Some descriptive research efforts are quite extensive. For example, the National Center for Health Statistics (NCHS) and the Centers for Disease Control and Prevention (CDC) collect voluminous amounts of data each year to describe the health status of Americans.

Predictive research focuses on prediction or making projections about what may occur in the future or in other settings. Insurance companies, for example, make use of sophisticated actuarial schemes to predict the risks involved with insuring people or property. Based on past descriptive research concerning deaths and injuries, they can project how long people with certain characteristics are likely to live or the degree of likelihood that they will suffer injuries. Such projections also can be made by the NCHS. For example, the NCHS can project that infants and children with particular social characteristics will have an increased likelihood of being undernourished or of suffering from infectious or parasitic diseases. Armed with this information, it is possible to devise preventive healthcare programs that are targeted at the high-risk groups.

Explanatory research involves explanation or determining why or how something occurred. Explanatory research, for example, would go beyond describing rates of juvenile delinquency or even predicting who will engage in delinquent acts. Explanatory research would focus on *why* certain people become delinquents. The goal of explanation may appear to be quite similar to that of prediction, but there is a difference: one can make predictions without an accompanying explanation. Insurance companies, for example, make actuarial predictions based on past statistical associations but often without knowing why those associations occurred.

Evaluation research focuses on evaluation or the use of scientific research methods to plan intervention programs, to monitor the implementation of new programs and the operation of existing ones, and to determine how effectively programs or clinical practices achieve their goals. Evaluation research can also determine whether a program has unintended consequences, whether desirable or undesirable. In the past few decades, a vast array of social programs has emerged—relating to poverty, child development, crime, alcoholism, delinquency, and the like—that attempts to ameliorate undesirable social conditions. Program directors often are required to justify and defend their programs in terms of cost-effectiveness. Thus, evaluation research has become part of human service programs.

Arleth and Byrnes's research most clearly falls under the category of descriptive research as their goal was to describe the extent to which police stops mirror the population at large. If their goal had been to evaluate the effectiveness of a police officer training aimed at reducing officer bias, this may have been an example of evaluation research. If their research had also involved an examination of police officers' decision-making processes that might explain decisions about stops, this could also have been an example of explanatory research.

Applications of Research

Some social research is called **basic research** (or **pure research**) in that its purpose is to advance knowledge about human behavior with little concern for any immediate, practical benefits. Many sociologists and psychologists conduct basic research. Research in the human services, however, is more likely to be **applied research**—that is, research designed with a practical outcome in mind and with the assumption that some group, or society as a whole, will gain specific benefits from it. The disproportionality example is clearly applied research as the researchers' goal was to apply what they learned to improving policing and police and community relations in the area. Although we distinguish between basic and applied research, it is important to recognize that the line between the two is vague and, in fact, that pure research can have applications in the human service field just as applied research can advance our knowledge of human behavior.

So the focus of this book is primarily on applied social research and, especially, on the linkage of social research with the human services. Human service fields such as social work or criminal justice focus on two important issues—practice and policy—and research can be utilized in each of these areas to produce more effective outcomes. Human service practice involves the direct provision of services to clients, such as individuals, families, or other groups, in order to assist them in dealing with some difficulties. While not every human service activity falls into one of these two categories, practice and policy constitute the bulk of human service work.

To make these distinctions between basic and applied research and between human service practice and policy more concrete, it is useful to identify five focal areas or applications where research is used in the human services: understanding human functioning in social environments, policy planning and development, assessment of client functioning, program evaluation, and practice effectiveness evaluation. We do not claim that this is the only way to divide the human service field or that our list of areas of application is exhaustive. These five categories, however, are a helpful aid as we analyze the links between research and practice. Here, we review each area briefly.

Behavior and Social Environments. Human service providers do many things: link people to resources they can use, enhance people's coping abilities, improve the operation of social systems, and participate in the development of social policy, to name only a few. All these activities rest on an understanding of the behavior of the people to whom services are provided and on a comprehension of the social environment in which they function. Social research can provide much of this knowledge. For example, the police captain mentioned earlier may turn to research on minority groups' view of police as he creates plans for improving policy and community relations. Although this research may be conducted without specific practice or policy goals in mind, it can still be applied in both realms.

Policy Planning and Development. Human service professionals gain direction from policies that are intended to advance the well-being of individuals, families, and society as a whole. Human service policy involves working through the political, governmental, and legal systems in order to establish programs, laws, administrative procedures, and other interventions that will deliver desired outcomes to individuals or groups. Policies can be thought of as a set of rules that govern what types of resources will be available to people to assist them in achieving goals, maximizing potential, and alleviating distress (Herrick, 2014). Many police departments as well as child welfare agencies across the United States, for example, have created policies mandating that all officers complete diversity awareness training to address potential biases. Research can be conducted to discover the positive and negative consequences of such a policy. This research can help policy makers in the original development of the policy as well as in deciding whether to change or eliminate the policy after it has been in operation for some time. In this way, social research can be used to help develop, evaluate, and if necessary change policies.

Assessment of Client Functioning. In the provision of human services, assessing the level of functioning of clients is often necessary. How well do members of a family communicate with one another? How capable is a teenage parent in dealing with the stresses of motherhood or fatherhood? How skilled is a person in negotiating a job interview? Practitioners often make such assessments, but the danger is that they will be made unsystematically. The past 20 years have seen extensive development of systematic and, in some cases, quantitative assessment tools that can be used for both research and practice tasks. The results of these assessment tools can be compared at different times to see if any change or improvement has occurred. Examples of such client assessment tools can be found in Sheafor and Horejsi (2015).

Program Evaluation. The term *policy* refers to broad directions or goals, whereas the term *program* refers to the organized delivery of services to people or groups. Programs represent the implementation of a policy or policies whereas policies determine what programs will exist and what they will look like. In the past few decades, many large, ambitious, and expensive programs intended to cope with social problems and to provide services to individuals have been developed. Along with the growth of these programs has emerged an increasing concern over their results: Do they achieve their intended goals? These programs are costly, and some evaluation is needed to assess whether resources are, indeed, being used effectively. Equally important, a program that fails to achieve its goals leaves a problem unsolved or an effective service undelivered. *Program evaluation* is an appraisal using scientifically sound methods of organizational processes or outcomes that have a social purpose (Grinnell, Williams, & Unrau, 2018). It is crucial that human service providers understand when program evaluation is called for and when it is possible to conduct an effective evaluation. In addition, many practitioners likely will find themselves participating in programs that include evaluation as one of their goals. (Given the close link between policy and program, there is much overlap between the two: Program evaluation is often a part of a policy evaluation.)

Practice Effectiveness Evaluation. Whereas program evaluation focuses on the assessment of entire programs or policies, the concern of human service professionals often is considerably more specific—namely, "Is what I am doing right now with this particular client working?" For this reason, practitioners are often disenchanted with the utility of evaluation research as a direct aid to helping clients. In recent years, however, major advances have occurred in the ability of research to answer professionals' questions about the efficacy of intervention efforts on specific clients. One such advance is a form of research called *single-system design,* in which practitioners devise a way to repeatedly measure the occurrence of a problem and monitor the behavior of a single client, group, family, or larger system for a period of time. Intervention then begins, and the behavior is again monitored. Comparison between the baseline and intervention periods permits the practitioner to make more accurate assessments of progress than the informal assessment on which human service professionals traditionally have relied. Through such careful monitoring of behavior and measuring of intervention effects, human service workers not only can enhance their own effectiveness but also can contribute to the development of an intervention technology that others can successfully apply.

Obvious similarities exist between program evaluation and practice effectiveness research. For example, both are concerned with the effectiveness of certain practices. The difference, however, is in the scope of the efforts. Program evaluation focuses on complete programs, whereas practice effectiveness emphasizes the assessment of some particular aspect of a practice situation in a way that will not necessarily affect the entire program.

Evidence-Based Practice

A theme that underlies many recent developments in the human services, and that shows great promise for linking practice and research, is encapsulated by the term **evidence-based practice.** According to Rubin and Bellamy (2012), evidence-based practice is a *process* for making practice decisions in which practitioners integrate best research evidence available with their practice expertise and with client attributes, values, preferences, and circumstances.

It is important to note that this conceptualization of evidence-based practice emphasizes processes for decision making. What makes a practice an evidence-based practice is not that it has been labeled as such by an official organization or other entity, but that it was arrived at deliberately by a practitioner who judiciously evaluated evidence. In most cases, the "best evidence" is knowledge that has been gained via the scientific research process. As the insert shows, this approach has been called a number of different things over the years by different practitioners, although "evidence-based practice" seems to have emerged as the most widely used designationo. The evidence-based approach is inherently critical, which means that it is always questioning whether particular practices or policies are effective. Just because a practice method has been routinely used in the past does not mean that it is necessarily effective. Just because a practice method has worked with clients with certain characteristics (e.g., based on age, race, or gender) or in some contexts (within some types of organizations and communities) does not mean that it will work on other clients. The evidence-based practitioner constantly questions the efficacy of methods, and the primary yardstick used in resolving these questions is the evidence provided by scientific research (Gray, Joy, Plath, & Webb, 2012).

Let us think back to the issue of policing and disproportionality. Captain Arleth was concerned about both the possibility of racial disproportionality in police stops and arrests as well as relationships between the police department and communities they serve. He knew his first step was to systematically collect evidence to assess the problem objectively. Seeing the problems lay more in disproportionality in arrest due to outstanding warrants than in police stops, Arleth and his research partner, Byrnes, began collecting evidence from other police units across the United States examining strategies for helping people clear up outstanding warrants. They are currently collecting information from other cities on strategies for improving relationships and communication between communities and police. While some might have been satisfied with the finding that there were not disproportional stops of minorities, Arleth and Byrnes continue to focus on ways the department can improve, and systematically reviewing evidence from other areas is an important step in this process.

The evidence-based practice approach has emerged, in part, because there is now a growing body of research evidence—some of it basic and some of it applied—that can provide guidance to human service practitioners and policy makers. In the past century, researchers in the social sciences and human services have developed more sophisticated research techniques and have used them to produce a large and complex body of knowledge about human social and psychological behavior. This body of knowledge now provides human service practitioners and policy makers with scientifically grounded evidence about what works and what does not. So, it is much more feasible today—than it was, say, 50 years ago—to base practice and policy on scientific evidence.

Another reason for the emergence of the evidence-based approach is that some startling criticisms of human service practice surfaced a few decades ago that concluded that such practice is not very effective at achieving its goals—or at least that we do not have much proof that it is effective other than the claims of the practitioners themselves. In response, in the intervening decades, human service researchers and practitioners focused their attention on producing research that would provide such proof. The resulting collaboration of researchers and practitioners has produced a body of research that provides us with evidence about what is effective in practice and what is not.

Evidence comes in many different forms, of course. The observations that a practitioner makes of a single client in his or her office are "evidences," as is the complex statistical analysis done on the observations of thousands of people in a

highly controlled experimental study. So, a central part of the evidence-based approach is to critically evaluate research studies to determine how much confidence we have in their conclusions and thus whether we want to use them as evidence in particular practice or policy settings. The purpose of this text is to provide students in the human services with an introduction to research methods so that they are in a better position to understand and participate in this critical evaluation. Although an understanding of research methods in general certainly contributes to becoming a more effective human service practitioner, we link research methods specifically with evidence-based practice in a number of chapters where the linkage is especially relevant.

Diversity and Research: The Impact of Diversity and Difference on Research

Human service professionals recognize that diversity and difference—whether they arise from variations in race, ethnicity, gender, or something else—are powerful influences on people and social life. Diversity and difference can lead some groups to suffer disproportionately from the problems that human service workers attempt to alleviate, such as poverty, inequality, or discrimination. So, human service practice devotes special attention to diversity and difference. Issues of diversity and difference also need to be addressed when conducting research in the human services. Because of the position of minorities in society, conducting research that produces accurate and complete data on them can be a challenge. In fact, in some circumstances, the standard research methods used in human service research result in misleading and, in some cases, outright false conclusions regarding a minority. In those circumstances, the research methods need to be modified.

This problem is sufficiently important to human service research that we devote special attention to it throughout the book. In each chapter, where relevant, we point out particular ways in which problems or biases in research on minorities can occur and provide strategies for overcoming them. The goal is to create sensitivity to the fact that research methods can have built-in biases when focused on

PRACTITIONER PROFILE 1.1 Brad Arleth, Captain, Spokane Police Department, Washington

Brad Arleth is a captain in the Spokane Police Department. According to Arleth, "I've been in the department in Spokane almost 27 years. I've worked every rank in the department and been in just about every bureau, from investigations to hiring to specialty units." Arleth has a Master of Science degree in criminal justice from the University of Louisville. As a student, Arleth took several research method courses, which has been helpful in his career. As he explains, "At work there's a lot of research and other academic material used, whether it is studies on use of force or internal research, to analyze calls for service by hour, or personnel and staffing." Arleth sees lots of connections between police work and research. "The field of research has a lot of applicability to what we do but at the local level and across all police forces in the U.S.," he explains. "We don't always make the best use of research," he continues. Arleth believes that police departments that are closely aligned with universities and social researchers do better than others in building trust with the communities they serve. "Research is critical to trust-building, creating policies based on best practices and just keeping current with social issues," he explains.

Arleth sees research as especially critical to law enforcement professionals. "Law enforcement professionals can deprive people of liberty, freedom and even life. The stakes are high," he explains. High stakes, Arleth contends, are why it is so important that policies and procedures and even street-level decisions reflect current research and best practices. Arleth also sees research as critical to innovation, which is important when working with communities to address existing problems. "It is critical to engage communities," Arleth explains,

> When others are involved in the process of finding solutions they feel respected. That can go a long way in developing solutions to complicated problems. There are no easy solutions to what we do and it helps when those we serve understand that too.

Arleth believes that students today have an amazing opportunity to learn from multiple fields of practice and sees the importance of interprofessional collaboration to develop policy and practice innovations:

> For students who are preparing for professional careers and doing research, your goal should be to figure out new innovations, to improve practice, to help us grow. You don't want to just stay in your lane, you want to overlap with others. See where partnerships can develop.

particular minority groups and that care must be exercised to detect and avoid this.

PARALLELS AND LINKAGES BETWEEN RESEARCH AND PRACTICE

Although scientific research is different in many respects from human service practice, important parallels exist between the two. In fact, researchers and practitioners use many of the same strategies in approaching their problems. After reviewing the steps in conducting research, we point out parallels that can be found in practice.

Steps in Conducting Research

Although each research project is unique in some fashion, some general steps characterize virtually every project. The research process can be divided into six identifiable stages: problem formulation, research design development, data collection, data analysis, drawing conclusions, and public dissemination of results.

Problem Formulation. The first step in conducting social research is to decide on the problem to research. When first encountering the issue of problem formulation, students commonly question its importance. So many problems exist that it would appear to be a simple matter to select one on which to conduct research. However, such a casual view of scientific problem formulation is erroneous. For example, some problems about which we might desire answers are not scientific questions at all, and no amount of research will answer them. Other problems, though possibly interesting and intriguing, might prove to be impractical from a methodological, ethical, or financial standpoint.

Another element of problem formulation is to shape a concern into a specific researchable question. In the policing example described earlier, for example, Arleth and Byrnes began with a concern about perceived differences in the treatment of minorities and Whites by police. After much discussion, they decided their main concern was potential biases by police officers that might result in disproportional stops of minorities. Eventually they settled on evaluating traffic and pedestrian stops that involve police officers exercising discretion in formally stopping someone (versus giving a verbal reprimand without making an official stop). This is a suitable issue for research in part because it can be answered through the examination of police records. (In Chapter 4, we outline the many issues involved in this process.)

Research Design Development. Having successfully established a researchable problem, we must develop a **research design,** which is a detailed plan outlining how observations will be made. This plan is followed by the researcher as the project is carried out. Research designs always address certain key issues such as who will be studied, how these people will be selected, and what information will be gathered from or about them. In fact, the research design spells out, in considerable detail, what will occur during the following stages of the research process. (Chapters 7–12 describe the different kinds of research designs and issues that must be considered in their development.)

Data Collection. A part of any research design is a description of what kinds of data will be collected and how this will be done. The data collected at this stage constitute the basic information from which conclusions will be drawn, so great care must be exercised in this step.

Two aspects of data collection, *pretests* and *pilot studies*, illustrate just how careful scientists are about this. The **pretest**, as the name implies, is a preliminary application of the data-gathering technique to determine its adequacy. It certainly would be risky and unwise to jump prematurely into data gathering without first knowing that all the data-collection procedures are sound. For example, if our study were a needs assessment of homemakers to determine how many would make use of occupational training services, we would choose a small group of homemakers and collect the same data from them that we plan to collect in the final project. A pretest is, in a sense, a trial run—and unless we are very good or very lucky, some modifications in the data-collection technique are likely to be required based on the results of the pretest. After these modifications are made, the technique is pretested again. Additional pretests are always desirable after any modifications in the data-gathering technique to assess whether the modifications handle the problems encountered in the previous pretest.

In some cases, it may even be necessary to do a **pilot study**, which is a small-scale trial run of all the procedures planned for use in the main study. In addition to administering the data-gathering instrument, a pilot study might include such things as a test of the procedures for selecting the sample and an application of the statistical procedures to be used in the data-analysis stage.

It is this kind of care in data collection that improves the validity of the data collected and bolsters confidence in the conclusions drawn.

The policing example does not necessarily involve new data collection because the data used to assess police stops is based on existing records already collected by the department. Follow-up research that Arleth and Byrnes intend on conducting related to minority residents' unresolved (or outstanding) warrants may involve new data collection protocols as this will likely involve in-depth interviews with residents and various officials.

Data Analysis. As with data collection, data analysis is spelled out in the research design and can be the most challenging—and interesting— aspect of a research project. It is challenging because data in raw form can be quite unrevealing. Data analysis is what unlocks the information hidden in the raw data and transforms it into something useful and meaningful. During data analysis, researchers learn whether their ideas are confirmed or refuted by empirical reality. In this step, researchers often make use of statistical tools that can range from simple percentages to complex statistical tests, which require much training to understand and master. These statistics aid in communicating the findings of the researchers to others. Once a researcher has learned the special language and interpretations of statistics, he or she can be more effective in communicating research findings in a clear, concise manner than when using conventional English. (Chapters 14–16 review some of the basic data-analysis and data-manipulation techniques that are used in social research.)

The policing example involved substantial quantitative data analysis (conducted by Ed Byrnes) to evaluate differences in rates of police stops and arrests of members of different racial groups.

> Having actual hard data can help bring the police and community together. We can review the data together and see that while there are problems the issue wasn't simply racist cops. It was more complicated than that. The numbers help us tell a more complicated and nuanced story. They also helped us see where we can work together to make a difference.

Drawing Conclusions. The next step in conducting social research is to draw some conclusions from the data analysis. The form this takes depends partly on the goals of the research project. A descriptive study, for example, simply presents what was found, possibly in a summarized form to make it more easily understood. Predictive and explanatory research, on the other hand, usually has hypotheses, or statements of what the researchers expect to find, presented before the data are collected. In this case, a major element of drawing conclusions is to assess how much support exists for the hypotheses. The support that the data provide for the hypotheses can range from strong to weak to none, and researchers have an obligation to those who might use their research to accurately represent the strength of their findings. Finally, in evaluation research, drawing conclusions usually involves making a judgment about the adequacy and effectiveness of programs and any changes that might improve conditions.

Often, research discovers some things that do not relate directly to any specific hypothesis or even things that are completely unanticipated. When drawing conclusions, the researchers should make note of the implications of any findings that are of sufficient importance to warrant mention. When complete, the conclusions should clearly indicate what has been learned by conducting the research and the impact of this new knowledge.

In the police example, the conclusions reached were basically that minorities were not disproportionately stopped by police but that arrest rates following stops were higher among minorities. Further examination of arrests showed that most arrests were due to outstanding warrants and did not involve police officers exercising discretion in arresting minorities at a higher rate. (Among those who were stopped, minorities were more likely than Whites to have outstanding warrants.) As Byrnes explained, "The data were interesting and important, but they weren't going to support community activists' nor the department's working impressions. There was a problem for sure, but it was more complex and systematic than anyone had thought."

Public Dissemination of Results. Research findings are of little value if they remain the private property of the researchers who produce them. A crucial stage of social research is the public dissemination of findings by publication in a book or professional journal or presentation to a professional organization. This shares the newly created knowledge with those who can put it to use or can build on it in future research. In fact, public dissemination of knowledge is a major mechanism for scientific advancement. (As we discuss further in Chapters 2 and 3, public dissemination makes it possible for others to reanalyze or replicate the research and to confirm the findings or identify cases of error-filled, biased, or fraudulent research.)

Both Arleth and Byrnes understood that they had to disseminate what they learned. As Arleth explained, "We have an obligation to the public to share what we did and what we found." Byrnes stressed the politics of their study: "We weren't going to make everyone happy with our results. There is a problem, yes, but it is a complicated one and not one that is easily fixed by changing how a few people do their jobs." Ultimately Arleth and Byrnes wrote a research report, gave several interviews on local news and radio programs, and helped community forums to share what they learned, their recommendations, and next steps.

Steps in Practice Intervention

Just as the research process can be organized as a series of steps, the process of human service practice also often is conceptualized as a series of stages. In fact, the stages of practice intervention demonstrate the parallels and linkages between practice and research (see Figure 1.1).

Problem Assessment. In much the same way that social researchers must decide on the problem to research, practitioners must specify the precise problem with which they are concerned, which factors might contribute to the problem, and which aspects of the problem will be given priority. In problem formulation, researchers make judgments concerning the feasibility of researching a particular phenomenon. Likewise, in problem assessment, practitioners must pose answerable questions. The initial step in evidence-based practice involves crafting questions for searching electronic databases so that the relevant information can be retrieved. A well-formed question describes the client, course of action, alternate courses of action, intended result, and whether effective intervention is possible.

Formulation of an Intervention Strategy. Just as researchers develop a research design, practitioners develop a strategy for intervention that will be effective in alleviating the problem specified during the assessment stage. Whereas researchers choose among a variety of research methods, practitioners choose among a variety of intervention strategies such as crisis intervention, behavior modification, or vocational training. Just as researchers may use more than one research technique over the course of a project, practitioners also may use more than one intervention strategy in attacking a problem. Tracking down the research studies and other data that will help one to evaluate intervention strategies requires access to relevant electronic databases and specialized skills in their efficient use. In addition to general web-searching tools and library databases, databases that relate specifically to medicine and human service practice are being developed to aid in the access and use of practice-related studies.

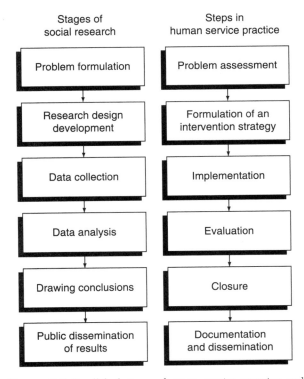

Figure 1.1 Parallels between human service practice and social research.

As you will learn through the course of studying research methods, however, all research results are not of equal value. Some research designs generate more convincing evidence of causation than others. Determining how valid and useful the results of any given study are is approached in a systematic way so that the so-called best evidence is given more weight than the results of other studies. At this stage, the practitioner must organize the results, consider conflicting findings, and determine which practice interventions show the most promise.

Implementation. Following the development of the research design, researchers proceed to put it into practice. In a similar fashion, practitioners implement the intervention strategies outlined during the preceding stage. Normally, researchers' activities are limited to data collection; they do not attempt to change the people they are studying. Practitioners, on the other hand, may collect data as a part of the implementation stage, but they are concerned primarily with the effectiveness of the intervention strategy in creating some changes in clients or in the systems that affect them.

Evaluation. Once researchers have collected their data, they analyze it to determine what their study has found. Similarly, evidence-based practice evaluates the effectiveness of the intervention strategy that was implemented during the preceding stage. Were the goals of the plan achieved? What were the costs of the strategy? Were any undesirable side effects brought about by the intervention? Which aspects of the intervention process seemed to be most important in producing the change that resulted? The evidence-based model emphasizes the employment of single-system designs and other systematic assessment strategies in contrast to the more casual observation that is associated with traditional practice. The results of these systematic assessments can help shape future research studies and may serve as evidence in their own right for guiding practice decisions.

Closure. Termination of intervention is an important part of the helping process. The extent to which the intervention has been effective must be determined, as well as the degree to which the goals of the intervention cannot be—and possibly will never be—achieved. Researchers may make suggestions for future research, which might be helpful in further clarifying the relationships found in the study. Likewise, practitioners might suggest other sources of help that the client could use to cope with any problems left unresolved by the intervention. In other words, for both researchers and practitioners, the conclusion is a time to review what has been accomplished and look forward to directions and alternatives for the future.

Documentation and Dissemination. We have made the point that both the process and the results of research must be carefully documented; the same can be said for human service practice. At a minimum, this stage includes meeting agency requirements for record keeping and case documentation, such as preparing treatment plans and case-closing reports. Although such agency-mandated reporting may serve a useful quality-control function, practitioners also have a responsibility to share with others the knowledge gained from their practice. This may take the form of case conferences within the agency, workshop presentations, or formal articles published in appropriate journals. As a consequence of subjecting practice to the scrutiny of supervisors and peers, deficits are identified, intervention techniques refined, and advances made in the delivery of human services.

By this point, you should be gaining an appreciation for the parallels and linkages between social research and human service practice. The parallels involve the similarities between the activities of researchers and those of practitioners. The linkages involve the contributions that research can make to practice endeavors, and vice versa.

THE PLAN OF THE BOOK

This first chapter has discussed the extent to which research is fundamental to the delivery of human services. As with Chapter 1, all chapters feature an extended vignette based on interviews with human service professionals and researchers to help readers better understand practice applications of research methods and concepts. After each vignette is introduced, we raise critical thought questions for students to consider as they study the chapter. These questions pertain to the core themes and competencies addressed in each chapter. Each of these questions is revisited at the end of the chapter in a **Critical Thinking** section where we revisit the chapter's main themes, discuss implications for practice, and introduce potential topics for further discussion in class. Each chapter also includes an **Evaluating Competency** section where we suggest activities and assignments for evaluating student competency in Council on Social Work Education (CSWE) competency areas (from the 2015 Educational Policy and Accreditation Standards [EPAS]). Chapters end with a **Main Points** section, summarizing key concepts, a list of **Important Terms for Review,** a list of questions for students to take a **Self-Assessment** on their knowledge of key concepts from the chapter (answers are found on the back of each **Self-Assessment** page), and a list of sources for students to read further titled **For Further Reading.**

In addition, we feature a human service professional in each chapter within **Practitioner Profile** boxes, highlighting ways in which professionals from various practice areas have integrated research into their work. Finally, each chapter contains a **Practice Competency** feature in which we describe knowledge, skills, behaviors, and ethics human service professionals should demonstrate in the field that pertain to each chapter.

The remainder of the book discusses how research is applied to the human services. Chapters 2–6 present some of the important issues that underlie research, including the role of hypotheses and theories, and ethical problems that researchers are likely to confront. We also address the issue of how to formulate a research problem and select a scientifically sound sample on which observations will be made.

With Chapter 7, we begin the first of five chapters on specific research methods. Chapter 7 covers *survey research,* which is a widely used data-collection technique based on obtaining people's responses to questions. In Chapter 8, we discuss the use of *available data* in research. Though not used as commonly as surveys, available data can be helpful to human service researchers. For example, the records kept by prisons, hospitals, or social service agencies would fall into the category of available data that could be used for research. Chapter 9 presents *field research* and *observational methods,* which involve the direct observation of people's behavior, often in the natural settings where people lead their everyday lives. This also is a common research technique in the human services, because human service practitioners typically make observations of the everyday lives of clients during the course of intervention. In Chapter 10, we discuss *experiments,* which are research techniques designed to assess the effect of one factor on another. Although human service providers only occasionally may conduct conventional experiments, they often are in a position to carry out *single-system research,* the topic of Chapter 11. Single-system research involves assessing the impact of some factors on the feelings or actions of a client, and it derives its basic logic from the experimental designs discussed in Chapter 10.

The next five chapters focus on issues that may have to be addressed irrespective of which specific research method is used in a particular study. *Evaluation research,* discussed in Chapter 12, refers to assessing how well a particular policy, program, or practice achieves its goals. This has become an increasingly important element in the human services, and evaluation researchers often use some—or all—of the five research techniques discussed in the preceding chapters. In Chapter 13, we analyze how to develop *indices* and *scales,* which are measuring devices that derive a single composite score from a number of other scores that measure something of interest. Chapters 14–16 offer an introduction to *data analysis* or what to do with numerical and non-numerical data once they are collected. Chapter 17 is an introduction to the *grant-seeking process,* or how to find financial support for research, including how to write grant proposals and research reports.

REVIEW AND CRITICAL THINKING

Main Points

- The human services are those professions with the goal of enhancing the relations between people and societal institutions to enable people to maximize their potential and alleviate distress.
- While the primary goal of the human services is to deliver services to clients, research has become a fundamental part of such service delivery. In fact, a major theme of this book is the important parallels and linkages between research and human service practice.
- A knowledge of research is necessary for both consumers of social research and those who produce it.
- Social research is a systematic examination of empirical data, collected firsthand, concerning the social or psychological forces operating in a situation.
- Social research seeks to achieve the goals of description, prediction, explanation, and evaluation.
- Social research also can involve basic research or applied research.
- The links between social research and human service practice can be identified in five focal areas: understanding human functioning in social environments, policy planning and development, assessment of client functioning, program evaluation, and practice effectiveness evaluation.
- The evidence-based practice approach to the human services emphasizes the use of the best evidence in deciding which policy and practice interventions to implement.
- Conducting accurate and unbiased research on members in the context of diversity and difference causes social researchers to confront special problems.
- Research and practice follow similar, parallel paths in approaching a problem. Research, for example, follows a series of steps that have parallels to the steps in practice intervention.
- Many human service professions have established core competencies that all practitioners in the profession should be skilled at; some of these competencies have to do with social research and research-related skills and activities.

IMPORTANT TERMS FOR REVIEW

Applied research
Basic research
Descriptive research
Evaluation research
Evidence-based practice

Explanatory research
Human services
Pilot study
Predictive research
Pretest

Pure research
Research design
Social research

CRITICAL THINKING

The term *critical thinking* refers to a mode of assessment or a reflective process that helps you assess information and decide on courses of action (Browne & Keeley, 2015; Paul, 1993). It is a careful and purposeful assessment that follows certain procedures or guidelines for gaining knowledge or making decisions. The logic of research that is presented in this book provides one set of procedures for critical thinking. The kind of analysis that is used in scientific work can be adapted for use in evaluating information in the realms of human service practice and policy as well as in your daily lives and everyday world. Even with evidence-based practice, where scientific research serves as a key source of direction, scientific evidence is rarely perfect, complete, or unambiguous. Practitioners must still engage in inference, interpretation, and judgment in order to determine appropriate applications. In our everyday world, we are confronted with much information—some of it contradictory and some of it incomplete. In all these cases, the critical thinking procedures provided by scientific reasoning provide some assistance in deciding how to proceed. They offer logical and organized procedures for sifting through this information and extracting some sense from it.

The following are critical thinking questions raised at the beginning of the chapter and some ideas for how they relate to social work practice. Students are encouraged to develop their own answers to these questions. In some chapters, we only present questions for students, many of which require students to apply critical thinking questions (topics) to practice scenarios.

How does research impact human services? Obviously human service professionals rely on research to inform their practices, whether this be related to policies that guide services, program design, or street-level decisions by those working directly with clients. Human service professionals assess the best available evidence in making decisions and in doing so engage in the evidence-based practice process. They also rely on various research methods in evaluating the services they provide.

What are the goals of social research and how do they relate to the goals of human services? The goals of social research are to describe, predict, or explain social phenomena, and/or evaluate efforts (policies, programs, or services) to help people. Human service professionals serve individuals, groups, and communities while helping to address their personal, social, economic, safety, and other goals. Social workers, police officers, nurses, and other professionals' primary aim is to serve others and research is rarely their primary activity. They rely on research and research skills, methods, and concepts to help describe phenomena pertaining to their practice, make predictions about outcomes pertaining to their interventions, explain issues facing people they serve, and evaluate the effectiveness of their programs, policies, and services.

What lessons can you learn while studying research methods that can be applied to the planning and delivery of human services? Ideally the study of research methods and the scientific process can help human service professionals develop critical thinking skills that can be used in assessing problems and resources to address them, creating service plans based on critical assessments of available evidence, evaluating the effectiveness of services and approaches to services, and improving services and related policies based on new evidence.

How can research be used to help reduce bias in human services? One of the core concepts of research is that conclusions should only be made after a careful and objective consideration of available evidence. Further, available evidence should be scrutinized to determine whether it is sufficient to answer a given question. We all have biases and preconceptions and these can impact how we view issues and problems and our preferences for how to address them. If unchecked, our biases can lead us to make errors in judgments. Studying research methods and scientific processes can give us tools to help us make more objective assessments and critically evaluate our perceptions and the extent to which they are based on sufficient evidence. They can help us arrive at decisions based on objective assessments of available evidence. Studying research may also lead us to constantly question our beliefs and perceptions as we understand that we rarely have complete information on anything.

EVALUATING COMPETENCY (FROM THE COUNCIL ON SOCIAL WORK EDUCATION [CSWE] 2015 EDUCATIONAL POLICY AND ACCREDITATION STANDARDS [EPAS])

Competency 1: Demonstrate Ethical and Professional Behavior

Both the CSWE 2015 EPAS and the National Association of Social Workers (NASW) *Code of Ethics* stress the importance of critical thinking, continuous learning, and competence.

- Why do you think both the CSWE and NASW view critical thinking, continuous learning, and competent practice as ethical imperatives?
- What roles might research and evidence-based practice play in ethically sound professional service delivery?

Competency 2: Engage Difference and Diversity in Practice

- How might reviewing research help human service professionals better understand various forms of oppression and privilege and their impact on different groups of people? What types of research do you believe would be most helpful in understanding oppression and privilege?
- Why might it be important for social researchers to include members of marginalized populations in research studies? How might their inclusion help create services that are more responsive to the needs of marginalized groups?

Competency 4: Engage in Practice-Informed Research and Research-Informed Practice

- Social workers and other human service professionals have stressed an appreciation for "multiple ways of knowing" to emphasize the importance of knowledge gained from practice and life experiences, instincts and intuition, and from scientific processes. Identify instances where you have relied on multiple forms of knowledge, including scientific methods or use of research findings, to understand something. How did research contribute to your understanding? Did it conflict with other forms of knowledge?
- Why is it important for human service professionals to get involved in the creation of research based on issues they see and experience in practice?

Competency 9: Evaluate Practice With Individuals, Communities, Groups, Organizations, and Communities

- Why is it important for individual professionals, organizations delivering human service programs, and policy makers to evaluate their services, programs, and policies?
- How might challenges be associated with objectively evaluating services, programs, and policies and making changes based on findings?

SELF-ASSESSMENT
. . . .

1. Linkages between research and practice refer to:
   a. The presence of evaluation teams within human service agencies.
   b. The idea that research can contribute to the goals of practice and properly conducted practice can contribute to the goals of research.
   c. Social researchers' reliance on professionals to recruit research subjects.
   d. Meetings that include teams of researchers and practitioners.
2. Social research involves:
   a. Systematic examination of empirical data, collected by someone firsthand, concerning the social or psychological forces impacting people.
   b. Any examination of phenomena related to groups of people.
   c. Collections of studies from scholarly journals in the social sciences.
   d. Research that involves collaboration between multiple researchers.
3. Predictive research:
   a. Involves predictions about what areas of practice will be examined next.
   b. Is problematic because we can never predict what will happen in social situations.
   c. Focuses on making projections about what may occur in the future or in other settings.
   d. Is the easiest form of research because it cannot be verified.

4. Applied research refers to:
a. Research that involves the application of an existing theory to a new practice context.
b. Research designed with a practical outcome in mind for the benefit of a specific group or society as a whole.
c. Research that has been funded after a successful application to a foundation.
d. Research conducted by human service practitioners as opposed to professional researchers.

5. Research design refers to:
a. Tables and graphs for displaying research findings.
b. Detailed plans for how research observations will be made.
c. Quantitative data collection formats.
d. The examination of existing studies to generate ideas for new research.

6. During data analysis researchers learn:
a. Whether their ideas are confirmed or refuted by empirical reality.
b. Whether or not they will successfully publish study reports.
c. How their findings will be applied in practice settings.
d. Whether or not they are strong researchers.

7. Public dissemination of results:
a. Should be avoided because research results are proprietary.
b. Should be avoided to protect the confidentiality of research subjects.
c. Is necessary so researchers can get credit for their work.
d. Is necessary so future research can build on it.

8. The results of evaluations in practice can:
a. Describe both costs and effectiveness of services.
b. Impact future practice.
c. Shape new research studies.
d. a, b, and c are all corect.

9. A pilot study is:
a. A small-scale trial run of all the procedures planned for use in the main study.
b. A design used in studying World War I fighter pilots, which has been borrowed to study social welfare among marginalized populations.
c. What occurs in the early stages of any large research project.
d. A technique used with quantitative research.

10. Parallels between research and practice:
a. Refer to similarities between the work of researchers and human service professionals.
b. Imply that research and practice are separate and should not intersect.
c. Show that researchers should have greater control and authority over human services.
d. Help ensure that research and practice maintain necessary distance between one another.

ANSWER KEY FOR SELF-ASSESSMENT QUIZ

1. **b.** The idea that research can contribute to the goals of practice and properly conducted practice can contribute to the goals of research.
2. **a.** Systematic examination of empirical data, collected by someone firsthand, concerning the social or psychological forces impacting people.
3. **c.** Focuses on making projections about what may occur in the future or in other settings.
4. **b.** Research designed with a practical outcome in mind for the benefit of a specific group or society as a whole.
5. **b.** Detailed plans for how research observations will be made.
6. **a.** Whether their ideas are confirmed or refuted by empirical reality.
7. **d.** Is necessary so future research can build on it.
8. **d.** a, b, and c are all correct.
9. **a.** A small-scale trial run of all the procedures planned for use in the main study.
10. **a.** Refer to similarities between the work of researchers and human service professionals.

FOR FURTHER READING

Brownson, R. C., Baker, E. A., Leet, T. L., Gillespie, K. N., & True, W. R. (2011). *Evidence-based public health* (2nd ed.). New York, NY: Oxford University Press. This text provides a case for evidence-based public health and practical guidance on how to choose, implement, and evaluate evidence-based programs and policies in public health settings. Extensive formal training in public health sciences is not required to grasp the presentation.

Hayes, S. C., Barlow, D. H., & Nelson-Gray, R. O. (1999). *The scientist–practitioner: Research and accountability in the age of managed care* (2nd ed.). Boston, MA: Allyn & Bacon. This is an excellent book on the linkage of research and practice. Although it focuses on psychology, it will be of interest to any professional attempting to establish a scientist–practitioner model.

Hoover, K. R., & Donovan, T. (2011). *The elements of social scientific thinking* (10th ed.). Belmont, CA: Wadsworth, Cengage. This book is an initiation to social science research intended for those who use the results of research or who are just beginning as researchers. Through several editions, it has remained to the point and up to date.

Kemeny, J. G. (1959). *A philosopher looks at science*. Princeton, NJ: Van Nostrand. A discussion of the philosophical underpinnings of science and scientific research. To truly understand research, you need some knowledge of the basic logic of science, a field generally referred to as the "philosophy of science."

Kirk, S. A., & Reid, W. J. (2002). *Science and social work: A critical appraisal*. New York, NY: Columbia University Press. The authors analyze major efforts to integrate social work research and practice, including scientifically based practice, computer-assisted social work practice, research-based practice (evidence-based practice), and research dissemination and utilization.

Lindsey, D., & Shlonsky, A. (Eds.). (2008). *Child welfare research: Advances for practice and policy*. New York, NY: Oxford University Press. An excellent source on research methods applied to the field of child welfare, this book provides a sound discussion of evidence-based practice in child welfare. It should be of particular interest to social workers; it provides many illustrations of linkages between practice and research.

Roberts, A. R., & Yeager, K. R. (Eds.) (2006). *Foundations of evidence-based social work practice*. New York, NY: Oxford University Press. The authors provide a concise introduction to evidence-based social work practice, highlighting the central role of research in it. The book includes definitions of key evidence-based practice terminology and discusses the importance of evidence-based practice and critical thinking.

Rossman, G. B., & Rallis, S. F. (2011). *Learning in the field: An introduction to qualitative research* (3rd ed.). Thousand Oaks, CA: Sage. This text provides a comprehensive overview of qualitative research, discussing both when it is preferred to quantitative research and how it is conducted.

Somekh, B., & Lewin, C (Eds.). (2011). *Research methods in the social sciences* (2nd ed.). Thousand Oaks, CA: Sage. This book provides a good overview of social science research and a balanced discussion of both theory and practical application in social research. The book provides insights into the nuances of particular approaches but also demonstrates how methods complement one another.

REFERENCES

Browne, M. N., & Keeley, S. M. (2015). *Asking the right questions: A guide to critical thinking* (11th ed.). New York, NY: Pearson.

Byrnes, E., & Arleth, B. (2015). Officer contacts with civilians and race in the City of Spokane: A quantitative analysis. Retrieved from https://static.spokanecity.org/documents/news/2015/03/19/ewu-spd-release-report-on-officer-contacts-with-civilians-race/civilian-police-encounter-analysis-spokane-police-department-eastern-washington-university-march-17-2015.pdf

Grinnell, R. M., Williams, M., & Unrau, Y. A. (2019). *Research methods for social workers: An introduction* (12th ed.). Kalamazoo, MI: Pair Bond Publications.

Gray, M., Joy, E., Plath, D. & Webb, S.A. (2013). Implementing Evidence-Based Practice: A Review of the Empirical Research Literature. Research on Social Work Practice 23(2),157–166. doi:10.1177/1049731512467072

Herrick, J. (2014, June 2). Social Policy: Overview. In C. Franklin, P. Allen-Meares, T. B. Bent-Goodley, A. J. Detlaff, S. Gehlart, L. M. Healy . . . F. Reamer (Eds.), *Encyclopedia of Social Work*. Retrieved from http://oxfordre.com/socialwork/view/10.1093/acrefore/9780199975839.001.0001/acrefore-9780199975839-e-607

Okpych, N. J., & Yu, J. L. (2014). A historical analysis of evidence-based practice in social work: The unfinished journey toward an empirically grounded profession. *Social Service Review, 88* (1), 3–58. doi:10.1086/674969

Paul, R. (1993). *Critical thinking: What every person needs to survive in a rapidly changing world*. Rohnert Park, CA: Foundation for Critical Thinking.

Rubin, A., & Bellamy, J. (2012). *Practitioners' guide to using research for evidence-based practice*. Hoboken, NJ: John Wiley & Sons.

Sheafor, B. W., & Horejsi, C. R. (2015). *Techniques and guidelines for social work practice* (10th ed.). Boston, MA: Pearson.

2
THE LOGIC OF SOCIAL RESEARCH

INTRODUCTION

Sydney Torrie (age 23) recently graduated with her bachelor of social work degree. She works at "A New Hope," a domestic violence treatment center in the rural community of Harristown, West Virginia. Sydney interned at this agency for a year and upon graduation was hired full time. The center currently provides Batterer Intervention Programs (BIPs) for three different surrounding counties to approximately 100 offenders a year. A BIP is an abuser treatment program that addresses participants' violent behaviors and provides support for developing new methods of interacting with their intimate partner and family member(s). All participants at the center are court-ordered for treatment. Sydney states, "Throughout the year the center will get many different types of offenders from partner abuse to child abuse, and it can be challenging to find interventions that meet all of our clients' different needs" (S, Torrie, personal communication, April 10, 2018). These programs explore the abuse of power and control used to inflict violence on their partners and children.

Treatment delivery is at an individual and group therapy level. Each treatment group has no more than 12 individuals at a time. These groups consist of all-male or all-female offenders.

The agency recently went through a change with hiring Samantha, their new executive director. Samantha asked Sydney to lead a project that is looking into what BIPs (interventions) are currently working at reducing violent behaviors. Samantha is ultimately interested in what program(s) are most effective at reducing domestic abuse among their clients.

Sydney is both excited and overwhelmed with leading this project. However, with being a recent graduate, much of her course work is still fresh in her memory. Sydney reflects on a systematic process of answering questions through observation including how you get from one fact to another. This chapter addresses the logic of research. As we present sources of knowledge and the use of theory, hypotheses, and perspectives on science, consider the following critical thinking questions: (a) What strengths do social workers possess that will help in determining program or intervention effectiveness? (b) What framework is referred to as "a systematic process of answering questions through observation including how you get from one fact to another" and why is this process important for her to follow? (c) What information is needed to begin to evaluate program effectiveness? (d) What resources would be helpful in evaluating program effectiveness?

After dashing through the looking-glass house to view its garden, Alice says:

> I should see the garden far better . . . if I could get to the top of that hill: and here's a path that leads straight to it—at least, no, it doesn't do *that* . . . but I suppose it will at last. But how curiously it twists! It's more like a corkscrew than a path! Well this turn goes to the hill, I suppose—no it doesn't! This goes straight back to the house! Well then, I'll try it the other way. (Carroll, 1946, pp. 21–22)

Understanding the world—especially human behavior—sometimes bears a striking resemblance to Alice's convoluted and frustrating journey in Wonderland. People do what we least expect, and without any apparent rhyme or reason: someone who was released on parole after being incarcerated appeared to be adjusting well back into life on the outside but suddenly commits another offense and goes back to jail; a marriage of 25 years that seemed to be quite solid suddenly ends in divorce; a respected and successful business executive commits suicide. Human service providers, in particular, are familiar with experiences such as these, and the path to understanding often mirrors Alice's corkscrew.

Science, however, provides a method for mapping and understanding that corkscrew. In this chapter, we discuss the basic logic underlying scientific research, beginning with an assessment of how science differs from other ways of gaining knowledge. Then, we analyze the importance of theories and their role in scientific research, drawing a parallel with the use of theories in human service practice. Following this, we discuss the role of concepts and hypotheses, showing how hypotheses serve to link theory and research. Finally, we analyze the nature of causality, because research is, at its core, a search for cause-and-effect relationships among phenomena.

SOURCES OF KNOWLEDGE

Human service practice is based on knowledge of human behavior and the social environment. There are numerous ways of gaining such knowledge, but all sources of knowledge have their pitfalls. We argued in Chapter 1 that practice knowledge should be grounded in scientific research. This does not mean that science is infallible, but science does have advantages as a source of knowledge that makes it superior to other ways of gaining knowledge.

To see why this is the case, we contrast science with four other common sources of knowledge: tradition, experience, common sense, and journalism. We then discuss how science can improve professional practice.

Tradition

Traditional knowledge is knowledge based on custom, habit, and repetition. It is founded on a belief in the sanctity of ancient wisdom and the ways of our forebears. People familiar with the musical *Fiddler on the Roof* will recall how the delightful character Tevye, a dairyman in the village of Anatevka, sang the praises of tradition:

> Because of our traditions, we've kept our balance for many, many years. Here in Anatevka we have traditions for everything—how to eat, how to sleep, how to wear clothes. . . . You may ask, how did this tradition start? I'll tell you—I don't know! But it's a tradition. Because of our traditions, everyone knows who he is and what God expects him to do. Tradition. Without our traditions, our lives would be as shaky as—as a fiddler on the roof! (Stein, 1964, pp. 1, 6)

For Tevye and the villagers of Anatevka, where traditions come from is unimportant. Traditions provide guidance; they offer "truth"; they are the final word. Traditions tell us that something is correct because it has always been done that way.

Traditional knowledge is widespread in all societies. For example, many people believe that the racial or ethnic match between parents and children is critical to children's healthy development and social adjustment. As a result, many states' child welfare systems aimed to match adoptive parents and children by race and ethnicity. Traditional knowledge is sometimes flawed, however. A Colorado-based study, for example, found that there is no clear evidence that matching children and adopting families by ethnicity leads to more successful adoptions. In fact, data show there are some cases where ethnic matches are associated with greater likelihood of post-adoption referrals back to child welfare systems (Orsi, 2015). This is not to suggest that child welfare systems should avoid facilitating adoptions between children and adoptive parents of the same race or ethnicity. Rather, it supports the idea that ethnic and racial match may not be the most important factor in predicting successful adoptions.

Human service providers can be affected in other ways by traditional beliefs. For example, the works of a Sigmund Freud or an Erik Erikson might be accepted without question, and emphasis might be placed on remaining true to their words rather than on assessing the accuracy or utility of their ideas.

Tradition can be an important source of knowledge, especially in areas such as moral judgments or value decisions, but it can have some major disadvantages. First, tradition is extremely resistant to change, even for those cases in which change might be necessary because new information surfaces or new developments occur. Second, traditional knowledge easily confuses knowledge (an understanding of what *is*) with values (a preference for what *ought to be*). For many people, the traditional emphasis on the two-parent family actually is based on a value regarding the preferred family form rather than on a knowledge of the effect that such a family has on child development.

Experience

Experience as a source of knowledge refers to firsthand, personal observations of events. **Experiential knowledge** is based on the assumption that truth and understanding can be achieved through personal experience and that witnessing events will lead to an accurate comprehension of those events.

Experience is a common source of knowledge for human service workers, who have numerous opportunities to make firsthand observations of children experiencing emotional disturbance, people with physical disabilities, foster children, and other service populations. From these contacts, practitioners can develop an understanding—not necessarily an accurate one—of what motivates their clients and what social or psychological processes have influenced them.

For example, a person working in a domestic violence shelter will have considerable contact with women whose partners have physically and psychologically abused them. Because of this, the worker likely is sensitive to the harm that can come to women from their partners. After seeing women and other people who have been severely abused, this worker may conclude that marital counseling with such spouses cannot work in a climate of violence and anger and may even be dangerous.

This experiential knowledge about family dynamics and abuse may be reinforced by traditional knowledge about the importance of family life. Armed with this knowledge, a practitioner might shape an intervention effort that focuses on individual counseling or on marital counseling.

Experiential knowledge, however, has some severe limitations that can lead to erroneous conclusions. First, human perceptions are notoriously unreliable. Perception is affected by many factors, including the cultural background and the mood of the observer, the conditions under which something is observed, and the nature of what is being observed. Even under the best conditions, some misperception is likely; thus, knowledge based on experience often is inaccurate.

Second, human knowledge and understanding do not result from direct perception but, rather, from *inferences* that are made from those perceptions. The conclusion that marital counseling does not work is an inference—that is, it is not directly observed. All that has been observed is that people, often women, have been abused by their partners. There is no observation of the effectiveness of any type of counseling. (We discuss making inferences from observations in more detail when we address the issue of causality later in this chapter.)

Third, the very people in positions to experience something directly frequently have vested interests in perceiving that thing in a certain way. Teachers, for example, observe that the students who do poorly are the ones who do not pay strict attention during class. However, teachers have a vested interest in showing that their teaching techniques are not the reason for poor performance among students. Therefore, teachers probably would be inclined to attribute students' failings to the students' lack of effort and inattentiveness rather than to their own inadequacies as educators.

A final limitation on experiential knowledge is that it is difficult to know if the people directly available to you are accurate representatives of all the people about whom you wish to draw conclusions. If they are not, then any conclusions drawn from your observations may be in error. To use our earlier example, are the women experiencing partner violence who contact a domestic violence shelter representative of all people experiencing partner violence? If the women who contact a shelter are different in some way, and if these differences influence the effectiveness of counseling in the shelter, then you cannot generalize conclusions from their outcomes in counseling to the experiences of all women in domestic violence situations. Battered women who go to a shelter may be more affluent or less isolated and, therefore, might evidence different outcomes in counseling than less affluent or more isolated women would.

Common Sense

The accumulation of knowledge from tradition and experience often blends to form what people call **common sense**: practical judgments based on the experiences, wisdom, and prejudices of a people. People with common sense are presumed to be able to make sound decisions even though they lack any specialized training and knowledge. Yet, is common sense a very accurate source of knowledge? Consider the following contradictory examples. Common sense tells us that people with similar interests and inclinations will be likely to associate with one another. When we see a youngster who smokes marijuana associating with others who do the same, we may sagely comment, "Birds of a feather flock together." Then, however, we see an athletic woman become involved with

a bookish, cerebral man, and we say, "Opposites attract."

In other words, common sense often explains everything—even when those explanations contradict one another. This is not to say that common sense is unimportant or always useless. Common sense can be valuable and accurate, which is not surprising, because people need sound information as a basis for interacting with others and functioning in society. However, common sense does not normally involve a rigorous and systematic attempt to distinguish reality from fiction. Rather, it tends to accept what "everyone knows" to be true and to reject contradictory information. Furthermore, common sense often is considered to be something that people either have or do not have, because it is not teachable. In fact, it often is contrasted with "book learning." This discourages people from critically assessing their common-sense knowledge and tempering it with knowledge acquired from other sources. For this reason, commonsense knowledge should be accepted and used cautiously. As a basis for human service practice, knowledge needs to be based on the rigorous and systematic methods used in scientific research. Common sense or a vague feeling of "helping" is not enough.

Journalism

The materials prepared by journalists for newspapers, magazines, television, websites, or other media are another important source of knowledge about the world for most people. With the explosion of news sources available on cable television and the Internet, people now have access to vast amounts of journalistic information. Though some journalism consists of opinion pieces based on the speculations and inferences of the journalist, much of it, like science, is grounded in observation: Reporters interview people or observe events, and they write their reports based on those observations. In addition, with modern technology, journalists often are in a position to provide a video and/or audio record of what happened at a scene.

So it may seem, at first glance, that science and journalism have much in common as sources of knowledge, and significant similarities between the two endeavors can be identified. Both use observation to seek out accurate knowledge about the world. In fact, some journalism can, at times, take on many of the characteristics of social science research. Some journalistic output, for example, can look a lot like the in-depth interviews and case studies we discuss in Chapter 9. However, although scientific standards require that scientists use the systematic procedures discussed in this book, journalism can—and often does—fall far short of meeting these standards.

A key difference between science and journalism is that the observations of scientists are much more systematic in nature. This means that scientists utilize far more careful procedures than journalists to reduce the chances that their conclusions will be inaccurate. For example, a journalist interested in the experiences of prison inmates probably will interview a few inmates who are made available to him or her by prison authorities and then use these interviews to draw conclusions, at least implicitly, about the experiences of all prisoners. Social scientists would recognize that prisoners selected by the authorities are likely to differ from other prisoners in some important ways: They may have been selected because they committed less serious offenses or were model prisoners. Their experience of prison also is likely to be very different from that of a more serious offender or that of someone who has chronic confrontations with prison authorities. Recognizing this, social scientists would be very careful about how they selected inmates on whom to make observations and usually would not accept a sample selected by prison authorities. The best sampling procedures, which are discussed in Chapter 6, would be those that ensure that all types of prisoners have a chance to appear in the sample. This could be done, for example, by interviewing all prisoners or, if that were not feasible, interviewing a randomly selected group of prisoners. If sampling procedures fall short of these standards, then social scientists have reduced confidence in the arrived-at conclusions. Journalists often do not use such rigorous sampling procedures.

A second key difference between science and journalism is that journalism is not concerned with theory building and verification as a way of developing an abstract explanation of people's behavior. Journalists are much more focused on, as the saying goes, "just the facts." However, journalists can provide a higher standard of work than social media. Journalists have professional standards, which they follow when reporting. Social media does not have these standards and is much of the time individual people discussing their ideas. Scientists, on the other hand, recognize that facts often do not speak for themselves—they need to be interpreted in the context of a theoretical understanding to fully comprehend what the facts mean.

Scientific Method

Winston Churchill, the prime minister of Britain during World War II, is reported to have said that democracy is an imperfect form of government but that it is far superior to all other forms. Many scientists have a similar view of science: They realize that it is imperfect and limited, but they also recognize that it is far superior to other sources of knowledge for gaining an understanding of the world. **Science** is a method of obtaining objective knowledge about the world through systematic observation. (The term *science* is also used to refer to the accumulated body of knowledge that results from scientific inquiry.) In the "A New Hope" example at the beginning of the chapter, Sydney needs to follow a systematic process to determine program effectiveness so that the agency will be able to determine if BIP is effective for their clients. The scientific method provides a systematic process that has five distinguishing characteristics that, taken together, set it apart from the other sources of knowledge.

First, science is *empirical*, which simply means that science is based on direct observation of the world. Science is not only founded in theorizing, philosophizing, or speculating. At times, scientists do all these things, but eventually, they must observe the world to see whether their theories or speculations agree with the facts. Observation can be accomplished through many different means, which are discussed in further detail in future chapters. These different types of observation can be conducted through direct observation. Types of direct observation consist of collecting surveys and field research. Science is always growing and changing based on observation. Facts that we know today were not considered as facts years ago, but because of science are now seen as everyday facts. For instance, in the 1980s and early 1990s it was commonly believed that someone could contract HIV through touching, kissing, or even being in the presence of someone who was infected with either HIV or AIDS. We now know that was incorrect and we know this because of science.

Second, science is *systematic,* meaning that the procedures used by scientists are organized, methodical, public, and recognized by other scientists. One dimension of the systematic nature of science is that scientists report, in detail, all the procedures used in coming to a conclusion. This enables other scientists to assess whether the inferences and conclusions drawn are warranted given the observations made. A second dimension of the systematic nature of science is *replication*—that is, repeating studies numerous times to determine if the same results can be obtained. Scientists are very cautious about drawing hard-and-fast conclusions from a single observation or investigation. In fact, and quite at variance with experiential knowledge, scientists assume that a single direct observation is as likely to be incorrect as it is to be correct. Only repeated observations can reduce the chance of error and misinterpretation (Rosenthal, 1991).

Third, science is *the search for causes.* Scientists assume that there is order in the universe, that there are ascertainable reasons for the occurrence of all events, and that scientists can discover the orderly nature of the world. If we assumed that there was no order, no pattern, then there would be no need to search for it. We could write off events as the result of chance or the intervention of some benevolent (or malevolent, or indifferent) otherworldly force that we can never understand.

Fourth, science is *provisional,* which means that scientific conclusions are always accepted as tentative and subject to question and possible refutation. There are no ultimate, untouchable, irrevocable truths in science. There are no scientists whose work is held in such esteem that it cannot be criticized or rejected. As the philosopher Jacob Bronowski (1978) put it, "Science is not a finished enterprise. . . . The truth is [not] a thing that you could find . . . the way you could find your hat or your umbrella" (pp. 121–122). Science is a process of continuous movement toward a more accurate picture of the world, and scientists fully realize that we will never achieve the ultimate and final picture.

Finally, science strives for *objectivity,* which means that scientists try to avoid having their personal biases and values influence their scientific conclusions. This is a controversial and complicated characteristic of science, because many social scientists would argue that true objectivity is impossible for human beings to achieve. We discuss this issue at a number of points in this book, but it is sufficient to say here that all scientists are concerned that their scientific conclusions are not solely (or merely) a product of their own personal biases and values. This does not mean that scientists should be devoid of values. Quite the contrary, they can be as passionate, concerned, and involved as any other group of citizens. However, they realize that their values and biases can—and probably will—lead to erroneous scientific conclusions. To address this problem, science incorporates mechanisms to reduce the likelihood of biased observations becoming an accepted part of the body of scientific knowledge. For example, publicizing all research procedures enables others to assess whether the research was conducted in a way that justifies the conclusions reached. Furthermore, such detailed reporting permits replication so that other researchers, with different values, can see if they come to the same conclusions regarding a set of observations.

Despite these checks, of course, values and biases will still be found in research. The very decision of what topics to investigate, for example, often is shaped by the researcher's values: One person studies family violence because a close friend was the victim of spousal abuse, and another studies factors contributing to job satisfaction because of a personal belief that work is central to identity. Values and biases also enter research through the interpretation of observations. For personal reasons, one researcher may desperately want to show that the criminal justice system rehabilitates (or does not rehabilitate). This may well influence how he or she goes about conducting research and interpreting the results. There are even a few cases (most commonly in biomedical research) of outright falsification of data to show a certain conclusion. The point is that values and biases commonly intrude on scientific research, but the overall scientific enterprise is organized to reduce their impact on the body of scientific knowledge.

The scientific method, then, with the characteristics just described, is viewed by scientists as preferable to other ways of gaining knowledge, because it is more likely to lead to accurate knowledge of the world. To return to our earlier example of single-parent families and adoption, science views all knowledge regarding the family as provisional and open to question, and there have been many scientific investigations of the role of the family in these matters. Child adjustment and development in two-parent and single-parent families have been compared in both adoptive and biological families as well as in stepfamilies.

The conclusion from these various studies is that the traditional, two-parent family does not seem to play the indispensable role that much commonsense knowledge would accord it—or at least that the role of parents in families is more complicated than was once thought. For example, the research shows that adoption by a single parent is not always detrimental when compared with two-parent adoptive settings; some adoptees with one parent do quite well (Haugaard, Palmer, & Wojslawowicz, 1999). A related finding is that nontraditional family structure (having one rather than two parents) probably is less critical to children's development than is family process (warm relationships and low conflict between parents and children). The negative consequences often associated with single-parent families may arise from the conflict that often accompanies divorce, because divorce is how many single-parent families are produced (Golombok & Tasker, 2015). Also, single-parent families often experience certain negative factors: low income, inadequate parental guidance, and less access to community resources. Single-parent families that overcome these difficulties do as well as other family forms in raising children (McLanahan & Sandefur, 1994). So, the common sense or traditional view that the two-parent family is always superior to the

single-parent setting is shown by research to be vastly oversimplified at best.

In this fashion, then, scientific knowledge overcomes many of the weaknesses of traditional, experiential, and commonsense knowledge. In particular, it enables us to accumulate accurate information despite the personal biases of individual researchers or practitioners. These positive attributes of science do not mean, however, that science is perfect. Scientists do make errors. But, as Jacob Bronowski (1978) so aptly put it, "Science is essentially a self-correcting activity" (p. 122). If proper scientific procedures are followed, then today's errors will be corrected by researchers in the future, whose errors in turn will be corrected by still more research.

Scientific Practice

With this more detailed understanding of science and its characteristics, we can return to the concept of evidence-based practice introduced in Chapter 1 and elaborate on what this approach says about the parallels between science and practice. Basically, this approach argues that effective human service practice should have characteristics that parallel those of science (Hayes, Barlow, & Nelson-Gray, 1999; Rosen, 1996). Human service practice would be enhanced if it is shaped by a consideration of each of the five characteristics of science just discussed. First, practice, like science, should be *empirical,* stressing problem assessment involving direct observation of client problems, actual counts of behaviors, and independent observations from multiple data sources. Such data are less subject to distortion and bias than self-reports, speculations, and philosophizing. Second, practice, like research, should be *systematic.* To the extent that practice procedures are well organized, clearly specified, and made public, they can be replicated and tested by others. Practitioner Profile 2.1 illustrates the practical transparent nature of research procedures and how one could replicate and test similar studies. In this manner, ineffective procedures can be eliminated, and promising ones can be refined and improved. One of the recurring criticisms of many human service interventions is that the intervention itself is not well specified. Consequently, research evaluating the intervention cannot clearly

PRACTITIONER PROFILE 2.1 Benjamin Sibley, Associate Professor Appalachian State University

Dr. Ben Sibley is an assistant professor at Appalachian State University and trains future physical education (PE) teachers. He works on offering high quality PE programs so that students can learn to be healthy and physically active. The research he conducts directly informs how to get people motivated to exercise and works on best teaching practices to assess students' overall health. This all has a direct application to what PE professionals do. Ideally, the results of his studies influence practice, because PE teachers can read them and apply best practice.

According to Dr. Sibley, the connection between social sciences and PE is natural because all educators and staff are interested in the physical health of their students. This can take place in many different ways. For instance, educators could learn best health practices for themselves; they can then role-model them for their students and talk about the positive aspects of these practices through stress management.

Dr. Sibley has recently been working on a project with elementary students to increase their health outcomes. Ben states that a good PE program needs to have fitness testing so that students can see their current level of fitness. This testing also provides information to their overall health now and in the future. There are many different ways PE educators measure fitness; however, Dr. Sibley has recently become interested in power, which is moving and exerting force explosively. Power is associated with different aspects of health, such as bone health and muscle fitness. Dr. Sibley explains that jumping is an excellent example of power because you are exerting force in a fast way and that people with power have stronger and healthier bones. There is currently not a health-related fitness test to measure power in PE. Since power is a new development of health, there are no fitness measures for PE educators. His research is meant to address this need. Using a tablet, researchers can enter a participant's height, weight, and vertical jump, which will calculate the power in watts that they produce during their jump. Comparing that to their raw score of vertical jumps enables us to know how much power a student is using when he or she jumps. The problem with raw scores when jumping is that heavier students use much more power, but they might not get as high with their jump. PE teachers and anyone trained on how to calculate power can calculate a student's score. Future research needs to look at the range of power that falls in a healthy fitness zone. Mental health and physical health have a strong link to each other. There are links between exercise and physical activity with depression, anxiety, and sleep quality. Research has also shown that exercise can be as effective at treating depression as antidepressants. All health professionals should be prescribing healthy activity and good nutrition to their patients to help their mental health along with their physical health.

indicate what did (or did not) work. Practice models also involve *causality* in terms of specifying a clear link between cause and effect or in explaining why a proposed intervention should work with the particular identified problem. Again, a criticism of human service projects in the past has been that many of them have consisted of a conglomeration of intervention efforts without a clearly articulated linkage between cause and effect.

Practice theory, like science, should be *provisional*. All practice models and techniques should be viewed as fair game for criticism and refutation. Through such a process of testing and challenging existing practices, healthy growth can occur in practice methodology.

Finally, human service professionals must deal with the problem of professional *objectivity*. The determination of the utility and effectiveness of practice procedures needs to be done under objective conditions. Just as the researcher must attempt to safeguard against the intrusion of values into the conduct of research, so practitioners must guard against the intrusion of values into practice. This issue of values and objectivity is particularly difficult for human service practitioners, who often approach problems with a strong set of values, both personal and professional. Personally, practitioners may have strong feelings about such matters as abortion, alcohol use, or domestic violence that may clash with those of the groups with which they work. Furthermore, some human service providers are conventional and middle class in their personal lives, which may influence what they see as successful social functioning. In addition to these personal values, human service practice itself is heavily imbued with professional values. In fact, as one human service educator put it, "Social work is among the most value based of all professions. . . . [It] is deeply rooted in a fundamental set of values that ultimately shapes the profession's mission and its practitioners' priorities" (Reamer, 2006, p. 3).

At times, these values may emphasize a conservatism or a pressure to preserve the status quo; at other times, the values may reflect a commitment to support vulnerable or oppressed populations. In either event, the recommendation that human service providers not let their values intrude into the provision of services to clients is challenging to satisfy. In fact, it probably is impossible to mount an effective change effort without some imposition of values, either implicit or explicit. Even more, some therapeutic approaches, such as those of Carl Rogers, Albert Ellis, and Hobart Mowrer, include as one of their goals the acceptance by the client of new—and more realistic—values.

So, even though professional practice in the human services is clearly oriented toward the fulfillment of certain values, practicing in the profession requires that the worker establish checks on the intrusion of values into practice, much as the researcher does in the conduct of research. In later chapters, we discuss research techniques that are less subject to biases in observation and measurement. Application of these principles in practice can also help restrict the unwanted intrusion of personal values into service delivery. Another way to control the influence of values is to do research on the role of values in practice and to design agency procedures that help provide services objectively. As Research in Practice 2.1 illustrates, the influence of values on the actual conduct of practice cannot be totally eliminated. However, by relying on a practice approach that is empirically based, employing procedures supported by research, and incorporating rigorous evaluation procedures, it is possible to sensitize professionals to the impact of their value positions and, thus, enhance the objectivity of service delivery.

THEORIES IN RESEARCH AND PRACTICE

Theory is a word that is misunderstood by many people. To the neophyte, theories often are associated with the abstract, the impractical, or the unreal. In reality, nothing could be further from the truth. In both research and practice settings, theories play a critical role in our understanding of reality and in our ability to cope with problems. In fact, people commonly use theories in their daily lives without recognizing that they do so.

What Is a Theory?

A **theory** is a set of interrelated, abstract propositions or statements that offers an explanation of some phenomenon (Skidmore, 1979). Three key elements in this definition are important to understanding theories. First, theories are made up of **propositions**, which are statements about the relationship between some elements in the theory. For example, a proposition from the differential association theory of crime is that a person becomes a criminal because of an excess of definitions favorable to the violation of the law over definitions unfavorable to the violation of the law. Elements in this proposition include "criminal" and "definitions favorable to the violation of the law" (Sutherland, 1939). Behavior modification theory also contains numerous propositions, such as: behavior change can occur through a reorganization of the environmental cues that reward and punish behavior (Brady & Kotkin, 2011). The elements in this proposition include "behavior change," "environmental cues," and "reward and punish behavior."

A second important part of our definition of theory is that theories are *abstract* systems, meaning they link general and abstract propositions

RESEARCH IN PRACTICE 2.1 Practice Effectiveness: Providing Services to Gays and Lesbians

Human service practitioners often deal with clients or situations that involve value-laden controversies. One area where this clearly is the case is the issue of whether gays or lesbians should be permitted to have custody of their children or to adopt. Traditional—and, in some cases, religious—values lead some people to the conclusion that only intact, heterosexual, married couples provide a suitable environment for child rearing and that being raised by a gay or lesbian parent would be harmful to a child. The difficult problem for the human service provider is how to serve clients within the context of one's own personal and professional values.

The movement toward evidence-based practice in the human services suggests that it is possible to use scientific research to assess whether personal or professional values are unreasonably influencing the services provided to clients. One of the primary features of evidence-based practice involves identifying general trends gleaned from a review of studies that are applicable to practice. The provision of child welfare services to gay and lesbian clients offers an excellent example of this feature. A human service professional charged with making recommendations about child custody and adoption would approach this situation by systematically searching the literature and asking the question: How well do gays and lesbians perform in the role of parent?

Marcus Tye (2003) summarizes the theoretical and empirical evidence currently available to answer this question. Over the past quarter century, beginning with the work of Karen Lewis (1980), a considerable body of research has accumulated on the development and experiences of the children of lesbians and gay men (Stacey & Biblarz, 2001). For the most part, this research does not support the negative developmental outcomes for the children that would be predicted by much traditional and experiential knowledge or some people's personal values. Children raised by gay or lesbian parents do not differ in their sexual orientation or personal development from children raised by heterosexual parents (Goldberg, 2009; Gottman, 1990).

By the 1990s, the research focus had shifted from looking at the quality of family life after a parent had acknowledged his or her homosexuality toward the examination of gay men and lesbians who, often in the context of a committed homosexual relationship, were opting to have children via the processes of adoption, artificial insemination, or surrogate mothers. This research also has found no negative effects for adopted children raised in gay- or lesbian-headed families. These adoptive families exhibited a level of family functioning that, by many measures, was at least as high as that found in other types of families (Erich, Leung, Kindle, & Carter, 2005; Leung, Erich, & Kanenberg, 2005).

So this evidence-based review suggests that children can be reared into healthy adults in families parented by homosexuals and sexual orientation should not preclude individuals from serving as adoptive or foster parents. Thus the general trends in the existing data help provide direction for shaping agency policy. Science cannot inform human service workers regarding what their personal values ought to be, but it can point out practice situations in which personal values seem to be unreasonably intruding on intervention decisions. Such research also safeguards against the danger that decisions based on personal values will masquerade as "in the client's best interest" by providing an empirical knowledge base for decision making.

to particular, testable events or phenomena. In many cases, these abstract systems are *deductive* systems, a general set of propositions that can be used to deduce further, more concrete relationships between the elements of the theory. Differential association theory is again illustrative. As noted, this theory relates definitions favorable to the violation of the law with the greater likelihood of criminal behavior. This means that the theory is supposed to apply to *all* specific types of crimes, such as robbery, larceny, and auto theft. So, it would be logical to deduce from the theory that greater exposure to definitions favorable to the violation of the law would be associated with higher incidences of robbery, larceny, and auto theft. Theories are abstract, because they have this deductive power: The broader and more abstract the propositions and their related concepts, the more numerous the specific relationships that can be deduced from them.

The third key aspect of theories is that they provide *explanations* for the phenomena they address. Indeed, the ultimate purpose of a theory is to explain *why* something occurred. In differential association theory, the phenomenon to be explained is criminal behavior, and the explanation is that criminality is learned through much the same process as noncriminal behavior is. The content of what is learned—namely, definitions favorable to violation of the law—makes the difference. Thus, differential association provides an explanation for the development of criminal behavior.

In comprehending theories and the roles they play, it is helpful to realize that we all use theories in our everyday lives, although we may not call them *theories* or even be consciously aware of using them. Nonetheless, we base our decisions and behavior on our past experiences and what we have learned from others. From these experiences, we generalize that certain physical, psychological, and social processes are operative and will continue to be important in the future, with predictable consequences. This is our "commonsense theory" about how the world operates and forms the basis for our decisions. For example, most people have certain general notions—that is, personal theories—about what causes poverty. Some personal theories emphasize poverty as an

individual problem: People are poor because of their individual characteristics, such as laziness, low intelligence, poor education, or lack of marketable skills. Others' theories of poverty emphasize structural features of the American economy dictating that, even in times of economic expansion, some people will be left impoverished through no fault of their own. Which of these theories people identify with most closely determines, in part, how they react to poor people and which public policy provisions toward poverty they support. Advocates of the individualistic theory might be hostile toward the poor and programs to aid them, because they believe the poor are undeserving people who suffer only from their own shortcomings. Supporters of the structural theory may view the poor as victims and tend to be more benevolent toward them.

Personal theories like these concerning poverty may be extreme and misleading, because they are based on casual observations, personal experience, or other information lacking the rigorous concern for accuracy of scientific investigations. Unlike commonsense theories, the theories in research and practice are precise, detailed, and explicit. It is important, however, to recognize that a theory is always tentative in nature—that is, any theory is best viewed as a *possible* explanation for the phenomenon under investigation. By conducting research, scientists gather evidence that either supports or fails to support a theoretical explanation or practice intervention. No theory stands or falls on the basis of one trial. Theories are tested over a long period of time by many investigations. Only with the accumulation of research outcomes can one begin to have confidence concerning the validity of a theory.

The Functions of Theories

We have all heard the refrain "It's only a theory" or "That's your theory." Such phrases often are used in the context of deflating an argument. Actually, these comments, though often intended in a disparaging sense, convey some truth regarding theories. In particular, they point out that theories are sometimes *untested* (but testable) assertions about reality and that theories are not the end product of scientific investigation but, rather, a part of the process of science. Theories have particular purposes in both research and practice settings. In fact, the same theories often are used in both research and practice, because both researchers and practitioners turn to them for similar reasons. We can identify three major functions of theories in research and practice.

Explanation of Phenomena. As we have seen, theories provide an explanation for phenomena. They say not only what will happen under certain conditions (which is what hypotheses also do, but more concretely) but also why it will happen. This provides a much more powerful understanding of human behavior. In differential association theory, for example, the phenomenon to be explained is criminal behavior, and the explanation is that criminal behavior is a product of learning appropriate behaviors from others who are important to us. Thus, differential association theory provides a broad, abstract explanation for the development of criminal behavior that links such behavior with general processes of conformity and group process. People learn to be criminals in the same way they learn to be doctors, nurses, or lawyers—namely, by learning through association with other people.

Guide for Research and Practice. Theories guide and direct research and practice. They focus attention on certain phenomena as relevant to the issues of concern. If we were to dispense with theories altogether, as some would suggest, then what would we study? What data would be collected? What intervention strategy would be adopted? Theories help us find answers to these questions.

Imagine that a counseling center wants to find solutions to combat the problem of teenage alcohol consumption at a particular high school and the staff decides to study the problem. Where to begin? What variables are important? As a first step, it is essential to fall back on some theory related to these issues. We might, for example, use the theory of differential association, which posits that alcohol consumption results from attitudes and patterns of behavior that are learned in

association with other people, particularly peers. To test this theory, we could determine whether alcohol consumption is more common when it is viewed as an acceptable form of behavior among peers. We are then in a position to collect data on attitudes toward alcohol and patterns of alcohol consumption in peer groups. If the theory is confirmed, then it supports the idea that effective intervention will need to focus on attitudes toward alcohol consumption in peer groups.

We could have selected a different theory regarding alcohol consumption. For example, some theories posit an inherited predisposition toward alcoholism. Other theories suggest that alcoholism results from a nutritional deficiency that is satiated by alcohol consumption. We do not presume to suggest which theory is more accurate—future research will settle that issue, one hopes. The same thing occurs in practice intervention. If a practitioner used crisis intervention theory to deal with the disruption caused by an alcoholic parent, then the theory would direct attention to such factors as family coping strengths and emotional adaptation. Community-organization practice theory, on the other hand, would focus on the community resources available to recovering alcoholics and community services for their families. The point is that the theories used by researchers and practitioners guide their approaches and focus their attention on particular phenomena.

Integration of Multiple Observations. Theories help integrate and explain the many observations made in diverse settings by researchers and practitioners. They tell us *why* something happened, and they enable us to link the outcomes of numerous studies and interventions made in a variety of settings. As long as the findings of these efforts remain individual and isolated, they are not particularly valuable to science. Recall that a single observation is viewed with considerable skepticism. Single research findings may be in error, may be passed over and forgotten, or their broader implications may be missed entirely. A familiarity with differential association theory would suggest that the social learning processes important in teenage drinking also may be relevant in unwanted pregnancies among teenagers. If this is the case, then practitioners working in one area may be able to borrow strategies for intervention from the other area. Thus, theories integrate the findings from independent research endeavors and provide implications for intervention strategies.

Theories, then, play an important part in both research and practice, but one point needs to be reiterated: The utility of theories must be based on their *demonstrated* effectiveness. Theories should never be allowed to become "sacred cows," the use of which is based on tradition or custom. Most authorities would agree with this conclusion: "The most important criterion to consider is the extent to which a given theory has been supported by empirical research" (Hepworth & Larsen, 1990, p. 18). In other words, has the intervention been shown to produce the desired results? In scientific research, this is called the **verification** of theories. Researchers approach the problem of verification by developing and testing hypotheses. This process of verification is diagrammed in Figure 2.1, which also shows a parallel process as it occurs in human service practice.

CONCEPTS AND HYPOTHESES

Defining Concepts

An important part of theories is **concepts**: mental constructs or images developed to symbolize ideas, persons, things, or events. Concepts are the elements of theories discussed earlier; they are the building blocks that are interrelated in propositions to form the explanatory statements of a theory (Alford, 1998). Some of the concepts

in behavior modification theory, for example, are reinforcement, conditioning, learning, and behavior change.

Concepts are similar in function to the words we use during everyday communication. The word *automobile,* for example, is the agreed-on symbol for a particular object that is used as a mode of transportation. The symbol or word is not the object itself but, rather, something that stands for or represents that object. Scientific concepts, like words in everyday language, also are symbols that can refer to an extremely broad range of referents. They may refer to something fairly concrete, like height or age, or to something highly abstract, like reinforcement or cohesion.

Despite the similarities between scientific concepts and ordinary words, some differences are critical to the scientific endeavor. In particular, concepts used in scientific research must be defined very carefully. With the words we use for everyday communication, we can get along quite well having only a general idea of how these words are defined. In fact, it is doubtful whether most people could give a dictionary-perfect definition of even the most commonly used words. Such imprecision in the use of scientific concepts, however, is totally inadequate. Scientists, who are widely scattered both geographically and temporally, carry on research that tests various aspects of theories. For these disconnected research projects to produce information of maximum utility, all the bits of knowledge need to be integrated into an explanatory scheme—namely, a theory. This accumulation of knowledge is severely hampered—in fact, it becomes practically impossible—if these isolated scientists use different definitions of the same concepts.

For example, many studies of the relationship between reinforcement and learning have been

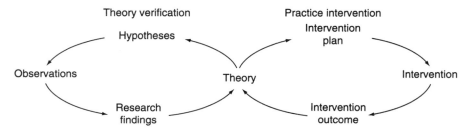

Figure 2.1 The process of theory verification in research compared with practice intervention.

conducted. If the results of different studies are to be comparable, then the concepts of reinforcement and learning should be defined the same way. Learning, for instance, can be defined in *behavioral* terms (as the performance of a new behavior) or in *cognitive* terms (as the understanding of how a particular behavior might be performed). When defined in these two different ways, the concept refers to something quite different in the world, and the results from two investigations using the different definitions would not be directly comparable. Perhaps, for example, behavioral learning occurs under quite different conditions than cognitive learning does.

Scientific analysis involves two types of definitions of concepts, each functioning at a different level of analysis and each serving a different purpose. At the theoretical or abstract level, concepts are given **nominal definitions**: verbal definitions in which scientists agree that one set of words or symbols will be used to stand for another set of words or symbols. Nominal definitions are directly analogous to the dictionary definitions of ordinary words in which a phrase is designed to give meaning to the word or concept being defined (Cohen & Nagel, 1934). For example, a nominal definition of "poverty" might be a deficiency in resources to the extent that people are not able to maintain a lifestyle considered to be minimally acceptable in a particular society (Sullivan, 2012, p. 148).

An important step in moving from the abstract level of theory to the concrete level of research is to give concepts **operational definitions**: definitions that indicate the precise procedures or operations to be followed in measuring a concept. For example, Mollie Orshansky developed one of the most widely used operational definitions of poverty for the Social Security Administration (Ruggles, 1990). Her measure, still used by the government as a basis for policy decisions, is based on what it costs to purchase a low-budget, nutritious diet for a family. If we use U.S. Department of Agriculture figures, the poverty line is determined by the cost of food, the size of the family, and other factors. This operational definition of poverty yields a series of income cutoffs below which families are defined as poor. This is a precise definition that

lists the exact operations—in this case, mathematical operations—to follow in defining poverty. Anyone using this definition measures the same thing in the same way.

The process of moving from nominal to operational definitions can be complex, because concepts are very general and abstract and controversy often arises over exactly what they refer to. Some concepts that have been a part of the literature for decades have yet to be operationalized in a way that is fully satisfactory. For example, "alcoholism" has proved to be extremely difficult to operationalize, especially in terms of establishing where social drinking leaves off and alcoholism begins (Lau-Barraco & Collins, 2011; Schuckit, 2006). Because of substantial individual and cultural differences, simple measures relying on the amount and frequency of consumption are inadequate. Researchers have been forced to operationalize alcoholism on the basis of such symptoms as family or work problems, morning drinking, poor eating, and recurrent blackouts. Whereas symptom-based measures of alcoholism avoid the errors inherent in consumption measures, substantial controversy remains concerning which symptoms are the best indicators, how many symptoms must be evident, and how serious they must be before the label of *alcoholic* may be meaningfully applied.

Even the concept of poverty, which may seem straightforward and easy to operationalize, has proven to be controversial. There is, of course, the issue of where to set the income cutoffs. Orshansky's cutoffs are based on the assumption that the average American family spends one third of its income on food; some critics have argued that this results in poverty thresholds that are too low. Furthermore, Orshansky's definition sets a fixed income level as the poverty level; thus, it is unaffected by changing levels of affluence within society as a whole. Some have argued for a relative definition of poverty that defines as poor those who earn one third or one half of the median family income (Bell, 1987). With such a definition, the poverty thresholds would rise automatically if the affluence of society as a whole increased. So, it should be evident that operationalizing concepts can be difficult, complex, and, sometimes, controversial. The process of moving from the nominal to the operational level is called *measurement,* and it is treated extensively in Chapters 5 and 13.

Developing Hypotheses

A common strategy in scientific investigations is to move from a general theory to a specific, researchable problem. A part of this strategy is to develop **hypotheses**, which are testable statements of presumed relationships between two or more concepts. Hypotheses state what we expect to find rather than what has already been determined to exist. A major purpose of developing hypotheses in research is to test the accuracy of a theory (see Figure 2.1). The concepts and propositions of which theories are composed usually are too broad and too abstract to be directly tested. Concepts such as *reinforcement* and *learning,* for example, need to be specified empirically through operational definitions before they are amenable to testing. Once operationally defined, these concepts generally are referred to as **variables**, or things that are capable of taking on more than one value. If hypotheses are supported, then this supplies evidence for the accuracy of the theory on which they are based.

In the construction of hypotheses, the relationship between variables is stated in one of two possible directions: a positive relationship, or a negative (also called an inverse) relationship. In a *positive relationship,* the values of the variables change in the *same* direction, such as both increasing or both decreasing. For example, we might hypothesize that the acceptance of the use of alcohol among an adolescent's peers will lead to an increased likelihood that the adolescent will consume alcohol. In other words, as acceptance of the use of alcohol by one's peers increases, so does the adolescent's own use of alcohol. In a *negative relationship,* or an *inverse relationship,* the values of variables change in *opposite* directions. We might hypothesize, for example, that, among adolescents, reduced parental supervision will lead to an increase in the likelihood of substance abuse. In this case, as the value of one variable (parental supervision) declines, the value of the other (substance abuse) is predicted to increase.

Useful guidelines to keep in mind for developing hypotheses include the following:

1. *Hypotheses are linked to more abstract theories.* Although generating hypotheses without deriving them from theories is possible, hypotheses are always linked to theories, because the theories provide explanations for why things happen.

2. *It is important that the independent and dependent variables in hypotheses be clearly specified.* The **independent variable** is the presumed active or causal variable—that is, it is the one believed to be producing changes in the dependent variable. The **dependent variable** is the passive variable, or the one that is affected. In the previous examples, peer acceptance of alcohol and parental supervision are the independent variables, and alcohol use and substance abuse are the dependent variables.

3. *It is important that the precise nature and direction of the relationship between variables be specified in the hypothesis.* Students sometimes are tempted to state hypotheses like this: "Parental supervision will have an effect on teenage alcohol use." However, although this statement says that there *is* a relationship, it does not say *what the nature or direction of the relationship is.* A proper hypothesis, as in the preceding, would state how changes in one variable will be associated with particular changes in the other: "As parental supervision decreases, teenage alcohol use increases."

4. *Hypotheses should be stated in such a way that they can be verified or refuted.* If this is not the case, then they are not hypotheses. Hypotheses, after all, are statements about which we can gather empirical evidence to determine whether they are correct or false. A common pitfall is to make statements that involve judgments or values rather than issues of empirical observation. For example, we might hypothesize that investigations should be increased to reduce the incidence of welfare fraud. On the surface, this statement might appear to be a hypothesis, because it relates to investigations and welfare fraud in a negative direction. As stated, however, it is not a testable hypothesis. The

problem is the evaluative "should be." What should—or should not—be social policy has no place in hypotheses. However, the statement can be modified so that it qualifies as a testable hypothesis: "Increased levels of investigation tend to reduce the incidence of welfare fraud." The hypothesis now makes an empirical assertion that can be checked against fact.

5. *All the concepts and comparisons in hypotheses must be clearly stated.* For example, consider the following hypothesis: "Southern Baptists have superior moral standards." The concept of "moral standards" is so abstract and vague that it is impossible to know what it means. This would have to be clearly specified in terms of what is considered to be a moral standard. In addition, to say that someone's standards are superior requires a referent for comparison: superior to whom or what? It could mean higher than some other religious group, or it could mean higher than some chosen, absolute standard.

Developing hypotheses from theories is a *creative* process that depends, in part, on the insight of the investigator. Because hypotheses link theories to particular, concrete settings, the researcher's insight often is the trigger for making such connections. In addition, researchers, at times, combine two or more theories to develop hypotheses that neither theory alone is capable of generating.

Concepts and Operational Definitions Among Minority Populations

When conducting research on minority populations, considerable opportunity for bias exists if concepts and operational definitions are not carefully developed. This has been a chronic problem with research on crime. For example, many people believe that non-Whites commit crimes at a higher rate than we would expect, given their numbers in the population. Although this is partly true, it greatly oversimplifies a complex reality, and it reflects how crime is typically operationalized. Official crime statistics from the Federal Bureau of Investigation (FBI, 2012) are an important source of data on crime. The FBI operationalizes some

crimes as "offenses cleared by arrest" and others as "offenses known to the police." In other words, an occurrence is not officially considered to be a crime until it is "known to the police" or "cleared by arrest." These official crime statistics show that non-Whites commit more crimes, proportionate to their numbers in the population, than Whites do. However, this is a function, in part, of how the official statistics operationalize the concept of crime. We know that non-Whites are more likely to be arrested for a given offense, suggesting that it may be arrest that is more common among non-Whites rather than the actual commission of crimes. It has been proposed that non-Whites also are more likely to commit highly visible crimes, such as armed robbery or assault, that are more frequently reported to the police and result in an arrest. Some suggest that Whites, on the other hand, commit more "hidden" crimes, such as embezzlement or fraud, that are less likely to come to the attention of the police. Research suggests that there may be no class difference in the number of hidden crimes that are committed (Eschholz, Chiricos, & Gertz, 2003). In addition, there are other ways to operationalize crime, such as through victimization studies (asking people if they have been a victim of a crime) and self-reports (having people anonymously report their own involvement in crime). Studies based on these operational definitions tend to show much smaller differences between White and non-White crime rates.

Another area in which poorly constructed operational definitions have produced misleading conclusions is that of intimate partner violence (Lockhart, 1991). Most studies have found rates of intimate partner violence to be considerably higher among African Americans than among Whites. Typically, these studies have used one of the following as an operational definition for the occurrence of abusive violence: a homicide involving a domestic killing, a battered woman seeking care in an emergency room or social service setting, a wife-abuse claim handled by a domestic court, or a domestic dispute call to a police department. It is well known, however, that African Americans are overrepresented among people who come to the attention of police, emergency room personnel, or social service workers. Because they generally are overrepresented among these populations, they will appear to have higher rates of abuse than Whites will when abuse is operationalized in this fashion. These problems can be reduced by selecting a sample of people from a community and having them answer questions about the amount of conflict and violence that occurs in their own families. This avoids the biased effect of looking only at certain locales. The National Family Violence Resurvey, for example, employed a sampling strategy that selected about 6,000 cases representing all racial and ethnic groups (Straus & Gelles, 1988).

The Committee on the Status of Women in Sociology (1986) has indicated another area in which operational definitions have led to misleading results: studies of work and social contribution. Often, work is operationalized in terms of paid employment, but this excludes many other types of work from consideration, such as community service or home-based work. With this kind of operational definition, if an employee of a carpet cleaning company shampoos the carpets in a home for a fee that is counted as work, but if a woman does the same activity on her own time in her own home, this is not classified as work. Such an operationalization of work tends to underestimate the extent of productive activity engaged in by women, because women are less likely than men to be paid for their social contributions.

So, in developing operational definitions, care must be taken to assess whether these definitions might lead to a distorted view of minorities. In some cases, this calls for careful consideration of what a concept is intended to mean. For example, is the focus of the research on paid employment, or is it on social contribution? In other cases, it calls for careful assessment of whether a definition will lead to an inaccurate, over- or underrepresentation of minorities.

PERSPECTIVES ON SCIENCE

Up to this point in these first two chapters, we have presented science as if it is a coherent, unified activity about which all scientists are in agreement. It is not. Or, more accurately, we should say that some people believe it is a coherent and unified

activity, whereas others are critical of that claim. Scientists vigorously debate a number of issues concerning the best ways to engage in scientific work. One such debate is whether science should be deductive or inductive in nature.

Deduction Versus Induction

We mentioned earlier that theories often are deductive systems. This means that hypotheses can be logically derived from the propositions that make up a theory. So, **deductive reasoning** involves deducing or inferring a conclusion from some premises or propositions. If the propositions—or the theory—are correct, then hypotheses logically derived from them also will be correct. In Figure 2.1, deduction involves moving from the level of theory to that of hypotheses or an intervention plan. Deductive reasoning is central to the scientific process.

Inductive reasoning, however, enables us to assess the validity of the hypotheses and the theory. **Inductive reasoning** involves inferring something about a whole group or class of objects from our knowledge of one or a few members of that group or class. We test one or a few hypotheses derived from a theory, and then we infer something about the validity of that theory as a whole. Thus, inductive reasoning carries us from the observations or interventions in Figure 2.1 to some assessment regarding the validity of the theory. The logic of scientific analysis involves an interplay between deduction, or deriving testable hypotheses, and induction, or assessing theories based on tests of hypotheses derived from the theories.

At times, inductive research is conducted without the benefit of previous deductive reasoning. This occurs in descriptive or exploratory research, where no theory exists from which to deduce hypotheses. In the absence of theory, we begin to make observations and then develop some theoretical propositions that would be plausible given those observations. For example, practitioners may observe that clients with problem pregnancies tend to come from families with low socioeconomic status. Based on the assumption that the parent–child bond is weaker in low socioeconomic families and, therefore, that such parents have less control over their children, the practitioners could inductively conclude that a weak parent–child bond leads to an increased risk of unwanted pregnancy. In other words, the observations are used to infer a proposition regarding the causes of unwanted pregnancies. In fact, as we explore in more detail in Chapter 9, some researchers claim that such inductive approaches can be superior to deductive approaches, because the former can involve fewer hidden assumptions or preconceived notions on the part of the scientist. Some of these inductive approaches permit the data to shape the theory rather than having a preconceived theory impose meaning on the data. Inductive research of this sort can serve as a foundation for building a theory, and that theory, in turn, can serve as a source of testable hypotheses through deductive reasoning. Thus, induction and deduction are key links in the chain of scientific reasoning, and they parallel the reasoning process that is found in practice intervention.

Research in Practice 2.2 describes research projects that highlight many of the issues discussed in the previous two sections regarding the use of theories and hypotheses in research and the importance of inductive and deductive reasoning.

RESEARCH IN PRACTICE 2.2 Practice Effectiveness: Social Theory and Burnout Among Social Workers

A social worker: I began to despise everyone and could not conceal my contempt.

A psychiatric nurse: Sometimes you can't help but feel "Damn it, they want to be there, and they're fuckers, so let them stay there." You really put them down . . .

A social worker: I find myself caring less and possessing an extremely negative attitude.

[Quoted in Maslach, 1979, p. 217]

These are hardly the caring, empathic reactions one would expect from human service workers, yet negative attitudes toward clients are expressed at some point by many social workers, nurses, psychologists, and others. The problem of burnout is of considerable concern to human service professionals, because it can impair their ability to deal with client problems. *Burnout* refers to a service worker's emotional disengagement from clients, dissatisfaction with the job, feelings of worthlessness, and physical and interpersonal problems (Arches, 1991). Commonsense approaches often focus on the personal abilities of human service workers to explain why they suffer burnout: They lack sufficient emotional strength or distance from clients, or they overidentify or overempathize with their clients. Rather than relying on such intuition, scientific researchers turn to theories for direction in identifying variables that might play a part.

When social work researcher W. David Harrison (1980) approached these issues, he turned to *role theory*, which views human behavior as resulting from conformity to expectations that are associated with particular roles. One of the tenets of role theory is that role expectations should be clear, unambiguous, and achievable. Furthermore, the various expectations associated with a role should not conflict with one another. Previous research suggested that situations in which role expectations are conflicting, incompatible, or unclear lead to personal stress and dissatisfaction. Role theory enabled Harrison to identify two different kinds of role difficulty: *Role conflict* refers to a situation in which conflicting and incompatible demands are placed on a person in a role, and *role ambiguity* refers to a lack of clarity in terms of what is expected of a person in a particular role. Harrison's research on child protective service workers showed that role difficulties, especially role ambiguity, produced job dissatisfaction and burnout among these social workers.

(continued)

In contrast, Joan Arches (1991) turned to *theories of organizational structure and change*, reasoning that recent developments in social service organizations might have an impact on burnout. These theories suggest that increasing bureaucratization and centralization in organizations can reduce workers' feelings of autonomy, and in turn, this can contribute to the job dissatisfaction that often is a part of burnout. Arches's research then provided evidence that this was the case, offering further verification for those organizational theories.

Burnout continues to be a topic of interest to social scientists and human service practitioners throughout the world. Peter Janssen and his colleagues at Utrecht University in the Netherlands reviewed the extensive body of research on burnout that has accumulated over the past few decades and designed a study of Dutch nurses (Janssen, Schaufeli, & Houkes, 1999). Their research examined work-related and individual determinants of burnout by using *conservation of resources theory* as a framework. This theory focuses on the impact of work-related demands and resources on different dimensions of burnout. They found that a scarcity of resources, in the form of excess job demands and work overload, increased emotional exhaustion (one dimension of burnout) but not depersonalization (another dimension of burnout).

Thus, the theoretical considerations of role theory, organizational theory, and conservation of resources theory do not point toward excessive empathy or emotional weakness as the culprits in burnout among human service workers. Rather, the organizational and role structures that surround them are important. These investigations illustrate the importance of grounding research in theory, because it is theory that suggests which variables might be important and how they might relate to one another. Theory also shows how hypotheses can be developed through deductive reasoning. Once confirmed, the hypotheses of these researchers provide support, through inductive reasoning, for the interpretations of these theories in regard to the causes of burnout in the human services. Based on this slow, methodical accumulation of knowledge, we should eventually establish a solid foundation from which to develop programs to alleviate the problem of burnout among human service workers.

Types of Explanations

Beyond deciding whether to use deductive or inductive approaches, scientists also need to decide what type of explanations will be contained in the theory. Earlier in this chapter, we defined theories as involving explanations of some phenomena. An explanation is one way of gaining knowledge of something; it tells why something happens or specifies the conditions under which something occurs. Theories can focus on two different types of explanations (Miller, 1986; Nagel, 1961).

Nomothetic Explanations. Nomothetic explanations focus on a class of events and attempt to specify the conditions that seem common to all those events. We will use the social control theory of deviant behavior as an illustration. Social control theory argues, in part, that delinquent behaviors such as shoplifting are produced by weak attachments to parents. A nomothetic explanation, then, might attempt to prove that all juveniles who shoplift have weak attachments to their parents. The focus of the explanation is on understanding the entire category of youth who shoplift. These explanations do not focus on understanding all the causes of a phenomenon. In fact, control theory would recognize that a complex behavior such as shoplifting probably has many causes other than weak social bonds and that other theories would be necessary to locate and identify those factors. For nomothetic explanations, knowledge results from an understanding of a particular cause in relation to a class of events.

Nomothetic explanations attempt to develop knowledge that can be generalized beyond a single study or set of circumstances. In a sense, a nomothetic explanation is designed to produce the conclusion that weak attachment to parents in all cases increases the likelihood that shoplifting will result. This does not mean that every person who experiences weak attachment will shoplift; however, it does mean that those people have a higher probability of engaging in shoplifting. To put it another way, a randomly selected group of teens with weak parental attachments will have a higher rate of shoplifting than a randomly selected group with strong attachments will. The explanation or knowledge that is gained is probabilistic in nature: It tells us something about the probability of events occurring. The knowledge gained is about the aggregate, or the whole group, rather than about specific individuals in the group.

Once you understand what nomothetic explanations consist of, you can begin to see their weaknesses. One weakness is that you cannot say for sure what will happen in any particular case or to any specific person. You cannot say whether Joe Smith, who has experienced weak parental attachment, will become a shoplifter. A second weakness is that you cannot make any claims of knowing the totality of causes that produced some event or phenomenon. So, the knowledge, though valuable, is incomplete. There may be, for example, some key factors that must occur in combination with weak parental attachments to produce shoplifting.

Idiographic Explanations. Idiographic explanations focus on a single person, event, or situation and attempt to specify all the conditions that helped produce it. An idiographic explanation of shoplifting, for example, might focus on one juvenile who shoplifts and attempt to understand the multiple factors that contributed to bringing about the shoplifting behavior in that person. The focus of the explanation is on a particular, unique individual or situation. These explanations do not attempt to understand all instances of shoplifting; in fact, they recognize that other shoplifters may be propelled by a different combination of causes. For idiographic explanations, knowledge results from a thorough understanding of the particular.

Idiographic explanations see causality in terms of a complex pattern of factors that combine over a period of time to produce an outcome. To truly understand something, researchers need

to comprehend that whole patterned sequence, the whole complex context in which something occurs. When the nomothetic approach isolates particular variables for study, knowledge is incomplete for two reasons. First, some factors or variables have not been included in the investigation. Second, the isolating approach cannot see how the combination of, or the interaction among, the various elements plays a critical role in producing an outcome. It may be, for example, that weak parental bonds produce shoplifting only when they combine or interact with a host of other factors. In fact, it may be that the particular combination of factors that produces shoplifting in one person is unique and does not occur in other cases. It also may be that each distinct case of shoplifting is produced by a unique combination of factors. In other words, the explanation or knowledge that we gain is idiosyncratic.

Nomothetic explanations are probabilistic in nature, but idiographic explanations are deterministic in that the event being studied, such as shoplifting, actually did occur in the case being studied. In addition, the idiographic explanation identifies the causes that determined that outcome.

As with nomothetic explanations, idiographic explanations have weaknesses. One major fault is their limited generalizability. With such explanations, it is difficult to determine whether knowledge can be extended beyond the particular case or situation being studied.

Combining Explanations. Because each type of explanation has its strengths and its limitations, you might have guessed that our conclusion is going to be that neither type is inherently better than the other. As we alluded to in the beginning of this chapter with the excerpt from *Through the Looking Glass,* numerous routes to gaining knowledge about the world exist, and each type of explanation provides us with a valuable, though incomplete, route. In later chapters, we will see that some research methodologies, such as surveys and experiments, tend to be used to develop nomothetic explanations and that other methodologies, such as field research, in-depth interviewing, and historical comparative research, often are used to develop idiographic explanations. The point is to understand the logic of each type of explanation and to be aware that conclusions supported by research using both types of explanations are more complete than if the research only uses one type.

Paradigms in Science

Over the centuries, philosophers and scientists have debated the nature of reality and how people can know that reality (Couvalis, 1997; Miller, 1986). These have been controversial issues for scientists who study the physical world, but they are even more contentious among social scientists, who study human beings and their psychological and social reality. Part of the reason for this heightened contention is the belief that human beings are different from the natural world of physical objects and events. People emote, remember, speculate, love, and hate—they think about what is happening to them and have feelings about it. People refuse to behave the way a scientist hypothesizes that they might. People do the unexpected or the unpredictable. Atoms, molecules, and chemical compounds do not have these elusive properties, and this is one of the reasons why natural scientists often can make certain nonprobabilistic predictions about what will happen: Under a certain set of conditions, all water molecules, for example, will freeze when the temperature drops below 0°C. Thus far, however, social scientists have been unable to make such statements about social reality.

Another reason that the issue of how we know the world has been controversial among social scientists is that the scientists who study social reality are people themselves, with personal values, goals, desires, and reactions to what they observe. These personal matters may interfere with their ability to comprehend the world accurately. Going a step further, the scientific endeavor is itself a social process, part of the social world that social scientists attempt to understand. After all, scientific work can advance one's career, help one make a living, and move one up (or down) in the stratification system. In doing their scientific work, scientists may be influenced by a variety of social and psychological factors that routinely influence other human beings in their social endeavors.

What does all this mean? For one thing, science is a much more complicated—and, in many respects, a much messier—enterprise than many people recognize. For another, a number of competing perspectives exist concerning the issues of how society works and what implications this has for how the scientific endeavor works. In fact, historian Thomas Kuhn (1970), in a groundbreaking study of scientific work over many centuries, concluded that scientific activity is shaped by **paradigms**, which are general ways of thinking about how the world works and how we gain knowledge about the world. Paradigms are fundamental orientations, perspectives, or world views that often are not questioned or subjected to empirical tests. People may not even be aware that their thinking about the world is shaped by an orientation or world view. In his study of the history of science, Kuhn discovered that, although paradigms change over time, scientific research at any given moment was shaped by the paradigm that was dominant at that time. Research that fell outside that paradigm was considered to be inappropriate, irrelevant, oddball, or just plain wrong. In a sense, the world of paradigms falls outside the scientific realm in that issues are not accepted or rejected on the basis of empirical evidence; instead, some things are considered to be true—and others false—because it is obvious that that is how things work. Evidence supporting the paradigm will be accepted and competing evidence either ignored or rejected.

At the risk of oversimplification, we can classify the paradigms in the social sciences into two general categories: *positivist approaches*, and a number of different approaches that we will call *nonpositivist approaches* (Alford, 1998; Benton, 1977; Prasad, 2015; Smart, 1976). Keep in mind that these viewpoints are not necessarily mutually exclusive; people may adopt ideas from more than one of them at the same time. In addition, one could agree with some parts of a paradigm but disagree with other parts of the same paradigm. We address this issue early in the book, because it is a debate that arises repeatedly as we discuss different research methodologies.

Positivist Approaches. Positivism (sometimes also called **logical empiricism**) argues that the world exists independently of people's perceptions of it and that science uses objective techniques to discover what exists in the world (Blaikie, 2007; Durkheim, 1938; Halfpenny, 1982). Astronomers, for example, use telescopes to discover stars and galaxies, which exist regardless of whether we are aware of them. So, too, scientists can study human beings in terms of observable behaviors that can be recorded using objective techniques. Recording people's sex, age, height, weight, or socioeconomic position is a legitimate and objective measurement technique—the equivalent of the physicist measuring the temperature, volume, or mass of some liquid or solid. For the positivist, quantifying these measurements—for example, assessing the average age of a group or looking at the percentage of a group that is male—is merely a precise way of describing and summarizing an objective reality. Such measurement provides a solid, objective foundation for understanding human social behavior. Limiting study to observable behaviors and using objective techniques, positivists argue, is most likely to produce systematic and repeatable research results that are open to refutation by other scientists.

The natural and social world is governed by natural and social rules and regularities that give it pattern, order, and predictability. The goal of research in the natural and social sciences is to discover laws about how the world works and to express those discovered regularities in the deductive theories and propositions that are discussed in this chapter. As scientists conduct research, they move progressively closer to the truth, which involves uncovering the laws and patterns that underlie objective reality. So, at least in its ideal form, science is an objective search for the truth in which human values are a hindrance whose impact should be limited if not eliminated. Values can only interfere with the objective search for truth. For example, Emile Durkheim, an early sociologist, was a strong believer that sociologists could study the social world in much the same way that physical scientists could study the physical world. Durkheim believed that there were "social facts" that social scientists could observe and then use those observations to discover the social laws that govern the social world. He believed that once we

discover these social laws, we will be able to both explain and predict human social behavior.

Of the various paradigms that we will review, positivism clearly is the most widely held view among natural scientists and, to a lesser degree, among social scientists. Among social scientists, those who adopt the positivist stance often tend to use certain kinds of research methodologies. For example, they tend toward **quantitative research**, which involves measurement of phenomena using numbers and counts. They also tend to use deductive and nomothetic explanations, experimental designs, and survey research. It is important not to oversimplify the link between a paradigm and the preferred research methodology, however, because positivists at times use **qualitative research**, which involves data in the form of words, pictures, descriptions, or narratives rather than numbers and counts. They also use inductive or idiographic explanations and field observations when these are appropriate to a research question.

Despite the popularity and dominance of the positivist paradigm, it has been subject to considerable criticism over the years. Some of this criticism arises out of empirical studies by social scientists of exactly how science operates (Bhattacharya, 2017; Galison & Stump, 1996; Lynch & Bogen, 1997; Shapin, 1995). What many of these researchers find is that what scientists actually do looks quite different from what the positivist paradigm says science should look like. This has led some critics to conclude that the positivist model is an idealized conception of science rather than an accurate description of it. Based on these and other concerns, alternative paradigms have emerged.

Nonpositivist Approaches. One prominent nonpositivist approach to science is what is called the interpretive approach. **Interpretive approaches** (also called interactionist or *Verstehen* approaches) posit that social reality has a subjective component that arises out of the creation and exchange of social meanings during the process of social interaction. Social science must have ways to understand this subjective reality (Flood, 2010; Holstein & Gubrium, 1994; Smith, 1989; Wilson, 1970). Interpretivists argue that the objective, quantitative approaches of positivism miss this very important part of the human experience: the subjective and personal meanings that people attach to themselves and what they do. Reality is seen as something emergent and in constant flux that arises out of the creation and exchange of social meanings during the process of social interaction. Rather than seeing reality as something apart from human perceptions, interpretive social science sees reality—or, at least, social reality—as created out of human perception and the interpretation of meaning. These kinds of ideas led many 19th-century and early 20th-century theorists, such as Wilhelm Dilthey, Ernst Troeltsch, and Max Weber, to conclude that social life cannot be understood by the same method that is used to study the natural world (Barnes, 1948).

Weber, for example, argued that we need to look not only at what people do but also at what they think and feel about what is happening to them (Weber, 1925/1957). This "meaning" or "feeling" or "interpretive" dimension cannot be adequately captured through objective, quantitative measurement techniques. Researchers need to gain what Weber called *Verstehen,* or a subjective understanding. They need to view and experience the situation from the perspective of the people themselves, "to walk a mile in their shoes." They need to talk to the people at length and immerse themselves in their lives so that they can experience the highs and lows, the joys and sorrows, the triumphs and tragedies as seen from the perspective of the people being studied. Researchers need to see how individuals experience and give meaning to what is happening to them. Interpretive research methods provide an understanding through empathy or fellow feeling, whereas positivist methods provide understanding through abstract explanation. Yet, the important point is that both methods provide an understanding of the world, and both are a part of the scientific enterprise.

Qualitative research methods attempt to gain access to that personal, subjective experience; for interpretivists, quantitative research by its very nature misses this important dimension of social reality. Positivists, for their part, do not necessarily deny the existence or importance of subjective experiences, but they do question whether the subjective interpretations of the *Verstehen* method have scientific validity.

According to the interpretivist approach, regularity and pattern in social life does not result from objective social laws that exist apart from the human experience and are discovered by scientists. Instead, pattern and predictability arise out of mutually created systems of meaning that emerge from social interaction (De Jaegher, Peräkylä, & Stevanovic, 2016; Rabinow & Sullivan, 1987; Roscoe, 1995). Regularity and pattern are created and maintained by people; they are not imposed by external force. Proponents of interpretive approaches argue that qualitative research methods enable the researcher to approximate *Verstehen,* an understanding of the subjective experiences of people. Of course, actual access to such experience is impossible; thoughts and feelings, by their very nature, are private. Even when someone says how he or she feels, the speaker has objectified that subjective experience into words and, thus, changed it. Researchers, however, can gain some insight into subjective experiences by immersing themselves in the lives and daily experiences of the people they study. By experiencing the same culture, the same values, the same hopes and fears, researchers are in a better position to take on the point of view of these people. Despite its focus on subjective experiences, however, such research is still empirical in the sense that it is grounded in observation. Qualitative researchers consider their qualitative observations and conclusions to be no less systematic or scientific than the more positivistic quantitative research techniques. Although positivists would argue that subjective meaning is difficult to quantify and study objectively, interpretive researchers would argue that it is, nonetheless, a key part of human social reality.

Another important difference between positivists and interpretivists has to do with the role of science: Positivists argue that scientists merely discover what exists in the world, but some interpretivists claim that scientists actually help create social reality through their scientific work (Knorr, 1981; Scotland, 2012). As researchers make observations, gather data, and draw conclusions, their activities contribute to the construction of patterns of meaning. Scientific principles and laws about social behavior become another aspect of reality that can influence people's behavior. Even something as simple as computing the average age of a group creates a new reality: Instead of recognizing that some people in the group are 22 years old, others 34 years old, and still others 43 years old, we now say that the "average age of the group is 36.7 years." This summary statement gives the impression—and creates the reality—that the group members share something in common in terms of age and that we know something very precise about their ages. That sense of commonality or precision, however, comes from the numbers created by the scientist, not from reality. In addition, though the average appears to be very precise, it actually is less precise than listing all the ages of the group members.

The interpretive approach focuses more on inductive and idiographic theory construction than on deductive and nomothetic approaches, considering the theories to emerge out of people's experiences rather than viewing them as abstractions developed by scientists. Understanding and truth come from an empathic grasp of the social meanings of a setting rather than from statistical analysis and abstract generalization to large numbers of cases. Once again, however, the link between paradigms and research approaches is not mutually exclusive. At times, interpretive social scientists do deductive and nomothetic theory construction, and they have even been known to use quantitative methods when appropriate.

Other nonpositivist characterizations of science exist as well. For example, critical and feminist approaches to research argue that science is inevitably linked to inequitable distributions of power and resources. These approaches posit that groups can and do use science to enhance their position in society and that patterns of dominance and subordination may exist between researchers and those on whom they conduct research. Other nonpositivist critiques are addressed in later chapters. At this point, we simply want to raise the controversy regarding positivist and nonpositivist views of science to stress that science and scientific research are more complicated than you might have originally thought. The goal for the student should not be to attempt to resolve these disputes or to choose

among the paradigms. Instead, the goal should be to understand the dimensions of the debate, to recognize how the paradigms are similar to or different from one another, and to comprehend the implications of each paradigm for the research process. In addition, the paradigms are not completely exclusionary of one another. All the paradigms agree with much of what will be covered in this book. For example, all the paradigms base their search for knowledge on systematic observation, and all agree that scientific work should be open and public. Of course, they may not always agree on what makes observations systematic, but there is not total agreement within each paradigm about that issue, either.

Another reason why the student need not adopt a preferred paradigm is that many researchers do not choose a particular perspective to follow exclusively (Alford, 1998). Many researchers find that each of the approaches offers some insights into social life and the scientific process that the others ignore. They move back and forth among the paradigms, using the best that each has to offer in understanding a particular aspect of human social life.

CAUSE-AND-EFFECT RELATIONSHIPS

One of the more important yet difficult tasks in scientific research is the search for causes—that is, the reasons *why* particular forms of behavior occur. Why do child abuse and spousal abuse occur? Why do some juveniles become delinquent, whereas others present no behavior problems? Why do some people exhibit symptoms of mental illness and others appear to be psychologically stable?

Discovering causal relationships is a difficult task, because causality cannot be directly observed. Rather, it must be inferred from the observation of other factors. Because of this, the philosopher John Kemeny has labeled causality "the mysterious force" (Kemeny, 1959, p. 49). We cannot see it, feel it, or hear it, but we often assume that it is there—and many scientists search for causality with hopefulness and tenacity. This search is a controversial task, because some philosophers, notably Bertrand Russell (1953), have argued for excluding the notion of causality from scientific investigation altogether. These people opt for restricting ourselves to description and analysis of "associations" without the implication that a "mysterious force" called causality lurks behind the scenes and orchestrates the actions of people and things. This controversy is long-standing; we do not presume to resolve it here. Nonetheless, it is important to understand the criteria that need to be satisfied if one wants to infer that one event caused another.

By **causality**, we mean that some independent variable (X) is the factor, or one of several factors, whose change produces variation in a dependent variable (Y). As noted, causality can only be inferred. We can observe the relationships among things in the world, and from that, we can infer or deduce that changes in one factor are causing changes in another. However, it is always an inference. To infer the existence of a causal relationship, one must demonstrate the following:

1. A statistical association between the independent and dependent variables must exist.
2. The independent variable must occur prior in time to the dependent variable.
3. The relationship between independent and dependent variables must not be spurious; that is, the relationship must not disappear when the effects of other variables are taken into account.

We will consider each requirement of causal inference in the context of an issue that is much in the news today—the campaign to reduce cigarette smoking. Over the years, there have been reports in the media about the negative impact of cigarette smoking on people's health. Some argue that making these reports public as part of a health campaign can motivate people to quit smoking. Table 2.1 presents hypothetical data that seem to show a link between reading such reports about smoking and actually quitting smoking: 50% of those who read the reports quit smoking, compared to only 27% of those who do not read the reports. Finding such a statistical relationship satisfies the first criterion for establishing a causal relationship.

The second requirement, that the independent variable occurs prior in time to the dependent,

TABLE 2.1 Effectiveness of Reading Media Reports on Smoking Cessation

		Person Reads Report	
		Yes	No
Person Quits Smoking	Yes	200 (50%)	135 (27%)
	No	200 (50%)	365 (73%)
	Totals	400 (100%)	500 (100%)

often is not as easy to establish. A major factor in this is the nature of the study. Some research techniques, such as the experiment or participant observation, are inherently *longitudinal*, which means that the researcher is in a position to trace the development of behavior as it unfolds over time. In these cases, establishing the time sequence of events generally is simple. Questions of temporal order are more difficult to resolve when dealing with *cross-sectional* data, such as surveys, in which measurements of the independent and dependent variables occur at the same time. This is especially true if the question of temporal sequence is not addressed until after the data have been collected. It sometimes is possible to sort out the time sequence of variables in survey data by asking additional questions. If the researcher does not gather the necessary information at the time of the survey, however, then establishing the appropriate time order of the variables may be impossible—hence the emphasis on the importance of carefully considering issues of data analysis when originally developing a research design.

The data in our illustration may suffer from this problem. One interpretation is that reading reports is the independent variable that influences whether people quit smoking, the dependent variable. For this interpretation to be correct, the reports would have to have been publicized before the people quit smoking. If the respondents were not asked when they quit smoking, then it would be impossible to say whether they quit smoking before or after reading the reports. Obviously, if they quit smoking before reading the reports, then such health campaigns could not have caused their change in behavior. In our example, without knowing the temporal sequence, one could argue logically for either factor being the cause of the other. Obviously, the health campaign could encourage people to quit smoking if they become frightened by learning the dire consequences of their habit. However, those who quit smoking also could be happy with and proud of their victory and might enjoy reading reports on what could have happened to them had they not quit smoking. In this second scenario, quitting smoking would be the independent variable that increases the likelihood that people will read reports about the health threat of smoking, the dependent variable.

The final criterion necessary for inferring causality is that the relationship between the independent and dependent variables not be *spurious,* or disappear when the effects of other variables are considered. The logic of causal and spurious relationships is compared in Figure 2.2. This often is the most difficult of the three criteria to satisfy. In fact, one is never *totally* sure that some other variable—one you have not even considered—might not confound an apparent causal relationship. All that can be accomplished is to rule out as many extraneous variables as we can, to the point where it is unlikely a variable exists that could render a given relationship spurious or noncausal.

Considerable effort is expended during the design stage of research to control as many potentially troublesome extraneous variables as possible.

Experiments, for example, are particularly good for avoiding spurious relationships because of the high degree of control that the experimental situation affords the researcher. Surveys, on the other hand, provide far less control, such that several variables capable of producing spuriousness typically have to be considered during data analysis. Several statistical techniques exist to control extraneous variables when the data are analyzed.

Returning to our example of smoking cessation, suppose we had solved the time sequence problem and, thus, had satisfied the first two requirements for establishing a causal relationship. We would now begin to consider variables that might render the relationship spurious. One variable that might do this is the level of education of the people studied. (The logic of this is outlined in Figure 2.3.) Considerable research links education with health behavior. Generally, people with higher levels of education engage in more health-promoting activities, such as quitting smoking or getting regular exercise. How do we determine whether the link between report reading and smoking cessation is spurious? We introduce the level of education as a control variable, which is illustrated with our hypothetical data in Table 2.2, in which we have divided the respondents in Table 2.1 into those with at least a high school education and those with less than a high school education. First, we can see by examining the row totals in each table that education is related to health behavior: 60% of the better educated group have quit smoking, compared to only 19% of the less educated group. However, we are really interested in what happens

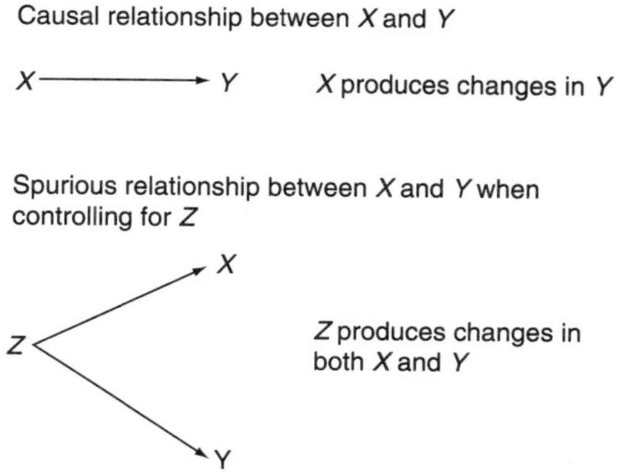

Causal relationship between X and Y

$X \longrightarrow Y$ X produces changes in Y

Spurious relationship between X and Y when controlling for Z

Z produces changes in both X and Y

Figure 2.2 Causal and spurious relationships.

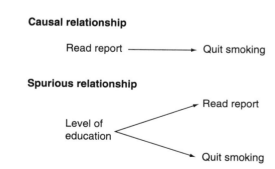

Figure 2.3 Causal and spurious relationships between reading a report and quitting smoking.

TABLE 2.2 Effectiveness of Reading Media Reports on Smoking Cessation, Controlling for Education

		Less Than High School Education		
		Person Reads Report		
		Yes	**No**	**Totals**
Person Quits Smoking	Yes	20 (20%)	75 (19%)	95 (19%)
	No	80 (80%)	325 (81%)	405 (81%)
	Totals	100 (100%)	400 (100%)	500

		High School Education or More		
		Person Reads Report		
		Yes	**No**	**Totals**
Person Quits Smoking	Yes	180 (60%)	60 (60%)	240 (60%)
	No	120 (40%)	40 (40%)	160 (40%)
	Totals	300 (100%)	100 (100%)	400

to the link between report reading and smoking cessation, and Table 2.2 shows that the relationship largely disappears: Within each educational group, the same percentage of people quit smoking among those who read the report as among those who did not. So, educational level, not whether one has read the report, influences a person's likelihood of quitting smoking. Furthermore, in our hypothetical example, educational level also influences whether one reads the report: 300 out of 400, or 75%, of those with a high school education read the report, compared with only 100 of 500, or 20%, of those with less than a high school education. So, in our example, the link between reading the report and quitting smoking is spurious; it occurs only because each of those two variables is affected by the same third variable.

If we had found the link between report reading and smoking cessation to be nonspurious when we controlled for education, could we conclude that the relationship was causal? The answer is no. We could not come to that conclusion—at least not yet. All that we would know was that the relationship remained when *one* alternative explanation was ruled out. Any other variables that could render the relationship spurious also would have to be investigated—and the relationship still hold—before we could argue with any confidence that it was, in fact, causal. (More intricacies of this sort of analysis are addressed in Chapter 15.)

We said at the outset that establishing the existence of causal relationships is difficult. Statistical relationships are easy to find but, on further investigation, all too frequently turn out to be spurious. The appropriate time sequence also can be problematic, especially with survey data. All in all, establishing causal relationships is a difficult but an important and challenging task.

REVIEW AND CRITICAL THINKING

Main Points

- Science is one source of knowledge, along with tradition, experience, common sense, and journalism, but it is a superior source of objective and accurate knowledge about the world.
- The five key characteristics of science are that it is empirical, systematic, provisional, objective, and searches for the causes of events. These crucial characteristics also are central features of scientifically based practice.
- Theories are sets of interrelated, abstract propositions that explain phenomena. Theories perform three major functions: They provide explanations, they guide research and practice, and they integrate observations from research.
- Concepts are mental constructs that symbolize ideas, persons, things, or events and form the basis for propositions and theories.
- Concepts are given both nominal definitions, which explain their meaning, and operational definitions, which indicate how they are measured. Care must be taken in developing operational definitions in research on minorities to ensure that such definitions do not lead to a distorted view of these populations.
- Hypotheses are statements that predict relationships between two or more variables and are tested through research.
- Theories are developed and elaborated by going back and forth between the abstract, conceptual level and the concrete, empirical level, using either deductive reasoning or inductive reasoning.
- Theories also differ in the types of explanations they seek, some nomothetic and others idiographic.
- Two paradigms, or ways of understanding how we know the world, are predominant in the social sciences: positivism and nonpositivism. Each tends to be associated with particular research methodologies. The goal for the student in this debate should be to understand the dimensions of the debate, to recognize how the paradigms are similar to or different from one another, and to comprehend the implications of each paradigm for the research process.
- Causality means that some independent variable produces variation in a dependent variable.
- To demonstrate a causal relationship, one must establish a statistical association between two variables, show that the independent variable occurs first temporally, and demonstrate that the relationship is not spurious.

IMPORTANT TERMS FOR REVIEW

Causality	Dependent variable	Independent variable
Common sense	Experiential knowledge	Inductive reasoning
Concepts	Hypotheses	Interpretive approaches
Deductive reasoning	Idiographic explanations	Logical empiricism

Nominal definitions
Nomothetic explanations
Operational definitions
Paradigms
Positivism

Propositions
Qualitative research
Quantitative research
Science
Theory

Traditional knowledge
Variables
Verification
Verstehen

CRITICAL THINKING

This chapter covers some of the building blocks of the scientific method: theories, propositions, hypotheses, concepts, variables, and so on. In using these building blocks, scientists try to be very careful when describing and analyzing the world in order to avoid misunderstanding. You can utilize some of these same building blocks in trying to critically analyze information for policy or practice purposes or for your everyday life. The following are critical thinking questions raised at the beginning of the chapter and some ideas for how they relate to social work practice. Students are encouraged to develop their own answers to these questions.

What are the different ways humans gain knowledge and know truth? There are multiple ways of knowing facts; however, some are more accurate than others are. These can be based on experience, ideology, books, dogma, philosophy, journalist's opinions, and many more. Although there are many different ways to know things, the scientific method stands as the gold standard for knowing truth, because it is a systematic way of obtaining knowledge.

What are the different steps in the scientific method? The scientific method consists of the following concepts: It is a method to gain knowledge. Everything is open to question. Knowledge is subject to refutation. Empirical evidence is based on observation, and evidence is systematic and comprehensive. Finally, it emphasizes the pursuit of objectivity.

How does knowing the scientific method help the relationship between research and practice? Social workers use the scientific method to understand evidence (that is, the body of knowledge from scientific inquiry) that is pertinent to their client and/or agency. This evidence helps social workers know which best practices are available for their clients that would do the least amount of harm.

EVALUATING COMPETENCY (FROM THE COUNCIL ON SOCIAL WORK EDUCATION [CSWE] 2015 EDUCATIONAL POLICY AND ACCREDITATION STANDARDS [EPAS])

Competency 2: Engaging Diversity and Difference in Practice

- Why is it important for social researchers to use theories that empower marginalized and oppressed populations?

Competency 4: Engaging in Practice-Informed Research and Research-Informed Practice

- Why is it important to use the scientific method when conducting research to inform practice?
- How does the scientific method help social research improve practice and practice improve research?

Competency 9: Evaluate Practice With Individuals, Families, Groups, Organizations, and Communities

- How does science help improve practice with individuals, families, groups, organizations, and communities?

SELF-ASSESSMENT
. . . .

1. The scientific method involves:
   a. Obtaining objective knowledge about the world through systematic observation.
   b. The accumulation of knowledge from experience.
   c. Knowledge based on habit, custom, and repetition.
   d. A closed system of beliefs and values that shapes the understanding and behavior of those who believe in it.
2. Humans gain knowledge and truth through:
   a. Experience, tradition, common sense, journalism, and the scientific method.
   b. Research osmosis.
   c. Authority figures.
   d. Discipline, hard work, and integrity.
3. Theories are:
   a. A set of ideas that are not related.
   b. Impossible to discover and understand.
   c. A set of interrelated, abstract propositions or statements that offers an explanation of some phenomenon.
   d. Experiences that are generalized from what we learn from others.
4. What are research paradigms?
   a. General ways of thinking about how the world works and how we gain knowledge about the world and in research are known as positivism and interpretivism.
   b. A lens you look through.
   c. A collection of research over time about different people.
   d. Research that eliminates perspectives and world views.
5. Hypotheses refers to:
   a. A general theory of research open to questions.
   b. An examination of a series of research questions.
   c. A testable statement of presumed relationships between two or more concepts.
   d. A new idea and phenomenon.

6. The purpose and functions of theories are:
   a. To prove a concept or idea.
   b. A testable assertion about reality guided by research, which is continually being added to.
   c. Only relatable to research and not practice.
   d. To prove ideas are not correct.
7. Developing hypotheses refers to:
   a. A series of questions based on a researcher's experiences.
   b. Testable statements of the relationship between two or more concepts.
   c. Testing unrelated concepts and variables.
   d. Something a researcher thinks of after the analysis of his or her study.
8. Deduction refers to:
   a. Inferring a conclusion from some premises or proposition.
   b. Inferring something about an entire group based on our knowledge.
   c. Researchers using graphs and charts to prove their position.
   d. No theory or ideas before research begins.
9. Causality means:
   a. An independent variable is the factor, or one of several factors, whose change produces variation in a dependent variable.
   b. A variable can be directly observed.
   c. A researcher knows that one variable must cause the other variable to change.
   d. An assumption that change has happened, because you can feel it.
10. Scientific practice refers to which of the following?
    a. Effective human service practice should have characteristics that parallel those of science.
    b. Human service practice should engage in research, but should leave that up to researchers to do.
    c. Practice should always come first before science.
    d. Science and human service practice would be better served to stay separate.

ANSWER KEY FOR SELF-ASSESSMENT QUIZ

1. **a.** Obtaining objective knowledge about the world through systematic observation.
2. **a.** Experience, tradition, common sense, journalism, and the scientific method.
3. **c.** A set of interrelated, abstract propositions or statements that offers an explanation of some phenomenon.
4. **a.** General ways of thinking about how the world works and how we gain knowledge about the world and in research are known as positivism and interpretivism.
5. **c.** A testable statement of presumed relationships between two or more concepts.
6. **b.** A testable assertion about reality guided by research, which is continually being added to.
7. **b.** Testable statements of the relationship between two or more concepts.
8. **a.** Inferring a conclusion from some premises or proposition.
9. **a.** An independent variable is the factor, or one of several factors, whose change produces variation in a dependent variable.
10. **a.** Effective human service practice should have characteristics that parallel those of science.

FOR FURTHER READING

Averett, P., Hegde, A., & Smith, J. (2017). Lesbian and gay parents in early childhood settings: A systematic review of the research literature. *Journal of Early Childhood Research, 15*(1), 34–46. doi:10.1177/1476718x15570959

Bengtson, V. L., Acock. A. C., Allen, K. R., Dilworth-Anderson, P., & Klein, D. M. (Eds.). (2005). *Sourcebook of family theory and research.* Thousand Oaks, CA: Sage. This reference work on theory and methods for family scholars demonstrates how the development of theory is crucial to the future of family research. The work focuses on the process of theory building and designing research.

Glaser, B. G., & Strauss, A. L. (1967). *The discovery of grounded theory.* New York, NY: Aldine. An excellent book about the virtues and procedures of developing theoretical propositions from data. This approach emphasizes qualitative research and induction.

Hoover, K. R., & Donovan, T. (2011). *The elements of social scientific thinking* (10th ed.). Belmont, CA: Wadsworth/Cengage Learning. A brief and readable initiation into social science thinking and research. It is intended for those who use the results of research and for those just getting into the field.

Merton, R. K. (1968). *Social theory and social structure* (2nd ed.). New York, NY: Free Press. A classic statement by a sociologist of the relationship between theory and research.

Ponterotto, J. G. (2005). Qualitative research in counseling psychology: A primer on research paradigms and philosophy of science. *Journal of Counseling Psychology, 52*(2), 126–136. doi:10.1037/0022-0167.52.2.126

Shoemaker, P. J., Tankard, J. W., Jr., & Lasorsa, D. L. (2004). *How to build social science theories.* Thousand Oaks, CA: Sage. This book traces theories from their most rudimentary building blocks (terminology and definitions) through multivariable theoretical statements, models, the role of creativity in theory building, and how theories are used and evaluated. The book includes a discussion of concepts and their theoretical and operational definitions.

Turner, J. H. (Ed.). (1989). *Theory building in sociology: Assessing theoretical accumulation.* Newbury Park, CA: Sage. In this collection of essays, one of the foremost U.S. theoreticians in sociology addresses a key assertion of the positivist approach: Does knowledge accumulate through the deductive approach of theory building and hypothesis testing?

Van de Ven, A. H. (2007). *Engaged scholarship: A guide for organizational and social research.* Oxford, UK: Oxford University Press. The author is a leading management researcher and writes from that perspective, but the issues he addresses are relevant to human service research as well. He especially addresses the issue of whether research findings and knowledge should be useful for science, practice, and policy. He also discusses how such research should be designed, carried out, and disseminated to achieve the twin goals of rigor and relevance.

Watts, D. J. (2011). *Everything is obvious* (*Once you know the answer).* New York, NY: Crown. This is an entertaining and insightful exploration of common sense as a source of knowledge—pointing to its weaknesses and failures as a foundation for thinking, reasoning, and planning.

REFERENCES

Alford, R. R. (1998). *The craft of inquiry: Theories, methods, evidence.* New York, NY: Oxford University Press.

Arches, J. (1991). Social structure, burnout, and job satisfaction. *Social Work, 36,* 202–206.

Barnes, H. E. (Ed). (1948). *An introduction to the history of sociology.* Chicago, IL: University of Chicago Press.

Bell, W. (1987). *Contemporary social welfare* (2nd ed.). New York, NY: Macmillan,

Benton, T. (1977). *Philosophical foundations of the three sociologies.* Boston, MA: Routledge & Kegan Paul.

Bhattacharya, K. (2017). *Fundamentals of qualitative research: A practical guide.* New York, NY: Routledge

Blaikie, N. (2007). *Approaches to social enquiry: Advancing knowledge.* Cambridge, UK: Polity Press.

Brady, J., & Kotkin, R. (2011). Creating lasting behavioral change through the generalization analysis worksheet. *Contemporary School Psychology, 15*(1), 131–137.

Bronowski, J. (1978). *The origins of knowledge and imagination.* New Haven, CT: Yale University Press.

Carroll, L. (1946). *Through the looking glass.* New York, NY: Random House.

Cohen, M. R., & Nagel, E. (1934). *An introduction to logic and scientific method.* New York, NY: Harcourt.

Committee on the Status of Women in Sociology. (1986). *The treatment of gender in research.* Washington, DC: American Sociological Association.

Couvalis, G. (1997). *The philosophy of science: Science and objectivity.* London, UK: Sage.

De Jaegher, H., Peräkylä, A., & Stevanovic, M. (2016). The co-creation of meaningful action: Bridging enaction and interactional sociology. *Philosophical Transactions of the Royal Society B: Biological Sciences, 371*(1693), 20150378. doi:10.1098/rstb.2015.0378

Durkheim, E. (1938). *Rules of the sociological method* (S. Solovay, Trans. & J. Mueller, Ed.). Chicago, IL: University of Chicago Press.

Erich, S., Leung, P., Kindle, P., & Carter, S. (2005). Gay and lesbian adoptive families: An exploratory study of family functioning, adoptive child's behavior, and familial support networks. *Journal of Family Social Work, 9,* 17–31. doi:10.1300/j039v09n01_02

Eschholz, S., Chiricos, T., & Gertz, M. (2003). The racial typification of crime and support for punitive measures. *Social Problems, 50,* 395–415. doi:10.1525/sp.2003.50.3.395

Federal Bureau of Investigation. (2012). *Uniform crime reports: Crime in the United States, 2011.* Washington, DC: U.S. Government Printing Office.

Flood, A. (2010). Understanding phenomenology. *Nurse Researcher, 17*(2), 7–15. doi:10.7748/nr2010.01.17.2.7.c7457

Galison, P., & Stump, D. (Eds.). (1996). *The disunity of science: Boundaries, contexts, and power.* Stanford, CA: Stanford University Press.

Goldberg, A. E. (2009). *Lesbian and gay parents and their children: Research on the family life cycle.* Washington, DC: American Psychological Association.

Golombok, S., & Tasker, F. (2015). Socioemotional development in changing families. In M. E. Lamb (Vol. Ed.), *Handbook of child psychology and developmental science: Vol. 3, Socioemotional processes* (7th ed., pp. 419–463). Retrieved from https://onlinelibrary.wiley.com/doi/10.1002/9781118963418.childpsy311

Gottman, J. S. (1990). Children of gay and lesbian parents. In F. W. Bozett & M. B. Sussman (Ed.), *Homosexuality and family relationships.* New York, NY: Harrington Park Press.

Halfpenny, P. (1982). *Positivism and sociology: Explaining social life*. London, UK: Allen & Unwin.

Harrison, W. D. (1980). Role strain and burnout in child-protective service workers. *Social Service Review, 54*, 31–44. doi:10.1086/643802

Haugaard, J. J., Palmer, M., & Wojslawowicz, J. C. (1999). Single-parent adoptions. *Adoption Quarterly, 2*(4), 65–74. doi:10.1300/j145v02n04_05

Hayes, S. C., Barlow, D. H., & Nelson-Gray, R. O. (1999). *The scientist practitioner: Research and accountability in the age of managed care* (2nd ed.). Boston, MA: Pearson.

Hepworth, D. H., & Larsen, J. (1990). *Direct social work practice*. Belmont, CA: Wadsworth.

Holstein, J. A., & Gubrium, J. F. (1994). Phenomenology, ethnomethodology, and interpretive practice. In N. Denzin & Y. Lincoln (Ed.), *Handbook of qualitative research*. Thousand Oaks, CA: Sage.

Janssen, P. P., Schaufeli, W.B., & Houkes, I. (1999). Work-related and individual determinants of the three burnout dimensions. *Work and Stress, 13*(1), 74–86. doi:10.1080/026783799296200

Kemeny, J. G. (1959). A philosopher looks at science. Princeton, NJ: Van Nostrand.

Knorr, K. (1981). *The manufacture of knowledge: An essay on the constructivist and contextual nature of science*. Oxford, UK: Pergamon Press.

Kuhn, T. (1970). *The structure of scientific revolutions* (2nd ed.). Chicago, IL: University of Chicago Press.

Lau-Barraco, C., & Collins, R. L. (2011). Social networks and alcohol use among nonstudent emerging adults: A preliminary study. *Addictive Behaviors, 36*, 47–54. doi:10.1016/j.addbeh.2010.08.017

Leung, P., Erich, S., & Kanenberg, H. (2005). A comparison of family functioning in gay/lesbian, heterosexual, and special needs adoptions. *Children and Youth Services Review, 27*, 1031–1044. doi:10.1016/j.childyouth.2004.12.030

Lewis, K. G. (1980). Children of lesbians: Their point of view. *Social Work, 25*, 198–203. doi:10.1093/sw/25.3.198

Lockhart, L. L. (1991). Spousal violence: A cross-racial perspective. In R. L. Hampton (Ed.), *Black family violence: Current research and theory*. Lexington, KY: Lexington Books.

Lynch, M., & Bogen, D. (1997). Sociology's asociological "Core": An examination of textbook sociology in light of the sociology of scientific knowledge. *American Sociological Review, 62*(3), 481–493. doi:10.2307/2657317

Maslach, C. (1979). Burned-out. In J. R. Folta & E. S. Deck (Eds.), *A sociological framework for patient care* (2nd ed.). New York, NY: Wiley.

McLanahan, S., & Sandefur, G. (1994). *Growing up with a single parent: What hurts, what helps*. Cambridge, UK: Harvard University Press.

Miller, L. P. (1986). The application of research to practice: A critique. *American Behavioral Scientist, 30*(1), 70–80. doi:10.1177/000276486030001008

Nagel, E. (1961). *The structure of science*. New York, NY: Harcourt, Brace & World.

Orsi, R. (2015). Predicting re-involvement for children adopted out of a public child welfare system. *Child Abuse and Neglect, 39*, 175–184. doi:10.1016/j.chiabu.2014.10.005

Prasad, P. (2015). *Crafting qualitative research: Working in the postpositivist traditions*. New York, NY: Routledge.

Rabinow, P., & Sullivan, W. M. (Eds.). (1987). *Interpretive social science: A second look*. Berkeley: University of California Press.

Reamer, F. G. (2006). *Social work values and ethics* (3rd ed.). New York, NY: Columbia University Press.

Roscoe, P. B. (1995). The perils of "Positivism" in cultural anthropology. *American Anthropologist, 97*(3), 492–504. doi:10.1525/aa.1995.97.3.02a00080

Rosen, A. (1996). The scientific practitioner revisited: Some obstacles and prerequisites for fuller implementation in practice. *Social Work Research, 20*(2), 105–111. doi:10.1093/swr/20.2.105

Rosenthal, R. (1991). Replication in behavioral research. In J. Neuliep (Ed.), *Replication research in the social sciences*. Newbury Park, CA: Sage.

Ruggles, P. (1990). *Drawing the line: Alternative poverty measures and their implications for public policy*. Washington, DC: Urban Institute Press.

Russell, B. (1953). On the notion of cause, with applications to the free-will problem. In H. Feigel & M. Brodbeck (Ed.), *Readings in the philosophy of science*. New York, NY: Appleton-Century-Crofts.

Schuckit, M. A. (2006). *Drug and alcohol abuse: A clinical guide to diagnosis and treatment* (6th ed). New York, NY: Springer Verlag.

Scotland, J. (2012). Exploring the philosophical underpinnings of research: Relating ontology and epistemology to the methodology and methods of the scientific, interpretive, and critical research paradigms. *English Language Teaching, 5*(9), 9–16. doi:10.5539/elt.v5n9p9

Shapin, S. (1995). Here and everywhere: Sociology of scientific knowledge. *Annual Review of Sociology, 21*(1), 289–321. doi:10.1146/annurev.soc.21.1.289

Skidmore, W. (1979). *Theoretical thinking in sociology.* Cambridge, UK: Cambridge University Press.

Smart, B. (1976). *Sociology, phenomenology, and Marxian analysis: A critical discussion of the theory and practice of a science of society.* Boston, MA: Routledge & Kegan Paul.

Smith, M. F. (1989). *Evaluability assessment: A practical approach.* Boston, MA: Kluwer Academic.

Stacey, J., & Biblarz, T. J. (2001). (How) does the sexual orientation of parents matter? *American Sociological Review, 66,* 159–183. doi:10.2307/2657413

Stein, J. (1964). *Fiddler on the roof.* New York, NY: Crown.

Straus, M., & Gelles, R. J. (1988). How violent are American families? Estimates from the national family violence resurvey and other studies. In G. Hotaling, D. Finkelhor, J. Kirkpatrick, & M. Straus (Ed.), *Family abuse and its consequences: New directions in research.* Newbury Park, CA: Sage.

Sullivan, T. J. (2012). *Introduction to social problems* (9th ed.). Boston, MA: Allyn & Bacon.

Sutherland, E. (1939). *Criminology.* Philadelphia, PA: Lippincott.

Tye, M. (2003). C. Lesbian, gay, bisexual, and transgender parents: Special considerations for the custody and adoption evaluator. *Family Court Review, 41,* 92–103. doi:10.1177/1531244502239355

Weber, M. (1957). *The theory of social and economic organization* (trans. A. M. Henderson & T. Parsons). New York, NY: Free Press. (Original work published 1925).

Wilson, T. (1970). Normative and interpretive paradigms in sociology. In J. Douglas (Ed.), *Understanding everyday life: Toward the reconstruction of sociological knowledge.* New York, NY: Aldine.

3

ETHICAL ISSUES IN SOCIAL RESEARCH

INTRODUCTION

About 10 years ago, two of the authors of this textbook (Timothy Hilton and Cornell DeJong) began a research project examining rural homelessness. They were faculty members at a university in a very rural area, Michigan's Upper Peninsula. When multiple community members and students raised the issue of homelessness in the local area (Marquette, Michigan), Hilton and DeJong decided this might be an interesting research topic. There was some discussion in the community about the need for a shelter. Some saw it as necessary. Others suggested there was no need for one because the homeless population in the area was small. Some feared a shelter might attract homeless from other communities to the community. A few community members even argued that a homeless shelter might reinforce "bad behavior" among young adults who would have an alternative to living at home and under their parents' rules.

Hilton and DeJong decided a good first step would be to identify homeless adults in the area and speak to them about their lives. This could help them better understand who was homeless in the area, how homeless adults survived in a rural area with limited human service and a harsh climate, which human services they used, their relationships with family and friends, and what unmet service needs they had. What they envisioned was a descriptive, qualitative research project with the goal of painting a picture of homelessness in the area. Ideally this research would help the community, including human service providers, better understand the homeless in the area so that they can be more responsive to their needs.

After designing a qualitative study consisting of in-depth interviews with homeless adults they began to think about submitting an application to their university's Institutional Review Board (IRB), which oversees compliance with ethical standards in research and helps ensure research subjects (here homeless adults completing an interview) have voluntarily consented to participate (without coercion) and are not subject to any unnecessary or excessive hardships, pain, or discomfort as a result of their participation.

Hilton began writing an application to the IRB. At first he thought this would be an easy process because all that was involved in this study were conversations with people about their day-to-day lives. They did not intend to ask particularly sensitive or personal information and they could easily keep the identities of people they interviewed hidden.

As he spoke with his colleagues and others about their study, however, he began to think more about potential risks to those participating in interviews. This was a small, tight-knit community. It is possible that reports, presentations, or articles they wrote based on these interviews would reveal details about the lives of some of the research participants that would clue some people into their identities. The researchers had planned to buy each participant lunch and pay them $20 in return for their participation. Some argued that this may be a form of coercion for potential participants who might otherwise decide not to share their stories but feel compelled to do so because they are desperate for food and money. Some people suggested that even simple conversations about day-to-day life can be hard for some homeless as they are forced to actively take stock of their lives or relive painful memories related to their current situations. Others suggested that we, as researchers, have an ethical obligation to give homeless participants information about resources in the area that might be useful to them. A few even suggested that the researchers may be obligated to give interviewees resources for counseling because the process of reflecting on their difficult lives may lead to painful emotions and conjure up difficult memories.

As Hilton and DeJong's experiences demonstrate, there are always risks and ethical considerations when doing research. On the other hand, research also has the potential to help people and communities address important issues. In this chapter, we address several ethical considerations in conducting research while focusing on strategies to minimize risks to participants. As you read this chapter, please consider the following questions: (a) What should researchers do to ensure they are engaging in ethically sound research? (b) How should risks and benefits be weighed when conducting research? (c) How do ethical standards and procedures used in research pertain to human service practitioners?

People are the subjects of social research, and because people have rights and feelings, special considerations apply in social research that do not confront the chemist studying molecules or the physicist investigating gravity. The Hilton and DeJong homeless study is a good example. As discussed earlier, this research involved some level of risk for participants, but it also had the potential to create some good for participants, the community at large, and perhaps even human services overall. Should this research proceed?

This question can be answered only by referring to some cultural, professional, or personal values that help us decide what is right and proper behavior. In the United States, three such values have been articulated in the Belmont Report (National Commission, 1978), a document that is considered to be a pillar of human research ethics. These principles are:

1. *Respect for persons:* We recognize the personal dignity and autonomy of individuals, and we should provide special protection of those persons with diminished autonomy.
2. *Beneficence:* We have an obligation to protect persons from harm by maximizing anticipated benefits and minimizing possible risks of harm.
3. *Justice:* The benefits and burdens of research should be distributed fairly.

Viewing the homelessness study in this context, some might argue that people's rights to autonomy and privacy preclude asking homeless persons detailed questions about their lives, especially in an in-depth interview. Is such an invasion of the privacy of homeless adults proper or acceptable? What about these individuals' right to confidentiality? Even if the researchers agree to remove names and other identifying information from any reports or presentations stemming from the research, there is always some chance that someone may recognize the research participant based on what he or she said. It is also possible, however unlikely, that participating in the research could bring harm to the research participant (perhaps stemming from emotional distress associated with discussing one's difficult life). As discussed earlier, this research has potential to help this community, but this benefit may come at a cost. A fundamental question that researchers should ask before conducting any study is who bears the cost of, and who benefits from, such research?

These are complicated issues. We do not presume that our statement of values is the final word or that the application of these values to particular cases is easy or straightforward. They do serve as an introduction, however, to the discussion of ethical issues in social research.

Ethics is the study of what is proper and improper behavior, of moral duty and obligation (Drewry, 2004). Moral principles can be grounded in philosophy, theology, or both. For social researchers, ethics involves the responsibilities that researchers bear toward those who participate in research, those who sponsor research, and those who are potential beneficiaries of research. It covers many specific issues. For example, is it ever permissible to harm people during the course of a research project? Should people who participate in a research project ever be deceived? Is it appropriate to suppress research findings that cast a sponsor's program in a negative light? Should researchers report to the police crimes they uncover while conducting a research project? The ethics of a given action depends on the standards used to assess the action, and those standards are grounded in human values. Because of this, ethical questions have few simple or final answers and no scientific tests that can show us whether actions are ethical. In fact, debate continues among scientists about ethical issues, because such issues involve matters of judgment and assessment.

Our purpose in this chapter is to identify the basic ethical issues in social research and to suggest some strategies for making sure that ethical considerations are attended to in the conduct and use of research.

THE MINORITY EXPERIENCE: THE NEED FOR ETHICAL STANDARDS

Ethical issues do not exist in a vacuum but, rather, within the context of a particular society and its historical development. Two events in the 20th century—one abroad and the other in the United States—served as major catalysts for efforts to codify a set of ethical standards for research.

The first event occurred in Europe during World War II: the heinous series of medical experiments conducted by the Nazis on Jews and others in concentration camps (Beauchamp, Faden, Wallace, & Walters, 1982). Prior to this, there had been no codification of scientific ethics, and researchers had been left largely to their own devices in deciding how to conduct their studies. The revelation of the German atrocities by the Nuremberg trials of 1945 and 1946 shocked the sensibilities of the world and left an indelible imprint on research ethics. The cruelty of these experiments is almost inconceivable. Healthy people were intentionally infected with such serious diseases as spotted fever or malaria to observe the course of the disease with and without medication. Others were used as subjects to test the effects of various poisons. Some had parts of their bodies frozen to test new treatments. Still others were deliberately wounded to study

new antibiotics and other treatments. Perhaps most evil of all were the excruciating decompression studies designed to test reactions to high-altitude flight (Katz, 1972). These gruesome experiments brought home exactly how far people would go in using research to further their own ends. They also brought home the vulnerability of minorities to exploitation in research, especially when the resources and authority of powerful groups support researchers with few ethical standards. Public outrage over these experiments led to heightened concern to establish codified standards for the ethical conduct of medical research on human subjects.

The second event that influenced the development of a codified set of ethical standards was an infamous study of syphilis conducted by the U.S. Public Health Service (PHS). This study began in 1932 with Black males from Tuskegee, Alabama—425 of them with syphilis and 200 of them without syphilis. All were poor and only semiliterate. None was told that he had syphilis. The intent was to observe the men over a span of years to learn how the disease progressed. When the study began, there was no cure for syphilis. Fifteen years later, penicillin was discovered to be an effective cure for this affliction, but the PHS continued the syphilis study for an additional 25 years, withholding treatment from all but a fortunate few who discovered its existence on their own and requested it. The justification for deceiving the men was that, because they were poor and semiliterate, they would in all likelihood not seek treatment even if they knew of it. Left untreated, syphilis can cause paralysis, insanity, blindness, and heart disease. Ultimately, it can even be fatal. Yet, these men were allowed to spread the disease to their wives and lovers. Many of the afflicted participants in the Tuskegee study suffered serious physical disorders or died as a result of not receiving treatment for the disease (Jones, 1992; Reverby, 2000).

Most Americans today—and especially those in the human services—would agree that the actions of the PHS were repugnant, racist, and unethical in the extreme. In fact, President Bill Clinton issued an apology on behalf of the nation for the Tuskegee Syphilis Study during a White House ceremony in 1997 (Eckenwiler, 1999). When the study began, however—and even when effective treatment for syphilis became available—the subordinate position of Blacks and poor people in American society resulted in their receiving fewer political, economic, and even medical rights than Whites and more affluent citizens received. It is unlikely that well-to-do Whites would have been treated in the same arrogant fashion, and one would hope that no such debacle would be seriously contemplated today. Yet we should keep in mind that the PHS study continued into the 1970s—an era we like to consider as more enlightened regarding human rights—and ended only when it received public notoriety. This further documents the extent to which minorities (and others) can be at risk of dangerous and inhumane treatment from researchers who are not governed by clear and enforceable ethical standards.

The immoral treatment of some minorities in research during the 20th century, especially the Nazi and PHS episodes, brought home the need to codify standards for ethical conduct so that researchers would have guidelines available and the research subjects would be afforded some protection. The first effort along these lines was the Nuremberg Code, developed in 1946 in direct response to the atrocities committed during World War II. The Nuremberg Code was limited to issues of ethics in medical research. In 1966, the PHS established ethical regulations for medical research that emphasized the following: (a) full disclosure of relevant information should be made to the participants; (b) the decision to participate must be completely voluntary; and (c) researchers must obtain documented, informed consent from participants (Gray, 1982; Reynolds, 1979). In 1974, the U.S. Department of Health, Education, and Welfare (DHEW, now the U.S. Department of Health and Human Services [DHHS]) decreed that the PHS guidelines would apply to social science research. Furthermore, the DHEW recognized that codes of conduct alone would not ensure ethical research without some oversight procedures in place. To this end, the DHEW required research institutions, such as universities, to establish IRBs, which would review research proposals and ensure that the guidelines were followed. These regulations have been broadened to apply not only to those projects directly funded by that agency but also to any research carried on in organizations

that obtain DHHS funding. Today, some research is conducted by researchers or agencies that are not a part of a university or another organization that has IRB services. For these researchers, there are nonaffiliated IRBs that are not owned or operated by a university or other research organizations. There is also an accreditation process for these independent IRBs, which serves as a check on the quality of their services.

The DHHS regulations are codified in Title 45, Part 46, of the Code of Federal Regulations (Protection of Human Subjects, 2018). Those basic regulations became final in 1981 and were subsequently revised in 1983, 1991, and in July 2018. The 1991 revision was especially important, because it involved the adoption of the Federal Policy for the Protection of Human Subjects that had been set forth in the Belmont Report. Those principles of respect, beneficence, and justice are now accepted as the three quintessential requirements for the ethical conduct of research involving human subjects. Although few would take issue with the basic ethical principles that had been expressed in the 1974 DHEW policy, the fact that those regulations initially originated in the context of medical research did cause concern for social scientists. A common feeling is that the risks to participants in most social science research are minimal and different from the risks to participants in medical research (Murray, Donovan, Kail, & Medvene, 1980). In social science research, breach of confidentiality, not direct harm, is the most likely ethical problem. There was concern that the original regulations would obstruct important research, hinder response rates, and reduce the validity and generalizability of findings.

In response to these concerns, the DHHS, under a policy issued in 1981, exempted the following research methodologies from IRB review: evaluation of teaching procedures or courses, educational testing, survey or interview techniques, observation of public behavior, and documentary research (Huber, 1981). The only exceptions are research dealing with "sensitive" behavior, such as drug and alcohol use, illegal behavior, or sexual conduct. In assessing social science research that is not exempt from IRB review, the IRBs have tended to subscribe to a risk–benefit doctrine (Smith,

1981). This means that questionable practices, such as deception or disguised observation, may be used if the purpose of the study is viewed as sufficiently important to justify them.

The 2018 planned revisions were written in part to responses to concerns about uses of biomedical samples. In one highly publicized case in 2003, the Havasupai Indian tribe in Arizona banished Arizona State researchers from their reservation for using blood samples from tribal members for purposes for which they had not given consent. Blood samples had been taken from many members of the tribe to help with research for high rates of diabetes in the tribe. The tribe had taken exception to researchers using the samples to evaluate other things such as mental health and the tribe's geographic origins (Harmon, 2010). The 2018 revisions will establish new policies to allow researchers to gain "broad consent" to cover several potential uses of data. The new policies will also require additional privacy safeguards related to the collection of personal data and biospecimens.

Although the DHHS regulations exempt much social science research from IRB review, many universities and other research institutions require that *all* research projects be reviewed to determine whether they are legitimately exempt. Furthermore, it has become common for private foundations to require IRB review as a prerequisite for funding. When planning research, an application to conduct the research should routinely be submitted to the appropriate IRB to determine whether the research is exempt and, if it is not, to gain permission to conduct the research. Box 3.1 lists the content that the DHHS expects to find on an IRB application form. As you read the rest of this chapter, you will see that many of the ethical issues discussed are addressed by the criteria listed for such applications. Even if a project is exempt from IRB review, researchers are not exempt from ethical concerns. Whether one's research will be reviewed or not, one still has the responsibility to consider the impact of the research on those who participate and on those who might benefit from it. As we will see, ethical guidelines do not eliminate the controversy that surrounds ethical issues because guidelines need to be interpreted and applied to specific contexts. Much debate surrounds such interpretation and application.

The debate over the Nazi experiments is not over. Controversy persists in terms of whether the data from that research are valid and reliable and, if so, whether those data should be used today (Moe, 1984; Palmer, 2010; Schafer, 1986). Some have argued that use of the data is justified if the data are scientifically valid and no other source of such data exists. If the data are used, it is argued, one should feel compelled to express horror and regret at the manner of collection. On the other side, some argue that our collective outrage at the treatment of minorities by the Nazis should be so great that use of the data is repulsive. In this view, refusing to use these data is a symbolic denunciation of such atrocities, and using the data might be interpreted as an acceptance of the methods that were used to collect them—or at least a willingness to let the importance of the Holocaust diminish with the passage of time. Between these two extremes, some researchers argue that the data should be used only if any overriding need demands it, and the objective of using the data overrides our symbolic rejection of the manner in which the data were collected.

Recent assessments suggest that the data from the Nazi experiments are seriously flawed—even fraudulent in some cases—and therefore should not be used, regardless of the ethical issues surrounding how the data were obtained (Berger, 1994). This controversy remains long-lasting and deeply rooted in ethical research issues.

ETHICAL ISSUES

Seven basic ethical issues arise in social science research: informed consent, deception, privacy (including confidentiality and anonymity), physical or mental distress, problems in sponsored research, scientific misconduct or fraud, and scientific advocacy. The unique situation confronting the human service researcher raises two additional considerations: protecting vulnerable clients and withholding treatment for research purposes.

Informed Consent

Informed consent refers to telling potential research participants about all aspects of the

---

BOX 3.1 Criteria for IRB Approval of Research

In order to approve research covered by this policy, the IRB shall determine that all of the following requirements are satisfied:

1. Risks to subjects are minimized:
   i. By using procedures that are consistent with sound research design and that do not unnecessarily expose subjects to risk
   ii. Whenever appropriate, by using procedures already being performed on the subjects for diagnostic or treatment purposes
2. Risks to subjects are reasonable in relation to anticipated benefits, if any, to subjects, and the importance of the knowledge that may reasonably be expected to result. In evaluating risks and benefits, the IRB should consider only those risks and benefits that may result from the research (as distinguished from risks and benefits of therapies subjects would receive even if not participating in the research). The IRB should not consider possible long-range effects of applying knowledge gained in the research (e.g., the possible effects of the research on public policy) as among those research risks that fall within the purview of its responsibility.
3. Selection of subjects is equitable. In making this assessment, the IRB should take into account the purposes of the research and the setting in which the research will be conducted and should be particularly cognizant of the special problems of research involving vulnerable populations such as children, prisoners, pregnant women, mentally disabled persons, or economically or educationally disadvantaged persons.
4. Informed consent will be sought from each prospective subject or the subject's legally authorized representative, in accordance with and to the extent required by §46.116.
5. Informed consent will be appropriately documented in accordance with, and to the extent required by, §46.117.
6. When appropriate, the research plan makes adequate provision for monitoring the data collected to ensure the safety of subjects.
7. When appropriate, there are adequate provisions to protect the privacy of subjects and to maintain the confidentiality of data.

Source: Adapted from Protection of Human Subjects, 45 C.F.R. § 46.111 (2018).

---

research that might reasonably influence the decision to participate. Very often, people are asked to sign a *consent form*, which describes the elements of the research that might influence a person's decision to participate (see Box 3.2). General agreement exists concerning the desirability of informed consent in behavioral science research, primarily because in the United States, cultural values place great emphasis on freedom and self-determination. Whether the issue is who to marry, what career to pursue, or whether to participate in a research project, we value the right of individuals to assess information and weigh alternatives before making their own judgments. To deceive potential research participants is to deny them the ability to determine their own destinies.

Although consensus exists about the general principle of informed consent, the debate regarding exactly how far the obligations of researchers extend in this realm is still a hot issue. At one extreme, researchers known as *ethical absolutists* argue that people should be fully informed of all aspects of the research in which they might play a part (Baumrind, 1985; Dunaway, 2017; Elms, 1982; Kimmel, 1988). Even when research is based on the public record, such as agency documents, or on observations of behavior in public,

---

BOX 3.2 Basic Elements of an Informed Consent Form

The following information shall be provided to each subject:

1. A statement that the study involves research, an explanation of the purposes of the research and the expected duration of the subject's participation, a description of the procedures to be followed, and identification of any procedures that are experimental
2. A description of any reasonably foreseeable risks or discomfort to the subject
3. A description of any benefits to the subject or to others which may reasonably be expected from the research
4. A disclosure of appropriate alternative procedures or courses of treatment, if any, that might be advantageous to the subject
5. A statement describing the extent, if any, to which confidentiality of records identifying the subject will be maintained
6. For research involving more than minimal risk, an explanation as to whether any compensation and an explanation as to whether any medical treatments are available if injury occurs and, if so, what they consist of, or where further information may be obtained
7. An explanation of whom to contact for answers to pertinent questions about the research and research subjects' rights, and whom to contact in the event of a research-related injury to the subject
8. A statement that participation is voluntary, refusal to participate will involve no penalty or loss of benefits to which the subject is otherwise entitled, and that the subject may discontinue participation at any time without penalty or loss of benefits to which the subject is otherwise entitled.

Source: Protection of Human Subjects, 45 C.F.R. § 46 (2018).

---

some absolutists argue that people about whom the observations have been made should be informed of the research. Otherwise, they do not have the full right to decide whether to participate.

Rigid adherence to the absolutist position, however, makes social research much more difficult to conduct. First, such adherence rules out many practices that some researchers consider to be important or essential. Many experiments, for example, rely on some degree of deception, at least to the extent of not telling participants the true research hypotheses. The reason for this is that people might respond differently if they knew about these hypotheses. All such studies would be unacceptable to the absolutists, however, and could not be conducted. Absolutists also would disallow disguised observation, during which people in public settings are not aware they are being observed. No longer could researchers engage in such effective strategies as infiltrating organizations—unless, of course, they told all employees what they were doing. The net result would be to make social science research highly conservative and very limited. It would become the study of people who volunteer to be studied, and research shows that people who volunteer differ in many ways from people who do not volunteer. This would seriously reduce the generalizability of research findings.

Second, the absolutist approach would call for obtaining informed consent in all research projects, and research has shown that obtaining written consent can reduce people's willingness to participate in research (De Oliveira, Vissoci, Machado, Rodrigues, & Limkakeng, 2017). One study found that formally requesting informed consent prior to conducting an interview reduced the rate of cooperation by 7% in comparison to cases in which a formal request was not made (Singer, von Thurn, & Miller, 1995). Because any reduction in response rate will reduce the generalizability of the findings, as we explain in Chapter 7, obtaining informed consent in survey research can have serious, negative consequences in terms of the validity of the research.

Written informed consent probably reduces people's willingness to participate because it appears to some respondents to contradict the researcher's assurance of confidentiality. One minute people are being told that their answers will remain confidential, and the next they are being asked to put their names on a consent form! Even though signing a consent form need not impede the maintenance of confidentiality, it is not surprising that respondents may not perceive it that way. Anything that undermines the belief of respondents in the confidentiality of their answers will reduce the response rates. Signing a consent form also may affect the quality of the data obtained, because those who do give consent may be less candid in their responses than they otherwise might have been.

Because of these problems with the absolutist approach to informed consent, many researchers take a less extreme position. They argue, first of all, that people should be informed of factors that might reasonably be expected to influence their decision to participate, such as any harm that might occur or how much time and effort will be involved. However, they also use a risk–benefit approach: questionable research strategies, such as deception, are appropriate if they are essential to conduct the research, if they will bring no harm to participants, and if the outcome is sufficiently important to warrant the research. Lively debate continues over the use of questionable practices and their routine approval by IRBs (Baumrind, 1985; Ortmann, 1997; Wendler, 1996).

A final issue regarding informed consent has to do with the possibility that a person might feel pressured to agree or might not understand precisely what he or she is agreeing to. After all, asking a person to participate in a study can involve social pressures not unlike those in other settings. We often feel pressured to help others when they ask for our assistance, and some people find it difficult to say no to a face-to-face request. In addition, scientific researchers represent figures of

some authority and status, and people often are disinclined to refuse their requests. In other cases, people may be temporarily confused about what is being asked of them.

To resolve these problems, a study involving institutionalized elderly people used a two-step consent procedure (Ratzan, 1981). In the first step, people were told what their participation would involve, what risks were entailed, and that several days later, they would be asked whether they were willing to participate. This was meant to reduce any immediate pressures to agree and to enable people to talk with others and clarify any confusing issues. The second step, occurring a few days later, involved obtaining the actual consent. In that study, all those who were asked refused to participate. This probably resulted from the fact that a part of the study involved having a needle inserted in a vein continuously for 8 days to take blood samples. However, some of the people might have agreed to participate had they been asked to sign a consent form during the first interview. Yet, it is questionable whether any consent obtained at that time would have been as informed and considered as it should have been. The goal of obtaining informed consent is not to pressure people into participating in the research but, rather, to gain participation that is truly informed.

In the homelessness study, Hilton and DeJong ultimately created an informed consent form that detailed potential risks and benefits to participation in their study. Because their study included audiotaping of interviews, they also created a separate consent form asking for permission to audiotape interviews, which allowed some participants to give consent to be interviewed but not to be audiotaped. Nearly all potential participants who sat through their explanation of the study agreed to be interviewed and nearly all who were interviewed agreed to be audiotaped, although several asked to use a different name during the interview to help ensure confidentiality. Ironically, the main concern participants had prior to participation was that they were required to print and sign their full names on the informed consent form, which detailed their rights to confidentiality.

Deception

Despite its status as a controversial strategy, deception is still fairly common in some areas of social science research such as social psychology (Kimmel, Smith, & Klein, 2011). One reason for this is that some research would be difficult—or even impossible—to conduct without some level of deception. At a minimum, many experiments necessitate not telling the participants the true research hypotheses; this withholding of information is a form of deception. As another example, field research sometimes uses disguised observation, where people in public settings are observed but are not aware that such observation is occurring. Some argue that this involves an implicit deception of those being observed. Other types of field research can involve more explicit deception to gain the cooperation of those who are being observed.

Richard Leo (1996), in his field study of police interrogators, withheld or concealed information regarding his own views about crime, punishment, homosexuality, and other issues from the police that he observed. In fact, he dubbed what he did the "chameleon strategy": "I consciously reinvented my persona to fit the attributes, biases, and worldview of my subjects" (Leo, 1995, p. 120). Before the detectives, he feigned opposition to abortion, support for the death penalty, and antipathy toward gays. He created this persona to gain their cooperation and to encourage them to act openly and naturally in front of him. If the police interrogators had known his true views on these issues, Leo claims, they might have distrusted him and not acted openly in front of him. Because his observations produced groundbreaking sociological research on this topic, he felt that the deception was warranted, given that little harm came to the police officers.

Ethical absolutists would rule out all such deception on the grounds that it is unethical to deceive other human beings deliberately (Erikson, 1967). Kimmel et al. (2011) compare deception in research to "white lies." They write,

> Deception in research is morally permissible to the extent that it is consistent with certain principles, a position akin to how lying is

treated in everyday life. White lies are considered permissible because they are harmless, if not beneficial; lies to avoid greater harms are also often considered permissible. (p. 4)

They also explain that deception is generally tolerated when four conditions are met: (a) researchers show respect for human dignity and are committed to voluntary participation and informed consent, (b) participants are reminded that participation is voluntary and that they can withdraw from the study at any time, (c) deception is used only where remedial measures meant to minimize risks associated with deception are used, including debriefing, and (d) deceptions are not harmful to the participant.

Debriefing is when participants are told the true purposes of the research and are informed of any deceptions that were used. This should be done in a positive and supportive way so that the participants feel they were joint partners in a worthwhile enterprise rather than dupes of the researchers. Usually, this can be achieved by explaining the reasons for the deception and the impossibility that anyone could have detected the deceptions before being informed of them. In some research, of course, debriefings are not possible, such as in disguised observations in field settings where the researcher never has a chance to contact the participants after the observations are made.

Hilton and DeJong's homelessness study did not include any use of deception. Over time, however, the researchers discovered that their interviews, which focused primarily on seemingly simply and mundane topics like food, healthcare, use of human services, and daily schedules, often led to highly emotional and personal testimonials. This led the researchers to develop warning statements prior to interviews telling participants that they may feel uncomfortable with some interview topics and reminding them of their right to end the interview at any time (without losing their payment for the interview). They also began informal debriefing sessions after each interview in which they thanked the interviewees for their time, explained the value of their participation to the study and to the provision of services, and directing participants to counseling and other services as necessary.

The Right to Privacy: Anonymity and Confidentiality

The right to privacy is one of the key values and ethical obligations mentioned at the beginning of this chapter. **Privacy** refers to the ability to control when and under what conditions others will have access to your beliefs, values, or behavior. Intrusions on our privacy have become endemic in modern society; with the growth of social research during the past century, the danger of even greater intrusion arises. Virtually any attempt to collect data from people raises the issue of privacy and confronts investigators with the dilemma of whether threats to privacy are warranted by the research. One well-known research project illustrates the complexity of this issue.

The sociologist Laud Humphreys (1970), in an effort to understand a particular type of sexual behavior, made observations of men having quick and impersonal sexual encounters with other men in public restrooms. To gather his data without arousing suspicion, Humphreys played the role of the "watch queen"—that is, someone who keeps watch and warns participants of approaching police or "straight" males who might disrupt the activities. None of the men who went to the restrooms to engage in sex was aware that a researcher was recording his behavior. Humphreys also noted the license plates on the cars of these men and was able to find their home addresses through public motor-vehicle records. He then interviewed them in their homes but did not inform them of the real reason for the interviews or that he had observed them earlier in the restrooms.

Humphreys was heavily criticized for using deception, for not obtaining informed consent, and for violating the privacy of these men who were engaging in highly stigmatized actions that, were they to be made public, might disrupt their family lives or threaten their jobs. Many sociologists believe that research on such sensitive topics is not simply a matter of confidentiality—that is, of not letting people's identities become known. Rather, these sociologists believe such data should not even be collected at all, because these men obviously were trying to conceal their actions. Social science researchers, it is argued, should respect that privacy.

Humphreys defended his research on the grounds that the confidentiality of his subjects was maintained and the results of the study were of significant scientific value. In fact, no one else has devised another method to study such sexual behavior. Humphreys discovered that the men who engage in this type of sexual activity were not unusual or deviant in the rest of their lives and, for the most part, were normal, respectable citizens with a rather unusual sexual outlet. Humphreys believed that the greater understanding of what had been considered to be deviant sexual conduct justifies the threat to privacy that these men experienced. In addition, the public setting in which they performed their acts, he argued, reduced their right to claim privacy.

The homeless study example described earlier offers another illustration of potential threats to privacy. While Hilton and DeJong were able to remove obvious identifiers in reports and presentations there were several times when they had to carefully consider how data were presented to address privacy concerns. For example, in the initial report-writing stages when the researchers introduced quotes from individual participants they attributed each quote to a man or woman and categorized that person by his or her living situation—staying at a shelter, doubling up with family or friends (or couch-surfing), or living outdoors or in a car. They also provided a brief description of the size of the community in which the person resided (because they were interested in differences between coping tactics within larger and smaller communities). They soon realized, however, that in this very sparsely populated region it might be possible for some people (especially service providers) to put all of this information together to identify specific interviewees. To avoid this, they went back to each quote included and removed some of these descriptions to help mask participants' identities.

Single-system research requires particular caution in this regard. As we explain in Chapter 11, single-system research involves observing changes in the feelings or behavior of an individual over a period of time. Furthermore, the clients in these studies often suffer from some conditions, such as a mental disorder, that might lead to stigmatization should others find out about it. Therefore, great care must be taken to ensure that people's identities are not unintentionally revealed in the process of describing the case. Researchers often must tread a fine line between providing sufficient case details and minimizing the risk of identifying a client. Final reports should always be written with sensitivity to this issue.

As these two case studies show, the right to privacy often is a difficult ethical issue to resolve. Researchers have come up with three major ways to deal with the problem of protecting people's privacy: (a) let subjects edit their data, (b) keep the data anonymous, and (c) keep the data confidential.

Editing the Data. One very effective way to protect privacy is to offer participants the opportunity, after the data has been collected, to destroy any data they wish to remain private. This has been done in studies of couples and family problems that use audio or video recordings of interactions between family members (Margolin et al., 2005). Even though the couples and families consent to the recording, investigators, sensitive to the issue of privacy, sometimes offer the opportunity for participants to review the recordings and edit out anything they wish. The assumption is that, despite agreeing to participate, family members might do something on the spur of the moment that they would prefer not be made public. Surprisingly, few family members exercise this option. This and other research suggests that people are generally more tolerant of invasions of privacy than researchers might expect. Nonetheless, it should always be the research subject's decision; the researcher should never assume that people will be tolerant of invasions or breaches of their privacy.

Anonymity. A second means of ensuring privacy is to accord the participants **anonymity,** which means that no one, including the researcher, can link any data to a particular respondent. This can be accomplished by not including any identifying names or numbers with the data collected. This method of protecting privacy is ideal, because the data are collected in such a way that it is impossible for anyone to determine which data came from which individual. In many research

situations, however, it is not possible or feasible to collect data in this fashion, so researchers turn to confidentiality.

Confidentiality. A third way of protecting privacy is through **confidentiality,** which means ensuring that information about or data collected from those who participate in a study are not made public in a way that can be linked to an individual. Researchers, of course, commonly release their data to the public, but usually only in aggregate forms—that is, reporting on how a whole group responded rather than how specific individuals responded. In many studies, the data are not of a sensitive nature and, thus, confidentiality would seem to be less important, but it is impossible to predict what bits of data all participants will want to be kept confidential. Because aggregate and anonymous reporting of results is all that is necessary in most research studies, confidentiality is routinely extended to encourage people's participation and honest responses.

It is worth pointing out that anonymity and confidentiality are quite distinct. With confidentiality, the researcher can link responses to particular respondents but does not release this information publicly; with anonymity, even the researchers cannot link responses to particular respondents. So, if a researcher sends out mailed questionnaires that are returned with no names or other identifiers on them, then the respondents have true anonymity. If the same questionnaires are mailed back with a name or any other identifier on them, however, then only confidentiality is possible, because the researcher can link responses to respondents. Even if the identifiers are removed as soon as the questionnaire is received, it would still be ethical to make promises of confidentiality only, because the researcher could link responses to respondents at the point when the questionnaires are received. Obviously, it is unethical to tell respondents that they will have confidentiality when they will not, but it is also wrong to claim that responses will be anonymous when all that will actually be protected is confidentiality.

In some cases, confidentiality can be breached merely by a person's involvement in a research project becoming known. If it becomes known, for example, that an individual was part of a study on homelessness, then knowledge that the individual is homeless has become public even if none of the data collected from that individual has been made public. So, one aspect of confidentiality is to ensure that the identities of those who are research subjects, especially when that research is sensitive, are kept hidden.

Confidentiality can also be threatened when third parties, such as the people sponsoring the research or the courts, seek to identify research participants. Intrusion by a sponsor is relatively easy to avoid, however. When establishing a research agreement with a sponsoring agency or an organization, one should make clear in the agreement that identities will not be revealed under any circumstances. If the sponsor objects, then researchers should refuse to accept the agreement. We have more to say about sponsors and ethics later in this chapter.

Court and Legislative Challenges to Confidentiality. The courts as well as some laws and statutes pose a more complicated threat to confidentiality. Most communications that physicians, lawyers, and clergy have with their clients are protected from judicial subpoena. Social workers in their clinical capacity are also afforded such protection in many instances, although the degree of protection varies with agency settings and jurisdictions. Social researchers, however, do not have a legal protection of privileged communication with the people from whom they gather data (Kimmel, 1988; Wiles, Crow, Heath, & Charles, 2008). In addition, physicians, most human service professionals, and, in some cases, researchers are required by many state laws to report to public agencies when they observe evidence for mistreatment of children or older adults. Thus, courts or public agencies may subpoena research data that reveal participants' identities, and failure to comply with such a subpoena renders researchers open to charges of contempt of court. Actually, social science researchers have been treated somewhat inconsistently by the courts in civil cases. During a civil suit in California, for example, the court refused to force a researcher to reveal the identities of respondents in confidential interviews

(Smith, 1981). In a more recent case, researchers associated with Boston College were forced by a U.S. court to hand over recordings of interviews of Irish Republican Army and loyalist paramilitary members collected as part of a study of violence in Northern Ireland (www.theguardian.com/uk-news/2016/apr/25/boston-college-ordered-by-us-court-to-hand-over-ira-tapes).

In criminal cases, however, the courts generally have held that the right of the public to be protected from criminal activity or the right of suspects to a fair trial supersedes any assurance of confidentiality in research. In one case, for example, the researcher had been making field observations in a restaurant when it was heavily damaged by a suspicious fire (Brajuha & Hallowell, 1986). Police wanted the researcher's field notes to determine whether any evidence of arson could be substantiated. One court squashed a subpoena for the field notes, but another upheld it. Eventually, a compromise was reached: The researcher's field notes were considered to be subject to a subpoena, but the researcher was allowed to remove any material that would have violated confidentiality. With rulings like this, the courts seem to recognize that the confidentiality a legitimate social science researcher establishes in a research relationship should be protected, if that can be done while still protecting the rights of the public and criminal suspects.

In another case, a sociologist actually spent time in jail because he refused to give information in court that he believed violated his promise of confidentiality to his research subjects. Rik Scarce (2005) conducted research on activists in the animal liberation movement during the 1990s. A federal grand jury was investigating break-ins by such activists at university laboratories, and some of the activists in whom the grand jury was interested had been interviewed by Scarce as part of his research. Scarce refused to answer certain questions about these activists that were put to him by the grand jury because he thought it would violate the confidentiality he had extended to the people he interviewed. He was jailed for 4 months on contempt-of-court charges. In his study of police interrogators described earlier in this chapter, Leo was compelled to testify in court under threat of contempt-of-court charges. As these cases illustrate, the courts generally have held that confidential communication between a researcher and a research participant is not protected in criminal cases; however, some courts have also recognized that the confidential relationship is an important and special one and that efforts should be made not to violate it. Because of cases like these, some researchers have called for federal legislation to give social science researchers protection—even if limited—from being compelled to violate their confidential relationships (Leo, 1995; Scarce, 2005).

Concern over a possible subpoena of their research data has led some researchers to adopt elaborate measures to protect that data. For example, it is common to establish computer files with the data identified only by numbers rather than by names. Often, it is unnecessary to retain name identification for research purposes once the data have been collected. In such cases, the names should be destroyed. If name identification is required—for example, because you want to interview the same people at a later time—the names should be stored in a separate computer file. This procedure reduces the possibility of unauthorized persons linking names with data.

One of the best means of securing confidentiality for sensitive research, such as that dealing with substance abuse or criminal behavior, is to use certificates of confidentiality, which were made available by the Public Health Service Act Amendments of 1974 (Beskow, Dame, & Costello, 2008; Bonnie & Wallace, 2003). Certificates of confidentiality are issued by the National Institutes of Health (NIH) and other Health and Human Service offices to protect identifiable research information from forced disclosure. They allow the investigator and others who have access to research records to refuse to disclose identifying information about research participants in any civil, criminal, administrative, legislative, or other proceedings, whether at the federal, state, or local level. By some interpretations, the certificates of confidentiality supersede even laws that require mandatory reporting of instances of mistreatment involving children and older adults. Certificates generally are awarded only for research on sensitive topics, such as

illegal drug use or sexual behavior, and regardless of whether the research project receives federal funding. While some believe that the certificates provide almost complete protection, some courts have insisted on at least partial disclosure of some information that the certificates were meant to protect. While courts take the certificates seriously, they also tend to view them as only one factor that influences how civil and criminal legal disputes should be resolved. At least some courts have taken the position that the constitutional rights of a plaintiff or defendant may supersede the legal protections offered by the certificates (Beskow et al., 2008; Check, Wolf, Dame, & Beskow, 2014; National Cancer Institute, 1998).

So, intrusion by courts is a real danger with research, especially regarding some topics, although it is not terribly common. Nonetheless, researchers have an obligation to inform potential subjects accurately about any possible threats to confidentiality that might arise, including what would likely happen should their data be subpoenaed by the courts. The lengths to which investigators will go to protect privacy indicate the importance of this ethical issue. The bottom line is that no one should be threatened with harm to themselves or their reputation as a result of participating in a scientific study.

Harm, Distress, and Benefit

Researchers should avoid exposing participants to physical or mental distress or danger. If the potential for such distress exists in a research investigation, then the participants should be fully informed, the potential research findings should be of sufficient importance to warrant the risk, and no possibility should exist of achieving the results without this risk. People should never be exposed to situations that might cause serious or lasting harm.

Research in the human services rarely involves physical danger, but there are research settings in which psychological distress may be an element. Some studies, for example, have asked people to view such things as pornographic pictures, victims of automobile accidents, and the emaciated inmates of Nazi concentration camps. Certainly, these stimuli can induce powerful reactions—in some cases, emotions that the participants had not expected to experience. A strong emotional reaction, especially an unexpected one, can be very distressful. In some studies, people have been given false feedback about themselves to observe how they respond.

In the homeless study discussed earlier, for example, Hilton and DeJong found that several participants became distressed even when speaking about seemingly mundane topics as where they slept the night before or what they ate today. While their study focused primarily on topics that did not seem particularly sensitive, the researchers found that several participants had difficulty voicing details about their basic life circumstances to others. In some cases, Hilton and DeJong reminded participants that they were free to stop the interview or move on to other topics at any point.

Another area in which social science research contains the potential for harm to those who are studied is in field research of people engaging in stigmatized, deviant, or illegal behavior. The potential harm comes if the researcher says or does anything that might lead the research subjects to be sanctioned for the deviant or illegal behaviors they displayed in front of the researcher (Sieber & Tolich, 2013). This is a complex topic that is explored in detail in Chapter 10, but the problem can arise because field research often involves an implicit or explicit agreement between the researcher and those being observed. In this agreement, the observed consent to letting the researcher join them and make observations on them; in return, they expect the researcher will support their illegal or deviant behavior—or at least not do anything to get them in trouble for it. For example, if police interrogations of suspects are likely to include some harsh or even illegal treatment of the suspects, then police officers would be unlikely to let a researcher observe the interrogations unless they believed that the researcher would support their actions or not report them to authorities or testify against them in court. In other words, the police would likely expect the researcher, in return for being permitted to observe them, to act like fellow officers and support them in their actions.

In developing a relationship with the police, the researcher may give the impression that he or she understands this, or the police may just assume that the researcher understands. This actually creates a moral dilemma for the researcher, because either of these choices is morally compromised. If the researcher supports the police and does not report the harsh treatment of the suspect, then the suspect is harmed by the researcher's actions, but if the researcher supports the suspect and reports the actions, then the police are harmed both by having their implicit agreement with the researcher violated and by being sanctioned for their behavior. This kind of ambiguous dilemma is inherent in some field research on deviant lifestyles and is part of what Leo meant by his comment that field work is "a morally ambiguous enterprise" (Leo, 1996, p. 125).

Assuming that the scientific benefits warrant the risk of distress and that the participants are fully informed, it is then the researcher's obligation to alleviate the impact of whatever distress actually does occur. As with problems created by deception, alleviating problems related to harm or distress often is accomplished through a debriefing that assesses people's psychological and emotional reactions to the research.

For some social scientists, an ethical standard that rests only on avoiding harm is far too limited. They would argue that those on whom we conduct research also should gain some positive benefit from their participation. This stance has been put forth most clearly by feminist, queer, and collaborative researchers (Browne & Nash, 2010; Nyden, Figert, Shibley, & Burrows, 1997; Reinharz, 1992). Viewing research as a two-way street, they argue that both the researcher and the research subject should gain something positive from the project. Researchers, of course, get data from the research that enable them to publish books and articles, which advances their careers, but what do the research subjects get? This raises the ethical issue of what the research community owes to the research subjects. These subjects could be paid for their time and effort, or the research results could be translated into social policies or practices that benefit the community from which the research subjects come. Or, by participating in the research, the subjects might develop knowledge or skills that will enable them to make their own lives better. The point is that, from this perspective, researchers have an ethical obligation not only to not leave research participants worse off but also to compensate them for their time and effort and, in some way, leave them better off for having participated in the research.

While Hilton and DeJong found that some homeless participants experienced distress as they discussed their lives, many more explained that they felt that the interviewing process had a therapeutic quality. Several explained that they were grateful to have someone listen to them for an extended period without judging them. (Many homeless felt they were constantly being judged by others.)

Sponsored Research

Because much social research is conducted under the auspices of a third-party sponsor, certain ethical considerations arise from that relationship. When research is sponsored, some type of research agreement—essentially, a contract—is developed. Researchers and sponsors alike should exercise great care in drafting this agreement. The potential for ethical problems to arise later is reduced when the research agreement clearly specifies the rights and obligations of the parties involved.

Three areas are of particular concern in sponsored research (King, Henderson, & Stein, 1999). First, it is common for sponsors to want to retain control over the release of the collected data. The precise conditions of release should be specified in the research agreement to avoid conflicts. One limitation that should not be tolerated, however, is the conditional publication of results—that is, agreeing to publish results only if they turn out a certain way (usually so when they support the preconceived notions of the sponsor). Such conditional publication violates the integrity of the research process and the autonomy of the researcher (Wolfgang, 1981). If the researcher agrees to some other type of limitation on release, however, it must be honored. To do otherwise would be a breach of the agreement and, therefore, unethical.

The second major concern in sponsored research is the nature of the research project itself. The precise purpose and procedures of the study should be specified in the agreement. Ethical questions arise if the researcher heavily modifies the study to cover matters not in the agreement. Often, sponsors will allow researchers to use the data gathered for scientific purposes beyond the needs of the sponsor, but it is unethical to agree to do a study that a sponsor wants and then change it for personal reasons so that it no longer meets the expectations of the sponsor.

A third area of ethical concern in sponsored research relates to the issue of informed consent—namely, revealing the sponsor's identity to participants. Although controversy exists in this regard, some researchers take the stance that truly informed consent can be given only if one knows who is sponsoring the study and for what purpose the study is being conducted. Some people might object, for example, to providing data that would help a company better market a product, a political party to better present a candidate, or the government to propagandize its citizens. In fact, studies show that people are less likely to participate in research they know to be sponsored by commercial organizations, which suggests that information about sponsorship can influence the decision of whether to participate (Fox, Crask, & Kim 1988; Rithchie et al., 2013). Each researcher, then, must carefully consider whether to make the sponsorship of a research project explicit. At a minimum, to deceive people regarding the sponsorship of a study to gain their participation is certainly unethical.

Scientific Misconduct and Fraud

When a research project reaches the final stage—that is, the dissemination of results—the primary consideration regarding ethical conduct shifts from avoiding harm to the participants in research to making sure the consumers of the research are not adversely affected. Results of a study typically are communicated in the form of a report to a sponsoring organization, a publication in a professional journal or, possibly, a news release to the media. The preeminent ethical obligation in this regard is not to disclose inaccurate, deceptive, or fraudulent results. To do so risks misleading scientists who depend on previous research to guide their own work. Ethical violations concerning disclosure of results undermine the very nature of the scientific process, which, as we saw in Chapter 2, depends upon building future knowledge on the foundation of existing knowledge. If we cannot depend on the accuracy of existing knowledge, then the scientific endeavor is threatened. In that case, the credibility of all research is damaged by such violations. Furthermore, deceptive or fraudulent disclosures of research results can cause human service practitioners to design useless—or even dangerous—interventions based on previous faulty studies.

Many ethical violations can occur in the process of reporting research (Gibelman & Gelman, 2001). **Fraud** is the deliberate falsification, misrepresentation, or plagiarizing of the data, findings, or ideas of others. These include such things as falsifying data, embellishing research reports, reporting research that has not been conducted, or manipulating data in a deceptive way. **Misconduct** is a broader concept that includes not only fraud but also carelessness or bias in recording and reporting data, mishandling data, and incomplete reporting of results. Other questionable practices are irresponsible claims of authorship (listing coauthors who did not really make contributions to the research) and premature release of results to the public without peer review.

Estimates regarding the actual amount of scientific misconduct that occurs suggest that the problem is relatively small. The Office of Research Integrity of the DHHS, which keeps track of such matters, reports that 100 to 200 new cases of alleged misconduct are brought to its attention each year, and many of these allegations prove to be unfounded (Office of Research Integrity, 2010). Of course, underreporting could hide a larger problem, but even if the number of cases is small, any misconduct in research can still damage the credibility of all research and place human service clients—and, by extension, human service providers—at risk.

The issue of who has the responsibility for detecting scientific misconduct is still very controversial (Gibelman & Gelman, 2001). For many years, government agencies that fund research pushed this responsibility onto the shoulders of the universities and other institutions where research was actually conducted. By the late 1980s, however, both the NIH and the DHHS had established their own offices to watch for misconduct. Yet, most scientists still consider protection against misconduct to be primarily a responsibility of the scientific community, which uses two major mechanisms to detect fraud: *peer review* and *replication*. There are, however, limitations to each of these mechanisms, as illustrated by a case of fraud in medical research involving Dr. Robert Slutsky (Engler, Covell, Friedman, Kitcher, & Peters, 1987).

The prolific Dr. Slutsky had authored or coauthored 137 articles on cardiological and radiological research over a 7-year period. During an evaluation of his appointment as a researcher at a university, questions were raised about duplicate data in two of his papers. In the ensuing investigation, 12 articles were deemed to be fraudulent and 48 were considered to be questionable. In some cases, articles described experiments that had never been conducted. How is it that these articles eluded the net of peer review by respected medical journals? There seem to have been two problems: First, peer review of article submissions cannot detect plausible, internally consistent fabrications. Second, the sheer number of research articles submitted to publications for review requires a large number of qualified reviewers who understand both the methodology and the content of the article.

If peer review does not detect and deter fraud, then will replication solve the problem? It might. The effectiveness of replication, however, has been severely crippled by the modern research system, because research funds often are not appropriated for replication. Agencies prefer to fund research efforts that delve into new areas. Furthermore, when replication does occur, it tends to be reserved for projects that have produced unusual results. Fraudulent studies that enhance the prestige of researchers but do not run counter to accepted findings in a field are not likely to arouse enough attention to warrant replication (Engler et al., 1987).

Beyond peer review and replication, there are several ways of reducing the chances of fraud or, if it occurs, detecting it. One is to supervise novice researchers until they demonstrate good practices, ethical conduct, and technical competency. Second, organizations need to guard against overly pro-lific researchers. Senior researchers and coauthors should not simply allow their names to be associated with research reports without carefully examining the work. Third, journals can reduce fraud by requiring more complete data to be submitted to reviewers, even if all the data cannot be included in the published article. When fraud is detected, journals have a responsibility to make the fraud public so that others will not unsuspectingly base research or treatments on the fraudulent material.

Though not as unethical as purposeful deception, careless errors in research have the same effect of creating misinformation. Social researchers owe the scientific community carefully conducted research that is as free of error as possible. As with fraud, errors are discovered and corrected either through critical review of research and reanalysis of data or through replication. For example, a study from the 1980s claimed to document substantial negative economic consequences of divorce for women; this study was an important foundation for developing social policy. Partly because these findings were somewhat at variance with the results of other studies, a reanalysis of the data was undertaken (Peterson, 1996). This reanalysis showed that the original conclusions were partly the result of errors in the original analysis. The reanalysis showed that women do suffer economically after divorce but not nearly as severely as the original analysis had suggested. Had the original research conclusions not been based on an inaccurate analysis, the subsequent policy development might have been different.

Beyond the problems of fraud and carelessness, researchers also have an obligation to report their results thoroughly. Researchers must take care to ensure that what they report does not give a distorted picture of the overall results. In addition, researchers should point out any limitations that might qualify their findings. Researchers also must be concerned with how the findings are applied to human service practice and policy decisions. Research projects on the effectiveness of arrest as a deterrent to intimate partner violence (see Chapter 10 for a detailed discussion) are excellent examples. A study conducted in Minneapolis has been singled out as a primary catalyst for widespread adoption of pro-arrest policies. Critics have argued that propaganda generated by some of the participating agencies was a key factor in the study's impact on policy, an impact they say was unjustified by a single study. Subsequent replications in several cities failed to support the findings of the Minneapolis study and have underscored the call for caution in rushing to apply findings to practice (Sherman, 1992). This was not a case of publishing fraudulent results or of misrepresenting data but, rather, an issue of the researcher's role in applying the research findings.

Any type of fraud can have serious consequences in both research and practice, so detecting and limiting fraud is important. Practitioner Profile 3.1 offers an example of how research methods can be used to help detect fraud.

PRACTITIONER PROFILE 3.1 Anne Gavin, Director, Evaluation, Planning and Support, Office of the Inspector General, Washington, DC

Anne Gavin is Director of Evaluation, Planning and Support for the Office of the Inspector General (OIG), Evaluation and Inspections unit. She has a master of arts in public policy from the University of Chicago and has been with the OIG for more than 10 years. During this time her main focus at OIG has been evaluating and monitoring DHHS funded programs. Earlier in her career Gavin directly evaluated DHHS programs, collecting and analyzing data, and writing reports. Now, as a supervisor, she is more focused on strategic planning, report review, and recommendation follow-up.

Gavin's educational background prepared her well for this work. "The public policy program was research intensive. I took some pretty intense research methods and statistics courses and I am glad I did," she explained. (Based on a personal communication on May 11, 2018.)

Like many of the other people in the program I went into public policy because I wanted to make a difference. One thing I learned was that if we are going to improve services for people we have to have a good sense of what is working and what is not. That requires having good data and making good use of it.

Gavin is currently involved in a project to identify cases of fraud in Medicaid and Medicare prescription drug programs. As she explains,

The OIG has been really involved in responding to the opioid crisis. To help detect fraud, OIG deploys state-of-the-art data analytics to identify the most egregious providers for possible investigation by OIG or our partners.

The evaluation office's role has been to analyze Medicare and Medicaid prescription drug claims and flag claims that may fit patterns associated with abuse.
As Gavin explains,

We have massive data sets and we cannot possibly look through every Medicaid or Medicare claim in the entire country. We have statisticians with very sophisticated data system skills who develop programs to identify potential problem claims. For example, we might flag specific types of drugs, in certain quantities and over certain time frames that seem to be associated with fraud.

While this work is very statistics heavy, Gavin also explains there is a qualitative side to this work as well.

We speak with folks from the Center[s] for Disease Control and other expert medical professionals to understand what are best practices and acceptable standards for pain management and other uses for various opiates. This gives us a picture of what we should expect to see in insurance claims and what might be out of the ordinary. It helps to learn the perspectives of those within medicine because they have knowledge of medical conditions and treatments that we don't. We use their expertise to develop better filters to find problem claims and identify patterns in problem claims.

Gavin likes her work and believes it can help the government do a better job of promoting positive health outcomes. As she explains,

Ultimately, we write reports that contain recommendations for DHHS, Congress, and the public with timely, useful, and reliable information on significant issues. These reports provide practical recommendations for improving program operations within DHHS.

In fact, Gavin contributed significantly to the production of the DHHS OIG's "Solutions to Reduce Fraud, Waste, and Abuse in HHS Programs: Top Unimplemented Recommendations" of 2018.

Scientific Advocacy

Scientific knowledge rarely remains the exclusive domain of the scientific community but, typically, finds its way into public life in the form of inventions, technological developments, or social policy. This raises potential ethical dilemmas in terms of the role of researchers as advocates for particular uses of their research results. What responsibility, if any, do scientists have for overseeing the use to which their results are put? To what extent should scientists become advocates for applying knowledge in a particular way? Quite naturally, disagreements arise on how to resolve these issues. This controversy is compounded in the case of human service researchers, because their research normally is initiated with some explicit, clinical application in mind. The classic approach to these issues derives from the exhortations of the sociologist Max Weber (1922/1946) that science should be "value-free." Social scientists, according to Weber, should create knowledge, not apply it. Therefore, they have no special responsibility for the ultimate use to which that knowledge is put. Furthermore, according to Weber, they are under no obligation to advocate particular uses of scientific knowledge. Indeed, advocacy is frowned on as threatening objectivity, which is a central concern of science. So, although remaining value-free is difficult, many argue that abandoning the effort would be disastrous, for it would prevent us from acquiring an accurate body of knowledge about human social behavior and might threaten the researcher's credibility as a disinterested expert (Gibbs, 1983; Gordon, 1988; Halfpenny, 1982).

Karl Marx (1848/1964) originally developed the opposite stance in this controversy. Marx championed the cause of the poor and downtrodden; he believed that social researchers should bring strong moral commitments to their work and strive to change unfair or immoral conditions. Following Marx, some modern researchers believe that social research should be guided by personal and political values and directed toward alleviating social ills (Brunswick Heinemann, 1981; Fay, 1987). Furthermore, scientists should

advocate for uses of their research by others that would help accomplish these personal goals.

Sociologist Alvin Gouldner (1976) developed a compromise position on the value-free controversy. Gouldner pointed to the obvious—namely, that scientists have values just as other human beings do. Furthermore, he noted, those values can influence research in so many subtle ways that their effects can never be totally eliminated. So, instead of denying or ignoring the existence or impact of these personal values, scientists need to be acutely aware of and upfront about them in research reports. Being thus forewarned, consumers of their research are then better able to assess whether the findings have been influenced by personal bias. In addition, Gouldner argued that social scientists have not only the right but also the duty to promote the constructive use of scientific knowledge (Gouldner, 1976). Because someone will make decisions concerning the use of scientific knowledge, scientists themselves are best equipped to make those judgments. As Gouldner states, technical competence would seem to provide a person with some warrant for making value judgments. People who take this position view the value-free stance as a potentially dangerous dereliction of a responsibility that accrues to scientists by virtue of their expertise and role in developing new knowledge.

Clinician–researchers, in particular, may be attracted by this stance. Because their research is conducted, in part, to advance the practice goals of the profession, they would probably view ensuring that any clinical application of the results be faithful to the outcome of the research as being one of their duties. Thus, human service researchers are more likely than many other behavioral scientists to take a strong stand in favor of advocacy.

Nothing is wrong with researchers openly pressing for the application of scientific knowledge in ways they deem to be desirable—so long as their advocacy is tempered with respect for objectivity. The danger of advocacy is that scientists can come to feel so strongly about the issues they promote that those feelings hamper the objective collection and analysis of data.

In the homeless study example, Hilton and DeJong began their research with the hope that their study would allow the community and sur-rounding region and rural areas in general to develop services to meet unmet needs of homeless adults. As such, they approached their research as advocates for homeless services. They also knew, however, that it would be unethical to portray research participants inaccurately or to paint an overly sympathetic picture of them (e.g., discount-ing or downplaying use of drugs or alcohol) for the sake of generating support for the cause of homeless services. What they found is that pro-viding accurate and detailed accounts of research participants' (interviewees') lives ultimately helped draw attention to the issue because it helped give a human face to the problem.

Protecting Vulnerable Clients

Human service clients, because they often are involuntary recipients of services, may find themselves vulnerable against pressures to coop-erate in research projects conducted by the orga-nizations that provide them with services. Such clients are likely to be sought out as research subjects, either because they often are viewed as being deviant in some way and, therefore, interesting to study or because they may be eas-ier than other groups to locate and keep track of during a research project.

Welfare recipients, children in day-care settings, patients in public mental hospitals, and partici-pants in job-training programs, to name only a few, are likely candidates for participation in social research projects. In fact, it is common for oper-ators of new or special programs to be required by their funding sources to research the effects of their programs as a condition for receiving those funds. Although such safeguards as codes of ethics and governmental regulations may serve as useful guides, special obligations fall on human service practitioners to safeguard their clients from unrea-sonable pressures to participate in research.

A crucial issue in this regard is the matter of voluntary and informed consent. Can clients actually give consent freely? This is one of the reasons that much research using prison inmates as subjects has been discontinued: It is debat-able how free inmates really are to give consent.

If participation in the research brings significant rewards in the form of separate living quarters or greater privacy, then these rewards may be almost coercive in the Spartan, degrading, and often dangerous world of the prison inmate. Although participation in the research is, on the face of it, voluntary, inmates may not seriously weigh the disadvantages or dangers of the research when their participation is perceived as a means of avoiding assault or rape.

Similar ethical questions also arise with research on people who have significant psychopathologies. If the psychopathology involves defective compre-hension or impaired insight, then the subjects may be unable to give truly informed consent. Research on such a population would have to be approached very carefully and could be justified only if it could not be done on a less vulnerable group. If the same research goals could be accomplished with a less vulnerable group, then that would be the route to follow. If it were decided to do research on a group with significant psychopathology, then informed consent should be approached in ways that pro-tect potential participants from even covert coer-cion. For example, consent could be sought by some party other than the researchers (to avoid the force of authority), or it could be sought in the presence of a relative, friend, or another advocate for the individual (to provide the social support to allow a refusal). If the psychopathology completely impairs the ability to consent, then most forms of research would be unethical unless it could be shown that either the patient or society would benefit significantly and that the research could be done in no other way (Oeye, Bjelland, & Skorpen, 2007).

The problem of voluntary consent may be somewhat more subtle among other recipients of human services. Even if refusal to participate is not linked to termination of benefits, clients might not be sure of this and, thus, might be disinclined to take the risk of finding out. In addition, the read-ing level of clients receiving public assistance often is less than that of the eighth grade, yet the read-ing level necessary to comprehend many welfare documents is above 13 years of education. Thus, it may be that clients who are accustomed to being confused by welfare requirements might not aggressively seek to determine their right to refuse participation in a research project. We are not suggesting that research never be conducted on prisoners or recipients of public welfare. Rather, clinician–researchers need to exercise additional caution—and, in some cases, possibly forgo valuable research projects—in the interests of ensuring truly voluntary informed consent.

As discussed earlier briefly, Hilton and DeJong's study of homeless adults in rural Michigan raised some issues related to informed consent. Some of their colleagues, including some on the IRB at their university, argued that some potential participants might look at their offer of providing a meal during an interview, $20 in cash, and a gift card for another meal as so enticing that even those who might otherwise wish to avoid talking with researchers about their homelessness might feel compelled to participate. Hilton and DeJong made an argument that if this benefit is acceptable for other groups, participants from other studies who provide an hour long interview should be considered suitable for homeless research subjects. To offer less, they argued, would be equivalent to discounting the value of the interview because the subject is poor. Ultimately they were able to offer $20 payment and the gift card to those who agreed to participate, but only if they gave the participants these benefits directly after the informed consent process (and not waiting until after the interview was complete). This helped reinforce the idea that anyone who felt uncomfortable answering a question or wanted to stop the interview at any time could do so without penalty (and keep the gift card and money).

Withholding Treatment for Research Purposes

An issue of particular concern to human service providers is the research practice of withholding treatment from a control group to assess whether a given treatment is effective. The **control group** serves as a comparison group. If a group receiving the treatment shows more improvement than the control group over a certain span of time, then we can feel justified in claiming that the treatment brought about the improvement. With no control group, however, we cannot say with confidence that the improvement shown by the treatment group was the result of the treatment. It could be that the improvement would have occurred even in the absence of the treatment. The control group, which is comparable to the treatment group in all ways except that it does not receive the treatment, helps in ruling out this possibility. Control groups thus are very important to the ability to state whether an independent variable causes change in a dependent variable (see Chapters 2 and 10). In fact, the evidence-based practice (EBP) approaches discussed in Chapter 1 give the most credence to evidence resulting from research designs that use random assignment of people to treatment and control groups. These EBP approaches argue that such research designs provide the "best" evidence.

Presumably, research is being conducted on some treatment because that treatment is believed to be effective. Herein lies the ethical dilemma: Some service providers believe it is unethical to withhold a treatment that might help people. They believe that withholding treatment deprives people in the control group of the possibility of improvement. This is a serious problem that is not easy to resolve, but there are a number of issues to consider: First, we might ask whether it is ethical to use untested treatments. We pointed out in Chapter 1 that evidence-based approaches to human service professions explicitly caution against the use of treatments without proven effectiveness. Providing services is expensive and time-consuming, and it also raises clients' expectations for improvement. Is it ethical to do this when no evidence documents that the treatment will be beneficial? For the most part, we would not think of marketing new medicines without a thorough test of their effects, both positive and negative. We should expect no less from the human services we offer.

Alternatives sometimes can be found to withholding treatment. One alternative would be to offer the control group a treatment that is known to be effective and then see whether the new treatment provides more or less improvement. In this way, all clients are receiving a treatment that is either known to be or suspected of being effective. In the study of the effectiveness of suicide intervention programs, for example, one certainly would be reluctant to evaluate a new intervention by using a control group that received no intervention at all. One study of outpatient interventions targeting suicidal young adults used a randomized experiment in which subjects were assigned either to a new experimental treatment or to a control group that received a treatment that had been commonly used for these interventions. Although both groups showed improvement, the experimental treatment was more effective in retaining the highest risk participants (Rudd, Rajab, & Orman, 1996).

Another alternative to withholding treatment would be to delay giving the treatment to the control group and make the comparisons between those receiving treatment and the control group over this period of time. For example, in a study of two different approaches to controlling people's smoking, all participants in the study were told that, if they were randomly placed in the group that would not receive immediate treatment, not only would they receive treatment when the study was over, they would receive whichever treatment the study showed to be most effective (Coehlo, 1983). This resolves the ethical problem by ensuring that all participants will receive treatment at some point.

In cases without such alternatives, however, clinician–researchers must use the risk–benefit approach: Does the benefit to be gained from the research outweigh the risks of withholding treatment from the people in the control group? If we were studying people at high risk of suicide, we would be cautious about withholding treatment. In the treatment of nonassertiveness, on the other hand, we might decide that a delay of a few weeks in treatment

would not be terribly detrimental and that whatever damage occurred could be undone once treatment was initiated. As with so many other ethical issues, this is ultimately a judgmental one over which clinician–researchers will continue to agonize.

CODES OF ETHICS

A point emphasized in this chapter is that ethical judgments are difficult and often controversial, because they involve interpretation and assessment. Most professional organizations establish written codes of ethics to serve as guides for their members to follow. These codes by no means settle all debate, but they do stand as a foundation from which professionals can begin to formulate ethical decisions. These codes can be found at the websites and in publications of the major organizations of professionals who conduct research in the social sciences and human services. See, for example, the web pages of these organizations:

- American Sociological Association (www.asanet.org)
- National Association of Social Workers (www.socialworkers.org)
- Association for Applied and Clinical Sociology (www.aacsnet.net)
- American Association for Public Opinion Research (www.aapor.org)

The codes of ethics of other social science and human service professions would be similar to these.

REVIEW AND CRITICAL THINKING

Main Points

- What is ethical in research and practice is based on human values and varies as those values change.
- The mistreatment of minorities in research has been a major impetus to the development of ethical standards for research in the United States and abroad.
- Social research typically is evaluated in terms of risks versus benefits, with some "questionable practices" allowed if the research promises sufficient benefits.

- Informed consent ensures participants the ability to determine their own destiny but may prevent the use of some research methods and force the study of only those persons who volunteer.
- Some level of deception is sometimes used in research, but whether or under what conditions deception is acceptable has been highly controversial.
- Research subjects have a right to privacy, which can be protected by letting them edit data about themselves from a data set, keeping the data anonymous, or keeping the data confidential.
- Confidentiality and anonymity are not the same thing. Intrusion by third parties, such as courts of law, occasionally can be a threat to the guarantee of confidentiality.
- Exposing subjects to physical or mental distress should be kept to a minimum and should never be done without fully informed consent. Subjects should be thoroughly debriefed at the conclusion of the research.
- When conducting research for a sponsor, many ethical difficulties can be avoided by a detailed research agreement that covers and reveals such topics as the purpose and nature of the research, the rights of publication, and the sponsor of the research.
- Researchers have an obligation to report their results fully and honestly and to avoid any kind of scientific misconduct or fraud. Replication is a major tool of science for correcting research errors and fraudulent reports.
- It is the researcher's own decision regarding the degree to which he or she will become an advocate; however, caution is required so that objectivity is not undermined.
- Because of their disadvantaged status, human service clients often are vulnerable to coercion to participate in research projects and, therefore, require special protection.
- Withholding treatment from control groups raises an ethical dilemma, but it often is justified when testing unproved approaches.
- Most professional organizations have established codes of ethics that provide useful guidelines for making ethical decisions.

IMPORTANT TERMS FOR REVIEW

Anonymity	Ethics	Misconduct (scientific)
Confidentiality	Fraud (scientific)	Privacy
Control group	Informed consent	

CRITICAL THINKING

1. Imagine you are working at an agency providing mental health counseling. You are conducting a survey and conduct interviews with 10 to 15 clients. What research ethics considerations should you consider? What steps should you take to help ensure you are engaging in ethically sound research?

2. As with all research, surveys and interviews like those from the preceding question involve some level of risk to research participants. (Here these are clients of your agency.) What risks might clients face through participation in a survey or interview? How might you help minimize or address these risks?

3. Evaluations conducted by social service agencies are not typically subject to review by IRBs. Why would it be important for you (as a practitioner conducting a program evaluation) to adhere to ethical standards and procedures pertaining to research?

EVALUATING COMPETENCY (FROM THE COUNCIL ON SOCIAL WORK EDUCATION [CSWE] 2015 EDUCATIONAL POLICY AND ACCREDITATION STANDARDS [EPAS])

Competency 1: Demonstrate Ethical and Professional Behavior

- As practitioners you may be asked to help researchers complete studies by recruiting study participants, sharing your professional experiences or expertise, or sharing data with researchers. In most cases, the researchers with whom you work will be well versed in ethical standards for research and received IRB approval for their studies. Still it is possible that your participation could create risk for you, your agency, and your clients. What might you (as a human service professional) do to minimize these risks?

- As professionals we are committed to lifelong learning and continuously upgrading our knowledge and skills. How do these commitments relate to conducting, consuming, and participating in research?

Competency 2: Engage Difference and Diversity

- Why would it be important to include a diverse sample of clients, including clients from marginalized populations, when completing a program evaluation (as in the preceding question)? What should you do to help ensure that members of marginalized populations are treated ethically when conducting this research?

- How can practitioners use their knowledge of vulnerable clients and mechanisms of oppression they face in advocating for their ethical treatment in research?

Competency 3: Advance Human Rights and Social and Economic Justice

- Social workers and other human service professionals advocate for marginalized and otherwise disadvantaged populations. We know that objectivity is crucial to research, but can be challenging when deeply engaged in advocacy. How might you engage in high-quality research related to social issues while also promoting social and economic justice and the proliferation of human rights?

- Is it possible to engage in objective research related to social issues while also pushing an agenda of increased social justice?

Competency 9: Evaluate Practice With Individuals, Families, Groups, Organizations, and Communities

- Social workers and other human service professionals are expected to evaluate services and programs. At times these evaluations may show that services or programs are ineffective or have not been properly implemented. Reporting these findings may impact some professionals' jobs or programs' funding. Should social workers and other professionals report negative findings?
- How can findings from program evaluations be used to improve services? What roles should social workers and other professionals play in this process?

SELF-ASSESSMENT
. . . .

1. Ethical questions (including research ethics questions):
   a. Generally have few simple or final answers and no scientific tests that can show us whether actions are ethical.
   b. Are easily answerable when ethical guidelines and scientific tests are followed.
   c. Should not be asked because researchers and research subjects feel uncomfortable.
   d. Can only be answered by licensed professionals.
2. Requirements in research studies that full disclosure of relevant information should be made to the participants; voluntary participation in research must be completely voluntary; and informed consent were products of:
   a. The Belmont Report
   b. The Nuremberg Code
   c. Institutional Review Boards
   d. The U.S. Public Health Service
3. The risk–benefit doctrine holds that:
   a. Risks must be avoided for research subjects unless the research provides sufficient benefits for disadvantaged populations.
   b. Risks are generally high for research subjects, which is why they must be compensated for their time.
   c. Questionable practices may be used if the purpose of the study is viewed as sufficiently important to justify them.
   d. There are higher benefits to researchers who take greater risk.
4. Informed consent:
   a. Is always required in research and does not impede researchers' abilities to collect and analyze data.
   b. Is required in many cases because it helps protect research participants' rights, but can negatively impact researchers' abilities to collect and analyze data.

    c. Is a good idea but should be up to researchers to determine whether or not it is needed.

    d. Is required by law for all social research.

5. Ethical absolutists would:

    a. Argue that it is wrong to include humans in social research because there are always risks associated with any research.

    b. Never publish research results unless completely sure their findings are valid.

    c. Vigorously campaign against funding for research that is contrary to their stances on social issues.

    d. Rule out all deception in research on the grounds that it is unethical to deceive other human beings deliberately.

6. Privacy and confidentiality:

    a. Are different but related concepts.

    b. Are antonyms.

    c. Are synonyms.

    d. Are not required in social research.

7. Anonymity is achieved when:

    a. Only one researcher can link data to an individual research participant (subject).

    b. Data are deleted from computer files.

    c. No one, including the researcher, can link data to individual research participants.

    d. Pseudonyms are used in reports and presentations to mask research participants' identities.

8. Certificates of confidentiality:

    a. Are given to research participants/subjects so that they are not required to disclose personal information.

    b. Are time limited.

    c. Protect researchers from being forced to disclose identifiable research information.

    d. Are required for all research funded by the federal government.

9. Which of the following are ethical considerations of sponsored research?

    a. Control over the release of data.

    b. The purpose and nature of the research.

    c. Informed consent and the disclosure of the sponsoring organization.

    d. All of the above.

10. Research fraud:

    a. Generally happens by accident.

    b. Can be avoided by undergoing an IRB review prior to engaging in research.

    c. Is the deliberate falsification, misrepresentation, or plagiarizing of data, findings, or ideas of others.

    d. Almost never happens in academic settings or when professional researchers conduct studies.

ANSWER KEY FOR SELF-ASSESSMENT QUIZ

1. **a.** Generally have few simple or final answers and no scientific tests that can show us whether actions are ethical.
2. **b.** The Nuremberg Code.
3. **c.** Questionable practices may be used if the purpose of the study is viewed as sufficiently important to justify them.
4. **b.** Is required in many cases because it helps protect research participants' rights, but can negatively impact researchers' abilities to collect and analyze data.
5. **d.** Rule out all deception in research on the grounds that it is unethical to deceive other human beings deliberately.
6. **a.** Are different but related concepts.
7. **c.** No one, including the researcher, can link data to individual research participants.
8. **c.** Protect researchers from being forced to disclose identifiable research information.
9. **d.** All of the above.
10. **c.** Is the deliberate falsification, misrepresentation, or plagiarizing of data, findings, or ideas of others.

FOR FURTHER READING

Caplan, A. L. (Ed.). (1992). *When medicine went mad.* Totowa, NJ: Humana Press. This volume contains articles relating to the research conducted by the Nazis during World War II. Although it deals with an extreme situation, it does provide an illustration of what can happen when science "goes mad."

Citro, C. F., Ilgen, D. R., & Marrett, C. B. (Eds.). (2003). *Protecting participants and facilitating social and behavioral sciences research.* Washington, DC: National Academies Press. This report examines three key issues related to human participation in social research: obtaining informed, voluntary consent from prospective participants; guaranteeing the confidentiality of information collected from participants; and using appropriate review procedures for "minimal-risk" research.

Corey, G., Corey, M. S., & Callanan, P. (2011). *Issues and ethics in the helping professions* (8th ed.). Belmont, CA: Brooks/Cole, Cengage. A comprehensive review of ethical issues in the many realms of human service practice. Given the linkage between research and practice, the analysis of practice ethics is relevant to clinician–researchers in the human services.

Crossen, C. (1994). *Tainted truth: The manipulation of fact in America.* New York, NY: Simon & Schuster. An enlightening book by a journalist about the many frauds that can be perpetrated by scientists. The author shows how frauds can be artfully crafted and how they can adversely affect us all.

Lee, R. (1993). *Doing research on sensitive topics.* Newbury Park, CA: Sage. Ethical issues become especially important and complicated when doing research on sensitive topics, and this author suggests ethical guidelines for navigating such treacherous waters.

Mertens, D. M., & Ginsberg, P. E. (Eds.). (2009). *The handbook of social research ethics.* Thousand Oaks, CA: Sage. The handbook provides a comprehensive understanding of the history, theory, philosophy, and implementation of applied social research ethics through a collection of writings by eminent, international scholars across the social and behavioral sciences and education. It also examines the ethical dilemmas that arise in the relationship between research practice and social justice issues.

Washington, H. A. (2006). *Medical apartheid: The dark history of medical experimentation on Black Americans from colonial times to the present.* New York, NY: Doubleday. The author provides a comprehensive history of medical experimentation on African Americans. The book details the way both slaves and freedmen were used in hospitals for experiments conducted without a hint of informed consent—a tradition that the author argues continues today within some Black populations.

Zimbardo, P. G. (2007). *The Lucifer effect: Understanding how good people turn evil.* New York, NY: Random House. The researcher who conducted the now-famous Stanford prisoner experiment addresses the question: What makes good people do bad things? Although research ethics is not the primary subject, the author's discussion of his controversial study provides rich illustrations of research ethics.

REFERENCES

Baumrind, D. (1985). Research using intentional deception. *American Psychologist, 40*(2), 165–174. doi:10.1037//0003-066x.40.2.165

Beauchamp, T. L., Faden, R. R., Wallace, Jr., R. J., & Walters, L. (Eds.). (1982). *Ethical issues in social science research.* Baltimore, MD: Johns Hopkins University Press.

Berger, R. L. (1994). Ethics in scientific communication: Study of a problem case. *Journal of Medical Ethics, 20*, 207–211. doi:10.1136/jme.20.4.207

Beskow, L. M., Dame, L., & Costello, E. J. (2008). Research ethics: Certificates of confidentiality and compelled disclosure of data. *Science, 322*, 1054–1055. doi:10.1126/science.1164100

Bonnie, R. J., & Wallace, R. B. (Eds.). (2003). *Elder mistreatment: Abuse, neglect, and exploitation in an aging America.* Washington, DC: National Academies Press.

Brajuha, M., & Hallowell, L. (1986). Legal intrusion and the politics of fieldwork. *Urban Life, 14*, 454–479. doi:10.1177/0098303986014004005

Browne, C. J., & Nash, K. (Eds.). (2010). *Queer methods and methodologies: Intersecting queer theories and social science research.* New York, NY: Routledge.

Brunswick Heineman, M. (1981). The obsolete scientific imperative in social work research. *Social Service Review, 55*, 371–397. doi:10.1086/643939

Check, D. K., Wolf, L. E., Dame, L. A., & Beskow, L. M. (2014). Certificates of confidentiality and informed consent: Perspectives of IRB chairs and institutional legal counsel. *IRB: Ethics and Human Research, 36*(1), 1–8.

Coehlo, R. J. (1983). *An experimental investigation of two multi-component approaches on smoking cessation* (Unpublished doctoral dissertation). Michigan State University.

De Oliveira, L. H., Vissoci, J. N., Machado, W. L., Rodrigues, C. G., & Limkakeng, A. T. (2017). Are well-informed potential trial participants more likely to participate? *Journal of Empirical Research on Human Research Ethic, 12*(5), 363–371. doi:10.1177/1556264617737163

Drewry, S. (2004). The ethics of human subjects protection in research. *The Journal of Baccalaureate Social Work, 10*, 105–117. doi:10.18084/1084-7219.10.1.105

Dunaway, B. (2017). Ethical vagueness and practical reasoning. *Philosophical Quarterly, 67*(266), 38–60. doi:10.1093/pq/pqw038

Eckenwiler, L. A. (1999). Pursuing reform in clinical research: Lessons from women's experience. *Journal of Law, Medicine & Ethics, 27*, 158–170. doi:10.1111/j.1748-720X.1999.tb01448.x

Elms, A. C. (1982). Keeping deception honest: Justifying conditions for social scientific research strategies. In T. L. Beauchamp, R. R. Faden, R. J. Wallace, Jr., & L. Walters (Eds.), *Ethical issues in social science research* (pp. 232–245). Baltimore, MD: Johns Hopkins University Press.

Engler, R. L., Covell, J. W., Friedman, P. J., Kitcher, P. S., & Peters, R. M. (1987). Misrepresentation and responsibility in medical research. *New England Journal of Medicine, 317*(22), 1383–1389. doi:10.1056/NEJM198711263172205

Erikson, K. T. (1967). A comment on disguised observation in sociology. *Social Problems, 14*, 366–373. doi:10.2307/798850

Fay, B. (1987). *Critical social science: Liberation and its limits.* Ithaca, NY: Cornell University Press.

Fox, R. J., Crask, M. R., & Kim, J. (1988). Mail survey response rate: A meta-analysis of selected techniques for inducing response. *Public Opinion Quarterly, 52*, 467–491. doi:10.1086/269125

Gibbs, L. (1983). Evaluation researcher: Scientist or advocate? *Journal of Social Service Research. 7*, 81–92. doi:10.1300/J079v07n01_06

Gibelman, M., & Gelman, S. R. (2001). Learning from the mistakes of others: A look at scientific misconduct in research. *Journal of Social Work Education, 37*, 241–254. doi:10.1080/10437797.2001.10779051

Gordon, M. M. (1988). *The scope of sociology.* New York, NY: Oxford University Press.

Gouldner, A. (1976). The dark side of the dialectic: Toward a new objectivity. *Sociological Inquiry, 46*, 3–16. doi:10.1111/j.1475-682X.1976.tb00743.x

Gray, B. H. (1982). The regulatory context of social and behavioral research. In T. L. Beauchamp, R. R. Faden, R. J. Wallace, Jr., & L. Walters (Eds.), *Ethical issues in social science research* (pp. 329–355). Baltimore, MD: Johns Hopkins University Press.

Halfpenny, P. (1982). *Positivism and sociology: Explaining social life.* London, UK: Allen & Unwin.

Harmon, A. (2010). Indian tribe wins fight to limit research of its DNA. *New York Times.* Retrieved from https://www.nytimes.com/2010/04/22/us/22dna.html?pagewanted=all&_r=0

Huber, B. (1981). New human subjects policies announced; Exemptions outlined. *ASA Footnotes, 9,* 1.

Humphreys, L. (1970). *Tearoom trade: Impersonal sex in public places.* Chicago, IL: Aldine-Atherton.

Jones, J. H. (Ed.). (1992). *Bad blood: The Tuskegee syphilis experiment.* New York, NY: Free Press.

Katz, J. (1972). *Experimentation with human beings.* New York, NY: Russell Sage Foundation.

Kimmel, A. (1988). *Ethics and values in applied social research.* Newbury Park, CA: Sage.

Kimmel, A. J., Smith, N. C., & Klein, J. G. (2011). Ethical decision making and research deception in the behavioral sciences: An application of social contract theory. *Ethics & Behavior, 21*(3), 222–251. doi:10.1080/10508422.2011.570166

King, N. M. P., Henderson, G. E., & Stein, J. (Eds.). (1999). *Beyond regulations: Ethics in human subjects research.* Chapel Hill: University of North Carolina Press.

Leo, R. A. (1995). Trial and tribulations: Courts, ethnography, and the need for an evidentiary privilege for academic researchers. *American Sociologist, 26,* 113–134. doi:10.1007/BF02692013

Leo, R. A. (1996). The ethics of deceptive research roles reconsidered: A response to Kai Erikson. *American Sociologist, 27,* 122–128. doi:10.1007/BF02692002

Margolin, G., Chien, D., Duman, S. E., Fauchier, A., Gordis, E. B., Oliver, P. H., . . . Vickerman, K. A. (2005). Ethical issues in couple and family research. *Journal of Family Psychology, 19,* 157–167. doi:10.1037/0893-3200.19.1.157

Marx, K. (1964). *Selected writings in sociology and philosophy* (T. B. Bottomore, Trans. & M. Rubel, Ed.). Baltimore, MD: Penguin. (Original work published 1848).

Moe, K. (1984). Should the Nazi research data be cited? *Hastings Center Report, 14,* 5–7. doi:10.2307/3561733

Murray, L., Donovan, R., Kail, B. L., & Medvene, L. J. (1980). Protecting human subjects during social work research: Researchers' opinions. *Social Work Research and Abstracts, 16,* 25–30. doi:10.1093/swra/16.2.25

National Cancer Institute. (1998). *Certificates of confidentiality: Background information and application procedures.* Washington, DC: U.S. Department of Health and Human Services.

National Commission for the Protection of Human Subjects of Biomedical and Behavioral Research. (1978). *The Belmont report: Ethical principles and guidelines for the protection of human subjects of research.* Washington, DC: Department of Health, Education, and Welfare.

Nyden, P., Figert, A., Shibley, M., & Burrows, D. (1997). *Building community: Social science in action.* Thousand Oaks, CA: Pine Forge Press.

Oeye, C., Bjelland, A. K., & Skorpen, A. (2007). Doing participant observation in a psychiatric hospital—research ethics resumed. *Social Science & Medicine, 65,* 2296–2306. doi:10.1016/j.socscimed.2007.07.016

Office of Research Integrity. (2010). *Annual Report 2009.* Washington, DC: Department of Health and Human Services.

Ortmann, A., & Hertwig, R. (1997). Is deception acceptable? *American Psychologist, 52*(7), 746–747. doi:10.1037/0003-066X.52.7.746

Palmer, B. (2010). Mein Data: Did any useful science come out of the Nazi concentration camps? *Slate.* Retrieved from http://www.slate.com/articles/news_and_politics/explainer/2010/06/mein_data.html

Peterson, R. R. (1996). A re-evaluation of the economic consequences of divorce. *American Sociological Review, 61,* 528–536. doi:10.2307/2096363

Protection of Human Subjects, 45 C.F.R. § 46 (2018).

Ratzan, R. M. (1981). The experiment that wasn't: A case report in clinical geriatric research. *Gerontologist, 21,* 297–302. doi:10.1093/geront/21.3.297

Reinharz, S. (1992). *Feminist methods in social research.* New York, NY: Oxford University Press.

Reverby, S. M. (Ed.). (2000). *Tuskegee's truths: Rethinking the Tuskegee syphilis study.* Chapel Hill: University of North Carolina Press.

Reynolds, P. D. (1979). *Ethical dilemmas and social science research.* San Francisco, CA: Jossey-Bass.

Ritchie, J., Lewis, J., Nicholls, C. M., & Ormston, R. (2013). *Qualitative research practice: A guide for social science students and researchers.* Newbury Park, CA: Sage.

Rudd, M. D., Rajab, M. H., & Orman, D. T. (1996). Effectiveness of an outpatient intervention targeting suicidal young adults: Preliminary results. *Journal of Consulting and Clinical Psychology*, *64*, 179–190. doi:10.1037/0022-006X.64.1.179

Scarce, R. (2005). *Contempt of court: A scholar's battle for free speech from behind bars.* Lanham, MD: Altamira Press.

Schafer, A. (1986). On using Nazi data: The case against. *Dialogue, 25*, 413–419. doi:10.1017/S0012217300020862

Sherman, L. (1992). *Policing domestic violence: Experiments and dilemmas.* New York, NY: Free Press.

Sieber, J. E., & Tolich, M. B. (2013). *Planning ethically responsible research* (Vol. 31). Los Angeles, CA: Sage.

Singer, E., von Thurn, D. R., & Miller, E. R. (1995). Confidentiality and response: A quantitative review of the experimental literature. *Public Opinion Quarterly, 59*, 446–459. doi:10.1086/269458

Smith, H. W. (1981). *Strategies of social research* (2nd ed.). Englewood Cliffs, NJ: Prentice Hall.

Weber, M. (1946). Science as a vocation. In H. H. Garth & C. W. Mills (Eds.), *Max Weber, essays in sociology* (pp. 129–156). New York, NY: Free Press. (Original work published 1922).

Wendler, D. (1996). Deception in medical and behavioral research: Is it ever acceptable? *The Milbank Quarterly, 74*(1), 87–4114. doi:10.2307/3350434

Wiles, R., Crow, G., Heath, S., & Charles, V. (2008). The management of confidentiality and anonymity in social research. *International Journal of Social Research Methodology, 11*(5), 417–428. doi:10.1080/13645570701622231

Wolfgang, M. E. (1981). Confidentiality in criminological research and other ethical issues. *Journal of Criminal Law and Criminology, 72*, 345–361. doi:10.2307/1142913

4

PROBLEM FORMULATION: DEVELOPING A WELL-BUILT ANSWERABLE QUESTION

INTRODUCTION

Stephen Fraser works at "Recovery Community," which is a sexual assault recovery center in San Antonio, Texas. Recovery Community is a center to empower those who have been victimized by sexual violence through advocacy, crisis intervention, and to educate the community about the impact of sexual assault. Stephen has worked at the center for over 3 years in a variety of positions. He started working at the center after he received his master's in social work. His first job at the center was working the crisis line and he has since moved into outreach and education. In his current role, he delivers violence prevention programming to many different high schools and middle schools in the area. Stephen states, "Prevention work can be challenging when there are many schools that want and need the program, but because of funding we cannot hire more educators and that leaves us turning away some schools" (S. Fraser, personal communication, May 12, 2018). The center has recently received news from their grantor that they will no longer be able to fund program delivery of the violence prevention program if the center cannot provide data showing effectiveness.

In the past, the center has only collected data on the presenter of the program and not the actual participants of the program. Stephen's boss has requested that he explore what strategies are effective for reducing dating violence through prevention efforts. Two different (but comparable) high schools are willing to let Stephen and the center test out program effectiveness in their health classes. The two high schools are similar in demographic makeup of their students.

This chapter addresses issues in problem formulation and the process of developing research questions. All good research projects require constructing a well-built answerable question. As you read this chapter, consider Stephen's situation and keep the following critical thinking questions in mind: (a) What different skills and resources do social workers possess to accomplish this project? (b) What is the first task a social worker needs to complete when starting a research project? (c) What information is needed to build an answerable research question? and (d) What additional resources would be helpful to successfully formulate a well-built research question?

Suppose you were required, as many students in social research courses are, to design and conduct a research project. Our experience teaching research courses in the social sciences and human services is that some students respond to this assignment by drawing a total blank. Others, however, grasp eagerly onto a topic, such as best practices for supporting people with substance use disorders, and rush off with total confidence that they are about to solve this enduring problem. In each case, the student is having difficulty adequately formulating a research problem. In the first case, the difficulty is in locating a problem to investigate, whereas in the second, the trouble lies in formulating a problem sufficiently specific that it is amenable to scientific research.

We assure you this problem is not unique to students. Every researcher must grapple with problem formulation. Because it is the initial step and provides the basis for the complete research project, problem formulation is of crucial importance. Many potentially serious difficulties can be avoided—or at least managed—by careful problem formulation. In this chapter, we present:

- How to formulate a well-built question
- How to select a problem on which to conduct research
- How to refine the research question so that it can be answered through research
- Factors relating to the feasibility of research

SELECTING A RESEARCH PROBLEM

The first hurdle confronting a researcher is to select an appropriate topic for scientific investigation. In the "Recovery Community" example at the beginning of the chapter, Stephen needs to develop a good research question that will be helpful in successfully completing his project. Actually, this is not as difficult as it may first appear, because the social world around us is teeming with unanswered questions. Selecting a problem calls for some creativity and imagination, but researchers can turn to a number of places for inspiration.

Personal Interest

Research topics often are selected because a researcher has an interest in some aspect of human behavior, possibly owing to some personal experience. One social scientist, for example, conducted research on battered women and women's shelters in part because of her own earlier experience of being abused by her husband; another researcher, who had grown up in the only African American family of a small rural town, did research on prejudice, discrimination, and the experience of minorities (Higgins & Johnson, 1988).

Researchers who select topics from their personal interests must be careful to demonstrate the scientific worth of their projects. Recall from Chapter 1 that the goals of scientific research are to describe, to explain, to predict, and to evaluate. The purpose of research is to advance our knowledge, not just satisfy personal curiosity. For example, in her study of female strippers, psychologist Tania Israel (2002) was interested in learning how people adapt to a job that many consider to be deviant. Such a focus placed her research firmly in an established area of study and amplified its scientific contribution. A researcher who chooses a topic based on personal interest—especially if it deals with what some may deem atypical behavior—should be prepared for the possibility that others will fail to see the worth of that research. Even though Israel, as noted, established a legitimate scientific rationale for her study of strippers, she was subjected to considerable criticism by those who failed to appreciate its scientific value; critics derided her research as lacking in rigor, illegitimate, and embarrassing.

Social Problems

In selecting a topic, researchers often need to look no farther than the daily news, which is full of the many social problems that our society faces. Such problems as crime, delinquency, poverty, pollution, overpopulation, drug abuse, alcoholism, mental illness, sexual deviance, discrimination, domestic violence, and political oppression have all been popular sources of topics for social research. The Society for the Study of Social Problems—a professional organization to which many social scientists and human service providers belong—publishes the journal *Social Problems,* whose sole purpose is to communicate the results of scientific investigations into current social problems.

Each of these general categories of social problems encompasses a range of issues for study. Many studies, for example, focus on the sources of a problem. Others are concerned with the consequences these problems have for individuals or for society. Still others deal with the outcomes of social programs and other intervention efforts intended to ameliorate these problems. People in the human services, who are routinely involved with many of these problems, can find opportunities for research that are directly related to their professional activities.

Testing Theory

Some researchers select problems based on their use in testing and verifying a particular theory. We noted in Chapter 2 that theoretical concerns should be at issue to some degree in all research. Nearly all research has some implications for existing theory. Certain research topics, however, are selected specifically to test some aspect of a given theory. Many theories relevant to the human services have not been thoroughly tested. In some cases, this means that we do not know how valid the theories are; in others, it means that we do not know how wide the range of human behavior is to which the theory can be applied.

Prior Research

One of the most fruitful sources of research problems is prior research because the findings of all research projects have limitations. Some questions are answered, but others always remain. In addition, the findings may raise new questions. It is, in fact, common for investigators to conclude research reports with a discussion of the weaknesses and limitations of the research, including suggestions

for future research that follow from the findings that have been presented. Focusing on these unanswered questions, or expanding on previous research, is a good way to find research problems.

Prior research can also lead to new research problems if we have reason to question the findings of the original research. As emphasized in Chapter 2, it is imperative that we not complacently accept research findings, especially when conclusions are based on a single study, because opportunities exist for error or bias to influence results. If we have reason to suspect research findings, we have a ready-made problem on which to conduct research ourselves. One of our own students, in fact, found his topic in just this way when faced with the course assignment of conducting a research project. The student had read a research article suggesting a number of differences between the social settings in which marijuana is used and those in which alcohol is used. The student disagreed, partly because of his own experiences, believing instead that the social environments in which the two substances were used were, in fact, quite similar. He designed a study that allowed him to determine whether his hypotheses—or those presumably verified by the previous investigation—would better predict what he would observe. As it turned out, many of his hypotheses were supported by his findings.

Program Evaluation and Policy Implementation

Program evaluation focuses on assessing the effectiveness or efficiency of some policy, program, or practice. As noted in Chapter 1, program and practice effectiveness evaluations have become increasingly important activities for human service professionals. Today, agencies or organizations that fund the human services typically demand that evaluation research be conducted if funding is to be granted or continued. Such research, developed for practical reasons, can take many forms. Practitioner Profile 4.1 illustrates a practical example of how program evaluation and implementation can be conducted in communities. A social agency, for example, may require some needs assessment research to gather information about its clients if it is to deliver services to them

PRACTITIONER PROFILE 4.1 Timothy Jones, Program Manager and Evaluation Coordinator, Appalachian District Health Department, North Carolina

Tim Jones is currently working as the program manager and evaluation coordinator for the Appalachian District Health Department, which serves multiple counties in the state of North Carolina, and he is currently managing two grants for the Positive Parenting Project and the Initiative Positive Parenting program, which are being implemented in North Carolina. These programs are used to deter child maltreatment and help individuals become better parents by using four levels of intervention that are structured to meet the needs of clients. Tim states, "The data collected prior to treatment and then after intervention is vital to the state and is an evidence-based approach to social work practice." North Carolina is the first state in the country to conduct the Positive Parenting Program, which Tim states, "I am excited to have the opportunity to be at the forefront of evaluating the program in the U.S."

Tim holds a bachelor's and master's degree in social work, which are staples in his passion to help others and are essential for effectiveness at his job. Tim states that he was "suffering from burnout as a chef, and had a desire to help people beyond his current job of serving in culinary capacity" (T. Jones, personal communication, June 1, 2018). His initial aspirations were to become a substance abuse counselor; however, that changed when he began taking research classes in his undergraduate studies. Tim states, "I learned about the international influence social work has on various populations and how research is needed to inform social work practice." He further stated the first step in research is "understanding that all research begins with an answerable research question that is geared around the problem and population served."

Tim works as a community social researcher and implements change at a macrolevel by using research to inform policies that would affect community healthcare. Tim, when discussing the importance of research, stated, "seeing how the importance of data, data utilization, and confidentiality were in research, I became more astute by applying research to community health assessments and implementing change at the community level at the health department."

Tim uses different health assessments to identify health problems that are relative to the community; they assess for an array of community health problems such as environmental factors, water quality, infant mortality rate, and rates of child abuse. The importance of *data feedback loops*, or the feedback cycle of research and community data collected, helps solve community problems. He states, "The feedback loop tells a story of the data, and it uses organic approach because that's what people connect to, thus making it more relatable." Research encompasses all of Tim's work as a project manager and evaluation coordinator.

efficiently. Or, a practitioner may need to know which intervention strategy—group work, psychotherapy, behavior therapy, or some other—will be most effective with a particular problem. Prison officials need to know which criminal offenders are the riskiest to parole. Home healthcare workers need information about how to ensure that people will take medications as prescribed. In all these cases, the practical information required by an agency or practitioner determines the focus of the research effort.

The ability to find problems in practice settings that could be the focus of program evaluation research is limited only by the creativity and imagination of the practitioner. This was brought home to us by two of our students during a recent social research course. They were doing a field placement in a community mental health clinic while taking our research course, so they decided to search for some problem at the clinic to serve as the focus of their research paper. These students noticed that one problem the clinic faced was the failure of clients to show up for appointments. In addition to creating difficulties in achieving effective intervention, this also resulted in an inefficient use of staff resources because counselors were left idle by missed appointments. The students designed a very simple investigation in which some clients were given a reminder phone call a day or so before their appointment and other clients were not contacted, as had been the previous practice. The researchers' concern was to establish whether the reminder call increased the rate at which people showed up for their appointments. After implementing this procedure for a while, the students concluded that the phone call did help and would be a useful and efficient addition to the functioning of the agency.

Human Service Practice

The linkage between human service practice and evaluation research is obvious, but service delivery can serve as the catalyst for basic research as well. During the course of working in human service programs, practitioners confront social problems and human diversity daily as they interact with clients who are struggling with life problems. The protective service worker who faces child abuse and neglect may derive research questions about parent–child bonding or human development. Hospice staff may generate questions about the dying process and grieving. Although answers to these questions may have practice implications, research that addresses issues such as these also has important implications for social science theory.

It is not only the behavior or characteristics of clients that generate research questions in practice settings; the mode and process of human service practice itself may even be the topic of research. For example, the mechanisms by which some human service agencies differentially allocate services according to social class or race might be a research issue. In fact, study of the human service delivery system has generated many of the major theoretical advances in our understanding of human behavior and social environments. For instance, Glaser and Strauss (1965) based their classic studies concerning death and social worth on observations of hospital patient care. More

recently, controversy has surfaced in the human services over what appears to be the intergenerational transmission of family violence, suggesting that experiencing or observing violence during childhood results in subsequent violent behavior as a parent or spouse. Not only does research into this issue have practical implications for intervention programs, it also is directly relevant to developing our understanding of learning, human development, the family, and society as well (Burgess & Youngblade, 1988).

Minorities in Research: The Political Context of Problem Selection

From the preceding discussion of how to select a research problem, one could get the impression that the problem selection process is largely a matter of personal preference. Guided by personal interest or experience, the prospective researcher identifies a worthy problem and then sallies forth in the pursuit of knowledge. Like most other types of human activity, however, problem selection cannot be explained solely in such individual terms. In fact, if we asked students in research courses why they chose the term paper topics they did, we might find that, in addition to personal interest, theoretical orientation, or practice interest, their choices were governed by factors such as these: "My instructor had a data set available on this problem." "I got financial aid to work as a research assistant." "I knew my prof was interested in this topic, so I hoped studying it might help me get a better grade." In other words, issues of political efficacy can influence problem selection as well.

In the world of professional research, the situation is not unlike that of the student. The stakes are much higher, however, and the consequences are much greater. Although the number of possible research problems may be infinite, the resources that society can allocate to research them are not. Research is a major societal enterprise in which universities, governmental organizations, private research corporations, and independent researchers compete with each other for limited resources. At the same time, societal forces are working to make sure that the concerns of vested interest groups receive attention from the research community. Thus, problem selection is very much a political issue, and the problems that affect minorities and other groups with little clout may not receive the research attention they deserve.

Consider the example of spousal abuse. Men have been assaulting their wives since long before there was social research. Before the 1970s, however, one would have been hard-pressed to find much research on the topic. Today, the social science and human service literature is replete with studies on spousal abuse, and the research endeavor in this area has expanded into a focus on intimate-partner violence. What explains the change? There is no single answer, but a major factor has been the rise of the women's movement. Before the 1960s, women as a group had considerably less political power than they have today, and the special problems of this minority group often received little research attention. Woman and intimate-partner violence is now an important issue to the women's movement, and this politically powerful group has been able to translate its concerns into public policy. Partly because of its pressure, the government has allocated money specifically for research on intimate-partner violence. In addition, with the changing roles of women in society, more women during the past three decades have chosen to pursue careers as researchers in the social sciences. One result of more women in research positions is that, given the role of personal interest in the selection of research topics, women are more likely to identify woman and intimate-partner violence as a problem warranting research investigation. As the topic gained more prominence in the social science and human service fields, editors of journals became more receptive to publishing research articles on the topic. All these factors, over time, had a snowball effect. The availability of funds, the potential for publication, and the desire to contribute knowledge to an area of public concern attracted to this area researchers seeking problems to study.

So, one major factor influencing the allocation of research funds is the existence of a powerful, articulate, and effective interest group that can push for research on a particular problem (Breton

et al., 2017; Lally, 1977; Varmus, 1999). Other factors include the following:

- Support for research by influentials at the national policy-making levels
- Definition of a condition as a social problem by national influentials
- Public awareness of, and concern about, the condition
- Severity, extent, and economic costs of the condition
- Amount of publicity about the condition
- Amount of support for research on the condition by the major funding agencies

On this last point, it is important to recognize that major agencies of the government, such as the Department of Health and Human Services (DHHS) and the National Science Foundation (NSF), dispense millions of dollars for research each year. Support of congressional leaders and key personnel in these major departments is essential for problem areas to be deemed worthy of financial backing for research. Typically, funding sources publish *requests for proposals* (RFPs), which outline the organization's funding priorities and requirements. Researchers are invited to submit proposals for competitive consideration. Proposals may be for millions of research dollars, and the competition for funding is as intense and high-pressuring as any major business deal.

Given that the political process plays a major role in determining which problems are sufficiently important to warrant research attention, it is not surprising that those people who lack access to social power in our society also are those whose interests are least likely to be served by the research conducted. One recent—and particularly disturbing—example of minority status influencing funding was with AIDS research. During the early years of the spread of AIDS in the United States, almost all people contracting the virus were men who had sex with other men. Today, this has changed: Currently, only 68% of new HIV infections involve male-to-male sexual contact or intravenous drug use, and 31% result from heterosexual contact (Centers for Disease Control and Prevention [CDC], 2018). In the earlier years, however, AIDS was associated in many people's minds with two groups of people—homosexuals and intravenous drug users—who were seen as marginal and highly stigmatized by many Americans, especially those in positions of power. In fact, people widely defined AIDS for a number of years as a "gay disease" and, thus, as something that most Americans need not worry about. The attitude of many was summed up by the comment of a person who was later to be a staff member at the White House: "Those poor homosexuals. They have declared war on nature, and nature is exacting an awful retribution" (quoted in Shilts, 1987, p. 311). As long as AIDS was defined as a disease of deviants, funds for research on its cause and prevention were slow in coming.

Other reasons for the delayed response to the AIDS crisis existed beyond the marginality and stigma the early victims suffered (Shilts, 1987). For instance, the Reagan administration, which entered office in 1981, expressed as policy the emphasis on smaller government and austerity in social and health programs. The first AIDS victims in the United States appeared in 1980. The competition for government funds during the early 1980s was fierce, and AIDS researchers typically lost the battle, partly because those suffering from AIDS had less clout in the policy-making process than other groups competing for dwindling funds.

In short, society's response to the minority status of those afflicted with AIDS, along with other political factors, contributed to a significant delay in attacking the problem. It was not until AIDS began to threaten the supply of blood available for transfusions and fear arose that AIDS was entering the heterosexual population that considerable research support was forthcoming.

The selection of research problems is thus a highly political process. Although powerful interest groups will always play a role in this process, researchers need to avoid the perceptual blinders that often hinder the ability of the powerful to see which problems are sufficiently important or serious to warrant attention. Human service professionals, whether they actually conduct research or not, can play an important role in the political issues surrounding problem selection. In the course of practice, human service providers deal directly with those experiencing poverty, persons labeled as deviant, minority populations, and persons with limited power in society. This puts these providers in a position to serve as advocates for inclusion on the societal research agenda of problems relevant to their clientele.

We have discussed numerous sources of research topics for practitioner–researchers. Although we have discussed them separately, more than one of these factors often influence a given choice of a research topic. Finding a research topic, however, is only the first step in problem formulation. The next step is to shape it into a problem that empirical research can solve.

SHAPING AND REFINING THE PROBLEM

As we mentioned, a frustrating trap in which novice researchers often become ensnarled is choosing a topic that is so broad and encompassing that, by itself, it offers little guidance in terms of how to proceed. Finding the "causes of juvenile delinquency" sounds intriguing, but these topics provide little direction concerning where to begin to look. The next step in the research process, then, is to begin translating a general topical interest into a precise, researchable problem by narrowing the scope of the problem to manageable proportions. A single investigation is unlikely to uncover the causes of juvenile delinquency, but it might provide some insight regarding the influence of particular variables on the emergence of particular delinquencies. Refining, narrowing, and focusing a research problem do not occur all at once but, rather, form a continuous process involving multiple procedures.

Conceptual Development

In Chapter 2, we discussed the role of theories and hypotheses in the research process, pointing out that concepts are one of the central components of theories. In the refining of a research problem, one of the key steps is *conceptual development*: identifying and properly defining the concepts on which the study will focus. In exploratory studies, of course, we are entering areas where there is little conceptual development, and a major purpose of the research itself may be to identify and define concepts. In cases where theory and research already exist, however, some conceptual development occurs as a part of formulating a research problem. One part of this process, already discussed in Chapter 2, is to clearly define the meaning of concepts. Another part of the process is to narrow the focus of the concept so that it encompasses a topic that is feasible to research in a single study. For example, practitioners in a youth home who had an interest in juvenile delinquency might ask themselves, "Are we interested in all forms of delinquent behavior or only in some types?" In reality, the concept of delinquency is an extremely broad category that includes all actions by juveniles that violate criminal or juvenile codes. We have no reason to assume that a single cause can explain all types of delinquency. The focus of the research therefore might be narrowed to include only certain behaviors, such as violence or truancy. The goal of this specification process, then, is to make clear exactly what the focus of the research effort is.

Once the key concepts are clearly defined, the next consideration is their measurability. Only concepts that are in some way measurable can be used in the research process. Eventually, of course, concepts will have to be operationalized, as discussed in Chapter 2, so any that cannot be readily measurable will have to be dropped. Measuring concepts sometimes can be difficult, as we note in more detail in Chapter 5. In fact, theories at times include concepts that are difficult to operationalize. However, if the concepts in a proposed study cannot be measured, then some modification in the project—and, possibly, in the theory—is necessary. This process of refining and developing concepts as a part of the research process illustrates a point made in Chapter 2 regarding the interplay between theory and research: Theories provide concepts and hypotheses for research, whereas research modifies theories through conceptual development.

Question Development

A widely used framework for developing a research question is the acronym PICO, which stands for population or people of interest, intervention, comparison, and outcome.

- P—Population or people of interest. The characteristics of the population explored. For example, women who have survived intimate-partner violence or university students.
- I—Intervention. The intervention should be specified as clear as possible. For instance, dating violence prevention or cognitive behavioral treatment.
- C—Comparison. This should include any comparisons to the intervention explored. For example, treatment as usual or solution focus therapy.
- O—Outcome. This is the desired outcome from the research question. For example, decrease in violent attitudes and behaviors or an increase in mental health.

This framework can help provide a road map to help develop an answerable question. Exhibit 4.1 is a tool to help students develop an answerable research question using the PICO framework.

Review of the Literature

With concepts clarified and deemed to be measurable, we are ready to conduct a review of previous research that relates to our research problem. This review of the literature is a necessary and important part of the research process (Collins, Leech, & Onwuegbuzie, 2012; Locke, Silverman, & Spirduso, 2010). We do it to familiarize ourselves with the current state of knowledge regarding the research problem and to learn how others have delineated similar problems. Unless we are planning a replication, it is unlikely that we will formulate our problem precisely like any one of these previous studies; rather, we are likely to pick up ideas from several that we can integrate to improve our own. Through reviewing the relevant literature, we can further narrow the focus of the research project and ensure that we do not unnecessarily duplicate what others have already

EXHIBIT 4.1 Building a PICO Question

| Problem | | Intervention or | | |
Client Type	Client Problem	Action	Comparison	Outcome

In a complete sentence, write your PICO question in the following:

```



```

PICO, population, intervention, comparison, and outcome.

done. Researchers undoubtedly will find that pit-falls can be avoided by learning from others' experiences. For example, suppose that one or more specific approaches to a topic have proven to be unproductive—that is, several studies have failed to find significant results or strong relationships. In this case, unless there is good reason to believe that these earlier studies contained methodological weaknesses, the same approach is likely to lead to failure once again. Future research is likely to be more productive if it focuses on studies that have achieved some positive results.

A thorough literature review calls for familiarity with basic library utilization skills (including how to locate books, professional journals, and public documents) as well as online search skills. In a literature review, we conduct a systematic search of each research report for certain kinds of information. First, the reviewer pays attention to *theoretical and conceptual issues*: What concepts and theories are used, how well developed are they,

and have they been subjected to empirical tests before? If the theories and concepts are well developed, then they can serve as an important guide in designing the planned research and in explaining the relationships between variables. If they are not well developed, then one will have to rely more on personal insight and creativity. In this case, researchers sometimes consider doing exploratory research, which may involve loosely structured interviews and less quantitative measuring devices, as a way of advancing conceptual and theoretical development.

The *research hypotheses*, including identification of the *independent* and *dependent variables*, are the second component of a literature review. Are the hypotheses clearly stated and testable? Are they related to the variables and hypotheses being considered in the planned study? Existing research can provide some fairly specific direction in terms of already tested relationships between independent and dependent variables.

The *measurement* and the *operational definitions* used in previous research are the third focus of a literature review. As noted, successful operationalization of concepts often is difficult. Previous work in this area is invaluable in finding workable measures for concepts. Past measures may require modification to meet current needs, of course, but making these modifications probably is easier than developing completely new measures, which is a difficult and time-consuming process.

A literature review also informs us about the fourth important element of research—the most appropriate *research technique* for a particular research problem. Successful approaches by others should be noted and unsuccessful approaches avoided. It is of the utmost importance that the problem determines the research technique that is used, and not the other way around. Many data-gathering techniques exist because no single method is always best. As we note in subsequent chapters, each technique has its own strengths and weaknesses, and each is suitable for answering some questions but not others.

The *sampling strategy* is the fifth element of a literature review. Previous research can be useful in determining the sampling strategy to use and in avoiding sampling problems that others have encountered. For example, suppose that the study we propose calls for the use of mailed questionnaires. An ever-present problem with mailed questionnaires is making sure that a sufficient number of people complete and return them. It would be useful for us to know what other investigators have experienced with people like those we plan to survey. Not all groups respond to mailed questionnaires with the same degree of enthusiasm. If the group that we are proposing to sample has exhibited notoriously low return rates during the previous studies, we have to plan accordingly: We would probably increase the number of questionnaires mailed, and we would certainly use all available means of obtaining the highest possible response rate. Or, if we anticipate very low return rates, we may want to search for another group to study—or even consider whether this particular project is feasible at all.

Statistical technique is the sixth element of a literature review. In Chapters 5, 14, and 15, we discuss issues relating to appropriate use of statistics. In the literature review, we must be aware of procedures and what constraints the concepts, variables, and hypotheses placed on the kind of statistics that would be appropriate.

Finally, a literature review notes the *findings and conclusions* of the studies that are examined. Which hypotheses were confirmed, and what guidelines for future research were presented? One aspect of the findings to watch for is the *effect size*, which refers to how big an effect an independent variable has on a dependent variable. Although we discuss this concept more fully in Chapter 15, we need to assess whether a dependent variable is affected in only a small but measurable way or whether the impact is dramatic (Gibbs, 1991).

A thorough literature review involves evaluating and comparing many research reports, identifying where they used similar procedures and reached similar outcomes, and where there were discrepancies between studies. This can be a complicated process, especially when hundreds of studies may be involved. It sometimes is helpful to produce a summary table, such as Table 4.1, to make comparisons. Notice that the table cites each separate study in the left-hand column, along with a brief description of the intervention model used in the study. The next two columns give information about the research design, sampling procedures, and measurement devices. Then, a column contains a summary of the results of each study. The final column on the right addresses any limitations found in the research. A systematic literature review of this sort provides the most useful information from previous studies. One can see at a glance how many studies came to similar conclusions and how commonly certain measuring devices were used. The ability to compile and summarize succinctly the features of studies in this fashion is essential to formulating a research problem and refining it into a research question that can be empirically investigated.

Units of Analysis

An important element in the process of shaping and refining a research problem is the decision regarding the unit of analysis to be investigated.

TABLE 4.1 A Summary Table of a Literature Review of Research on Rural Homelessness

Authors (Area)	Methods	Measures	Sample	Results	Limitations
Mondello, Bradley, McLaughlin, and Shore (2009) (service use and costs)	Use of available data (human service agency records of actual costs of services)	Cost comparisons of housing and other services (before and after supportive housing) based on the actual costs recorded in agency files	Availability sample: all chronically homeless Maine residents with disabilities living in permanent supportive housing (163 agreed to participate)	Costs of services were greater for those individuals and families prior to supportive housing than after supportive housing placement (when factoring both housing and other services' costs)	Limited to Maine residents (in rural areas). Limited to those with service records (including cost records) both before and after supportive housing placement
First, Toomey, and Rife (1990) (demographics, coping behaviors)	Survey research (from in-person interviews)	Survey questions measure living arrangements, use of services, mental health and psychiatric assessments; Homeless Permanent Survey Instrument; Psychiatric Status Schedule	Snowball sample of 921 homeless adults in 21 rural counties in Ohio, located through homeless advocates, advisors, and contact persons who were knowledgeable of each county	Minorities are greatly overrepresented in rural homeless population. Roughly 40% were living in shelters, 14% outdoors or other substandard shelters, and 46% were staying with family and friends	Conducted in 1990. Limited to Ohio residents.
Hilton and DeJong (2010) (coping behaviors, felt experiences)	Qualitative (semistructured interviews)	Open-ended interview questions provide data on living arrangements, use of services, social relationships, self-perceptions of felt experience of homelessness	Snowball sample of 55 homeless adults in Michigan's Upper Peninsula	Four main types of coping patterns identified: shelter users, couch hoppers, campers (living outdoors), and mixed (multiple forms of coping). Implications for social relationships and felt experiences discussed	Limited to Michigan's Upper Peninsula; representativeness of the sample unknown

Units of analysis are the specific objects or elements whose characteristics we wish to describe or explain and about which we will collect data. Although there are many units of analysis, five that are commonly used in human service research are individuals, groups, organizations, programs, and social artifacts (see Table 4.2). Different units of analysis are used in studying documents; these are discussed in Chapter 8.

Much social research focuses on the *individual* as the unit of analysis. The typical survey, for example, obtains information from individuals about their attitudes or behavior. Whenever we define a population of inquiry with reference to some personal status, we are operating at the individual level of analysis. For example, single parents, welfare recipients, children with developmental delays, and similar categories all identify individuals with reference to a status they occupy.

If we identify our unit of analysis as individuals, then it is important to recognize that the entire analysis will remain at that level. For the sake of describing large numbers of individuals, it is necessary to use summarizing statistics, such as averages. For example, we might, as part of a study of single parents, note that their average age when giving birth was 16.8 years. Aggregating data in this fashion in no way changes the unit of analysis. We are still collecting our data about individuals.

Social scientists sometimes focus on social *groups* as their unit of analysis and collect data on some group characteristic or behavior. Some groups consist of individuals who share some social relationship with the other group members. For example, in families, peer groups, occupational groups, or juvenile gangs, the members have some sense of membership or belonging to the group. If we study families in terms of whether or not they are intact, then we are investigating the characteristics of a group—the family—and not the characteristics of individuals. Other groups of

TABLE 4.2 Possible Units of Analysis in Research on Juvenile Delinquency

Unit of Analysis	Example	Appropriate Variables	Research Problem
Individuals	Adolescents arrested for larceny	Age, sex, prior arrests	Do males receive different penalties from females for similar offenses?
Groups	Delinquent gangs	Size, norms on drug use	Are gangs involved in drug trafficking more violent than other gangs?
Organizations	Adolescent treatment agencies	Size, auspices, funding level	Do private agencies serve fewer minority and lower class delinquents than public agencies?
Programs	Delinquency prevention programs	Theoretical model, type of host setting	What services are most frequently included in prevention programs?
Social artifacts	Transcripts of adjudication hearings	Number of references to victim injury	To what extent does the level of violence in the offense affect the kind of penalty imposed?

interest to social scientists are merely aggregates of individuals with no necessary sense of membership, such as census tracts, cities, states, or members of a particular social class. For example, we might study the relationship between poverty and delinquency by comparing rates of delinquency in census tracts with low income and those with high income. In this case, we have collected data regarding the characteristics of census tracts rather than data regarding individuals.

Social scientists also deal with *organizations* as the unit of analysis. Formal organizations are deliberately constructed groups that are organized to achieve some specific goals. Examples of formal organizations include corporations, schools, prisons, unions, government bureaus, and human service agencies. For example, our experience may lead us to suspect that organizations providing substance abuse services can more effectively serve their clients if they have an open and democratic communication structure rather than a closed and rigidly stratified one. If we compare the success rates of organizations with different communication structures, then our study would use organizations, not individuals or groups, as the unit of analysis. Although individuals may experience success at overcoming substance abuse, only organizations can have a *success rate*.

Research in the human services can also focus on *programs* as the basic unit of analysis. The program may provide services for individuals, and it may exist as part of an organization. It is still, however, a separate unit of analysis about which data can be collected. Like organizations, programs can have success rates or be assessed in terms of overall costs. For example, one research project investigated 25 programs that provided services for pregnant and parenting teenagers (Fernandez & Ruch-Ross, 1998). This research assessed each program according to its overall success rate: A successful program was one in which the clients were more likely to stay in school or stay employed and less likely to get pregnant than were clients in the other programs. Note that a program can have a success rate (in other words, a certain proportion of their clients succeeding) but an individual can only succeed or fail (rather than showing a rate of success).

The researchers compared the programs to determine the characteristics of successful and unsuccessful programs. Programs might cut across a number of different organizations, such as social service agencies, in which case the unit under observation is the effectiveness of the combination of services provided by these organizations.

Finally, the unit of analysis may be *social artifacts,* which are simply any material products that people produce. Examples are virtually endless: newspapers, buildings, movies, books, magazines, tablets, automobiles, songs, graffiti, and so on. Of all the units of analysis, social artifacts are the least frequent focus of human service research, but as reflections of people and the society that produces the artifacts, analysis of social artifacts is useful. Books and magazines, for example, can be used as artifacts in the assessment of gender-role stereotyping. Children's books have been attacked for allegedly reinforcing traditional gender roles through their presentations of men and women (Crabb & Bielewski, 1994; Gee & Jackson, 2006). Any kind of legal or administrative statute also is an artifact worthy of study. One effort, for instance, used state juvenile codes as the independent variable in a study of whether legal statutes made a difference in how courts handled juvenile cases (Grichting, 1979).

Clearly specifying the unit of analysis in research is important in avoiding a serious problem: an illegitimate shift in the analysis from one unit to another. Jumping from one level to another can result in erroneous conclusions being drawn. One way this can happen is called the **ecological fallacy:** inferring something about individuals based on data collected at higher units of analysis, such as groups. In other words, a mismatch occurs between the unit of analysis about which data are collected and about which conclusions are drawn. Suppose, for example, a study found that census tracts with high rates of teenage drug abuse also had a large percentage of single-parent families. We might be tempted to conclude that single-parent families are a factor promoting teenage drug abuse. Such a conclusion, however, represents an illegitimate shift in the unit of analysis. The data have been collected about census tracts, which are at the group level. The conclusion being drawn, however, is at the individual level—namely, that teenage drug abusers live in single-parent families. The data, however, do not show this. In fact, the data only show the association of two rates—substance abuse and single parenthood—in census tracts. (Perhaps two-parent families are a minority in a census tract, but a high proportion of children in these families abuse drugs.) It is, of course, possible that relationships found at the group level will hold at the individual level but they may not. In our hypothetical study, some other characteristic of census tracts may lead to both high rates of drug abuse *and* single-parent families. The error comes in the automatic assumption that correlations at the group level necessarily reflect relationships at the individual level.

Fallacious reasoning can occur in the opposite direction as well; in this case, it is called the **reductionist fallacy**: inferring something about groups, or other higher levels of analysis, based on data collected from individuals. Suppose we collected data from individual teenagers about their drug use and family environments and found an association—namely, that teens from single-parent families are more likely to abuse drugs. Could we then conclude that communities with high rates of single-parent families would have high rates of teenage drug abuse? The answer, once again, is that we could not draw that conclusion about the group level (communities) with any certainty, because the data we have is about social process at the individual level (what happens in the lives of individual teens). It may well be that the social process that produces high rates of drug abuse in communities is different from the social process that leads individuals to use drugs. When data are collected at one level of analysis, it is always an empirical question as to whether conclusions can be drawn from that data about other levels of analysis. A clear awareness of the unit of analysis can help ensure that we do not make such illegitimate shifts.

A final point needs to be made about the unit of analysis in contrast to the source of data. The unit of analysis refers to the element *about which* data are collected and inferences made, but it is not necessarily the source *from which* data are collected. A common example is the U.S. Census, which reports data for *households*. We speak of household size and income, but households do not fill out questionnaires—people do. In this case, individuals, such as the heads of households, are the *source* of the data, but the household is the unit of analysis *about which* data are collected. When the unit of analysis is something other than the individual, attention must be paid to the source of that data, because this might introduce bias into the data analysis. For example, when the household is the unit of analysis, we often collect data from one member of the household. In single-parent families, headed primarily by women, we would be gathering data mostly from women. In two-parent heterosexual parent families, we would be obtaining data from both men and women, because either could be the head of the household. In some cases, men might be the majority of those we collect data from. If men tend to answer some questions differently from women, then there could be a gender bias in the results even though our unit of analysis was not linked to gender. A difference that we attribute to single-parent as compared to two-parent families may result from the fact that the former involves mostly women answering questions and the latter involves mostly men.

Reactivity

The issue of reactivity is another consideration in refining a research problem. The term **reactivity** refers to the fact that people can react to being studied and may behave differently than when they do not think they are being studied. In other words, the data we collected from people who know they are the objects of study might be different from the data we collected from the same people if they do not know. So, a reactive research technique changes the very thing that is being studied. Suppose, for example, that you are a parent. A researcher enters your home and sets up videotaping equipment to observe your interactions with your children. Would you behave in the same way that you would if the observer were not present? You might, but most people would feel strong pressures to be "on their toes" and present themselves as good parents. You might be more forgiving of your child, for instance, or give fewer negative sanctions.

Reactivity in research can take many forms, and it is a problem for virtually all sciences. It is especially acute in social research, however, because human beings are self-conscious and aware of what is happening to them. Refining a research problem and choosing a research design are done with an eye toward reducing as much as possible the extensiveness of reactivity. We consider this in assessing the various research strategies during later chapters.

Qualitative Versus Quantitative Research

Another aspect of refining a research problem is to decide whether to use one of two broad strategies toward research: *qualitative research* or *quantitative research*. **Qualitative research** involves data in the form of words, pictures, descriptions, or narratives. **Quantitative research** uses numbers, counts, and measures of things (Berg & Lune, 2012; Wakefield, 1995). In general, two factors come into play in deciding whether to conduct qualitative or quantitative research: the state of our knowledge on a particular research topic, and the individual researcher's position regarding the nature of human social behavior. Regarding the first factor, when knowledge is sketchy or there is little theoretical understanding of a phenomenon, it may be impossible to develop precise hypotheses or operational definitions. In such cases, researchers often turn to qualitative research, because it can be more exploratory in nature. The research can be descriptive, possibly resulting in the formulation of hypotheses rather than the verification of them. When enough previous research exists on a topic, however, it may be more feasible to state precisely concepts, variables, and hypotheses. It also may be possible to develop quantifiable operational definitions of what the researcher is interested in, which then allows research to take on a more quantitative nature.

The second consideration in choosing between quantitative and qualitative research stems from a more fundamental controversy over the nature of human social behavior. We saw in Chapter 2 that the choice between qualitative and quantitative research is related to whether one follows positivist or nonpositivist paradigms toward science. This complicated issue, which is discussed in more detail in Chapters 2 and 9, basically involves debate over whether we can meaningfully reduce the human experience to numbers and measures. Some social scientists argue that the human experience has a subjective dimension—that is, the personal meanings and feelings that people have about themselves and what they do. These meanings or feelings cannot be captured very well through numbers or measures. Instead, narrative descriptions of people going about their daily routines or lengthy and broad-ranging interviews with them better express those meanings and feelings. Such techniques are better able to capture the critical subjective meanings that are an essential element of understanding human behavior. Quantitative research, on the other hand, provides us with much more precise statements about human behavior.

The line between qualitative and quantitative approaches is not always completely clear, and the choice between the two can be difficult. Many research projects incorporate both approaches to gain the most benefit.

Cross-Sectional Versus Longitudinal Research

In addition to deciding on the unit of analysis to investigate, refining a research problem also requires a decision about the time dimension. Here, the basic issue is whether the researcher wants a single snapshot in time of some phenomenon or an ongoing series of photographs over time. The former is called **cross-sectional research**, and it focuses on a cross section of a population at one point in time. Many surveys, for example, are cross-sectional in nature.

Although researchers collect all the data in cross-sectional research at one time, we can use such studies to investigate the development of some phenomena over time. For example, to study the developmental problems of children of alcoholic parents, one could select groups of children of varying ages—say, one group at age 5, another group at age 10, and a third group at age 15. By observing differences in developmental problems among these groups, we may infer that a single youngster would experience changes as he or she grew up similar to the differences observed among these three groups. Yet, one of the major weaknesses of such cross-sectional studies is that we have not actually observed the changes that an individual goes through; rather, we have observed three different groups of individuals at one point in time. Differences among these groups may reflect something other than the developmental changes that individuals experience. Because of this disadvantage, researchers sometimes resort to the other way of handling the time issue: longitudinal studies.

Longitudinal research involves gathering data over an extended period, such as months, years, or even, in a few cases, decades. One type of longitudinal approach is the **panel study**, in which the same people are studied at different times. This allows us to observe the actual changes these individuals go through over time. For example, a study of the social, psychological, and familial characteristics that influence whether drug addicts can successfully remain free of drugs followed the same 354 narcotic addicts for more than 24 years, collecting data on their family experiences, employment records, and a host of other factors (Bailey, Hser, Hsieh, & Anglin, 1994). Another longitudinal approach is the **trend study**, in which different people are observed at different times. Public opinion polling and research on political attitudes often are trend studies.

Both the nature of the research problem and practical considerations typically determine the decision about whether to use a longitudinal or a cross-sectional approach. Longitudinal studies, especially panel studies, have the advantage of providing the most accurate information regarding changes over time. A research question regarding such changes, then, probably would benefit from this approach. A disadvantage of panel studies is that they can be reactive: People's responses or behavior at one time may be influenced by the fact that they have been observed earlier. For example, a person who stated opposition to abortion in one survey may be inclined to respond the same way 6 months later so as not to appear inconsistent or vacillating, even if his or her attitudes had changed in the interim. Another disadvantage

of panel studies is that people who participated early in a panel study may not want to—or may be unable to—participate later. People die, move away, grow uninterested, or become unavailable in other ways as panel studies progress. This loss of participants can adversely affect the validity of the research findings. The disadvantages of all longitudinal studies are that they can be difficult and expensive to conduct, especially if they span a very long period of time.

Cross-sectional research is cheaper and faster to conduct, and one need not worry about the loss of participants. However, cross-sectional research may not provide the most useful data for some research questions. Thus, the decision regarding the issue of the time dimension should be based on considerations of both the nature of the research problem and practical issues. There are times, of course, when practical feasibility plays a large part in the decision.

FEASIBILITY OF A RESEARCH PROJECT

By the time researchers have selected, shaped, and refined a research problem, the problem should be sufficiently clear that a consideration of practical issues involving the feasibility of the project is in order. Practical considerations of what the research can reasonably accomplish given the time and resources available can force researchers to reduce—sometimes painfully—the scale of a project. A careful and honest appraisal of the time and money required to accomplish a project is useful in determining the feasibility of that project as envisioned, and it can reveal if a change in goals is called for. In making a feasibility assessment, one should keep in mind a couple of axioms that apply to research projects: "Anything that can go wrong will" (Murphy's Law), and "Everything will take longer than possibly imagined."

The practical aspects of a project's feasibility center primarily on two related concerns: time and money (Kelly & McGrath, 1988).

Time Constraints

In developing a research project, one of the major considerations is whether there will be sufficient time to adequately complete what you hope to do. In later chapters, as we consider specific research techniques, we will see how different techniques vary in terms of how much time they take. Here, we want to mention some of the major factors related to time considerations.

One factor concerns the population that is the focus of the research. If that population has characteristics that are fairly widespread, then a sufficient number of people will be readily available from which to collect data. For instance, if we were studying the differing attitudes of men and women toward work-release programs for prison inmates, we could select a sample of men and women from whatever city or state we happened to be in. If, however, our study focuses on people with special characteristics that are somewhat rare, problems may arise. In general, the smaller the number of people who have the characteristics needed for inclusion in a study, the more difficult and time-consuming it will be to contact a number sufficient to make scientifically valid conclusions. For example, a study of incestuous fathers, even in a large city, may encounter problems obtaining enough cases, because relatively few such people will be openly known.

A second problem relating to time constraints involves the proper development of measuring devices. Researchers should test all techniques used for gathering data before the actual study is conducted, and this can be very time-consuming in itself. A pretest, as we saw in Chapter 1, refers to the preliminary application of the data-gathering techniques to assess their adequacy. A pilot study is a small-scale, "trial run" of all the procedures planned for use in the main study. In some studies, we may need to conduct several pretests as we modify data-collection devices based on the results of earlier pretests. All in all, the refining of data-gathering procedures can consume a lot of time.

A third major factor related to time considerations is the amount of time required for actual data collection, which can range from a few hours for a questionnaire administered to a group of "captive" students to the years that are necessary in many longitudinal studies. Because the amount of time required for data collection is so variable, the

issue of time requires close scrutiny when addressing the question of the feasibility of a particular research design.

A fourth consideration related to the time issue is the amount of time necessary to complete the analysis of the data. In general, the less structured the data, the more time will be required for its analysis. The field notes that serve as the data for some observational studies, for example, can be very time-consuming to analyze (see Chapter 9). Likewise, videotapes collected during an experiment or during single-subject research may need several viewings before they are adequately understood (see Chapters 10 and 11). Highly structured data in quantified form, however, also can be time-consuming to analyze (see Chapters 14 and 15). Although some quantitative data can be quickly entered into a computer file if it is in a form that can be optically scanned or submitted from a website, other data must be manually entered. Even optically scanned or web data require considerable advance programming and preparation before the data can actually be submitted. Also, raw data often must be manipulated and transformed before they are ready for analysis, and this can be time-consuming as well. So, the time needed for data analysis requires careful consideration owing to wide variation in the amount of time that may be necessary.

The fifth area in which time becomes a factor is the writing of the report itself. The amount of time this consumes depends on the length and complexity of the report and on the skills of the investigator. Each researcher is in the best position, based on past writing experiences, to assess the amount of time that he or she requires. As a final reminder, it will likely take longer than you expect.

Financial Considerations

The financial expenditures associated with a research project are another constraint on feasibility. Good research is not always expensive. In many instances, students and human service practitioners can get by with only modest costs, because data are easy to obtain, analysis procedures are simple, and the labor is either voluntary or provided at no additional charge. Even small projects, however, are likely to require money for telephone calls, typing and duplicating questionnaires, computer equipment, Internet access, and other services that can quickly stress the tight resources of a small human service agency. At the other extreme, it is not unusual for the price tag of major research and demonstration projects in the human services to run into six figures or more. For example, between 1997 and 2003, the National Institute of Justice (2003) provided annual grants of about $1 million for the development and evaluation of educational programs to assist teenagers in developing skills to avoid drug use or other forms of delinquency and to avoid becoming victims of crime. Table 4.3 shows the budget for a hypothetical survey research project of modest scale and indicates some of the general expenditure categories to consider when assessing the feasibility of any project.

The salaries of those who conduct the study are potentially the most expensive item, especially for studies that require large interviewer staffs. Such expenses include not only the interviewers' wages but also transportation costs and living expenses, which can be sizable. Interviewers may require

hours of training before they can begin to collect data. If respondents are not available, callbacks may be necessary, which further increases the cost of each interview. To get the work done in a timely fashion and to ensure reliability, investigators may need to hire people or contract with an organization to code the raw data into an analyzable format.

Computer expenses also can be formidable. A few decades ago, data analysis comprised the bulk of computer costs, but now computing services of one kind or another are used for questionnaire design, project management, data collection, literature searches, and report preparation. A significant cost here is for the software packages and Internet access that actually perform these procedures, in addition to the cost of the computer itself and peripherals like printers, scanners, zip drives, and so on.

Another major cost consideration is expenditures for office supplies and equipment. Under this category are such items as paper, envelopes, postage, tape, printing, and the like. Paper products might seem to be inexpensive at first glance, but given the large samples that are used for some surveys, this cost can be substantial. For example,

TABLE 4.3 An Illustrative Budget for Conducting Face-to-Face Interviews of 400 People

Elements of the Interview	Cost	% of Total
Materials for Interview: print or electronic maps; interviewer manuals; printed questionnaires	$500	2%
Interviewer Training Sessions: 2 days of training, wages for trainer and interviewers	$2,400	9.8%
Conduct Interview: Travel Costs: travel to and locate residence (including 60 callbacks for people not home); 1 hour per interview; $10 per completed interview	$4,000	16.3%
Conduct Interview: contact respondent; 1.5 hours per interview	$9,000	36.7%
Clerical and Data Entry Tasks: code or transcribe interviews; enter data into an electronic data file (1 hour per interview at $10 per hour)	$4,000	16.3%
Professional Supervision: coordinating and supervising all of the aforementioned tasks (160 hours at $60,000 total annual compensation)	$4,620	18.8%
TOTAL	$24,520	100%

suppose we conduct a survey of approximately 500 people. Each person receives a large envelope containing a letter of introduction; a professionally printed, four-page questionnaire; and a postage-paid return envelope. In addition, all members of the sample receive a reminder letter urging them to respond, and about 250 nonrespondents receive a second questionnaire. The cost for printing, envelopes, and postage could easily exceed $2,000. Different kinds of studies present different cost issues. For example, studies based on direct observation of behavior may necessitate high-cost equipment, such as video cameras, recorders, and videotape. Unless these are already available, the project will require substantial outlays.

Providing incentives to ensure the cooperation of people in the study also may be a cost factor. This may range from giving stickers or balloons to schoolchildren for completing a questionnaire to paying respondents in recognition of the large time commitment required for a longitudinal study. A study evaluating the effectiveness of advocacy services to women leaving their abusive partners (Sullivan, 1991) illustrates participant incentive costs. Women were interviewed before the program and at 5, 10, and 20 weeks following the program. Not only was it difficult to maintain contact with this highly mobile population, completing a survey form was a low priority for these women, given the stress and disruption in their lives. To encourage the women to participate, the 46 participants were paid $10, $20, $30, and $40, respectively, for the four interviews, for a total cost of $4,600. Payment of subjects is more of an issue in experiments that require more time investment and greater commitment from participants than usually is required in most surveys or observational studies.

Dissemination of research findings also generates costs. Besides the additional printing and office supplies for preparing reports, this expense category may include travel to professional meetings to present papers. Program evaluation studies also may entail hosting workshops or conferences with sponsors and other interested parties to ensure that the findings are incorporated into the policy and intervention planning process.

Finally, some costs associated with a research project are difficult to specify. When research is conducted under the auspices of a university, a human service agency, or a research center, some organizational resources will partially or indirectly support the research. For example, money will be spent to heat and light the building where the research project is housed, but this cost is difficult to assess precisely. A major factor in awarding a research project to a particular organization may be the fact that the organization has an extensive research library, sophisticated computer facilities, or an extensive research laboratory. The organization maintains these facilities for general use, not just for a particular research project, so it is difficult to ascertain how much of the overall cost of supporting the facilities should be assigned to a given project. Consequently, the concept of "indirect cost," typically a percentage of the total grant request, is employed to cover these real but hard-to-specify costs. Each organization negotiates its rate with the granting agency on the basis of the facilities and equipment that the organization has for research. The amount charged to indirect costs varies from 15% to well in excess of 100% of the basic grant.

Anticipating and Avoiding Problems

Problems related to time and financial considerations arise during virtually all research projects, but their impact on the outcome of the research can be minimized if they are anticipated as much as possible, especially during the planning stage, when the details of the project are easier to change. A number of steps can be taken to anticipate problems. First, learn as much as possible from the experiences of others through the studies consulted during the literature review. We mentioned earlier that finding problems other researchers encountered is one purpose of the literature review. Also, solicit personal advice from experienced researchers who might be available for consultation. A knowledgeable researcher may be able to identify potential trouble spots in the plans and suggest modifications to avoid them.

Second, obtain whatever permissions or consents may be needed early in the planning stages of the project. Depending on the people the researcher wishes to study, it may be necessary to obtain permission from them to collect data. For example, some studies are aimed at school-age children and seek to gather data while the children are in school. To protect students from undue harassment and themselves from parental complaints, school administrators frequently are cool to allowing researchers into their schools. It may take considerable time to persuade whatever authorities are involved to grant the permissions needed—if they are granted at all. It certainly is wise to obtain any needed permissions before expending effort on other phases of the project, which might be wasted if these permissions cannot be obtained.

The final—and, perhaps, most important—suggestion for avoiding problems is to conduct a pilot study. As noted, a pilot study is a preliminary run-through, on a small scale, of all the procedures planned for the main study. For surveys, contact and interview a small part of the sample—say, 20 people. Then, analyze the data as you would for the complete project. In experiments, the researcher should run a few groups through all procedures, looking for any unexpected reactions from participants. Observational researchers should visit the observation sites and make observations as planned for the larger study. The focus is, again, on problems that might force modifications in research plans. Deal with any problems that surface during the pilot study before the main project is launched.

Given all the pitfalls that a project might encounter, it is quite possible that, at some point, the researcher may conclude that the project is not feasible as planned. Before calling it quits, however, give careful consideration to possible modifications that would enhance the project's feasibility. If inadequate time or money is the problem, perhaps the project can be scaled down. It might be possible to reduce the sample size or the number of hypotheses tested to make the experiment manageable. If face-to-face interviews were originally planned, consider a mailed questionnaire or even a telephone survey as cost-cutting and time-reducing measures. If the problem is with procedures, such as may occur in an experiment, consider how they might be changed so that the project can proceed. The point is that a project should not be abandoned until all efforts to make it feasible have been investigated.

REVIEW AND CRITICAL THINKING

Main Points

- Suitable topics for research come from a variety of sources, including personal interest, social problems, theory testing, prior research, program evaluation and policy implementation, and human service practice.
- Political factors also influence problem selection: Powerful interest groups encourage the expenditure of research resources on issues that are of interest to them and that may not serve the interests of less advantaged or minority groups.
- A general topic for research must be narrowed and focused into a precise, researchable problem.
- An important part of refining a research problem is conceptual development: identifying and defining the concepts on which the study will focus.
- Reviewing previous research related to the selected topic is a crucial step in problem development and preparing to conduct a research project. This review should produce information about theoretical and

conceptual issues, research hypotheses and variables, measurement and operational definitions, research techniques, sampling strategies, statistical techniques, and findings and conclusions.

- The units of analysis must be clearly specified as individuals, groups, organizations, programs, or social artifacts.
- Continual awareness of the operative unit of analysis ensures avoidance of such errors as the ecological fallacy and the reductionist fallacy.
- Reactivity refers to the fact that people may behave differently when they are being watched than when they are not being watched, and the effects of reactivity must be considered when shaping a research problem.
- Qualitative research emphasizes the description of how people experience the world; it relies on data in the form of words, pictures, descriptions, and narratives. Quantitative research uses numbers, counts, and measures to assess statistical relationships between variables.
- Cross-sectional research is based on data collected at one point in time, which makes accurate conclusions about trends or behavioral changes difficult. Longitudinal studies are based on data collected over a period of time and are particularly useful for studying trends or behavioral changes.
- Once fully refined, the practical feasibility of a proposed research project requires realistic assessment.

IMPORTANT TERMS FOR REVIEW

Cross-sectional research	Qualitative research	Trend study
Ecological fallacy	Quantitative research	Units of analysis
Longitudinal research	Reactivity	
Panel study	Reductionist fallacy	

CRITICAL THINKING

Critical thinking calls for the careful assessment of the nature, extent, and various facets of a problem to be addressed. So, human service practitioners, policy makers, and people in their everyday lives need to devote attention to formulating, shaping, and refining a problem. It does not have to be a scientific problem, which is the focus of this book; it could be a problem confronting an individual, a family, or an organization. The following are critical thinking questions raised at the beginning of the chapter and some ideas for how they relate to social work practice. Students are encouraged to develop their own answers to these questions.

Why is it important to refine a research problem in conceptual development? Problem formation—identifying the social work problem and its research question—is of crucial importance, because all other steps of evidence-based practice (EBP) rely on a good research question.

Posing a specific question is defined first with reference to a client-oriented, practical problem.

How do you first start creating a research question and what should you consider when constructing this question? Designing a research project can initially be a daunting task. But, understanding the building blocks that are needed in a research project can help the project be less overwhelming. The first step in a research project is formulating an answerable research question that is drawn from a research problem. Areas to consider are your population, an intervention of interest, and what outcome you are looking for.

What is the importance of developing a clear and specific research question? Before you start developing a research question, you first select an appropriate topic for scientific investigation. Selecting a problem will take creativity; you may consider searching social work concepts of human behavior or possibly personal experience or expertise. For example, if you are interested in exploring intimate-partner violence you may want to explore if there are programs that are effective at decreasing violence or preventing violence.

EVALUATING COMPETENCY (FROM THE COUNCIL ON SOCIAL WORK EDUCATION [CSWE] 2015 EDUCATIONAL POLICY AND ACCREDITATION STANDARDS [EPAS])

Competency 2: Engaging Diversity and Difference in Practice

- How might understanding how to formulate a research question help with marginalized and oppressed populations? What types of research questions would be most helpful in understanding these populations?

Competency 4: Engage in Practice-Informed Research and Research-Informed Practice

- How does understanding how to construct a well-built answerable question help improve research to practice and practice to research?

Competency 9: Evaluate Practice With Individuals, Families, Groups, Organizations, and Communities

- What challenges might a social researcher face when developing a research question for different organizations?
- What knowledge does a social researcher need to understand how to build a research question for agencies in the community?

SELF-ASSESSMENT

• •

1. Problem formation involves:
   a. Something that is only for researchers.
   b. Identifying a clear and specific social problem, an intervention, comparison intervention, and desired outcome.
   c. A general set of social problems a population faces.
   d. Social researchers' good intentions to improve a population's quality of life.

2. Selecting a research problem refers to:
   a. Social researchers selecting an appropriate topic or current social problem, a desire to test a theory, based on prior research, and service delivery.
   b. Research that involves looking into a personal interest only.
   c. Research that is general and more difficult to answer because of social problems' complex nature.
   d. A problem that is very specific and has little flexibility.

3. Qualitative research involves:
   a. Research that includes numbers and graphs.
   b. Research that has a large amount of previous research to draw from.
   c. Research that provides a thick description of data, narratives, and quotes from participants.
   d. Research that includes statistical analysis.

4. Quantitative research involves:
   a. Research that includes numbers, measurements, and statistical analysis.
   b. Research that includes participants' stories.
   c. Research that provides a deeper understanding of participants.
   d. Research that is more exploratory in nature.

5. Feasibility of a research project refers to:
   a. A fast process of turning out results of a study.
   b. Research that is completed with not too much effort.
   c. Research that is shortsighted, but adapts as the project gets going.
   d. A set of considerations for the project that include time constraints, fiscal costs, lack of cooperation, and ethical dilemmas in research.

6. Cross-sectional research involves:
   a. Observing participants multiple times to explore a phenomenon.
   b. Research that involves following one participant over a short time period to track his or her behavior change.
   c. Research that is exploring a snapshot in time using multiple measurements focusing on a population at one time.
   d. Research that is collecting data over a long period to explore change in participants.

7. Longitudinal research involves:
   a. Research that gathers data over an extended period of time to evaluate change in participants.
   b. Research that is collected all at one time.

   c. Research that can affect an area of social interest over a long period of time.
   d. Research that explores multiple groups in a single setting.
8. Review of the literature involves:
   a. A review that only takes place once a study is complete.
   b. A review of previous research by searching databases that relate to our research problem and question.
   c. A review that is helpful, but nonessential.
   d. A process of perusing literature to gain a fast understanding of the problem.
9. Program evaluation refers to:
   a. An extensive process of assessing effectiveness of a program or practice.
   b. A researcher's personal experience of working with a program.
   c. An explanation of why a program is important for a specific population.
   d. A program that appears to work because it makes sense.
10. Units of analysis refers to:
   a. Research that provides outcome analysis of a study.
   b. An analysis with statistical significance.
   c. An analysis of the people or things whose characteristics social researchers observe, describe, and explain.
   d. An analysis that focuses on graphs and charts.

ANSWER KEY FOR SELF-ASSESSMENT QUIZ

1. **b.** Identifying a clear and specific social problem, an intervention, comparison intervention, and desired outcome.
2. **a.** Social researchers selecting an appropriate topic or current social problem, a desire to test a theory, based on prior research, and service delivery.
3. **c.** Research that provides a thick description of data, narratives, and quotes from participants.
4. **a.** Research that includes numbers, measurements, and statistical analysis.
5. **d.** A set of considerations for the project that include time constraints, fiscal costs, lack of cooperation, and ethical dilemmas in research.
6. **c.** Research that is exploring a snapshot in time using multiple measurements focusing on a population at one time.
7. **a.** Research that gathers data over an extended period of time to evaluate change in participants.
8. **b.** A review of previous research by searching databases that relate to our research problem and question.
9. **a.** An extensive process of assessing effectiveness of a program or practice.
10. **c.** An analysis of the people or things whose characteristics social researchers observe, describe, and explain.

FOR FURTHER READING

Berg, B. L., & Lune, H. (2012). *Qualitative research methods for the social sciences* (8th ed.). Boston, MA: Pearson. Although this book focuses primarily on how to conduct good qualitative research, it also contains a good comparison of qualitative and quantitative research and assesses when each is the most appropriate design.

Bransford, J. D., & Stein, B. S. (1995). *The ideal problem solver: A guide to improving thinking, learning, and creativity* (2nd ed.). New York, NY: Freeman. Sound thinking combined with creativity clearly is important to formulating research problems. This guide assists in improving thought processes, drawing logical deductions, enhancing creativity, and even improving communication skills.

Gross, R. (1993). *The independent scholar's handbook.* Berkeley, CA: Ten Speed Press. This book contains many examples of how successful scholars developed personal hunches and notions into serious research inquiries. It is also filled with practical advice about such things as obtaining resources and communicating with other researchers who share similar research interests.

Higgins, P. C., & Johnson, J. M. (1988). *Personal sociology.* New York, NY: Praeger. This book includes many illustrations of how personal life events and experiences shaped the research interests of a variety of sociologists.

Hunt, M. M. (1985). *Profiles of social research: The scientific study of human interactions.* New York, NY: Basic Books. As its title implies, this book presents a series of descriptions of major research projects. Follow these projects from inception to completion, and see successful social scientists at work.

Lipowski, E. E. (2008). Developing great research questions. *American Journal of Health-System Pharmacy, 65*(17), 1667–1670. doi:10.2146/ajhp070276

Locke, L. F., Silverman, S. J., & Spirduso, W. W. (2010). *Reading and understanding research* (3rd ed.). Thousand Oaks, CA: Sage. This is an excellent and thorough overview of how to do a good literature review and extract the appropriate information from it in an organized fashion.

Menard, S. (2002). *Longitudinal research* (2nd ed.). Newbury Park, CA: Sage. This book provides a readable overview of both longitudinal and cross-sectional research. It discusses when each is an appropriate design and some of the problems that arise in doing good longitudinal research.

Reinharz, S. (1992). *Feminist methods in social research.* New York, NY: Oxford University Press. This book is a massive compilation of examples for all types of research conducted by researchers identified as feminists. Anyone interested in conducting research from this perspective is well advised to consult this impressive work.

REFERENCES

Bailey, R. C., Hser, Y.-I., Hsieh, S.-C., & Anglin, M. D. (1994). Influences affecting maintenance and cessation of narcotics addiction. *Journal of Drug Issues, 24*(2), 249—272. doi:10.1177/002204269402400204

Berg, B. L., & Lune, H. (2012). *Qualitative research methods for the social sciences* (8th ed.). Boston, MA: Pearson.

Breton, M., Brousselle, A., Champagne, G., Contandriopoulos, D., Larouche, C., & Rivard, M. (2017). Policy-making: Polarization and interest groups influence. *The European Journal of Public Health, 27*(3), 63–64. doi:10.1093/eurpub/ckx187.166

Burgess, R., & Youngblade, L. (1988). Social incompetence and the intergenerational transmission of abusive parental practices. In G. Hotaling, D. Finkelhor, J. Kirkpatrick, & M. Strauss (Eds.), *Family abuse and its consequences: New directions in research.* Newbury Park, CA: Sage.

Centers for Disease Control and Prevention. (2018). HIV surveillance report: Diagnosis of HIV infection in the United States and dependent areas, 2017. (Vol. 29). Atlanta, GA: U.S. Department of Health and Human Services. Retrieved from https://www.cdc.gov/hiv/pdf/library/reports/surveillance/cdc-hiv-surveillance-report-2017-vol-29.pdf

Collins, K. M., Leech, N. L., & Onwuegbuzie, A. J. (2012). Qualitative analysis techniques for the review of the literature. *The Qualitative Report, 17*(28), 1–28.

Crabb, P. B., & Bielawski, D. (1994). The social representation of material culture and gender in children's books. *Sex Roles, 30*(1–2), 69–79. doi:10.1007/bf01420740

Fernandez, M., & Ruch-Ross, H. S. (1998). Ecological analysis of program impact: A site analysis of programs for pregnant and parenting adolescents in Illinois. *Journal of Applied Sociology, 15,* 104–133.

First, R., Toomey, B., & Rife, J. (1990). Preliminary findings on rural homelessness in Ohio. Columbus: The Ohio State University College of Social Work.

Gee, S., & Jackson, S. (2006). "Look Janet," "No, you look John": Constructions of gender in early school reader illustrations across 50 years. *Gender and Education, 17*(2), 115–128. doi:10.1080/0954025042000301410

Gibbs, L. (1991). *Scientific reasoning for social workers: Bridging the gap between research and practice.* New York, NY: Macmillan.

Glaser, B., & Strauss, A. (1965). *Awareness of dying.* Chicago, IL: Aldine.

Grichting, W. L. (1979). Do laws make a difference? *Journal of Social Service Research, 2*(3), 245–265. doi:10.1300/j079v02n03_01

Higgins, P. C., & Johnson, J. M. (1988). *Personal sociology.* New York, NY: Praeger.

Hilton, T., & DeJong, C. (2010). Homeless in God's country: Coping behaviors and felt experiences of the rural homeless. *Journal of Qualitative and Ethnographic Research, 5*(1), 12–30.

Israel, T. (2002). Studying sexuality: Strategies for surviving stigma. *Feminism & Psychology, 12*(2), 256–260. doi:10.1177/0959353502012002013

Kelly, J. R., & McGrath, J. E. (1988). *On time and method.* Beverly Hills, CA: Sage.

Lally, J. J. (1977). Social determinants of differential allocation of resources to disease research: A comparative analysis of crib death and cancer research. *Journal of Health and Social Behavior, 18*(2), 125–138. doi:10.2307/2955377

Locke, L. F., Silverman, S. J., & Spirduso, W. W. (2010). *Reading and understanding research* (3rd ed.). Thousand Oaks, CA: Sage.

Mondello, M., Bradley, J., McLaughlin, T., & Shore, N. (2009). Cost of rural homelessness: Rural permanent supportive housing cost analysis: State of Maine. Retrieved from https://shnny.org/uploads/Cost_of_Rural_Homelessness.pdf

National Institute of Justice. (2002). *Funding opportunities: National Institute of Justice Awards in fiscal year.* Retrieved from https://ojp.gov/about/offices/nij.htm

Shilts, R. (1987). *And the band played on: Politics, people, and the AIDS epidemic.* New York, NY: St. Martin's Press.

Sullivan, C. (1991). The provision of advocacy services to women leaving abusive partners. *Journal of Interpersonal Violence, 6*(1), 41–54. doi:10.1177/088626091006001004

Varmus, H. (1999). Evaluating the burden of disease and spending the research dollars of the National Institutes of Health. *New England Journal of Medicine, 340*(24), 1914–1915. doi:10.1056/nejm199906173402411

Wakefield, J. C. (1995). When an irresistible epistemology meets an immovable ontology. *Social Work Research, 19*(1), 9–17. doi:10.1093/swr/19.1.9

5

THE PROCESS OF MEASUREMENT

CHAPTER OUTLINE

Important Terms for Review

Critical Thinking

Evaluating Competency (From the Council on Social Work Education [CSWE] 2015 Educational Policy and Accreditation Standards [EPAS])

    Competency 1: Demonstrate Ethical and Professional Behavior

    Competency 2: Engage Diversity and Difference in Practice

    Competency 3: Advance Human Rights and Social, Economic, and Environmental Justice

    Competency 5: Engage in Policy Practice

    Competency 7: Assess Individuals, Families, Groups, Organizations, and Communities

    Competency 9: Evaluate Practice With Individuals, Families, Groups, Organizations, and Communities

Self-Assessment

Answer key for Self-Assessment Quiz

For Further Reading

References

INTRODUCTION

The Northwest School of Innovative Learning (NWSOIL) is an alternative school for children in kindergarten through high school who for any number of reasons have not been able to be successful in traditional public schools. Many NWSOIL students have behavioral, social, and emotional issues and require behavioral modification and therapy in addition to academic instruction.

NWSOIL operates a token economy they refer to as a Positive Behavioral Interventions and Support (PBIS) program. Students can earn credits to "purchase" various things ranging from special foods to increased freedoms, including the ability to take academic electives, moving between classrooms without chaperones, or playing outside on the playground without a monitor standing next to the student.

Kelsey Johansen, an administrator at NWSOIL, described the school's need for data prior to creating the PBIS program.

We could not justify our behavior intervention and treatment plans because we didn't have data. We didn't have information to back up what we were saying in meetings—like why some students should be transitioning out of the program. We didn't have any information to back that up. We started talking about the need for student data to be more credible and evidence-based. We wanted the school districts that contract with us to see we were using real-time data to help with Individual Education Plan (IEP) goals and the completion of behavior and treatment plans. We needed functional behavioral assessments that were accurate for the students' behaviors. (Based on personal communication on April 16, 2018.)

NWSOIL staff developed a behavioral tracking system to record and track students' behaviors. Johansen explained that the initial goal for students is to help them remain seated at their desks because until then there is little opportunity to make academic progress. She and her staff helped develop a behavioral tracking tool that evaluates students' behaviors every 15 minutes. Teachers and paraeducators record students' positive and negative behaviors on a data sheet that is divided into different columns. Behaviors that are recorded are those that have been identified as target behaviors on students' IEPs. During each 15-minute stretch, students earn between 0 and 3 points depending on the behaviors they exhibit (positive and negative). Each day students can earn up to 75 points. Their daily behavioral percentage scores are calculated based on the total points earned divided by 75.

NWSOIL have found the behavioral tracking system to be a major help in working with children with behavioral disorders. Johansen described her work with one student who had intermittent explosive disorder. "Over time we saw that most of his behaviors would occur in the early morning. He was coming in every morning and blowing up. He'd tell everyone he hates them as soon as he arrived each morning." Teachers and staff decided to give the student 30 minutes to himself each morning. This allowed the medication he took each morning to take effect. After this 30-minute period he would go to class and typically scored 100% for a behavior score for the day.

NWSOIL's PBIS program rests on its ability to evaluate or measure students' daily behavioral performance. **Measurement** refers to the process of describing abstract concepts in terms of specific indicators by assigning numbers or other symbols to these indicants in accordance with rules. At the very minimum, one must have some means of determining whether a variable is either present or absent. NWSOIL, for example, developed classifications of positive and negative student behaviors for various grade levels. They also developed processes for evaluating behaviors and criteria by which various behaviors would be classified. In some cases, measurement can be much more complex and involves assessing how much, or to what degree, a variable is present. While NWSOIL's PBIS system is largely based on numbers of positive and negative behaviors within different time frames, their measures of students' academic performance are more elaborate and include more sophisticated evaluations of students' performance in various academic subjects.

In this chapter, we discuss measurement in social research while continuing to highlight the NWSOIL example. As you read, try to consider the applicability of measurement concepts and techniques to human service practice and reflect on the following questions:

1. Measurement requires being careful and precise and linking the abstract world of concepts and ideas to the concrete world of observations. How does this differ from the ways in which most people describe social phenomena?
2. How do scientists (including social scientists) evaluate whether something exists and/or how much of it exists? What lessons can we draw from this process that might be applied to our work as human service professionals?
3. Reliability and validity are key measurement concepts. What challenges might human service professionals face in creating reliable and valid measures (in assessment, monitoring progress, tracking outcomes, and summarizing performance)?

Measurement is a part of the process of moving from the abstract or theoretical level to the concrete. Recall from Chapter 2 that scientific concepts have two types of definitions: *nominal* and *operational*. Before research can proceed, researchers must translate nominal definitions into operational ones. The operational definitions indicate the exact procedures, or operations, that the researchers will use to measure the concepts. Measurement is essentially the process of operationalizing concepts. In the NWSOIL example, administrators and staff needed to create nominal and operational definitions of various positive and negative behaviors so that teachers and paraeducators could accurately describe students' behavioral performance. Operational definitions of concepts like "bullying" allowed those who were tracking and recording students' behaviors throughout the day to determine whether an interaction between students was a display of bullying or some other behavior like "minor teasing" or "appropriate humor." Figure 5.1 illustrates the place of measurement in the research process.

In this chapter, we discuss the general issues that relate to all measurements, beginning with some of the different ways in which we can make measurements. We then analyze how measurements that are made at different levels affect the

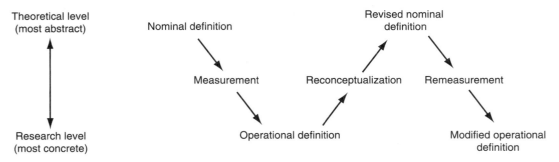

Figure 5.1 The measurement process.

mathematical operations that can be performed on them. Finally, we present ways of evaluating measures and determining the errors that can occur in the measurement process.

WAYS OF MEASURING

From Concepts to Indicators

Normally, we cannot observe directly the concepts and variables that are the focus of both research and practice. We cannot see such things as poverty, social class, developmental delays, and the like; we can only infer them from something else. Take something as seemingly obvious as child abuse. Can you directly observe child abuse? Not really. What you directly observe is a bruise on a child's back, an infant's broken leg, or a father slapping his daughter. And even the slap may not relate to child abuse, because parents sometimes slap their children without its being a case of child abuse. However, all these things—the bruise, the broken leg, the slap—may be used as *indicators* of child abuse. In research and in practice, an **indicator** is an observation that we assume is evidence of the attributes or properties of some phenomenon. What we observe are the indicators of a variable, not the actual properties of the variable itself. Emergency room personnel may assume that a child's broken leg is an indicator of child abuse even though they have not observed the actual abuse.

Child abuse represents a good illustration of the difficulties of moving from nominal to operational definitions with variables involving social and psychological events. At the nominal level, we might define child abuse as an occurrence in which a parent or caretaker injures a child not by accident but in anger or with deliberate intent (US Department of Health and Human Services, 2018; Gelles, 1987; Korbin, 1987). What indicators, however, would we use to operationalize this definition? Some things would obviously seem to indicate child abuse, such as a cigarette burn on a child's buttock, but what about a bruise on the arm? Some subcultures in our own society view hitting children, even to the point of bruising, as an appropriate way to train or discipline them. Furthermore, some people would argue that a serious psychological disorder a child suffers is an indicator of child abuse, because it shows the parents did not provide the proper love and affection for stable development. In short, one of the problems in operationalizing child abuse, as with many other variables in human service research, is that its definition is culture-bound and involves subjective judgments. This illustrates the importance of good conceptual development and precise nominal definitions for research. It also shows how the theoretical and research levels can mutually influence one another: As we shape nominal definitions into operational ones, the difficulties that arise often lead to a reconceptualization, or a change, in the nominal definition at the theoretical level (see Figure 5.1).

The example of child abuse also illustrates another point about measurement—namely, that more than one indicator of a variable may exist. The term **item** is used to refer to a single indicator of a variable. Items can take numerous forms, such as an answer to a question or an observation of a behavior or characteristic. Asking a person her age or noting her sex, for example, would both produce items of measurement. In many cases, however, the process of operationalizing variables involves combining a number of items into a composite score called an **index** or a **scale**. (Although scales involve more rigor in their construction than indices do, we can use the terms interchangeably at this point; Chapter 13 presents some distinctions between them.) Attitude scales, for example, commonly involve asking people a series of questions, or items, and then summarizing their responses into a single score that represents their attitude on an issue.

A major reason for using scales or indices rather than single items is that scales enable us to measure variables in a more precise and, usually, more accurate fashion. To illustrate the value of scales over items, consider your grade in this course. In all likelihood, your final grade will be an index, or a composite score, of your answers to many questions on many tests throughout the semester. Would you prefer that your final grade be determined by a one-item measure, such as a single multiple-choice or essay question? Probably not, because that item would not measure the full range of what you have learned. Furthermore, an error on that item would indicate that you had not learned much in the course, even if the error were the result of ill health or personal problems on the day of the exam. For these reasons, then, researchers usually prefer multiple-item measures to single-item indicators.

We began this discussion by noting that because variables are abstract, we normally cannot observe them directly. Variables differ in their degree of abstraction, however, and this affects the ease with which we can accomplish measurement. In general, the more abstract the variable, the more difficult it is to measure. In the NWSOIL example, the daily rating of student behavior is relatively simple. While it does involve composites of behavioral scores from multiple time frames, these scores are based on straightforward categorizations of behavior as either positive or negative. If, however, staff were asked to evaluate more complex phenomena like students' "self-concept" or the extent to which a student has positive or negative feelings about him- or herself, they would have to develop more sophisticated nominal and operational definitions than used in their behavioral scale. This is because "self-concept" is a much more abstract idea than whether or not students are displaying positive or negative behaviors in class. Highly abstract concepts usually have no single empirical indicator that is clearly and obviously preferable to others as a measure of the concept.

We have emphasized the point that measurement involves transition from the abstract and conceptual level to the concrete and observable level, and this is what most typically occurs in research. Exploratory studies, however, can involve measurement in the opposite direction: First, we observe empirical indicators and then formulate theoretical concepts that those indicators presumably represent. In Chapter 2, we called this *inductive reasoning*. In a sense, you might think of Sigmund Freud or Jean Piaget as having done this when they developed their theories of personality and cognitive development, respectively. Piaget, for example, observed the behavior of children for many years as he gradually developed his theory about the stages of cognitive development, including concepts like egocentrism, object permanence, and reversibility (Ginsburg & Opper, 1988; Oesterdiekhoff, 2016). Piaget recognized that the behaviors he observed could be understood only if placed in a more abstract, theoretical context. In a sense, he measured something before he knew what it was he had measured. Once his theories began to develop, he then developed new concepts and hypotheses, and he formulated different measuring devices to test them deductively. The point is that whether one shifts from the abstract to the concrete, or vice versa, the logic is the same, involving the relationship between theoretical concepts and empirical indicators.

Techniques of Measuring

We will discuss specific techniques for measuring variables in other chapters in this book, but we find that discussing these techniques briefly at this point helps make clear the issues surrounding measurement. Measurement techniques in the social sciences and human services vary widely, because the concepts we measure are so diverse. These techniques, however, mostly fall into one of three categories (see Figure 5.2).

1. *Verbal reports.* This is undoubtedly the most common measurement technique in social research. It involves people answering

Verbal reports	Measuring school performance:	

Verbal reports

People answering questions, being interviewed, or responding to verbal statements

Measuring school performance:

Ask students to tell us what their grades are or how much they know about a particular subject

Researcher

Observation

Directly watch people at school, work, or other setting and make note of what they say and do

Measuring school performance:

Directly observe their behavior in the classroom, noting how often they answer questions posed by teachers, how often their answers are correct, and how they get along with teachers and students

Researcher

Archival reports

Review available recorded information

Measuring school performance:

Use the school records to locate students' grades, performance on exams, attendance records, and disciplinary problems

Researcher

Figure 5.2 The major strategies used by social scientists to measure variables.

questions, being interviewed, or responding to verbal statements (see Chapters 7 and 9). For example, research on people's attitudes typically uses this technique by asking people how they feel about commercial products, political candidates, or social policies. Similarly, a social worker might assess a client's risk of homelessness by asking questions about the stability of his or her current living situation.

2. *Observation.* Social researchers also measure concepts by making direct observations of some phenomena (see Chapter 9). NWSOIL's assessments of students' positive and negative behaviors are good examples of measurement through observation. Teachers and paraeducators observe students' behaviors in class at several points each day and categorize behaviors as positive or negative.

3. *Archival records.* Researchers also use a variety of available recorded information to measure variables (see Chapter 8). These records might take the form of statistical records, governmental or organizational documents, personal letters and diaries, newspapers and magazines, or movies and musical lyrics. All these archival records are the products of human social behavior and can serve as indicators of concepts in the social sciences. In the study of school performance, for example, a researcher could use school records to locate students' grades, performance on exams, attendance records, and disciplinary problems as measures of how well they are doing in school.

These are the major ways that social scientists measure concepts. Researchers must specify exactly what aspects of verbal reports, observations, or available data will serve as indicators of the concepts they want to measure. In addition, researchers use some key criteria to help them decide whether a particular indicator is a good measure of some concept. These criteria are discussed later in this chapter.

Positivist and Nonpositivist Views of Measurement

Much of the foundation for measurement and operationalization in the social sciences derives from the work of statisticians, mathematicians, philosophers, and scientists in a field called *classical test theory* or *measurement theory* (Bohrnstedt, 1983; Stevens, 1951), which provides the logical foundation for issues discussed in this chapter and derives largely from the positivist view of science discussed in Chapter 2. The logic of measurement can be described by the following formula:

$$X = T + E.$$

In this formula, X represents our observation or measurement of some phenomenon; it is our indicator. It might be the grade on an exam in a social research class, for example, or a response to a self-esteem scale (see Table 5.1). Also in this formula, T represents the true, actual phenomenon that we are attempting to measure with X; it would be what a student actually learned in a social

research class or what his or her true self-esteem is. The third symbol in the formula, E, represents any measurement error that occurs, or anything that influences X other than T. It might be the heat and humidity in the classroom on the day of the social research exam, which made it difficult to concentrate, or it could reflect the fact that a subject incorrectly marked a choice on the self-esteem scale, inadvertently circling a response that indicated higher or lower self-esteem than he or she actually possessed.

The formula is very simple—but also very profound and important: Our measurement of any phenomenon is a product of the characteristics or qualities of the phenomenon itself and any errors that occur in the measurement process. What we strive for is measurement with no error:

$$E = 0$$

and, therefore,

$$X = T.$$

The ideal to strive for is a measurement of the phenomenon that is determined only by the true state of the phenomenon itself. Scientists recognize, however, that they normally cannot achieve this ideal state in its entirety. In reality, we attempt to reduce E as much as possible. Later in this chapter, we complicate this measurement formula a bit, but for now, it can stand as a shorthand way of understanding the process of measurement.

TABLE 5.1 Elements in the Process of Measurement

X	=	T	+	E
Observation	**=**	**True Phenomenon**	**+**	**Error**
Reading on a weight scale	=	Your actual weight	+	Clothing you are wearing; heavy object in your pocket
Grade on an examination in social research class	=	Actual knowledge you acquired in social research class	+	Heat and humidity in test room; distraction due to fight with partner
Score on a scale measuring self-esteem	=	Your actual level of self-esteem	+	Incorrectly marking a self-esteem scale; questions on self-esteem scale that are difficult to understand

Before going deeper into the process of measurement, it is important to consider the nonpositivists' critique of classical measurement theory. Many nonpositivists argue that we have not examined a huge assumption in this at all, one that may render the entire topic somewhat problematic. The assumption is that the phenomenon being measured (*T*) exists objectively in the world and that our measurement device is merely discovering it and its properties. Some things do exist in the world independently of our perceptions and our judgments about them. The computer monitor on which these words are being written, for example, has a screen that is 15 inches tall—we just measured it with a ruler. Our measurement of it was a discovery of its properties, and the measurement process did not create or change those properties. Now, however, think about a social science concept, such as self-esteem. We measure it by asking subjects to agree or disagree with a series of statements. We score a "strongly agree" response as "4" and a "strongly disagree" response as "1"; then, we sum up those responses to all the separate items in the scale and give a self-esteem score that ranges from 10 to 40. What, however, is the objective reality behind this measurement? If a subject receives a score of 32 on our measurement device, what does that 32 correspond to in his or her subjective world, or mind, or consciousness? The 32 is the *X* in our measurement formula, but what is the *T* that it corresponds to? Is the link between the measurement of a computer screen and its actual length as direct as the link between the score of 32 on the self-esteem measure and the actual subjective experience of self?

Nonpositivists argue that many social science concepts do not have such clear and objective referents in the world. Our concepts are based on an intuitive and theoretical understanding of what parts of the world are like. In other words, we are *constructing* the world, not just *discovering* it. We believe that something like self-esteem exists, but it is our construction of it that we measure with the self-esteem scale, not the thing itself (if the thing itself even exists). This does not make measurement theory useless, but it does suggest that the whole process is more complicated—and not nearly as objective—as the positivists suggest. Nonetheless, many nonpositivists agree that some

social science measurement can follow the model of measurement theory. Some social phenomena, such as age and sex, do have some objective existence in the world. A person's age has something to do with how many times the Earth has circled the sun since his or her birth, and sex has something to do with a person's physical genitalia. The social significance of these characteristics is another matter, of course, but in many cases, the measurements of age and sex can follow classical measurement theory.

A major problem in most measurements has to do with which indicators to use in a particular research project. This depends in part, of course, on theoretical concerns, but there are other matters to consider as well. One such matter has to do with whether a particular measure permits one to perform mathematical operations on it; we turn to this issue next.

LEVELS OF MEASUREMENT

We have seen just a few of the many ways of measuring phenomena, such as asking questions or noting observations. Measures differ from one another in terms of what is called their **level of measurement**, or the rules that define permissible mathematical operations that can be performed on a set of numbers produced by a measure. There are four levels of measurement: *nominal, ordinal, interval,* and *ratio.* If we keep in mind that variables can take on different values, then measurement basically involves assessing the value or category into which a particular entity falls. Measuring age, for example, is the process of placing each person into a particular age category.

Nominal Measures

Nominal measures classify observations into mutually exclusive and exhaustive categories. They represent nominal variables at the theoretical level. Variables such as sex, ethnicity, religion, or political party preference are examples. Thus, we might classify people according to their religious affiliation by placing them into one of five categories: Protestant, Catholic, Jewish, other, or no religious affiliation. These are mutually exclusive categories because membership in one precludes membership in another. They are exhaustive categories because there is a category for every possible case (for this measure of religious affiliation, the "other religion" and "no religion" categories ensure this). For purposes of data analysis, we might assign numbers to represent each of the categories. We could label Protestant as 1, Catholic as 2, Jewish as 3, other as 4, and no religious affiliation as 5. It is important to recognize, however, that the assignment of numbers is purely arbitrary; the numbers making up a nominal measure have none of the properties, such as ranking, ordering, and magnitude, that we usually associate with numbers. None of the usual arithmetic operations, such as adding, subtracting, multiplying, or dividing, can legitimately be performed on numbers in a nominal scale. The reason for this is that the numbers in a nominal scale are merely symbols or labels used to identify a category of the nominal variable. We could just as easily have labeled Protestant as 2 rather than 1.

In the NWSOIL example, the classification of various classroom behaviors (e.g., bullying, talking out of turn, disrespecting another student) is a good example of nominal level measurement as is the categorization of these behaviors as either positive or negative. The assigning of a score between 0 and 3 for each 15-minute increment, however, is a higher level of measurement, which we discuss next.

Ordinal Measures

When variables can be conceptualized as having an inherent order at the theoretical level, we have an ordinal variable and, when operationalized, an ordinal measure. **Ordinal measures** are of a higher level than nominal measures, because in addition to having mutually exclusive and exhaustive categories, the categories have a fixed order. Socioeconomic status, for example, constitutes an ordinal variable, and measures of socioeconomic status are ordinal scales. Table 5.2 illustrates how we might divide socioeconomic status into ordinal categories. With ordinal measurement, we can speak of a given category as ranking higher or lower than some other category; lower-upper class, for example, is higher than middle class but not as high as upper-upper class. It is important

TABLE 5.2 Ordinal Ranking of Socioeconomic Status

Category	Ranks
Upper upper	7
Lower upper	6
Upper middle	5
Middle	4
Lower middle	3
Upper lower	2
Lower lower	1

to recognize that ordinal measurement does not assume that the categories are equally spaced. For example, the distance between lower-upper class and upper-upper class is not necessarily the same as between lower-middle class and middle class, even though in both cases the classes are one rank apart. This lack of equal spacing means that the numbers assigned to ordinal categories do not have the numerical properties that are necessary for arithmetic operations. Like nominal scales, we cannot add, subtract, multiply, or divide ordinal scales. The only characteristic they have that nominal scales do not is the fixed order of the categories.

Back to the NWSOIL example, teachers and paraeducators assign scores to students between 0 and 3 for each 15-minute time slot during the school day. (They then add these numbers together to calculate a total score for the day—out of a possible 75.) This is an example of ordinal level measurement. The value or distance (in terms of the positive nature of behavior) between a score of 0 and 1 is not necessarily the same as the value or distance between a 1 and a 2, or a 2 and a 3.

Interval Measures

The next highest level of measurement is interval. **Interval measures** share the characteristics of ordinal scales—mutually exclusive and exhaustive categories and an inherent order—but have equal spacing between the categories. Equal spacing comes about because some specific unit of measurement, such as a degree on a temperature scale, is a part of the measure. Each of these units has the same value, which results in the equal spacing. We have an interval scale if the difference between scores of, say, 30 and 40 is the same as the difference between scores of, say, 70 and 80. A 10-point difference is a 10-point difference regardless of where on the scale it occurs.

The common temperature scales, Fahrenheit and Celsius, are true interval scales. Both scales have, as units of measurement, degrees and the equal spacing that is characteristic of interval scales. A difference of 10 degrees is always the same, no matter where it occurs on the scale. These temperature scales illustrate another characteristic of true interval scales: The point on the scale labeled zero is arbitrarily selected. Neither 0°C nor 0°F is absolute zero, the complete absence of heat. Because the zero point is arbitrary in true interval scales, we cannot make statements concerning ratios—that is, we cannot say that a given score is twice or thrice as high as some other score. For example, a temperature of 80°F is not twice as hot as a temperature of 40°F. Despite not having this ratio characteristic, interval scales have numbers with all the other arithmetic properties. If we have achieved interval level measurement, then we can legitimately perform all the common arithmetic operations on the numbers.

Considerable controversy exists over which measures used in behavioral science research are true interval measures; only a few measures are clearly of interval level. For example, one that is relevant to the human services is intelligence as measured by IQ tests. The IQ tests have specific units of measurement—points on the IQ scale— and each point on the scale is mutually exclusive. Furthermore, the distance between IQs of 80 and 90 is equivalent to the distance between IQs of 110 and 120. An IQ scale has no absolute zero point, however, so we cannot say that a person with an IQ of 150 is twice as intelligent as a person with an IQ of 75. As with temperature scales, the IQ scale is, in part, an arbitrary construction that allows us to make some comparisons but not others.

Beyond a few measures such as intelligence, however, the debate ensues. Some researchers

argue, for example, that we can treat attitude scales as interval scales. The questions that make up attitude scales commonly involve choosing one of five responses: strongly agree, agree, uncertain, disagree, or strongly disagree. The argument is that people see the difference between "strongly agree" and "agree" as roughly equivalent to the distance between "disagree" and "strongly disagree." This perceived equidistance, some argue, makes it possible to treat these scales as interval measures. Other researchers argue that there is no logical or empirical reason to assume that such perceived equidistance exists and, therefore, that we should always consider attitude scales as ordinal rather than interval measures (Harpe, 2015).

We do not presume to settle this debate here. Rather, we raise the issue because the level of measurement influences which statistical procedures to use at the data-analysis stage of research (see Chapters 14 and 15). The results of research in which the researcher used an inappropriate statistical procedure for a given level of measurement should be viewed with caution.

Ratio Measures

The highest level of measurement is ratio. **Ratio measures** have all the characteristics of interval measures, but the zero point is absolute and meaningful rather than arbitrary. As the name implies, with ratio measures, we can make statements to the effect that some score is a given ratio of another score. For example, one ratio variable with which human service workers are likely to deal is income. With income, the dollar is the unit of measurement. Also, as many are all too well aware, there is such a thing as no income at all, so the zero point is absolute. Thus, it is perfectly legitimate to make statements such as this about income: An income of $20,000 is twice as much as $10,000 but only one-third as much as $60,000. (We recognize, of course, that income is a ratio measure only as an indicator for the *amount* of money that is available to a person; if income is used as a measure of a person's *social status,* for example, then a difference between $110,000 and $120,000 does not necessarily represent a shift in status equivalent to that between $10,000 and $20,000.) Given that ratio scales have all the characteristics of interval scales, we can, of course, perform all arithmetic operations on them.

As we previously stated, the measurements used by NWSOIL administrators and staff in their PBIS token economy system are primarily ordinal level measures. When analyzing students' behavior over time, however, they may also look at numbers of certain behaviors seen within a given time period. For example, they may evaluate numbers of bullying behaviors displayed in a given month. This is an example of a ratio level measure. Zero recorded behaviors have a real meaning and two behaviors in a month would be a 50% decrease from four behaviors in a month.

We summarize the characteristics of the four levels of measurement in Table 5.3. Keep in mind that, even though researchers have no control over the nature of a variable, they do have some control over how they define a variable, at both the nominal and operational levels, and this affects the level of measurement. It sometimes is possible to change the level of measurement of a variable by redefining it at the nominal or the operational level. This is important, because researchers generally strive for the highest possible level of measurement: Higher levels of measurement generally enable us to measure variables more precisely and to use more powerful statistical procedures (see Chapters 14 and 15). It also is desirable to measure at the highest possible level because it gives the researcher the most options: The level of measurement can be reduced during the data analysis, but it cannot be increased. Thus, choosing a level of measurement that is too low introduces a permanent limitation into the data analysis.

The primary determinant for the level of measurement, however, is the nature of the variable we want to measure. The major concern is an accurate measure of a variable (a topic we discuss at length in the next section). Religious affiliation, for example, is a nominal variable, because that is the nature of the theoretical concept of "religious affiliation." There is no way to treat religious affiliation as anything other than a merely nominal classification, but by changing the theoretical variable somewhat, we may open up higher levels of measurement. If, instead of religious *affiliation,* we were to measure *religiosity,* or the strength of religious beliefs, then we would have a variable that we could conceptualize and measure as ordinal and, perhaps, even as interval. On the basis of certain responses, we could easily rank people into ordered categories of greater or lesser religiosity. Thus, the theoretical nature of the variable plays a large part in determining the level of measurement. This illustrates, once again, the constant interplay between theoretical and research levels (see Figure 5.1). The decision regarding level of measurement at the research level might affect the conceptualization of variables at the theoretical level.

Finally, note that nominal variables are not inherently undesirable. The impression that variables capable of measurement at higher levels are always better than nominal variables is wrong. The first consideration is to select variables on theoretical grounds, not on the basis of their possible level of measurement. Thus, if a research study really is concerned with religious affiliation and not with religiosity, then the nominal measure is the correct one to use and not a measure of religiosity

TABLE 5.3 The Characteristics of the Four Levels of Measurement

| Level of Measurement | Mutually Exclusive and Exhaustive | Characteristics of Categories | | |
		Possesses a Fixed Order	Equal Spacing Between Ranks	True Zero Point
Nominal	Y			
Ordinal	Y	y		
Interval	Y	y	y	
Ratio	Y	y	y	y

(even though it is ordinal or, possibly, interval). Also, researchers do strive for more accurate and powerful measurement. Other things being equal, a researcher who has two measures available, one ordinal and one ratio, generally prefers the ratio measure.

Discrete Versus Continuous Variables

In addition to considering the level of measurement of a variable, researchers also distinguish between variables that are *discrete* or *continuous*. **Discrete variables** have a finite number of distinct and separate values. A perusal of a typical client fact sheet from a human service agency reveals many examples of discrete variables, such as sex, household size, number of days absent, or number of arrests. Household size is a discrete variable because households can be measured only in a discrete set of units, such as having one member, two members, and so on; no meaningful measurement values lie between these distinct and separate values. **Continuous variables,** at least theoretically, can take on an infinite number of values. Age is a continuous variable because we can measure age by an infinite array of values. We normally measure age in terms of years, but theoretically, we could measure it in terms of months, weeks, days, minutes, seconds, or even nanoseconds! There is no theoretical limit to how precise the measurement of age might be. For most social science purposes, the measurement of age in terms of years is quite satisfactory, but age is nonetheless a continuous variable.

Nominal variables are, by definition, discrete in that they consist of mutually exclusive or discrete categories. Ordinal variables also are discrete. The mutually exclusive categories of an ordinal variable may be ranked from low to high, but there cannot be a partial rank. For example, in a study of the military, rank might be ordered as 1 = private, 2 = corporal, and so on, but it would be nonsensical to speak of a rank of 1.3. In some cases, interval and ratio variables are discrete. For example, family size and number of arrests are whole numbers or discrete intervals. (We can summarize discrete interval and ratio data by saying, for example, that the average family size is 1.8 people, but this is a summary statistic, not a measurement

of a particular household.) Many variables at the interval and ratio level are continuous, at least at the theoretical level. A researcher may settle for discrete indicators either because the study does not demand greater precision or because no tools exist that can measure the continuous variable with sufficient reliability. In some cases, researchers debate over whether a particular variable is discrete or continuous in nature. For example, we used social class as an illustration of an ordinal variable, suggesting that several distinct classes exist. Some argue that social class is inherently a continuous interval variable and that we only treat it as ordinal because of the lack of instruments that would permit researchers to measure it reliably as a true continuous, interval variable (Borgatta & Bohrnstedt, 1981).

A variable, then, is continuous or discrete by its very nature, and the researcher cannot change that. It is possible to measure a continuous variable by specifying a number of discrete categories, as we typically do with age, but this does not change the nature of the variable itself. Whether variables are discrete or continuous may influence how we use them in data analysis. Knowing the level of measurement and whether variables are discrete or continuous has implications for selecting the best procedures for analyzing the data.

EVALUATING MEASURES

We have seen that there normally are a number of indicators, sometimes a large number and at different levels of measurement, that we can use to measure a variable, but how do we choose the best of these measures for a particular study? A number of factors come into play in making this decision, including matters of feasibility (discussed in Chapter 4). Here, we want to discuss two additional and very important considerations in this regard—that is, the validity and reliability of measures (Alwin, 2007).

Validity

Validity refers to the accuracy of a measure: Does it accurately measure the variable it is intended to measure? If we were developing a measure of self-concept, a major concern would be whether our measuring device measures the concept as it is theoretically defined. There must be a fairly clear and logical relationship between the way that a variable is nominally defined and the way that it is operationalized. For example, if a group of social workers trying to identify families at risk of becoming homeless propose to measure housing stability on the basis of how stylishly their children dress, then we probably would have an invalid measure. Many factors influence the way that people dress at any given time. The slight possibility that one of these factors might have something to do with self-concept is not sufficient to make the suggested measure valid. The validity of measures is very difficult to demonstrate with any finality. Several approaches to the question of validity exist, however, and they can offer evidence regarding the validity of a measure.

Face validity involves assessing whether a logical relationship exists between the variable and the proposed measure. It essentially amounts to a rather commonsense comparison of what makes up the measure and the theoretical definition of the variable: Does it seem logical to use this measure to reflect that variable? We might measure child abuse in terms of the reports that physicians or emergency room personnel make concerning injuries suffered by children. This is not a perfect measure, because health personnel might be wrong. It does, however, seem logical that an injury such people report might reflect actual abuse.

No matter how carefully done, face validity clearly is subjective in nature. All we have is logic and common sense as arguments for the validity of a measure. This makes face validity the weakest demonstration of validity, and it usually should be considered as no more than a starting point. All measures must pass the test of face validity. If they do, then we should attempt one of the more stringent methods for assessing validity.

An extension of face validity is called **content validity**, or **sampling validity**, which has to do with whether a measuring device covers the full range of meanings or forms that are included in a variable to measure. In other words, a valid measuring device provides an adequate, or representative, *sample* of all *content*, or *elements*, or *instances*, of the phenomenon being measured. For example, if one were measuring a person's job satisfaction (the extent to which he or she is satisfied with his or her job), it would be important to recognize that job satisfaction includes more than the extent to which they like the actual work involved (see Liziano & Mor Barak, 2015). It can also pertain to the extent to which people believe they are fairly compensated for their work, the perceived recognition they receive from their employers for the work they do, the extent to which they enjoy the social aspects of the job (i.e., relationships with coworkers), and the extent to which the job allows them to manage both work and home life demands. A valid measure of job satisfaction, then, would take that variability into account. If a measure of job satisfaction consisted of a series of statements to which people expressed degrees of agreement, then a valid measure would include statements that relate to those many settings in which job satisfaction might be expressed. If all the statements in the measuring device had to do, say, with actual work tasks, then it would be a less valid measure of overall job satisfaction.

Content validity is a more extensive assessment of validity than is face validity, because it involves a detailed analysis of the breadth of the measured concept and its relationship to the measuring device. Content validity involves two distinct steps: (a) determining the full range or domain of the content of a variable and (b) determining whether all those domains are represented among the items that constitute the measuring device. It is still a somewhat subjective assessment, however, in that someone has to judge what the full domain of the variable is and whether a particular aspect of a concept is adequately represented in the measuring device. There are no agreed-on criteria that determine whether a measure has content validity. Ultimately, it is a judgment, albeit a more carefully considered judgment than occurs with face validity.

One way to strengthen confidence in face or content validity is to gather the opinions of other investigators, especially those who are knowledgeable about the variables involved, regarding whether particular operational definitions are logical measures of the variables. This extension of face or content validity, which sometimes is referred to as **jury opinion**, is still subjective, of course. Because more people serve as a check on bias or misinterpretation, however, jury opinion is superior to individual tests of face or content validity.

Criterion validity establishes validity by showing a correlation between a measurement device and some other criterion or standard that we know or believe accurately measures the variable under consideration. Or, we might correlate the results of the measuring device with some properties or characteristics of the variable that the measuring device is intended to measure. For example, a scale intended to measure risk of suicide, if it is to be considered valid, should correlate with the occurrence of self-destructive behavior. The key to criterion validity is to find a criterion variable against which to compare the results of the measuring device.

Criterion validity moves away from the subjective assessments of face validity and provides more objective evidence of validity. One type of criterion validity is **concurrent validity**, which compares the instrument under evaluation to some already existing criterion, such as the results of another measuring device. (Presumably, any other measuring devices in this assessment have already been tested for validity.) Lawrence Shulman (1978), for example, used a form of concurrent validity to test an instrument intended to measure the practice skills of human service practitioners. This instrument consisted of a questionnaire in which clients rated the skills of practitioners. Shulman reasoned that clients would view more skilled practitioners as more helpful and that those practitioners would have more satisfied clients. Thus, Shulman looked for correlations between how positively clients rated a practitioner's skills and the perceived helpfulness of practitioners or satisfaction of clients. These correlations offered evidence for the validity of the measure of practitioners' skills.

Numerous existing measures can help establish the concurrent validity of a newly developed measure. (Following are only some of the compilations of such measures available in the social sciences and the human services: Bloom, Fischer, &

Orme, 2009; Fischer & Corcoran, 2007; Fredman & Sherman, 1987; Hays, 2014; Magura & Moses, 1986; McDowell, 2006; Miller & Salkind, 2002; Robinson, Shaver, & Wrightsman, 1991; Schutte & Malouff, 1995; Strainer, Norman, & Cairney, 2015; Touliatos, Perlmutter, Strauss, & Holden, 2001.) More measures can be found in research articles in professional journals. In addition, the Consulting Psychologists Press and other organizations publish catalogs of measures they make available to assess a wide array of skills, behaviors, attitudes, and other variables. (This also suggests, as pointed out in Chapter 4, that a thorough review of the literature, undertaken before going through all the work of creating a new measure, may unearth an existing measure that meets one's needs and has already been demonstrated to have adequate validity and reliability.) Then, it is a matter of applying both measures to the same sample and comparing the results. If a substantial correlation is found between the measures, we have reason to believe that our measure has concurrent validity. As a matter of convention, a correlation of $r = .50$ is considered to be the minimum required for establishing concurrent validity.

The inherent weakness of concurrent validity is the validity of the existing measure that is used for comparison. All we can conclude is that our measure is about as valid as the other one. If the measure that we select for comparison is not valid, then the fact that ours correlates with it hardly makes our measure valid. For this reason, researchers should use only those measures that have been established as being valid by research for comparison purposes in concurrent validity.

A second form of criterion validity is **predictive validity**, in which an instrument predicts some future state of affairs. In this case, the criteria that are used to assess the instrument are certain future events. For example, homeless service providers across the United States have adopted a measurement tool, the Vulnerability Index-Service Prioritization Decision Assistance Tool (VI-SPDAT) for use in prioritizing which clients (or potential clients) are most in need of the most intensive homeless services. (The VI-SPDAT is often used by service providers to identify clients for housing first programs designed to quickly move the neediest chronically homeless persons into housing.) This assessment tool is designed to help predict which clients are most at risk of death without housing and other assistance (Stafford & Wood, 2017).

Ultimately, the SPDAT's ability to make accurate predictions about mortality and other health-related issues can validate that measure. Because this may require numerous applications and many years, scales like the SPDAT can be assessed initially for validity on the basis of their ability to differentiate between high and low health risks.

If we know that certain groups are likely to differ substantially on a given variable, then we can use a measure's ability to discriminate between these groups as an indicator of validity. This variation on predictive validity is the *known groups* approach to validity. Suppose, for example, we were working on a measure of food insecurity. We might apply the measure to a group of upper middle class professionals, whom we would expect to be low in food insecurity, and to a group of welfare recipients, whom we would expect to be high in prejudice. If these groups differed significantly in how they responded to the measurement instrument, then we would have reason to believe that the measure is valid. If the measure failed to show a substantial difference, we would certainly have doubt about its validity.

Despite the apparent potential of the known groups approach, it does have its limitations. Frequently, no groups are known to differ on the variable that we are attempting to measure. In fact, the purpose of developing a measure often is to allow the identification of groups that do differ on some variable. Thus, we cannot always use the known groups' technique. When we do, we also have to consider a further limitation—namely, that it cannot tell us whether a measure can make finer distinctions between less extreme groups than those used in the validation. Perhaps the measure of food insecurity just described shows the welfare recipients to be high in food insecurity and the upper middle class professionals to be low. With a broader sample, however, the measure may show that *only* the welfare recipients score high and that *everyone else,* not just professionals, scores low. Thus, the measure can distinguish between groups only in a very crude fashion.

Construct validity, the most complex of the types of validity that we discuss here, involves relating an instrument to an overall theoretical framework to determine whether the instrument is correlated with all the concepts and propositions that comprise the theory (Cronbach & Meehl, 1955). In this case, instruments are assessed in terms of how they relate not to one criterion but, rather, to the numerous criteria that can be derived from some theory. For example, if we develop a new measure of socioeconomic status, we can assess construct validity by showing that the new measure accurately predicts the many hypotheses that can be derived from a theory of occupational attainment. In the theory, numerous propositions would relate occupational attainment and socioeconomic status to a variety of other concepts. If we do not find some or all of the predicted relationships, then we may question the validity of the new measuring instrument. (Of course, it may be that the theory itself is flawed; this possibility must always be considered when assessing construct validity.)

Construct validity takes some very complex forms. One is the **multitrait–multimethod approach** (Campbell & Fiske, 1959). This is based on two ideas: First, two instruments that are valid measures of the same concept should correlate rather highly with each other even though they are different instruments. Second, two instruments, even if similar to each other, should not correlate highly if they measure different concepts. This approach to validity involves the simultaneous assessment of numerous instruments (multimethod) and numerous concepts (multitrait) through the computation of intercorrelations. Wolfe et al. (1987) used this technique to assess the validity of children's self-reports about negative emotions, such as aggressiveness and depression. The point is that assessing construct validity can become highly complex, but this complexity offers greater evidence for the validity of the measures.

The types of validity we have discussed so far—face, content, criterion, and construct—involve a progression in which each builds on the previous one. Each type requires more information than the prior ones but provides a better assessment of validity. Unfortunately, many studies limit their assessment to content validity, with its heavy reliance on the subjective judgments of individuals or juries. Although this sometimes is necessary, measures subjected only to content validity should be used with caution.

Practitioner Profile 5.1 offers an example of one school's efforts to create valid and reliable measures of student behavior. While this is a practice and not a research example, the principles of measurement are the same.

Reliability

In addition to validity, measures also are evaluated in terms of their **reliability**, which refers to a measure's ability to yield consistent results each time it is applied. In other words, reliable measures only fluctuate because of variations in the variable being measured. An illustration of reliability can be found at any carnival, where there usually is

---

PRACTITIONER PROFILE 5.1 Kelsey Johansen, School Supervisor, Northwest School of Innovative Learning, Washington (Based on personal communication on April 16, 2018.)

Kelsey Johansen is school supervisor of the Northwest School of Innovative Learning (NWSOIL) in Redmond, Washington. She began at NWSOIL about 5 years ago as an intern and worked her way up to the school supervisor position. She has an undergraduate degree in sociology and psychology and a master's degree in counseling psychology. NWSOIL is a therapeutic day school for students who require Individual Education Plans (IEPs). Most students have severe behavioral disabilities and mental health diagnoses. They contract with area school districts to serve children who are not able to succeed in traditional school settings.

Kelsey always had an interest in research and especially implementing research findings into practice. Since her time as an intern at NWSOIL she had a desire to create an evidence-based practice within the school.

As I worked my way up the program I saw that we were not always able to justify behavioral intervention and treatment plans. We didn't have data, we didn't have information to back up what we were saying in meetings and why students should be transitioning out of the program. We started tracking student data because we needed to be more credible and evidence-based. We wanted the school districts to see we were using real-time data to track progress toward IEP goals and behavior and treatment plans. We needed to have functional behavioral assessments that were accurate.

As detailed in the chapter vignette, Kelsey helped to develop a behavioral tracking and token economy system at NWSOIL. The next step, she explains, is to move to an electronic system that allows teachers and paraeducators to enter data using a Kindle tablet:

Now we're switching over to tablets to track real-time data. We'll be able to record whether children are bullying or showing kindness or any number of other behaviors. So we'll be able to see by lunch—visually with charts and graphs—how these kids' days are going. There's going to be a consequence tab that our behavioral intervention specialist can monitor, and go and check with the kids. They will be adding monetary value based on behaviors they are displaying. At the end of the week we'll be able to determine whether children were being safe this week. Our program needs to be able to show that. We really run on data.

(continued)

Ensuring reliability of the behavioral tracking system requires substantial effort. As Kelsey explains,

> We have our new paraeducational assistants training with our seasoned staff members to make sure that data is being tracked accurately. When we bring new staff on, we talk about how important documentation is at the school because it determines what services students receive.

Shae Sunwold, a former paraeducator at NWSOIL and current Master of Social Work student, explains that there are processes to help ensure consistency in recording students' behaviors.

> Every classroom is different, and organized by age and behaviors. One nice fallback is that the paraeducator, who records most of the behaviors, can ask the teacher whether a particular behavior should be considered bullying or if we should just ignore it. The teacher is in there every day so she knows how to record each circumstance. We also have behavioral intervention specialists who float between classrooms. When I had that position I would look through the data to find errors or discrepancies. For example, a student may have been sleeping but was given full points for that period of the day. That's not necessarily how we should be recording sleeping behavior, so we would go and have a talk with whoever recorded that and assigned points.

Another strategy for creating reliable measures is using notes to summarize (qualitatively) a behavior or set of behaviors. These notes are later shared with other staff who discuss how teachers and paraeducators should record the behavior—whether it is positive or negative and what points might be assigned to it.

One of the biggest advantages to having a sophisticated data tracking system is that it helps create buy-in with school districts that contract with NWSOIL as well as parents. "Districts love having data because it isn't subjective. They like being able to see an IEP and then see exactly how much progress has been made toward achieving the goals within it," she explained. "Parents are a little different."

> When they come to our school, they tend to see it either as a gift or a very difficult school placement. If there is resistance to the placement, then they might try to fight the data. When they feel that it has been a gift to their kid, they embrace the data.

Eventually, Kelsey explains, many parents end up embracing the school and our data system because they see it works. Parental buy-in, she believes, is critical to the school's success.

> I think that we see more success with our students when the parents collaborate with our teachers. Parents sometimes connect students' privileges at home with their privileges here at school. For example when a student has a 60% day, compared to an 80% day, they may lose their privileges at home. Parent involvement is key to success.

When asked about the ultimate goal of her data tracking efforts Kelsey said that she hopes the majority of students can eventually leave NWSOIL and succeed in traditional school settings.

(continued)

> We don't want this to be a forever school. We want it to be a chapter for these kids to learn how to be a functioning student. We'll look at the data to move them through our program, through our levels system to get them to our transition class. We can start transitioning them back to their comprehensive schools that will offer them experiences that we can't offer due to our population. Some of the successes we have seen are kids sending us pictures of them in their suit when they went to a dance, or calling us and telling us that they are graduating high school. I had one student come back recently that is in college. He came back here to do an interview about the IEP and mental health processes.

a booth with a person guessing people's weights within a certain range of accuracy—say, plus or minus three pounds. The customer essentially bets that the carnival worker's ability to guess weights is sufficiently unreliable that his or her estimate will fall outside the prescribed range, and if so, the customer will win a prize. A weight scale, of course, is a reliable indicator of a person's weight because it records roughly the same weight each time the same person stands on it, and the carnie provides such a scale to assess his or her guess of the customer's weight. Despite the fact that carnies who operate such booths become quite good at guessing weights, they do occasionally guess wrong—influenced, perhaps, by aspects of the customer other than his or her actual weight, such as loose clothing that obscures a person's physique.

In general, a valid measure is reliable. So, if we were certain of the validity of a measure, then we would not need to concern ourselves with its reliability. Evidence of validity, however, is always less than perfect, and this is why we turn to other ways of evaluating measures, including reliability. Reliability gives us more evidence for validity, because a reliable measure may be valid. Fortunately, we can demonstrate reliability in a more straightforward manner than we can demonstrate validity. Many specific techniques exist for estimating the reliability of a measure, but all are based on one of two principles—namely, stability and equivalence. *Stability* is the idea that a reliable measure should not change from one application to the next, assuming that the concept being measured has not changed. *Equivalence* is the idea that all items that make up a measuring instrument should measure the same thing and, thus, be

consistent with one another. The first technique for estimating reliability, test–retest reliability, uses the stability approach; the others discussed use the equivalence principle.

Test–Retest. The first and most generally applicable assessment of reliability is called *test–retest*. As the name implies, this technique involves applying a measure to a sample of people and then, somewhat later, applying the same measure to the same people again. After the retest, we have two scores on the same measure for each person, as illustrated in Table 5.4. We then correlate these

TABLE 5.4 Hypothetical Test–Retest Data

Subjects	Initial Test	Retest
1	12	15
2	15	20
3	22	30
4	38	35
5	40	35
6	40	38
7	40	41
8	60	55
9	70	65
10	75	77
$r = .98$		

two sets of scores with an appropriate statistical measure of association (see Chapter 15). Because the association in test–retest reliability involves scores obtained from two identical questionnaires, we fully expect a high degree of association. As a matter of convention, a correlation coefficient of .80 or better normally is necessary for a measure to be considered as reliable. In Table 5.4, the *r* means that the particular statistic used was Pearson's correlation coefficient, and the value of .98 indicates that the measurement instrument is highly reliable according to the test–retest method.

Lawrence Shulman (1978), in addition to subjecting his measure of practice skills to the tests of validity mentioned earlier, also tested its reliability. He did so by sending versions of the questionnaire to a set of clients and then sending an identical questionnaire 2 weeks later to the same clients. This provided him with a test–retest assessment of reliability, and he obtained a correlation coefficient of .75. When a reliability coefficient is close to the conventional level, such as in this case, then the researcher must make a judgment about whether to assume that the instrument is reliable (and the low coefficient is a result of factors other than the unreliability of the instrument) or to rework the instrument to obtain higher levels of association.

In actual practice, we cannot simply use the test–retest method as suggested, because exposing people to the same measure twice creates a problem known as *multiple-testing effects* (Campbell & Stanley, 1963). Whenever we apply a measure to a group of people a second time, they may not react to it the same as they did the first time. They may, for example, recall their previous answers, and that could influence their second response. People might respond as they recall doing the first time to maintain consistency, or people might purposely change responses for the sake of variety. Either case can have a confounding effect on testing reliability. If people strive for consistency, then their efforts can mask actual unreliability in the instrument. If they deliberately change responses, then a reliable measure can appear to be less reliable.

A solution to this dilemma is to divide the test group randomly into two groups: an experimental group to test twice, and a control group to test

TABLE 5.5 Design for Test–Retest

	Initial Test	Retest
Experimental group	Yes	Yes
Control group	No	Yes

only once. Table 5.5 illustrates the design for such an experiment. Ideally, the measure will yield consistent results in all three testing sessions; if it does, then we have solid reason to believe the measure is reliable. On the contrary, substantial differences among the groups may indicate unreliability. If, for example, the experimental group shows consistency in both sets of responses to the measurement instrument but the control group differs, then the measure may be unreliable and the consistency of the experimental group might result from the multiple-testing effects. However, if the experimental group yields inconsistent results but the control group shows responses similar to those of the experimental group's initial test, this outcome also may be caused by multiple-testing effects and result from the experimental group's changing answers during the retest. Despite the inconsistency in the experimental group, the measure still might be reliable if we observe this outcome. Finally, we may see that the results of all three testing sessions appear to be inconsistent. Such an outcome would suggest that the measure is not reliable. If either of the outcomes that leave the reliability of the measure in doubt occurs, researchers should conduct a second test–retest experiment with the hope of obtaining clearer results. If the same result occurs, then we should redesign the instrument.

The test–retest method of assessing reliability has both advantages and disadvantages. Its major advantage is that we can use it with many measures, which is not true of alternative tests of reliability. Its disadvantage is that it is slow and cumbersome to use, with two required testing sessions and the desirability of a control group. In addition, as we have seen, the outcome may not be clear, leading to the necessity of repeating the whole procedure. Finally, we cannot use the test–retest method on measures of variables whose value might have changed during the interval between tests. For example, people's attitudes can change for reasons that have nothing to do with the testing, and a measure of attitudes might appear to be unreliable when it is not.

Multiple Forms. If our measuring device is a multiple-item scale, as often is the case, we can approach the question of reliability through the technique of multiple forms. When developing the scale, we create two separate but equivalent versions made up of different items, such as different questions. We then administer these two forms successively to the same people during a single testing session. We correlate the results from the forms, as in test–retest, using an appropriate statistical measure of association, with the same convention of $r = .80$ or better required for establishing reliability. If the correlation between the two forms is sufficiently high, then we can assume that each scale is reliable.

Multiple forms have the advantages of requiring only one testing session and of needing no control group. These may be significant advantages if using either multiple-testing sessions or a control group is impractical. In addition, we need not worry about changes in a variable over time, because both forms are administered at the same time.

The multiple-forms technique relies on the two forms appearing to the respondents as though they were only one, long measure so that the respondents do not realize they are really taking the same test twice. This necessity of deluding people points out one of the disadvantages of multiple forms: To maintain the equivalence of the forms, the items in the two forms probably will be quite similar— so similar, in fact, that people may realize they are responding to essentially the same items twice. If this occurs, it raises the specter of multiple-testing effects and casts doubt on the accuracy of the reliability test. Another disadvantage of multiple forms is the difficulty of developing two measures with different items that really are equivalent. If we obtain inconsistent results from the two forms, it may be caused by differences in the forms rather than by the unreliability of either one. In a way, it is questionable whether multiple forms really test reliability and not just our ability to create equivalent versions of the same measure.

Internal Consistency Approaches. Internal consistency approaches to reliability use a single scale that is administered to one group of people to develop an estimate of reliability. For example, in the *split-half approach* to reliability, the test group responds to the complete measuring instrument. We then randomly divide the responses to the instrument into halves, treating each half as though it were a separate scale. We correlate the two halves by using an appropriate measure of association. Once again, we need a coefficient of $r = .80$ or better to demonstrate reliability. In his study of practice skills mentioned earlier, Shulman (1978) used a split-half reliability test on his instrument in addition to the test–retest method. He divided each respondent's answers to his questions about practitioners' skills into two roughly equivalent sets, correlated the two sets of answers, and found a correlation (following a correction, to be mentioned shortly) of .79. This is an improvement over the reliability that he found with the test–retest method, and it comes very close to the conventional level of .80.

One complication in using the split-half reliability test is that the correlation coefficient may understate the reliability of the measure because, other things being equal, a longer measuring scale is more reliable than a shorter one. Because the split-half approach divides the scale into two, each half is shorter than the whole scale and, thus, will appear to be less reliable than the scale as a whole. To correct for this, we can adjust the correlation coefficient by applying the Spearman–Brown formula, which Shulman did:

$$r = \frac{2r_i}{1 + r_i},$$

where r_i = uncorrected correlation coefficient and r = corrected correlation coefficient (reliability coefficient).

To illustrate the effect of the Spearman–Brown formula, suppose we have a 20-item scale with a correlation between the two halves of $r_i = .70$, which is smaller than the minimum needed to demonstrate reliability. The Spearman–Brown formula corrects as follows:

$$r = \frac{(2)(.70)}{1+.70} = \frac{1.40}{1.70} = .82.$$

It can be seen that the Spearman–Brown formula has a substantial effect, increasing the uncorrected coefficient from well below .80 to just over it. If we had obtained these results with an actual scale, we would conclude that its reliability was now adequate.

Using the split-half technique requires two preconditions that can limit its applicability. First, all the items in the scale must measure the same variable. If the scale in question is a jumble of items measuring several different variables, then it is meaningless to divide it and compare the halves. Second, the scale must contain a sufficient number of items so that, when it is divided, the halves do not become too short to be considered as scales themselves. A suggested minimum is 8 to 10 items per half (Goode & Hatt, 1952, p. 236). Because many measures are shorter than these minimums, however, it may not be possible to assess their reliability with the split-half technique.

A number of other approaches to internal consistency reliability sometimes are used to overcome the weaknesses of the split-half approach. After all, the split-half approach only uses one random separation of the scale into two halves. Randomly dividing the items of a scale into halves could result in many different arrangements of items, and each would yield a slightly different correlation between the halves. One common approach to this problem is to use Cronbach's alpha, which may be thought of as the average of all possible split-half correlations. Theoretically, the scale is divided into all possible configurations of two halves. Then, a correlation is computed for each possibility, and the average of those correlations is computed to derive alpha (Cronbach, 1951). This is not actually how Cronbach's alpha is calculated, but it does describe the logic of the procedure.

Another approach to internal consistency reliability is to correlate each item in the scale with every other item and then use the average of these correlations as the measure of reliability. This also is done by correlating each item with the overall scale score.

(Statistical packages such as SPSS contain procedures that will produce Cronbach's alpha as well as other reliability tests based on inter-item correlations.)

Internal consistency reliability tests have several advantages. They require only one testing session and no control group. They also give the clearest indication of reliability. For these reasons, researchers prefer to use these methods of assessing reliability whenever possible. The only disadvantage, as we noted, is that we cannot always use them. Shulman's approach teaches a lesson, however: Use more than one test, if possible, to assess both reliability and validity. These issues are sufficiently important that the expenditure of time is justified.

Measurement With Diverse Populations

Researchers often first assess the validity and reliability of measuring instruments (for research and practice) by applying them to White, non-Hispanic respondents, because they find such people to be the most accessible. We should almost never assume, however, that such assessments can be generalized to culturally diverse populations (Mushquash & Bova, 2007; Venter & Buys, 2016). The development of such instruments typically does not consider the unique cultural characteristics and attitudes of minorities. For some minorities, such as Asians, Latinos, and Aboriginals, language differences mean that an English-language interview would have some respondents answering in a second language. Researchers cannot assume that such a respondent will understand words and phrases as well as—or in the same way as—a person for whom English is his or her first language. In addition, some concepts in English do not have a precise equivalent in another language.

It is important, therefore, to refine measuring instruments to ensure that they are valid and reliable measures among minorities. Many researchers have pointed out, for example, that studies of health issues and healthcare needs within communities have failed to include items pertaining to issues and needs pertaining to transgender people (Feldman et al., 2016). One of the authors of this textbook, Timothy Hilton, conducted a study of Native Americans transitioning from prisons to their home communities with one of his students, Joseph Masters. One of the interview questions they asked study participants was whether their communities welcomed them back when they returned or spurned them because of their past crimes. The researchers were surprised that time after time interviewees were confused by the question and were unable to answer it. Finally one respondent explained that this was not a question Native Americans on reservations would understand because all tribal members are always welcomed because they belong to the community. It is their right of membership (Masters & Hilton, 2014). (We will discuss this study in more depth in Chapter 16.)

These illustrations should make clear that measurement in social research must be culturally sensitive. When conducting research on a group with a culture different from that of the researchers, the researchers can take a number of steps to produce more valid and reliable measurement instruments (Marin & VanOss Marin, 1991; Tran & Williams, 1994; Wardale, Cameron, & Li, 2015):

1. Researchers can immerse themselves in the culture of the group under study, experiencing the daily activities of life and the cultural products as the natives do.
2. Researchers should use key informants, people who participate routinely in the culture of the group under study, to help develop and assess the measurement instruments.
3. When translating an instrument from English into another language, researchers should use the most effective translation methods, usually *double translation* (translate from English into the target language and then back into English by an independent person), to check for errors or inconsistencies.
4. After developing or translating measurement instruments for use with minority populations, researchers should test the instruments for validity and reliability on the population they intend to study.
5. At times, using mixed methods approaches to data collection (that include both quantitative and qualitative data collection) can help researchers better understand how diverse research participants interpret measures, allowing them to make necessary adjustments.

ERRORS IN MEASUREMENT

The range of precision in measurement is quite broad—from the cook who measures in terms of pinches, dashes, and smidgens to the physicist who measures in angstroms (0.003937 millionths of an inch). No matter whether a measurement is crude or precise, it is important to recognize that *all* measurements involve some component of error (Alwin, 2007). There is no such thing as an exact measurement. Some measurement devices in the social sciences are fairly precise. Others, however, contain substantial error components, because most of our measures deal with abstract and shifting phenomena, such as attitudes, values, or opinions, which are difficult to measure with a high degree of precision. The large error component in many of our measurements means that researchers must pay close attention to the different types and sources of error. In measurement, researchers confront two basic types of error: *random* and *systematic*. In fact, we can modify the formula from the measurement theory introduced earlier in this chapter with the recognition that the error term in that formula, E, is actually made up of two components:

$$E = R + S,$$

where R refers to random error and S refers to systematic error. Now, our measurement formula looks like this:

$$X = T + R + S.$$

Our measurement or observation of a phenomenon is a function of the true nature of that phenomenon along with any random and systematic error that occurs in the measurement process.

Random Errors

Random errors are those that are neither consistent nor patterned; the error is as likely to be in one direction as in another. Essentially, random errors are chance errors that, in the long run, tend to cancel themselves out. In fact, in measurement theory, mathematicians often assume that $R = 0$ in the long run. For example, a respondent may misread or mismark an item on a questionnaire; a counselor may misunderstand and, thus, record incorrectly something said during an interview; a computer operator may enter incorrect data into a computerized data file. All these are random sources of error and can occur at virtually every point in a research project. Cognizant of the numerous sources of random error, researchers take steps to minimize them. Careful wording of questions, convenient response formats, and "cleaning" of computerized data all keep random error down. Despite researchers' best efforts, however, the final data may contain some component of random error.

Because of their unpatterned nature, random errors are assumed to tend to cancel each other out. For example, the careless computer operator mentioned earlier would be just as likely to enter a score that was lower than the actual one as to enter a score that was higher. The net effect is that the random errors at least partly offset each other. The major problem with random error is that it weakens the precision with which a researcher can measure variables, thus reducing the ability to detect a relationship between variables when one is, in fact, present. For example, consider a hypothetical study concerning the relationship between empathy on the part of human service workers and client satisfaction with treatment. Assume that higher levels of client satisfaction actually are associated with higher levels of empathy. For such a study, measurements would be taken of the level of empathy that a worker expressed and of client satisfaction. Suppose we monitor five client interviews by each of five workers—a total sample of 25 cases—for the level of worker empathy and client satisfaction. To the extent that random error is present in our measures, some interviews will be scored too high and some too low, even though the overall mean empathy and satisfaction scores can be expected to be quite close to the true averages. In terms of individual cases, however, random measurement will produce some empathy scores that are erroneously low for their associated satisfaction scores. Conversely, random error will produce some empathy scores that are high for their associated satisfaction scores. Thus, the random error tends to mask the true correlation between empathy and satisfaction. Despite the fact that worker empathy and client satisfaction really are correlated, too much of this type of random measurement error may result in the conclusion that the relationship between these variables does not exist.

Fortunately, researchers can combat random error with a variety of strategies. One is to increase the sample size. Instead of using five workers and five interviews per worker, the researcher might use 10 workers and 10 interviews per worker, for a total sample of 100. A second strategy is to increase the "dose," or "contrast," between levels of the independent variable. For example, researchers might select workers for the study according to their empathy skills to ensure some cases with low expression of empathy and some with high expression. Finally, the researcher might increase the number of items on the measurement scales or, in other ways, more precisely refine the tools. Such strategies can reduce the impact of random error, but the same is not true for systematic error.

Systematic Errors

Systematic error is consistent and patterned. Unlike random errors, systematic errors may not cancel themselves out. If there is a consistent over- or understatement of the value of a given variable, then the errors will accumulate. For example, we know that systematic error occurs when measuring crime using official police reports; the Uniform Crime Reports (UCR) of the Federal Bureau of Investigation (FBI) count only crimes that are reported to the police. The Department of Justice supplements these statistics with the National Crime Victimization Survey (NCVS), which measures the number of people who claim to be the victims of crime. Comparisons of these two measures consistently reveal a substantial amount of hidden crime—that is, crimes that are reported by victims but never brought to the attention of the police. Guitierez and Kirk (2017) found that there is substantially less reporting of crimes within communities with high percentages of noncitizen and foreign-born community members, suggesting there may be barriers to reporting crimes for some groups, creating systematic measurement error.

Systematic errors are more troublesome to researchers than random errors, because they are more likely to lead to false conclusions. For example, official juvenile delinquency statistics consistently show higher rates of delinquency among children of families with lower socioeconomic status. Self-report studies of involvement with delinquency suggest, however, that the official data systematically overstate the relationship between delinquency and socioeconomic status (Binder, Geis, & Bruce, 1988; Piotrowska, Stride, & Rowe, 2015). It is easy to see how the systematic error in delinquency data could lead to erroneous conclusions regarding possible causes of delinquency as well as to inappropriate prevention or treatment strategies.

Improving Validity and Reliability

When a measurement device does not achieve acceptable levels of validity and reliability—that is, when much error occurs—researchers often attempt to redesign the device so that it is more valid and reliable. We will discuss how to develop valid and reliable measuring devices at length in other chapters, when we discuss how to design good measurement tools. Here, however, we mention a few techniques as a preview of what happens when a measurement device does not yield adequate validity and reliability:

1. *More extensive conceptual development.* Often, validity and reliability are compromised because the researcher is not sufficiently clear and precise about the nature of the concepts being measured and their possible indicators. Rethinking the concepts often helps in revising the measuring instrument to make it more valid.
2. *Better training of those who will apply the measuring devices.* This is especially useful when a measuring device is based on someone's subjective assessment of an attitude or state. Researchers show the people applying the device how their judgments can be biased or produce error and how they can guard against it in their assessments.
3. *Interview the subjects of the research about the measurement devices.* Those under study may have some insight regarding why the verbal reports, observations, or archival reports are not producing accurate measures of their behavior. They may, for example, comment that the wording of questions is ambiguous or that members of their subculture interpret some words differently than the researcher intended.
4. *Higher level of measurement.* This does not guarantee greater validity and reliability, but a higher level of measurement can produce a more reliable measuring device in some cases. So, when the researcher has some options in terms of how to measure a variable, it is worth considering a higher level of measurement.
5. *Use more indicators of a variable.* This also does not guarantee enhanced reliability and validity, but a multiple-item measuring device can, in some cases, produce a more valid measure than a measuring device with fewer items can.
6. *Conduct an item-by-item assessment of multiple-item measures.* If the measuring device consists of a number of questions or items, perhaps only one or a few items are the problem: These are the invalid ones that are reducing the validity and reliability of the instrument, and deleting them may improve validity and reliability.

After revising a measuring device based on these ideas, researchers must, of course, subject the revised version to tests of validity and reliability.

CHOOSING A MEASUREMENT DEVICE

We have seen that we can use a number of indicators, sometimes a large number and at different levels of measurement, to measure a variable. How do we choose the best of these measures to use in a particular study? If we are developing a new measuring device, how do we decide whether it is good or not? It is a complicated and sometimes difficult decision for researchers, but a number of factors, discussed in this or in earlier chapters, can serve as guidelines for making this decision:

1. Choose indicators that measure the variables in ways that are theoretically important in the research, as discussed in Chapter 2.
2. Choose indicators based on their proven validity and reliability.
3. If two measuring instruments are equivalent in all other ways except for the level of measurement, choose the indicator at the higher level of measurement.
4. Choose indicators that produce the least amount of systematic and random error.
5. Choose indicators with matters of feasibility, as discussed in Chapter 4, in mind.

REVIEW AND CRITICAL THINKING

Main Points

- Measurement is the process of describing abstract concepts in terms of specific indicators by assigning numbers or other symbols to them.
- An indicator is an observation that we assume to be evidence for the attributes or properties of some phenomenon. Social research measures most variables through verbal reports, observation, or archival records. Positivists and nonpositivists disagree about the nature of measurement.
- The four levels of measurement are nominal, ordinal, interval, and ratio.
- The nature of the variable itself and the way that it is measured determines the level of measurement achieved with a given variable.
- Discrete variables have a limited number of distinct and separate values. Continuous variables theoretically have an infinite number of possible values.
- Validity refers to a measure's ability to measure accurately the variable it measures.
- Face validity, content or sampling validity, jury opinion, criterion validity, and construct validity are techniques of assessing the validity of measures.
- Reliability refers to a measure's ability to yield consistent results each time it is applied.
- Test–retest, multiple forms, and internal consistency, such as split-half, are techniques for assessing the reliability of measures.
- Measurement in social research must be culturally sensitive; researchers should never assume a measurement instrument that is valid and reliable for a majority group will be so for minorities.
- Random errors are neither consistent nor patterned and can reduce the precision with which variables are measured.
- Systematic errors are consistent and patterned and, unless noted, can potentially lead to erroneous conclusions.
- Researchers can take a number of steps to improve the validity and reliability of measurement devices.
- Measurement devices are chosen on the basis of theoretical considerations, their validity and reliability, their level of measurement, the amount of systematic and random errors, and feasibility.

IMPORTANT TERMS FOR REVIEW

Concurrent validity	Interval measures	Predictive validity
Construct validity	Item	Random errors
Content validity	Jury opinion	Ratio measures
Continuous variables	Level of measurement	Reliability
Criterion validity	Measurement	Sampling validity
Discrete variables	Multitrait–multimethod	Scale
Face validity	approach	Systematic error
Index	Nominal measures	Validity
Indicator	Ordinal measures	

CRITICAL THINKING

1. How does social research measurement differ from the ways in which most people describe social phenomena? What can we learn from social scientists that might help us better describe the social world?
2. How do scientists (including social scientists) evaluate whether something exists and/or how much of it exists? What lessons can we draw from this process that might be applied to our work as human service professionals?
3. Consider the ways in which we evaluate human service outcomes like "housing stability" or "prosocial behavior." How do we know whether or not these exist for clients and/or their magnitude?
4. Reliability and validity are key measurement concepts. What challenges might human service professionals face in creating a reliable and valid measure (in assessment, monitoring progress, tracking outcomes, and summarizing performance)?
5. Identify a human service outcome that may be meaningful to you (from your current work, field placement, or your future career).
6. What steps could you and your colleagues do to create a reliable and valid measure for this outcome?

EVALUATING COMPETENCY (FROM THE COUNCIL ON SOCIAL WORK EDUCATION [CSWE] 2015 EDUCATIONAL POLICY AND ACCREDITATION STANDARDS [EPAS])

Competency 1: Demonstrate Ethical and Professional Behavior

- The 2015 EPAS states that social workers "use reflection and self-regulation to manage personal values and maintain professionalism in practice situations." How might well-designed measures help social workers and other human service professionals manage personal biases that might interfere with the ways they evaluate clients and practice and program outcomes?

Competency 2: Engage Diversity and Difference in Practice

- Think about an area of practice that interests you. Identify two or three measures that are important to this area of practice. (This may be related to assessment, client goals, client outcomes, or program outcomes.) Are these measures universal from a cultural standpoint? (Do they have the same meaning for all groups of people?) If not, how might these measures be changed so they have meaning to all groups that you serve?

Competency 3: Advance Human Rights and Social, Economic, and Environmental Justice

- Human service agencies typically identify goals for their programs. Typically outcome measures reflect these goals. Think about a human service program that is important to you and identify the outcome measures associated with it. To what extent do these outcome measures pertain to the advancement of human rights and social, economic, or environmental justice?
- Thinking about the outcome measures from the aforementioned example, what additional outcome measures might the human service agency adopt that might help the agency evaluate the extent to which the program promotes the advancement of human rights and social, economic, and environmental justice?

Competency 5: Engage in Policy Practice

- Identify a policy (national, state, or local) that is important to you. What are the policy's goals? How are these goals evaluated? What measures are used to evaluate the policy's success? Are these measures a good reflection of the policy goals? Do they allow policy makers and other interested parties to track policy performance over time?
- What challenges might policy makers have in creating reliable and valid measures when evaluating policy performance?

Competency 7: Assess Individuals, Families, Groups, Organizations, and Communities

- Identify a human service program or activity that you care about. (This may be a program in which you work or within an area of practice with which you hope to be involved.) How are clients, communities, and/or social issues assessed within this program (or activity)?
- What measures are used in assessing these clients or communities (and/ or social issues)? Are these valid and reliable assessment measures? If not, what changes would improve their validity and reliability?

Competency 9: Evaluate Practice With Individuals, Families, Groups, Organizations, and Communities

- Identify a human service program that is important to you. What are the program's goals? What outcome measures are evaluated? Are these reliable and valid measures? Are they reflective of the program's goals?
- What roles do human service professionals have in generating the program goals identified earlier? To what extent are the outcome measures a reflection of the human service professionals' job performance? What else (besides outcome measures) should agency administrators evaluate when considering the job performance of professionals involved in this program?

SELF-ASSESSMENT
. . . .

1. Measurement refers to:
  a. The extent to which a client feels he or she improved after participating in a human service program.
  b. Assigning numbers to represent clients' progress.
  c. The process of describing concepts in terms of specific indicators.
  d. The consistency of outcomes.

2. Which of these is the term that means an observation that social researchers and practitioners assume is evidence of the attributes or properties of some phenomenon?
  a. Nominal definition
  b. Operational definition
  c. Reliability
  d. Indicator

3. If a measure involves an index or scale we know that the measure:
  a. Is highly reliable.
  b. Is a composite score based on multiple items.
  c. Is valid because it includes multiple concepts.
  d. Requires professional training to administer.

4. Age is an example of:
  a. A continuous variable because it can take on an infinite number of values.
  b. A discrete variable because it can take on an infinite number of values.
  c. A continuous variable because it can take on a finite number of values.
  d. A discrete variable because we need only consider people living to a reasonable age.

5. Social science and human service measures can be based on:
  a. Direct observation only (because we must observe phenomena directly for it to have real value).
  b. Self-reports only (since clients' experiences are the most important).
  c. Archival records only (because if it was not recorded it did not happen).
  d. Self-reports, observations, and archival records.

6. Which of these is considered the highest level of measurement?
  a. Ordinal
  b. Ratio
  c. Interval
  d. None of the above. All measurements are equally valuable and useful.

7. A ratio level measurement:
  a. Has all the characteristics of an ordinal level measurement.
  b. Has all the characteristics of an interval level measurement.
  c. Includes a zero value that is not arbitrary.
  d. All of the above are true.

8. Nonpositivists might argue that:
    a. Social phenomena are constructed by people as opposed to discovered by them.
    b. Social and psychological reality is universal, which allows for precise and objective measurement of social phenomena.
    c. We can never be certain about our measures so it is best not to measure social phenomena.
    d. Description is the only worthwhile form of measurement.
9. Systematic errors:
    a. Are not as serious as random errors because they are more precise.
    b. Are consistent and patterned.
    c. Are a result of chance.
    d. Can be overcome by moving away from self-report measures and using more observed measures.
10. Interviewing the subjects of research about measurement devices:
    a. Can help researchers gain insights that may allow them to create more valid and reliable measures.
    b. Is not advisable because it may create new measurement biases, essentially replacing researcher biases with respondent biases.
    c. Is advisable because it gives research subjects the opportunity to carefully consider their answers.
    d. Is unethical because it causes unnecessary burden for research subjects.

ANSWER KEY FOR SELF-ASSESSMENT QUIZ

1. **c.** The process of describing concepts in terms of specific indicators.
2. **d.** Indicator
3. **b.** Is a composite score based on multiple items.
4. **a.** A continuous variable because it can take on an infinite number of values.
5. **d.** Self-reports, observations, and archival records.
6. **b.** Ratio
7. **d.** All of the above are true.
8. **a.** Social phenomena are constructed by people as opposed to discovered by them.
9. **b.** Are consistent and patterned.
10. **a.** Can help researchers gain insights that may allow them to create more valid and reliable measures.

FOR FURTHER READING

Blythe, B. J., & Tripodi, T. (1989). *Measurement in direct practice.* Newbury Park, CA: Sage. This book looks at measurement issues from the standpoint of day-to-day efforts to apply successful interventions to help clients. It should be particularly useful for those who are currently in or planning to enter direct practice.

Campbell, D. T., & Russo, M. J. (2001). *Social measurement.* Thousand Oaks, CA: Sage. This book provides a user-friendly presentation of Campbell's essential work in social measurement. The book includes his arguments as to why qualitative approaches belong with quantitative ones as well as his debate with deconstructionists and social constructionists over measurement validity.

Geismar, L. L., & Camasso, M. (1993). *The family functioning scale: A guide to research and practice.* New York, NY: Springer Publishing. This book provides an excellent illustration of measurement in both research and practice as it explores development of a family functioning scale for use in both realms. It is a good example of both the parallels and linkages between research and practice.

Hersen, M. (Ed.) (2003). *Comprehensive handbook of psychological assessment* (Vols. 1–4). New York, NY: Wiley. These volumes provide essential information about developing and using the major types of psychological assessment instruments. These assessment instruments address the same kinds of measurement issues as instruments used in research do.

Hindelang, M. J., Hirschi, T., & Weis, J. G. (1980). *Measuring delinquency.* Beverly Hills, CA: Sage. A good description of the development of a measuring device related to a human service issue. The volume covers all the issues related to problems of measurement.

Kirk, J., & Miller, M. L. (1986). *Reliability and validity in qualitative research.* Beverly Hills, CA: Sage. This work presents the measurement issues of reliability and validity as they apply to qualitative research, such as field research (see Chapter 9). Unfortunately, reliability and validity often are presented only in the context of quantitative research.

Martin, L. L., & Kettner, P. M. (2009). *Measuring the performance of human service programs* (2nd ed.). Thousand Oaks, CA: Sage. This short book explains in detail how to measure and assess human service programs, especially with outcome measures. It includes such measures as levels of functioning scales and client satisfaction.

Miller, D. C., & Salkind, N. J. (2002). *Handbook of research design and social measurement* (6th ed.). Thousand Oaks, CA: Sage. A good resource work for scales and indices focusing on specific human service concerns.

REFERENCES

Alwin, D. F. (2007). *Margins of error: A study of reliability in survey measurement.* Hoboken, NJ: John Wiley & Sons.

Binder, A., Geis, G., & Bruce, D. (1988). *Juvenile delinquency: Historical, cultural, and legal perspectives.* New York, NY: Macmillan.

Bloom, M., Fischer, J., & Orme, J. G. (2009). *Evaluating practice: Guidelines for the accountable professional* (6th ed.). Boston, MA: Pearson.

Bohrnstedt, G. W. (1983). Measurement. In P. H. Rossi, J. D. Wright, & A. B. Anderson (Eds.), *Handbook of survey research* (pp. 69–121). New York, NY: Academic Press.

Borgatta, E., & Bohrnstedt, G. (1981). Levels of measurement: Once over again. In G. Bohrnstedt & E. Borgatta (Eds.), *Social measurement: Current issues.* Beverly Hills, CA: Sage.

Campbell, D. T., & Fiske, D. W. (1959). Convergent and discriminant validity by the multitrait–multimethod matrix. *Psychological Bulletin, 56*(2), 81–105. doi:10.1037/h0046016

Campbell, D. T., & Stanley, J. C. (1963). *Experimental and quasi-experimental designs for research.* Chicago, IL: Rand McNally.

Cronbach, L. J. (1951). Coefficient alpha and the internal structure of tests. *Psychometrica, 16*(3), 197–334. doi:10.1007/bf02310555

Cronbach, L. J., & Meehl, P. (1955). Construct validity in psychological tests. *Psychological Bulletin, 52*(4), 281–302. doi:10.1037/h0040957

Feldman, J., Brown, G. R., Deutsch, M. B., Hembree, W., Meyer, W., Meyer-Bahlburg, H. F. L., & Safer, J. D. (2016). Priorities for transgender medical and health care research. *Current Opinion in Endocrinology, Diabetes, and Obesity, 23*(2), 180–187. doi:10.1097/MED.0000000000000231

Fischer, J., & Corcoran, K. (Eds.). (2007). *Measures for clinical practice and research: A sourcebook* (4th ed.). New York, NY: Oxford University Press.

Fredman, N., & Sherman, R. (1987). *Handbook of measurements for marriage and family therapy.* New York, NY: Brunner/Mazel.

Gelles, R. J. (1987). What to learn from cross-cultural and historical research on child abuse and neglect: An overview. In R. J. Gelles & J. B. Lancaster (Eds.), *Child abuse and neglect: Biosocial dimensions.* New York, NY: Aldine de Gruyter.

Ginsburg, H., & Opper, S. (1988). *Piaget's theory of intellectual development* (3rd ed.). Englewood Cliffs, NJ: Prentice Hall.

Goode, W. J., & Hatt, P. K. (1952). *Methods in social research.* New York, NY: McGraw-Hill.

Gutierrez, C.M. & Kirk, D.S. (2017). Silence speaks: The relationship between immigration and the underreporting of crime. *Crime and Delinquency 63*(8), 926–950. doi:10.1177/0011128715599993

Harpe, S. E. (2015). How to analyze Likert and other rating scale data. *Currents in Pharmacy Teaching and Learning, 7*(6), 836–850. doi:10.1016/j.cptl.2015.08.001

Korbin, J. E. (1987). Child maltreatment in cross-cultural perspective: Vulnerable children and circumstances. In R. J. Gelles & J. B. Lancaster (Eds.), *Child abuse and neglect: Biosocial dimensions.* New York, NY: Aldine de Gruyter.

Liziano, E. L., & Mor Barak, M. (2015). Job burnout and affective wellbeing: A longitudinal study of burnout and job satisfaction among public child welfare workers. *Children and Youth Services, 55*, 18–28. doi:10.1016/j.childyouth.2015.05.005

Magura, S., & Moses, B. S. (1986). *Outcome measures for child welfare services: Theory and applications.* Washington, DC: Child Welfare League of America.

Marin, G., & VanOss Marin, B. (1991). *Research with Hispanic populations.* Newbury Park, CA: Sage.

Masters, J., & Hilton, T. (2014). Return to the rez: Native American parolees' transitions to community life. In S. Bowan (Ed.), *Critical perspectives on race, ethnicity and the prison system.* Santa Barbara, CA: ABC Clio.

McDowell, I. (2006). *Measuring health: A guide to rating scales and questionnaires* (3rd ed.). New York, NY: Oxford University Press.

Miller, D. C. & Salkind, N.J. (2002). *Handbook of research design and social measurement* (6th ed.). Thousand Oaks, CA: Sage.

Mushquash, C. J., & Bova, D. L. (2007). Cross-cultural assessment and measurement issues. *Journal of Developmental Disabilities, 13*, 53–65.

Oesterdiekhoff, G. W. (2016). Is a forgotten subject central to the future development of sciences? Jean Piaget on the interrelationship between ontogeny and history. *Personality and Individual Differences, 98*, 118–126. doi:10.1016/j.paid.2016.03.098

Piotrowska, P. J., Stride, C. B., & Rowe, R. (2015). Socioeconomic status and antisocial behaviour among children and adolescents: A systematic review and meta-analysis. *Clinical Psychology Review, 35*, 47–55. doi:10.1016/j.cpr.2014.11.003

Robinson, J., Shaver, P., & Wrightsman, L. (Eds.). (1991). *Measures of personality and social psychological attitudes.* San Diego, CA: Academic Press.

Schutte, N. S., & Malouff, J. M. (1995). *Sourcebook of adult assessment strategies*. New York, NY: Plenum.

Shulman, L. (1978). A study of practice skills. *Social Work, 23*, 274–280. doi:10.1093/sw/23.4.274

Stafford, A., & Wood, L. (2017). Tackling health disparities for people who are homeless? Start with social determinants. *International Journal of Environment Research and Public Health, 14*(12), 1660–4601. doi:10.3390/ijerph14121535

Stevens, S. S. (Ed.). (1951). *Handbook of experimental psychology*. New York, NY: Wiley.

Strainer, D., Norman, G., & Cairney, J. (2015). *Health measurement scales: A practical guide to their development and use* (5th ed.). New York, NY: Oxford University Press.

Touliatos, J., Perlmutter, B. F., Strauss, M. A., & Holden, G. W. (Eds.). (2001). *Handbook of family measurement techniques*. Thousand Oaks, CA: Sage.

Tran, T. V., & Williams, L. F. (1994). Effect of language of interview on the validity and reliability of psychological well-being scales. *Social Work Research, 18*, 17–25. doi:10.1093/swr/18.1.17

U.S. Department of Health and Human Services. (2018). *Child Welfare Information Gateway*. Retrieved from https://www.childwelfare.gov/topics/can/defining/federal

Venter, E., & Buys, E. (2016). Evidence-based assessment: The answer to challenges of assessment in educational psychology practice in diverse societies? *Journal of Psychology, 7*(2), 77–85. doi:10.1080/09764224.2016.11907847

Wardale, D., Cameron, R., & Li, J. (2015). Considerations for multidisciplinary, culturally-sensitive, mixed methods research. *Electronic Journal of Business Research Methods, 13*(1). Retrieved from http://www.ejbrm.com/issue/download.html?idArticle=397

Wolfe, V. V., Finch, A. J., Saylor, C. F., Blount, R. L., Pallmeyer, T. P., & Carek, D. J. (1987). Negative affectivity in children: A multitrait-multimethod investigation. *Journal of Consulting and Clinical Psychology, 55*, 245–250. doi:10.1037/0022-006x.55.2.245

6

SAMPLING

CHAPTER OUTLINE

Critical Thinking

Evaluating Competency (From the Council on Social Work Education [CSWE] 2015 Educational Policy and Accreditation Standards [EPAS])

  Competency 1: Demonstrate Ethical and Professional Behavior

  Competency 2: Engage Diversity and Difference in Practice

  Competency 4: Engage in Practice-Informed Research and Research-Informed Practice

Self-Assessment

Answer key for Self-Assessment Quiz

For Further Reading

References

INTRODUCTION

Charlene is a case management supervisor for a housing first program in a medium-sized city in the Midwestern United States. Housing first is an approach to homeless services that emphasizes moving homeless people directly into stable housing as opposed to progressing a series of housing programs—ranging from emergency shelters to transitional housing to supportive housing programs—while addressing a range of health, mental health, financial, and other needs along the way. The basic idea is that having a stable home base (i.e., housing) will allow clients to make progress in many areas. Further, housing first approaches prioritize the hardest to serve clients, the chronically homeless with a range of health, mental health, and addiction issues. Proponents of housing first stress that many chronically homeless adults have short life expectancies because of challenges associated with accessing healthcare and other services while homeless. Many proponents have also shown that this approach can create cost savings as fewer homeless people will have to rely on emergency rooms for basic healthcare needs.

There are approximately 200 adults receiving housing first services at Charlene's agency. Each of these adults has been placed in an apartment, half in buildings owned and operated by Charlene's agency and half in apartments scattered throughout the city and owned and managed by private landlords. While residents of the housing first apartments are not obligated to participate in services the agency provides, Charlene and her staff offer case management services to housing first clients. The primary goal of these services is to connect residents to healthcare, mental health treatment, substance abuse recovery, and other services. The case management team has noticed that as they develop relationships with clients more and more are interested in learning about service options and several have already begun to use these services and have made substantial gains in addressing health, mental health, and substance abuse concerns.

Charlene and her team believe the case management services and housing they provide benefit clients; however, they lack data to show that clients have made strides in improving their lives (aside from the fact that they are housed and not living on the streets). Charlene is interested in getting some data about clients in her program, specifically about their use of healthcare, mental health, and substance abuse treatment services. One challenge she faces is that many clients are unwilling to speak with her or her case managers about services or other aspects of their lives (as per program rules they do not have to). Some will only speak to her staff if there is an incentive to do so or if they are required to do so to keep their housing. Another challenge is that her staff do not have time to speak to every client to get this information, either through an interview or a survey.

Charlene sought assistance from her former social work professor and researcher. He explained that her dilemma required getting data from an appropriate sample of clients so that she can make conclusions about the program as a whole. This leads to an important question: Can knowledge gained from one or a few cases be considered knowledge about a whole group of people? The answer depends on whether those who are included (and who complete an interview or survey) are *representative* of all the clients of which those who participate are a "sample." Do they represent all clients in the program? Only clients in a particular type of housing? Just those who already have good working relationships with case managers? Or maybe those who agree to participate in an interview or survey about service usage are not representative of the larger group of housing first clients?

These issues are at the center of the problem of *sampling*, or selecting a few cases out of some larger grouping for study. All of us have had experience with sampling. Cautiously tasting a spoonful of soup is a process of sampling to see how hot it is; taking a bite of a new brand of pizza is a process of sampling to see if we like it. All sampling involves attempting to make a judgment about a whole something—a bowl of soup, a brand of pizza, or a housing first participation—based on an analysis of only a part of that whole. Scientific sampling, however, is considerably more careful and systematic than casual, everyday sampling.

In this chapter, we discuss the fundamentals of sampling along with the benefits and disadvantages of various sampling techniques. We will refer back to the housing first example several times. Please keep the following questions in mind as we present concepts of sampling and associated techniques: (a) Why do researchers and practitioners often rely on samples to make generalizations about larger groups of people? (b) What factors are important to consider when selecting a representative sample? (c) How confident are we

that a sample represents the group of people about which we would like to learn? and (d) Why is sampling important to human service practitioners as well as researchers?

THE PURPOSE OF SAMPLING

When we first encounter the subject of sampling, a common question is this: Why bother? Why not just study the whole group? A major reason for studying samples rather than whole groups is that the whole group sometimes is so large that studying it is not feasible. In the aforementioned housing first example, staff do not have the time or abilities to include all 200 clients in their study. Sampling, however, can allow them to study a workable number of cases from the larger group to derive findings that are relevant to all clients.

A second reason for sampling is that, surprising as it may seem, we can get better information from carefully drawn samples than we can from an entire group. This is especially true when the group under study is extremely large. For example, the United States takes a census of all residents at the beginning of each decade. Despite the vast resources that the federal government puts into the census, substantial undercounts and other errors occur. In fact, after recent censuses, numerous cities filed lawsuits complaining of alleged undercounts. Between the decennial censuses, the U.S. Census Bureau conducts *sample* surveys to update population statistics and collect data on other matters. The quality of the data gathered in these sample surveys actually is superior to the data in the census itself. The reason is that, with only a few thousand people to contact, the task is more manageable, involving better trained interviewers, greater control over the interviews, and fewer hard-to-find respondents. In fact, the U.S. Census Bureau even conducts a sample survey after each census as a check on the accuracy of that census. Indeed, were it not a constitutional requirement, the complete census might well be dropped and replaced by sample surveys.

Much research, then, is based on samples of people. Samples make possible a glimpse of the behavior and attitudes of whole groups of people, and the validity and accuracy of research results depend heavily on how samples are drawn. An improperly drawn sample renders the collected data virtually useless. So, an important consideration regarding samples is how *representative* they are of the population from which we draw them. A **representative sample** is one that accurately reflects the distribution of relevant variables in the target population. In a sense, the sample should be considered a small reproduction of the population.

Think back to the housing first example. Staff making conclusions about clients' use of various services based on a sample of clients want to ensure that their sample represents their clients at large. They might, for example, be concerned about the extent to which the sample represents clients in both the buildings owned and managed by the agency and those in scattered site apartments. They might also be concerned about whether those included represent both clients who communicate frequently with case managers and those who do not. Staff may also be concerned about including clients who have been in the program for a short period of time and those who have been in it for a longer period.

In short, a representative sample should have all the same characteristics as the population. The representative character of samples allows the conclusions that are based on them to be legitimately generalized to the populations from which they are drawn. As we see later in this chapter, nonrepresentative samples are useful for some research purposes, but researchers must always assess the representativeness of their samples to make accurate conclusions. Before comparing the various techniques for drawing samples, we define some of the major terms that are used in the field of sampling.

SAMPLING TERMINOLOGY
. . . .
Populations and Samples

A sample is drawn from a **population**, which refers to all possible cases of what we are interested in studying. In the human services, the target population often is people who have some particular characteristic in common, such as all Americans, all eligible voters, all school-age children, and so

on. A population need not, however, be composed of people. Recall from Chapter 4 that the unit of analysis can be something other than individuals, such as groups or programs. Then, the target population is all possible cases of our unit of analysis. A **sample** consists of one or more elements selected from a population. The manner in which we select elements for the sample has enormous implications for the scientific utility of the research based on that sample. To select a good sample, we need to clearly define the population from which to draw the sample. Failure to do so can make generalizing from the sample observations highly ambiguous and result in inaccurate conclusions.

The definition of a population should specify four things: (a) content, (b) units, (c) extent, and (d) time (Kish, 1965, p. 7). Consider the aforementioned housing first example. First, the *content* of the population refers to the particular characteristic that the members of the population have in common. In this example, the characteristic is that the members of the population being studied are participants in the housing first program at this specific agency. Second, the *unit* indicates the unit of analysis, which in this example is individual people, again participants of this housing first program. Third, the *extent* of the population refers to its spatial or geographic coverage. While the agency that runs this housing first program has programs across much of the United States, this study is limited to program participants in this one city (those receiving services from case managers that Charlene supervises). Finally, the *time* factor refers to the temporal period during which a unit must possess the appropriate characteristic to qualify for the sample. In this example, only those clients who are current participants in the housing first program at the time the study (or evaluation) is conducted will be considered for the sample.

With these four factors clearly defined, a population normally is adequately delimited. Then, we can construct what is called a *sampling frame*.

Sampling Frames

A **sampling frame** is a listing of all the elements in a population. In many studies, we draw the actual sample from this listing. The adequacy of the sampling frame is crucial in determining the quality of the sample, and the degree to which the sampling frame includes *all* members of the population is of major importance. Although an endless number of possible sampling frames exist, a few illustrations will describe some of the intricacies of developing good sampling frames.

In human service research, some of the most adequate sampling frames consist of lists of members of organizations. In the housing first example, the sampling frame is pretty straightforward and consists of all current participants in the agency's housing first program in that particular city. If we wanted to expand the study, we could draw a larger sample of housing first participants by including all housing first clients in programs operated by that agency across the United States. Alternatively, we could decide to create a sampling frame consisting of current clients of all housing programs (at multiple agencies) funded by the city government. Other examples of sampling frames based on organizational affiliation would be the membership rosters of professional groups, such as the National Association of Social Workers (NASW), the American Psychological Association, or the American Society of Criminology. These lists are not always perfectly accurate, however, because people who have very recently joined the organization might not appear on the official lists. Clerical errors also might lead to a few missing names. These errors, however, would have little effect on the adequacy of the sampling frame.

When using organizational lists as a sampling frame, we must exercise caution about what we define as the population and about whom we make generalizations. The population consists of the sampling frame, and we can make legitimate generalizations only about the sampling frame. Many social workers, for example, do not belong to the NASW. Thus, a sample taken from the NASW membership roster represents only NASW members and not all social workers. When using organizational lists as sampling frames, then, it is important to assess carefully who the list includes and who the list excludes. Sometimes, research focuses on a theoretical concept that is operationalized in terms of an organizational list that does not include all actual instances of what the concept intends. For example, a study of poverty could

operationalize the concept "poor" as those receiving some form of public assistance. Yet, many people with little or no income do not receive public assistance. In this case, the sampling frame would not completely reflect the population that the theoretical concept intended.

Some research focuses on populations that are quite large, such as residents of a city or a state. To develop sampling frames for household-based surveys of these populations, two types of listings could be considered: (a) telephone numbers and (b) lists of addresses in a community, which is referred to as "address-based sampling." A listing of telephone numbers in a geographic area can be considered a sampling frame of households, although there are a number of problems with using such a listing today. Even today, some people do not have telephone service (about 3% of households). Those without telephones tend to be concentrated among the poor, living in rural areas, and transient groups, such as the young. For a research project in which these groups are important, sampling based on telephone numbers could be very unrepresentative. Another problem is the growth in use of cell phones, with more than half of all households having cell phone service only (www.cbsnews.com/news/milestone-for-cellphones-vs-landline-phones). Cell phones are not as clearly tied to a particular household or geographic area as traditional landlines are. So, a person may live in a different geographic area from where the cell phone is registered. This makes it difficult to know what phone numbers are to be included in a sampling frame when selecting a random sample of households for a particular community. If cell phones are left out, it threatens the representativeness of the sample, because cell phone–only people tend to be younger, less affluent, and more transient. Telephone books do not provide a very good listing of telephone numbers because of the many unlisted numbers and cell phones that are not listed in phone books. Instead, if telephone numbers are to be used as a sampling frame, some random number selection technique, such as *random-digit dialing* (RDD), can ensure that every household with telephone service has a chance of appearing in the sample. Of course, RDD does nothing about noncoverage resulting from the lack of telephone service in some households or some of the problems created by cell phones.

An alternative to telephone numbers as a population listing for a particular geographic area would be a listing of all the addresses in the community—address-based sampling (Iannacchione, 2011; Link, Battaglia, Frankel, Osborn, & Mokdad, 2008; O'Muircheartaigh, 2018). One source of such household listings—called the "traditional listing method"—is lists developed by some private or nonprofit survey research organizations by having trained people walk through a community, physically locate every housing unit, and note its address. This is probably the most complete listing of households in a community, but it is also expensive—either to purchase or to develop.

A second source of such address-based lists is provided by the U.S. Postal Service (USPS) Computerized Delivery Sequence File, which is a listing of all residential addresses that it serves in an area. These listings can be purchased from sampling vendors who are approved by the USPS, but they also have problems of noncoverage: Households can request that their address not be sold by the post office, and many rural addresses do not show up on the listing. The sampling vendors who provide them sometimes make efforts to overcome some of these shortcomings, so the completeness of lists can vary from one vendor to another.

Another household listing sometimes used for sampling is a list of customers from a local electric utility. Although some households do not have telephone service, relatively few lack electricity, and the problem of noncoverage therefore is less significant. A major problem, however, comes from multiple-family dwellings, which often list utilities only in the name of the building's owner rather than in the names of all the individual residents. The young, the old, and the unmarried are more likely to inhabit these multiple-family dwellings. Unless we supplement the utility listings, samples will systematically underrepresent people in these groups. Visiting the dwellings and adding the residents to the list of utility subscribers can overcome this problem, but this is a time-consuming task.

Finally, city directories, criss cross directories, and other directories exist that are quite useful as household listings. Available in most libraries, and online, these directories contain, among other things, an alphabetical listing of streets and addresses with residents' names. This listing is fairly accurate, but it does exclude new construction. Some of these directories also include information on gender, age, length of residence, wealth, and other important characteristics.

Learning From Experience: Poor Sampling Frames

Some disastrous mistakes have occurred in past investigations because of inadequate sampling frames. A classic example of this was the attempt *Literary Digest* magazine made to predict the outcome of the 1936 presidential race between Alfred Landon and Franklin Roosevelt. When predicting an election, the target population is all likely voters. *Literary Digest,* however, did not use a sampling frame that listed all likely voters. Rather, they drew their sample from lists of automobile owners and from telephone directories. On the basis of their sample results, they predicted that Landon would win by a substantial margin, but of course, Roosevelt won the election easily. Why the error in prediction? A major part of the problem was a flawed sampling frame (Cahalan, 1989; Lohr & Brick, 2017; Squire, 1988). In 1936, with the Great Depression at its peak, a substantial proportion of eligible voters, especially poorer ones, did not own cars or have telephones. In short, the sample was drawn from an inadequate sampling frame and did not represent the target population. In addition, because the poor are more likely to vote Democratic, most of the eligible voters excluded from the sampling frame voted for the Democratic candidate, Roosevelt.

We can construct adequate sampling frames for many human service projects from existing listings, but we must exercise caution in using such lists because they may inadvertently exclude some people. In fact, human service research is especially vulnerable to this, because we often study populations that are difficult to enumerate. For example, undocumented aliens are, by definition, not listed anywhere. We know they make up a large segment of the population in such urban centers as Los Angeles, but a study of the poor in these areas that relied on a city directory or another such listing obviously would miss large numbers of such people. Early studies of gay men also fell prey to this problem (Bell & Weinberg, 1978; Hooker, 1957). In some of these studies, the sampling frame was homosexuals who were listed as patients by psychotherapists who participated in the research. The studies concluded that homosexuality was associated with personality disturbance. Yet, it does not take great insight to recognize that the sampling frames did not list many gay men—namely, those feeling no need to see therapists—and, thus, were strongly biased toward finding personality disorders among gays.

We must assess sampling frames carefully to ensure that they include all elements of the population of interest. The remainder of this chapter is a discussion of the different ways in which to select samples. First, we discuss probability samples, for which we are most likely to have a sampling frame from which to draw the sample. Researchers use probability samples in some types of human service research, such as needs assessment and evaluation research. Then, we discuss nonprobability samples, which researchers use in assessing client functioning and in evaluating the effectiveness of intervention strategies.

PROBABILITY SAMPLES

With luck, almost any sampling procedure could produce a representative sample, but that is little comfort to the researcher who wants to be as certain as possible that his or her sample is representative. Techniques that make use of probability theory can both greatly reduce the chances of getting a nonrepresentative sample and, more importantly, permit the researcher to estimate precisely the likelihood that a sample differs from the true population by a given amount. In these samples, known as **probability samples**, each element in the population has some chance of inclusion in the sample, and the investigator can determine the chances or probability of each element's inclusion (Scheaffer, Mendenhall, Ott, & Gerow, 2012). In their simpler versions, probability sampling techniques ensure that each element has an *equal*

chance of inclusion. In more elaborate versions, the researcher takes advantage of knowledge about the population to select elements with differing probabilities. The key point is that, whether the probabilities are equal or different, each element's probability of inclusion in a probability sample is nonzero and known. Furthermore, probability sampling enables us to calculate **sampling error**, which is an estimate of the extent to which the values of the sample differ from those of the population from which it was drawn.

Simple Random Sampling

The simplest technique for drawing probability samples is **simple random sampling** (SRS), in which each element in the population has an equal probability of inclusion in the sample. SRS treats the target population as a unitary whole. We might begin with a sampling frame containing a list of the entire population—or as complete a list as we can obtain. We would then number the elements in the sampling frame sequentially and select elements from the list using a procedure known to be random. If we computerized the sampling frame, we could accomplish random selection merely by programming the computer to select randomly a sample of whatever size we desired.

Although simple random samples have the desirable feature of giving each element in the sampling frame an equal chance of appearing in the sample, SRS often is impractical. A major reason for this is cost. Imagine doing a research project that calls for a national sample of 2,000 households. Even if one could obtain such a sample using SRS, which is unlikely, it would be prohibitively expensive to send interviewers all over the country to obtain the data. Furthermore, alternatives to SRS might be more efficient in terms of providing a high degree of representativeness with a smaller sample. Normally, SRS is limited to fairly small-scale projects that deal with populations of modest size for which we can obtain adequate sampling frames. The importance of SRS lies not in its wide application. Rather, SRS is the basic sampling procedure on which statistical theory is based, and it is the standard against which other sampling procedures are measured.

Systematic Sampling

A variation of SRS is called **systematic sampling**, which involves taking every *k*th element listed in a sampling frame. Systematic sampling uses the table of random numbers to determine a random starting point in the sampling frame. From that random start, we select every *k*th element into the sample. The value of *k* is called the *sampling interval,* and it is determined by dividing the population size by the desired sample size. For example, if we wanted a sample of 100 from a population of 1,000, then the sampling interval would be 10. From the random starting point, we would select every 10th element from the sampling frame for the sample. If the starting point is in the middle of the list, then we proceed to the end, jump to the beginning, and end up at the middle again.

In actual practice, dividing the population by the sample size usually does not produce a whole number, so the decimal is rounded upward to the next-largest whole number. This provides a sampling interval that takes us completely through the sampling frame. If we round downward, then the sampling interval becomes slightly too narrow, and we reach the desired sample size before we exhaust the sampling frame, which would mean that those elements farthest from the starting point have no chance of selection.

We commonly use systematic sampling when we draw samples by hand rather than by computer. The only advantage of systematic sampling over SRS is in clerical efficiency. In SRS, the random numbers will select elements scattered throughout the sampling frame. It is time-consuming to search all over the sampling frame to identify the elements that correspond to the random numbers. In systematic sampling, we proceed in an orderly fashion through the sampling frame from the random starting point.

Stratified Sampling

With SRS and systematic sampling methods, we treat the target population as a unitary whole when sampling from it. **Stratified sampling** changes this by dividing the population into smaller subgroups, called *strata,* before drawing the sample and then drawing separate random samples from each of the strata.

Reduction in Sampling Error. One of the major reasons for using a stratified sample is that stratifying reduces sampling error for a given sample size to a level lower than that of an SRS of the same size. This is so because of a very simple principle: The more homogeneous a population on the variables under study, the smaller the sample size needed to represent it accurately. Stratifying makes each subsample more homogeneous by eliminating the variation on the variable used for stratifying.

A gastronomic example will help illustrate this point. Imagine two large, commercial-size cans of nuts, one labeled "peanuts" and the other labeled "mixed nuts." Because the can of peanuts is highly homogeneous, only a small handful from it gives a fairly accurate indication of the remainder of its contents. The can of mixed nuts, however, is quite heterogeneous, containing several kinds of nuts in different proportions. A small handful of nuts from the top of the can cannot be relied on to represent the contents of the entire can. If the mixed nuts were stratified by type into homogeneous piles, however, then a few nuts from each pile could constitute a representative sample of the entire can.

In the housing first program example, the practitioner–researchers may decide to create a stratified sample by dividing the sampling frame (the participants of that agency's housing first program in that city) into those living in the agency owned building and those living in scattered site apartments. This would be especially important if there is reason to believe that these groups differ in an important way. For example, it may be that those placed in agency owned buildings were those staff believed were at greater risk of eviction due to noncompliance with landlords' expectations for tenants.

Although stratifying does reduce sampling error, it is important to recognize that the effects are modest. We expect approximately 10% to 20% (or less) reduction in comparison to an SRS of equal size (Henry, 1990; Sudman, 1976). Essentially, the decision to stratify depends on two issues: the difficulty of stratifying and the cost of each additional element in the sample. It can be difficult to stratify a sample on a particular variable if it is hard to get access to data on that variable. For example, we would find it relatively easy to stratify a sample of university students according to class level, because universities typically include class status as part of a database of all registered students. In contrast, we would find it difficult to stratify that same sample on the basis of whether the students had been victims of sexual abuse during childhood because these data are not readily available and getting them would require a major study in itself. So, stratification requires either that the sampling frame include information on the stratification variable or that the stratification variable is easily determined. Telephone surveys and stratification of respondents by gender illustrate the latter situation. Telephone interviewers can simply ask to speak to the man of the house to obtain the male stratum and request to speak to the woman of the house for the female stratum. If no one of the desired gender is available, then the interviewer drops that household and substitutes another. The process may require some extra phone calls, but the time and cost of doing this can pay for itself in the quality of the sample. As for the effect of cost issues on the decision of whether to stratify, if the cost of obtaining data on each case is high, as in an interview survey, then stratifying to minimize sample size probably is warranted. If each case is inexpensive, however, then stratifying to reduce cost may not be worth the effort unless it can be easily accomplished.

Proportionate Sampling. When we use stratification to reduce sampling error, we normally use *proportionate* stratified sampling, in which the size of the sample taken from each stratum is proportionate to the stratum's presence in the population. Consider a sample of the undergraduates at a college or university. Although the students differ on many characteristics, an obvious difference is their class standing. Any representative sample of the student body should reflect the relative proportions of the various classes as they exist at the college as a whole. If we drew an SRS, then the sample size would have to be quite large for the sample to reflect accurately the distribution of class levels. Small samples would have a greater likelihood of being disproportionate. If we stratify on class level, however, then we can easily make the sample match the actual class distribution, regardless of

the sample size. Table 6.1 contains the hypothetical class distribution of a university student body. If a researcher wanted a sample of 200 students with these proportions of students accurately represented, stratifying could easily accomplish it. The researcher would begin by developing a sampling frame with the students grouped according to class level, then would draw a separate SRS from each of the four class strata in numbers proportionate to their presence in the population: 70 freshmen, 50 sophomores, 40 juniors, and 40 seniors.

In actual practice, it is normal to stratify on more than one variable. In the case of a student population, for example, the researcher might want to stratify on sex as well as class level. That would double the number of separate subsamples from four to eight: senior men, senior women, junior men, and so on. Even though stratifying on appropriate variables always improves a sample, researchers should use stratification judiciously. Stratifying on a few variables provides nearly as much benefit as stratifying on many. Because the number of subsamples increases geometrically as the number of stratified variables and the number of categories increase, attempting to stratify on too many variables can excessively complicate sampling without offering substantially increased benefits in terms of a reduction in sampling error.

In the housing first example, for example, practitioner–researchers may be tempted to stratify the sample based on housing (agency owned or other

TABLE 6.1 Hypothetical Proportionate Stratified Sample of University Students

Proportion in University		Stratified Sample of 200	
Seniors	20%	Seniors	40
Juniors	20%	Juniors	40
Sophomores	25%	Sophomores	50
Freshmen	35%	Freshmen	70
	100%		200

landlord owned) and length of time in which participants have been in housing (e.g., less than or more than 6 months). Additional stratification may also be possible based on other characteristics—gender, age, race, mental health diagnosis, and so on. This may substantially complicate the sampling process, however, without necessarily creating a more representative sample.

Disproportionate Sampling. In addition to reducing error, we use stratified samples to enable comparisons among various subgroups in a population when one or more of the subgroups is relatively uncommon. For example, suppose the number of men in the housing first program greatly outnumbers the number of women, and staff are very interested in learning about service usage for both men and women. If women comprise just 10% or 20% of the 200 clients of the program, a sample that selects 20% of all clients would likely result in just four women being selected. This number is far too small to make meaningful comparisons between men and women. Stratifying in this case allows us to draw a larger sample of women to provide enough cases for reliable comparisons to men to be made. This is called *disproportionate* stratified sampling, because we do not sample the strata proportionately to their presence in the population. This type of sample is different from most probability samples, where we achieve representativeness by giving every element in the population an equal chance of appearing in the sample. With a disproportionate stratified sample, each element of a stratum has an equal chance of appearing in the sample of that stratum, but the elements in some strata have a better chance of appearing in the overall sample than the elements of other strata do.

Selection of variables on which to stratify depends on the reason for stratifying. If we were stratifying to ensure sufficient numbers of cases for analysis in all groups of interest, as in the example of women in the housing first program, then we would stratify on the variable that has a category with a small proportion of cases in it. This often is an independent variable and involves disproportionate stratified sampling. On the other hand, if the goal of stratifying is to reduce sampling error,

as is the case in proportionate stratified sampling, then we might use variables other than the independent variable. Stratifying has an effect in reducing sampling error only when the stratification variables relate to the dependent variables under study. So, we should select variables that we know or suspect of having an impact on the dependent variables. For example, a study concerning the impact of religiosity on delinquency might stratify on socioeconomic status, because studies have shown that this variable is related to delinquency involvement. Stratifying on a frivolous variable, such as eye color, would gain us nothing, because it is unlikely to relate to delinquency involvement. It is worth noting, however, that stratifying never hurts a sample. The worst that can happen is that the stratified sample will have about the same sampling error as an SRS of equivalent size, and that the stratifying efforts will have gone for naught.

Area Sampling

Area sampling (also called **cluster sampling** or **multistage sampling**) is a procedure in which we obtain the final units to include in the sample by first sampling among larger units, called *clusters,* that contain the smaller sampling units. A series of sampling stages are involved, working down in scale from larger clusters to smaller ones.

For example, imagine that we wanted to conduct a needs assessment survey that would determine the extent and distribution of preschool children with educational deficiencies in a large urban area. Simple random and systematic samples are out of the question, because no sampling frame listing all such children exists. We could, however, turn to area sampling, a technique that enables us to draw a probability sample without having a complete list of all elements in the population. The ultimate unit of analysis in this needs assessment would be households, because children live in households and we can create a sampling frame of households. We get there in the following way (see Figure 6.1). First, we take a simple random sample from among all census tracts in the urban area. (The U.S. Census Bureau divides urban areas into a number of census tracts, which are areas of approximately 4,000 people.) In the second stage,

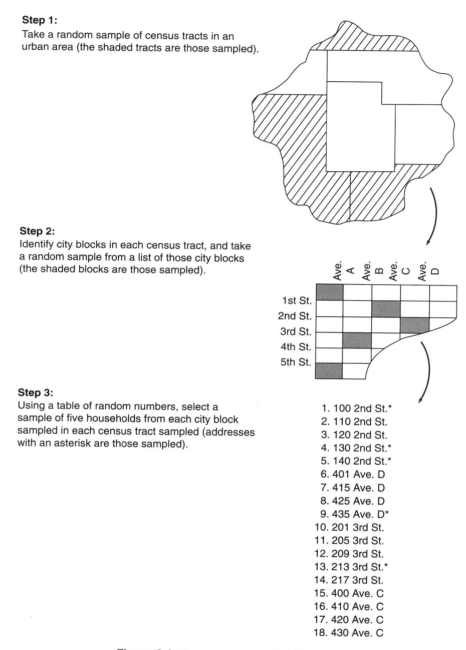

Step 1:
Take a random sample of census tracts in an urban area (the shaded tracts are those sampled).

Step 2:
Identify city blocks in each census tract, and take a random sample from a list of those city blocks (the shaded blocks are those sampled).

Step 3:
Using a table of random numbers, select a sample of five households from each city block sampled in each census tract sampled (addresses with an asterisk are those sampled).

1. 100 2nd St.*
2. 110 2nd St.
3. 120 2nd St.
4. 130 2nd St.*
5. 140 2nd St.*
6. 401 Ave. D
7. 415 Ave. D
8. 425 Ave. D
9. 435 Ave. D*
10. 201 3rd St.
11. 205 3rd St.
12. 209 3rd St.
13. 213 3rd St.*
14. 217 3rd St.
15. 400 Ave. C
16. 410 Ave. C
17. 420 Ave. C
18. 430 Ave. C

Figure 6.1 Drawing an area probability sample.

we list all the city blocks in each census tract in our sample, and then we select a simple random sample from among those city blocks. In the final stage, we list the households on each city block in our sample, and then we select a simple random sample of households on that list. With this procedure, we have an "area probability sample" of households in that urban area. (Public opinion polling agencies, such as Roper, typically use area sampling or a variant of it.) Finally, we interview each household in the sample regarding educational deficiencies among children in that household. If we were sampling an entire state or the whole country, then we would include even more stages of sampling, starting with even larger areas, but eventually working down to the household or individual level, whichever is our unit of analysis. Research in Practice 6.1 describes an important, national research study that uses sophisticated area sampling procedures and whose results will have long-ranging policy implications.

A number of factors can complicate area sampling. For example, selected blocks within an area often contain vastly different numbers of people—from high-density inner-city areas to the lower density suburbs. We must adjust the number of blocks and the number of households per block that are selected into the sample to take into account the differing population densities. Another complication involves the estimation of sampling error. Fairly straightforward formulas for estimating sampling error exist for the simpler sampling techniques. With area sampling, however, the many stages of sampling involved make error estimation exceedingly complex (Kish, 1965; Scheaffer et al., 2012).

Error estimation is quite important for area samples. These samples are subject to greater error than other probability samples, because some error is introduced at each stage of sampling: The more the number of stages involved, the more the sampling error accumulates. Other factors affecting sampling error are the size of the areas initially selected and their degree of homogeneity: The larger the initial areas and the greater their homogeneity, the greater the sampling error. This may seem odd, because with stratified sampling, greater homogeneity leads to less error. Remember, however, that with stratified sampling, we select a sample from *each stratum,* but with area sampling, we draw samples only from *a few areas.* If the few areas in a sample are homogeneous in comparison with the others, then they are less representative. Small, more numerous, heterogeneous clusters lead to more representative area samples. Despite the complexity, area sampling allows us to draw highly accurate probability samples from populations that, because of their size or geographical spread, we could not otherwise sample.

Estimating Sample Size

As we have seen, a key issue in selecting a sample is that it should *represent* the population from which it was drawn. People sometimes assume that a larger sample is more representative than a smaller one and, thus, that one should go for the largest sample possible. Actually, however, deciding on an appropriate sample size is far more complicated. Five factors influence the sample size: (a) research hypotheses, (b) precision, (c) population homogeneity, (d) sampling fraction, and (e) sampling technique.

Research Hypotheses. One concern in establishing the desired sample size is that we have a sufficient number of cases with which to examine our research hypotheses. Consider a hypothetical study with three variables containing three values each. For an adequate test of the hypotheses, we need a cross tabulation of these three variables, and this would require a $3 \times 3 \times 3$ table, or a table with 27 cells. If our sample were small, then many cells would have few or no cases in them, and we could not test the hypotheses. Johann Galtung (1967, p. 60) has suggested that 10 to 20 cases in each cell provides an adequate test of hypotheses. We might use disproportionate stratified sampling here to ensure an adequate number of cases in each cell. When that is not possible, Galtung suggests the following formula to determine sample size:

$$r^n \times 20 = \text{sample size,}$$

where r refers to the number of values on each variable and n refers to the number of variables. Thus, for our hypothetical study,

$$r^n \times 20 = 3^3 \times 20 = 27 \times 20 = 540.$$

So, we would need a sample size of 540 to feel reasonably assured that we had a sufficient number of cases in each cell. The formula works only if, as in our example, all variables have the same number of values. Furthermore, this technique does not guarantee an adequate number of cases in each cell. If some combination of variables is rare in the population, we may still find few cases in our sample.

Researchers often use statistical procedures in testing hypotheses, and most such procedures

RESEARCH IN PRACTICE 6.1 Policy Planning and Development: An Area Sample Using Address-Based Sampling in a National Children's Health Study

The National Children's Study (NCS) is a major investigation into the environmental factors that shape child health and development (Michael & O'Muircheartaigh, 2008; Montaquila, Hsu, Brick, English, & O'Muircheartaigh, 2009). It is sponsored by a variety of agencies, including the Department of Health and Human Services and the Environmental Protection Agency. It is a complex and ambitious effort that enrolls children into the study before they are born and continues to observe them until they are 21 years of age (a longitudinal panel study, as described in Chapter 4). The results of the study will be used to make recommendations for social policies that will impact the health and well-being of children for decades to come.

To provide the most valid information, the study designers must be very careful about the sampling techniques used to select people for the study. The NCS uses "address-based sampling" with the units to be sampled being the household or the housing unit and the sampling frame being a listing of all residential addresses in a particular area.

The NCS is an example of a "multistage area probability household sample," which simply means that areas are sampled at a number of different stages, with known probabilities of each area being selected, and that the household is the unit to be sampled. The first, or largest, sampling stage is the whole United States, from which is selected a sample of primary sampling units (PSUs). PSUs are usually counties (or clusters of counties where there is low population density). The second sampling stage is to select a sample of geographic areas within each PSU. The third sampling stage is to select a sample of "segments" within each geographic area, each segment being a contiguous block of 500 to 1,200 housing units or households. For the NCS, all households in this final stage (segment) are surveyed, except for some very densely populated segments where a sample of households were selected to be surveyed.

At each stage in the multistage sample, a sampling frame, or complete listing, of all the elements in that stage is necessary. So, the NCS needed a complete listing of all PSUs in the United States, all geographic areas in each PSU, all segments within each geographic area, and finally all households in each segment. The NCS uses what is called a "traditional listing" method of establishing this final sampling frame. With the traditional listing method, "listers" go through an area and locate all residences. This traditional listing method is considered to be the "gold standard": It produces a more complete and accurate sampling frame than does any other method.

A drawback of the "traditional listing" method is the expense: It is costly to hire "listers" and pay them to physically inspect the community. This has led the NCS to explore whether other sampling approaches—frame generation methods might be less expensive and equally as accurate (English, O'Muircheartaigh, Dekker, Latterner, & Eckman, 2009). For example, research has been done comparing the "traditional listing" method with the U.S. Postal Service Computerized Delivery Sequence File. Both sampling methods provide a fairly complete and accurate sampling frame, although the traditional listing method does a better job in some situations, such as in rural areas. In urban areas, the two methods were equivalent. The research also finds significant differences in coverage among sampling vendors who distribute the Computerized Delivery Sequence File (CDSF), with some providing a more complete list. The NCS found that the most complete sampling frame was provided by combining the listing developed using the traditional method with a list made available by the most effective sampling vendor.

This illustration of the sampling practices used in the NCS shows the complexity of sampling procedures—especially in large surveys such as this—and the care and effort that researchers devote to developing a complete sampling frame.

require some minimum number of cases to provide accurate results. What is the smallest legitimate sample size? This depends, of course, on the number of variables and on the values they can take. Generally, however, 30 cases is considered to be the bare minimum, and some researchers conservatively set 100 as the smallest legitimate sample size (Bailey, 1987; Champion, 1981). Anything smaller begins to raise questions about whether researchers can properly apply statistical procedures.

Precision. Another factor influencing sample size is the level of precision, or the amount of sampling error, that a researcher is willing to accept. Recall that sampling error refers to the difference between a sample value of some variable and the population value of the same variable. Suppose that the average age of all teenagers in a city is 15.4 years. If we draw a sample of 200 teenagers and calculate an average age of 15.1 years, then our sample statistic is close to the population value, but there is an error of 0.3 years. Remember, however, that the ultimate reason for collecting data from samples is to draw conclusions regarding the population from which we drew those samples. We have data from a sample, such as the average age of a group of teenagers, but *we do not have those same data for the population as a whole.* If we did, we would not need to study the sample, because we already would know what we want to know about the population.

If we do not know what the population value is, how can we assess the difference between our sample value and the population value? We do it in terms of the likelihood, or probability, that our sample value differs by a certain amount from the population value. (Probability theory is discussed in more detail in Chapter 15.) So, we establish a *confidence interval,* or a range in which we are fairly certain the population value lies. If we draw a sample with a mean age of 15.1 years and establish a confidence interval of ± (plus or minus) 1.2 years, then we are fairly certain that the mean age in the population is between 13.9 and 16.3 years of age. Probability theory also enables us to be precise about how certain we are. For example, we might be 95% certain, which is called the *confidence level.*

(The computation of confidence intervals and confidence levels is beyond the scope of this book.) Technically, this means that if we draw a large number of random samples from our population and compute a mean age for each of those samples, then 95% of those sample means would have confidence intervals that include the population mean and 5% would not. What is the actual population mean? We do not know, because we have not collected data from the whole population. We have data from only one sample, but we can conclude that we are 95% sure that the population mean lies within the confidence interval of that sample.

Precision is directly related to sample size: Larger samples are more precise than smaller ones. Thus, probability theory enables us to calculate the sample size that is required to achieve a given level of precision. Table 6.2 does this for simple random samples taken from populations of various sizes. As an example of how to read the table, a sample size of 1,024 would give you a 95% chance to obtain a sampling error of 3% or less with a population of 25,000 elements and a relatively heterogeneous population (a 50/50 split identifies a heterogeneous population, and an 80/20 split is a homogeneous population). In other words, a 95% chance exists that the population value is within 3% of the sample estimate. Again, to be technical, it means that if we draw many random samples and determine a confidence interval of 3% for each, then 95% of those confidence intervals will include the population value. Table 6.2 shows that sample size must increase when, other things being equal, the researcher wants less sampling error—that is, more precision—or the population size is larger or the population is more heterogeneous.

In actuality, of course, we draw only one sample. Probability theory tells us the chance we run of a single sample's having a given level of error. There is a chance—5 times out of 100—that the sample will have an error level greater than 3%. In fact, there is a chance, albeit a minuscule one, that the sample will have a large error level. This is a part of the nature of sampling: Because we are selecting a segment of a population, there is always a chance that the sample will be unrepresentative of that population. The goal of good sampling techniques is to reduce the likelihood of that error.

TABLE 6.2 Calculating Sample Size Based on Confidence Level, Sampling Error, Population Heterogeneity, and Population Size

Population Size	95% Confidence Level				99% Confidence Level			
	Sampling Error +/−3%		Sampling Error +/−5%		Sampling Error +/−3%		Sampling Error +/− 5%	
	50/50 Split	80/20 Split	50/50 Split	80/20 Split	50/50 Split	80/20 Split	50/50 Split	80/20 Split
1,000	517	407	278	198	649	542	400	299
2,500	749	537	334	224	1,062	802	525	364
5,000	880	601	357	245	1,347	955	586	422
10,000	965	640	370	240	1,557	1,056	623	408
25,000	1,024	665	379	244	1,717	1,127	647	418
50,000	1,045	674	382	245	1,778	1,153	655	422
100,000	1,056	679	383	246	1,810	1,166	660	423
1,000,000	1,066	683	384	246	1,840	1,179	664	425
10,000,000	1,067	683	385	246	1,843	1,180	664	425
100,000,000	1,068	683	385	246	1,843	1,180	664	425

"Split" has to do with the heterogeneity of the population. A "50/50 split" indicates a fairly heterogeneous population on some characteristic of interest (e.g., it is roughly half male and half female or half smokers and half nonsmokers). An "80/20 split" indicates a homogeneous population (e.g., most are males or most are smokers).

(Furthermore, one goal of replication in science, as discussed in Chapter 2, is to protect against the possibility that a researcher has unknowingly based the findings of a single study on a sample that contains a large error.)

If the 95% confidence level is not satisfactory for our purposes, then we can raise the odds to the 99% level by increasing the sample size. In this case, only 1 out of 100 samples is likely to have an error level greater than 3%. A sample size large enough for this confidence level, however, might be expensive and time-consuming. For this reason, professional pollsters normally are satisfied with a sample size that enables them to achieve an error level in the range of 2% to 4%. Likewise, most scientific researchers are forced to accept higher levels of error—often as much as 5% to 6% with

a 95% confidence level. At the other end of the spectrum, exploratory studies can provide useful data even though they incorporate considerably more imprecision and sampling error. So, the issue of sample size and error is influenced, in part, by the goals of the research project.

Population Homogeneity. The third factor affecting sample size is the variability of the sampled population. As we have noted, a large sample is more essential for a heterogeneous population than for a homogeneous one. Unfortunately, researchers may know little about the homogeneity of their target population and can make accurate estimates of population variability only *after* they draw the sample, collect the data, and at least partially analyze that data. On the surface, this would appear to preclude estimating the sample size in advance. In fact, however, probability theory allows sample size to be estimated by simply assuming maximum variability in the population. In Table 6.2, the assumption of "50/50 split" means that we assume maximum variability. Such estimates are, of course, conservative: This means that the sample size estimates are larger than needed for a given level of precision if the actual variability in the population is less than assumed.

Sampling Fraction. A fourth factor influencing sample size is the *sampling fraction*, or the number of elements in the sample relative to the number of elements in the population (or n/N, where n is the estimated sample size ignoring sampling fraction and N is the population size). With large populations, we can ignore the sampling fraction, because the sample constitutes only a tiny fraction of the population. In Table 6.2, for example, a population of 10,000 calls for a sample size of only 370 (5% sampling error and 50/50 split), which is less than 4% of the population. For such samples, the research hypotheses, sampling error, and population homogeneity are sufficient to determine the sample size. With smaller populations, however, a sample that meets these criteria may constitute a relatively large fraction of the whole population and, in fact, may be larger than it needs to be (Moser & Kalton, 1972). This is so because a sample that constitutes a large fraction of a population contains less sampling error than if the sample were a small fraction. In such cases, the sample size can be adjusted by the following formula:

$$\text{Adjusted sample size} = n/[1 + (n/N)],$$

where:
  n = estimated sample size ignoring the sampling fraction
  N = population size.

As a rule of thumb, this correction formula should be used if the sampling fraction is more than 5%. For example, suppose that a community action agency is conducting a needs assessment survey for a Native American tribal organization with 3,000 members. On the basis of the research hypothesis, sampling error, and population variance on key variables, it is estimated that a sample size of 600 is needed. The sampling fraction, then, is n/N = 600/3,000 = 0.2, or 20%. Because this is well over 5%, we apply the correction. (Here n is the adjusted sample size.)

$$n' = 600/[1 + (600/3,000)]$$

$$n' = 600/1.20$$

$$n' = 500.$$

Thus, instead of a sample of 600, we need only 500 to achieve the same level of precision. At costs that often exceed $50 per interview, the savings of this adjustment often are significant.

Sampling Technique. The final factor influencing sample size is the sampling technique employed. The estimates discussed thus far are for simple random samples. More complex sampling procedures change the estimates of sample size. Area sampling, for example, tends to increase sampling error in comparison with SRS. We can obtain a rough estimate of sample sizes for area samples by simply increasing the suggested sizes in Table 6.2 by one half (Backstrom & Hursh-Cesar, 1981). This estimate is crude and, probably, conservative, but it is simple to obtain. Stratified sampling, on the other hand, tends to reduce sampling error and to decrease the required sample size. Estimating sample sizes for stratified samples is relatively complex (Kish, 1965; Scheaffer et al., 2012; Singh & Musuku, 2014).

In an assessment of the implications of scientific work for clinical application, the issue of precision in sampling comes to the fore. Practitioners need to exercise judgment regarding how scientifically sound the research is and whether it is sufficiently valid to introduce into practice. As we have emphasized, practitioners should view single studies with caution—irrespective of how low the sampling error is. As numerous studies begin to accumulate, we must then assess them in terms of how much error we can expect, given the sample size and the sampling technique. If the sampling errors appear to be quite low, then a few replications might confirm that the findings from these samples reflect the state of the actual population. With large sampling errors, however, the probability increases that the samples do not represent the population. In such cases, confidence in the outcomes can result only if a number of studies arrive at the same conclusions. More studies mean the drawing of more samples, which in turn reduces the likelihood that *all* the samples contain large sampling errors.

NONPROBABILITY SAMPLES

Probability samples are not required—or even appropriate—for all studies. Some research situations call for **nonprobability samples**, in which the investigator does not know the probability of each population element's inclusion in the sample. Nonprobability samples have some important uses (Etikan, Musa, & Alkassim, 2016; O'Connell, 2000). First, they are especially useful when the goal of research is to see whether a relationship exists between independent and dependent variables, with no intent to generalize the results beyond the sample to a larger population. This sometimes is the case, for instance, in experimental research, where future research in other settings will establish generalizability (see Chapter 10).

A second situation where nonprobability samples are useful is in some qualitative research, where the goal is to understand the social process and meaning structure of a particular setting or group (Maxwell, 2012). In such qualitative research, the research goal often is only to develop an understanding of one particular setting or group of people; issues of generalizing to other settings are either irrelevant or an issue for future research projects. As we see in Chapters 9 and 16, some qualitative researchers see probability samples as inappropriate for, or at best irrelevant to, theoretically sound qualitative research.

A third situation in which nonprobability samples are useful is when it is impossible to develop a sampling frame of a population. With no complete list of all elements in a population, researchers cannot ensure that every element has a chance to appear in the sample. These populations sometimes are called "hidden populations," because at least some of their elements are hidden and either difficult or impossible to locate. In fact, the members

of hidden populations sometimes try to hide themselves from detection by researchers and others, because they engage in illegal or stigmatized behavior, such as drug use or criminal activity. Rather than giving up on the study of such populations, however, researchers use nonprobability samples.

Although nonprobability samples can be useful, they do have some important limitations. First, without the use of probability in the selection of elements for the sample, we can make no real claim of representativeness. There is simply no way of knowing precisely what population, if any, a nonprobability sample represents. This question of representativeness greatly limits the ability to generalize findings beyond the level of the sample cases.

A second limitation is that the degree of sampling error remains unknown—and unknowable. With no clear population represented by the sample, we have nothing with which to compare it. The lack of probability in the selection of cases means that the techniques employed for estimating sampling error with probability samples are not appropriate. It also means that the techniques for estimating sample size are not applicable to nonprobability samples. Of the five criteria used in considering sample size among probability samples, the only one that comes into play for nonprobability samples is the first—namely, that researchers select sufficient cases to allow the planned types of data analysis. Even population homogeneity and the sampling fraction do not come into play, because the researcher does not know the exact size or composition of the population.

A final limitation of nonprobability samples involves statistical tests of significance. These commonly used statistics, which we discuss in Chapter 15, indicate to the researcher whether relationships found in sample data are sufficiently strong to generalize to the whole population. Some of these statistical tests, however, are based on various laws of probability and assume a random process for selecting sample elements. Because nonprobability samples violate some basic assumptions of these tests, researchers should use these statistical tests with caution on data derived from such samples.

Back to the housing first program example, if Charlene and her staff were more interested in understanding the process and experiences of moving from homelessness to having stable housing and how this comes to impact clients' decisions about service usage than in learning how many clients are accessing these services, a carefully selected nonprobability sample might be appropriate. Charlene and her staff may, for example, decide to select 5 to 10 clients representing different demographic groups to participate in in-depth interviews so that they can learn more about this process. A nonprobability sample might also be used in this situation if they expect they will face substantial barriers in getting cooperation from many clients to participate in the study (survey or qualitative interviews). In this case a nonprobability sample would be the best option available to them. Of course, they would have to accept that the clients who do participate are not fully representative of the client group as a whole.

Availability Sampling

Availability sampling (also called **convenience sampling** or **accidental sampling**) involves the researchers taking whichever elements are readily available. These samples are especially popular—and appropriate—for research in which it is either difficult or impossible to develop a complete sampling frame. Sometimes it is too costly to do so; in other cases, it is impossible to identify all the elements of a population. Two of the authors of this textbook (Hilton & DeJong, 2010), for example, relied on an availability sample in their study of rural homelessness. Because it was practically impossible to develop a sampling frame of all homeless adults in the region they were studying, they turned to social service providers, law enforcement professions, and others for assistance. They asked these people to help them recruit homeless people to participate in the study. The limitation on generalizability, however, seriously reduces the utility of findings based on availability samples. It is impossible for Hilton and DeJong to argue, for example, that the people they interviewed were representative of all homeless adults. It may well be that only homeless adults with certain characteristics were likely to become a part of the sample. It could very well be, for example, that people who

were more likely to be connected to human service programs were overrepresented while those who tend to avoid services were underrepresented.

Availability samples often are used in experimental or quasiexperimental research. This is because it often is difficult to get a representative sample of people to participate in an experiment—especially one that is lengthy and time-consuming. For example, Ronald Feldman and Timothy Caplinger (1977) were interested in factors that bring about behavior changes in young boys who exhibit highly visible antisocial behavior. Their research design was a field experiment calling for the children participating in the study to meet periodically in groups over an 8-month period. Groups met an average of 22.2 times for 2 to 3 hours each time. Most youngsters could be expected to refuse such a commitment of time and energy. Had the investigators attempted to draw a probability sample from the community, they probably would have had such a high refusal rate as to make the representativeness of their sample questionable. They would have expended considerable resources and still had, in effect, a nonprobability sample. So, they resorted to an availability sample. To locate boys who had exhibited antisocial behavior, they sought referrals from numerous sources: mental health centers, juvenile courts, and the like. For a comparison group of boys who were not identified as antisocial, they sought volunteers from a large community center association. Given the purpose of experimentation, representative samples are less important. Experiments serve to determine *if* we can find cause-and-effect relationships; the issue of how generalizable those relationships are becomes important only after the relationships have been established.

Availability sampling probably is one of the more common forms of sampling used in human service research, both because it is less expensive than many other methods and because it often is impossible to develop an exhaustive sampling frame. You can readily grasp the problems of trying to develop a sampling frame in the following studies:

- Turning points in the lives of young inner-city men previously involved in violence, illegal drug marketing, and other crimes and now contributing to their community's well-being: The sample consisted of 20 young men, most of whom were referred by intervention programs, pastors, and community leaders.

- A study on methods for preventing HIV/AIDS transmission in drug-abusing, incarcerated women: The sample consisted of inmates at Rikers Island who were recruited with posted notices and staff referrals.
- A study on effectiveness of a program to reduce stress, perceived stigma, anxiety, and depression for family members of people with AIDS: Participants were recruited from an AIDS service program.
- Depression and resilience in elderly people with hip fractures: The sample consisted of 272 patients over age 65 who were hospitalized following hip fractures.

An exhaustive sampling frame that would make possible the selection of a probability sample in each of these studies might be, respectively, as follows:

- All reformed/rehabilitated young adult offenders
- All drug-abusing, incarcerated women
- All family members of people infected with AIDS
- All elderly people with hip fractures

Clearly, such probability sampling is beyond the realm of most investigators. Availability samples, though less desirable, make it possible for scientific investigation to move forward in those cases when probability sampling is impossible or prohibitively expensive.

Snowball Sampling

When a snowball is rolled along in wet, sticky snow, it picks up more snow and gets larger. This is analogous to what happens with **snowball sampling:** We start with a few cases of the type we want to study, and we let them lead us to more cases, which in turn lead us to still more cases, and so on. Like the rolling snowball, the snowball sample builds up as we continue to add cases. Because snowball sampling depends on the sampled cases

being knowledgeable of other relevant cases, the technique is especially useful for sampling subcultures where the members routinely interact with one another. Snowball sampling is also useful in the investigation of sensitive topics, such as child abuse or drug use, where the perpetrators or the victims might hesitate to identify themselves if approached by a stranger, such as a researcher, but might be open to an approach by someone who they know shares their experience or deviant status (Etikan, Musa, & Alkassim, 2016; Gelles, 1978).

In their rural homelessness study, Hilton and DeJong made use of snowball sampling toward the end of their study to recruit additional homeless adults who tend to avoid human services, including many who "rough it", surviving by camping in the woods. At the end of interviews with people who fit this description, they would often ask participants to refer other people they interact with while "roughing in" to participate in the study. This helped the researchers create a more diverse sample.

Snowball sampling allows researchers to accomplish what Norman Denzin (1989) calls *interactive sampling*—that is, sampling people who interact with one another. Probability samples are all noninteractive samples, because knowing someone who is selected for the sample does not change the probability of selection. Interactive sampling often is theoretically relevant, because many social science theories stress the impact of associates on behavior. To study these associational influences, researchers often combine snowball sampling with a probability sample. For example, Albert Reiss and Lewis Rhodes (1967), in a study of associational influences on delinquency, drew a probability sample of 378 boys between the ages of 12 and 16. They then asked each member of this sample to indicate his two best friends. By correlating various characteristics of the juveniles and their friends, the researchers were able to study how friendship patterns affect delinquency.

This interactive element, however, also points to one of the drawbacks of snowball sampling: Although it taps people who are involved in social networks, it misses people who are isolated from such networks. Thus, a snowball sample of drug users is limited to those users who are part of some social network and ignores those who use drugs in an individual and isolated fashion. It is possible that drug users who are involved in a social network differ from isolated users in significant ways. Care must be taken in making generalizations from snowball samples to ensure that we generalize only to those people who are like those in our sample.

Quota Sampling

Quota sampling involves dividing a population into various categories and then setting quotas on the number of elements to select from each category. Once we reach the quota for each category, we put no more elements from that category into the sample. Quota sampling is like stratified sampling in that both divide a population into categories and then take samples from the categories, but quota sampling is a nonprobability technique that often depends on availability to determine precisely which elements will be in the sample. At one time, quota sampling was the method of choice among many professional pollsters. Problems deriving from efforts to predict the very close 1948 presidential election between Harry S. Truman and Thomas E. Dewey, however, caused pollsters to turn away from quota sampling and to embrace the newly developed probability sampling techniques. With its fall from grace among pollsters, quota sampling also declined in popularity among researchers. Presently, the use of quota sampling is best restricted to those situations where its advantages clearly outweigh its considerable disadvantages. For example, researchers might use quota sampling to study crowd behavior, for which they cannot establish a sampling frame given the unstable nature of the phenomenon. A researcher who is studying reactions to disasters, such as a flood or a tornado, might use quota sampling where the need for immediate reaction is critical and takes precedence over sample representativeness.

Researchers normally establish quotas for several variables, including such common demographic characteristics as age, sex, race, socioeconomic status, and education. In addition, they commonly include one or more quotas directly related to the research topic. For example, a study of political behavior would probably include a quota on political party affiliation to ensure that the sample mirrored the population on the central variable in the study.

In quota sampling, interviewers do the actual selection of respondents. Armed with the preestablished quotas, interviewers begin interviewing people until they have their quotas on each variable filled. The fact that quota sampling uses interviewers to do the actual selection of cases is one of its major shortcomings. Despite the quotas, considerable bias can enter quota sampling because of interviewer behavior. Some people simply look more approachable than others, and interviewers naturally gravitate toward them. Interviewers also are not stupid. They realize that certain areas of major cities are less-than-safe places to go around asking questions of strangers, and protecting their personal safety by avoiding these areas can introduce obvious bias into the resulting sample.

While there is a risk of bias with quota samples, the technique does have some major positive attributes—namely, it is cheaper and faster than probability sampling. At times, these advantages can be sufficient to make quota sampling a logical choice. For example, if we wanted a rapid assessment of people's reactions to some event that had just occurred, quota sampling would probably be the best approach.

Purposive Sampling

In the sampling procedures discussed thus far, one major concern has been to select a sample that is representative of—and will enable generalizations to—a larger population. Generalizability, however, is only one goal, albeit an important one, of scientific research. In some studies, the issue of *control* may take on considerable importance and dictate a slightly different sampling procedure. In some investigations, control takes the form of choosing a sample that specifically *excludes* certain types of people, because their presence might confuse the research findings. Consider the housing first program example. If Charlene and her team were particularly interested in a few cases where clients had been able to access many services and made substantial progress in addressing health and other issues since securing housing, they might decide to select these few cases for the study. Perhaps, their main goal is not to get an overall impression of how many clients are accessing various services but to understand why these particular cases were so successful. Selecting these cases might help clue them into service outreach strategies or client and staff relationships that are most conducive to clients accessing services.

This would be an example of **purposive sampling,** or **judgmental sampling**: The investigators use their judgment and prior knowledge to choose for the sample people who best serve the purposes of the study. This is not "stacking the deck" in the researcher's favor, however. Consider the illustration given earlier: The basic purpose of the research is to help the team understand what service approaches are conducive to helping clients connect with services and make life improvements. If we select a random sample, the team will get variation based on age, sex, education, socioeconomic status, and a host of other variables that may not be of direct interest to Charlene and her team. Of course, there will be issues with respect to generalizability as those selected through this sampling method will not necessarily represent all clients in the program.

Research in Practice 6.2 illustrates some of the kinds of research problems we can approach with nonprobability samples and how a sampling strategy might actually involve a creative combination of some of the sampling types discussed here.

RESEARCH IN PRACTICE 6.2 Behavior and Social Environments: Using Nonprobability Samples to Study Hidden Populations

One of the major advantages of nonprobability samples is that they enable us to gain access to "hidden populations"—that is, people who are difficult to locate or who, for one reason or another, prefer to hide their identity or behavior from the prying eyes of authorities, social science researchers, and others (O'Connell, 2000). Typically, we cannot construct sampling frames for such groups. Area or cluster sampling is not feasible either, so probability samples are out of the question. Thus, studies of illicit drug users typically use nonprobability samples, with sampling strategies involving variants on or combinations of such strategies as snowball, quota, and purposive sampling. Douglas Heckathorn (1997), for example, used a variant of snowball sampling, which he called **respondent-driven sampling**, in a study of intravenous drug users and AIDS. He began with a small group of drug users, called "seeds," who were known to the researchers; each seed was asked to contact three other drug users he or she knew. The seeds received a payment for their interviews and an additional payment when each of the people they contacted came in for an interview. Each recruit interviewed then became a seed and was sent out to contact others. The procedure, especially the incentives, proved to be successful in recruiting other drug users and protected the privacy of the users, because the researchers did not learn anyone's name until he or she voluntarily came in for the interview.

One drawback of snowball samples is that they can produce "masking"—that is, when a respondent protects the privacy of others by *not* referring them to the researchers. Researchers must take care in making generalizations from snowball samples to ensure that we generalize only to those people who are like those in our sample. Actually, Heckathorn presents evidence to show that his respondent-driven sampling procedure substantially reduces the masking bias.

With all the incentives available in Heckathorn's study, consider that a subject might try to take advantage of the situation. Given the overlapping networks among drug users, it is highly likely that more than one recruiter might contact a single user, creating the possibility that one user could get interviewed twice by assuming a false identity at the second interview (and, thus, get two rewards). Heckathorn reduced the likelihood of this happening by recording visible identifying characteristics of each person interviewed: gender, age, height, ethnicity, scars, tattoos, and other characteristics that, in combination, identify a particular person. The concern

(continued)

here is less about money than about validity: If one person contributes multiple interviews, then the overall results become biased in the direction of that person.

Targeted sampling is a sampling strategy with similarities to both quota and purposive sampling; it involves strategies to ensure that people or groups with specified characteristics have an enhanced chance of appearing in the sample. In other words, researchers target specified groups for special efforts to bring them into the sample. We might identify the targeted groups for theoretical reasons because they would be especially useful for gathering certain kinds of information. Or, we might identify them during the data-collection process if we find that some groups are not showing up in the sample. So, targeted sampling is interactive, with the results of data collection possibly changing the method of sampling.

An example of targeted sampling is a study of injecting drug users conducted by John Watters and Patrick Biernacki (1989). They began by constructing an "ethnographic map" of the city in which they were conducting their research. This told them where drug users and drug activity tended to occur, in what amounts, and what the characteristics of the users in different locations were. This information provided the basis for deciding where to start recruiting people for participation in their study. This ethnographic map also told them that snowball sampling alone probably would not work, because the drug scene they found consisted of many nonoverlapping social networks. This meant that any network in which they could not find an initial informant probably would not show up in their sample.

Watters and Biernacki targeted neighborhoods in the city for sampling based partly on racial composition. They wanted to ensure adequate numbers of Black and Latino drug users in their sample. To enhance Latino participation, for example, they sent two Latino males who were familiar with the drug scene into the community to inform people of the research, to encourage their participation, and eventually, to drive people to the center where the data were collected. As data collection proceeded, Watters and Biernacki recognized that an insufficient number of female injecting drug users were showing up in the sample, so they revised the sampling techniques to enhance participation by women. One reason for the low participation by women, they learned, was that some of the female users were prostitutes, and going to the center to participate in the research meant that they lost time working the streets to earn money. To help alleviate this, the researchers established a "ladies first" policy at the data-collection sites: If there was a wait, women received precedence over men. This and other strategies were an effort to target women and get adequate numbers in the sample.

Heckathorn (1997), in his respondent-driven sampling, also used a form of targeted sampling to reduce bias problems that might arise because some groups of drug abusers are isolated from contact with others. He used "steering incentives" in the form of bonus payments for contacting drug users with special characteristics. For example, female users also were somewhat rare in his sample, so anyone contacting a female injector who then showed up for an interview received an extra $5.

So, even though nonprobability sampling techniques such as those presented here are not suitable for population studies in which the goal is to obtain precise estimates of population parameters, nonprobability approaches are extremely valuable for accessing hidden populations and increasing our understanding of these groups. With these techniques, researchers may not be able to compute sampling error as we could with random sampling, but we still can improve the representative quality of the sample with such techniques as targeted sampling and, thus, enhance the value of the study results. Given the goals of the study and the reality of accessing the population, a researcher's best option often is a nonprobability sampling strategy.

Dimensional Sampling

It often is expeditious—if not essential—to use small samples. Small samples can be very useful, but we must exercise considerable care in drawing the sample. (The smallest sample size, of course, is the single case, which we discuss in Chapter 11.) **Dimensional sampling** is a sampling technique for selecting small samples in a way that enhances their representativeness (Arnold, 1970). The two basic steps to dimensional sampling are these: First, specify all the important dimensions or variables. Second, choose a sample that includes at least one case that represents each possible combination of dimensions.

We can illustrate this with a study of the effectiveness of various institutional approaches in the control of juvenile delinquency (Street, Vinter, & Perrow, 1966). The population consisted of all institutions for delinquents. To draw a random sample of all those institutions, however, would have made a sample size that would tax the resources of most investigators. As an alternative, the researchers used a dimensional sample. The first step was to spell out the important conceptual dimensions. In terms of juvenile institutions, this investigation considered three dimensions, each containing two values, as illustrated in Table 6.3: organizational goals (custodial or rehabilitative), organizational control (public or private), and organizational size (large or small). In the second step, the researchers selected at least one case to represent each of the eight possibilities that resulted.

Dimensional sampling has a number of advantages that make it an attractive alternative in some situations. First, it is faster and less expensive than studying large samples. Second, it is valuable in exploratory studies with little theoretical development to support a large-scale study. Third, dimensional sampling provides more detailed knowledge of each case than we would likely gain from a large sample. With a large sample, data collection necessarily is more cursory and focused (which is justified if previous research has narrowed the focus of what variables are important).

Despite their limitations, nonprobability samples can be valuable tools in the conduct of human service research; however, we want to reiterate two points. First, some research uses both probability and nonprobability samples in a single research project, and we have given some illustrations of this. The point is that the two types of samples should not be considered as competitors for attention. Second, we should view findings based on nonprobability samples as being suggestive rather than conclusive, and we should seek opportunities to retest their hypotheses using probability samples.

SAMPLING WITH DIVERSE POPULATIONS

The key to selecting scientifically valid samples is to ensure their representativeness so that we can make valid generalizations. Accomplishing this is an especially difficult challenge when we are conducting research on populations that are diverse in terms of race, ethnicity, gender, or other characteristics. One problem is that some minorities have "rare event" status—that is, they constitute a relatively small percentage of some populations. African Americans and Hispanic Americans, for example, each constitute approximately 13% and 16% of the U.S. population, respectively, while Native Americans are about 1% (U.S. Census Bureau, 2012). This means that a representative sample of 1,500 Americans would, if it included the proper proportions of minorities, contain 195 African Americans, 240 Hispanics, and 15 Native Americans. These numbers are too small for many data analysis purposes. The Native Americans especially are so few that any analysis that breaks the sample down into subgroups would result in

TABLE 6.3 An Illustration of Institutional Dimensions for a Dimensional Sample

	Custodial Goals		Rehabilitative Goals	
	Public	**Private**	**Public**	**Private**
Large Size				
Small Size				

meaninglessly small numbers in each subgroup. Furthermore, these small numbers mean that the error rate becomes much higher for minority groups than for nonminority groups, because small samples are less reliable and have more error (Smith, 1987). These small sample sizes also make it difficult to assess differences of opinion or behavior within a minority group; thus, it is easy to conclude—falsely—that the group is homogeneous. As a consequence, we know little about gender, social class, regional, or religious differences among members of particular minorities. The outcome, according to Smith (1987), is "little more than a form of stereotyping, an *underestimation* of the variability of opinions among blacks. This leads to an *overestimation* of the contribution of race, per se, to black–white differences" (p. 445) in attitude and behavior.

Some minorities have rare event status in another way that can cause problems in sampling. Because of substantial residential segregation of minorities in the United States, minorities who live in largely White areas are relatively small in number, and researchers can easily miss them by chance even in a well-chosen, representative sample. The result is a biased sample that includes minorities living in largely minority communities but not minorities living elsewhere. Because minorities living in non-minority communities probably vary in terms of attitudes and behavior, such a biased sample gives a deceptively homogeneous picture of the minority.

So, efforts must be made in sampling to ensure that those rare events have a chance at selection for the sample. In some cases, we can employ disproportionate sampling, in which some individuals or households have a greater probability of appearing in the sample than other individuals or households do. Another way to avoid some of these problems is to use both probability and non-probability sampling techniques when studying minorities (Becerra & Zambrana, 1985; Schwartz et al., 2014). A dimensional sample of Latinos, for example, might specify an entire series of dimensions to cover in the sample. Thus, a researcher might specify certain age cohorts of Latino women (20–30, 31–40, and 41 and older) to include in the sample or some minimum number of single-parent and two-parent Hispanic families. This would ensure that sufficient people with certain characteristics are in the sample for valid data analysis. A study of mental health among Asian immigrants in the Seattle area used the snowball technique to ensure a complete sampling frame (Kuo & Tsai, 1986). Those researchers used local telephone directories and gathered names from ethnic and community organizations to develop part of the sampling frame. Then, given the dispersion of Asian Americans in the area, researchers added the snowball technique.

A NOTE ON SAMPLING IN PRACTICE

Human service practitioners do not routinely engage in sampling procedures like those used for research purposes, yet parallels exist between what occurs in practice and in research. We can apply some of the sampling principles in this chapter to providing client services. The needs and characteristics of a particular client typically guide the assessments and actions of practitioners, but to what extent are judgments about one client based on experiences with other clients? The issue here, of course, is that of *generalizability*. As human beings, we constantly dip into our own funds of experience to help us cope with situations that we confront. Practitioners use their past experience with clients—sometimes very effectively—to grapple with the problems of subsequent clients. The critical judgment to make in this regard is whether it is legitimate to generalize past outcomes to current situations.

Practice settings rarely involve dealing with probability samples, unless the research goal is an evaluation of a specific program and not to generalize to populations at large. Irrespective of whether the clients are welfare recipients, elderly people receiving nursing home care, child abusers, or individuals with problem pregnancies, practitioners have no way of knowing whether *all* people with such characteristics had a chance to be in the "sample"—that is, to be one of their clients—or how great that chance was. For all practical purposes, then, practitioners deal with nonprobability samples and all the limitations that they entail. In most cases, practitioners have an availability sample of people who happen to come to their attention because they are clients. This means that practitioners need to show caution in making generalizations from their observations, but this is no reason for despair. Remember that many scientific investigations are based on availability samples. We simply need to recognize their limitations and use care in generalizing.

If the main concern is to generalize to other clients with similar problems, then a reasonable assumption is that the clients are representative of others with similar problems who seek the aid of a practitioner, as with the housing first program example. Whatever propels people to see a particular practitioner is probably operative for many—if not all—of that practitioner's other clients. If the practitioner's research interest concerns all people experiencing a certain type of problem, like chronic homelessness, then agency clients are not an appropriate sample. Agencies both intentionally and unintentionally screen their prospective clients; thus, many people who could use services are not included in a sample of agency clients. The well-known study by Robert Scott (1975) on agencies that serve the blind is a classic example. Scott found that these agencies concentrate their efforts on young, trainable clientele, even though most blind people are elderly or have multiple handicaps. If workers in such an agency assumed that the agency clientele represented all blind people, then they would have a distorted perspective on the actual blind population.

Ways of checking on such distortions exist, of course. For example, practitioners can compare notes with each other. Do they find the same kinds of problems among their clients? If so, that is support for an assumption that one set of clients is representative of all people with similar problems. Practitioners also might consider using (at least informally) other sampling techniques, such as adopting a snowball technique by asking clients to recommend someone they know who has a similar problem but is not receiving any services. Especially with people whose problems may be of a sensitive nature, this snowball approach is a mode of entry with a considerable likelihood of success. Another possibly effective sampling technique is purposive sampling. For example, in an agency dealing with unplanned pregnancies among teenagers, suppose that all clients are members of ethnic minorities. It might appear that the clients' behavior, such as hostility toward practitioners, is caused either by the crisis of the pregnancy or by the animosity of a minority member toward the welfare bureaucracy. The problem is that the sample is homogeneous with respect to the two variables that are important: All clients have problem pregnancies, and all clients are members of an ethnic minority. To get around this problem, the researcher might begin to choose a purposive sample in which the problem pregnancies occur among nonminority teenagers and, thus, be in a better position to determine the source of the hostility.

Practitioner Profile 6.1 offers a good example of a human service professional who uses a variety of sampling techniques in her work to assess company employees' health, attitudes and preferences.

PRACTITIONER PROFILE 6.1 Lynn Bennett, Director of Benefits, Illinois (Based on a personal communication from May 30, 2018)

Lynn Bennett is Director of Benefits within the human resources department of a large multinational corporation. She has an MSW with a concentration in occupational social work. According to Bennett, "My interest in human resources came out of a paper I was assigned as an undergraduate about my career path. I was deciding between a career in business or social work when I learned about employee assistant programs (EAPs) and realized I could do both as an EAP counselor." (Based on personal communication from May 30, 2018.) EAPs, Bennett explained, provide case management and counseling services to employees on behalf of their employers. "When employees are struggling with personal problems EAPs connect them with resources. The idea is that they serve employees so they can stay in their jobs and be productive."

(continued)

Bennett has been in the human resources department for more than 25 years. As Director of Benefits she has global responsibilities for EAP and wellness programs and domestic (U.S.) responsibilities for benefits and the child care center at corporate headquarters. According to Bennett,

> Social work certainly cuts across all of the work I do. I attend to employees' needs and negotiate those with the corporation's needs. I also need to be able to conduct research and analyze statistics. Sometimes it seems like I look at numbers all day.

One of the research activities in which Bennett is involved is evaluating reasons employees use EAPs.

> We look at our EAP data over time to see why people access EAPs. One of the things we notice is that family issues are a major reason. We see that communication issues are often associated with use of EAPs. So we design programs to target communication—trainings, webinars, and other web-based programs. Then we evaluate whether people feel they work. We also look to see if rates of EAP use for family communication issues have changed after implementing these programs.

Healthcare data, Bennett explains, is also a powerful tool. "The healthcare provider can be useful in helping us target problems," she stated.

> For example, we've seen people who have treatments because of weight issues, lack of exercise, and sleep problems. We'll ask 'What factors are associated with various treatments?'. We looked at diabetes and weight, for example. So then we'll launch a new program to promote diet and exercise. We'll evaluate insurance claim data for employees—comparing preprogram and postprogram data. Then we'll take a look at claims one year after the program. We see if people lose weight in our programs, but then gain back. We also assess the long-term viability of these programs. We consider incentive packages for participating in weight loss challenges. We look at data to help determine how much weight we should expect people to lose before receiving reductions in healthcare costs or gift cards or some other rewards.

Healthcare use data also allows the company to evaluate impacts of various human resource initiatives.

> For example, if we give someone a $600 reduction in healthcare premiums, then we look at what we get for that $600 in terms of reductions in claims. Then we consider if that is a good investment for us or not.

Lynn also described a recent initiative at the corporation involving substance abuse treatment.

> The average length of stay at one of the inpatient substance abuse treatment facilities our insurance covers is 28 days. We recently invested in providing those in treatment with case management meetings prior to discharge and then again 24 hours after discharge. We also provide ongoing case management appointments for a week after discharge. We will be comparing readmission rates—for relapses–and compare rates of readmission

(continued)

prior to the new case management services to rates afterwards. It is too early to tell if this has worked. We'll look at this after six months and then after one year. We'll keep monitoring outcomes and determine whether or not it is cost effective.

Lynn explained her corporation also regularly conducts focus groups with carefully selected groups of employees to understand more about their concerns regarding benefits.

It is really important that we include people in focus groups who represent our employees at large, so we pay attention to age, gender, race, their job at the company and several other factors. I will contribute questions for the focus groups, but I don't conduct the groups because I may have a vested interest in the outcome.

Lynn described a recent set of focus groups where hourly employees described their sick time allotment.

They get 60 hours and many use most or all of this time. What we learned is that many employees were using this time not because they were sick but because a family member was sick and they had to take care of them. We wanted to extend the definition of sick time to include having to care for a child or partner, parent, and even in-laws, nieces and nephews. When we looked at the policy and the potential impact on our bottom line we decided to make the change. It was the right thing to do, employees felt they were heard and our analysis determined it would not hurt our bottom line. So we did it.

Bennett said she hoped other social workers would become comfortable with research and data analysis. "Knowing my numbers has really opened doors for me. There are not too many of us social workers working within corporations, but the social work training I've received has really helped me in this environment," she explained.

REVIEW AND CRITICAL THINKING

Main Points

- A population consists of all possible cases of whatever a researcher is interested in studying.
- A sample is composed of one or more elements selected from a population.
- A sampling frame is a list of the population elements that are used to draw some types of probability samples.
- The representativeness of a sample is its most important characteristic and refers to the degree to which the sample reflects the population from which it was drawn.
- Sampling error is the difference between sample values and true population values.
- Probability sampling techniques are the best for obtaining representative samples.
- The key characteristic of probability sampling is that every element in the population has a known chance of selection into the sample.

- Simple random, systematic, stratified, and area samples are all types of probability samples.
- Nonprobability samples do not ensure each population element a known chance of selection into the sample and, therefore, lack the degree of representativeness of probability samples.
- Availability, snowball, quota, purposive, and dimensional samples are all types of nonprobability samples.
- Data based on properly drawn probability samples are reliable and generalizable within known limits of error to the sampled populations.
- In studies of racial and other minorities, researchers must take care to ensure that sampling procedures do not result in unrepresentative samples, especially given the "rare event" status of many minorities.
- Cell phones have created sampling challenges for researchers because it is now more difficult to use telephone numbers as a sampling frame.

IMPORTANT TERMS FOR REVIEW

Accidental sampling	Nonprobability samples	Sample
Area sampling	Population	Sampling error
Availability sampling	Probability samples	Sampling frame
Cluster sampling	Purposive sampling	Simple random sampling
Convenience sampling	Quota sampling	Snowball sampling
Dimensional sampling	Representative sample	Stratified sampling
Judgmental sampling	Respondent-driven	Systematic sampling
Multistage sampling	sampling	Targeted sampling

CRITICAL THINKING

1. Why do researchers and practitioners often rely on samples to make generalizations about larger groups of people? Why do you think Charlene and her team of caseworkers in the housing first program would likely rely on a sample of clients to draw conclusions about use of services by housing first program participants?
2. What factors are important to consider when selecting a representative sample? If you were on Charlene's team what suggestions would you have for selecting a sample among the clients in the program? What factors do you think would be important to consider? Would this depend on what you hoped to learn, specifically?
3. How confident should researchers and practitioners be that a sample represents the group of people about which we would like to learn? Does this depend on the purpose of the research? The nature of the population to which you would like to generalize?
4. Why is sampling important to human service practitioners as well as researchers? Think about an area of practice that is important to you. What sampling issues might researchers studying issues related to that area of practice face? What do you think researchers would have to understand about those issues (and area of practice) to generate a good sample?

EVALUATING COMPETENCY (FROM THE COUNCIL ON SOCIAL WORK EDUCATION [CSWE] 2015 EDUCATIONAL POLICY AND ACCREDITATION STANDARDS [EPAS])

Competency 1: Demonstrate Ethical and Professional Behavior

- Human service professionals evaluating their programs or conducting or assisting in other research have an interest in generating samples that are representative of the larger groups (or populations) about which they hope to learn. At the same time, they have an ethical obligation to uphold clients' right to self-determination. Given that some clients may not want to participate in evaluations or research, what can human service professionals do to help generate good samples while also protecting this right?

Competency 2: Engage Diversity and Difference in Practice

- Why is it so important to include diverse groups of people (including marginalized populations) in research and evaluations pertaining to human service programs?
- What challenges does this create for researchers and practitioners?
- How can human service professionals aid researchers in creating more inclusive studies of human services?

Competency 4: Engage in Practice-Informed Research and Research-Informed Practice

- Suppose you were helping to design and implement a new program in your community. You have turned to research studies of human service programs to inform your work and are trying to determine which evidence is most applicable. Why is it important to carefully consider sampling techniques used in each study and the sample generated?
- What types of samples would you hope to find in the studies you examine (to convince you the findings might be applicable to your work)?

SELF-ASSESSMENT

1. Why do researchers and practitioners often use sampling as opposed to studying all members of a population?
   a. Sometimes it is not feasible to study all members of a population because the population is so large.
   b. At times researchers and practitioners can get better information from a carefully drawn sample than from an entire population.
   c. Both a and b are correct.
   d. None of the above.

2. A sampling frame is:
   a. The basic rationale behind a sampling strategy.
   b. A listing of all the elements in a population.
   c. Impossible to create in social research.
   d. Needed for nonprobability samples.
3. In a probability sample:
   a. Each element in a population is included in the sample.
   b. Each element in the population has the same chance of being included in the sample.
   c. Each element in the population has some chance of being included in the sample, and researchers can determine how likely it is that each will be included.
   d. Elements are chosen from a sample on a first come, first selected basis.
4. Simple random samples:
   a. Are probability samples.
   b. Are samples where each element has an equal chance of being selected into the sample.
   c. Both a and b are correct.
   d. Are preferred by all researchers because of their simplicity.
5. Dividing populations into subgroups or strata before drawing a sample and then drawing separate random samples from each strata is known as:
   a. Proportionate sampling
   b. Systematic sampling
   c. Snowball sampling
   d. Stratified sampling
6. Which is a procedure for obtaining final units to include in a sample by first sampling among larger units that contain the smaller sampling units?
   a. Disproportionate sampling
   b. Proportionate sampling
   c. Area sampling
   d. Homogeneous sampling
7. Sample size needed to create a representative sample:
   a. Increases as population heterogeneity increases.
   b. Increases as population homogeneity increases.
   c. Increases as both population heterogeneity and population homogeneity increase.
   d. Is the same regardless of the diversity within the population.
8. Probability samples are:
   a. Needed in all research but not necessary in human service evaluation.
   b. Are not required or even appropriate in all studies.
   c. Are always preferable to nonprobability samples, but not necessarily required.
   d. Only needed in quantitative research.
9. Quota sampling is an example of:
   a. A nonprobability sample.
   b. A probability sample.
   c. A convenience sample.
   d. A sampling frame.

10. Suppose a researcher turned to a human service program that provided services to a specific population (e.g., adults with substance abuse disorders) for help recruiting clients to serve as participants for a study where the goal was to make generalizations about that larger population (e.g., all adults with substance abuse disorders). What assumptions should the researcher make about the sample generated?

a. The sample will be perfectly representative of adults with substance abuse disorders because all study participants will have confirmed substance abuse disorders.

b. The sample will be useless since the sampling frame only includes clients of that agency.

c. The sample will be limited to adults with substance abuse disorders who are receiving treatment at this agency, so it is not perfectly representative of adults with substance abuse disorder.

d. The sample will be very representative of the study population but only if clients remain in treatment for the duration of the study.

ANSWER KEY FOR SELF-ASSESSMENT QUIZ

1. **c.** Both a and b are correct.
2. **b.** A listing of all the elements in a population.
3. **c.** Each element in the population has some chance of being included in the sample, and researchers can determine how likely it is that each will be included.
4. **c.** Both a and b are correct.
5. **d.** Stratified sampling
6. **c.** Area sampling
7. **a.** Increases as population heterogeneity increases.
8. **b.** Are not required or even appropriate in all studies.
9. **a.** A nonprobability sample.
10. **c.** The sample will be limited to adults with substance abuse disorders who are receiving treatment at this agency, so it is not perfectly representative of adults with substance abuse disorder.

FOR FURTHER READING

Daniel, J. (2012). *Sampling essentials.* Thousand Oaks, CA: Sage. This concise book is a handy guide to basic issues related to sampling. It also includes some interesting examples of research projects and the sampling procedures they used.

Fink, A. (2002). *How to sample in surveys* (2nd ed.). Thousand Oaks, CA: Sage. This book is also an excellent overview of the issues in sampling, with attention focused on sampling in survey research rather than in other kinds of research methodologies.

Kish, L. (1995). *Survey sampling.* New York, NY: Wiley-Interscience. Considered to be the mainstay regarding sampling issues in social research, this book assumes that the reader has an elementary understanding of statistics.

Maisel, R., & Persell, C. H. (1996). *How sampling works.* Thousand Oaks, CA: Pine Forge Press. This book provides an excellent and detailed overview of scientific sampling as well as software to assist students in learning through working problems.

Scheaffer, R. L., Mendenhall, W., Ott, R. L., & Gerow, K. G. (2012). *Elementary survey sampling* (7th ed.). Belmont, CA: Cengage, Brooks/Cole. As the name implies, this book is meant as an introductory text on the design and analysis of sample surveys. Limited to coverage of probability sampling techniques, it provides the information necessary to successfully complete a sample survey.

Stuart, A. (1987). *The ideas of sampling* (3rd ed.). New York, NY: Oxford University Press. This book is another good review of sampling strategies that can be used in many human service settings.

Sudman, S. (1976). *Applied sampling.* New York, NY: Academic Press. This book, along with the Kish work, will tell you almost all you need to know about sampling.

Wainer, H. (1986). *Drawing inferences from self-selected surveys.* New York, NY: Springer-Verlag. This book focuses on the issue of self-selection into samples and the problems this can create in terms of making inferences from samples to populations.

REFERENCES

Arnold, D. O. (1970). Dimensional sampling: An approach for studying a small number of cases. *American Sociologist, 5,* 147–150.

Backstrom, C. H., & Hursh-Cesar, G. D. (1981). *Survey research* (2nd ed.). New York, NY: Macmillan.

Bailey, K. (1987). *Methods of social research* (3rd ed.). New York, NY: Free Press.

Becerra, R. M., & Zambrana, R. E. (1985). Methodological approaches to research on Hispanics. *Social Work Research and Abstracts, 21,* 42–49. doi:10.1093/swra/21.2.42

Bell, A. P., & Weinberg, M. S. (1978). *Homosexualities: A study of diversity among men and women.* New York, NY: Simon & Schuster.

Cahalan, D. (1989). The *Digest* poll rides again! *Public Opinion Quarterly, 53,* 129–133. doi:10.1086/269146

Champion, D. J. (1981). *Basic statistics for social research* (2nd ed.). Scranton, PA: Chandler.

Denzin, N. (1989). *The research act: A theoretical introduction to sociological methods* (3rd ed.). Englewood Cliffs, NJ: Prentice Hall.

English, N., O'Muircheartaigh, C., Dekker, K., Latterner, M., & Eckman, S. (2009). Coverage rates and coverage bias in housing unit frames. In *JSM Proceedings, Survey Research Methods Section* (595–602). Alexandria, VA: American Statistical Association.

Etikan, I., Musa, S. A. & Alkassim, R. S. (2016). Comparison of convenience sampling and purposive sampling. *American Journal of Theoretical and Applied Statistics, 5*(1), 1–14. doi:10.11648/j.ajtas.20160501.11

Feldman, R. A., & Caplinger, T. E. (1977). Social work experience and client behavioral change: A multivariate analysis of process and outcome. *Journal of Social Service Research, 1,* 5–33. doi:10.1300/J079v01n01_02

Galtung, J. (1967). *Theory and methods of social research.* New York, NY: Columbia University Press.

Gelles, R. J. (1978). Methods for studying sensitive family topics. *American Journal of Orthopsychiatry, 48,* 408–424. doi:10.1111/j.1939-0025.1978.tb01331.x

Heckathorn, D. D. (1997). Respondent-driven sampling: A new approach to the study of hidden populations. *Social Problems, 44,* 174–199. doi:10.2307/3096941

Henry, G. (1990). *Practical sampling.* Newbury Park, CA: Sage.

Hilton, T., & DeJong, C. (2010). Homeless in God's country: Coping behaviors and felt experiences of the rural homeless. *Journal of Qualitative and Ethnographic Research, 5,* 12–30.

Hooker, E. (1957). The adjustment of the male overt homosexual. *Journal of Projective Techniques, 21,* 18–31. doi:10.1080/08853126.1957.10380742

Iannacchione, V. G. (2011). Research synthesis: The changing role of address-based sampling in survey research. *Public Opinion Quarterly, 75,* 556–575. doi:10.1093/poq/nfr017

Kish, L. (1965). *Survey sampling.* New York, NY: Wiley.

Kuo, W. H., & Tsai, Y. (1986). Social networking, hardiness, and immigrants' mental health. *Journal of Health and Social Behavior, 27,* 133–149. doi:10.2307/2136312

Link, M. W., Battaglia, M. P., Frankel, M. R., Osborn, L., & Mokdad, A. H. (2008). A comparison of address-based sampling (ABS) versus random-digit dialing (RDD) for general population surveys. *Public Opinion Quarterly, 72,* 6–27. doi:10.1093/poq/nfn003

Lohr, S., & Brick, J. (2017). Roosevelt predicted to win: Revisiting the 1936 Literary Digest Poll. *Statistics, Politics and Policy, 8*(1), 65–84. doi:10.1515/spp-2016-0006

Maxwell, J. A. (2012). *Qualitative research design: An interactive approach* (3rd ed.). Thousand Oaks, CA: Sage.

Michael, R. T., & O'Muircheartaigh, C. (2008). Design priorities and disciplinary perspectives: The case of the U. S. National Children's Study. *Journal of the Royal Statistical Society: Series A, 171,* 465–480. doi:10.1111/j.1467-985X.2007.00526.x

Montaquila, J., Hsu, V., Brick, J. M., English, N., & O'Muircheartaigh, C. (2009). A comparative evaluation of traditional listing vs. address-based sampling frames: Matching with field investigation of discrepancies. In, *Proceedings of the Survey Research Methods Section, American Statistical Association* (pp. 4855–4862).

Moser, C. A., & Kalton, G. (1972). *Survey methods in social investigation* (2nd ed.). New York, NY: Basic Books.

O'Connell, A. A. (2000). Sampling for evaluation: Issues and strategies for community-based HIV prevention programs. *Evaluation and the Health Professions, 23,* 212–234. doi:10.1177/016327870002300206

O'Muircheartaigh, C. (2018). Address-based and list-based sampling. In D. Vannette & J. Krosnick (Eds.), *The Palgrave handbook of survey research* (pp. 363–372). Basingstoke, UK; Palgrave.

Reiss, A. K., & Rhodes. L. (1967). An empirical test of differential association theory. *Journal of Research in Crime and Delinquency, 4,* 28–42.

Scheaffer, R. L., Mendenhall, W., Ott, R. L., & Gerow, K. G. (2012). *Elementary survey sampling* (7th ed.). Belmont, CA: Thomson/Brooks Cole.

Schwartz, S. J., Syed, M., Yip, T., Knight, G. P., Umana-Taylor, A. J., Rivas-Drake, D., & Lee, R. M. (2014). Methodological issues in ethnic and racial identity research with ethnic minority populations: Theoretical precision, measurement issues and research designs. *Child Development, 85*(1), 58–76. doi:10.1111/cdev.12201

Scott, R. A. (1974). The selection of clients by social welfare agencies: The case of the blind. In Y. Hasenfeld & R. A. English (Eds.), *Human service organizations* (pp. 485–498). Ann Arbor: University of Michigan Press.

Singh, A. S., & Musuku, M. B. (2014). Sampling techniques and determination of sample size in applied statistics research: An overview. *International Journal of Economics, Commerce and Management, 2*(11). Retrieved from http://citeseerx.ist.psu.edu/viewdoc/download?doi=10.1.1.678.1300&rep=rep1&type=pdf

Smith, T. W. (1987). That which we call welfare by any other name would smell sweeter: An analysis of the impact of question wording on response patterns. *Public Opinion Quarterly, 51*, 75–83. doi:10.1086/269015

Squire, P. (1988). Why the 1936 Literary Digest poll failed. *Public Opinion Quarterly, 52*, 125–133. doi:10.1086/269085

Street, D., Vinter, R. D., & Perrow, C. (1966). *Organizations for treatment: A comparative study of institutions for delinquents*. New York, NY: Free Press of Glencoe.

Sudman, S. (1976). *Applied sampling*. New York, NY: Academic Press.

Watters, J. K., & Biernacki, P. (1989). Targeted sampling: Options for the study of hidden populations. *Social Problems, 36*, 416–430. doi:10.2307/800824

7

SURVEY RESEARCH

Evaluating Competency (From the Council on Social Work Education [CSWE] 2015 Educational Policy and Accreditation Standards [EPAS])

    Competency 1: Demonstrate Ethical and Professional Behavior

    Competency 2: Engage Difference and Diversity in Practice

    Competency 4: Engage in Practice-Informed Research and Research-Informed Practice

    Competency 9: Evaluate Practice With Individuals, Communities, Groups, Organizations, and Communities

Self-Assessment

Answer key for Self-Assessment Quiz

For Further Reading

References

INTRODUCTION

Martin McBride (age 28) holds a master's in social work and works for a state health coalition in Sioux Falls, South Dakota. He recently joined a committee at the state health coalition that is building a survey to explore violence rates and health disparities throughout the state. The state health coalition currently has access to the following standardized instruments for their survey: the Behavioral Risk Factor Surveillance System that measures health-related risk behaviors for adults, and the Conflict Tactic Scale that measures violent behavior toward an intimate partner. These instruments in their current state are only inclusive of those who are heterosexual. This is problematic for exploring all populations. Martin has the task of making these questions more inclusive of LGBTQ populations. The committee is interested in comparing health disparities and violence rates between heterosexual and LGBTQ populations. Understanding the difference between these populations will provide more information for the state to help underserved and underrepresented groups.

The committee at the state health coalition has four people, including Martin, and 2 months to develop the survey. Another important area of survey collection is access to populations. Martin states,

Gaining access to LGBTQ populations has been easy for us since we have many different agencies and groups that are willing to work with us from The Queer Alliance to The Pride Center. Having community partners is so important in this work to ensure we are including the voices who should be involved. (M. McBride, personal communication, June 5, 2018)

After the survey is developed, Martin will need to deliver the survey across the state. The survey has been turned into an electronic survey to help with reaching more people. He is going to use social media and listservs to deliver the survey online.

This chapter addresses survey research and how to collect data for different populations you are interested in working with. As you read this chapter on survey research, consider the following questions: (a) What strengths and resources do social workers have to develop surveys for different populations? (b) Where should social workers start when building a survey? (c) What are different ways social workers can recruit participants to participate in their survey to make sure they get a good sample? (d) What additional resources will social workers need to help accomplish building a good survey?

The term **survey** both designates a specific way of collecting data and identifies a broad research strategy. Survey data collection involves gathering information from individuals, called *respondents*, by having them respond to questions. We use surveys to gather data as a part of many of the research methods discussed in other chapters, such as qualitative studies, quantitative studies, experiments, field research, and program evaluations. In fact, the survey probably is the most widely used means of gathering data in social sciences research. A literature search in the online database *Sociological Abstracts* (SocAbs) for the 5-year period from 1998 to 2002 using the keyword search terms "social work" and "survey" identified more than 600 English-language journal articles. Surveys have been used to study all five of the human service focal areas discussed in Chapter 1. This illustrates a major attraction of surveys, namely flexibility.

As a broad research strategy, **survey research** involves asking questions of a sample of people, in a fairly short period of time, and then testing hypotheses or describing a situation based on their answers. As a general approach to knowledge building, the strength of surveys is their potential for generalizability. Surveys typically involve collecting data from large samples of people; therefore, they are ideal for obtaining data that are representative of populations too large to deal with by other methods. Consequently, many of the issues addressed in this chapter center around how researchers obtain quality data that are, in fact, representative.

All surveys involve presenting respondents with a series of questions to answer. These questions may tap matters of fact, attitudes, opinions, or future expectations. The questions may be simple, single-item measures or complex, multiple-item scales. Whatever the form, however, survey data basically are what people say to the investigator in response to a question. We collect data in survey research in two basic ways: with *questionnaires*, or with *interviews*. A **questionnaire** contains recorded questions that people respond to directly on the questionnaire form itself, without the aid of an interviewer. A questionnaire can be handed directly to a respondent; can be mailed or sent online to the members of a sample, who then fill it out on their own and send it back to the researcher; or can be presented via a computer, with the respondent recording answers with the mouse and keypad. An **interview** involves an interviewer reading questions to respondents and then recording their answers. Researchers can conduct interviews either in person or over the telephone.

Some survey research uses both questionnaires and interview techniques, with respondents filling in some answers themselves and being asked other questions by interviewers. Because both questionnaires and interviews involve asking people to respond to questions, a problem central to both is what type of question we should use. In this chapter, we discuss this issue first and then we analyze the elements of questionnaires and interviews separately. An important point to emphasize about surveys is that they only measure what people say about their thoughts, feelings, and behaviors. Surveys do not directly measure those thoughts, feelings, and behaviors. For example, if people report in a survey that they do not take drugs, then we have not measured actual drug-taking behavior—only people's reports about that behavior. In social research, this is referred to as "self-report." This is very important in terms of the conclusions that can be drawn: We can conclude that people report not taking drugs, but we cannot conclude that people do not take drugs. This latter is an inference we might draw from what people say. So, surveys always involve data on what people say about what they do, not what they actually do.

DESIGNING QUESTIONS

Closed-Ended Versus Open-Ended Questions

Two basic types of questions are used in questionnaires and interviews: *closed-ended* or *open-ended* (Sudman & Bradburn, 1982). **Closed-ended questions** provide respondents with a fixed set of alternatives from which to choose. The response formats of multiple-item scales, for example, are all closed-ended, as are multiple-choice test questions. **Open-ended questions** require that the respondents write their own responses, much as for an essay-type examination question.

The proper use of open- and closed-ended questions is important for the quality of data generated as well as for the ease of handling that data. Theoretical considerations play an important part in the decision about which type of question to use. In general, we use closed-ended questions when we can determine all the possible, theoretically relevant responses to a question in advance, and the number of possible responses is limited. For example, The General Social Survey question for marital status reads, "Are you currently—married, in a relationship, widowed, divorced, separated, or have you never been married?" A known and limited number of answers is possible. (Today, researchers commonly offer people an alternative answer to this question—namely, "living together" or cohabitating. Although cohabitation is not legally a marital status, it helps to accurately reflect the living arrangements currently in use.) Another obvious closed-ended question is about biological sex. To leave such questions open-ended runs the risk that some respondent will either purposefully or inadvertently answer in a way that provides meaningless data.

Open-ended questions, on the other hand, are appropriate for an exploratory study in which the lack of theoretical development suggests that we should place few restrictions on people's answers. In addition, when researchers cannot predict all the possible answers to a question in advance, or when too many possible answers exist to list them all, then closed-ended questions are not appropriate. Suppose we wanted to know the reasons why people moved to their current residence. So many possible reasons exist that such a question has to be open-ended. If we are interested in the county and state in which our respondents reside, then we can generate a complete list of all the possibilities and, thus, create a closed-ended question. This list would consume so much space on the questionnaire, however, that it would be excessively cumbersome, especially considering that respondents should be able to answer this question correctly in its open-ended form.

Some topics lend themselves to a combination of both formats. Religious affiliation is a question that usually is handled in this way. Although a great many religions exist, there are some to which only a few respondents will belong. Thus, we can list religions with large memberships in closed-ended fashion and add the category "other," where a person can write the name of a religion not on the list (see Question 4 in Exhibit 7.1). We can efficiently handle any question with a similar pattern of responses—numerous possibilities, but only a few popular ones—in this way. The combined format maintains the convenience of closed-ended questions for most of the respondents but also allows those with less common responses to express them. An example of this would be with sex and gender. This would be a two-part question that first asks a closed-ended question "What sex were you assigned at birth?" with set categories of male, female, and intersex, then following with an open-ended question: "Is your gender the same you were assigned at birth?" This question structure allows you to gain more accurate information from your participants.

When we use the option of "other" in a closed-ended question, it is a good idea to request that respondents write in their response by indicating "Please specify." We can then code these answers into whatever response categories seem to be appropriate for data analysis. Researchers should offer the opportunity to specify an alternative, however, even if, for purposes of data analysis, we will not use the written responses. This is done because respondents who hold uncommon views or memberships may be proud of them and desire to express them on the questionnaire. In addition, well-educated professionals tend to react against completely closed-ended questions as too simple, especially when the questions deal with complicated professional matters (Huby & Hughes, 2004; Sudman, 1985). The opportunity to provide a written response to a question is more satisfying to such respondents, and given this opportunity, they will be more likely to complete the questionnaire. Additionally, giving respondents the opportunity to self-identify through written responses can be a validating experience, especially for people who have marginalized identities.

Another factor in choosing between open- and closed-ended questions is the ease with which

EXHIBIT 7.1 Formatting Questions for a Questionnaire

Please indicate your response to the following questions by placing an X in the appropriate box.

1. Which of the following best describes where you live?
   - [X] In a large city (100,000 population or more)
   - [ ] In a suburb near a large city
   - [ ] In a middle-sized city or small town (under 100,000 population) but not a suburb of a large city
   - [ ] Open country (but not on a farm)
   - [ ] On a farm

2. Have you ever shoplifted an item with a value of $10 or more?
   - [ ] Yes
   - [ ] No

   Filter

   If Yes: How many times have you taken such items?
   - [ ] Once
   - [ ] 2 to 5 times
   - [ ] 6 to 10 times
   - [ ] More than 10 times

   Contingency Question

3. Do you belong to an organized religion?
   - [ ] Yes
   - [ ] No (If No, please skip to Section C, question 1)

4. Please indicate the religion to which you belong:
   - [ ] Protestant
   - [ ] Catholic
   - [ ] Jewish
   - [ ] Other (please specify):_____

we can handle each at the data analysis stage. Open-ended questions sometimes are quite difficult to work with. One difficulty is that poor handwriting or the failure of respondents to provide clear answers can result in data that we cannot analyze (Rea & Parker, 2005). Commonly, some responses to open-ended questions just do not make sense, so we end up dropping them from analysis. In addition, open-ended questions are more complicated to analyze by computer, because we must first code a respondent's answers into a limited set of categories; this coding not only is time-consuming but also can introduce error (see Chapter 14).

Another related difficulty with open-ended questions is that some respondents may give more than one answer to a question. For example, in a study of substance abuse, researchers might ask people why they use—or do not use—alcoholic beverages. As a response to this question, a researcher might receive the following answer: "I quit drinking because booze was too expensive and my wife was getting angry at me for getting drunk." How should this response be categorized? Should the person be counted as quitting because of the expense or because of the marital problems created by drinking? It may be, of course, that both factors were important in the decision to quit. Researchers usually handle data analysis problems like this in one of two ways: First, the researchers may accept all the individual's responses as data. This, however, creates difficulties in data analysis; some people give more reasons than others because they are talkative rather than because they actually have more reasons for their behavior. Second, the researchers may handle multiple responses by assuming that each respondent's *first* answer is the most important one and considering that answer to be the only response. This assumption, of course, is not always valid, but it does solve the dilemma systematically.

The decision about whether to use open- or closed-ended questions is complex, often requiring considerable experience with survey methods. It is an important issue that can have substantial effects on both the type and the quality of the data collected, as illustrated in a survey of attitudes about social problems confronting the United States. The Institute for Social Research at the University of Michigan asked a sample of people open- and closed-ended versions of essentially the same questions (Schuman & Presser, 1979). The two versions elicited quite different responses. For example, with the closed-ended version, 35% of the respondents indicated that crime and violence were important social problems, compared with only 15.7% in the open-ended version. With a number of other issues, people responding to the closed-ended questions were more likely to indicate that particular issues were problems. One reason that the type of question has such an effect on the data is that the list of alternatives in the closed-ended questions tends to serve as a "reminder" to the respondent of issues that might be problems. Without the stimulus of the list, some respondents might not even think of some of these issues. A second reason is that people tend to choose from the list provided in closed-ended questions rather than writing in their own answers, even when provided with an "other" category.

In some cases, researchers can gain the benefits of both open- and closed-ended questions by using an open-ended format in a pretest or pilot study and then, based on these results, designing closed-ended questions for the actual survey.

Wording of Questions

Because the questions that make up a survey are the basic data-gathering devices, researchers need to word them with great care, especially with questionnaires that allow the respondent no opportunity to clarify questions. Ambiguity can cause substantial trouble. We will review some of the major issues in developing good survey questions (Sudman & Bradburn, 1982). (In Chapter 13, we will discuss some problems of question construction having to do specifically with questions that are part of multiple-item scales.)

Researchers should subject the wording of questions, whenever possible, to empirical assessment to determine whether a particular wording might lead to unnoticed bias. Words, after all, have connotative meanings—that is, emotional or evaluative associations—that the researcher may not be aware of but that may influence respondents' answers to questions. In a study of attitudes about social welfare policy in the United States, for example, researchers asked survey respondents whether they believed the government should spend more or less money on welfare (Smith, 1987). Respondents, however, were asked the question in three slightly different ways. One group was asked about whether we were spending too much or too little on "welfare," a second group about spending too much or too little on "assistance for the poor," and a third group about money for "caring for the poor." At first glance, all three questions seem to have much the same meaning, yet people's responses to them suggested something quite different. Basically, people responded much more negatively to the question with the word "welfare" in it, indicating much less willingness to spend more money on "welfare" compared with spending money to "assist the poor." For example, 64.7% of the respondents indicated that too little was being spent on "assistance to the poor," but only 19.3% said we were spending too little on "welfare." This is a very dramatic difference in opinion, resulting from what might seem, at first glance, to be a minor difference in wording. Although the study did not investigate why these differing responses occurred, it seems plausible that the word *welfare* has connotative meanings for many people that involve images of laziness, waste, fraud, bureaucracy, or the poor as being disreputable. "Assisting the poor," on the other hand, is more likely associated with giving and Judeo-Christian charity. These connotations lead to quite different responses. In many cases, the only way to assess such differences is to compare people's responses with different versions of the same question during a pretest.

In general, researchers should state questions in the present tense. Specialized questions that focus on past experiences or future expectations, however, are an exception. In these situations, researchers should use the appropriate past or future tense. Of major importance is making sure that tenses are not carelessly mixed. Failure to maintain consistent tense of questions can lead to an understandable confusion on the part of respondents and, therefore, to more measurement error.

Researchers should keep questions simple and direct, expressing only one idea, and avoid complex statements that express more than one idea. Consider the following double-negative question that appeared in a Roper Organization poll conducted in 1992 about the Holocaust: "Does it seem possible or does it seem impossible to you that the Nazi extermination of the Jews never happened?" (Smith, 1995, p. 269). The results showed that 22% said "possible," 65% "impossible," and 12% "don't know." Could it be that more than one-fifth of Americans had doubts about the Holocaust and more than one-third questioned it or were uncertain that it had occurred? Considerable controversy erupted over the survey results. In a subsequent Gallup Poll, researchers asked respondents the same double-negative question with this follow-up question: "Just to clarify, in your opinion, did the Holocaust definitely happen, probably happen, probably *not* happen, or definitely *not* happen?" (Smith, 1995, p. 277). Of those who had said it

was possible that the Holocaust never happened in response to the first question, 97% changed their position to say that it did happen with the second question.

Statements that seem to be crystal clear to a researcher may prove to be unclear to many respondents. One common error is to overestimate the reading ability of the average respondent. For example, a national study of adult literacy found that more than 20% of adults in the United States demonstrate skills in the lowest level of prose, document, and quantitative literacy proficiencies. At this level, many people cannot total an entry on a deposit slip, identify a piece of specific information in a brief news article, or respond to many of the questions on a survey form (Calderon, Hays, Liu, & Morales, 2006; Kirsch, Jungeblut, Jenkins, & Kolstad, 1993). Such limited literacy skills are common among some clients of the human services, especially when English is a second language. Accordingly, the researcher should avoid the use of technical terms on questionnaires. For example, it would not be advisable to include such a statement as "The current stratification system in the United States is too rigid." The word *stratification* is a technical term in the social sciences that many people outside the field do not understand in the same sense that social scientists do.

Another practice to avoid is making reference to things that we cannot clearly define or that depend on the respondent's interpretation. For example, "Children who get into trouble typically have had a bad home life" is an undesirable statement, because it includes two sources of vagueness. The word *trouble* is unclear. What kind of trouble? Trouble with the law? Trouble at school? Trouble with parents? The other problem is the phrase "bad home life," because what constitutes a "bad home life" depends on the respondent's interpretation.

Finally, for the majority of questions designed for the general public, researchers should never use slang terminology. Slang tends to arise in the context of particular groups and subcultures. Slang terms may have a precise meaning within those groups, but such terms confuse people outside those groups. Occasionally, however, the target population for a survey is more specialized than the general population, and the use of their "in-group" jargon may be appropriate. It would demonstrate to the respondents that the researcher cared enough to "learn their language" and could increase rapport, resulting in better responses. Having decided to use slang, however, the burden is on the researcher to be certain that they use it correctly.

Once a survey instrument is developed, it must be pretested to see whether the questions are clearly and properly understood and are unbiased. We can handle pretesting by having people respond to the questionnaire or interview and then reviewing it with them to find any problems. The way that a group responds to the questions themselves also can point out trouble. For example, if many respondents leave a particular answer blank, then there may be a problem with that question. Once the instrument is pretested and modifications are made where called for, the survey should be pretested again. Any change in the questionnaire requires more pretesting. Only when it is pretested with no changes being called for is the questionnaire ready to use in research.

We present these and other problems that can arise in writing good survey questions in Table 7.1. One of the critical decisions in survey

TABLE 7.1 Common Errors in Writing Questions and Statements

Original Question	Problem	Solution
The city needs more housing for the elderly, and property taxes should be raised to finance it.	**Two questions in one:** Some respondents might agree with the first part but disagree with the second.	Questions should be broken up into two separate statements, each expressing a single idea.
In order to build more stealth bombers, the government should raise taxes.	**False premise:** What if a person does not want more bombers built? How does that person answer?	First ask for an opinion on whether the bomber should be built; then, for those who respond "Yes," ask the question about taxes.
Are you generally satisfied with your job, or are there some things about it that you do not like?	**Overlapping alternatives:** A person might want to answer "Yes" to the first part (i.e., he or she is generally satisfied) but "No" to the second part (i.e., there are also some things he or she does not like).	Divide this into two questions: One measures the respondent's level of satisfaction, while the other assesses whether there are things the respondent does not like.
How satisfied are you with the number and fairness of the tests in this course?	**Double-barreled question:** It asks about both the "number" and the "fairness," and a person might feel differently about each.	Divide this into two questions.
What is your income?	**Vague and ambiguous words:** Does "income" refer to before-tax or after-tax income? To hourly, weekly, monthly, or yearly income?	Clarify: What was your total annual income, before taxes, for the year 2000?
Children who get into trouble typically have had a bad home life.	**Vague and ambiguous words:** The words *trouble* and *bad home life* are unclear. Is it trouble with the law, trouble at school, trouble with parents, or what? What constitutes a *bad home life* depends on the respondent's interpretation.	Clarify: Specify what you mean by the words: *trouble* means "having been arrested" and *bad home life* means "an alcoholic parent."

research—and it is a complex decision—is whether to collect data through questionnaires or through interviews. We discuss both types of surveys with an eye on the criteria to use in assessing which is more appropriate for a particular research project.

QUESTIONNAIRES

Questionnaires are designed so that they can be answered without assistance. Of course, if a researcher hands a questionnaire to the respondent, as we sometimes do, the respondent then has the opportunity to ask the researcher to clarify anything that is ambiguous. A good questionnaire, however, should not require such assistance. In fact, researchers often mail questionnaires or send them online to respondents, who thus have no opportunity to ask questions. In other cases, researchers administer questionnaires to many people simultaneously in a classroom, auditorium, or agency setting. Such modes of administration make questionnaires quicker and less expensive than most interviews; however, they place the burden on researchers to design questionnaires that respondents can properly complete without assistance.

Structure and Design

Directions. One of the simplest—but also most important—tasks of questionnaire construction is the inclusion of precise directions for respondents. Good directions go a long way toward improving the quality of data that questionnaires generate. If we want respondents to click on a button or put an "X" in a box corresponding to their answer, then we tell them to do so. Questionnaires often contain questions requiring different kinds of answers as well, and at each place in the questionnaire where the format changes, we need to include additional directions.

Order of Questions. An element of questionnaire construction that requires careful consideration is the proper ordering of questions. Careless ordering can lead to undesirable consequences, such as a reduced response rate or biased responses to questions. Generally, questions that are asked early

in the questionnaire should not bias answers to those questions that come later. For example, if we asked several factual questions regarding poverty and the conditions of the poor, and we later asked a question concerning which social problems people consider to be serious, more respondents will likely include poverty than would otherwise have done so. When a questionnaire contains both factual and opinion questions, we sometimes can avoid these potentially biasing effects by placing opinion questions first.

Ordering of questions can also increase a respondent's interest in answering a questionnaire—this is especially helpful for boosting response rates with mailed questionnaires. Researchers should ask questions dealing with particularly intriguing issues first. The idea is to interest the recipients enough to get them to start answering, because once they start, they are more likely to complete the entire questionnaire. If the questionnaire does not deal with any topics that are obviously more interesting than others, then opinion questions should be placed first. People like to express their opinions, and for the reasons mentioned earlier, we should put opinion questions first anyway.

Question Formats. All efforts at careful wording and ordering of the questions will be for naught unless we present the questions in a manner that facilitates responding to them. The goal is to make responding to the questions as straightforward and convenient as possible and to reduce the amount of data lost because of responses that we cannot interpret.

When presenting response alternatives for closed-ended questions, we obtain the best results by having respondents indicate their selection by placing an "X" in a box (□) corresponding to that alternative, as illustrated in Question 1 of Exhibit 7.1. This format is preferable to open blanks and check marks, because it is easy for respondents to get sloppy and place check marks *between* alternatives, rendering their responses unclear and, therefore, useless as data. Boxes force respondents to give unambiguous responses. This may seem to be a minor point, but we can attest from our own experience in administering questionnaires that it makes an important difference.

Some questions on a questionnaire may apply to only some respondents and not others. These questions normally are handled by what are called *filter questions* and *contingency questions*. A **filter question** is a question whose answer determines which question the respondent goes to next. In Exhibit 7.1, Questions 2 and 3 are both filter questions. In Question 2, the part of the question asking about "how many items they have taken" is called a **contingency question**, because whether a person answers it depends on—that is, it is contingent on—his or her answer to the filter question. Notice the two ways in which the filter question is designed with a printed questionnaire. With Question 2, the person answering "Yes" is directed to the next question by the arrow, and the question is clearly set off by a box. Also in the box, the phrase "If Yes" is included to make sure the person realizes that this question is only for those who answered "Yes" to the previous question. With Question 3, the answer "No" is followed by a statement telling the person which question he or she should answer next. Either format is acceptable; the point is to provide clear directions for the respondent. (When questionnaires are designed by special computer programs to be answered on a computer screen or online, the computer program automatically moves the respondent to the appropriate contingency question once the person answers the filter question.) By sectioning the questionnaire on the basis of filter and contingency questions, we can guide the respondent through even the most complex questionnaire. The resulting path that an actual respondent follows through the questionnaire is referred to as the *skip pattern*. As is true of many aspects of questionnaire design, it is important to evaluate the skip pattern by pretesting the questionnaire to ensure that respondents complete all appropriate sections with a minimum of frustration.

In some cases, a number of questions or statements may all have identical response alternatives. An efficient way of organizing such questions is in the form of a **matrix question**, which lists the response alternatives only once; a box to check, or a number or letter to circle, follows each question or statement. Table 13.1 is an example of a matrix question. Multiple-item indexes and scales often use this compact way of presenting a number of items.

Researchers should use matrix questions cautiously, however, because these questions contain a number of weaknesses. One is that, with a long list of items in a matrix question, it is easy for the respondent to lose track of which line is the response for which statement and, thus, to indicate an answer on the line above or below where the answer should go. Researchers can alleviate this by following every third or fourth item with a blank line so that it is easier visually to keep track of the proper line on which to mark an answer. A second weakness of matrix questions is that they may produce *response set*. (We will discuss the problem of response set and techniques for alleviating it at length in Chapter 13.) A third weakness of matrix questions is that they may tempt the researcher, to be able to gain the efficiencies of the format, to force the response alternatives of some questions into that matrix format when another format would be more valid. Researchers should determine the response format of any question or statement by theoretical and conceptual considerations of what is the most valid way to measure a variable.

Response Rate

A major problem in many research endeavors is gaining people's cooperation so that they will provide whatever data are needed. In surveys, we measure cooperation by the **response rate**, or the proportion of a sample that completes and returns a questionnaire or that agrees to an interview. With interviews, response rates often are very high—in the area of 90%—largely because people are reluctant to refuse a face-to-face request for cooperation. In fact, with interviews, the largest nonresponse factor is the inability of the interviewers to locate respondents. With mailed or online questionnaires, however, this personal pressure is absent, and people feel freer to refuse. This can result in many *nonreturns*, or people who refuse to complete and return a questionnaire. Response rates for questionnaires (especially mailed ones) vary considerably, from an unacceptably low 20% to levels that rival those of interviews.

Why is a low response rate of such concern? The issue is the representativeness of a sample, as we discussed in Chapter 6. If we selected a representative sample and obtained a perfect 100% response, then we would have confidence in the representativeness of the sample data. As the response rate drops below 100%, however, the sample may become less representative. Those who refuse to cooperate may differ in some systematic ways from those who do return the questionnaire that can affect the results of the research. In other words, any response rate less than 100% may result in a biased sample. Of course, we rarely achieve a perfect response rate, but the closer the response rate is to that level, the more likely that the data are representative. Researchers can take a number of steps to improve response rates. Most apply only to questionnaires, but we also can use a few of them to increase response rates in interviews.

A Cover Letter. A properly constructed cover letter can help increase the response rate. A **cover letter** accompanies a questionnaire and serves to introduce and explain it to the recipient. With mailed or online questionnaires, the cover letter may be the researcher's only medium for communicating with the recipient, so the researcher must carefully draft the letter to include information that recipients will want to know and to encourage them to complete the questionnaire (see Table 7.2).

Researchers should feature the name of the sponsor of the research project prominently in the cover letter. Recipients want to know who is seeking the information they are being asked to provide, and research clearly indicates that knowledge of the sponsoring organization influences the response rate (Goyder, 1985; Rea & Parker, 2005). Questionnaires sponsored by governmental agencies receive the highest response rates. University-sponsored research generates somewhat lower response rates. Commercially sponsored research produces the lowest rates of all. Apparently, if the research is at all associated with a governmental agency, stressing that in the cover letter may have a beneficial effect on the response

TABLE 7.2 Items to Include in the Cover Letter of a Questionnaire or the Introduction to an Interview

Item	Cover Letter	Interview Introduction
1. Sponsor of the research	Yes	Yes
2. Address/phone number of the researcher	Yes	If required
3. How the respondent was selected	Yes	Yes
4. Who else was selected	Yes	Yes
5. The purpose of the research	Yes	Yes
6. Who will utilize or benefit from the research	Yes	Yes
7. An appeal for the person's cooperation	Yes	Yes
8. How long it will take the respondent to complete the survey	Yes	Yes
9. Payment	If given	If given
10. Anonymity/confidentiality	If given	If given
11. Deadline for return	Yes	Not applicable

rate. Researchers also can increase response rates of particular groups if their research is sponsored or endorsed by an organization that people in the group believe has legitimacy. For example, we can increase response rates of professionals if the research is linked to relevant professional organizations, such as the National Association of Social Workers, the American Nurses Association, or the National Education Association (Larson & Poist, 2004; Sudman, 1985).

The address, email address, and telephone number of the researcher also should appear prominently on the cover letter. In fact, using letterhead stationery for the cover letter is a good idea. Especially if the sponsor of the research is not well known, some recipients may desire further information before they decide to participate. Although relatively few respondents will ask for more information, including the address and telephone number gives the cover letter a completely open and honest appearance that may further the general cooperation of recipients.

In addition, the cover letter should inform the respondent of how people were selected to receive the questionnaire. It is not necessary to go into great detail on this matter, but people receiving an unanticipated questionnaire are naturally curious about how they were chosen to be part of a study. A brief statement, for example, that they were randomly selected or selected by computer (if this is the case) should suffice.

Recipients also want to know the purpose of the research. Again, without going into great detail, the cover letter should explain why the research is being conducted, why and by whom it is considered to be important, and the potential benefits that are anticipated from the study. Investigations have shown clearly that we can significantly increase the response rate if we emphasize the importance of the research to the respondent. We must word this part of the cover letter carefully, however, so that it does not sensitize respondents in such a way that it affects their answers to our questions. We can minimize sensitizing effects by keeping the description of the purpose general—certainly, do not suggest any of the research hypotheses. Regarding the importance of the data and the anticipated benefits, the researcher should resist the temptation

of hyperbole and, instead, make honest, straightforward statements. Respondents will see claims about "solving a significant social problem" or "alleviating the problems of the poor" as precisely what they are—exaggerated.

The preceding information provides a foundation for the single most important component of the cover letter, namely a direct appeal for the recipient's cooperation. General statements about the importance of the research are no substitute for a personal appeal to the recipient as to why he or she should take time to complete the questionnaire. Respondents must believe that their responses are important to the outcome (as, of course, they are). A statement to the effect that "your views are important to us" is a good approach that stresses the importance of each individual respondent and emphasizes that the questionnaire will allow the expression of opinions, which people like.

The cover letter also should indicate that the respondent will remain anonymous or that the data will be treated as confidential, whichever is the case. "Anonymous" means that *no one, including the researcher,* can link a particular respondent's name to his or her questionnaire. "Confidential" means that even though the researcher can match a respondent's name to his or her questionnaire, the researcher will treat the information collectively and will not link any individuals publicly to their responses.

With mailed questionnaires, two techniques assure anonymity (Sudman, 1985). The best is to keep the questionnaire itself completely anonymous, with no identifying numbers or symbols; instead, the respondent gets a separate postcard, including his or her name, to mail back at the same time that the individual mails back the completed questionnaire. This way, the researcher knows who has responded and need not send reminders, yet no one can link a particular respondent's name with a particular questionnaire. A second way to ensure anonymity is to attach a cover sheet to the questionnaire with an identifying number and assure the respondents that the researcher will remove and destroy the cover sheet once the receipt of the questionnaire has been recorded. This second procedure provides less assurance to the respondent, because an unethical researcher might retain the link between questionnaires and their identification numbers. The first procedure, however, is more expensive because of the additional postcard mailing, so a researcher may prefer the second procedure for questionnaires that do not deal with highly sensitive issues that sometimes make respondents more concerned about anonymity. If the material is not highly sensitive, then assurances of confidentiality are adequate to ensure a good return rate. No evidence indicates that assuring anonymity rather than confidentiality increases the response rate in nonsensitive surveys (Bangerter et al., 2014; Moser & Kalton, 1972).

Finally, the cover letter should include a deadline for returning the questionnaire, that is, a deadline calculated to take into account mailing time and a few days to complete the questionnaire. The rationale for a fairly tight deadline is that it encourages the recipients to complete the questionnaire soon after they receive it and not set it aside, where they can forget or misplace it.

Payment. Research consistently shows that we can also increase response rates by offering a payment or other incentives as part of the appeal for cooperation and that these incentives need not be large to have a positive effect. Studies find that, depending on the respondents, an incentive of between $2 and $20 can add 10% to a response rate (Singer & Ye, 2013; Warriner, Goyder, Gjertsen, Hohner, & McSpurren, 1996; Woodruff, Conway, & Edwards, 2000). For the greatest effect, researchers should include such payments with the initial mailing instead of promising payment on return of the questionnaire. One study found that including the payment with the questionnaire boosted the return rate by 12% over promising payment on the questionnaire's return (Berry & Kanouse, 1987; Johnson, VanGeest, & Welch, 2007). Researchers have used other types of incentives as well, such as entering each respondent in a lottery or donating to charity for each questionnaire returned, but these have shown mixed results as far as increasing response rates.

Mailing procedures also affect response rates. It almost goes without saying that researchers should supply a stamped, self-addressed envelope for returning the questionnaire to make its return

as convenient as possible for the respondent. The type of postage used also affects the response rate, with stamps bringing about a 4% higher return rate compared with bulk-printed postage (Yammarino, Skinner, & Childers, 1991). Presumably, the stamp makes the questionnaire appear more personal and less like unimportant junk mail. A regular stamped envelope also substantially increases the response rate in comparison with a business reply envelope (Armstrong & Luck, 1987; Campbell, Lavelle, & Todd, 2008).

Follow-Ups. The most important procedural matter affecting response rates is the use of follow-up letters or other contacts. A substantial percentage of those who do not respond to the initial mailing will respond to follow-up contacts. With two follow-ups, researchers can achieve 15% to 20% increases over the initial return (James & Bolstein, 1990; Woodruff et al., 2000). Such follow-ups are clearly essential; researchers can do them by telephone, if the budget permits and speed is important. With aggressive follow-ups, the difference in response rates between mailed questionnaires and interviews declines substantially (Goyder, 1985; Johnson et al., 2007).

In general, researchers use two-step follow-ups. Some send follow-up letters to nonrespondents that encourage return of the questionnaire once the response to the initial mailing drops off. This letter should include a restatement of the points in the cover letter, with an additional appeal for cooperation. When response to the first follow-up declines, the researcher then sends a second follow-up to the remaining nonrespondents and includes another copy of the questionnaire in case people have misplaced the original. After two follow-ups, we consider the remaining nonrespondents to be a pretty intransigent lot, because additional follow-ups generate relatively few further responses.

Length and Appearance. Two other factors that affect the rate of response to a mailed questionnaire are the length of the questionnaire and its appearance. As the length increases, the response rate declines. No hard-and-fast rule, however, governs the length of the mailed questionnaires. Much depends on the literacy of the respondents, the degree of interest in the topic of the questionnaire, and other such matters. It probably is a good idea, though, to keep the questionnaire to less than five pages, requiring no more than 30 min to fill out. Researchers must take great care to remove any extraneous questions, or any questions that are not essential to the hypotheses under investigation (Epstein & Tripodi, 1977). Although keeping the questionnaire to less than five pages is a general guide, researchers should not strive to achieve this by cramming so much material onto each page that the respondent has difficulty using the instrument—because, as mentioned, the appearance of the questionnaire also is important in generating a high response rate. As discussed earlier, the use of boxed response choices and smooth transitions through contingency questions help make completing the questionnaire easier and more enjoyable for the respondent, which in turn increases the probability that he or she will return it.

Other Influences on the Response Rate. Many other factors can work to change response rates. In telephone surveys, for example, the voice and manner of the interviewer can have an important effect (Drabble, Korcha, Trocki, Salcedo, & Walker, 2016; Oksenberg, Coleman, & Cannell, 1986). Interviewers with higher-pitched, louder voices and clear, distinct pronunciation have lower refusal rates. The same is true for interviewers who sound competent and upbeat. Reminders of confidentiality, however, can negatively affect the response rate (Frey, 1986): If an interviewer reminds a respondent of the confidentiality of the information partway through the interview, the respondent is more likely to refuse to respond to some of the remaining questions compared with someone who does not receive such a reminder. The reminder may work to undo whatever rapport the interviewer has already built up with the respondent.

A survey following all the suggested procedures should yield an acceptably high response rate. Specialized populations may, of course, produce either higher or lower rates. Because so many variables are involved, we offer only rough guidelines for evaluating response rates with mailed questionnaires. The desired response rate is 100%, of course. Anything less than 50% is highly suspectful as far as its representativeness is concerned. Unless some evidence of the representativeness can be presented, we should use great caution when generalizing from such a sample. In fact, it might be best to treat the resulting sample as a nonprobability sample from which we cannot make confident generalizations. In terms of what a researcher can expect, response rates in the 60% range are good; anything more than 70% is very good. Even with these response rates, however, we should use caution about generalizing and check for bias as a result of nonresponse. The bottom line, whether the response rate is high or low, is to report it honestly so that those who are reading the research can judge its generalizability for themselves.

Checking for Bias Due to Nonresponse

Even if researchers obtain a relatively high rate of response, they should investigate possible bias due to nonresponse by determining the extent to which respondents differ from nonrespondents (Groves, 2004; Miller & Salkind, 2002; Rea & Parker, 2005). One common method is to compare the characteristics of the respondents with the characteristics of the population from which they were selected. If a database on the population exists, then we can simplify this job. For example, if researchers are studying a representative sample of people receiving welfare in a community, the Department of Social Services is likely to have data regarding age, sex, marital status, level of education, and other characteristics for all people receiving welfare in the community. The researchers can compare the respondents with this database on the characteristics for which data have already been collected. A second approach to assessing bias from nonresponse is to locate a subsample of nonrespondents and interview them. In this way, we can compare the responses to the questionnaire by a representative sample of nonrespondents with those of the respondents. This is the preferred method, because we can measure directly the direction and the extent of any bias that results from nonresponse. It is, however, the most costly and time-consuming approach.

Any check for bias from nonresponse, of course, informs us only about those characteristics on which we make comparisons. It does not prove that the respondents are representative of the whole sample on any other variables, including those that might be of considerable importance to the study. In short, we can gather some information regarding such bias, but in most cases, we cannot *prove* that bias from nonresponse does not exist.

The proper design of survey instruments is important to collecting valid data. Research in

Practice 7.1 provides an illustration of a use to which survey research is commonly put by human service practice organizations today.

An Assessment of Questionnaires

Advantages. As a technique of survey research, questionnaires have a number of desirable features. First, they gather data far more inexpensively and quickly than interviews do. Mailed questionnaires require only 4 to 6 weeks, whereas obtaining the same data by personal interviews would likely take

---

RESEARCH IN PRACTICE 7.1 Behavior and Social Environment: Surveys as an Evidence-Based Foundation for Practice Delivery

Paul is a social worker with a master's degree. He is the youth development associate for a non-profit organization (GLCYD) whose mission is to provide various supports to other nonprofits that deliver services to youth. The goal of GLCYD is to increase the effectiveness of these other nonprofits through technical support and action-oriented research. One way GLCYD does this is through survey research.

Every 2 years, Paul oversees the administration of the Profiles of Student Life survey to 8th-, 10th-, and 12th-grade students in 16 school districts within a two-county area. Created by the Search Institute, a professional research firm, Profiles of Student Life evaluates 40 study assets, attitudes, and behaviors deemed beneficial to academic performance and overall social life. The survey also assesses levels of drug and alcohol use and experiences with violence, sex, and other behaviors considered risky. The availability of research firms such as the Search Institute has made sophisticated survey research available to and affordable by even small human service agencies. These firms provide a whole range of services—from design of the survey instrument to analysis of the resulting data—that only the larger agencies would have in-house staff to conduct.

While many of the students who take the survey as 8th graders will also take it as 10th and 12th graders, Paul is careful not to refer to this as a panel study (see Chapter 4). "Students who take the survey in 8th grade are not exactly the same group as those who take it two years later in 10th grade and again in 12th grade two years after that," he explained. "Still, the vast majority are the same students and I believe that comparing data year to year can give us a real sense of trends within the counties," he continued (based on personal communication, September, 2011).

The surveys are administered by teachers, guidance counselors, and social workers in each of the schools. Paul trains them to administer the survey, which includes 160 profile questionnaire items and an additional 30 items developed specifically for students in these counties. These additional questions are referred to as the "side bar" portion of the survey and include items pertaining to nutrition and exercise, prescription drug use, Internet use and safety, and future career plans.

(continued)

Completed surveys are sent to the Search Institute where results are tabulated and compiled in a report. As Paul explains, "My job is to then interpret results and decide what information people would like to know and what data I would want people to know." GLCYD's clients, which include school districts, nonprofits, and other community organizations, often use survey results when writing grant proposals to fund practice interventions. One local nonprofit, for example, used the survey's results in a recent grant proposal to argue for additional resources to support after-school programs. Substance abuse treatment agencies have used the data to tailor services for youth as patterns in drug use—specifically types of drugs consumed—have shifted in recent years. A domestic violence shelter and services agency uses the data to understand trends in youth victimization and adjust services accordingly.

According to Paul, one of the greatest outcomes of the survey project is positive publicity for young people.

Many people in the area see young people as dangerous. Others think they're all using drugs or alcohol. Our data help us "kill the boogeyman." We can portray an accurate snapshot of young people if the public understands that not everyone is drinking or doing drugs. In fact, it is a small minority of students who are doing these things and an even smaller group who do them regularly.

Paul also explained that parents have used the data in setting limits for their adolescent children.

Parents like to be able to have numbers to show that the limits they set for their kids are not unreasonable. They feel better about this when they can show their kids that not everyone their age is going to all night parties or doing any number of risky behaviors.

a minimum of several months. Mailed questionnaires also save the expense of hiring interviewers, interviewer travel, and other costs.

Second, mailed questionnaires enable the researcher to collect data from a geographically dispersed sample. It costs no more to mail a questionnaire across the country than it does to mail a questionnaire across the city. Costs of interviewer travel, however, rise enormously as the distance increases, making interviews over wide geographic areas an expensive process.

Third, with questions of a personal or sensitive nature, mailed questionnaires may provide more accurate answers than interviews. People may be more likely to respond honestly to such questions when they are not face to face with a person who they perceive as possibly making judgments about them. In practice, researchers may use a combination of questionnaires and interviews to address

this problem. Written questions, or computer-assisted self-interviewing, has been proved to generate more accurate information (Davies & Morgan, 2005; Newman, DesJerlais, Turner, & Gribble, 2002).

Self-administered questionnaires can sometimes elicit responses about topics people may be uncomfortable talking face to face with a stranger about. For example, in a previous General Social Survey, self-administered questionnaires increased reporting of male-to-male sexual activity over standard interview procedures (Anderson & Stall, 2002).

Finally, mailed questionnaires and/or surveys administered through anonymous online channels eliminate the problem of interviewer bias, which occurs when interviewers influence a person's response to a question by what they say, their tone of voice, or their demeanor. Because no interviewer is present when the respondent fills out the questionnaire, an interviewer cannot bias the answers to a questionnaire in any particular direction (Cannell & Kahn, 1968).

Disadvantages. Despite their many advantages, mailed questionnaires have important limitations that may make them less desirable for some research efforts (Moser & Kalton, 1972). First, mailed questionnaires require a minimal degree of literacy, which some respondents may not possess. Substantial nonresponse is, of course, likely with such people. Nonresponse because of illiteracy, however, does not seriously bias the results of most general-population surveys. Self-administered questionnaires are more successful among people who are better educated, motivated to respond, and involved in issues and organizations. Often, however, some groups of interest to human service practitioners do not possess these characteristics. If the survey is aimed at a special population in which the researcher suspects lower-than-average literacy, personal interviews are a better choice.

Second, all the questions must be sufficiently easy to comprehend on the basis of printed instructions. Third, there is no opportunity to probe for more information or to evaluate the nonverbal behavior of the respondents. The answers they mark on the questionnaire are final. Fourth, the researcher has no assurance that the person who should answer the questionnaire is the one who actually does. Fifth, the researcher cannot consider responses to be independent, because the respondent can read through the entire questionnaire before completing it. Finally, all mailed questionnaires face the problem of nonresponse bias.

INTERVIEWS

During an interview, the investigator or an assistant reads the questions directly to the respondents and then records their answers. Interviews offer the investigator a degree of flexibility that is not available with questionnaires. One area of increased flexibility relates to the degree of structure built into an interview.

The Structure of Interviews

The element of *structure* in interviews refers to the degree of freedom that the interviewer has in conducting the interview and that respondents have in answering questions. We classify interviews in terms of three levels of structure: (1) *unstandardized*, (2) *nonschedule-standardized*, and (3) *schedule-standardized*.

The *unstandardized interview* has the least structure. All the interviewer typically has for guidance is a general topic area, as illustrated in Exhibit 7.2. By developing their own questions and probes as the interview progresses, the interviewer explores the topic with the respondent. The approach is called "unstandardized" because each interviewer asks different questions and obtains different information from each respondent. There is heavy reliance on the skills of the interviewer to ask good questions and to keep the interview going; this can only be done if experienced interviewers are available. This unstructured approach makes unstandardized interviewing especially appropriate for exploratory research. In Exhibit 7.2, for example, only the general topic of coping behaviors of people experiencing homelessness guides the interviewer. The example also illustrates the suitability of this style of interviewing for exploratory research, where the interviewer is directed to search for as many types of coping behaviors as can be found.

Nonschedule-standardized interviews add more structure, with a narrower topic and specific questions asked of all respondents. The interview, however, remains fairly conversational; the interviewer is free to probe, to rephrase questions, or to ask the questions in whatever order best fits that particular interview. Note in Exhibit 7.2 that specific questions are of the open-ended type, allowing the respondent full freedom of expression. As in the case of the unstandardized form, success with this type of interview requires an experienced interviewer.

The *schedule-standardized interview* is the most structured type. An **interview schedule** contains specific instructions for the interviewer, specific questions to be asked in a fixed order, and transition phrases for the interviewer to use. Sometimes, the schedule also contains acceptable rephrasings

EXHIBIT 7.2 Examples of Various Interviewer Structures

The Unstandardized Interview

Interviewer Instructions: Identify coping behaviors used by homeless respondents. Coping behaviors refer to all methods of securing food, shelter, and clothing, including: reliance on family and friends, social service use, and self-help (e.g., camping, hunting, foraging, earning money through work or other means, etc.). Look for all of these and possibly others.

The Nonscheduled-Standardized Interview

Interviewer Instructions: Your task is to identify coping behaviors among homeless respondents. We are interested in behaviors and strategies that allow them access to food, shelter, and clothing. We would like to focus on several types of coping behaviors (shown in the following list); however, the initial question is broad and open-ended. This is designed to help you build a rapport with the interviewee and to help show your nonjudgmental attitude toward the homeless and your understanding of the day-to-day struggles associated with meeting basic needs.

1. Many people have described multiple challenges they have faced in surviving day-to-day while homeless. What sorts of challenges do you face? (Possible probes: What is your most pressing challenge right now? What, if anything, has been helpful in helping you address this issue?)
2. Let's focus on shelter.
   a. Do you receive shelter assistance from any social service agencies (e.g., shelter programs, temporary housing vouchers (including hotel coupons), transitional housing program assistance?
   b. Do you ever get shelter assistance from family members or friends (e.g., a place to live or at least sleep)?
   c. How else do you find a place to sleep? (Possible probes: Do you camp? Do you sleep outdoors? Do you sleep in cars? Do you ever sleep in abandoned buildings?)
3. Let's focus on food.
   a. Do you receive food assistance from any social service agencies (e.g., food stamps, meals at soup kitchens, food baskets or other donated foods from food pantries)?
   b. Do you ever get food assistance from family members or friends (e.g., meals, a place to prepare and/or store food)?
   c. How else do you get food? (Possible probes: Do you purchase food at stores? Where do you store food? How do you prepare it?)
4. Let's focus on clothing.
   a. Do you receive clothing assistance from any social service agencies (e.g., free clothing or shoes, discounted clothing)?
   b. Do you ever get clothing assistance from family members or friends (e.g., hand-me-downs, a place to store clothing)?
   c. How else do you get clothing? (Possible probes: Do you purchase clothing at stores? Where do you store clothing?)

The Schedule Standardized Interview

Interviewer explanation to the homeless respondent: We are interested in learning about the ways that homeless adults survive in rural areas. We want to understand how people access food, shelter, clothing, and other basic necessities while homeless. We are especially interested in learning about any help received from family, friends, and use of social services. In addition, we are interested in other strategies for surviving while homeless, including: living outdoors, cooking without a stove, and staying warm when it is cold outside. We have a checklist here of some of the possible ways that people access shelter while homeless. Think about the last month you were homeless and put a check to show how often you have accessed shelter using the tactic listed on each row. If you have never accessed shelter in any one of these ways then put the check in the column where it says "never."

(continued)

EXHIBIT 7.2 Examples of Various Interviewer Structures (*continued*)

(Hand the interviewee the first card dealing with shelter while saying "If you don't understand anything listed on the card, let me know and we'll talk about it." When the respondent completes this card, hand him or her the second card, saying, "Here is a list of ways that homeless adults might access food. Do the same thing with the list.")

Method	Never	Only Once	More Than Once	Many Times
Stayed with a family member				
Stayed with a friend				
Stayed in a shelter				
Slept outdoors (including in a tent)				
Slept in a car				
Slept in an abandoned building or another building without permission.				
Other shelter arrangements (please identify):				

for questions and a selection of stock probes. Schedule-standardized interviews are fairly rigid, with neither interviewer nor respondent allowed to depart from the structure of the schedule. Although some questions may be open-ended, most are closed-ended. In fact, some schedule-standardized interviews are quite similar to a questionnaire, except that the interviewer asks the questions rather than having the respondent read them. In Exhibit 7.2, note the use of cards with response alternatives handed to the respondent. This is a popular way of supplying respondents with a complex set of closed-ended alternatives. Note also the precise directions for the interviewer as well as verbatim phrases to read to the respondent. Relatively untrained, part-time interviewers can conduct schedule-standardized interviews, because the schedule contains nearly everything they need to say. This makes schedule-standardized interviews the preferred choice for studies with large sample sizes and many interviewers. The structure of these interviews also ensures that all respondents receive the same questions in the same order. This heightens reliability and makes schedule-standardized interviews popular for rigorous hypothesis

testing. Research in Practice 7.2 explores some further advantages of having more or less structure in an interview.

Contacting Respondents

As with researchers who mail questionnaires, those who rely on interviewers face the problem of contacting respondents and eliciting their cooperation. Many interviews are conducted in the homes of the respondents; locating and traveling to respondents' homes are two of the more troublesome—and costly—aspects of interviewing. It has been estimated that as much as 40% of a typical interviewer's time is spent traveling (Wagner & Olson, 2018; Sudman, 1965). Because so much time and cost are involved, and because researchers desire high response rates, they direct substantial efforts at minimizing the rate of refusal. The first contact of prospective respondents has a substantial impact on the refusal rate.

Two approaches to contacting respondents that might appear logical to the neophyte researcher have, in fact, an effect opposite of that desired. It might seem that *telephoning* to set up an

RESEARCH IN PRACTICE 7.2 Assessment of Client Functioning: Merging Quantitative and Qualitative Measures

That survey research is necessarily quantitative in nature probably is a common misconception. Virtually every edition of the evening news presents the results from one or more surveys, indicating that a certain percentage of respondents hold a given opinion or plan to vote for a particular candidate or offers other information that is basically quantitative or reduced to numbers. However, survey research is not limited to quantitative analysis. In fact, as we note in the discussion of Exhibit 7.2, interviews run the gamut from totally quantitative in the highly structured type to fully qualitative in the least structured variety—as well as any combination in between. Some researchers combine both quantitative and qualitative measures in individual studies to obtain the benefits of each approach.

Two studies of families experiencing homelessness headed by female researchers illustrate such a merging of interview styles. Thrasher and Mowbray (1995) interviewed 15 families from three homeless shelters, focusing primarily on the experiences of the mothers and their efforts to take care of their children. Timberlake (1994) based her study on interviews with 200 unhoused families not living in shelters and focused predominantly on the experiences of the children. In both studies, the researchers used structured interview questions to provide quantitative demographic information about the families experiencing homelessness, such as their race/ethnicity, length of homelessness, and employment status.

As important as this quantitative information might be, the researchers in both studies wanted to get at the more personal meaning of—and feelings about—being homeless. For this, they turned to the unstructured parts of the interviews (sometimes called ethnographic interviews), which were designed to get the subjects to tell their stories in their own words. The goal of both studies was to assess the needs of the families either to develop new programs to assist them or to modify existing programs to better fit their needs. The researchers felt that the best way to accomplish this goal was to get the story of being homeless, in as pure a form as possible, from the people who lived it, and without any distortion by the researchers' preconceived notions. The open-ended questions that Timberlake asked the children experiencing homelessness illustrate this unstructured approach: "Tell me about not having a place to live." "What is it like?" "What do you do?" "How do you feel?" "How do you handle being homeless?" "Are there things that you do or say?" (1994, pp. 9–20) The questions that Thrasher and Mowbray asked the mothers were similar. Both studies used probes as needed to elicit greater response and to clarify vague responses.

An example from Thrasher and Mowbray illustrates how responses to open-ended questions provide insight into what the respondent is experiencing. Those researchers found that a common experience of the women in the shelters was that, before coming to the shelter, they had bounced around among friends and relatives, experiencing a series of short-term and unstable living arrangements. The researchers present the following quote from 19-year-old "Nancy":

I went from friend to friend before going back to my mother and her boyfriend. And all my friends they live with their parents, and so you know, I could only stay like a night, maybe two nights before I had to leave. So, the only thing I could do was to come here to the shelter and so that's what I did. After all, there is only so many friends. I went to live once with my grandmother for a week who lives in a senior citizens' high rise. But they don't allow anyone to stay there longer than a week as a visitor. So, I had to move on. I finally went

(continued)

to my social worker and told her I don't have any place to stay. She put me in a motel first because there was no opening in the shelter. Then I came here. (1995, pp. 93–101)

As this example illustrates, hearing the experiences of people experiencing homelessness in their own words gives researchers greater insights into the experience. In cases like this, there are no substitutes for collecting meaningful data.

In part because of her much larger sample, Timberlake did not tape-record her interviews and so made no verbatim transcripts. Instead, she took field notes that summarized the responses of the children experiencing homelessness. This resulted in a different approach to analysis, because she did not have the long narratives that Thrasher and Mowbray had. Instead, she had a large number of summarized statements from her notes. She ended up doing a more quantitative analysis by categorizing the respondents' statements into more abstract categories. Timberlake found that the responses clustered around three themes: separation/loss, caretaking/nurturance, and security/protection. Within each theme were statements along two dimensions, which Timberlake refers to as "deprivation" and "restoration," respectively—the negative statements about what is bad about being homeless, and the positive statements about what the children have and how they cope. So, children's statements such as "we got no food" and "Daddy left us" were categorized as reflecting deprivation related to caretaking/nurturance. "Mama stays with us" and "I still got my clothes" were seen to reflect restoration related to separation/loss. Timberlake tabulated the number of each kind of statement. It seems rather indicative of the devastation of homelessness on the children that Timberlake found approximately three times as many deprivation statements as she did restoration statements. It is important to note that these categories and themes were not used by the respondents themselves but were created by Timberlake in an effort to extract some abstract or theoretical meaning from the narratives.

Neither of these studies used an interview format that would be suitable for interviewing a large, randomly selected sample of people experiencing homelessness with the purpose of estimating the demographic characteristics of the entire homeless population. Imagine trying to organize and summarize data from several thousand interviews like those conducted by Thrasher and Mowbray! To reasonably accomplish such a population estimate, a schedule-standardized interview format, producing quantitative data, is far more appropriate. If the goal of the research project is to gain an understanding of the personal experiences and reactions to being homeless, however, as in the two studies just discussed, then presenting results in the respondents' own words is more effective. However, if researchers wanted to design a schedule-standardized survey project to do a population description of the unhoused, studies such as the two discussed here would be invaluable for determining what concepts to measure and for developing the quantitative indicators that such a study would demand.

These two studies illustrate that both qualitative and quantitative approaches are essential to social research. Which approach is most appropriate in a given situation depends on the particular goals of the research; in some cases, a blend of both quantitative and qualitative approaches in the same project obtains the desired results.

appointment for the interview is a good idea. In reality, telephoning greatly increases the rate of refusal. In one experiment, for example, the part of the sample that was telephoned had nearly *triple* the rate of refusal of those who were contacted in person (Brunner & Carroll, 1967). Apparently, it is much easier to refuse over the relatively impersonal medium of the telephone than in a face-to-face encounter with an interviewer. *Sending people a letter* asking them to participate in an interview has much the same effect (Cartwright & Tucker, 1967). The letter seems to give people sufficient time before the interviewer arrives to develop reasons why they do not want to cooperate. Those first contacted in person, on the other hand, have only those excuses they can muster on the spur of the moment. Clearly, then, interviewers obtain the lowest refusal rates by contacting interviewees in person.

Additional factors also can affect the refusal rate (Gorden, 1987). For example, information regarding the research project should blanket the total survey population through the news media to demonstrate general community acceptance of the project. With a few differences, information provided to the media should contain essentially the same information as provided in a cover letter for a mailed questionnaire (see Table 7.2). Pictures of the interviewers and mention of any equipment they carry, such as laptop computers or video or audio recording devices, should also be included. This information assists people in identifying interviewers and reduces possible confusion of interviewers with salespeople or solicitors. In fact, it is a good idea to equip the interviewers with identification badges or something else that is easily recognizable so that they are not mistaken for others who go door to door. When the interviewers go into the field, they should take along copies or have electronic access to news coverage as well. Then, if they encounter a respondent who has not seen the media coverage, they can show newspaper clippings or video footage during the initial contact.

The timing of the initial contact also affects the refusal rate. It is preferable to contact interviewees at a time that is convenient for them to complete the interview without the need for a second call. Depending on the nature of the sample, predicting availability may be fairly easy or virtually impossible. For example, if interviewers can obtain the information that is required from any household member, then almost any reasonable time of day will do. On the other hand, if the interviewer must contact specific individuals, then timing becomes more critical. If we must interview the breadwinner in a household, for example, then we probably should make the contacts at night or on weekends (unless knowledge of the person's occupation suggests a different time of greater availability).

Whatever time the interviewer makes the initial contact, however, it still may not be convenient for the respondent, especially if the interview is lengthy. If the respondent is pressed for time, use the initial contact to establish rapport, and set another time for the interview. Even though callbacks are costly, this is certainly preferable to the rushed interview that results in inferior data.

When the interviewer and potential respondent first meet, the interviewer should give an introduction that includes most or all of the information listed in Table 7.2: basic information about the survey, the approximate length of the interview, the sponsor of the research, and so on. After the introduction, the interviewer should be prepared to elaborate on any points the interviewee questions. To avoid biasing responses, however, the interviewer must exercise care when discussing the purpose of the survey.

Conducting an Interview

A large-scale survey with an adequate budget often turns to private research agencies to train interviewers and conduct interviews. Often, however, smaller research projects cannot afford this and must train and coordinate their own team of interviewers, possibly with the researchers themselves doing some of the interviewing. It is important, therefore, to know how to conduct an interview properly.

The Interview as a Social Relationship. The interview is a social relationship designed to exchange information between the respondent and the interviewer. The quantity and quality of information exchanged depend on how astute and creative the interviewer is at understanding and managing that relationship (Fowler & Mangione, 1990; Holstein & Gubrium, 2003). Human service workers generally are knowledgeable regarding the properties and processes of social interaction; in fact, much human service practice is founded on the establishment of social relationships with clients. A few elements of the research interview, however, are worth emphasizing, because they have direct implications for conducting interviews.

A research interview is a secondary relationship in which the interviewer has a practical, utilitarian goal. It is easy, especially for an inexperienced interviewer, to be drawn into a more casual or personal interchange with the respondent. Especially with a friendly, outgoing respondent, the conversation might drift off to topics like sports, politics, or children. That, however, is not the purpose of the interview. The goal is not to make friends or to give the respondent a sympathetic ear but, rather, to collect complete and unbiased data following the interview schedule.

We all recognize the powerful impact that first impressions have on perceptions. This is especially true during interview situations, in which the interviewer and the respondent are likely to be total strangers. The first impressions that affect a respondent are the physical and social characteristics of the interviewer. So, we need to take considerable care to ensure that the first contact enhances the likelihood of the respondent's cooperation (Warwick & Lininger, 1975). Most research suggests that interviewers are more successful if they have social characteristics similar to those of their respondents. Thus, characteristics such as socioeconomic status, age, gender, sex, race, and ethnicity might influence the success of the interview, especially if the subject matter of the interview relates to one of these topics. In addition, the personal demeanor of the interviewer plays an important role; interviewers should be neat, clean, and businesslike but friendly.

After exchanging initial pleasantries, the interviewer should begin the interview. The respondent may be a bit apprehensive during the initial stages of an interview. In recognition of this, the interview should begin with fairly simple, nonthreatening questions. A schedule, if used, should begin with these kinds of questions. The demographic questions, which are reserved until the later stages of a mailed questionnaire, are good to begin an interview. The familiarity of respondents with this information makes these questions nonthreatening and a good means of reducing tension in the respondent.

Probes. If an interview schedule is used, then the interview progresses in accordance with it.

As needed, the interviewer uses **probes**, or follow-up questions, intended to elicit clearer and more complete responses. In some cases, the interview schedule contains suggestions for probes. In less-structured interviews, however, interviewers must develop and use their own probes. These probes can take the form of a pause in conversation that encourages the respondent to elaborate or an explicit request to clarify or elaborate on something. A major concern with any probe is that it not bias the respondent's answer by suggesting the answer (Bell, Fahmy, & Gordon, 2016; Fowler & Mangione, 1990).

Recording Responses. A central task of interviewers, of course, is to record the responses of respondents. The four most common ways are classifying responses into predetermined categories, summarizing key points, taking verbatim notes (by handwriting or with a laptop computer), or making an audio or video recording of the interview.

Recording responses generally is easiest when we use an interview schedule. Because closed-ended questions are typical of such schedules, we can simply classify responses into the predetermined alternatives. This simplicity of recording is another factor making schedule-standardized interviews suitable for use with relatively untrained interviewers, because no special recording skills are required.

With nonschedule-standardized interviewing, the questions are likely to be open-ended and the responses longer. Often, all we need to record are the key points the respondent makes. The interviewer condenses and summarizes what the respondent says. This requires an experienced interviewer who is familiar with the research questions who can accurately identify what to record and then do so without injecting his or her own interpretation, which would bias the summary.

Sometimes, we may want to record everything the respondent says verbatim to avoid the possible biasing effect of summarizing responses. If the anticipated responses are reasonably short, then competent interviewers can take verbatim notes. Special skills, such as shorthand, may be necessary. If the responses are lengthy, then verbatim note taking can cause difficulties, such as leading the interviewer to fail to monitor the respondent or to be unprepared to probe when necessary. It also can damage rapport by making it appear that the interviewer is ignoring the respondent. Making audio or video recordings of the interviews can eliminate problems such as this but also can increase the costs substantially, both for the equipment and for later transcription of the materials (Gorden, 1987; Markle, Rich, & West, 2011). Such recordings, however, also provide the most accurate account of the interview.

The fear some researchers have that audio recorders increase the refusal rate appears to be unwarranted (Gorden, 1987). If the recorder is explained as a routine procedure that aids in capturing complete and accurate responses, then only few respondents object.

Controlling Interviewers. Once interviewers go into the field, the quality of the resulting data depends heavily on them. It is a naive researcher, indeed, who assumes that, without supervision, they will all do their job properly, especially when part-time interviewers who have little commitment to the research project are used. Proper supervision begins during interviewer training by stressing the importance of contacting the right respondents and meticulously following established procedures.

Although sloppy, careless work is one concern, a more serious issue is **interviewer falsification**, or the intentional departure from the designed interviewer instructions, unreported by the interviewer, which can result in the contamination of data (American Association for Public Opinion Research Standards Committee [AAPOR], 2003). A dramatic illustration of this was discovered in a National Institutes of Health (NIH) survey of AIDS and other sexually transmitted diseases (Marshall, 2000). Eleven months into the study, a data-collection manager was troubled by the apparent overproductivity of one interviewer. A closer look revealed that, although the worker was submitting completed interviews, some were clearly falsified. For example, the address of one interview site turned out to be an abandoned house. The worker was dismissed, and others came under suspicion.

It took months to root out what was referred to as an "epidemic of falsification" on this research project. A cessation of random quality checks was identified as a major contributing factor to the problem.

Falsified data is believed to be rare, but survey organizations take this problem seriously and follow established procedures to address it. Factors that contribute to falsification include pressure on interviewers to obtain very high response rates and the use of long, complicated questionnaires that may frustrate both interviewer and respondent. The problem can be prevented by careful recruitment, screening, and training of interviewers; by recognizing incentives for falsification created by work quotas and pay structures; and by monitoring and verifying interviewer work (Biemer et al., 2016; Bushery, Reichert, Albright, & Rossiter, 1999).

Diversity and the Interview Relationship

Many respondents in surveys have different characteristics than those of the interviewers. Does it make a difference in terms of the quantity or quality of data collected? It appears that it does. In survey research, three elements interact to affect the quality of the data collected: (1) the characteristics of the interviewer, (2) the characteristics of the respondent, and (3) the content of the survey instrument. Researchers should carefully consider the interrelationships among these elements to ensure that the least amount of bias enters the data-collection process.

As we have emphasized, an interview is a social relationship in which the interviewer and the respondent have cultural and subcultural expectations for appropriate behavior. Practitioner Profile 7.1 illustrates an example of how an interviewer can ask culturally appropriate questions to their research. One set of expectations that comes into play is the social desirability of respondents' answers to questions. Substantial research documents a tendency for people to choose more desirable or socially acceptable answers to questions in surveys (DeMaio, 1984; Holstein & Gubrium, 2003; Tourangeau & Yan, 2007), in part from the

PRACTITIONER PROFILE 7.1 Leo Kattari, Consultant for LGBTQ Inclusivity Training, Denver, Colorado

Leo played an important role in Colorado's Youth Risk Behavior Survey, particularly making sure it includes the perspective of LGBTQ youth. He also uses data from Healthy Kids Colorado looking at youth and healthcare to educate community members and agencies on how to interpret data. He states, "Providing information on what statistical significance means is important so that providers can make informed decisions based on research findings" (L. Kattari, personal communication, June 8, 2018).

Another area Leo has worked with is LGBTQ health and providing data collection for One Colorado, which explores data for transgender healthcare. There is little to no research done in this area. He states, "In 2014 there was basically nothing that looked at transgender health and needs." Transgender individuals are an underrepresented group in healthcare research and service provision. Leo helped develop surveys to explore what transgender individuals were experiencing around health risks compared to the general population. He and his team modeled this survey after the Behavioral Risk Factor Surveillance System (an adult risk factor assessment survey). However, they added specific questions for transgender people so that it was not only looking at risk, but also the larger overall experience. Leo posits, "We asked questions around inclusivity of healthcare providers for transgender people." Online surveys, hard copy surveys, and social media outlets were utilized to recruit and gain access to transgender populations.

After the data were collected, they made a report which compared transgender populations to the general population of the state and made recommendations based on these results. Although service providers felt they provided good care to transgender individuals, results indicate that transgender individuals feel they do not receive inclusive treatment from their healthcare providers. This information not only helped service providers understand that they can be more inclusive, but also provided data for transgender advocates to push for inclusive changes within healthcare. Findings from this survey also revealed health disparities between transgender populations and the general population. Leo states, "suicide rates and negative mental health rates were higher for this population." Finally, transgender individuals who have healthcare providers who offer inclusive treatment have better health outcomes. This survey provided an opportunity for transgender populations who are invisible and more vulnerable in our healthcare system to have their voices heard.

desire to appear sensible, reasonable, and pleasant to the interviewer. In all interpersonal contacts, including an interview relationship, people typically prefer to please someone rather than to offend or alienate. For cases in which the interviewer and the respondent are from different racial, ethnic, or sexual orientation groups, respondents tend to give answers that they perceive to be more desirable—or, at least, less offensive—to the interviewer; this is especially true when the questions are related to race, ethnicity, or sexual orientation. A second set of expectations that comes into play and affects responses during interviews is the social distance between the interviewer and the respondent, or how much they differ from each other on important social dimensions, such as age or marginalized status. Generally, the less social distance between people, the more freely, openly, and honestly they will talk. Race, sexual orientation, and ethnic group differences often indicate a degree of social distance.

The impact of cross-race interviewing has been studied extensively with African American and White respondents (Anderson, Silver, &

Abramson, 1988; Bachman & O'Malley, 1984; Dailey & Claus, 2001; Gibson & Abrams, 2003). African American respondents, for example, express more warmth and closeness for Whites when interviewed by a White person and are less likely to express dissatisfaction or resentment over discrimination or inequities against African Americans. White respondents tend to express more pro-Black attitudes when the interviewer is African American. This race-of-interviewer effect can be quite large, and it occurs fairly consistently. Some research concludes that it plays a role mostly when the questions involve race or other sensitive topics, but recent research suggests that its effect is more pervasive, affecting people's responses to many questions on a survey, not just the racial or sensitive questions (Davis, 1997; Davis & Silver, 2003).

Issues with respect to differences between researchers and interviewees are not limited to African Americans and Whites. Many recent studies have revealed that differences with respect to ethnicity, cultural identity, nation of origin, socioeconomic status, and age impact researchers' access to many types of populations and their abilities to gain participants' trust and discuss a variety of issues (Arean, Alvidrez, Nery, Estes, & Linkins, 2003; Becerra & de Anda, 1999; Clark, 2006; Hyman, 1954; Manderson, Bennett, & Andajani-Sutjahjo, 2006).

Innes (2009), for example, found that being a Plains Cree tribal member gave him unique access to Native American research subjects, helped him develop trust with other tribal members, and also increased participants' interest in his research. Alternatively, some researchers have argued that being "outsiders" and acknowledging lack of cultural knowledge within an interview can elicit more detailed responses from questions, minimize respondents' fears of researchers, allow researchers to ask sensitive questions that insiders may be expected to avoid, and help maintain critical distance between the researcher and the subject matter (Tinker & Armstrong, 2008).

Many researchers have argued that gender dynamics are always present within research interviews (e.g., Gibson & Abrams, 2003; Pini, 2005). Pini explains that when analyzing interviews, it is critical to consider not only the genders of the interviewer and respondent, but also their age, topics being discussed, and physical settings. In her study of Australian cane growers, for example, she found that when young, female graduate students interviewed male farmers in very rural areas where there are often few women, the interviews tended to portray the men in ways that exaggerated their masculinity. Another study (Wilson, Brown, Mejia, & Lavori, 2002) found that men were less likely to report sex with strangers when interviewed by women than when interviewed by men. The study also found that women were less likely to report oral sex to older interviewers.

Some researchers recommend routinely matching interviewer and respondent for race, ethnicity, or gender in interviews on racial or sensitive topics, and this generally is sound advice. Sometimes, however, a little more thought is called for. The problem is that we are not always sure in which direction bias might occur. If White respondents give different answers to White as opposed to Black interviewers, which of their answers most accurately reflect their attitudes? For the most part, we are not sure. We generally assume that same-race interviewers gather more accurate data (Caldwell, Couper, Davis, Janz, & Resnicow, 2010; Fowler & Mangione, 1990). A more conservative assumption, however, is that the truth falls somewhere between the data that the two interviewers of different race collect.

When people speak a language different from that of the dominant group, conducting the interview in the dominant group's language can affect the quality of data collected (Abma, Deeg, Jonsson, & Van Ness, 2010; Marin & VanOss Marin, 1991). For example, a study of Native American children in Canada found that these children expressed a strong White bias in racial preferences when the study was conducted in English; however, this bias declined significantly when interviewers used the children's native Ojibwa language (Annis & Corenblum, 1986). This impact of language should not be surprising, considering that language is not just a mechanism for communication but also reflects cultural values, norms, and a way of life. So, when interviewing groups in which a language other than English is widely used, it is appropriate to consider conducting the interviews in that other language.

An Assessment of Interviews

Advantages. Personal interviews have several advantages compared with other data-collection techniques. First, interviews can help *motivate* respondents to give more accurate and complete information. Respondents have little motivation to be accurate or complete when responding to a mailed questionnaire; they can hurry through it if they want to. The control that an interviewer affords, however, encourages better responses, which is especially important as the information sought becomes more complex.

Second, interviewing offers an opportunity to *explain* questions that respondents may not otherwise understand. Again, if the information being sought is complex, then this can be of great importance, and interviews virtually eliminate the literacy problem that may accompany mailed questionnaires. Even lack of facility in English can be handled with multilingual interviewers. (When we conducted a needs assessment survey in some rural parts of Michigan's Upper Peninsula several years ago, we employed one interviewer who was fluent in Finnish, because a number of people in the area spoke Finnish but little or no English.)

Third, the presence of an interviewer allows *control* over factors that are uncontrollable with mailed questionnaires. For example, the interviewer can ensure not only that the proper person responds to the questions, but also that he or she does so in sequence. Furthermore, the interviewer can arrange to conduct the interview so that the respondent does not consult with and is not influenced by other people before responding.

Fourth, interviewing is a more *flexible* form of data collection than questionnaires. The style of interviewing can be tailored to the needs of the study. A free, conversational style, with much probing, can be adopted in an exploratory study. In a more developed study, a highly structured approach can be used. This flexibility makes interviewing suitable for a far broader range of research situations compared with mailed questionnaires.

Finally, the interviewer can add *observational information* to the responses. What was the respondent's attitude toward the interview? Was he or she cooperative? Indifferent? Hostile? Did the respondent appear to fabricate answers? Did he or she react emotionally to some questions? This additional information helps us better evaluate the responses, especially when the subject matter is highly personal or controversial (Gorden, 1987).

Disadvantages. Some disadvantages associated with personal interviews may lead the researcher to choose another data-collection technique. The first disadvantage is cost. Researchers must hire, train, and equip interviewers and also pay for their travel. All these expenses are costly.

The second limitation is time. Traveling to respondents' homes requires a lot of time and limits each interviewer to only a few interviews each day. In addition, to contact particular individuals, an interviewer may require several time-consuming call-backs. Project start-up operations, such as developing questions, designing schedules, and training interviewers, also require considerable time.

A third limitation of interviews is the problem of interviewer bias. Especially in unstructured interviews, the interviewers may misinterpret or misrecord something because of his or her personal feelings about the topic. Furthermore, just as the interviewer's characteristics affect the respondent, so the characteristics of the respondent similarly affect the interviewer. Gender, sex, age, race, social class, and a host of other factors may subtly shape the way in which the interviewer asks questions and interprets the respondent's answers.

A fourth limitation of interviews, especially less structured interviews, is the possibility of significant but unnoticed variation in wording either from one interview to the next or from one interviewer to the next. We know that variations in wording can produce variations in response, and the more freedom that interviewers have in this regard, the more of a problem this is. Wording variation can affect both reliability and validity (see Chapter 5).

TELEPHONE SURVEYS

Face-to-face interviews tend to be a considerably more expensive means of gathering data than either mailed questionnaires or telephone surveys (Rea & Parker, 2005). Mail or telephone surveys require no travel time, fewer interviewers, and fewer supervisory personnel. Although telephone charges are higher in telephone surveys, these costs are far outweighed by other savings. The cost advantages of the less-expensive types of surveys make feasible much research that otherwise would be prohibitively expensive.

The speed with which a telephone survey can be completed also makes it preferable at times. If we want people's reactions to a particular event, for example, or repeated measures of public opinion, which can change rapidly, then the speed of telephone surveys makes them preferable in these circumstances.

Certain areas of the country and many major cities contain substantial numbers of non-English-speaking people. Mail questionnaires and personal interviews that seek to capture non-English-speaking respondents should be designed to accommodate the population. Because of this, it is important to know what language respondents speak ahead of time. We can adapt surveys for non-English-speaking people fairly easily, with telephone surveys. All we need are a few multilingual interviewers. (Spanish speakers account for the vast majority of non-English-speaking people in the United States.) If an interviewer contacts a non-English-speaking respondent, then he or she can simply transfer that respondent to an interviewer who is conversant in the respondent's language. Although multilingual interviewers can be—and are—used in personal interviews, this process is far less efficient, probably involving at least one callback to arrange for an interviewer with the needed language facility. A final advantage of telephone interviews is that supervision is much easier. The problem of interviewer falsification is eliminated, because supervisors can monitor the interviews at any time. This makes it easy to ensure that specified procedures are followed and any problems that might arise are quickly discovered and corrected.

Despite these considerable advantages, telephone surveys have several limitations that may make the method unsuitable for many research purposes. First, telephone surveys must be quite short in duration. Normally, the maximum length is about 20 min, and most are even shorter. This is in sharp contrast to personal interviews, which can last for an hour or longer. The time limitation obviously restricts the volume of information that interviewers can obtain and the depth to which they can explore issues. Telephone surveys work best when the information desired is fairly simple and the questions are uncomplicated.

A second limitation stems from the fact that telephone communication is only voice to voice. Lack of visual contact eliminates several desirable characteristics of personal interviews. The interviewer cannot supplement responses with observational information, for example, and it is harder for an interviewer to probe effectively without seeing the respondent. Furthermore, a phone interview precludes the use of cards with response alternatives or other visual stimuli. The inability to present complex sets of response alternatives in this format can make it difficult to ask some questions that are important.

Finally, as we noted in Chapter 6, surveys based on samples drawn from listings of telephone numbers may have considerable noncoverage, because some people do not have telephones at all, others have unlisted numbers, and still others have cell phones, which may have unlisted numbers and are not linked to specific geographic locations, such as a household. In addition, some people today have both a cell phone (sometimes more than one) and a landline; this means that, even with random-digit dialing, people with multiple phones have a greater likelihood of being selected for a sample than people with only one phone (or no phone) do. Although modern telephone sampling techniques, such as random-digit dialing, eliminate some problems, sampling bias remains a potential problem when using telephone numbers as a sampling frame. Because some human service clients are heavily concentrated in the population groups that are more likely to be missed in a telephone sample, we should exercise special care when using a telephone survey.

Computer-mediated communications technologies now assist survey research through **computer-assisted interviewing**, or using computer technology to assist in designing and conducting questionnaires and interviews. One important form this takes is **computer-assisted telephone interviewing** (CATI), where an interview is conducted over the telephone: In CATI, the interviewer reads questions from a computer monitor instead of a clipboard and records responses directly into the computer via the keyboard instead of a paper form. Superficially, CATI replaces the paper-and-pencil format of interviewing with a monitor-and-keyboard arrangement, but the differences are much more significant. Some of the special techniques possible with CATI include personalizing the wording of questions based on answers to previous questions and automatic branching for contingency questions. These features speed up the interview and improve accuracy. CATI software enters the data from respondents directly into a data file for analysis. CATI programs help prevent errors from entering the data during the collection phase. For example, with a question that requires numerical data, such as "How old are you?" the program can require that only numerical characters be entered. Range checks also catch errors. Assuming one is interviewing adults, the age range might be set to 18 to 99 years. Any response outside that range would result in an error message or a request to recheck the entry.

ONLINE SURVEYS

The emergence of the Internet has led to the growth of surveys conducted online rather than in person, through the mail, or by telephone. "Internet surveys," or "Web surveys," sometimes are sent as email or an email attachment or are made available at a website. Online surveys are similar to other surveys in many respects, in that the basic data still involves people's answers to questions. The differences, however, are sufficiently important that they need to be discussed.

Online surveys have many advantages. Among the major advantages are their speed, low cost, and ability to reach respondents anywhere in the world (Couper, Kapteyn, Schonlau, & Van Soest, 2009; Fricker & Schonlau, 2002; Schonlau et al., 2004). Most studies find that compared with mailed or telephone surveys, online surveys can be done much less expensively and that the responses are returned much more quickly.

Another advantage of online surveys is the versatility and flexibility offered by the technology. The questionnaire text can be supplemented with a variety of visual and auditory elements, such as color, graphics, images (static and animated), and even sound (Conrad, Couper, & Tourangeau, 2007; Couper, Tourangeau, & Kenyon, 2004). (This is discussed in Chapter 13 as a measurement issue.) The technology also can provide randomized ordering of questions for each respondent, error checking, and automatic skip patterns so that respondents can move easily through the interview. In addition, the data can be entered directly into a database once the respondent submits it.

The anonymity and impersonal nature of online interaction also may have advantages in research. For example, we discuss in this chapter the problem of interviewer effects, that is, how interviewer characteristics, such as race or gender and behavior, may influence people's responses to questions. When answering questions online, there is no interviewer to produce such effects (Duffy, Smith, Terhanian, & Bremer, 2005). Similarly, the absence of an interviewer reduces the impact of social desirability, that is, respondents' concerns about how their responses appear to other people. Researchers may even find computer surveys to be a more ethical approach in terms of minimizing the harm associated with revealing sensitive data, such as child maltreatment (Black & Ponirakis, 2000; Bokström, Dahlberg, Fängström, & Sarkadi, 2016). It also provides a good way to contact and collect data from groups that are difficult to access in other ways, possibly because they are relatively rare in the population or because of their involvement in undesirable or deviant interests or activities (Duffy et al., 2005; Koch & Emrey, 2001). In fact, people seem to be more likely to admit their involvement in undesirable activities during online surveys compared with other types of surveys.

Online surveys also have their disadvantages, of course. Sampling and representativeness are especially problematic (Duffy et al., 2005; Kaplowitz, Hadlock, & Levine, 2004; Schonlau et al., 2004). One problem is that not everyone has access to or actually uses the Internet. A second problem is that, even among those with Internet access, not everyone chooses to respond to requests to fill out an online survey. Given these problems, some argue that online surveys should be considered to be convenience samples rather than probability samples, with all the limitations in statistical analysis and generalizability that this implies (see Chapter 6). The population of people who use the Internet tends to be skewed toward those who are affluent, well educated, young, and male. So, unless the research has a clearly defined population, all of whose members have access to the Internet, questions about the representativeness of online respondents are difficult to resolve. Even with a clearly defined population and sampling frame, nonresponse can significantly distort results. For example, an online survey of the faculty members at a university probably would involve a population where all members have Internet access; however, it may be the younger faculty or those from particular academic disciplines who are most likely to respond. Thus, researchers need to scrutinize the issues of response rate and representativeness, just as they do with other types of surveys. For needs assessment surveys, however, and some kinds of qualitative research where probability samples are not critical, researchers may find online surveys quite useful.

Strategies are being developed to deal with these problems of sampling and representativeness. One approach uses the random selection of telephone numbers to identify a probability sample of people who are representative of a particular population. These people are then contacted and asked to participate. Those who agree are supplied with Internet equipment and an Internet service connection (or they can use their own equipment). This panel of study members can then be repeatedly contacted by email and directed to a website to complete a survey.

Another difficulty with online surveys is formatting: Different computer systems can change formatting in unpredictable ways. A survey that looks fine on the designer's computer screen may become partially unintelligible when emailed to a respondent's computer. Or, a web browser may not support all the design features in some web page design software. Earlier in this chapter, we mentioned the importance of survey appearance in terms of achieving high response rates and gathering complete and valid responses. If respondents with various computers receive differently formatted surveys, this may influence their willingness to participate or their responses (and introduce error into the measurement).

FOCUS GROUPS

Research situations sometimes arise in which the standardization found in most surveys and interviews is not appropriate and researchers need more flexibility in the way they elicit responses to questions. One area in which this is likely to be true is exploratory research. Here, researchers cannot formulate questions into precise hypotheses, and the knowledge of some phenomena is too sketchy to allow precise measurement of variables. This is also true in research on personal and subjective experiences that are unlikely to be adequately tapped by asking the same structured questions of everyone.

In such research situations, the **focus group**, or **group depth interview**, is a flexible strategy for gathering data (Krueger & Casey, 2008; Morgan, 1996). As the name implies, this is an interview with a whole group of people at the same time. Focus groups originally were used as a preliminary step in the research process to generate quantitative hypotheses and to develop questionnaire items, and they are still used in this way. Survey researchers, for example, sometimes use focus groups as tools for developing questionnaires and interview schedules. Now, however, researchers also use focus groups in applied research as a strategy for collecting data in their own right, especially when the researchers are seeking people's subjective reactions and the many levels of meaning that are important to human behavior. Today, tens of millions of dollars are spent each year on focus groups in applied research, marketing research, and political campaigns. One example of this is a study of the barriers that women confront in obtaining medical care to detect and treat cervical cancer, a potentially fatal disease that is readily detected and treated if women obtain Pap smears on a regular basis and return for follow-up care when necessary. These researchers decided that a focus group "would allow free expression of thoughts and feelings about cancer and related issues" and would provide the most effective mechanism to probe women's motivations for not seeking appropriate medical care (Dignan et al., 1990, p. 370).

A focus group usually consists of at least one moderator and up to 10 respondents, and it lasts for up to 3 h. The moderator follows an interview guide that outlines the main topics of inquiry and the order in which they will be covered, and they may have a variety of props, such as audiovisual cues, to prompt discussion and elicit reactions. Researchers select focus group members on the basis of their usefulness in providing the data called for in the research. Researchers chose the women for the study on cervical cancer, for example, because, among other things, all had had some previous experience with cancer. Normally, focus group membership is not based on probability samples, which Chapter 6 points out as the most likely to be representative samples. This, therefore, can throw the generalizability of focus group results into question. In exploratory research, however, such generalizability is not as critically important as it is in other research. In addition, most focus group research enhances its representativeness and generalizability by collecting data from more than one focus group. The cervical cancer study, for example, involved four separate focus groups of 10 to 12 women each, and some research projects use 20 or more focus groups.

The moderator's job in a focus group is to initiate discussion and facilitate the flow of responses. Following an outline of topics to cover, the moderator asks questions, probes unclear areas, and pursues lines of inquiry that seem fruitful. A focus group, however, is not just 10 in-depth interviews. Rather, the moderator uses knowledge of group dynamics to elicit data that an interviewer might not have obtained during an in-depth interview. For example, a status structure emerges in all groups, including focus groups; some people

become leaders and others followers. The moderator uses this group dynamic by encouraging the emergence of leaders and then using them to elicit responses, reactions, or information from other group members. Group members often respond to other group members differently than they respond to the researcher/moderator. People in a focus group make side comments to one another—something obviously not possible in a one-person interview—and the moderator makes note of these comments, possibly encouraging group members to elaborate. In fact, in a well-run focus group, the members may interact among themselves as much as they do with the group moderator. In a standard interview, the stimulus for response is the interviewer's questions; in contrast, focus group interviews provide a second stimulus for people's responses, namely the group experience itself.

The moderator also directs the group discussion, usually from more general topics in the beginning to more specific issues toward the end (Krueger & Casey, 2008). For example, in the focus group study of cervical cancer, the moderators began with questions about general life concerns and the perceived value of health, and they ended with specific questions about cancer, cancer screening, and Pap smears. The general questions provided a foundation and a context, without which the women might not have been as willing—or as able—to provide useful answers to the more specific questions. Group moderators take great care in developing these sequences of questions. The moderator also observes the characteristics of the participants in the group to ensure effective participation by all members. For example, the moderator constrains a "rambler" who talks a lot but does not say much and encourages "shy ones" who tend to say little to express themselves. In short, moderating a focus group is a complex job that calls for both an understanding of group dynamics and skills in understanding and working with people.

During a focus group session, too much happens too fast to engage in any useful data analysis on the spot. The focus group produces the data, which are preserved on video recording devices for later analysis. During this analysis, the researcher makes field notes from the recordings and then prepares a report summarizing the findings and presenting conclusions and implications. Data from a focus group usually are presented in one of three forms (Krueger & Casey, 2008). In the *raw data format,* the researcher presents all the comments that group participants made about particular issues, thus providing the complete range of opinions the group expressed. The researcher offers little interpretation other than to clarify some nonverbal interaction or nuance of meaning that could be grasped only in context. The second format for presentation is the *descriptive approach,* in which the researchers summarize in narrative form the kinds of opinions expressed by the group, with some quotes from group members as illustrations. This calls for more summary on the part of the researcher, but it also enables him or her to cast the results in a way that best conveys the meaning communicated during the group session. The third format is the *interpretive model,* which expands on the descriptive approach by providing more interpretation. The researcher can provide his or her own interpretations of the group's mood, feelings, and reactions to the questions. This may include the moderator's impression of the group members' motivations and unexpressed desires. The raw data model is the quickest manner of reporting results, but the interpretive model provides the greatest depth of information from the group sessions. Of course, the interpretive approach, because it does involve interpretation, is more likely to contain some bias or error.

Focus groups have major advantages over more structured, single-person interviews: The focus groups are more flexible, cost less, and can provide quick results. In addition, focus groups use the interaction between people to stimulate ideas and to encourage group members to participate. In fact, when run properly, focus groups have high levels of participation and, thus, elicit reactions that interviewers might not have obtained in a one-on-one interview setting. Unfortunately, focus groups also have disadvantages: The results are less generalizable to a larger population, and the data are more difficult and subjective to analyze. Focus groups also are less likely than interviews to produce quantitative data; in fact, focus group data

may more closely resemble the field notes that are produced in field research, which we will discuss in Chapter 9.

PRACTICE AND RESEARCH INTERVIEWS COMPARED

The interview is undoubtedly the most commonly employed technique in human service practice. Therefore, it is natural for students in the human services to wonder how research interviewing compares with practice interviewing. The fundamental difference is the *purpose* of the interview. Practitioners conduct interviews to help a particular client, whereas researchers conduct interviews to gain knowledge about a particular problem or population. The practitioner seeks to understand the client as an individual and, often, uses the interview to effect change; the researcher uses the data collected on individuals to describe the characteristics of and variations in a population. To the practitioner, the individual client system is central. To the researcher, the respondent is merely the unit of analysis, and the characteristics and variability of the population are of primary concern.

The difference in purpose is the basis for the differences between practice and research interviewing. Whereas we select *respondents* to represent a population, we accept *clients* because they have individual needs that the agency serves. Research interviews typically are brief (often single encounters); practice relationships are often intensive, long-term relationships. Clients (or clients' needs) often determine the topic and focus of a practice interview, whereas the nature of the research project predetermines the content of the research interview. The ideal research interview presents each respondent with exactly the same stimulus to obtain validly comparable responses. The ideal practice interview provides the client with a unique situation that maximizes the potential to help that individual.

An emphasis on the differences between the two forms of interviewing, however, should not obscure their similarities. Both require that the interviewer make clear the general purpose of the interview. Both require keen observational skills and disciplined use of self according to the purpose of the interview. This last point is crucial to answering another question about interviewing: Do practitioners make good research interviewers? The answer depends on the nature of the particular interview task and on the interviewer's capacity to perform that task. Interviewers who display warmth, patience, compassion, tolerance, and sincerity best serve some situations; other situations require reserved and controlled interviewers who bring an atmosphere of objective, detached sensitivity to the interview (Kadushin & Kadushin, 1997). Some researchers have found that verbal reinforcement—both positive comments to complete responses and

negative feedback to inadequate responses—results in obtaining more complete information from respondents (Vinokur, Oksenberg, & Cannell, 1979). Although successful in terms of the amount of information gained, such techniques might be foreign to the style of interviewing that a practitioner uses. Thus, for the structured, highly controlled interview, a practitioner who is used to improvising questions and demonstrating willingness to help may be a poor choice as an interviewer. In situations requiring in-depth, unstructured exploratory interviews, however, that same practitioner's skills might be ideal. Again, the purpose of the interview and the nature of the task determine the compatibility of human service skills with the research interview.

REVIEW AND CRITICAL THINKING

Main Points

- Surveys are of two general types: (1) questionnaires completed directly by respondents, and (2) interviews with the questions read and the responses recorded by an interviewer.
- Closed-ended questions provide a fixed set of response alternatives from which respondents choose.
- Open-ended questions provide no response alternatives, leaving respondents complete freedom of expression.
- Once developed, survey instruments should be pretested for clearly understood and unbiased questions; after changes are made in the instrument, it should be pretested again.
- Questionnaires must provide clear directions, both to indicate what respondents should do and to guide them through the questionnaire.
- Researchers should order questions so that early questions maximize the response rate but do not affect the responses to later questions.
- Obtaining a high response rate (the percentage of surveys actually completed) is very important for representativeness in survey research.
- The cover letter, use of payments and follow-up letters, and length and appearance of the questionnaire are all central in efforts to maximize the response rate with the mailed questionnaire.
- Interviews are classified by their degree of structure as unstandardized, nonschedule-standardized, or schedule-standardized.
- Probes elicit clearer and more complete responses during interviews.
- Telephone surveys offer significant savings in terms of time and cost compared with interviews or mailed questionnaires and, in many cases, are a suitable alternative.

- Online surveys are fast and inexpensive compared to other surveys and permit flexible formatting and design, but they raise serious questions regarding sampling and representativeness.
- Focus groups rely on group dynamics to generate data that would not be discovered using a standard questionnaire or interview format.
- Websites are now widely available that will conduct surveys from beginning to end—from designing the survey instrument to the analysis of the data and the preparation of a report.

IMPORTANT TERMS FOR REVIEW

Closed-ended questions
Computer-assisted
 interviewing
Computer-assisted
 telephone interviewing
Contingency question
Cover letter

Filter question
Focus group
Group depth interview
Interview
Interview schedule
Interviewer falsification
Matrix question

Open-ended questions
Probes
Questionnaire
Response rate
Survey
Survey research

CRITICAL THINKING

The research techniques discussed in this chapter involve observations of what people say about the thoughts, feelings, or behaviors of themselves or others. This kind of research technique has advantages, but it also has drawbacks. Practitioners and policy makers, as well as people in their everyday lives, need to be cautious when confronted with information or conclusions based on similar data. The following are critical thinking questions raised at the beginning of the chapter and some ideas for how they relate to social work practice. Students are encouraged to develop their own answers to these questions.

Why is it important to understand how to develop questions for a survey? Open-ended and closed-ended questions require respondents to answer questions differently. Open-ended questions allow the participants the ability to write their own responses, which can be harder to code for analysis. Closed-ended questions have a fixed set of alternatives that respondents can choose from, which can lead to a more straightforward way of coding for analysis. However, both provide essential information that could be useful when analyzing data.

What are key considerations for developing a questionnaire and why is this important for social researchers? Questionnaires or surveys are a staple in social research for collecting information on participants. The design of these questionnaires is essential because respondents complete these without assistance. Therefore, the flow and design needs to be easy with simple direction and careful working and ordering of questions.

Explain how different types of research interviews affect the desired goals of a study. In social research, there are many different approaches to collecting information through interviews. These interviews follow a structure similar to a questionnaire, but the researcher is usually asking the question over the phone or in focus groups. This type of research is still quantitative even though the researcher is asking the questions, because he or she is recording the participant's responses in a survey.

EVALUATING COMPETENCY (FROM THE COUNCIL ON SOCIAL WORK EDUCATION [CSWE] 2015 EDUCATIONAL POLICY AND ACCREDITATION STANDARDS [EPAS])

Competency 1: Demonstrate Ethical and Professional Behavior

- Why is ethics so important when conducting research with human subjects?
- What ethical duties do social researchers have when administering a survey?

Competency 2: Engage Difference and Diversity in Practice

- How might social researchers capture diverse groups when conducting survey research?
- Why is it important for social researchers to have inclusive language in surveys to understand marginalized populations?

Competency 4: Engage in Practice-Informed Research and Research-Informed Practice

- True evidence-based practice should flow from practice-to-inform-research and research-to-inform-practice to gain best practice. How would a social researcher construct a survey when working with a practitioner? How can a social researcher work with practitioners to ensure their expertise is included in the research?
- Why is it important for practitioners and social researchers to work together when conducting research?

Competency 9: Evaluate Practice With Individuals, Communities, Groups, Organizations, and Communities

- Why is it important for social researchers to evaluate individuals, communities, groups, organizations, and communities?
- When conducting research with community members, what "road blocks" might you find?

SELF-ASSESSMENT

. . . .

1. Open-ended questions refer to:
   a. Participants writing their own responses, which are more like an essay-type survey.
   b. Questions that elicit short responses.
   c. Participants selecting answers from a long list of provided questions.
   d. Questions only used when conducting an interview.
2. Closed-ended questions refer to:
   a. Questions that provide participants with the ability to write down their own answers.
   b. Questions only used in self-administered surveys.
   c. Questions that provide participants with a fixed set of alternatives to choose.
   d. Questions that provide a space for respondents to write an answer.
3. Designing a questionnaire involves:
   a. A set of questions where participants have to ask questions to finish the questionnaire.
   b. Good directions, cover letter, and ordering of questions, which are all straightforward and convenient.
   c. Multiple sections that can lead participants to miss some questions.
   d. A set of questions that have abbreviations, small font, and use as few pages as possible.
4. Survey interview consists of:
   a. The researcher reading and then summarizing the questions to participants for their response.
   b. Following little to no structure while letting the respondent decide the direction of the interview.
   c. The researcher reading the questions directly to respondents and then recording the answers.
   d. A quick process that provides no flexibility.
5. Online surveys involve:
   a. Conducting surveys through email or social media, which are fast, have low cost, and reach participants all over the world.
   b. Surveys that are face-to-face and in-person.
   c. Surveys that can be inconvenient.
   d. Higher cost and little flexibility.
6. Telephone surveys involve:
   a. Higher cost than face-to-face interviews.
   b. Faster response rates and capture a larger sample than face-to-face or mail surveys.
   c. Surveys that are longer than other types of surveys.
   d. Surveys that are fast and can capture everyone.
7. Focus groups in survey research involve:
   a. Social research that is mainly explanatory.
   b. Multiple people at once and the researcher follows an interview guideline that outlines main topics that will be covered.

c. Flexibility where participants can come and go as they please during the interview.

d. A quick process that usually takes 30 min or less.

8. Practice interviews refer to:

a. An interview that has the same purpose as a research interview.

b. An interview where a practitioner seeks to understand the client and uses the interview to effect change.

c. An interview that is meant to collect data for data analysis.

d. A one-time interview where the respondent will not have any interaction with the practitioner again.

9. Research interviews refer to:

a. An interview where a researcher gains knowledge about a particular problem or population and uses data analysis.

b. An interview where the researcher wants to know the participant's individual needs.

c. An interview where the participant decides the direction of the questions.

d. An interview where the researcher asks personal questions to help provide immediate help to the respondent.

10. A survey refers to:

a. A process where a researcher talks with individuals, but does not collect data.

b. A specific way of collecting data and identifies a broad research strategy through gathering information from individuals.

c. The process of researchers developing research questions.

d. A method that is not used in data collection.

ANSWER KEY FOR SELF-ASSESSMENT QUIZ

1. **a.** Participants writing their own responses, which are more like an essay-type survey.
2. **c.** Questions that provide participants with a fixed set of alternatives to choose.
3. **b.** Good directions, cover letter, and ordering of questions, which are all straightforward and convenient.
4. **c.** The researcher reading the questions directly to respondents and then recording the answers.
5. **a.** Conducting surveys through email or social media, which are fast, have low cost, and reach participants all over the world.
6. **b.** Faster response rates and capture a larger sample than face-to-face or mail surveys.
7. **b.** Multiple people at once and the researcher follows an interview guideline that outlines main topics that will be covered.
8. **b.** An interview where a practitioner seeks to understand the client and uses the interview to effect change.
9. **a.** An interview where a researcher gains knowledge about a particular problem or population and uses data analysis.
10. **b.** A specific way of collecting data and identifies a broad research strategy through gathering information from individuals.

FOR FURTHER READING

Dillman, D. A., Smyth, J. D., & Christian, L. M. (2009). *Internet, mail, and mixed-mode surveys: The tailored design method* (3rd ed.). New York, NY: Wiley. This is an excellent introduction to survey research, and it also provides the most up-to-date overview of how to conduct surveys through the mail and on the Internet.

Gorden, R. L. (1992). *Basic interviewing skills*. Itasca, IL: Peacock. This useful how-to book on interviewing covers everything from developing questions to motivating good responses to evaluating respondents' nonverbal behavior.

Gubrium, J. F., & Holstein, J. A. (2001). *Handbook of interview research: Context and method*. Thousand Oaks, CA: Sage. This complete handbook covers many forms of interviewing, including survey, qualitative, in-depth, and therapy. The book addresses technical issues, distinctive respondents, and analytic strategies.

Kadushin, A., & Kadushin, G. (1997). *The social work interview: A guide for human service professionals* (4th ed.). New York, NY: Columbia University Press. This is the standard text for social work interviewing. It covers all aspects of the helping interview, and it presents a solid comparison for the survey interview.

Krueger, R. A., & Casey, M. A. (2008). *Focus groups: A practical guide for applied research* (4th ed.). Thousand Oaks, CA: Sage. This book is the standard for learning how to conduct a focus group. The third edition compares market research, academic, nonprofit, and participatory approaches to focus group research, and it describes how to plan focus group studies and do the analysis, including step-by-step procedures.

McInroy, L. B. (2016). Pitfalls, potentials, and ethics of online survey research: LGBTQ and other marginalized and hard-to-access youths. *Social Work Research, 40*(2), 83–93. doi:10.1093/swr/svw005. This article provides important considerations for online surveying methods with a focus on marginalized youth populations that frequently engage with the Internet.

Salant, P., & Dillman, D. A. (1994). *Conducting surveys: A step-by-step guide to getting the information you need*. New York, NY: Wiley. As the title states, this is a very useful guide to all the steps in conducting sound survey research.

Schuman, H., & Presser, S. (1996). *Questions and answers in attitude surveys: Experiments on question form, wording, and context.nt* Thousand Oaks, CA: Sage. This is a comprehensive handbook on the rules, problems, and pitfalls of designing survey questions. It goes far beyond what this chapter is able to cover on this important topic.

Sue, V. M., & Ritter, L. A. (2012). *Conducting online surveys* (2nd ed.). Los Angeles, CA: Sage. This volume is a comprehensive guide to the creation, implementation, and analysis of email and Web-based surveys. The authors specifically address issues unique to online survey research such as selecting software, designing Web-based questionnaires, and sampling from online populations.

REFERENCES

Abma, T., Deeg, D., Jonsson, H., & Van Ness, F. (2010). Language differences in qualitative research: Is meaning lost in translation? *European Journal of Ageing, 7*(4), 313–316. doi:10.1007/s10433-010-0168-y

American Association for Public Opinion Research Standards Committee. (2003). *Interviewer falsification in survey research: Current best methods for prevention, detection, and repair of its effects* (3rd draft). Retrieved from https://www.aapor.org/AAPOR_Main/media/MainSiteFiles/falsification.pdff

Anderson, B., Silver, B., & Abramson, P. (1988). The effects of the race of the interviewer on race-related attitudes of Black respondents in SRC/CPS National Election Studies. *Public Opinion Quarterly, 52*(3), 289–324. doi:10.1086/269108

Anderson, J. E., & Stall, R. (2002). Increased reporting of male-to-male sexual activity in a national survey. *Sexually Transmitted Diseases, 29*(11), 643–646. doi:10.1097/00007435-200211000-00005

Annis, R. C., & Corenblum, B. (1986). Effect of test language and experimenter race on Canadian Indian Children's racial and self-identity. *Journal of Social Psychology, 126*(6), 761–773. doi:10.1080/00224545.1986.9713658

Arean, P. A., Alvidrez, J., Nery, R., Estes, C., & Linkins, K. (2003). Recruitment and retention of older minorities in mental health services research. *The Gerontologist, 43*(1), 36–44. doi:10.1093/geront/43.1.36

Armstrong, J. S., & Luck, E. J. (1987). Return postage in mail surveys: A meta-analysis. *Public Opinion Quarterly, 51*(2), 233–248. doi:10.1086/269031

Bachman, J. G., & O'Malley, P. M. (1984). Yea-saying, nay-saying, and going to extremes: Black–White differences in response styles. *Public Opinion Quarterly, 48*(2), 491–501. doi:10.1086/268845

Bangerter, A. K., Grill, J. P., Murdoch, M., Noorbaloochi, S., Partin, M. R., Polusny, M. A., & Simon, A. B. (2014). Impact of different privacy conditions and incentives on survey response rate, participant representativeness, and disclosure of sensitive information: A randomized controlled trial. *BMC Medical Research Methodology, 14*(1). 90. doi:10.1186/1471-2288-14-90

Becerra, R. M., & de Anda, D. (1999). Can valid research on ethnic minority populations only be conducted by researchers from the same group? In D. de Anda (Ed.), *Controversial issues in multiculturalism* (pp. 110–118). Boston, MA: Allyn & Bacon.

Bell, K., Fahmy, E., & Gordon, D. (2016). Quantitative conversations: The importance of developing rapport in standardised interviewing. *Quality & Quantity, 50,* 193–212. doi:10.1007/s11135-014-0144-2

Berry, S. H., & Kanouse, D. H. (1987). Physician response to a mailed survey: An experiment in timing of payment. *Public Opinion Quarterly, 51*(1), 102–114. doi:10.1086/269018

Biemer, P., Day, O., Hsieh, Y. P., Murphy, J., Stringer, C., & Thissen, R. (2016). Interviewer falsification: Current and best practices for prevention, detection, and mitigation. *Statistical Journal of the IAOS, 32*(3), 313–326. doi:10.3233/sji-161014

Black, M. M., & Ponirakis, A. (2000). Computer-administered interviews with children about maltreatment: Methodological, developmental, and ethical issues. *Journal of Interpersonal Violence, 15*(7), 682–695. doi:10.1177/088626000015007002

Bokström, P., Dahlberg, A., Fängström, K., & Sarkadi, A. (2016). In my shoes: Validation of a computer assisted approach for interviewing children. *Child Abuse & Neglect, 58,* 160–172. doi:10.1016/j.chiabu.2016.06.022

Brunner, G. A., & Carroll, S. J. (1967). Effect of prior telephone appointments on completion rates and response content. *Public Opinion Quarterly, 31*(4), 652–654. doi:10.1086/267564

Bushery, J. M., Reichert, J. W., Albright, K. A., & Rossiter, J. C. (1999). Using date and time stamps to detect interviewer falsification. In *Proceedings of the Survey Research Method Section, American Statistical Association* (pp. 316–320).

Calderon, J. L., Hays, R. D., Liu, H., & Morales, L. S. (2006). Variation in the readability of items within surveys. *American Journal of Medical Quality: The Official Journal of the American College of Medical Quality, 21*(1), 49–56. doi:10.1177/1062860605283572

Caldwell, C. H., Couper, M. P., Davis, R. E., Janz, N. K., & Resnicow, K. (2010). Interviewer effects in public health surveys. *Health Education Research, 25*(1), 14–26. doi:10.1093/her/cyp046

Campbell, M., Lavelle, K., & Todd, C. (2008). Do postage stamps versus pre-paid envelopes increase responses to patient mail surveys? A randomised controlled trial. *BMC Health Services Research, 8*, 113. doi:10.1186/1472-6963-8-113

Cannell, C. F., & Kahn, R. L. (1968). Interviewing. In G. Lindzey & E. Aronson (Eds.), *The handbook of social psychology* (2nd ed., Vol. 2, pp. 526–595). Reading, MA: Addison-Wesley.

Cartwright, A., & Tucker, W. (1967). An attempt to reduce the number of calls on an interview inquiry. *Public Opinion Quarterly, 31*(2), 299–302. doi:10.1086/267524

Clark, J. (2006). Field research methods in the Middle East. *PS: Political Science and Politics, 39*(3), 417–424. doi:10.1017/s1049096506060707

Conrad, F. G., Couper, M. P., & Tourangeau, R. (2007). Visual context effects in web surveys. *Public Opinion Quarterly, 71*(4), 623–634. doi:10.1093/poq/nfm044

Couper, M., Kapteyn, A., Schonlau, M., & Van Soest, A. (2009). Selection bias in web surveys and the use of propensity scores. *Sociological Methods & Research, 37*(3), 291–318. doi:10.1177/0049124108327128

Couper, M. P., Tourangeau, R., & Kenyon, K. (2004). Picture this! Exploring visual effects in web surveys. *Public Opinion Quarterly, 68*(2), 255–266. doi:10.1093/poq/nfh013

Dailey, R. M., & Claus, R. E. (2001). The relationship between interviewer characteristics and physical and sexual abuse disclosures among substance users: A multilevel analysis. *Journal of Drug Issues, 31*(4), 867–888. doi:10.1177/002204260103100404

Davies, M., & Morgan, A. (2005). Using computer-assisted self-interviewing (CASI) questionnaires to facilitate consultation and participation with vulnerable young people. *Child Abuse Review, 14*(1), 389–406. doi:10.1002/car.925

Davis, D. W. (1997). Nonrandom measurement error and race of interviewer effects among African Americans. *Public Opinion Quarterly, 61*(1), 183–207. doi:10.1086/297792

Davis, D. W., & Silver, B. D. (2003). Stereotype threat and race of interviewer effects in a survey on political knowledge. *American Journal of Political Science, 47*(1), 33–45. doi:10.1111/1540-5907.00003

DeMaio, T. J. (1984). Social desirability and survey measurement: A review. In C. F. Turner & E. Martin (Eds.), *Surveying subjective phenomena* (2nd ed., pp. 257–282). New York, NY: Russell Sage Foundation.

Dignan, M., Michielutte, R., Sharp, P., Bahnson, J., Young, L., & Beal, P. (1990). The role of focus groups in health education for cervical cancer among minority women. *Journal of Community Health, 15*(6), 369–375. doi:10.1007/bf01324299

Drabble, L., Korcha, R. A., Trocki, K. F., Salcedo, B., & Walker, P. C. (2016). Conducting qualitative interviews by telephone: Lessons learned from a study of alcohol use among sexual minority and heterosexual women. *Qualitative Social Work: Research and Practice, 15*(1), 118–133. doi:10.1177/1473325015585613

Duffy, B., Smith, K., Terhanian, G., & Bremer, J. (2005). Comparing data from online and face-to-face surveys. *International Journal of Market Research, 47*(6), 615–639. doi:10.1177/147078530504700602

Epstein, I., & Tripodi, T. (1977). *Research techniques for program planning, monitoring, and evaluation.* New York, NY: Columbia University Press.

Fowler, F., Jr., & Mangione, T. (1990). *Standardized survey interviewing.* Newbury Park, CA: Sage.

Frey, J. H. (1986). An experiment with a confidentiality reminder in a telephone survey. *Public Opinion Quarterly, 50*(2), 267–269. doi:10.1086/268980

Fricker, R. D., & Schonlau, M. (2002). Advantages and disadvantages of Internet research surveys: Evidence from the literature. *Field Methods, 14*(4), 347–367. doi:10.1177/152582202237725

Gibson, P., & Abrams, L. (2003). Women in qualitative research: Racial difference in engaging, recruiting, and interviewing African Americans. *Qualitative Social Work, 2*(4), 457–476. doi:10.1177/1473325003024005

Gorden, R. L. (1987). *Interviewing: Strategies, techniques, and tactics* (4th ed.). Chicago, IL: Dorsey Press.

Goyder, J. (1985). Face-to-face interviews and mailed questionnaires: The net difference in response rate. *Public Opinion Quarterly, 49*(2), 234–252. doi:10.1086/268917

Groves, R. M. (2004). *Survey errors and survey costs*. New York, NY: Wiley.

Holstein, J. A., & Gubrium, J. F. (Eds.). (2003). *Inside interviewing: Conceptual issues and methodological considerations*. Thousand Oaks, CA: Sage.

Huby, M., & Hughes, R. (2004). The construction and interpretation of vignettes in social research. *Social Work & Social Sciences Review, 11*(1), 36–51. doi:10.1921/17466105.11.1.36

Hyman, H. (1954). *Interviewing in social research*. Chicago, IL: University of Chicago Press.

Innes, R. A. (2009). Wait a second, who are you anyways? The insider/outsider debate of American Indian studies. *American Indian Quarterly, 33*(4), 440–461.

James, J., & Bolstein, R. (1990). The effect of monetary incentives and follow-up mailings on the response rate and response quality in mail surveys. *Public Opinion Quarterly, 54*(3), 346–361. doi:10.1086/269211

Johnson, T. P., VanGeest, J. B., & Welch, V. L. (2007). Methodologies for improving response rates in surveys of physicians: A systematic review. *Evaluation & the Health Professions, 30*(4), 303–321. doi:10.1177/0163278707307899

Kadushin, A., & Kadushin, G. (1997). *The social work interview: A guide for human service professionals* (4th ed.). New York, NY: Columbia University Press.

Kaplowitz, M. D., Hadlock, T. D., & Levine, R. (2004). A comparison of web and mail survey response rates. *Public Opinion Quarterly, 68*(1), 94–101. doi:10.1093/poq/nfh006

Kirsch, I. S., Jungeblut, A., Jenkins, L., & Kolstad, A. (1993). *Adult literacy in America: A first look at the results of the National Adult Literacy Survey*. Washington, DC: U.S. Department of Education.

Koch, N. S., & Emrey, J. A. (2001). The Internet and opinion measurement: Surveying marginalized populations. *Social Science Quarterly, 82*(1), 131–138. doi:10.1111/0038-4941.00012

Krueger, R. A., & Casey, M. A. (2008). *Focus groups: A practical guide for applied research* (4th ed.). Thousand Oaks, CA: Sage.

Larson, P. D., & Poist, R. F. (2004). Improving response rates to mail surveys: A research note. *Transportation Journal, 43*(4), 67–74.

Manderson, L., Bennett, E., & Andajani-Sutjahjo, S. (2006). The social dynamics of the interview: Age, class, and gender. *Qualitative Health Research, 16*(10), 1317–1334. doi:10.1177/1049732306294512

Marin, G., & VanOss Marin, B. (1991). *Research with Hispanic populations*. Newbury Park, CA: Sage.

Markle, D. T., Rich, P. J., & West, R. E. (2011). Beyond transcription: Technology, change, and refinement of method. *Forum: Qualitative Social Research, 12*(3), Art. 21.doi:10.17169/fqs-12.3.1564

Marshall, E. (2000). How prevalent is fraud? That million-dollar question. *Science, 290*(5497), 1662–1663. doi:10.1126/science.290.5497.1662

Miller, D. C., & Salkind, N. J. (2002). *Handbook of research design and social measurement* (6th ed.). Thousand Oaks, CA: Sage.

Morgan, D. L. (1996). *Focus groups as qualitative research* (2nd ed.). Thousand Oaks, CA: Sage.

Moser, C. A., & Kalton, G. (1972). *Survey methods in social investigation* (2nd ed.). New York, NY: Basic Books.

Newman, J. C., DesJerlais, D. C., Turner, C. F., & Gribble, J. (2002). The differential effects of face-to-face and computer interview modes. *American Journal of Public Health, 92*(2), 294–297. doi:10.2105/ajph.92.2.294

Oksenberg, L., Coleman, L., & Cannell, C. F. (1986). Interviewers' voices and refusal rates in telephone surveys. *Public Opinion Quarterly, 50*(1), 97–111.

Pini, B. (2005). Interviewing men: Gender and the collection and interpretation of qualitative data. *Journal of Sociology, 41*, 201–216. doi:10.1177/1440783305053238

Rea, L., & Parker, R. (2005). *Designing and conducting survey research* (3rd ed.). San Francisco, CA: Jossey-Bass.

Schonlau, M., Zapert, K., Simon, L. P., Sanstad, K. H., Marcus, S. M., Adams, J., . . . Berry, S. H. (2004). A comparison between responses from a propensity-weighted web survey and an identical RDD Survey. *Social Science Computer Review, 22*(1), 128–138. doi:10.1177/0894439303256551

Schuman, H., & Presser, S. (1979). The open and closed question. *American Sociological Review, 44*(5), 692–712. doi:10.2307/2094521

Singer, L., & Ye, C. (2013). The use and effects of incentives on surveys. *The Annals of the American Academy of Political and Social Science, 645*(1), 112–141. doi:10.1177/0002716212458082

Smith, T. W. (1987). That which we call welfare by any other name would smell sweeter: An analysis of the impact of question wording on response patterns. *Public Opinion Quarterly, 51*(1), 75–83. doi:10.1086/269015

Smith, T. W. (1995). The Polls—A review: The Holocaust denial controversy. *Public Opinion Quarterly, 59*(2), 269–295. doi:10.1086/269473

Sudman, S. (1965). Time allocation on survey interviews and other field occupations. *Public Opinion Quarterly, 29*(4), 638–648. doi:10.1086/267367

Sudman, S. (1985). Mail surveys of reluctant professionals. *Evaluation Research, 9,* 349–360. doi:10.1177/0193841x8500900306

Sudman, S., & Bradburn, N. M. (1982). *Asking questions.* San Francisco, CA: Jossey-Bass.

Timberlake, E. M. (1994). Children with no place to call home: Survival in cars and on the streets. *Child and Adolescent Social Work Journal, 5*(4), 268.

Tinker, C., & Armstrong, N. (2008). From the outside looking in: How an awareness of difference can benefit the qualitative research process. *The Qualitative Report, 13*(1), 53–60.

Thrasher, E., & Mowbray, C. (1995). A strengths perspective: An ethnographic study of homeless women with children. *Health and Social Work, 20*(2), 93–101. doi:10.1093/hsw/20.2.93

Tourangeau, R., & Yan, T. (2007). Sensitive questions in surveys. *Psychological Bulletin, 133*(5), 859–883. doi:10.1037/0033-2909.133.5.859

Vinokur, A., Oksenberg, L., & Cannell, C. (1979). Effects of feedback and reinforcement on the report of health information. In C. Cannell, L. Oksenberg, & C. Converse (Eds.), *Experiments in interviewing techniques.* Ann Arbor: University of Michigan Institute for Social Research.

Wagner, J., Olson, K. (2018). An analysis of interviewer travel and field outcomes in tow field surveys. *Journal of Official Statistics, 34*(1), 211–237.

Warriner, K., Goyder, J., Gjertsen, H., Hohner, P., & McSpurren, K. (1996). Charities, no; lotteries, no; cash, yes: Main effects and interactions in a Canadian incentives experiment. *Public Opinion Quarterly, 60*(4), 542–562. doi:10.1086/297772

Warwick, D. P., & Lininger, C. (1975). *The sample survey: Theory and practice.* New York, NY: McGraw-Hill.

Wilson, S. R., Brown, N., Mejia, C., & Lavori, P. W. (2002). Effects of interviews characteristics on reported sexual behavior of California Latino couples. *Hispanic Journal of Behavioral Sciences, 24*(1), 38–62. doi:10.1177/0739986302024001003

Woodruff, S. I., Conway, T. L., & Edwards, C. C. (2000). Increasing response rates to a smoking survey for U.S. Navy enlisted women. *Evaluation and the Health Professions, 23*(2), 172–181. doi:10.1177/016327870002300203

Yammarino, F. J., Skinner, S. J., & Childers, T. L. (1991). Understanding mail survey response behavior: A meta-analysis. *Public Opinion Quarterly, 55*(4), 613–639. doi:10.1086/269284

8

ANALYSIS OF AVAILABLE DATA

Evaluating Competency (From the Council on Social Work Education [CSWE] 2015 Educational Policy and Accreditation Standards [EPAS])

Competency 2: Engage Diversity and Difference in Practice, and

Competency 3: Advance Human Rights and Social, Economic, and Environmental Justice

Competency 4: Engage in Practice-Informed Research and Research-Informed Practice

Competency 9: Evaluate Practice With Individuals, Families, Groups, Organizations, and Communities

Self-Assessment

Answer key for Self-Assessment Quiz

For Further Reading

References

INTRODUCTION

Homeless Management Information Systems (HMIS) are locally operated information technology systems used for collecting client-level data pertaining to the provision of homeless services. Each local or regional homeless services network that receives federal funding from the Department of Housing and Urban Development (HUD) is required to develop an HMIS. The basic rationale behind this requirement is that it helps create referral and information networks among homeless services providers. HMIS databases allow service systems to maintain centralized client intake, referral, assessment, and reporting systems. They also help homeless service system administrators (generally local or county government agencies) to meet regulatory guidelines and create more seamless and streamlined systems among service providers. Beyond these benefits, these systems give researchers and human service professionals a critical resource, data.

According to David Lewis, the HMIS Manager for Spokane County (WA), "Data is the most powerful tool we have to manage a social problem like homelessness" (All quotes are based on personal communication from April 5, 2018). He explains, "Having a well-structured database

and a well-designed methodology for collecting and using data is critical. It makes your planning more efficient and it gives you a clear picture of the actual problem." Prior to the creation of HMIS systems in Spokane and elsewhere there was less coordination of services and, as Lewis explains, less learning from past mistakes.

Although people had good intentions and put lots of effort into planning, we were limited by a lack of data. We ended up making some mistakes time and time again or attempting what seemed like a novel, new solution, but was really something we'd already tried before. On top of all that, the knowledge we did collect was often siloed [sic], so we didn't always learn from one another.

Spokane and other communities have made better use of HMIS over time. According to Lewis,

The evolution of the HMIS follows community partners' becoming more comfortable with data to make informed decisions. What started out as a simple reporting platform required by HUD has turned into something completely different and better. People began using it because they were required to use it. In time more people began to think 'Well this is helpful'. That sparked a revolution of sorts. Now agencies and practitioners are talking about how to make data portable. They're working with [City government] to build data platforms that allow users to communicate with one another via news bulletin boards and chat rooms where they discuss how to interpret HMIS data. It has gone beyond basic cold demographic information on clients and become an active case management tool. That is where we are at now."

Lewis sees the next step in creating a more useful data tool is further integration with other social services data systems. He explains, "Where we are headed is even more integration of what I would call community data, not just all of the things people think about when they think of homeless services, but also criminal justice, and hospital data, and other segments of our social safety net that absolutely play a role in whether or not someone is successfully housed and whether they can stay stable. They're now part of this system too. So we have a complete profile of what each individual's challenges are that are preventing them from being successful. I have clients in the system that we have been storing for 8 or 9 years. Now a social worker can look at that data and say, 'Wow, we've put you through this system three times and it's not working. What is your need that we're not meeting?'"

There are multiple groups using HMIS data in creating plans to address homelessness. The homeless services Continuum of Care Board and several subgroups focused on veterans, chronically homeless adults, and youth use HMIS to get data on people seeking services. As Lewis explains,

In a sense, the HMIS becomes our central nervous system. You can't make a decision if you don't have the inputs and a means to process them. We look at our datasets to see where needs are greatest and where data are lacking. We also bring in experts to review the data to help us identify priority areas for area.

Recent data have pointed toward the need to better address chronic homelessness among families.

When you look at our client level data and our housing data one of the clearest bright line trends is that we have been de-prioritizing transitional housing. As we rushed to respond to demands to move to housing first approaches, stressing quick placements into permanent housing, we defunded transitional housing that served a very specific need. It is pretty clear that we should have also stuck with these services longer because some clients, especially chronically homeless families, seem to benefit from transitional housing.

When asked about how homeless services have changed since the creation of HMIS databases, Lewis remarked that the problem of homelessness has remained more or less the same, but that responses have become more effective and efficient. He explains,

I don't know that homelessness itself has changed that much. The same factors that contribute to becoming homeless are still present. As a community, we are doing a better job addressing these challenges as best we can. We're making decisions based on information. We are well poised to do that and doing more of that every day. Income inequality, unequal access to resources and other problems are still there. Maybe they will always be there. What we can do is to make sure that where people do fall there really is a safety net to get them back on their feet as quickly as possible. It's about reducing the duration and the frequency of episodes of homelessness.

More about David Lewis and his use of available data of clients and services in guiding policymaking and program development can be found in Practitioner Profile 8.1.

Normally, researchers prefer to organize and direct the collection of the data themselves. This enables them to tailor the nature and form of the data collected to their research hypotheses and to the state of knowledge in the field (see Chapter 4). In some cases, however, this is far

PRACTITIONER PROFILE 8.1 David Lewis, Homeless Management Information System (HMIS) Program Manager for Spokane County (WA)

David Lewis has a master's degree in Public Administration from Eastern Washington University. He has always viewed information technology and computer programming as a hobby, but his main passion is social justice and advocacy for disadvantaged populations, especially the poor. After an internship with the Spokane Low Income Housing Consortium in which he helped the agency create an agency database that allowed them to extract useful data, he was hired to take over the City of Spokane's HMIS database. He has worked in this position for the last 9 years. According to Lewis, "Everybody who goes to work in government has the goal of fixing problems, but we all approach this in different ways. For me, I view data as the most powerful tool we have to address our social problems. That includes everything from homelessness to opiate addictions." Lewis also explained that he finds that in a lot of communities a lot of effort goes into planning services systems, but that planning processes go awry from lack of data. "People are well intentioned, but I think they are often limited by a lack of data. . . . On top of all that our collective knowledge is siloed. We all have different skill sets, and areas of expertise that never cross pollenate."

Lewis explained that Spokane's HMIS evolved as service providers, system administrators (government agencies), and policy makers became more comfortable using data.

What started off as a simple reporting platform required by the Department of Housing and Urban Development had turned into something completely different. The evolution feels organic. As people use it and become comfortable with it they begin to say 'Well this is useful. We are centralizing this information so it is helpful for our It funders. How do we make it useful for us?'

This evolution led to what Lewis calls a revolution in human services. As he explains,

People started to suggest that we establish scan cards that clients can have to make their data portable. Let's create a platform for agencies to communicate with one another via news bulletin boards. . . . It went beyond basic, cold demographic information on a client to a useful case management tool, which is where are at now. It was a database that was built to serve one role, that is, at a minimum serving two roles. And where we're headed is even more integration of what I call community data.

Lewis explained that the initial HMIS platform was open to partners that HUD required be involved, especially government administrators and homeless services providers. Now, there is a strong desire in the community to include new entities from outside of homeless services and further integration with other systems, including state welfare and child welfare agencies, employment services, criminal justice, and health and mental care systems.
"We're not having to drag people along anymore," Lewis explains.

People see it as useful and they see the roles that many groups play—from those who spot and recruit new clients to those who do intakes to those who provide housing to those who provide food assistance. We're even reaching out to people in criminal justice and getting interest there too.

(continued)

At least part of the excitement for further use of data and integration of new systems into HMIS, Lewis admits, is because new funding entities, including private foundations, will only fund agencies that are involved in the HMIS system. "These funders are catching on to the fact that HMIS is a valuable tool and important to creating a cohesive services system—so that people are not falling through the cracks."

too costly and time-consuming. In other cases, it is either impractical or unnecessary. HMIS databases, for example, have also been used by many researchers studying homelessness and homeless services. Fargo et al. (2012), for example, used HMIS databases from seven cities to examine changing rates of homelessness among veterans (2012). Similarly Cronley, Strand, Patterson, and Gwaltney (2009) used one city's HMIS database in a study comparing services outcomes for homeless adults caring for an animal (generally a pet) and those who did not. In both these cases, using the HMIS databases gave researchers access to rich data without the expense and time of collecting it firsthand. While these databases do not necessarily contain records for every person who lacks housing in each area studied (because HMIS systems are based on counts of homeless adults and often miss many who do not seek services), these are the most complete and official records of homeless people and services in their respective areas.

Data of this type are called **available data:** observations collected by someone other than the investigator for purposes that differ from the investigator's but that, nonetheless, are available. In the case of HMIS databases, for example, data that were collected by service agencies and system administrators for the purposes of tracking client outcomes, generating referrals between service providers, and making reports for funders is now used by both practitioners and researchers to answer larger questions about services and populations served. This chapter will focus on the use of available data for research, including applied research and evaluation (as with the HMIS example). As we present

the use of available data please consider the following questions: (a) Why might researchers use available data as opposed to collecting data themselves? (b) What are advantages and disadvantages of relying on available data to answer research questions? and (c) What are sources of available data that can be accessed by human services professionals in conducting applied research and evaluation?

A vast array of this type of data exists for scientific analysis. In some cases, such data take the form of *statistical data,* or quantified observations of some element of human behavior. For example, various branches of government collect large amounts of statistical data and provide quantified information about crime, health, birth rates, death rates, and so on. *Documents* are another form of available data and refer, in their broadest sense, to any form of nonquantitative communication. Documents include such items as books, magazines, letters, memoranda, diaries, Web pages, and other communication media, such as radio, television, movies, and plays. Documents also can make up a part of the records maintained by various institutions, such as military records, police records, court records, and social agency records. Some such records, of course, include both statistical and nonstatistical data.

Available data are a rich source for human service research and, sometimes, are used in conjunction with data collected from other sources, such as surveys. Furthermore, researchers often can treat available data as if they were data the researchers had collected themselves. Available data, however, do present researchers with some new problems, and these problems are also covered in this chapter.

STATISTICAL DATA

Human service professionals often complain about the mountains of paperwork associated with the procedures of trying to help people, but the facts and figures that these procedures generate can be a rich source of data for research. Sometimes this agency data can be deficient in some critical respects as research data. However, an important contribution that research-knowledgeable human service professionals can make to both practice and research is to help develop data-collection procedures in agencies that generate useful statistical data. To make such a contribution, however, human service professionals must have an understanding of how researchers use available statistical data and of what qualities enhance the usefulness of available data for research.

Sources of Statistical Data

Statistical data are collected for many reasons, and much of these data are available to human service researchers. First, some statistical data are collected as part of many research projects. Many research organizations, such as the Institute for Social Research at the University of Michigan or the Institute for Research on Poverty at the University of Wisconsin, collect large amounts of useful data that others may reanalyze with different research questions in mind. In this way, data collected for one project may be reanalyzed by a number of different people in the years that follow. This reanalysis of data collected for some other research project is called **secondary analysis** (Riedel, 2000; Sieber, 1991). Today, a number of national and international organizations have developed **data archives,** which are essentially libraries that lend or sell data sets as much as libraries or bookstores lend or sell books. Among the better known are the Inter-University Consortium of Political and Social Research (ICPSR) at the University of Michigan, the Roper Center at Cornell University, and Networked Social Science Tools and Resources (NESSTAR). These organizations increasingly use the advantages of the Web to make it easy to publish, locate, and access statistical data.

Some private organizations also have created data archives in specialized areas. The Sociometrics Corporation, for example, offers numerous data sets from studies focusing on adolescent pregnancy issues. Many individual researchers also make data sets available to those with legitimate secondary uses for the data. Some funders of research, such as the National Science Foundation (NSF), now require, as a stipulation for receiving research funds, that the data eventually be delivered to a public archive. Data collected for research purposes and available for secondary analyses tend to be of fairly high quality, because professional researchers collected them. Nonetheless, such data still suffer from some of the problems to be discussed shortly.

A second source of statistical data is the federal, state, and local human service agencies that collect data for either administrative or client service purposes. Community mental health centers, Head Start programs, departments of social services, and health and educational institutions are repositories of vast amounts of available data. Unfortunately, data from human service agencies often are not efficiently cataloged and indexed and, therefore, often are difficult for investigators to locate and use. Nonetheless, such data, including HMIS databases described earlier, have grown to voluminous proportions over the decades.

A third source of statistical data is the organizations and governmental agencies that collect data as a public service or to serve as the basis for social policy decisions. The Federal Bureau of Investigation (FBI) and the National Center for Health Statistics, for example, collect vast amounts of data, as do state and local governments. The U.S. Census Bureau also collects enormous amounts of data to use for establishing and changing the boundaries of political districts and for allocating government funds that are based on population size. Often, researchers can use data from these sources in conjunction with other types of data—from questionnaires, for example, or from agency records—to test hypotheses. One of the authors of this textbook and his research partner, for example, used both original data from in-depth interviews with homeless families and data from Washington State's Healthy Youth Survey (HYS) in examining the impacts of homelessness and housing instability on school performance. Data from the Healthy Youth Survey allowed them to show statistical connections between homelessness and housing instability and various social, psychological, and academic outcomes. Data from qualitative interviews with homeless parents helped the researchers explain how homelessness and housing instability impacted children and their experiences in school.

Data collected by private organizations are distributed less widely than government statistics and, for that reason, may be more difficult to locate. Professional associations, such as the American Medical Association, the American Bar Association, and the National Association of Social Workers (NASW), produce statistics relating to their membership and issues of concern to their members. Additionally, research institutes and commercial polling firms also produce statistical data.

Using Statistical Data

When we use available statistical data, remember that most such data were not collected for research purposes—or at least not for the specific research questions for which we now intend to use them. They were compiled to meet the needs of whatever agency, organization, or researcher originally collected them, and the form in which the data were collected limits the analysis. This leads to some special problems that call for caution.

Missing Data. For a variety of reasons, a data set may not include complete data for every person studied or may fail to collect data from the entire population or sample of interest. For example, a person may refuse to answer certain questions, which results in a gap in his or her data set. Or, researchers may not have collected data in a particular neighborhood, which was considered to be too dangerous for interviewers to enter. Such gaps in a data set are referred to as **missing data**, and they appear, to some degree, practically in all studies. The problem when using available data files is that we have no control over this failure to collect a complete set of data. Missing data result in

incomplete coverage, which, if extensive, questions the representativeness of the data. Furthermore, because statistical procedures are based on the assumption of complete data, missing data can result in misleading statistical conclusions.

As we dig into data from the past, it is not uncommon to find data for whole periods missing. This can occur for many reasons, such as data destroyed by fire, lost data, changes in policy, and the like. Finding data that cover only a portion of a target population also is quite common. HMIS databases are a good example. While what they typically offer are the most complete records of homeless populations and related services, they neither fully capture all homeless persons nor services provided through area human services agencies. As previously mentioned, many people who choose to not seek services and those who may be hidden from point-in-time counts of homeless people within an area are very unlikely to be present in these databases. Furthermore, these databases are typically limited to people who meet federal definitions of homelessness and often omit people forced to double-up with family or friends or "couch-hopping" between different friends and relatives' residences.

Another example comes from a study of changes in work–family conflict over time based on statistical available data from two national surveys of adults, one done in 1977 and the other in 1997 (Nomaguchi, 2009). The sample in the 1977 survey did not include people who worked fewer than 20 hours per week. Although such people were included in the 1997 survey, they had to be excluded from the analysis since they were missing in the 1977 survey. These missing cases meant that conclusions about work–family conflict could be drawn only about those who work longer hours, and such people also tend to have more skilled jobs and are thus higher in socioeconomic status. So, when working with data that suffer from noncoverage, we should assess the implications of noncoverage for the results of the research.

Inductive Versus Deductive Analysis. In research investigations that collect data firsthand, we commonly use a deductive approach. That is, hypotheses are deduced from a theory, variables in the hypotheses are operationally defined, and data are collected based on these operational definitions. In short, research moves from the abstract to the concrete: The theory and hypotheses that we are testing determine the kind of data that we collect (see Chapter 2). In the analysis of available data, however, such a deductive approach often is impossible, because the data necessary to measure the variables derived from a theory may not have been included when the original data were collected. For example, a theory regarding caseworker effectiveness with clients might include the variable of the intensity of the casework relationship. Although intensity of relationship is a crucial concept in interpersonal helping, it is, unfortunately, not the type of variable that is included in routine agency data-collection procedures or in system-wide databases like HMIS systems. In circumstances like this, it is not possible to operationalize the variable in the way that is most appropriate to the theory. If this difficulty is encountered, a compromise often is made. As shown in Chapter 5, the measurement process often calls for modifying nominal and operational definitions (refer back to Figure 5.1). So, we revise operational definitions and, in some cases, hypotheses so that we can test them with the data available (see Figure 8.1). In the example of caseworker effectiveness, we might measure intensity of relationship by looking at the amount of time a worker spent with a given client over the course of treatment, frequency of contacts, or duration of contacts. Although none of these variables may be the best measure for "intensity of relationship," we can readily derive them from the worker time sheets that are mandatory in many agencies. We may use total contact time, frequency of contact,

duration of contact, or some combination of these, even though they are not thoroughly accurate measures of the variable of interest.

In other words, we modify our research to fit the data. When this occurs, research takes on a somewhat inductive character. In inductive research, we move from the concrete to the abstract: Starting with the data collected, we develop hypotheses and theories to explain what we find. The situation we have described is actually somewhere in between induction and deduction. We have begun with theories and hypotheses, but we also have had to let the available data influence how we test the hypotheses. This is a frequent problem in the analysis of available statistical data.

Validity. Recall from Chapter 5 that *validity* refers to whether a measurement instrument actually measures what it is intended to measure. Many data in the existing statistical files are valid indicators of certain characteristics that they describe directly, such as age, sex, and racial profiles of clients, along with the amounts of different kinds of services provided. Validity problems, however, frequently arise in three areas.

First, many elements of agency operation, such as achievement of goals, success of programs, or satisfaction of clients, may not be measured directly by any data that are normally collected by an agency. To study these, we would have to search for indirect measures among the agency data that might enable us to infer such things as goal achievement, success, or satisfaction. These situations create the same kinds of validity problems that confront researchers using other methods, except that when we use available data, we cannot consider and resolve validity problems *before* we

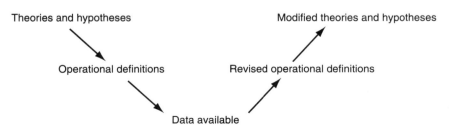

Figure 8.1 The measurement process with available statistical data.

collect the data. Because someone else has already collected the data, these problems are entrenched.

A second area in which validity problems frequently arise is data analysis that becomes inductive—that is, when we change operational definitions so that we can measure variables with the available data. The more the definitions are changed, the more the validity of the measures is called into question. Sometimes, the operational definitions may be changed so drastically that they no longer measure the theoretical concepts they were first intended to measure.

Finally, validity questions arise when the procedures that an agency or organization uses in gathering data change over the years. Changing modes of collecting data, such as dropping some questions or developing new definitions of something, are quite common in any agency or organization. These procedural changes, however, can affect the comparability of data collected at various times and the validity of using the same operational definitions. Crime statistics are a good example. Researchers commonly use data from the Uniform Crime Reports (UCR) compiled by the FBI as a measure for the volume of crimes in the United States, and Research in Practice 8.1 explores some of the problems that can arise when using this particular set of data.

RESEARCH IN PRACTICE 8.1 Policy Planning and Development: Hazards in Estimating the Crime Problem From Available Data

Combating crime is a key objective for many human service programs, whether it is running a neighborhood watch to increase safety for the elderly, providing late-night basketball for inner-city youths, or offering treatment groups for offenders. Whenever an organization embarks on an effort to design and implement a program like one of these, the planning process commonly requires that program planners demonstrate the need for the program by documenting the seriousness of the crime problem in a community. It is unlikely that most human service organizations have either the resources or the capacity to gather crime data themselves, so available data are an appealing alternative. As we noted in this chapter, one of the advantages of conducting research with available data is that somebody else paid to collect that data. It is, however, important to make serious inquiries about exactly how the data were collected and the numbers were produced.

The human service agency that uses available crime data faces several possible pitfalls. The Federal Bureau of Investigation (FBI) produces one of the most widely used sources of crime data. The Uniform Crime Reports (UCR) is published annually and is available in libraries and online (www.fbi.gov). On the surface, it might seem that data produced by an agency of the federal government, with all its authority and resources, would be reliable—and within limits, they are. Those limitations, however, can cause problems if they are not understood.

One of the most basic questions about crime is: How much crime exists? The UCR data cannot answer well even this apparently simple question. For an event to be recorded as a crime in the UCR, it must come to the attention of some police official. In a minority of cases, police chance across a crime taking place, so it gets officially recorded. Most often, however, police must rely on citizens who are victimized by crime to report it—and herein lies one of the problems with the UCR data. A large percentage of even serious crime never gets reported to the police. A recent estimate by the Bureau of Justice Statistics suggests that only 42% to 56% of all violent and property crimes are reported to the police and make their way into the UCR data (Gramlich, 2017). Clearly, this reporting gap causes the UCR data to significantly understate the true impact of criminal activity in the United States.

(continued)

You may be wondering how such an estimate of unreported crime can be made. Another measure of criminal activity is the National Crime Victimization Survey (NCVS). The NCVS is conducted every year on a representative sample of more than 100,000 citizens, inquiring if they have been victims of crimes. The disparity between the NCVS data and the UCR data provides an indicator of the amount of crime that goes unreported by the UCR and, thus, gives a clearer picture of the actual criminal activity. Another possible pitfall awaiting users of the UCR data is that reporting to the FBI is voluntary on the part of local law enforcement agencies, and this leads to a number of possible misinterpretations of the data. For example, researchers cannot compare different regions or localities and conclude with any certainty which area has the higher or the lower crime rate. Any differences noted might be real, or they might merely be differences in the willingness of local officials to report to the FBI.

A related problem confronts anyone who is interested in longitudinal analysis. Over the long history of the UCR, the percentage of police agencies that report their numbers has steadily increased. This, of course, means that any comparison over time has a built-in problem. Even if crime has not increased over time, it will appear to have increased because of the higher rate of reporting in more recent years.

Yet another problem stems from the fact that during the first several decades of the UCR, crime rates were computed not from updated population estimates but from the most recent census count. The census is conducted only once every 10 years, and this meant that, for years, the basis for computing crime rates stayed the same for a decade, until the numbers from a new census became available. Of course, however, a population does not remain stagnant and then suddenly explode every 10 years. The population steadily increases from year to year, meaning that there are more people to commit crimes and to become crime victims. Using the same census number to compute crime rates meant that apparent increases in crime from year to year were inevitable. Then, when a new census number was used, there would appear to be a substantial drop in crime. Obviously, this "drop" was not the result of a real decline in criminal activity but, rather, of the census number used to compute the crime rate catching up with the population increase. This is no longer a problem with the UCR data, because the UCR now uses yearly population estimates, which are quite accurate, in computing the crime rates. It does, however, typify the kind of traps that may await the unsuspecting researcher using other people's data.

Finally, when working with data collected over a long period of time, such as the UCR data, an important question is this: Have definitions or categorizations changed over time that would hamper meaningful comparisons? Again, the UCR is illustrative. According to Barlow (1996), during the history of the UCR, the FBI's classification system for counting crime has changed several times. In fact, in 1979, the FBI added an additional crime, arson, to those that make up the "crime index"—that is, the crimes that are tracked and used to compute the general crime rate. In addition to arson, the index crimes are homicide, aggravated assault, sexual assault, robbery, burglary, larceny, and auto theft. Naturally, when arson was added to the index, it appeared that crime had suddenly—and dramatically—increased when, of course, the change in measurement primarily caused the change in the numbers.

As illustrated by the UCR data, a researcher who uses available data must be careful not to fall into possible traps hidden in that data. Such risks do not mean that we should avoid available data but, rather, that we should use such data with caution. For example, the UCR data are not without value, because they reflect changes in people's willingness to report crime to the police. In some periods, the UCR data have shown a marked increase in the number of reported rapes, whereas the NCVS data have shown no such increase. This difference is evidence for an increased willingness of victims to report the crime to the police.

CONTENT ANALYSIS

Whenever activity is recorded in some document— whether a book, diary, case record, film, or tape recording—it is amenable to scientific analysis. Although the data discussed in the previous section were already quantified when they were made available for research, the documents we now discuss contain basically *qualitative* data that researchers must quantify. Consider the following research studies by various social scientists:

- A study of websites marketing e-cigarettes shows that marketers frequently make untrue or unsubstantiated claims about health risks and smoking cessation benefits of e-cigarettes (Grana, Popova, & Ling, 2014).
- A study of propaganda videos created by terrorists groups found that leaders of terrorist networks tend to favor significantly less indiscriminate violence than their operators commit (Abrahms, Beauchamp, & Mroszczyk, 2017).
- A study of magazine advertisements determines whether the behavior displayed in advertisements is different for men and women and assesses whether stereotypical portrayals of men and women have changed over the past two decades (Kang, 1997).
- A study of how emotions are expressed and interpreted in different settings reviews audiotapes of emergency 911 calls (Whalen & Zimmerman, 1998).

Content analysis refers to a method of transforming the symbolic content of a document, such as words or other images, from a qualitative, unsystematic form into a quantitative, systematic form (Franzosi, 2008; Neuendorf, 2002). In the previous examples, the "documents" consist of marketing websites, recruitment videos, magazine advertisements, and 911 audiotapes. Content analysis is a form of *coding,* a practice we discuss in Chapters 7 and 9 as a way of transforming data in some surveys and observational research. **Coding** refers to categorizing behaviors or elements into a limited number of categories. In surveys and observational research, we perform coding on data the investigator collects firsthand

for particular research purposes. In content analysis, coding is performed on documents produced for purposes other than research but then made available for research purposes. In both survey data coding and content analysis, we develop categories and coding schemes to quantify verbal or symbolic content.

Coding Schemes

A major step in content analysis is to develop a coding scheme for analyzing the documents at hand. Coding schemes in content analysis, like coding schemes in observed behavior, are quite variable, and their exact form depends on the documents being studied and the hypotheses being tested in the research project.

Existing Coding Schemes. In some cases, researchers can find existing coding schemes for content analysis. For example, Robert Bales (1950) developed a set of coding categories for the analysis of social interaction in groups, and this coding scheme has been widely used in research. Bales's coding scheme emerged from his analysis of social processes and interactional strategies common to all groups. In particular, he argued that all behavior in groups relates to either "task" issues (instrumental or goal-oriented behavior) or "social–emotional" issues (having to do with feelings, emotions, or morale). Within each of those categories, he identified three specific behavioral forms it could take. For task issues:

1. Gives or asks for suggestions or directions.
2. Gives or asks for opinions or evaluations.
3. Gives or asks for orientation (information, clarification).

For social–emotional issues:

1. Shows solidarity or antagonism.
2. Shows tension or tension release.
3. Agrees or disagrees.

Each behavior of a person can then be classified into one of these categories. Over the years, researchers have used this coding scheme to test hypotheses about how common certain kinds of strategies are, the conditions under which they occur, and how effective they are at producing certain outcomes.

Some human service researchers have developed a somewhat analogous coding scheme to analyze the content of a clinician's responses to patients in interviews (Duehn & Proctor, 1977). In a study of the impact of clinicians' responses on whether clients continued with treatment, researchers developed a coding system using three categories:

1. *Substantive congruent responses:* clinician responses that referred to the client's immediately preceding response or that contained some elements of that response.
2. *Nonsubstantive congruent responses:* clinician responses, such as "I see" or "Yes," that indicate the clinician is aware of and paying attention to the client's verbalizations.
3. *Incongruent responses:* clinician responses that appear to be unrelated to what the client has said.

Others interested in similar aspects of the practitioner–client interview might use the same coding scheme.

In conducting content analysis, then, we find it beneficial to search for an existing coding scheme that applies to the research problem at hand. The use of an existing coding scheme results in considerable savings for the researcher in terms of time, energy, and money. It also serves to make the research project comparable with other studies that use the same coding system.

We can find coding schemes in the many journals that report research relevant to the human services or in books, such as those by Holsti (1969) and Krippendorff (2019), that are devoted to the study of content analysis.

Characteristics. Like categories in any measurement process, those used in content analysis should be exhaustive and mutually exclusive. Categories are *exhaustive* when a category is available for every relevant element in the documents. If there are only a few possibilities and they can be clearly defined, then an exhaustive set of categories is not difficult to develop. If what we are trying to measure is rather open-ended, however, and has

many possibilities, then developing an exhaustive set of categories is difficult. For example, researchers have analyzed presidential speeches in terms of the values expressed, but so many values exist that developing an exhaustive list is unlikely. One such list contained 14 value categories, which undoubtedly cover the most important or commonly mentioned values (Prothro, 1956). It is doubtful whether even that many categories are really exhaustive, however. If it is impossible to be exhaustive, then we use the most common or most important categories and make available a residual category ("other") for those items that do not fit any of the categories.

Coding categories should also be *mutually exclusive,* which means that each coded item can fall into one—and only one—category. This requirement forces researchers to provide precise definitions for each category so that no ambiguity exists concerning which items it includes and which it does not. Failure to meet this requirement can totally befuddle the measurement process, because coders who are confused by overlapping categories will place items every which way. Lack of mutual exclusiveness likely will show up in low levels of reliability as the coders disagree on the placement of items into categories.

Units of Analysis

With the categories established, the next research decision concerns precisely what aspects of the documents to record. Generally, there are four units of analysis: a word, a theme, a major character, or a sentence or paragraph. (We discussed the units of analysis commonly found in research other than content analysis in Chapter 4.) An often-convenient unit of analysis is a *single word,* because we can code the presence of certain words in documents easily and with a high degree of reliability. If a single word qualifies as a valid indicator of what we wish to measure, then it is a good choice for the unit of analysis. For example, as part of their study of colonial families, Lantz, Schmitt, Britton, and Snyder (1968) counted the frequency with which the word *power* was associated with men or women in colonial magazines. In this context, the single word was used as a measure of the perceived distribution of power between men and women during colonial times. When using single words as the unit of analysis, it often is helpful to make use of a *context unit,* which is the context in which the single word is found. The words surrounding the word being used as the unit of analysis modify it and further explain its meaning. We then take this contextual information into account when coding the unit of analysis. For example, in the study just mentioned, the investigators needed to know whether the word *power* referred to men or to women. The context surrounding the word supplied this crucial information. The amount of context needed to explain the use of a given word adequately is, of course, variable.

The *theme* as a unit of analysis refers to the major subject matter of a document or part of a document. An entire document can be characterized as having a primary theme. Novels, for example, can be described as mysteries, science fiction, historical, and so on. In a study of the images of LGBT-themed children's books and their gender roles, parenting, and race, Lester (2014) found that despite presenting LGBT characters favorably, stories and characters also reinforced traditional gender roles, favored people with vested interests in parenting (as opposed to choices to not raise children), and presented primarily White and upper class lifestyles). Themes, however, can be difficult to delineate. The overall theme may or may not be clear, or there may be multiple themes. Coder reliability is likely to be lower than when easily identifiable words are the unit of analysis.

A third unit of analysis in documents is the *main character.* The use of this unit of analysis is, of course, limited to documents that have a cast of characters, such as plays, novels, movies, or television programs. A study of television programs on the Disney Channel, Cartoon Network, and Nickelodeon, for example, used the major character as the unit of analysis. That study found that 66% of major characters were males and that stereotypical gender-specific behaviors by major characters differed significantly by network (Hentges & Case, 2013).

The fourth unit of analysis is a *sentence* or *paragraph.* The study described earlier regarding congruency in clinician–client interaction used a similar unit of analysis: Each clinician's response,

preceded and followed by a client comment, was considered to be the unit to code, as either congruent or incongruent. A paragraph or even a single sentence, however, often contains more than one idea, and this may make these larger units more difficult to classify while maintaining mutually exclusive categories and intercoder reliability. Indeed, reliability often is lower than with the word or main character units. Yet, the larger units often are more theoretically relevant in the human services. In clinician–client interaction, for example, it makes little conceptual sense to characterize an interchange as congruent on the basis of one word. Meaning in social interaction normally arises from a whole block of words or sentences. So, as we emphasized when discussing units of analysis in Chapter 4, the primary consideration in selecting a unit of analysis is theoretical—that is, which unit seems to be preferable given theoretical and conceptual considerations.

Manifest Versus Latent Coding

In content analysis, researchers distinguish between *manifest coding* and *latent coding.* The term **manifest coding** refers to coding the more objective or surface content of a document or medium (Holsti, 1969). One example of manifest coding notes each time a particular word appears in a document. Another example occurs in a study of the portrayal of African Americans in children's picture books, which observed whether Blacks, Whites, or people of other racial groups appeared in the pictures (Pescosolido, Grauerholz, & Milkie, 1997). In some cases, it may be difficult to judge the race of a particular character—certainly more difficult than deciding whether a particular word appears in a document. This is still manifest coding, however, because there is a fairly direct link between the image in the document and the coding category.

Latent coding, on the other hand, inherently involves some inference in which the coder has to decide whether the representation in the document is an instance of some broader category of phenomena. Coders assess the representations in the document for what they say about a more abstract or implicit level of meaning. The study just mentioned also used latent coding to judge the nature of the Black representations in the picture books and of the Black–White interactions portrayed. So, the coders made judgments about how central the Black characters were in the pictures and about how intimate or egalitarian the Black–White interactions were. "Centrality," "intimacy," and "egalitarianism" are qualities that a coder must infer on the basis of a judgment or assessment of the materials.

Another example that used both manifest and latent coding was a study of resiliency and relational patterns of Maori, Pacific, and European families (Waldegrave et al., 2016). The study examined Maori, Pacific, and European families that were identified as resilient. Manifest coding was fairly straightforward coding of respondents' questions regarding relationship- and socially oriented sources of their resiliencies. Latent coding proceeded in an inductive approach and involved identifying and describing types of external supports associated with various themes identified in the manifest coding. This latent coding required researchers to make subjective judgments about the nature of various supports and their relationships to family resiliency, which does raise some issues pertaining to reliability. On the other hand, identifying and describing these supports and their relationships to participants' identified belief systems, organizational patterns, and communication styles that support resiliency allowed the researchers to develop new hypotheses pertaining to social factors that foster family resiliency. As these two examples illustrate, manifest coding generally is more reliable than latent coding, but latent coding often is a more valid way to get at some fairly complex and theoretically important social processes and characteristics.

ISSUES IN CONTENT ANALYSIS

When developing coding categories for content analysis, researchers confront several issues. Remember that content analysis is a form of measurement—that is, measurement of aspects of a document's contents. As such, we encounter the familiar concerns regarding validity and reliability, along with problems of choosing a level of measurement and a sample (see Chapters 5 and 6).

Validity

In content analysis, *validity* refers to whether the categories we develop and the aspects of the content coded are meaningful indicators of what we intend to measure. Developing coding schemes that are valid indicators can be challenging. For example, Anne Fortune (1979) reported on an effort to study communication patterns between social workers and their clients in which recordings of interviews were content analyzed. The goal of the research was to discover which interview techniques bring about cognitive and affective changes in clients. Fortune particularly wanted to know how techniques varied when the clients were adults rather than children. First, she developed a typology of communication techniques based on William Reid's work regarding task-centered casework. Because there are many ways to execute a particular verbal technique in a therapeutic setting, it was impossible to base the content analysis on a single word or phrase. Instead, Fortune provided coders with a description of each technique and examples of the verbal forms that each technique might take. For example, the communication technique of "exploration" was described as "communication intended to elicit information, including questions and restatements or 'echoes' of client's communications." Examples of this technique provided to the coders included such phrases as "What class was that?" and "You said your son misbehaved. . . . " The communication technique of "direction" was exemplified by "I think the first step would be to talk this over with your daughter" (Fortune, 1979, p. 391). By providing specific examples of how to code comments, she hoped the resulting coding would have greater validity than if the coders were left on their own.

Depending on the nature of the research and the documents to analyze, researchers might apply any of the methods for assessing validity discussed in Chapter 5. The logical approaches of content validity and jury opinion are the most generally used assessments of validity in content analysis, although researchers sometimes use criterion validity. For example, in a content analysis of suicide notes, one study attempted to identify aspects of the content of real suicide notes that would differentiate them from simulated ones written by people who had not actually attempted suicide (Jones & Bennell, 2007). The researchers compared the genuine notes with the simulated ones and found, among other things, that genuine notes used shorter sentences, gave more instructions to survivors about such things as financial matters, and expressed more positive affect than did the simulated notes. Using these criteria, people who did not know which notes were real and which were simulated were able to predict correctly the genuine notes with a high level of accuracy. The results suggest that the identified content of the notes were valid indicators of the authenticity of the notes.

Researchers must be able to argue convincingly that indicators are valid to attain acceptance of their scientific outcomes. Even though most content analyses do not go beyond content validity or jury opinion, it is important to remember that these are the weakest demonstrations of validity. Whenever possible, more rigorous tests should be attempted.

Reliability

Reliability refers to the ability of a measure to yield consistent results each time we use it. In content analysis, reliability relates to the ability of coders to apply the coding scheme consistently. The question is this: Can several workers code the documents according to the coding scheme and obtain consistent results? Reliability in content analysis depends on many factors, including the skill of the coders, the nature of the categories, the rules guiding the use of the categories, and the degree of clarity or ambiguity in the documents (Franzosi, 2008; Holsti, 1969). The clarity of the documents in any given study is largely fixed, so our discussion of control over reliability is limited to coders and categories used.

First, researchers can enhance reliability by thoroughly training the coders and having them practice applying the coding scheme. Anyone who continually deviates from the others in his or her coding during this practice period should not be

relied on as a coder. We must be cautious, however, about eliminating coders without assessing whether their deviation indicates poor performance or an ambiguous coding scheme.

Second, the nature of the categories to be applied to the document also is important for reliability. The simpler and more objective the categories, the higher the reliability. Vaguely defined categories or those requiring substantial interpretation decrease reliability, because they create greater opportunity for disagreement among the coders.

Measuring reliability in content analysis is much the same as measuring reliability when coding observed behavior (see Chapter 9). One simple method is to calculate the percentage of judgments on which coders agree out of the total number of judgments they must make:

$$\text{percent of agreement} = \frac{2 \times \text{number of agreements}}{\text{total number of observations recorded by both observers}}$$

Accepted levels of reliability are 75% or better agreement between coders. Well-trained coders using well-constructed coding schemes should achieve better than 85% agreement.

A certain tension exists between validity and reliability in content analysis. The simplest coding schemes, such as those employing word frequency counts, produce the highest reliability, because they are very easy to apply in a consistent manner. As noted, however, word frequency counts may not validly measure what we want to measure. We may have to sacrifice some degree of reliability for the sake of validity. Researchers often end up performing a balancing act between the dual requirements of validity and reliability.

Level of Measurement

Like other methods of collecting data, content analysis involves a decision about the level of measurement to use (see Chapter 5). The level of measurement achieved depends on the variable being measured and the process being used to measure it. The variable being measured puts an upper limit on the level of measurement that we can reach. For example, if we rate main characters in a book according to marital status, the highest level of measurement would be nominal, because marital status is a nominal variable. No amount of measurement finesse can change this once we have selected the key variables. Researchers do have some control over the level of measurement, however, depending on the process being used to measure the variables. The important factor is how we quantify the unit of analysis in the coding process. Coding systems in content analysis generally fall into one of four categories: (1) presence or absence of an element, (2) frequency of occurrence of an element, (3) amount of space or time devoted to an element, or (4) intensity of expression.

The simplest rating system is merely to indicate *the presence or the absence of an element* in a document. For example, we might rate interviews as to whether the clinician mentions certain subjects, such as sexual behavior or parent–child relationships. This simple system yields nominal data and conveys a minimum of content information. Several important questions remain unanswered. We do not know whether the clinician addressed the subject in a positive or a negative light, nor do we know how the client reacted. Also unknown is how much time was devoted to that subject and how frequently it was repeated. Consideration of these factors would make the study more informative.

Frequency counts are common methods of rating: We simply count how often an element appears. For example, Jack Levin and James Spates (1970) sought to compare the dominant values expressed in middle-class publications with those in the so-called underground press. The investigators rated the frequency with which statements of various values appeared in the two types of publications. On the basis of the frequency counts, the study concluded that the underground press emphasized values related to self-expression, whereas the middle-class publications stressed values related to various types of personal achievement. Frequency counts reveal more information about the document than a simple present-or-absent approach does and they open the way for more sophisticated statistical analysis, because with the appropriate theoretical concepts, they can achieve an interval- or ratio-level of measurement.

Coding systems based on *the amount of space or time devoted to an element* have proved useful for analyzing the mass media. In newspapers or magazines, the normal approach is to measure column inches. The equivalent for films or television is time. For example, in a study about the contribution of social work writers to the development of professional knowledge, Merlin Taber and Iris Shapiro (1965) counted the number of column inches that selected social work journals devoted to a discussion of different types of knowledge, such as theoretical versus empirical knowledge. We could measure, over a period of years, the amount of space devoted to a topic, such as family violence or the problems of lesbian mothers, to assess the impact of popular trends or political events on professional concern about various issues. The major attraction of space/time measures is their ease of use. We can measure the amount of space devoted to a given topic far more rapidly than we can measure word frequency counts or even whether key words are present or absent. Because each document takes only a short time to analyze, space/time measures allow a larger sample size and, possibly, lead to greater representativeness. Space/time measures also can yield interval- or ratio-level measurement with theoretical concepts that are amenable to such a level of measurement.

Qualitative data analysis software programs like Nvivo and Atlasti have tools to assist researchers with frequency counts and analyses of time or space devoted to a particular element. Word counts for specific words or phrases within written documents or transcripts, for example, can be calculated instantly as can analyses of the proportion of document space (or audio or video space for Nvivo) devoted to various themes or ideas (assuming they have already been coded by researchers).

Unfortunately, space/time measures are still somewhat crude. Other than the volume of space devoted to the particular topic in question, they reveal nothing further about the content. For example, time measures applied to the network news could tell us which types of news are allotted the most coverage but nothing about more subtle issues, such as whether the news coverage was biased. As Ole Holsti (1969) notes, "A one-to-one relationship between the amount of space devoted to a subject and the manner in which it is treated cannot be assumed" (p. 121).

The most complex rating systems involve a *measure of intensity*, that is, the forcefulness of expression in the documents. Developing intensity measures is difficult, however. Intensity of expression often is quite subtle and dependent on many aspects of word usage, which makes it extremely difficult to specify clearly the conditions for coding content elements. Coders have to make many judgments before deciding how to categorize the content, and this leads to disagreements and low reliability.

Developing intensity measures that produce reliable results is quite similar to constructing measurement scales, as we discuss in Chapter 13. We could, for example, have coders rate documents along a scale (as in the semantic differential or the Likert scales). Newspaper editorials dealing with public assistance programs might be rated as (a) very unfavorable, (b) unfavorable, (c) neutral, (d) favorable, or (e) very favorable. The options for intensity scales are nearly endless given the vast variety of intensity questions that can arise concerning the contents of documents. Despite their complexity, intensity measures are the most revealing about a document's contents.

Sampling

In document analysis, the number of documents often is too vast for all of them to be analyzed; in this case, we have to take a sample from a group of documents. For example, we might want to study the extent to which concern for child abuse has changed among human service providers between the 1950s and the 2000s. We could do this by studying the extent of coverage of the topic in human service journals during those years. Considering the number of journals and thousands of pages involved, sampling clearly is necessary to make such a project feasible.

As with other types of sampling, representativeness is a critical issue. To generalize the findings of our document analysis, the sampling procedure must be likely to yield a representative sample, which often is difficult to achieve with

documents. One problem is that the elements of the population of documents may not be equal. In studying child abuse, for example, some journals are more likely than others to publish articles on that topic—*Child Welfare* or the *Journal of Interpersonal Violence,* for example. A more general journal, like *Social Service Review,* would include a much smaller proportion of child abuse articles. Likewise, a journal specializing in a different area, such as the *Journals of Gerontology,* probably would not publish any articles on child abuse. A random sample of all human service journals, then, might include only a few journals most likely to publish articles on this topic. In other words, this random sample would be dominated by journals having a small likelihood of publishing family violence articles, making it more difficult to measure changes in practitioner concern for family violence. We can solve this problem by choosing our sample from among those journals specializing in areas related to family violence. Or, we can stratify the journals by type, and then select a stratified random sample, taking disproportionately more journals that are likely to publish articles on family violence (see Chapter 6).

A second issue in sampling documents is the difficulty in defining the population of documents. For example, a study on doctoral dissertations completed by social work students used content analysis to examine the proportion of dissertations that focused on social work interventions. The researchers had to determine where to locate abstracts of dissertations to create a sample. Ultimately they limited dissertations to those written by students from schools that were members of the Group of the Advancement of Doctoral Education (GADE) because they believed these schools were most likely to have well-established, high-quality programs. They accessed dissertations from the ProQuest Dissertations and Abstract and Theses database using the key word "social work" and limiting the search to dissertations and theses. This resulted in 790 abstracts, which was then cut to 445 when master's theses were excluded. When they further limited analysis to students from GADE member schools they ultimately came to a final sample size of 252 (Horton & Hawkins, 2010).

Assuming that we can adequately define the population to sample, we can apply to documents the normal procedures of sampling discussed in Chapter 6. Of those, simple random sampling probably is most common and most generally applicable (Scott, 1990). As we have seen, however, researchers may require stratified sampling to avoid bias when sampling from a population of unequal elements. We should approach systematic sampling cautiously, because it is easy to be trapped by periodicity in documents (see Chapter 6). *Periodicity* is the problem in which elements with certain characteristics occur at patterned intervals throughout the sampling frame. For example, both the size and the content of newspapers vary substantially with the days of the week. If the sampling interval were seven or a multiple of seven, then a systematic sample would include only papers published on the same day of the week and could be very biased, depending on the aspects of content under study.

Sampling documents often involves multistage sampling. As in all multistage sampling, we start with large units and work down through a series of sampling stages to smaller and smaller units. The sample of the underground press by Levin and Spates (1970) illustrates multistage sampling. In the first stage, the researchers selected a sample of publications from the membership of the Underground Press Syndicate by choosing the top five publications in terms of circulation. In the second stage, they randomly selected a single issue of each publication for every other month from September 1967 to August 1968. This produced six sample issues for each of the five publications, for a total of 30 issues. In the final stage, Levin and Spates selected for analysis every other nonfiction article appearing in the sample issues. The resulting sample contained 316 articles to represent the underground press.

ASSESSMENT OF AVAILABLE DATA ANALYSIS

Like other research techniques, the use of available data has both advantages and disadvantages. A consideration of these helps determine when such analysis is the most appropriate and points out some potential problems as well. The Research in Practice 8.2 section also discusses some ethical issues directly related to using available data.

RESEARCH IN PRACTICE 8.2 Information Technologies and Ethical Research

Developments in information technologies have brought new twists to the conduct of ethical research. For example, we now have inexpensive and portable data storage devices in the form of memory sticks and laptop computers. We can also easily transmit large amounts of data electronically over the Internet. In addition, medical and social service records are now often stored electronically. So, it is now relatively easy for researchers to access and transmit these data sets. In addition, propelled in part by the demands of government funders of medical and social services, the data collection instruments are increasingly uniform across agencies and even states. All of these developments make it possible for researchers to archive, or combine, these data sets to include cases from multiple organizations, states, and time periods, resulting in multiorganizational and longitudinal research that can overcome some of the weaknesses of more traditional secondary analysis of statistical data. Such data sets can also answer many more questions relevant to evidence-based social policy than can more limited data sets (Jonson-Reid & Drake, 2008).

One of the advantages of such nonreactive, available data is that the researcher confronts fewer ethical dilemmas as compared to gathering data directly from people. Ethical concerns do arise, however, especially in trying to maintain the privacy (confidentiality and anonymity) of

(continued)

these data. For example, the easy portability of these storage devices makes it tempting to bring data home or to another location that is not secure. There have been cases where data stored on a memory stick or laptop computer was lost or stolen. Some research falls under the purview of government agencies and legislation, such as the Family Educational Rights and Privacy Act (FERPA) or Health Insurance Portability and Accountability Act (HIPAA), and this can provide some guidance regarding how to handle these privacy concerns. The HIPAA Privacy Rule, for example, suggests procedures for protecting the privacy of people whose health data will be used in available-data research (Centers for Disease Control and Prevention [CDC], 2003; Office for Civil Rights [OCR], 2009). One approach is to use a "de-identified" data set, which means that 18 specified identifiers have been removed from the data set (such as names and telephone numbers). Such a data set would presumably have no information that could identify a particular individual. Another approach is to use a "limited" data set, in which most of these identifiers have been removed but a few are retained (such as some geographic identifiers or birth dates). However, the identifiers that remain in a limited data set must be essential to the research and must not be used to re-identify the individual.

With research that involves available data spanning many organizations or time periods, there must be a way to identify particular individuals so that their data from different organizations or time periods can be connected. One way to handle this is to de-identify the final, or "use," database and subject it to limited security because it poses no threat to privacy (Jonson-Reid & Drake, 2008). Then, the working, or "core," data set would have identifiers and would be used when new cases need to be added to the file and linked with previous cases. This core data set would require higher levels of security. For example, research organization rules might prohibit saving the core data set on a memory stick or other easily transportable device. Or there might be a security code required to open or save the core data set.

Various federal agencies provide guidelines for how to gather and share such available data while meeting ethical standards (CDC, 2005). Researchers review these guidelines carefully for insight while designing their research.

Advantages

Lower Costs. Document analysis is one of the least costly forms of research, and using available statistical data can help reduce the costs of a research project. The producers of the documents or statistics bear the major expense of data gathering rather than the researcher. The sheer volume of data that the U.S. Census Bureau, the NASW, or the many local and state social agencies collects is so massive that only the best-endowed research projects could possibly duplicate their efforts. Document analysis becomes expensive if the documents of interest are widely scattered and difficult to obtain or if very large samples are employed. Also, the more complex the coding process, the more expensive the study. Overall, however, available data offer an opportunity to conduct valuable research at reasonable cost.

For practitioners and policy makers, using available data to evaluate services, assess the effectiveness of specific strategies or approaches, and gauge responsiveness to various populations can be tremendously beneficial. It helps us avoid natural tendencies to forget past mistakes and only seek data that reinforces our existing beliefs. Examining hard data can also help various entities reach consensus in establishing priorities and agreement about areas where improvements are needed.

Nonreactivity. Like hidden observation and unobtrusive measures, available data are nonreactive (see Chapters 4 and 9). Unlike surveys or experiments, in which the participants are aware that they are being studied, producers of documents normally do not anticipate a researcher coming along at a later date to analyze those documents. The contents of the documents are, therefore, unaffected by the researcher's activities. This does not mean, of course, that those who produced the documents did not react to some elements that might have biased the documents. For example, a social worker might be more likely to substantiate a case of abuse or neglect following an investigation when the parent or parents in a family are non-White than when they are White, thus generating data that make non-Whites appear to be more abusive and neglectful. In addition, people who compile documents may be reacting to how people other than researchers, such as a supervisor or a politician, may respond to their document. Likewise, the preparer's hope for a "place in history" can shape the preparation of a document. Despite all this, researchers are not a source of reactivity with available data.

Inaccessible Subjects. When properly cared for, documents can survive far longer than the people who produce them. Document analysis allows us to study the ways of society long ago and the behaviors of people long dead. The study of the colonial family by Lantz et al. (1968) and the study of suicide notes by Jones and Bennell (2007) dealt with the behavior of people quite inaccessible by research techniques other than document analysis.

Longitudinal Analysis. Many statistical data and documents are collected routinely over a period of years—or even centuries. This contrasts sharply with the typical one-shot, cross-sectional survey data. With such longitudinal data, we can accomplish trend analysis—that is, looking for changing patterns over time. For example, Reynolds Farley (1984) used a longitudinal analysis of available data in an evaluation of the progress of African Americans in the United States since the 1950s. Using census data from the 1950s, 1960s, and 1970s, Farley compared the position of African Americans relative to Whites over three decades, and he found mixed results. The census data revealed that African Americans as a whole had made substantial gains in quality of employment, family earnings, and educational attainment. Other indicators, such as residential integration, unemployment rate, and school integration, were less encouraging, however, showing little or no improvement. This type of research obviously is

valuable in putting today's conditions into historical perspective; just as obviously, researchers can conduct this type of longitudinal analysis of past trends only through the analysis of available data. (Existing statistical data often lend themselves to the kind of time-series analysis that we will describe in Chapter 10.)

Sample Size. Many types of documents are abundant. As mentioned when discussing sampling, a researcher is likely to confront far more documents than he or she can analyze rather than too few. This means that a researcher can employ large samples to increase confidence in the results. The low cost associated with document analysis also contributes to the researcher's ability to use substantial sample sizes without encountering prohibitive costs.

Disadvantages

Variable Quality. Because documents are produced for purposes other than research, their quality for research purposes is quite variable. Unless researchers know the limitations of the documents, as with crime statistics, they may have little idea of the conditions under which the data were collected or the attention to quality that went into them. Researchers should, of course, investigate the issue of quality when possible to discover any deficiencies in the data. When we cannot do this, we simply have to draw conclusions cautiously.

Incompleteness. Documents, especially those of a historical nature, frequently are incomplete. Gaps of weeks, months, or even years are not uncommon. In addition, data may be missing in available statistics. The effect of these gaps on a study often is impossible to know, except that such gaps reduce confidence in the findings. Incompleteness is simply a common characteristic plaguing available data that researchers have to work around if they can.

Lack of Comparability Over Time. Even though documents are commonly used in longitudinal analysis, this can be problematic, because change over time may create statistical artifacts in the data and render comparisons useless. With crime statistics, for example, changes in how the FBI collects data make it misleading to compare crime statistics over long periods of time. Researchers need to be careful of similar kinds of changes in other data.

Bias. Because documents are produced for purposes other than research, there is no assurance that they are objective. Data from private sources, for example, may be intentionally slanted to present a particular viewpoint. A researcher who blindly accepts such data can walk into a trap. Nonstatistical documents may suffer from biased presentation as well. A good example is the corporate annual report to stockholders, filled with glowing praise for management, impressive color photographs, and bright prospects for the future and presenting anything negative either in the most favorable light or camouflaged in legalese.

Sampling Bias. Bias may creep into otherwise objective data during the sampling process. As we have noted, sampling documents often is difficult because of unequal population elements and hard-to-define populations. We also have commented that document sampling frequently is complex, requiring several stages. Errors or bad decisions made during the sampling process can result in a highly biased sample that will produce misleading results.

Using Available Data in Research on Minorities

When studying emotionally charged topics, such as racism or sexism, reactivity can be a very serious problem, because people are inclined to disguise true feelings or motives that might result in disapproval. Even though they may feel prejudice that influences their behavior, people may deny feelings of prejudice toward minorities or women when a survey researcher asks about such feelings. One of the major benefits of available data, however, is that they often are less reactive than other data used to study behavior. Therefore, available data may be the preferred research method—or a valued adjunct to other research methods—when studying such emotion-laden topics.

Consider, for example, some of the uses to which researchers have put available data in the study of racism and sexism. If we ask people whether they are racists or sexists or whether they treat women or minorities unfairly, most people deny it, especially in the contemporary environment that frowns upon such attitudes and practices. Yet, the records of agencies and organizations might contain evidence of sexism or racism despite the denial of those who run those organizations. Are Whites or males found disproportionately in the more prestigious or better-paying positions in an organization? Do Whites or males earn substantially higher salaries than women or minorities in the organization do? Such organizational practices suggest sexism or racism in the organization. It often is less reactive and more valid to measure the consequences of organizational decisions than to ask people about such things directly.

Another way to detect the persistence of prejudices and stereotypes is to study the portrayal of people in various cultural products, such as books, magazines, or movies. Two or more decades ago, the images of males and females that were presented in school textbooks, for example, typically reinforced traditional stereotypes: Males were pictured far more often than females; males were pictured in many occupations and women in few; and female pronouns, such as *her*, were uncommon. Things have improved, especially when efforts are made to produce materials that are nonsexist in their presentation, but stereotyping persists. More recent studies of children's picture books, for example, find that, although they are portrayed more often than in the past, women are still shown less often than men are (only one third of the illustrations are of women); women are still shown in fewer occupations than men; women are still likely to be portrayed in traditional gender roles associated with household work; and women are still portrayed as less brave and adventurous and more helpless (Crabb & Bielawski, 1994; Koss, 2015; Owen & Padron, 2016; Peterson & Lach, 1990; Purcell & Stewart, 1990). Even college textbooks are not immune to these influences. Studies of the pictorial content of texts for college-level psychology and sociology courses found that women appear less often than men and are depicted more passively and negatively than men are (Collins & Hebert, 2008; Ferree & Hall, 1990; Manza & Van Schyndel, 2000; Peterson & Kroner, 1992). For example, the psychology texts portray women as the victims of mental disorders and as the clients in therapy while picturing men as the therapists. Thus, cultural products, like books or newspapers, can serve as available data to detect gender stereotyping that might be undetectable by other research methods.

REVIEW AND CRITICAL THINKING

Main Points

- Available data include both statistical data collected by others and documents, which include any form of communication.
- Content analysis quantifies and organizes the qualitative and unsystematic information contained in documents.
- Content analysis is essentially a form of measurement, making the issues of validity and reliability paramount. Available data also must be analyzed carefully in terms of level of measurement, which is determined by the nature of the variable being measured as well as by the process being used in measuring it from the available data used.
- Document analysis normally includes some form of sampling procedure, which must be performed carefully for the sake of representativeness.
- Document analysis offers the advantages of low cost, nonreactivity, ability to study otherwise inaccessible subjects, easy longitudinal analysis, and often, large samples.
- Problems in using available data include the variable quality of the data, incomplete data, changes in data over time, possible bias in data, and possible sampling bias.
- The analysis of available data often is less reactive than other research methods, which can make it useful in the study of emotionally charged topics, such as racism and sexism, where people may be inclined to hide their true feelings and emotions.

IMPORTANT TERMS FOR REVIEW

Available data	Data archives	Missing data
Coding	Latent coding	Secondary analysis
Content analysis	Manifest coding	

CRITICAL THINKING

1. Why might researchers use available data as opposed to collecting data themselves? Identify and describe a human services practice (intervention) or policy scenario where available data could be used to address a practice or policy concern (like the HMIS example where the database was used to identify service gaps and priority populations).

2. What are advantages and disadvantages of relying on available data to answer research questions? Does using available data help researchers and practitioners create more valid and reliable measures of variables? Does this depend on the nature of the data? Refer back to the scenario in Question 1. What variables might you measure with the available data? Would this be a valid and reliable measure?

3. What are sources of available data that can be accessed by human services professionals in conducting applied research and evaluation? What additional data would help you (as a future practitioner) better address issues that are important to you (and better serve your clients)? How could this data be collected in the future (and by whom)? What are challenges to collecting these data?

EVALUATING COMPETENCY (FROM THE COUNCIL ON SOCIAL WORK EDUCATION [CSWE] 2015 EDUCATIONAL POLICY AND ACCREDITATION STANDARDS [EPAS])

Competency 2: Engage Diversity and Difference in Practice, and Competency 3: Advance Human Rights and Social, Economic, and Environmental Justice

- Social workers understand that there are mechanisms of oppression and injustice that marginalize some populations and that human services systems have played and may even continue to play a role in marginalizing some groups (e.g., in human resources practices, in treatment of clients or potential clients, and in disproportionality of program or treatment outcomes). Identify an area of practice where some groups may have been treated unjustly (or different than other groups).
- What sources of data might be helpful in examining these injustices? What would you look to in these data (specifically) to assess unjust treatment of minorities and other disadvantaged populations?

Competency 4: Engage in Practice-Informed Research and Research-Informed Practice

- Human service professionals often have access to substantial program, agency, and human services system data. How might professionals work collaboratively with researchers and one another to analyze these data to create more effective and efficient services?
- Human service professionals are typically very busy meeting their clients' needs and often have little time to review available data to inform program or policy changes. Given time constraints, what can practitioners do to make better use of available data to improve services?

Competency 9: Evaluate Practice With Individuals, Families, Groups, Organizations, and Communities

- Human services professionals engaged in direct practice are typically focused on client outcomes while administrators and policy makers are typically focused on agency-level and system-level outcomes. How can direct practitioners, administrators, and policy makers work together to assess relationships between individual, agency, and system outcomes? How might using available data help in this process?
- Think about an area of practice in which you are passionate (or in which you are currently working). What types of data tend to get recorded in program, agency, or system-wide databases? To what extent are these data reflective of individual, program, agency, and system-wide performance? What other data would need to be collected to give researchers and others the opportunity to assess the extent to which individuals, programs, agencies, and systems as a whole are effective?

SELF-ASSESSMENT

1. Quantified observations of some element of human behavior are known as:
   a. Meta-analyses.
   b. Spreadsheets.
   c. Statistical data.
   d. Scatterplots.
2. Examples of data that can be collected without approval from an Institutional Review Board include:
   a. Observations collected by someone other than the investigator for purposes that differ from the investigator's.
   b. Data obtained from other researchers.
   c. Data collected from interviews with clients at an agency where the researcher has worked as a social worker.
   d. Data obtained from hidden or disguised observations.
3. This reanalysis of data collected for some other research project is called:
   a. Post hoc analysis.
   b. Tertiary analysis.
   c. Convenience sampling.
   d. Secondary analysis.
4. Which of the following circumstances can result in threats to measurement validity when using available data from a human services agency?
   a. Some elements of agency operation, such as achievement of goals, success of programs, or satisfaction of clients, may not be measured directly by any data that are normally collected by an agency.
   b. Researchers change operational definitions so that they can measure variables with the available data.

    c. Procedures that an agency or organization uses in gathering data change over time.

    d. All of the above.

5. Which of these terms refers to a method of transforming the symbolic content of a document, such as words or other images, from a qualitative, unsystematic form into a quantitative, systematic form?

    a. Operationalization

    b. Content analysis

    c. Surveying

    d. Criterion validity

6. Categorizing behaviors or elements into a limited number of categories is known as:

    a. Transcription.

    b. Ration level of measurement.

    c. Inductive reasoning.

    d. Coding.

7. Like categories in any measurement process, those used in content analysis should be:

    a. Exhaustive and mutually exclusive.

    b. Exhaustive but not necessarily mutually exclusive.

    c. Mutually exclusive but not necessarily exhaustive.

    d. Neither mutually exclusive nor exhaustive.

8. Which of these is a unit of analysis that refers to the major subject matter of a document or part of a document?

    a. Element

    b. Category

    c. Theme

    d. Indicator

9. Which type of coding in content analysis inherently involves some inference in which the coder has to decide whether the representation in the document is an instance of some broader category of phenomena?

    a. Manifest coding

    b. Manifest destiny

    c. Likert scaling

    d. Latent coding

10. Using available data in research has advantages with respect to measurement validity because the contents of the documents are unaffected by the researcher's activities. This is known as:

    a. Criterion validity.

    b. Concurrent validity.

    c. External validity.

    d. Nonreactivity.

ANSWER KEY FOR SELF-ASSESSMENT QUIZ

1. **c.** Statistical data
2. **a.** Observations collected by someone other than the investigator for purposes that differ from the investigator's.
3. **d.** Secondary analysis
4. **d.** All of the above.
5. **b.** Content analysis
6. **d.** Coding
7. **a.** Exhaustive and mutually exclusive
8. **c.** Theme
9. **d.** Latent coding
10. **d.** Nonreactivity

FOR FURTHER READING

Larose, D. (2005). *Discovering knowledge in data: An introduction to data mining.* Hoboken, NJ: Wiley InterScience. This book introduces students to several statistical methods used for exploring and analyzing existing quantitative data sets.

Lee, R. M. (2000). *Unobtrusive methods in social research.* Philadelphia, PA: Open University Press. This book provides an excellent overview of the different types of unobtrusive or nonreactive measures as well as the advantages and problems in using them.

McCulloch, G. (2004). *Documentary research in education, history, and the social sciences.* New York, NY: Routledge Falmer. This book offers an overview of documentary research. The chapters explore a wide range of documentary source materials that are available for researchers in the social sciences: Policy reports, autobiographies, diaries, committee papers, correspondence, school magazines, textbooks, log books, newspapers, local registers, and visual sources such as photographs and paintings.

Murnane, R. J., & Willett, J. B. (2010). *Methods matter: Improving causal inference in educational and social science research.* New York, NY: Oxford University Press. This book examines ways in which researchers can help policy makers and other decision makers make more informed decisions when using existing data while critically examining data collection and other research methodologies used in creating data sets.

Riedel, M. (2000). *Research strategies for secondary data: A perspective for criminology and criminal justice.* Thousand Oaks, CA: Sage. Although it focuses on the field of criminology, this useful guide to the many sources of data available for secondary analysis also reviews some of the methodological issues that are important to consider in doing such data analysis.

West, M. D. (2001). *Applications of computer content analysis.* Westport, CT: Ablex. This is a basic introduction to the procedures used in conducting content analysis research, with special emphasis on the role of computers.

REFERENCES

Abrahms, M., Beauchamp, N., & Mroszczyk, J. (2017). What terrorist leaders want: A content analysis of terrorist propaganda videos. *Studies in Conflict & Terrorism, 40*(11), 899–916. doi:10.1080/1057610X.2016.1248666

Bales, R. F. (1950). *Interaction process analysis.* Cambridge, MA: Addison-Wesley.

Barlow, H. (1996). *Introduction to criminology* (7th ed.). New York, NY: Harper Collins.

Centers for Disease Control and Prevention. (2003). HIPAA privacy rule and public health: Guidance from CDC and the U.S. Department of Health and Human Services. *Morbidity and Mortality Weekly Review, 52,* 1–12. Retrieved from https://www.cdc.gov/mmwr/preview/mmwrhtml/m2e411a1.htm

Centers for Disease Control and Prevention. (2005). CDC/ATSDR Policy on releasing and sharing data. *Manual GUIDE: General Administration, CDC-GA-2005-14.* Atlanta, GA: Author. Retrieved from https://www.cdc.gov/maso/policy/releasingdata.pdf

Collins, J., & Hebert, T. (2008). Race and gender images in psychology textbooks. *Race, Gender & Class, 15,* 300–307. Retrieved from https://www.jstor.org/stable/41674666

Crabb, P. B., & Bielawski, D. (1994). The social representation of material culture and gender in children's books. *Sex Roles, 30*(1–2), 69–79. doi:10.1007/bf01420740

Cronley, C., Strand, E. B., Patterson, D. A., & Gwaltney, S. (2009). Homeless people who are animal caretakers: A comparative study. *Psychological Reports, 105*(2), 481–499. Retrieved from https://doi.org/10.2466/PR

Duehn, W. D., & Proctor, E. K. (1977). Initial clinical interaction and premature discontinuance in treatment. *American Journal of Orthopsychiatry, 47*(2), 284–290. doi:10.1111/j.1939-0025.1977.tb00983.x

Fargo, J., Metraux, S., Byrne, T., Munley, E., Montgomery, A. E., Jones, H., & Culhane, D. (2012). Prevalence and risk of homelessness among US veterans. *Preventing Chronic Disease, 9*(45), 110112. doi:10.5888/pcd9.110112

Farley, R. (1984). *Blacks and Whites: Narrowing the gap.* Cambridge, MA: Harvard University Press.

Ferree, M., & Hall, E. (1990). Visual images of American society: Gender and race in introductory sociology textbooks. *Gender and Society, 4*(4), 500–533. doi:10.1177/089124390004004005

Fortune, A. E. (1979). Communication in task-centered treatment. *Social Work, 24*(5), 390–397.

Franzosi, R. (Ed.). (2008). *Content analysis.* Thousand Oaks, CA: Sage.

Gramlich, J. (2017). Most violent and property crimes in the U.S. go unsolved. Retrieved from http://www.pewresearch.org/fact-tank/2017/03/01/most-violent-and-property-crimes-in-the-u-s-go-unsolved

Grana, R. A., Popova, L., & Ling, P. M. (2014). A longitudinal analysis of electronic cigarette and smoking cessation. *JAMA Internal Medicine, 174*(5), 812–813. doi:10.1001/jamainternmed.2014.187

Hentges, B., & Case, K. (2013). Gender representations on Disney Channel, Cartoon Network, and Nickelodeon broadcasts in the United States. *Journal of Children and Media, 7*(3), 319–333. doi:10.1080/17482798.2012.729150

Holsti, O. R. (1969). *Content analysis for the social sciences and humanities.* Reading, MA: Addison-Wesley.

Horton, E. G., & Hawkins, M. (2010). A content analysis of intervention research in social work doctoral dissertations. *Journal of Evidence-Based Social Work, 7*(5), 377–386. doi:10.1080/15433710903344066

Jones, N. J., & Bennell, C. (2007). The development and validation of statistical prediction rules for discriminating between genuine and simulated suicide notes. *Archives of Suicide Research, 11*(2), 219–233. doi:10.1080/13811110701250176

Jonson-Reid, M., & Drake, B. (2008). Multisector longitudinal databases: An indispensable tool for evidence-based policy for maltreated children and their families. *Child Maltreatment, 13*(4), 392–399. doi:10.1177/1077559508320058

Kang, M. (1997). The portrayal of women's images in magazine advertisements: Goffman's gender analysis revisited. *Sex Roles, 37*(11–12), 979–996. doi:10.1007/bf02936350

Koss, M. D. (2015). Diversity in contemporary picture books: A content analysis. *Journal of Children's Literature, 41*(1), 31–42.

Krippendorf, K. (2019). *Content analysis: An introduction to its methodology* (4th ed.). Thousand Oaks, CA: Sage.

Lantz, H. R., Schmitt, R., Britton, M., & Snyder, E. C. (1968). Pre-industrial patterns in the colonial family in America: A content analysis of colonial magazines. *American Sociological Review, 33*(3), 413–426. doi:10.2307/2091915

Lester, J. Z. (2014). Homonormativity in children's literature: An intersectional analysis of queer-themed picture books. *Journal of LGBT Youth, 11*(3), 244–275. doi:10.1080/19361653.2013.879465

Levin, J., & Spates, J. L. (1970). Hippie values: An analysis of the underground press. *Youth and Society, 2*(1), 59–73. doi:10.1177/0044118x7000200104

Manza, J., & Van Schyndel, D. (2000). Still the missing feminist revolution? Inequalities of race, class, and gender in introductory sociology textbooks. *American Sociological Review, 65*(3), 468–475. doi:10.2307/2657468

Neuendorf, K. A. (2002). *The content analysis guidebook.* Thousand Oaks, CA: Sage.

Nomaguchi, K. M. (2009). Change in work-family conflict among employed parents between 1977 and 1997. *Journal of Marriage and Family, 71,* 15–32. doi:10.1111/j.1741-3737.2008.00577.x

Office for Civil Rights. (2009). Health information privacy. Retrieved from https://www.hhs.gov/ocr/hipaa

Owen, P. R., & Padron, M. (2016). The language of toys: Gendered language in toy advertisements. *Journal of Research on Women and Gender, 6,* 67–80.

Pescosolido, B. A., Grauerholz, E., & Milkie, M. A. (1997). Culture and conflict: The portrayal of Blacks in U.S. children's picture books through the mid- and late-twentieth century. *American Sociological Review, 62*(3), 443–464. doi:10.2307/2657315

Peterson, S., & Kroner, T. (1992). Gender biases in textbooks for introductory psychology and human development. *Psychology of Women Quarterly, 16*(1), 17–36. doi:10.1111/j.1471-6402.1992.tb00237.x

Peterson, S., & Lach, M. (1990). Gender stereotypes in children's books: Their prevalence and influence on cognitive and affective development. *Gender and Education, 2*(2), 185–197. doi:10.1080/0954025900020204

Prothro, J. W. (1956). Verbal shifts in the American presidency: A content analysis. *American Political Science Review, 50*(03), 726–739. doi:10.2307/1951555

Purcell, P., & Stewart, L. (1990). Dick and Jane in 1989. *Sex Roles, 22*(3–4), 177–185. doi:10.1007/bf00288190

Riedel, M. (2000). *Research strategies for secondary data: A perspective for criminology and criminal justice.* Thousand Oaks, CA: Sage.

Scott, J. (1990). *A matter of record: Documentary sources in social research.* Oxford, UK: Polity Press.

Sieber, J. (Ed.). (1991). *Sharing social science data: Advantages and challenges.* Newbury Park, CA: Sage.

Taber, M., & Shapiro, I. (1965). Social work and its knowledge base: A content analysis of the periodical literature. *Social Work, 10*(4), 100–107. doi:10.1093/sw/10.4.100

Waldegrave, C., King, P., Maniapoto, M., Tamases, T. K., Parsons, T. L., & Sullivan, G. (2016). Relational resilience in Maori, Pacific, and European sole parent families: From theory and research to social policy. *Family Processes, 55*(4), 673. doi:10.1111/famp.12219

Whalen, J., & Zimmerman, D. H. (1998). Observations on the display and management of emotion in naturally occurring activities: The case of "Hysteria" in Calls to 9-1-1. *Social Psychology Quarterly, 61*(2), 141–159. doi:10.2307/2787066

9

FIELD RESEARCH AND QUALITATIVE METHODS

INTRODUCTION

Jane is a mental health therapist who provides a treatment to a variety of clients ranging from adults with clinical depression to children with attention deficit hyperactivity disorder. She is seeing a new client, Jeremy, today. He is a 45-year-old man who has come to her agency because he says he is feeling depressed. Jeremy arrives 15 minutes late for his appointment and when Jane meets him at the reception desk he immediately apologizes for being late. On the way to her office he tells her that he was late because he was debating whether or not to come and that he only left the house to come because his wife insisted on it. Jeremy was wearing casual business attire, but it was obvious that his shirt was not clean and his pants were excessively wrinkled. He did not have a beard, but it appeared he had not shaved in at least 2 days. His hair was uncombed and he had dark circles under his eyes. After sitting down in Jane's office he yawned twice. He immediately apologized and admitted he had not slept the night before, partially because he was stressed about both his work and family and because he was nervous about coming to this appointment.

As you read the start of this vignette you are likely already beginning to make some mental notes about Jeremy. You may also be thinking about some potential areas you would like to explore and perhaps even some questions you would like to ask him. As a good mental health therapist Jane has also noticed several things, starting with Jeremy's being late to his somewhat disheveled appearance. She has also noted that he has already apologized to her twice. No doubt she has taken note of the fact that he has not slept and reports feeling stressed about both his work and family. She has also already decided that at some point she would like to ask him about his relationship with his wife as it already appears there may be some conflict within the relationship. While there are no outward signs of alcohol or drug use she has also begun to wonder whether Jeremy may be drinking or using drugs to cope with his stress and what she believes may be depression as well. Still she is careful not to make too many assumptions about Jeremy before she has more information.

While Jane is not a researcher and her work with Jeremy is not research, her training as a mental health therapist has taught her an important skill that is critical to both researchers and practitioners, observation. In research, **observational techniques** refer to the collection of data through direct visual or auditory experience of behavior. With observational techniques, which can include video or audio recordings of behavior, the researcher actually sees or hears the behavior or words that are the data for the research. Observational techniques can be either quantitative or qualitative in nature.

While not conducting research, Jane's observations of Jeremy have many parallels to qualitative observations in research. She has taken notice of his appearance and behaviors. She has also studied his words, tone, and voice. She is beginning to develop some questions she would like to explore further as she begins to assess Jeremy and understand his life and mental state. Of course she is careful not to draw conclusions too quickly and to continue to collect new information while allowing her mental picture of Jeremy to develop over time. This approach is very much like a qualitative researcher conducting grounded theory research.

In this chapter, we will present field research and qualitative research methods. Throughout the chapter, we will discuss parallels between field and qualitative research, and mental health counseling, particularly assessment. Please keep the following questions in mind as you read this chapter: (a) What types of research and practice questions or problems are best answered through qualitative as opposed to quantitative research? (b) How can researchers and practitioners increase the reliability of their qualitative measures? and (c) Why is context so important in understanding social phenomena and how can qualitative research methods help researchers and practitioners better understand the importance of context?

As we discussed in Chapter 1, qualitative research basically involves research in which the data come in the form of words, pictures, narratives, and descriptions rather than in numerical form. A second way that observational techniques differ from one another is whether the observations are done in a naturalistic setting or in a laboratory or contrived setting. A *naturalistic setting* is a "real-life" situation in which people behave as they routinely would if they were not the subjects of scientific observation. In fact, in some cases, people in naturalistic settings may not even know that they are under observation. Contrived settings are created by the researcher and would not have occurred were it not for the research project. This chapter focuses on observation done in naturalistic, or field, settings. (We will discuss observation in contrived settings, such as laboratory experiments, in Chapter 10.)

Field research involves observations made of people in their natural settings as they go about their everyday life. Surveys involve people's reports to the researcher about what they said, did, or felt. With surveys and available data, the researcher does not directly observe what will be the focus of the research. With field research, on the other hand, the researcher actually sees or hears the behaviors that are the data for the research. Field research is most closely associated, in many people's minds, with the work of anthropologists, who live among indigenous peoples for extended periods and write ethnographic reports that summarize people's way of life. Yet, researchers in other social sciences and the human services also find field research to be a useful way to gather data.

This chapter focuses mostly on qualitative field research, but it also explores methods of collecting quantitative data in the field and some other types of qualitative methods. It is helpful to begin with a quick overview of some of the characteristics that set qualitative research methods apart from quantitative research methods.

In the mental health analogous example, Jane is not able to view Jeremy in his naturalistic work or home settings, so she is forced to make judgments about his life based on what he does and says in a therapeutic setting. Of course this means Jane must be aware that what Jeremy does or says in this setting may not be a perfect reflection of himself in the outside world.

CHARACTERISTICS OF QUALITATIVE METHODS

Contextual Approach

Chapters 2 and 4 introduced the distinctions between positivist and nonpositivist approaches to science and between qualitative and quantitative research. Although qualitative research methods at times might be conducted by people who take a positivist approach and might involve collecting some quantitative data, qualitative research has been closely associated over the years with nonpositivist or interpretive paradigms. Proponents of such paradigms argue that qualitative and contextual approaches offer access to a valuable type of data—namely, a deeper and richer understanding of people's lives and behavior, including some knowledge of their subjective experiences (Benjafield, 2002; Benton, 1977; Gubrium & Holstein, 1997; Lincoln, Lynham, & Guba, 2011). This is the reason why we offer to present the analogy of mental health treatment as we present qualitative research methods, because both qualitative researchers and mental health practitioners are often interested in understanding individuals' subjective experiences.

Positivism argues that the world exists independently of people's perceptions of it and that scientists can use objective techniques to discover what exists in the world (Cupchik, 2001; Durkheim, 1938; Halfpenny, 1982). Astronomers, for example, use telescopes to discover stars and

galaxies, which exist regardless of whether we are aware of them. So, too, researchers can study human beings in terms of behaviors that can be observed and recorded using some kind of objective techniques. Recording people's gender, age, height, weight, or socioeconomic position are legitimate and objective measurement techniques—the equivalent of the physicist measuring the temperature, volume, or velocity of some liquid or solid. For the positivist, quantifying these measurements—that is, assessing the average age of a group or looking at the percentage of a group that is male—is simply a precise way of describing and summarizing an objective reality. Such measurement provides a solid and objective foundation for understanding human social behavior. Limiting study to observable behaviors and using objective techniques, positivists argue, is most likely to produce systematic and repeatable research results that are open to refutation by other scientists. Some mental health practitioners, including those relying on behaviorists models, may limit their assessments of clients to observable and even quantifiable behaviors. Most, however, also tend to be focused on clients' subjective and felt experiences, including Jane in the previous example.

Subjectivism (also called the *interpretive,* or *verstehen, approach*) provides a more nonpositivist perspective on these issues. It is argued that these "objective" measures miss an important part of the human experience, namely the subjective and personal meanings that people attach to themselves, to what they do, and to the world around them (Wilson, 1970). Max Weber, an early proponent of this view, argued that we need to look not only at what people do but also at what they think and feel about what is happening to them (Weber, 1925/1957). Researchers cannot adequately capture this "meaning," or "feeling," or "interpretive" dimension through objective, quantitative measurement techniques; they need to gain what Weber called **verstehen,** or a subjective understanding. They need to view and experience the situation from the perspective of the people themselves. To use a colloquialism, the researchers need "to walk a mile in the shoes" of the people being studied. They need to talk to these people at length and immerse themselves in their subjects' lives so that they can experience the highs and lows, the joys and sorrows, the triumphs and the tragedies from the perspective of the people they are studying.

Researchers need to see how the individuals experience and give meaning to what is happening to them. Qualitative research methods are an attempt to gain access to that personal, subjective experience. These qualitative approaches stress the idea that knowledge, especially of the subjective dimension, best emerges when researchers understand the full context in which people behave. For interpretivists, quantitative research, by its very nature, misses this important dimension of social reality. Positivists, for their part, do not necessarily deny the existence or importance of subjective experiences, but they do question whether qualitative methods, with their emphasis on the subjective interpretations of the *verstehen* method, have any scientific validity.

This idea is similar to what many social workers and other human services professionals refer to as "starting where the client is at." That is to say these mental health and other professionals espouse that it is often as or even more important to understand how a client experiences and views his or her life than to offer an objective outside view of it. Back to Jane and her work with Jeremy, Jane is mindful that her assessment of Jeremy must also include at least some focus on how Jeremy views himself and his life.

Grounded Theory Methodology

Many qualitative methods are closely grounded in the data, in that they let meaning, concepts, and theories emerge from the raw data rather than being imposed by the researcher. In many research methodologies in the social sciences, the role of theories parallels the positivist approach and the deductive model that we discussed in Chapter 2. Theories are abstract explanations containing a variety of concepts and propositions. From these theories, the researcher derives testable hypotheses and operational definitions of concepts. Then, he or she makes observations to determine whether the hypotheses are true. This deductive approach, however, is not always appropriate—or even

useful: Some research projects are exploratory in nature, meaning that there is little existing theory, concepts, or propositions from which to shape hypotheses or develop operational definitions. Another reason such a deductive approach is not useful for some research projects is that it involves the scientists, through theory and measurement, imposing structure, categorization, and meaning onto reality rather than letting the structure and meaning emerge from reality.

So, proponents of more inductive approaches to theory development argue that deducing hypotheses from existing theories sometimes is limiting, especially during the early stages of theory development, when the theory may not include some relevant variables (Charmaz, 2006). If the variables are not in the theory, they cannot be part of hypotheses and, thus, may be ignored. In other words, strict adherence to deductive hypothesis construction might blind researchers to some key phenomena. One of the more widely used approaches to these issues is called **grounded theory,** which is a research methodology for developing theory by letting the theory emerge from, or be "grounded" in, the data. With this method, there is a continual interplay between data collection, data analysis, and theory development. In the positivist model, these three elements are sequenced: data collection, followed by data analysis, which in turn is followed by theory development. Using a grounded theory method, these three elements can occur simultaneously as one goes constantly back and forth among them. Thus, theory development occurs in the midst of data collection rather than following it.

In the absence of theory, researchers begin by making observations. Those who use grounded theory often do qualitative research by making direct observations or conducting interviews in field settings. Without the restrictions of a preexisting theory, they describe what happens, identify relevant variables, and search for explanations of what they observe. Beginning with these concrete observations, researchers develop more abstract concepts, propositions, and theoretical explanations that would be plausible, given those observations. Inductive research of this sort can serve as a foundation for building a theory, and the theory that emerges can later serve as a guide for additional research and, possibly, even as a source of testable hypotheses through deductive reasoning.

Proponents of qualitative methods argue that concepts and theories produced by such grounded approaches provide a more valid representation of some phenomena, because they emerge directly from the phenomena being studied. In fact, in positivist science, we can engage in theory development without engaging in any data collection or data analysis at all. This is impossible in grounded theory, because the theory emerges from the data or observations. Theory produced in this manner, however, also could be subject to further verification by deducing and testing hypotheses. In fact, a common misconception of grounded theory is that it is entirely inductive in nature. To the contrary, grounded theory does, at times, use existing theory to understand and explain data, and it does include procedures for verifying theories. Thus, some of the considerations of more positivist approaches are relevant to grounded theory: Grounded theory uses evidence to verify theories, rigorously follows precise procedures, makes efforts at replication, and as one of its goals, generalizes about social processes across a variety of social settings.

Reflecting back to our mental health treatment analogous example, Jane may have adopted a specific theoretical and treatment framework for understanding human behavior and treating mental health conditions. For example, she may have been trained as a cognitive behavioral therapist and view Jeremy's thoughts and behavior as possibly deriving from issues pertaining to how he processes and responds to information and other inputs from his environment. This would be analogous to deductive reasoning as Jane tests hypotheses about Jeremy stemming from cognitive behavioral theory. Her tests may involve cognitive behavioral treatments designed to evaluate and possibly alter thought processes and their connections to behaviors. Alternatively, Jane may adopt a more humanistic or person-centered approach in which her goal is to understand Jeremy's world as he understands it, showing empathy and positive regard as she supports his own self-reflection and individualized goal setting. This would be

analogous to inductive reasoning and grounded theory as at least one function of therapy is to begin to understand Jeremy and his world as he understands it and help him create a better life based on his own vision of positive growth.

We will discuss grounded theory in more detail in Chapter 16, in the context of analyzing qualitative data. It is helpful, however, to review these ideas about the contextual and grounded nature of qualitative research to recognize the commonalities among the different types of qualitative methods that we will explore.

FIELD RESEARCH

Field research is one of the more common types of qualitative methods in the social sciences and human services. A number of different approaches to conducting field research exist. Although there is some overlap among them, each introduces some special techniques of data collection.

Participant Observation

One technique for doing field research is **participant observation,** a method in which the researcher observes people in their natural environment (the "field") and the researcher is a part of and participates in the activities of the people, group, or situation being studied (DeWalt & DeWalt, 2011; Lofland, Snow, Anderson, & Lofland, 2006). Participant observation research is naturalistic and involves some participation by the investigator, although, as we will see, the degree of such participation varies. In some cases, the investigator may have belonged to the group before the start of the research and can use this position as a group member to collect data. For example, a social worker might be interested in staff adaptation to antidiscriminatory hiring legislation. If he or she is on the agency personnel committee, such a position might serve as the context for participant observation. As the agency hires new staff members, the social worker can observe the reactions of the other staff in dealing with the new regulations. In other cases, a researcher must first gain access to a group to be a participant observer.

Anthropologist Sue Estroff (1981) did this to learn more about the daily lives and problems of former mental patients. For two years, she joined in the lives of a group of deinstitutionalized mental patients, experiencing the drudgery and degradation of their daily routine. She worked at low-paying jobs, such as slipping rings onto drapery rods that were the lot of these ex-patients. She took the powerful antipsychotic drugs that were routinely administered to them and that had distinctive side effects, such as hand tremors and jiggling legs. She also experienced the extreme depression and despair that result when patients suddenly stop taking these potent drugs. From her position as a participant in their subculture, she could observe the con games that characterized the relationships between patients and mental health professionals.

Through this type of participant observation, practitioners have access to a view of client groups that they cannot gain during an interview or therapy session. Jane, for example, does not have a complete picture of Jeremy's family life because she has not observed him interacting with his family during individual therapy sessions and he has not experienced family dynamics because she has not been a part of them. Participant observation is a unique view because the researcher sees from the perspective of the client, which is especially valuable to anyone who works with groups that are stigmatized or commonly misunderstood by both practitioners and laypeople. Though many practitioners may not have the opportunity to engage in such observations personally, such research efforts by behavioral scientists can be used to develop a better understanding of client groups. Human service professionals should seek opportunities to conduct this kind of research themselves to understand particular groups or subcultures. In fact, practitioners might consider periodically engaging in participant observation of their clients, if possible, to detect ways in which the practitioner perspective may limit understanding of client groups.

Proponents of participant observation argue that it is the only method that enables the researcher to approximate *verstehen,* an empathic understanding of the subjective experiences of people. Of course, actual access to such experience is impossible; thoughts and feelings, by their very nature, are private. Even when someone talks about how he or she feels, the person has objectified that subjective experience into words and, thus, changed it. Participant observers, however, can gain some insight regarding those subjective experiences by immersing themselves in the lives and daily experiences of the people who they study. By experiencing the same culture, the same values, and the same hopes and fears, researchers are in a better position to take on the point of view of these people. Despite its focus on subjective experiences, however, participant observation is still empirical, in the sense that it is grounded in observation, and issues of reliability and validity also concern those who use this method. Researchers using participant observation consider it to be no less systematic or scientific than the more positivistic research techniques.

So, one reason that researchers select participant observation and qualitative methods is because they have determined that an interpretive approach best advances knowledge in a particular area. A second reason for choosing these research methods is because the research is exploratory in nature, and theoretical development does not enable researchers to spell out relevant concepts or to develop precise hypotheses. Participant observation permits the researcher to view human behavior as it occurs in the natural environment without the restrictions of preconceived notions or explanations. Through observation, the researcher can begin to formulate concepts, variables, and hypotheses that seem relevant to the topic and grounded in the actual behavior of people. Similarly, as a counselor, Jane may decide not to move to formal assessments and diagnoses of clients until she has had ample opportunity to interact with a client (like Jeremy)—to hear from the client, observe him or her, and develop some understanding of his or her behaviors and mental state within specific contexts.

It is important to recognize that, in participant observation, knowledge is gained from two distinct but linked kinds of observations. One is based on *participation,* where the researcher learns about the social world of those she observes by personally experiencing that world. This is the *verstehen* method proposed by Weber, and it provides understanding through empathic experience. This empathic experience is an important source of knowledge that offers an intersubjective understanding of other people's lives. The second is produced by *observation,* noting and recording how others behave and what occurs at a social setting. Observation provides understanding through a deep appreciation of the full context within which people live their lives. It enables social scientists to make rich descriptions of everyday social life.

Examples of Participant Observation. Some examples of participant observation can flesh out this discussion. In the mid-1980s, anthropologist Philippe Bourgois (1995), recently married at the time and looking for an apartment he could afford, moved into "El Barrio," an East Harlem neighborhood in New York. Although fieldwork was not his intent in moving there, he eventually used his residence as a springboard for doing research on the underground economy, social marginalization, and how the poor families in that community managed to survive. He lived there for three-and-a-half years and got to know many of the community members. He visited their homes often and attended parties and celebrations with them. He observed how people managed to get by when they could get either no jobs at all or only poorly paying ones. Most of El Barrio's residents were law-abiding, but a small, publicly visible portion were involved in the drug trade. Bourgois became friends with two dozen street dealers and their families. He spent many nights on the streets and in the crack houses with both dealers and addicts. He saw how the residents who had nothing to do with drugs coped with the vibrant and, sometimes, violent drug world that pervaded their community.

Sara Ababneh's study of the women's day-waged labor movement in Jordan in 2011–2012 also relied on participant observation in conjunction with other qualitative methods, including in-depth interviews and focus groups. Ababneh participated in multiple demonstrations associated with the movement, which allowed her to better understand how demonstrations were organized, and also how women participated in them. She was also able to see firsthand how ad hoc meetings

were conducted and how negotiations with government officials proceeded (Ababneh, 2016).

With participant observation, then, researchers can observe processes and grasp levels of meaning that other, more objective methods, such as surveys or available statistical data, cannot uncover. Researchers also can identify differences between what people say they do and their actual behavior.

Observer Roles. In many types of research, the relationship between the researcher and those participating in the research is fairly clear-cut. In surveys, for example, participants know who the researchers are and that, as respondents, they are providing data to those researchers. In observational research and, especially, in participant observation, the researcher–participant relationship becomes more problematic, in that it can take a number of different forms. Two critical issues arise: the extent to which the observer will change the setting under observation, and the extent to which people should be informed that they are being used for research purposes. The way in which a researcher resolves these issues determines the nature of the observer–participant relationship for a given research project.

In the therapy analogy, interactions with the client (Jeremy) help Jane, the therapist, better understand Jeremy—his problems, strengths, resources, and so on. These interactions can complicate Jane's assessment of Jeremy, however, if these interactions change the client substantially or if these interactions elicit responses from Jeremy that are removed from the issues for which he came to see her. At the very least these interactions can complicate her evaluation.

A participant observer is part of the activities being studied and, therefore, is in a position to influence the direction of those activities. For example, Sue Estroff might have wanted to organize the deinstitutionalized mental patients she studied into a lobbying group demanding better living conditions and improved treatment from mental health professionals. If she had done this early in her participant observation, however, would it have interfered with her research goals? Would she have learned all the sources of despair and degradation that these people experienced?

Would she have learned how such groups, without the benefit of an intervening anthropologist, adapt to their plight? The resolution of this issue concerning the extent of intervention, of course, rests partly on the research question. If Estroff were interested in how such groups adapt without outside aid, then she should limit her influence on the group, even though humanitarian values might push her toward involvement. However, if she wanted to assess effective strategies for improving the lot of these groups, then intervention on her part would be called for by the research question. Human service providers, in particular, need to be sensitive to this issue, because an important part of their role as practitioners is intervention. Providers need to recognize that intervention may, at times, be counterproductive to research goals.

This problem of the degree of intervention often is a question of whether the researcher is, first and foremost, a participant or an observer (Gold, 1958). Which of these two aspects should he or she emphasize? Let us look at each side of the issue. Those who emphasize the importance of participation by the observer argue that the investigator plays two roles—namely, that of scientist, and that of group member. To fully comprehend the activities of the group and the dynamics of the situation, the researcher must become fully involved in the group. Otherwise, group members may not confide in the researcher. In addition, the researcher who does not participate is hampered in achieving *verstehen,* an empathic understanding of the deep meanings and experiences that are important to the group. To become fully involved, the researcher must act like any other group member—and this means intervening during those situations in which other group members might do so.

On the other side of the issue, those who emphasize observation over participation argue that the more fully one becomes a group member, the less objective one becomes. The real danger is that researchers will become so immersed in the group that they take on completely the perspective of that group and no longer view the situation from a less-interested perspective (Shupe & Bromley, 1980). Any semblance of a scientific perspective or judgment will be lost. Most participant observers attempt to strike a balance between

total immersion and loss of objectivity on the one hand and total separation with its consequent loss of information on the other. After all, going native can assist in developing the empathic understanding that is one of the goals of field research. In a sense, the field researcher must be somewhere between a stranger and a friend; it requires some judgment to detect the point beyond which friendliness has more negative than positive consequences for the research.

Other critical issues in the researcher–participant relationship are both practical and ethical: To what extent should the people who are studied be informed of the investigator's research purposes and have a role in its design (Brunger & Wall, 2016; Calvey, 2008)? This is an especially troubling problem in participant observation, because in some cases, fully informing people undermines the researcher's ability to gather accurate data. For example, a study of staff treatment of patients in a mental hospital was conducted by having researchers admitted to the hospital as patients without informing the staff of their research purposes (Rosenhan, 1973). Undoubtedly, hospital staff would have behaved quite differently had they known they were under surveillance. Therefore, some researchers take the position that concealment sometimes is necessary to conduct scientific work and that researchers must judge whether the scientific gain justifies the deception and any potential injury—whether social or psychological—that might result. Others, however, hold adamantly to the position that any research on human beings must include "informed consent," that is, that the people involved must be fully informed about the purposes of the research, any possible dangers or consequences, and the credentials of the researchers. Anything less, they argue, is both unethical and immoral, because it tricks people into cooperation and may lead to undesirable consequences of which they are not aware. (We dealt with this complex ethical dilemma at greater length in Chapter 3.)

The analogous example of mental health therapy discussed earlier (Jane and Jeremy) is relevant to this ethical issue as well. As Jane interacts with Jeremy she is obviously gathering information that may be useful in her initial assessment of his functioning and ultimately a possible diagnosis of his condition. To what extent should she inform Jeremy of the processes and criteria by which she will be making such a diagnosis? Will all information that he shares be used? Jane and Jeremy may develop a therapeutic partnership and have a common goal of using as much information as possible to make the most accurate assessment and designing the best possible treatment plan. Still, it is also possible that Jeremy may wish to keep some information—including information that may pertain to past services he received, current relationship issues, or medical records—separate from this assessment. Perhaps he sees this information as inaccurate and not reflective of his current life circumstances. In any case, these issues may need to be discussed explicitly before they engage in this assessment process.

In a classic piece on observational research, Raymond Gold (1958) identified three distinct observer roles that can emerge depending on how

the issues of observer influence and informed consent are resolved: complete participant, participant-as-observer, and observer-as-participant. The distinguishing feature of the *complete participant* role is that the researcher's status as observer is not revealed to those who are being studied. The observer enters a group under the guise of being just another member and, essentially, plays that role while conducting the study. The researcher must be able to sustain this pretense for long periods of time, because studies using the complete participant role usually are characterized by lengthy involvement with the group studied. The complete participant role has proved to be valuable in studying groups, such as drug users or dealers, that otherwise might be closed to research if the observer's true identity were known. Research in Practice 9.1 provides an interesting illustration of the complete participant role being used to better understand life in prison.

RESEARCH IN PRACTICE 9.1 Behavior and Social Environment: The Complete Participant Role in a Prison

Field research can be difficult and complicated to conduct, and it can put the researcher in situations where it is difficult to know what the proper action is. In fact, sociologist Richard Leo (1996) put it this way: "Fieldwork is a morally ambiguous enterprise that is fraught with moral hazards, contingencies and uncertainties" (p. 125). A participant observation research study by James Marquart (2001) conducted in prisons illustrates some of these issues. Marquart's research also illustrates many of the steps in conducting field research discussed in this chapter.

Marquart first came into contact with the world of prisons while working on a project to evaluate the training of prison guards. He met a prison warden who invited him to visit his prison; Marquart did this a number of times over a period of a year or two. During these visits, Marquart came to know many of the guards and inmates, who encouraged him to learn what prison life was "really" like by working as a full-time prison guard. Marquart's specific research goal was to evaluate the effectiveness of a practice in the prison called the "building tender system," in which the prison used particularly dominant and aggressive inmates to control other inmates by meting out punishments, which included beatings. He recognized that becoming a prison guard and taking the complete participant role would give him a perspective on this system that he could gain in no other way. So, with the support of the warden, he began work as a full-time prison guard, a job he kept for about a year and a half.

One major issue that a field researcher confronts is what to tell the people he is observing in the field. Marquart's research was not truly disguised observation, because the warden and some

(continued)

of the guards knew that he was a sociologist making field observations of prison life. To those who knew of his research role, he never lied or misrepresented himself, yet he was not completely honest with them either. Although one of his major interests was in evaluating the building tender system, he did not tell the prison officials this, because he feared they would become defensive about a practice they had implemented and refuse him access. Instead, he stated his interests to be something more general, involving the study of guards and guard work. This is what Richard Leo calls an "act of omission" (withholding information) rather than an "act of commission" (intentionally giving false information). Leo and some other field researchers argue that acts of omission are morally acceptable in field research, because they often are necessary to get the research done (see Chapter 3). Marquart's belief was that, if he had not withheld certain information, he could not have done his research. Yet, he clearly recognized that intentional falsification was morally unacceptable.

Prison life is filled with fear, danger, paranoia, suspicion, and factionalism—for both inmates and guards. It is a challenging environment in which to attempt to gain the rapport that is so essential to good fieldwork. Both guards and inmates came up with all kinds of theories as to who Marquart was and why he was working in the prison: He was a government agent, a spy, or a close relative of the warden. Marquart did a number of things over a period of time to build rapport. He worked hard and took on difficult and dangerous assignments, such as breaking up inmate fights. He lifted weights, boxed, and jogged with inmates to gain their respect. He also got into some serious and dangerous physical altercations with inmates. All of this enabled him, gradually, to become "invisible," that is, perceived by both guards and inmates as just another prison guard.

One of the more difficult and morally ambiguous aspects of field research involves the researcher's responsibilities to those whom he or she observes in the field. In Marquart's case, the prison guards—and even the prisoners—let him into their world and their lives. What obligations did he have to them for doing this? When the guards accepted him in the role of prison guard, they expected him to perform that role well, and one part of that role was to provide support for other guards. This meant assisting the guards in their various tasks, coming to the aide of a guard attacked by a prisoner, and even, possibly, not informing on a guard who beats a prisoner. As Marquart put it, "The ability to 'keep one's mouth shut' was a highly prized asset and I quickly internalized this important value" (2001, p. 40). A good guard was expected to keep his mouth shut. Leo, Marquart, and some other field researchers argue that Marquart took on an implicit moral obligation when he moved into the role of prison guard. Implicit in the guards' and prisoners' acceptance of him is that he be a good guard and carry out all aspects of that role.

Prison is a violent place. Marquart observed prisoners brutalizing other prisoners. He watched guards beat inmates senseless with clubs as the inmates pleaded for mercy. He was so disturbed by some incidents he observed that he almost quit, yet he remained and developed a coping strategy of indifference. He also kept his mouth shut, not telling authorities outside the prison of any illegal or brutal actions he had observed. He respected the moral obligation he had incurred by going into the field, but it was surely a complex and ambiguous moral obligation. Other researchers might dispute the acceptability of his choices. Surely, there must be a line that can be crossed that nullifies the moral obligation. What if a guard killed an inmate? Some would argue that some of the actions Marquart observed crossed that line.

The *participant-as-observer* role differs from the complete participant role in that the researcher reveals his or her status as an observer to those who are being studied. In this role, the observer enters a group and participates in their routines but is known to be doing so for research purposes. As in the case of the complete participant role, the participant-as-observer spends a considerable amount of time observing in the group being studied. Community research often uses the participant-as-observer role, probably because of the large size of these groups and the need for direct access to information that the complete participant might find difficult or too time consuming to obtain while maintaining a disguise. Whyte's (1955) classic study, "Street Corner Society," is a fine example of the use of the participant-as-observer role.

The *observer-as-participant* role is similar to the participant-as-observer role in that the observer's true status is known to those being studied, but it differs with regard to the length of time that the observer spends with the group. The participant-as-observer role assumes a lengthy period of observation. The observer-as-participant role, however, involves a brief contact with the group being studied—possibly for as little as one day. This brief contact tends to preclude the deep, insightful results that characterize studies using the two previous roles. The observer-as-participant role is likely to generate shallower, superficial results. In fact, the brief contact that characterizes this role may lead the observer to misunderstand aspects of the group being studied. Because of these problems, the observer-as-participant role has been less popular for conducting serious social research. We do see assessments that are analogous to observer-as-participant roles in human services practice. For example, public child welfare agencies often create opportunities for parents of children in state custodial care to periodically visit their children. These visits are often supervised by child welfare staff, who directly observe the parent and child interactions, both to assess the nature of these interactions and indirectly parents' readiness to be reunited with their children and to ensure children's safety.

Unobtrusive Observation

Some research questions call for or require the investigator to refrain from participation in the group being investigated. This is the case when the intrusive impact of an outsider might change the behavior of group members in ways that are detrimental to the research question. In such cases, the relationship adopted by the investigator is what Gold (1958) labeled the *complete observer role*—that is, the observer has no direct contact with or no substantial influence on those who are being observed. One way of doing such nonparticipant observation is an observational technique called **unobtrusive observation** or **nonreactive observation:** Those under study are not aware that they are being studied, and the investigator does not change their behavior by his or her presence (Fritsche & Linneweber, 2006; Lee, 2000; Mortenson, Sixsmith, & Woolrych, 2015; Webb, Campbell, Schwartz, Sechrest, & Grove, 1981). Unobtrusive observation can be done in naturalistic or contrived settings and involves both quantitative and qualitative observations. Two forms that unobtrusive observation can take are hidden observation and disguised observation.

Hidden Observation. In some research projects, we can observe behavior from a vantage point that is obscured from the view of those under observation—through a one-way mirror, perhaps, or by videotaping with a hidden camera. For example, some studies of aggressive behavior among children use observations in naturalistic settings by videotaping, with the camera in a hidden location, children at play in school yards (Pepler & Craig, 1995). The camera can be set up in a classroom window, out of sight of the children, and zoom lenses make possible clear observation of children's behavior from long distances. As long as the children are not aware of the cameras and the fact that they are being observed, the research is truly nonreactive in nature. This naturalistic, hidden observation is important in the study of aggression among children, because children behave more normally under these conditions; in a contrived setting or an interview, it probably is impossible to make the same honest, natural observations.

In fact, one group of researchers of such behavior noted that "the use of knives on our school playground tapes was so covert that it often took several passes through the audiovisual tapes to discern their presence" (Pepler & Craig, 1995, p. 550). Because the children clearly attempted to hide the knives from others, they would have been extremely unlikely to display such aggressive behavior to researchers in surveys or a contrived setting. Naturalistic and hidden observations are key to making such discoveries.

A major problem with hidden observations is ensuring that the observations are, in fact, hidden and truly unobtrusive. The unobtrusive nature of the study of children's aggression just mentioned, for example, was compromised in two ways: First, the school principal, teachers, and other adults supervising the children at play knew about the observations. All people have a tendency to react differently when they are being observed—they put their best foot forward or behave in a fashion they think is acceptable to the observer. The adults supervising these children may well have done the same thing—watching the children more closely or reacting more quickly to behaviors that hinted of aggression. If these adults behaved differently with the children than they would have if the children were not being observed, then this would compromise the unobtrusive nature of the observations. A second compromise occurred because the researchers also wanted an audiotape of the children's conversations to fully understand the nature of their aggressive behavior. So, the children had wireless microphones clipped to their clothing while they played in the school yard, thus making them aware that they were being observed. The researchers decided that both of these compromises were essential and that they had only minor effects on the validity of the observations made. The adults, for example, did not know exactly which children on the playground were being observed at a given time, and after a short period of being aware of the microphone, the children seemed to ignore it and play naturally. Other research supports this idea that people often tend to forget they are being observed and to behave normally, especially if the observation occurs over a long period. This research on aggression among children does, however, illustrate the ways in which what appears at first to be hidden observation is not actually completely unobtrusive.

Disguised Observation. With some types of behavior, we can conduct what we call *disguised observation*: Researchers observe people in a naturalistic setting, but without participating and without revealing that they are observing them. Any setting in which one can be present and not participate without calling attention to oneself is a potential scene for disguised observation. The observer enters a group under the guise of being just another member and then plays that role while conducting the observations.

One setting, for example, that might lend itself to such disguised observation is a public establishment, like a bar or a tavern. A group of investigators interested in alcohol-related aggressive behavior (Graham, LaRocque, Yetman, Ross, & Guistra, 1980) conducted exactly this kind of disguised observation. They decided that they could best gather information through unobtrusive observation of the behavior of people as they consumed alcohol in various bars of Vancouver, British Columbia. Teams of observers spent from 40 to 56 hours per week making observations in drinking establishments. Each team consisted of a male–female pair who would enter an establishment, locate a table with a good view of the saloon, and order a drink. They made every effort not to influence the people in the bar in any way. We consider such research to be nonparticipant rather than participant, because the investigators made efforts to have no contact with or influence on the behavior of the patrons. At times, this was impossible—a patron would wander over to their table and engage them in a conversation. In those cases, they quickly terminated the observations and left the bar. In other ways, we might question the unobtrusive character of their observation: The female observer often was the only Caucasian female in the bar, the observers sometimes were the only people in the bar who were not at least slightly inebriated, and there often were social class differences between the dress and behavior of the observers and those being observed. Nonetheless, their impact on the behavior of the clientele probably was minimal, so we can consider this to have been disguised, nonparticipant observation.

STEPS IN FIELD RESEARCH

The exact steps taken in conducting field research vary depending on whether it is participant observation, unobtrusive observation, or some variant. Here, we will describe the steps taken in participant observation, recognizing that some parts of what follows may be unnecessary in other types of field research.

Problem Formulation

The first step in field research is to engage in problem formulation, including a literature review and conceptual development. From this assessment, the researcher establishes the specific goals of the research and decides whether field research is the most appropriate research strategy. A part of problem formulation also includes learning as much as we can about the people, groups, and settings that will be the focus of observation by reviewing previous research on the groups as well as any historical and literary materials that might enlighten us about the group and its culture. The more we learn before going into the field, the more effective we will be at making observations in the field.

Selecting a Field Setting

The second step is to decide which specific group to study. Whether we are studying deinstitutionalized mental patients, cocaine dealers, or motorcycle gangs, we have to decide exactly which group we will join and observe. One way to decide this is by finding a group that is accessible. Sometimes, a field setting presents itself as a by-product of some research or other activities. Barrie Thorne's (1993) participant observation in elementary schools arose because she was asked to assess issues of gender equity in the schools. She designed her field observations to achieve that goal, but she also obtained permission to make additional observations for her own research purposes. Clifford Stott was interested in how violence escalates among fans of British soccer teams, so this focus determined the necessity of making field observations of fans before, during, and after soccer matches (Stott & Reicher, 1998). A soccer fan himself, Stott joined other fans of the team he supported at international soccer matches, and these matches and fans became the focus of his participant observation. Anthropologist Nancy Scheper-Hughes (1992) selected a particular shantytown in Brazil as her field setting because she had lived there years earlier, before becoming an anthropologist, as a Peace Corps volunteer. Her earlier exposure had resulted in continuing ties with some people who lived there and made this shantytown a relatively accessible field setting for her.

Entering the Field

The third step is challenging: gaining entry into the group to be studied. In the complete participant role, this step is less of a problem, because the people do not know they are being studied—though we must be sufficiently like those being studied to gain access. In the other participant roles, however, where they know that we are outsiders and researchers, we must find some way to convince the people to accept our involvement as researchers. Several methods increase the likelihood that people will cooperate (Feldman, Bell, & Berger, 2003; Jorgensen, 1989; Roulet, Gill, Stenger, & Gill, 2017). One way is to win the support of those with more status or influence in the group and then use our relationship with them to gain access to others. It would be best, for example, to approach the directors of a mental health center and enlist their aid before contacting caseworkers and ward staff.

Another way to increase cooperation is to present our reasons for conducting the research in a way that seems plausible and makes sense in the subjects' frame of reference. Esoteric or abstract scientific goals are unlikely to appeal to an agency director or a struggling single parent on welfare. Instead, we should emphasize that our major concern is understanding their thoughts and behaviors as being legitimate, acceptable, and appropriate. Nothing closes doors faster than the hint that we intend to evaluate the group. The door of a welfare recipient may open if we say we are studying the difficulties confronting parents on welfare, but it will surely be slammed shut if we say we want to separate the good welfare recipients from the bad.

Cooperation also is enhanced if we have some means of legitimizing ourselves as researchers—perhaps through an affiliation with a university that supports the study or an agency with an interest in the research. One of the authors of this textbook (Hilton), for example, has done research and evaluation work related to homeless and homeless services. His affiliation with the university at which he is employed has been helpful in gaining access to several services agencies, including shelters, and enabled him to meet with staff and clients and observe services in action. This university affiliation, however, can also backfire. For example, previous research conducted by someone at the university that presented findings or resulted in policy decisions that were not favorable to an agency could make access more challenging.

Finally, we may need to use informants to gain entry into some groups. An *informant* is an insider who can introduce us to others in the group, ease our acceptance into the group, and help us interpret how the group views the world. Especially with informal subcultures, the informant technique is a valuable approach.

Sometimes it takes a bit of creativity—or even courage—to gain entry into some field settings. Sociologist Ruth Horowitz (1987) wanted to study Latino gangs in a particular city, but as a Jewish woman, she did not have easy entry into these groups. So, she sat on a bench in a park frequented by gang members until they approached her—an obvious outsider on their turf. Eventually, one of the leaders of the gang asked who she was. She told him that she wanted to write a book about Latino youth and then convinced him to introduce her to other members of the gang.

In some cases, the researcher may know members of the group being observed, and these personal contacts can ease the researcher's entry into the group. For example, in a study of violence among British soccer fans, the anthropologist doing the study selected a particular group of fans to join and observe because he had grown up and

gone to school with some of them (Armstrong, 1994). These personal contacts made it easier for the researcher to gain their cooperation.

Developing Rapport in the Field

The fourth step in participant observation is to develop rapport and trust with the people who are being studied so that they will serve as useful and accurate sources of information. This can be time-consuming, trying, and traumatic. It is a problem with which the human service professional can readily identify. The community organizer attempting to gain the trust of migrant workers, the substance-abuse worker dealing with a narcotics addict, and the child welfare worker running a group home for girls can all attest to the importance of establishing rapport. Although in many cases the human service worker can express a sincere desire to help as a means of establishing rapport, the researcher cannot always employ this approach, because the research goals may not include providing such help. During the initial stages of the research, people are likely to be distant if not outright distrustful. We are likely to make errors and social gaffes that offend the people we have joined. More than one participant observation effort has had to be curtailed because the investigator inadvertently alienated the people being studied.

Many elements are involved in developing rapport or trust with our informants (Feldman et al., 2003; Lane & Harris, 2015; Spano, 2006). Rapport can emerge if the informants and group members view the investigator as a basically nice person who will do them no harm. It matters little if the informants know of or agree with the research goals—only that they develop a positive attitude toward the investigator. Trust and rapport also can emerge if the investigator shows through behavior that he or she agrees with—or, at least, has some sympathy for—the group's perspective. If we join our field contacts in some of their routine activities, such as drinking beer or playing cards, they are likely to view us as someone who accepts them and as someone they can trust. Of course, the researcher must balance the need for acceptance against personal and professional standards of behavior. Another way to enhance trust and rapport is to reduce the social distance between the researcher and those who are being observed. Finally, researchers can enhance rapport if the relationship between investigator and group members is reciprocal—that is, both the observer and the group members have something the other needs and wants. We might, for example, gain scientific data from our informants, whereas they hope to gain some publicity and attendant public concern from the publication of our results.

Two of the authors of this textbook (Hilton and DeJong) have had to address issues of trust and rapport in gaining access to homeless adults in qualitative studies involving in-depth interviews. They found that emphasizing that they were not affiliated with any social service or other public agency was important in putting potential interview participants at ease. Being up front that the interview would not have any benefit or penalty in terms of services they might access helped remove any sense that they were important public authorities. Offering lunch and eating lunch with research participants during the interview also seemed to create more of a sense that we were peers as opposed to people who could hold something over this vulnerable group. Emphasizing our goal of making recommendations to policy makers to create policies and programs to better address homelessness was also helpful in developing rapport and gaining access.

Becoming Invisible

In field research, being "invisible" means that those who are present perceive the observer as a natural part of the setting, not as an outsider or as someone in any way unusual. Even in the participant-as-observer role, when the people know we are researchers, we can become invisible if the others begin to see us as "just one of them." This has something to do with rapport: As rapport develops, the observer comes to be seen as a natural part of the setting by the people being observed. Becoming invisible also is partly a matter of time: The longer a person is in the scene, the less that he or she is noticed as being unusual or as an outsider. Initially, the presence of the observer may change behavior, but this effect often dissipates as time passes. People also become invisible when they join in the routine activities in the setting, whether working side by side at some task, drinking beer or smoking marijuana with the others at the scene, or joining in on some illegal behavior. By doing these things, the group comes to see the observer as a routine part of their setting. Another way to become invisible is to develop friendships with those being observed. When this happens, the friendship role, in the eyes of those being observed, becomes more important than does the researcher role. As the friendship role becomes more salient, people become more open and honest and less guarded in their interactions with the observer. Research in Practice 9.2 explores more dimensions of ethical behavior in the field.

RESEARCH IN PRACTICE 9.2 The Moral Complexity of Research Work in Field Settings

Field researchers sometimes find themselves observing people who are doing something illegal, disreputable, or stigmatizing, such as dealing drugs, performing a strip tease dance, or engaging in deviant sexual behavior. On occasion, the subjects of the observation have asked or expected the researcher to participate in or in some fashion assist them in their illegal or deviant behavior, at least to the point of not interfering or not bringing any harm or punishment to them. What ethical obligations does a researcher have in such situations?

One solution to such ethical dilemmas, of course, is to not initiate field research among groups for whom such issues are likely to arise (Calvey, 2008). However, this is an extraordinarily limiting strategy in that it places many forms of social behavior beyond the reach of field research. In addition, one does not always know ahead of time when such ethical dilemmas will

(continued)

be an issue. In choosing to study police detectives, for example, one might not predict that those detectives might brutalize someone they have arrested. Should one avoid all field research on police? Again, that would remove extraordinary amounts of social life from the view of social science research.

Another solution to the dilemma rests on the purported value of the research and weighs that against the harm that might be caused by the deviant behavior of those being observed. By refusing to participate or by interfering, the researcher would likely threaten the rapport with the observed to the point where the research project becomes untenable. The observed may no longer cooperate or may become so restrained and inauthentic in their behaviors that few valid observations can be made. Or, even worse, they might reject the researcher outright. In either event, the argument goes, the researcher is justified in ignoring, or even in some cases supporting, the deviant behavior in order to protect the integrity of the research project. This assumes, of course, that the benefits of the research are considerable and the harm of the deviant behavior is not too substantial. Judgments about this must be considered carefully, possibly including consultations with others without a stake in the research project.

Carl Klockars (1979) suggests a third solution to the dilemma which is based on the idea that the people being observed have, by virtue of permitting the researcher into their lives and space, placed a confidence in the researcher:

> This confidence and the access which is granted based upon it is a complex set of understandings, some explicit and some tacit, some formal, some taken for granted. In any given field research relationship it is very difficult to describe the details of such understandings as roles evolve and the rules and responsibilities proceeding from them evolve with them. However, in all field research with deviant subjects that confidence begins with a promise by the researcher not to "blow the whistle" on his subjects . . . . (Klockars, 1979, p. 275)

Klockars argues that field researchers develop complex relationships with those they observe in the field, and those relationships involve a plethora of moral obligations. The field worker is placed into a particular field role by the agreements, either implicitly or explicitly, that are forged by researcher and subject. Police officers, for example, may cast the observer into the role of "fellow undercover cop," and they fully expect that the researcher will live up to that role, just as another officer would. A fellow cop would not blow the whistle on another cop who harasses or brutalizes suspects, and the police expect the fieldworker to live up to that role. In fact, Klockars argues, the police have let the fieldworker into their lives precisely because of the moral assumption that the researcher will live up to those role obligations. Even though nothing was explicitly said about it, such a belief is at the foundation of the relationship.

So, what does a researcher do if the police harass or brutalize someone in his or her custody? For Klockars, the resolution of the ethical dilemma is clear: "It is the immediate, morally unquestionable, and compelling good end of keeping one's promise to one's subjects" (Klockars, 1979, pp. 275–276). The researcher ignores and goes along. A civilian who is trying to be a "decent human being" might not ignore the deviance. But Klockars' answer to that is: "Decent human beings do not; morally competent fieldworkers do" (Klockars, 1979, p. 276). Not everyone would agree with Klockars' conclusion, and certainly police could cross a line that could not be ignored by a field researcher. However, whether one agrees with Klockars or not, his analysis does suggest the complexity of the relationships forged in the field and their implications for conducting ethical research.

Attitude of the Researcher

In positivist research, the researcher's attitude is presumed to be one of objectivity and detachment. In field research, however, researcher–subject relationships are more extensive, complex, and personal. As Philippe Bourgois put it, "in order to collect 'accurate data,' ethnographers violate the canons of positivist research; we become intimately involved with the people we study" (1995, p. 13). Another anthropologist put it this way: "The ethnographer must be intellectually poised between familiarity and strangeness, while socially, he or she is poised between 'stranger' and 'friend'" (Powdermaker, 1966, p. 20). So, the researcher's role may be that of friend or stranger—or somewhere in between. This complexity and ambiguity means that each field observer needs to address the issue of what his or her attitude should be toward those who are being observed.

Similarly, in mental health counseling the interaction between the therapist or counselor and the client is important. Different counselors may take different approaches in these relationships because they may change the nature of the therapeutic setting and even change the client and the counselor (or therapist) in important ways. Understanding the dynamics of client relationships is important, not just in terms of treatment outcomes, but also for evaluating the client. Counselors' and therapists' attitudes toward clients, which may emerge from interactions with them, may impact or even bias their assessments (which is one reason good therapists typically regularly review cases with peers).

In most field settings, the researcher's attitude probably should be one of *openness* to a wide range of types of behavior and of *respect* for the dignity of the research subjects. As the examples in this chapter show, field researchers sometimes find themselves observing behavior that they find morally offensive or politically unpalatable. The researcher's goal, however, is not to judge but, rather, to observe, record, and learn. Moral or political reactions can interfere with these goals and may threaten the rapport that is necessary to achieve good field research. Similarly, in mental health treatments the goal of many counselors is to withhold judgments of clients' behavior and ideas and

try to understand them from the clients' perspective. In research ethical principles (see Chapter 3) dictate that the people who let us into their lives should not be harmed, and taking moral or political offense can be a form of attack. Researchers who cannot achieve this attitude of openness and respect toward particular groups might be best served by not doing field research on those groups.

The researcher's attitude also needs to be *reciprocal*, recognizing that the subjects make as significant a contribution to the production and interpretation of knowledge as the researcher does. A dangerous attitude is one that Barrie Thorne (1993) calls "studying down," in which the researcher assumes that it is the researchers who produce or "discover" knowledge and that the subjects are less informed and less able to contribute to the production of knowledge. Thorne ran across this attitude in research on children; many researchers seemed to dismiss the possibility that the children being observed could teach the researchers something and that the children could help produce knowledge and understanding. Thorne approached her field observations "with an assumption that kids are competent social actors who take an active role in shaping their daily experiences. I wanted to sustain an attitude of respectful discovery, to uncover and document kids' points of view and meanings" (1993, p. 12).

Finally, the researcher needs to *balance* his or her attitude in terms of identifying both the positive and negative aspects of the settings or cultures being observed. Philippe Bourgois, in his field research on inner-city street culture, points out that:

[T]he methodological logistics of participant observation require researchers to be physically present and personally involved. This encourages them to overlook negative dynamics because they need to be empathetically engaged with the people they study and must also have their permission to live with them. (1995, p. 14)

This can produce an unwitting self-censorship when the researcher fails to notice or report on some of the negative aspects of the behavior or lifestyle of the subjects. Bourgois found aspects of the street culture that he studied to be violent, dangerous, and abhorrent. Yet, a balanced attitude requires that the researcher's overall picture is neither unrealistically negative nor unrealistically positive.

Observing and Recording in the Field

The center of attention in field research, of course, is observing and recording what occurs. This cannot truly begin, however, until we have accomplished the other steps just described. Although field researchers keep track of what they observe while entering the field and gaining rapport, the best observations depend on those things having been achieved. What observations to record and how to record them are discussed later in this chapter.

Exiting the Field

In most field research, the period of observations in the field ends because the researcher has collected sufficient data (or run out of grant money). When this time comes, the researcher must leave the field in a way that brings no negative consequences to the people being observed. Because field research involves the researcher living in some degree of intimacy with those being studied, it is not uncommon for some level of personal relationship to develop. Acquaintances, friendships, and maybe even more intense relationships can emerge. The researcher needs to sever these relationships in such a way that people don't experience significant social or emotional loss. This may mean that, throughout the period of being in the field, the researcher remains somewhat socially or emotionally distant so that complicating personal relationships do not develop to the point where difficulty in exiting the field occurs. This is one way to avoid expectations of excessive intimacy or permanency in a relationship. Of course, there is a balance here, because some level of friendly involvement may be essential to developing rapport. From the very beginning, however, the researcher has an eye on the exit in terms of developing relationships with respondents. There is an obvious parallel here to the mental health analogy. While the therapeutic relationship between counselor and client is an important element of treatment, counselors generally have an eye on healthy terminations throughout the therapeutic process.

RECORDING OBSERVATIONS IN FIELD RESEARCH

Field research is most closely associated with qualitative research, but observations made in the field can involve either qualitative or quantitative data or both. Accordingly, the manner in which field researchers record observations depends on whether the observations primarily are quantitative or qualitative in nature. Qualitative observation typically calls for less-structured *field notes,* whereas quantitative observation typically uses more-structured recording of data on *coding sheets.*

Qualitative Observation: Field Notes

Detailed, descriptive accounts of the observations made during a given period are called **field notes.** The precise nature of field notes varies greatly from one study to another, but all field notes should include six elements (Bogdan & Taylor, 1975; Lofland et al., 2006):

1. A *running description* makes up the bulk of the field notes. This is simply a record of the day's observations, with a primary concern of recording accurately the concrete events that were observed. The researcher should avoid analyzing persons or events while in the field, both because there is not the time and because it interferes with observation of the ongoing scene. Instead, he or she should concentrate on faithfully recording what occurs.

2. Field notes also include *accounts of previous episodes that were forgotten or went unnoticed* but that the investigator remembered while still in the field. When preparing the field notes from any observation session, it is likely that the researcher may forget or leave out certain events. Subsequent observations may bring the forgotten episodes back to mind. The researcher should record these events when remembered, with the proper notation concerning when they originally occurred.

3. *Analytical ideas and inferences* refer to spur-of-the-moment ideas concerning such things as data analysis, important variables, speculation regarding causal sequences, and the like. Researchers should record these "flashes of insight," regarding any aspect of the study, when they occur. Reviewing these ideas after the completion of observations can greatly benefit the final data analysis and writing of the report. Although most data analysis is reserved until after the observation period, no researcher wants to forget whatever analytical ideas occurred while in the field.

4. *Personal impressions and feelings* should be noted, because the possibility that bias might color our observations is always present. Recording personal impressions and feelings helps minimize this bias by giving a sense of the perspective from which the observer is viewing various persons, places, or events. Does the observer simply dislike a certain person in the setting? If so, the observer should honestly record such a feeling when it first occurs. This can prove to be beneficial when reviewing accounts relating to that person to see if the researcher's personal feelings influenced the description.

5. *Notes for further information* are notes that observers write to and for themselves: plans for future observations, specific things or persons to look for, and the like. It is risky to rely on memory for anything important relating to the study.

6. *Methodological notes* refer to any ideas that relate to techniques for conducting field research in this setting. As researchers, we should note any difficulties we have in collecting data, any biases that might be introduced by the data-collection techniques, or any changes in how we make and record observations. The purpose of this is to better prepare us to assess validity (to be discussed shortly) and to provide insight for future researchers who might make observations in similar settings.

How to Record. Field notes can take a number of different forms (Bernard, 2006; Lofland et al., 2006). For example, parts of field notes might consist of brief jottings where researchers make

note of something that is happening or something that occurs to them. Many field researchers carry a notepad at all times, even when not in the field, to make a note of things as they occur or as they think of them. Other parts of field notes might contain a more detailed and complete written record of what is happening in some setting. In some cases, instead of writing field notes, researchers use laptop or notebook computers or audiotapes to make their recordings. In other cases, conversations or interviews conducted in the field might be tape-recorded or videotaped for later analysis. The choice of which format to use depends on which most accurately preserves the record without interfering with rapport.

Recording field notes is particularly problematic for participant observers whose status as an observer is disguised. Because such observers must constantly guard against having their true identity revealed, they must take notes surreptitiously. In some settings, a bit of ingenuity on the part of the researcher can handle this problem quite nicely. For example, in her study of people's behavior in bars, Sheri Cavan (1966) solved the note-taking problem by making frequent trips to the restroom and recording her observations there. Given the well-recognized effect of alcoholic beverages on the human body, her trips probably raised little suspicion among the other bar patrons.

In many participant observation settings, no amount of innovation will allow the researcher to record observations on the scene. In these situations, there is no alternative but to wait and record observations after leaving the observational setting. Relying on memory in this fashion is less than desirable, however, because memory is fallible. The observer should record observations as soon as possible to minimize the likelihood of forgetting important episodes.

What to Record. For someone who has never conducted participant observation research, collecting data through field notes can be particularly frustrating and confusing. What should the researcher watch for? What should he or she include in the field notes? These are difficult questions even for veteran observers. In addition, because participant observation research may be exploratory, researchers often are only partially aware of what might be relevant. It is possible, nevertheless, to organize our thoughts around some general categories of things to observe and record (Bogdan & Biklen, 1992; Lofland et al., 2006; Runcie, 1980; Smith, Mountain, & Hawkins, 2016):

1. *The setting:* Field notes should contain some description of the general physical and social setting being observed. Is it a bar, a restaurant, or a ward of a mental institution? Are there any physical objects or barriers that might play a role during the social interaction in this setting? In some cases, it would be valuable to begin each day's field notes with a drawing or photograph of the physical layout being observed. Such things as time of day, weather, or the presence of others who are not the focus of your observations are useful information in some field research. In short, the field notes serve to remind us—when we review them weeks, months, or even years later—of the characteristics of the setting in which we observed behavior.

2. *The people:* Field notes should include a physical and social description of the main characters who are the focus of our observations. How many people are there? How are they dressed? What are their age, gender, and socioeconomic characteristics (as well as we can observe from physical appearance)? Again, field notes should tell us, for each separate day of observation, who was present, who entered and left the setting during observation, and how the cast changed from one day to the next.

3. *Individual actions and activities:* The central observations in most studies are the behaviors of the people in the settings. How do they relate to one another? Who talks to whom, and in what fashion? What sequences of behavior occur? In addition, we may want to record the duration and the frequency of these interactions. Do repetitive cycles of behavior occur? Is there a particular sequencing of behavior?

4. *Group behavior:* In some cases, the behavior of groups is an important bit of information. How long does a group of people remain on the scene? How does one group relate to another? It might be useful, for example, to know what cliques have formed in a setting. What we record here describes the social structure of the setting, such as the statuses and roles that various people occupy and the relationships between them.

5. *Meanings and perspectives:* Field researchers are sensitive to the subjective meanings that people give to themselves and their behavior, which is one of the reasons for doing qualitative field research. So, field notes should contain observations about these meanings and what words or behaviors are evidence of those meanings. *Perspectives* refers to general ways of thinking that people exhibit, evidence of which should appear in the field notes.

The mental health treatment analogy can be extended to the concept of field notes. Therapists typically write notes after meeting with clients to make a record of the session and describe what was discussed. They may also make notes about their thoughts and feelings during the session as well as ideas they may have related to their ongoing assessment of the client and possible next steps. Therapists sometimes also take some notes during the session; however, therapists should be careful that their note-taking does not interfere with the session or make the client feel uncomfortable.

Quantitative Observation: Coding Sheets

When it is possible to do quantitative observation in field research, such observation often involves a process of **coding,** or categorizing behaviors into a limited number of preordained categories. To do this, researchers specify, as clearly as possible, the behaviors to be observed or counted during data collection. When possible, use of coding sheets is desirable. A *coding sheet* is simply a form designed to facilitate the categorizing and counting of behaviors. For example, a typical coding sheet lists various behaviors with blanks following them for checking off the behaviors as they occur. If the duration of a behavior also is important, additional blanks record the timing.

The coding sheet for a particular research project is likely to be a unique, highly specific document that reflects the special concerns of that project. Nevertheless, a number of coding schemes have sufficient generality to use in a number of different settings. For example, Table 9.1 presents a coding scheme based on Robert Bales' theory about the interactional strategies that people use when they interact in groups, described in Chapter 8. Table 9.1 presents a coding scheme of some of Bales' interaction categories as they might be used to study interaction in a counseling group for intimate partner abusers. So, the column on the left of Table 9.1 shows a few of the conceptual categories that Bales uses to understand strategies used in social interaction. The middle column presents some concrete examples of what each category might look like in actual social interaction in order to assist the coders to categorize behaviors. The right-hand column shows the symbols that would be entered on the actual coding sheet to show that a particular interaction strategy had been displayed. The actual coding sheet is displayed in Table 9.2. Using the symbols from Table 9.1, each observer would indicate, for each member of the group, which interaction strategies were displayed during each 5-minute interval of the 30-minute counseling sessions. The result is a running account of the kinds of interaction strategies used by members of the group.

TABLE 9.1 Coding Categories for Bales' (1950) Theory of Social Interaction Strategies in Groups (See Chapter 8.) Illustrated With Interaction in a Counseling Group for Intimate Partner Abusers

Description of Interaction Categories	Example of Behavior	Symbol for Coding Sheet
Social–emotional behavior		
Shows solidarity	Gives other group members "high five" in response to member comment	1-1
Shows antagonism	Shouts, slams notebook on table	1-2
Shows tension release	Laughs and nods agreement when member pokes fun at his own childish behavior toward his girlfriend	1-3
Shows tension	Glares and refuses to talk when leader confronts him about denying responsibility	1-4
Task behavior		
Gives suggestion or direction	Tells other group member to try taking a "time out" when he starts getting agitated	2-5
Asks for suggestion or direction	Describes conflict; asks group members what he could have done differently	2-6
Gives opinion or evaluation	States that showing trust in partner is important	2-7
Asks for opinion or evaluation	Asks if how he handled situation when wife was late getting home was good	2-8

Note: First number of symbol indicates whether a social–emotional or task behavior; second number indicates type of social–emotional or task behavior.

TABLE 9.2 Coding Sheet Used to Record Data in 5-Minute Intervals During 30-Minute Counseling Sessions, Using Categories Described in Table 9.1

Time Intervals	:00 - :05	:06 - :10	:11 - :15	:16 - :20	:21 - :25	:26 - :30
Group Member ID #						
001	1-1	1-3	1-1; 1-4		1-1	1-1
002	1-3			2-5	2-7	2-7
003				1-4		
004	2-1	2-1; 1-4			1-4	

The development of an efficacious coding scheme requires considerable care. The coding categories should derive from the theories and hypotheses being tested in the research. In the example in Table 9.1, the researchers' concern was with the nature and quality of social interaction in a group, and the categories that were derived from Bales' theory reflect that focus. In addition, coding categories should be highly specific and behavioral. Obviously, the degree to which we can achieve this is limited, because overspecificity soon becomes cumbersome and meaningless. For example, in the study by intimate partner abusers, a category of "speaks" would be too general, because it does not inform us about the nature of verbal contribution. At the other extreme, a category such as "raises eyebrows" is so specific that we cannot determine the meaning of the behavior. Thus, we walk a fine line between being too specific and being too general in providing a coding scheme that enables us to answer our research questions. It is important to recognize that, although coding behavior with such schemes may appear to be quantifiable and objective, a considerable degree of subjective interpretation is involved. The coder must decide, for example, whether a given response is positive or negative and shows solidarity or antagonism; these judgments are necessarily subjective.

The use of coding schemes is not limited to situations in which a group is small, well organized, or engaging in highly structured behavior. If it is possible to specify concepts and hypotheses precisely—in other words, if the research clearly

is hypothesis testing rather than exploratory—then it may be possible to develop a precise coding scheme for data collection. In their disguised observation study of alcohol-related aggression, Kathryn Graham et al. (1980) were able to do this. Their basic hypothesis was that aggressive behavior among men when they drink resulted from situational factors as much as from psychological predispositions toward violence. They hypothesized that aversive stimuli in bars (their independent variable) serve as cues that allow or encourage aggressive behavior (the dependent variable). They coded the dependent variable using a dichotomous coding scheme: nonphysical aggression (swearing or other forms of abusive language), and physical aggression. Within the physical category, behavior was coded as physical threats or challenges to fight but no actual contact; aggressive but uninjurious physical contact, such as grabbing and pushing; and actual physical violence, such as punching and kicking.

The independent variable—situational factors eliciting aggression—was, needless to say, more complex to code. First, the researchers spent some weeks in the field observing and developing precise definitions and coding schemes for the situational variables. Here are a few of the coding categories they developed:

Location: 1 = downtown bar
             2 = suburban bar
Time of day: 1 = 9 a.m. to noon

	2 = noon to 3 p.m.
	3 = 3 p.m. to 6 p.m. and so on
Noise level:	1 = very quiet
	2 = medium quiet
	3 = medium loud
	4 = loud
Sexual bodily contact:	1 = none, very casual
	2 = discreet necking
	3 = heavy necking, touching
	4 = flagrant fondling
Friendliness to strangers:	1 = open, lots of conversation with strangers
	2 = closed, people talk only to members of their own group

Each two-person observation team spent between two and two-and-a-half hours in an establishment. Most recording of observations was done after leaving the establishment so that note taking would not attract attention.

This unobtrusive observation illustrates the manner in which field observers can use a precise, quantifiable coding scheme if the hypotheses to be tested are sufficiently developed. The investigators also found, however, that coding, although the major form of data collection, was not sufficient by itself. They needed to collect qualitative data as well, because while they were in the field, more variables of importance began to emerge. The researchers wanted to record descriptive accounts of aggressive incidents to ensure a complete record. This provides an illustration of a grounded theory approach, where data collection changes while still in process, because evaluation suggests that some new theoretical concepts are important.

Coding schemes can become highly complex, involving many categories of behavior, timing of behaviors, measures of intensity, and the like. We can only use more complex coding schemes, however, in situations where we can record accurately all that is necessary. The study described in Table 9.2 of a single, small, task-oriented group enabled the use of a complicated coding scheme. In the study by Graham and colleagues, this would have been considerably more difficult, because the group (the clientele of a bar) was large and shifting in composition, much was going on, and the actual recording of observations had to wait until after the observation period had concluded. This research setting necessitated a simpler coding scheme. Furthermore, investigations using complex coding schemes that require intense concentration on the part of the observer often require a number of observers, each of whom records for a short period and is then relieved by another observer. This reduces error caused by observer fatigue or fluctuations in concentration. In some investigations, group behavior is recorded on videotape to reduce error and allow researchers to view the group as often as needed to code behavior properly. In developing a coding scheme, in short, researchers must make sure that the scheme does not become so complex as to become unusable, given the resources at hand.

Coding schemes are not appropriate forms of recording observations in all field research. In some cases, as with exploratory research, we cannot develop hypotheses with sufficient precision to operationalize concepts through coding schemes, because the research is intended to explore and discover rather than to explain and predict. In other cases, a nonpositivist approach suggests that the nature of some phenomena does not lend itself to quantification; in fact, proponents of the nonpositivist approaches argue that quantification can lead to distortion and misunderstanding of what is going on. In these cases, the hypotheses involve variables and relationships that require considerable interpretive effort on the part of the observer in the field and cannot easily be condensed to a few coding categories. In still other cases, the complexity and lack of structure in the group being observed render coding schemes useless. In all these situations, the investigator is likely to turn to field notes as a means of recording observations.

While relatively few therapists use something like a coding sheet during therapeutic sessions, some may take notes about specific words or behaviors that clients use in sessions. The therapist, for example, might question a client asking why he or she used a specific word or phrase so frequently when describing a person or event. Having a notebook handy might allow the therapist to make a note about a word use or phrase and count the number of times it was used.

OTHER QUALITATIVE METHODS

In addition to field research, the social sciences and human services use a number of other important qualitative research methods—sometimes on their own, and sometimes as part of a field research study.

In-Depth Interviewing

Chapter 7 discussed the use of interviews in survey research, but those interviews generally are more structured and focused than the in-depth interviewing that often is used in qualitative research. **In-depth interviews,** or **ethnographic interviews,** are informal and unstructured interviews that explore a wide range of topics and that may last for a long time, even days or weeks. Often, they are more like a rambling conversation, with the interviewer relatively nondirective and the person being interviewed fairly unconstrained in what he or she talks about (Arnault & Shimabukuro, 2012; Fontana & Frey, 1994; Patton, 2002). Actually, there is some overlap between participant observation and in-depth interviewing, because participant observation often gathers some data through informal interviews with people in the field.

These interview data are a third source of data collected in participant observation, in addition to gathering data through participation and observation. Yet, in-depth interviewing and participant observation are distinct, because, in contrast to in-depth interviewing, true participant observation research also gathers data through participation

and observation. In addition, interviews can be a mechanism for collecting qualitative data apart from field research. For example, two of the authors of this textbook (Hilton & DeJong, 2010) studied homelessness among adults in the rural Upper Peninsula of Michigan. Their main data-gathering tools were unstructured interviews, which enabled the researchers to explore issues pertaining to their survival strategies and use of human services in great breadth and depth. The topic had been the focus of relatively little previous research, so the researchers had no existing knowledge base from which to derive meaningful concepts or to develop hypotheses. Instead, they wanted the concepts and hypotheses to emerge from the freewheeling and friendly conversations that were their unstructured interviews. These interviews were supplemented with interviews with social services providers and policy makers in the area. This research paved the way for subsequent research on homeless adults' use of extended family members for critical help (e.g., occasional shelter, food, and storage space), which was one of the themes that emerged from Hilton and DeJong's research (Trella & Hilton, 2014).

The researcher approaches an in-depth interview with some general topics of interest and asks questions that probe into those areas. The whole process, however, is much more interactive and collaborative and much less directive than that in survey interviews (Holstein & Gubrium, 1995). It is more like a conversation. The researcher talks, rather than just asking questions, to keep the conversation going. The researcher may talk about himself or herself and life and even respond to questions the respondent asks—something not normally done in a survey interview. The researcher also permits the interview to take unexpected directions if they appear to be rewarding in terms of the research question or essential to maintaining the rapport and interest of the respondent. In fact, the relationship between interviewer and respondent often becomes one of equals conversing rather than one of an expert gathering data from a subject. Yet, the general topics that the researcher needs to cover impose a structure, of sorts, on the interview. This is especially apparent when more than one person is interviewed, because the researcher must make sure that he or she covers the same general topics with each person.

The goal of the in-depth interview is similar to that of participant observation—namely, to explore how the world appears to the respondent without imposing inappropriate structure on the views that he or she expresses by using preestablished categories or an overly restrictive direction on what subjects to explore and how they express it. The respondent's perspective should unfold and be framed in ways that make sense to him or her; it should not be limited or constrained by the researcher's preconceived category systems or structures of meaning. The value of such in-depth interviewing is especially remarkable when studying behavior in very diverse cultures, as Practitioner Profile 9.1 illustrates.

Referring back to the mental health treatment analogy, an in-depth qualitative interview is much what many mental health counselors do in allowing the client to begin sessions (or at least the initial session) by discussing what is most pressing to her or him. Allowing the client to structure sessions gives assurances that the focus of the session concerns issues that are most pressing or important to the client. Therapists may vary in the extent to which they direct counseling sessions, largely depending on the therapeutic approach (and the nature of the problem and the preferences of both the therapist and the client).

PRACTITIONER PROFILE 9.1 Hasan Reza

Hasan Reza is a master's level social worker who has conducted several qualitative research projects in his home country of Bangladesh examining various social welfare issues impacting vulnerable populations. He has used his research to make policy and program recommendations to domestic and international advocacy and service organizations. According to Hasan,

> Most research on social welfare issues in Bangladesh has been conducted by professional researchers from other places. These tend to be highly qualified researchers, but the value of the research is limited because it is rarely grounded in actual fieldwork nor does it fully capture the complexity of factors that create and perpetuate social welfare issues in Bangladesh.

Over the past several years while receiving advanced training in research methods as a social work doctoral student at the University of Chicago, Hasan has remained committed to advancing understandings of social welfare issues in Bangladesh. As he explains,

> My goal is to use the theoretical and methodological training I have received in developing a research agenda that will help draw attention to the issues I have seen in my country. Truly understanding poverty and homelessness in a country like Bangladesh is very hard to do from a western perspective because these issues have different meanings there. For example, in poor households women are supposed to serve their husband first before they eat. The best part of the meal is usually consumed by him. Then children are served. Whatever is left is consumed by the wife, and in many cases this is very little. It is difficult for an outsider to understand this without in-depth knowledge about such cultural practices. Without understanding household dynamics of food distribution it is difficult to end women's poverty.

His dissertation project has focused on what he calls "street kids" in three cities in Bangladesh. According to Hasan, these children typically leave their homes at a young age and

(continued)

come to areas of cities where they can earn enough money to survive by doing a variety of odd jobs. While typically homeless, Hasan explains, these children very often report being better off than they were at home where they also commonly experience absolute poverty, food insecurity, and multiple forms of abuse.

As Hasan explains,

> The typical outside perspective on these street kids is that these kids leave home because the families are too poor to care for them and that if family poverty were alleviated these children could be reunited with their families. The real picture is much more complicated than that. These children often face tremendous abuse and neglect at home. Polygamy is common and this contributes to unstable family dynamics. Fathers often leave their families to find work in cities and marry new wives, sometimes abandoning the first wife and children. Early death is common for mothers because of poor healthcare and in many situations second wives are forced to care for children of previous wives. Stepmothers and fathers often resent these children and in many cases this contributes to abuse and neglect. Understanding these family and cultural factors helps in showing that these children are not just leaving home because their families are too poor to care for them. They leave because home life is unbearable for many reasons.

Hasan conducted at least two to three episodes of in-depth interviews with each of 75 street kids from three locations of Dhaka city, the capital of Bangladesh. All interviews were audio-recorded. They all focused on factors that led to their leaving home, transition experiences, and their survival on the streets, particularly the use of social networks in meeting basic needs. Hasan developed a visual aid, adapted from Antonucci (1986), to help these children map their social networks. He showed each of these children a chart with a series of concentric circles and cartoon pictures of Bengali children, men, and women. Inner circles, he explained, represented close contacts—those whom the children contacted regularly and relied heavily on to meet basic needs. Outer circles represented occasional contacts. Children were asked to give names to each of the cartoon characters who represented people in their social networks and explain why they were in each circle.

> What I found is that these kids create very strong social networks that allow them to survive and even thrive in many ways. Most say they are much happier on the streets than they were at home. There are very strong bonds between these street kids. Offering financial supports to one another is common. These kids often give one another money, make small loans, and purchase food for those who need it. They sleep near one another for protection. They share information about resources in the community and ways to earn money. They will also care for someone who is sick, even buying medicine for someone who needs it without expecting them to pay it back.

Hasan also explained that, despite sleeping outdoors, these children were better off in many ways than they were while they were housed.

> These kids have learned to survive on about fifty cents a day. The median daily income in my sample was just over a dollar fifty per day. These kids earn much more than they need to survive and actually save some money for when they need it for something

(continued)

like medicine. They do odd jobs like running errands for merchants in the market-place. Some pick up discarded fruits and vegetables from merchants at a public market and sell them someplace else. Others recycle bottles and cans—picking up discarded refuse and then selling them to businesses that need these materials. Few complain much about working and the majority report liking the freedom of working and living independently.

When asked what he hopes to do with his research, Hasan reported that he would like to present it to international children's development organizations and domestic [Bengali] service agencies so they have a more complete view of these children.

Many times these organizations will focus on reuniting these kids with their families or getting them into school. These are well-intentioned goals, but they may not be what these kids want or need. Few want to return home. School isn't attractive either if it means they can't work. These children definitely need help, but services should build on their current coping strategies, not replace them. Agencies offering drop-in type services—food, medicine, entertainment, a safe place to sleep on occasion, or just a place to spend time during the day—might have real success in developing relationships with these kids and offering real help. Education is needed, yes, but schools should be structured so that kids can both work and go to school. Without that, they are very unlikely to attend.

Hasan's work is a very good example of the importance of understanding social context in designing social policies, programs, and interventions to address social problems. It highlights the potential contributions of qualitative research in discovering the complex social meanings that are found in diverse cultures and in using that knowledge to inform policy and practice.

Case Studies, Life Histories, and Narratives

Another qualitative research technique is variously called *narrative inquiry, life histories,* or *case studies* (Clandinin & Connelly, 2000; Yin, 2009). Although there are some differences among these approaches, they all involve a detailed descriptive account of part or all of a particular individual's life or, in some case studies, of an organization or an event. The goal is to gain understanding through depth and richness of detail. The description in case studies and life histories is a detailed and what sometimes is called "thick" description—that is, a complete and literal accounting of the person or setting under study. Some quantitative data might be included, but the emphasis is on telling a story in prose or narrative. Researchers base case studies and life histories on direct observation, interviews, document analysis, organizational records, or some combination thereof—basically, any data that contributes to a description of the case under study.

Case studies and life histories share with participant observation a desire to understand how the social world looks from the perspective of the person being studied. Anthropologist Bourgois (1995), for example, used a life-history approach in his participant observation research in El Barrio: He tape-recorded long conversations with his informants to see how their current circumstances and behavior were part of the flow of their lives. One of the strengths of case studies and life histories is that they permit the people being studied to play a big part in framing and providing meaning for their lives rather than having meaning and interpretation imposed by the observer. Case studies take a much longer time perspective, however, because they typically explore a good part—if not the whole—of a person's life. Case studies and life histories have proven to be useful methodologies in feminist research and in interpretivist and critical approaches (Lawless, 1991).

The primary goal of most case studies and life histories is an idiographic explanation that focuses on an in-depth understanding of a particular case. Such an understanding might enhance our comprehension of other cases and situations, but the primary focus is description, not generalization. The advantage of these methods is the rich and detailed descriptions they provide of people's lives, experiences, and circumstances. In addition, the ability of these methods to allow people to speak in their own voices makes them valuable sources of data. Because they are based on a person's life, however, case studies and life histories are criticized on the grounds that the results are not generalizable beyond that one case. The data from such studies also contain a considerable element of subjectivity because of their dependence on the accounts of one individual. These methods also suffer from the normal errors of people's memories as well as from selective recall on the part of the individual. In fact, the data produced in narratives sometimes are the result of collaboration between researcher and subject, where the final story is one that they both find acceptable. To overcome some of these problems, people producing case histories sometimes check for errors or misinterpretations with others who are knowledgeable of the people or events in the case history. Of course, errors in memory or selective recall may be valuable data in themselves, in that we may learn as much about people from how they remember or reconstruct their past as we may from their actual past. In fact, proponents of case studies and life histories argue that a person's own story is important to understand, irrespective of the objective facts. A good analogy for case studies and life histories in mental health treatment is narrative therapy, because a major aspect of narrative therapy is understanding how clients tell their own story and the meanings they ascribe to various events in their lives.

Focus Groups

We discussed focus groups as a form of survey research in Chapter 7 because they involve interviewing people, but focus groups deserve mention here as a qualitative research method. Focus groups also are called *group depth interviews,* because they are like an in-depth interview with a number of people at the same time. The advantage of focus groups is that they are flexible forms of data collection that leave the participants free to frame their answers and construct meaning as they wish. Although some quantitative data are collected as part of focus groups, people are free to talk as much as they wish, and their complete responses serve as data for the research.

Another advantage of focus groups is the ability to see interactions between people. Sometimes, for example, one focus group member will introduce a topic or issue that jogs other members' memories or leads others to become interested in a topic. A parallel in mental health counseling is group therapy or treatment groups within which interactions between group members may become an integral part of the treatment process. In some cases conflicts between group members may create opportunities for conflict resolution and other breakthroughs.

ISSUES IN OBSERVATIONAL AND FIELD RESEARCH

Sampling

In most field research, it is difficult—if not impossible—to use probability samples, because we can establish no adequate sampling frame. In addition, the research questions that field research sometimes addresses do not call for probability samples. So, nonprobability samples are widely used in field research. Especially common are snowball sampling, targeted sampling, and purposive sampling. (In Chapter 6, we described a number of field studies that used one of these sampling strategies or some combination of them.) These samples make possible sampling procedures in situations where sampling frames do not exist, and they also encourage the researcher, especially with targeted and purposive sampling, to avoid samples that are biased as a result of some group being inadvertently missed by a particular sampling procedure.

In addition to the more common sampling issue of selecting participants for a project, observational and field researchers face another challenge—it often is impossible to conduct round-the-clock observation over the full length of the study, which may involve a considerable period of time. Participant observers record things as they happen, and more quantitative observers mark coding schemes for as long as an interchange or a social setting persists. In some situations, however, continuous data collection is costly and unnecessary. In addition, as we discussed with other forms of sampling in Chapter 6, it often is not necessary to collect data from *all* elements of a population. In studies of child development, for example, we may not need to record all that occurs during an hour, a day, or a week. Instead, we can gather valid data through **time sampling,** or making observations only during certain selected periods of time (Irwin & Bushnell, 1980; Smith, Anderson, & Pawley, 2017; Stadnick, Haine-Schlagel, & Martinez, 2016). For example, with an observational study of adolescents in a group home, the prime hours for observation are those when the residents are most likely to be at the home, such as weekdays from 3 p.m. until lights out at 11 p.m. (40 hours per week) and Saturdays and Sundays from 7 a.m. until 11 p.m. (32 hours per week). The researcher can construct a sampling frame consisting of a weekly list of these 72 one-hour time segments and then select a random sample of these elements. To be sure to include both weekdays and weekends, the researcher might specify eight hours during the week and four hours during the weekend. The resulting sample of 12 one-hour time segments would provide sufficient time coverage for observation while reducing biases that might occur if, say, the researcher made all observations on weekdays after 8 p.m., when many youths are tired at the end of the day.

Keep some guidelines in mind when conducting time sampling (Smith et al., 2017; Suen & Ary, 1986). The length of each time-sampling interval and the distance between intervals depend on the nature of the behaviors being observed: These behaviors should occur with sufficient frequency so as to appear during the sampled time periods;

very infrequent behaviors might call for continual observations. The more frequently a behavior occurs, the smaller the number of intervals we have to sample. Furthermore, the time interval should be long enough for the behavior to occur and for the observer to make whatever recordings are necessary.

Many of the considerations in time sampling are the same as those in sampling subjects or respondents as we discussed in Chapter 6. If our primary concern is to be assured of observing *some* occurrences of the behavior under study, then it is advisable to use the equivalent of a purposive sample. For example, in studying domestic violence, we want to observe instances of family quarreling. Observing at mealtime is one way to increase the probability of witnessing the sought after events. However, if we want to estimate accurately the frequency of occurrence of a particular event or to study the pattern of responses over a time period, then we should use the equivalent of a probability sample. For example, to observe nursing home residents for frequency of contacts with nonresidents, we could divide the week into hourly segments and then use a random selection of hours as the basis for the observations.

Particularly when the observation process is highly complex and difficult to sustain for long periods of time, some form of time sampling can help to improve the quality of the data collected.

Validity and Reliability

We assess observational techniques, like other forms of data collection, in terms of how valid and reliable they are (Kirk & Miller, 1986; Noble & Smith, 2015). Observation rests on human sense organs and human perceptions—both of which are notoriously fallible. This is an especially difficult and insidious problem, because we often are totally unaware of the ways in which our senses and our perspectives lead us to misperceived situations. Especially with observational methods, people say resolutely, "I was there. I saw it. I comprehend what was going on." Yet, as any trial lawyer will readily attest, eyewitnesses often are highly unreliable spectators to events, and considerable experimental evidence indicates that firsthand accounts of events often are partially inaccurate (Granot, Balcetis, Feigenson, & Tyler, 2018; Houston, Hope, Memon, & Don Read, 2013; Wells & Olson, 2003). Given these problems, we need to consider carefully the validity and reliability of observations.

Little question exists that observational techniques have greater face validity as measures of behavior and events than techniques relying on secondhand accounts do. Surveys depend on someone else's perception and recollection, which many factors beyond the control of the researcher can shape and cloud. Observational techniques, on the other hand, provide firsthand accounts of occurrences under conditions that the investigator at least partially controls. Misperception may still occur, of course, but the researcher is in a position to recognize its impact and, possibly, control its magnitude. For these reasons, observation has greater face validity than many other data-collection techniques.

As shown in Chapter 5, we sometimes can measure the validity of an instrument by correlating the results of the instrument with the results achieved by some other instrument already known to be a valid measure of the variable. Often, however, such direct measures of validity are not possible in qualitative field research; nevertheless, we can employ certain procedures in field research to enhance the validity of the observations:

1. *Be as thorough as possible in describing and interpreting situations.* This increases the likelihood that we will make important observations and produce a valid assessment of a situation. Observations that seem to be unimportant while in the field may later be recognized as important. Observations not recorded, of course, are lost forever as data. Obviously, observers cannot record everything that happens in a situation, but it is preferable to err on the side of being too complete rather than too skimpy.
   Similarly, mental health therapists often pay attention to many aspects of clients' behavior from what they say, to how they sit in their chair, to whether or not they show up on time for each session, to how they respond to critical feedback.

2. *Carefully assess our own desires, values, and expectations to see if these might bias our observations.* People's expectations—or lack of them—drastically shape their perceptions. If we expect something to occur, we are much more likely to observe it—whether it actually occurs or not. If we expect welfare recipients to be lazy, then we will be acutely aware of all those behaviors among welfare recipients that might be interpreted as laziness. Thus, validity of observations is reduced to the extent that our expectations—recognized or not—mold our perceptions. We should assiduously look for the *opposite* of what we expect to happen, and we should be careful and critical if what we expect to find seems to be happening. On the other side of the coin, a lack of expectations may lead us to miss something of importance in a setting.
   Extending the mental health analogy, therapists are trained to keep their personal biases in check when assessing and treating clients. When personal biases interfere with client assessments and treatments there is a major risk of misdiagnosis or even worse, providing ineffective or even harmful treatment.

3. *Have other observers visit the same group or setting to see if they come to the same conclusions.* If they do, this provides validation that our conclusions are a response to the actual setting rather than to our expectations or biases—especially if the other observers had different expectations or biases.
   Asking other mental health therapists to accompany them in a treatment session is relatively rare; however, therapists routinely consult other therapists when having difficulty assessing a client or where they suspect personal biases may cloud their judgment of a client.

4. *Compare the conclusions reached through field observations with the conclusions reached through other research methodologies.* These other research methodologies can be observational research in other settings or surveys, available data, or experimental research (Weinstein, 1982). This is a variation on criterion validity (discussed in Chapter 5). If the various methodologies yield the same conclusions, then we have greater confidence that the field

observations have validity. Field research whose conclusions are at wide variant with the results of other research requires careful review, especially if none of these other checks on validity are available.

While a therapist primarily relies on direct observations and interactions with clients in making assessments and creating treatment plans, where possible therapists will also collect information on clients' past treatment histories (even if just asking the client about past treatments and diagnoses). Where therapists' assessments are confirmed by clients' treatment histories they are more confident in diagnoses.

5. *Consider how the condition of the observer might influence observations and conclusions.* Hunger, fatigue, stress, or personal problems can lead to distorted perceptions and interpretations. Likewise, physical characteristics, such as the lighting in an establishment, may lead to invalid observations. (This is another good reason for keeping complete field notes—they allow us to assess, at a later time, field conditions affecting validity.) If a number of these conditions exist, then we may decide to terminate observation and resume when conditions are more favorable.

A parallel in mental health treatment is transference and countertransference whereby interactions between the therapist and client may elicit sets of responses in which the client may view the therapist as he or she has viewed others in his or her life. Here the therapeutic relationship itself impacts what the client says and does in treatment.

6. *Look for behavior that is illegal, stigmatizing, or potentially embarrassing or that risks punishment.* If people engage in these kinds of behaviors, especially when they know they are being observed, then they are probably acting naturally and not putting on a performance for the benefit of the observer. In his study of a sexually transmitted disease clinic, Joseph Sheley argued that the validity of his data was quite strong, because "staff members dropped their professional masks and displayed quite unprofessional behavior and ideas in the company of the researcher" (Sheley, 1976, p. 116). Under such conditions, we can assume that people are reacting to environmental stimuli that normally guide their behavior rather than shaping a performance for the benefit of the investigator. If the people being observed do not have *anonymity,* then their behavior may not be a true reflection of how they behave normally. Especially when controversial, sensitive, or potentially embarrassing issues are investigated, validity declines substantially if anonymity has not been ensured. For this reason, hidden or disguised observation as well as observation in which the researcher takes the complete participant role is more valid than other types of observation.

In a mental health treatment session, the therapist must be aware that clients may downplay or avoid discussion of behavior or thoughts that are unflattering or socially unacceptable. Depending on where these behaviors and thoughts are displayed in treatment, therapists may be especially attentive to them as they may be an indication of serious issues.

7. *If possible, make a video or audio recording of the scene.* Although such recordings have their weaknesses as records of what occurred, they do provide another way to check and validate our observations and conclusions. Others can review such recordings as well, offering yet further checks on possible bias or misinterpretation.

While this is not always possible in mental health treatment, some therapists may audio-record therapy sessions to ensure accuracy when reviewing a case, making an assessment or diagnosis, or planning next steps for treatment.

Thus, researchers should follow as many of these guidelines as possible in designing field research; the more we incorporate, the more confidence we have in the validity of the results. Although many of the conditions influencing validity are beyond our control as investigators, it is important to honestly assess their impact on the research so that we can make an accurate appraisal of the results.

As for reliability of observational research, an individual researcher who is studying a single group or setting through participant observation has no practical way to assess reliability (Kirk &

Miller, 1986; Roberts & Povee, 2014). With more structured observations, such as when using a coding scheme, we can readily assess reliability with tests of *intercoder reliability,* or the ability of observers to code behaviors consistently into the same categories of the coding scheme: Two or more observers code the same behavior, with the resulting codes then being correlated to determine the degree of agreement between them. For example, in their study of homelessness in Michigan's Upper Peninsula, Hilton and DeJong (two authors of this textbook) assessed intercoder reliability of their coding scheme for evaluating coping strategies for homeless adults. Using NVivo software to code audiotaped interviews, they evaluated the extent to which coding stripes for various coping strategies connected to interview segments from each of their independent analyses lined up with one another. They found their intercoder reliabilities were sufficient. Many experts suggest that structured observations should achieve an intercoder reliability of $r = 0.75$ or better (Bailey, 1987).

Reactivity

Reactivity, or the degree to which the presence of the researcher influences what is being observed, is a major concern in any research (Lee, 2000; Reynolds, Robles, & Repetti, 2016). To take an extreme example, suppose that a researcher enters a group for the purpose of studying it through participant observation. Suppose, in addition, that the researcher takes an active role in the group's proceedings by talking a great deal, offering suggestions, and so on. Clearly, an observer behaving in this fashion will exert considerable influence on what occurs in the group, making the observer's presence highly reactive. This affects the validity of the observations, because we do not know whether we have measured the group's *natural* activities or their *reactions* to the observer. We are never sure if events different from those actually observed might have taken place if the researcher had conducted the observation in a less reactive manner. Reactivity also relates to the generalizability of findings. If the observer's presence is reactive, it is difficult to generalize findings to similar groups that have not had an observer in attendance.

Researchers generally agree that participant observation generates the best results when reactivity is kept to a minimum. This is a major argument in favor of the complete observer role (unobtrusive observation) or the complete participant role in participant observation, where the observer's true status is concealed. It is logical to assume that observation affects a group less if they are unaware of the observer's role as an observer than if they are aware of it. Using the complete participant role does not, however, guarantee a lack of reactivity. Observers must play the role properly—that is, as passively as possible without raising suspicion. Even when a researcher accomplishes the beginning of an observational study without undue reactivity, he or she must be careful that reactivity does not increase during the course of the project.

ASSESSMENT OF FIELD TECHNIQUES AND QUALITATIVE METHODS

As this chapter has shown, observational techniques differ from one another in terms of how qualitative and naturalistic they are. Not surprisingly, the advantages and disadvantages of observational techniques also differ depending on whether they are qualitative or quantitative and contrived or naturalistic. The first two advantages described next would apply to all forms of observational research. The remainder of the advantages and disadvantages apply particularly to the more qualitative, naturalistic, or unstructured types of observational research.

Throughout this chapter, we have discussed parallels between qualitative research and mental health counseling, particularly in the assessment phase. The main goals within both are similar— to understand behavior or some aspect of social life within a natural setting and to complete deep meaningful assessments of abstract phenomena (e.g., happiness, depression, fulfillment, spirituality, etc.). Both often involve interactions with people as a way of evaluating and assessing their conditions and potential for change or growth. Unlike research, however, the goal of therapy is change. Researchers are not typically interested in changing others. In fact, they are generally careful that their presence does not change others.

Advantages

1. Unlike surveys, which are limited to dealing with verbal statements, observational research can focus on both verbal and nonverbal behavior. This is an advantage because we can study *actual behavior* in addition to people's *statements* about how they behave. By dealing with behavior, observational research avoids a potential source of error, namely the gap between what people say they do and what people actually do. The ability of observational techniques to consider both verbal and nonverbal behavior puts the researcher in a better position to link the verbal statements with behavior.

2. Much observational research is longitudinal in nature and, thus, enables researchers to make statements concerning changes that occur over the time of the research. In addition, by following activities over time, observers have less trouble establishing the correct causal sequence than they do with surveys. (As noted in Chapter 2, establishing the causal order with survey data sometimes can be difficult.)

3. The advantage most often claimed for observational research is that it provides deeper and more insightful data than most other methods generate. Especially with participant observation, researchers immerse themselves in the daily activities of those being studied to a greater degree than with other techniques. This places them in a position to gain information that they would likely miss with techniques such as questionnaires or interviews. This is especially true for the complete participant or those who have become "invisible": As accepted members of the group, they see people behaving freely and naturally, unaware that they are being studied. Even such techniques as in-depth interviews and case studies can produce a deep, rich understanding of people's lives. The survey interviewer, on the other hand, may generate more socially acceptable responses and a carefully orchestrated presentation of self, but the participant observer and the in-depth interviewer can go beyond

these public fronts and penetrate the behind-the-scenes regions of human behavior.

4. Observational research can study the behavior of groups that are closed to other forms of research. Many studies cited in this chapter involve groups that, for various reasons, are not open to research by other methods. These people may have something to hide, or they may view a stranger's intrusion as somehow threatening to their cohesion and values. The ability of the complete participant to conceal his or her identity and conduct research where we cannot otherwise go is a major advantage of this observational technique. Even participant observers and in-depth interviewers, whose status as researchers is known, may, over time, gain access to groups through the development of trust and rapport; the same groups might reject the more brief and superficial entreaties of an interviewer.

5. A frequently overlooked—but nevertheless significant—advantage of observational research is that the most qualified person often is directly involved in collecting data, because the senior researcher often is one of the observers (Denzin, 1989; Morrow, 2010). This is very different from surveys, for example, in which the project director rarely conducts interviews, leaving this task to part-time interviewers hired specifically for the job. Surveys place the most knowledgeable person farthest from the data-collection effort.

Disadvantages

Most of the disadvantages of observational research relate to the more qualitative, naturalistic, and unstructured types. With less structure, the quality of the results from an observational study depends heavily on the individual skills of the researcher, and this leads to several criticisms:

1. A nagging concern with participant observation research is the possible effect of observer bias on the results. Such research does not have the same structured tools of other methods to help reduce such bias. If researchers are not careful, personal attitudes and values can distort research findings, rendering them virtually useless for scientific purposes.

2. Closely related to the issue of observer bias is the problem of the observer going native, or overidentifying with those who are being studied. Because the observer frequently becomes a part of a group for a substantial period of time, this possibility is quite real.

3. The lack of structure also makes exact replication—an important part of scientific research—difficult if not impossible. Observational studies often are such individualized projects that the possibility for replication is slight. Any observer in a natural setting will be forced to record what occurs selectively because of the sheer volume of behaviors and events. There is little chance that a replication attempt would select precisely the same aspects of a given setting on which to focus.

4. The nature of the data gathered in some observational research makes them very difficult to quantify. Some participant observers generate field notes that are basically rambling descriptions; data in this form are difficult to code or categorize in summary form, which makes traditional hypothesis testing more difficult. As a result, many observational studies fail to get beyond a description of the setting. (Of course, some nonpositivist researchers consider this to be an advantage of qualitative research.)

5. Although unrelated to its lack of structure, some critics have called the ethics of participant observation into question, with the complete participant role generating the most controversy. Some social scientists see it as unethical to conceal one's identity for the purpose of conducting research, because it deprives people of the opportunity to give informed consent. Whether disguised observation is ethical remains an open controversy in the social sciences. (As noted in Chapter 3, disguised observation is considered to be a questionable practice that requires approval by an Institutional Review Board.) As long as the research is not trivial and the identities of participants are not revealed, however, disguised observation probably will be allowed.

6. As mentioned earlier, participant observation affords the researcher little control over the variables in the setting. A great deal may be happening that the researcher is not in a position to control or moderate. This often leads to situations in which the researcher is at a loss to select the important causal factors in a situation.

7. Because of the physical limitations on any researcher's observing capabilities, a participant observation study will almost certainly study a limited sample of people. Although we could, with a sufficient number of observers, study a large sample, we rarely do. Observation more commonly is limited to a small group, such as a family or a gang, or to one setting, such as a bar or a restaurant. The explanatory power that comes from a large sample size therefore is not available.

REVIEW AND CRITICAL THINKING

Main Points

- Observational techniques involve data collection through direct visual or auditory experience of behavior. In qualitative research, the data come in the form of words, pictures, narratives, and descriptions rather than in numerical form. Field research is one type of qualitative research. Two important characteristics of qualitative research are that it is contextual in nature and that it uses a grounded theory approach.

- One type of field research is participant observation, which is similar to the anthropologist's ethnographic research. Many field researchers base their work on the nonpositivist approach and often use the method of *verstehen*. Knowledge in participant observation is gained through both participation (empathic understanding) and observation (deep appreciation of context).

- A major decision for the participant observer is whether to reveal his or her status as an observer to those being studied. Also important is the extent to which the researcher's role will stress participation or observation.
- Unobtrusive observation, including both hidden observation and disguised observation, is designed to minimize reactivity.
- Steps involved in conducting field research include problem formulation, selecting a field setting, entering the field, developing rapport with people in the field, becoming invisible, observing and recording, and exiting the field.
- When variables cannot be easily quantified or when using the *verstehen* strategy, observers collect data in field research in the form of field notes, which are detailed, descriptive accounts of the observations made during a given period. When researchers can measure variables quantitatively in field research, they use coding schemes to measure and record observations. Coding sheets contain the categories of the coding scheme and facilitate the recording process.
- Another form of qualitative research is in-depth interviewing, an informal and unstructured interview that can explore a wide range of topics and may last for a long time, even days or weeks. It is quite different from the interviews done in survey research. Qualitative research also takes the form of narratives, life stories, or case studies, all of which involve a detailed descriptive account of part or all of a particular individual's life or, with some case studies, of an organization or an event. The goal is to gain understanding through the depth and richness of detail achieved with this method in comparison to quantitative methods. Focus groups also are a form of qualitative research.
- Time sampling in observational research reduces the volume of observations that researchers have to make. Validity and reliability in observational research mean that the observations correctly and accurately reflect reality.
- Some observational techniques, especially unobtrusive observation, minimize reactivity and, thus, are good for studying sensitive topics, such as racism and sexism.
- Observational techniques are relevant to both research and practice settings.

IMPORTANT TERMS FOR REVIEW

Coding	In-depth interviews	Reactivity
Ethnographic	Nonreactive	Time sampling
Interviews	Observation	Unobtrusive
Field notes	Observational	Observation
Field research	Techniques	*Verstehen*
Grounded theory	Participant observation	

CRITICAL THINKING

1. What types of research and practice questions (or problems) are best answered through qualitative as opposed to quantitative research? Think of a service-oriented question (i.e., a question pertaining to a professional service) that would be best answered through qualitative research. How might the data/information you collect be useful to you as a professional and to your employer/agency? Identify potential threats to validity and reliability with these data.

2. How can researchers and practitioners increase the reliability of their qualitative measures? Imagine you have the task of interviewing clients at your agency to determine what they like about services provided at the agency and what they do not like. What are some ways you could help ensure that the information (data) you collect and your report to your supervisors is valid and reliable?

3. Why is context so important in understanding social phenomena and how can qualitative research methods help researchers and practitioners better understand the importance of context? Think about the task outlined in Question 2. What contextual factors might be important to examine in your evaluation? How might you help ensure that contextual factors important to your clients are covered in the evaluation?

EVALUATING COMPETENCY (FROM THE COUNCIL ON SOCIAL WORK EDUCATION [CSWE] 2015 EDUCATIONAL POLICY AND ACCREDITATION STANDARDS [EPAS])

Competency 2: Engage Diversity and Difference in Practice

- Qualitative research is often used to understand the subjective experiences of other people (or how they experience, respond to, and feel about certain phenomena). Why might this approach be important to engaging diversity and difference in practice?
- In what ways might qualitative research be especially well suited to assessing the extent to which services meet the needs of marginalized populations?

Competency 4: Engage in Practice-Informed Research and Research-Informed Practice

- Social workers and other human services professionals are increasingly expected to engage in evidence-based practice—that is, to rely on research findings in designing services or creating programs. To what extent should qualitative research findings be used as a basis for designing services and creating new programs?

- What practice-related skills can also be applied when conducting qualitative research? In what ways might a qualitative research interview be similar to an assessment interview with a client? In what ways are qualitative research and assessment interviews different?

Competency 7: Assess Individuals, Families, Groups, Organizations, and Communities

- Think about a professional practice situation where you would have the task of assessing an individual client. What characteristics or contextual factors might you wish to assess quantitatively and which would you wish to assess qualitatively?
- How might it help to collect both quantitative and qualitative information (data) on some characteristics or contextual factors?

Competency 9: Evaluate Practice With Individuals, Families, Groups, Organizations, and Communities

- Think about a practice outcome associated with a professional service of interest to you. How would you measure this outcome? Would you incorporate any qualitative measures in your outcome measurement?
- Suppose you are interested in learning more about outcomes of a service or program that are important to clients but are not captured in existing program measures (or evaluations). What qualitative research methods might you use?

SELF-ASSESSMENT

1. Observing people in their natural settings as they go about their everyday life is known as:
   a. Systematic review.
   b. Field research.
   c. Program evaluation.
   d. Focus groups.
2. The perspective that the world exists independently of people's perceptions of it and that scientists can use objective techniques to discover what exists in the world is known as:
   a. Positivism.
   b. Nonpositivism.
   c. Optimism.
   d. Scientific advocacy.
3. The qualitative research method in which the researcher observes people in their natural environment (the "field") and the researcher is a part of and participates in the activities of the people, group, or situation being studied is known as:
   a. Focus groups.
   b. Participant observation.

    c. Grounded theory.
    d. Experimental design.

4. The distinguishing feature of a complete participant role is:
    a. The researcher's status as observer is not revealed to those who are being studied.
    b. The researcher is unaware of his or her role as a researcher.
    c. The researcher's status as a researcher is known to all participants.
    d. The researcher observes a social phenomenon but is careful not to actively participate in it.

5. In field research, being "invisible" means
    a. That those who are present cannot see the observer.
    b. That those who are present are aware of the observer but do not know his or her real identity.
    c. That those who are present perceive the observer as a natural part of the setting, not as an outsider.
    d. That the observer does not know the personal identities of those being observed.

6. Detailed, descriptive accounts of the observations made during a given period are called:
    a. Data points.
    b. Coding sheets.
    c. Recordings.
    d. Field notes.

7. Categorizing behaviors into a limited number of preordained categories is known as:
    a. Coding.
    b. Zoning.
    c. Narrative.
    d. Data entry.

8. Informal and unstructured interviews that explore a wide range of topics and that may last for a long time, even days or weeks, are known as:
    a. Extensive or elaborate interviews.
    b. Background interviews.
    c. Survey interviews.
    d. In-depth or ethnographic interviews.

9. Case studies and life histories involve detailed and what sometimes is called "thick" description, which refers to:
    a. A complete and literal accounting of the person or setting under study.
    b. Long written narratives that take up many pages.
    c. Descriptions based on interviews with all people in a social network.
    d. Descriptions that include an extensive vocabulary.

10. Focus groups are also known as:
    a. Table interviews.
    b. Group surveys.
    c. Group depth interviews.
    d. Semi-structured interviews.

ANSWER KEY FOR SELF-ASSESSMENT QUIZ

1. **b.** Field research
2. **a.** Positivism
3. **b.** Participant observation
4. **a.** The researcher's status as observer is not revealed to those who are being studied.
5. **c.** That those who are present perceive the observer as a natural part of the setting, not as an outsider.
6. **d.** Field notes
7. **a.** Coding
8. **d.** In-depth or ethnographic interviews
9. **a.** A complete and literal accounting of the person or setting under study.
10. **c.** Group depth Interviews

FOR FURTHER READING

Anderson, E. (1990). *Streetwise: Race, class, and change in an urban community.* Chicago, IL: University of Chicago Press. This is an excellent example of participant observation research in a community setting. In this case, changes in community life are described as the racial and social class composition of a neighborhood changes.

Berg, B. L., & Lune, H. (2012). *Qualitative research methods for the social sciences* (8th ed.). Boston, MA: Allyn & Bacon. Berg provides more detail on the qualitative research methods discussed in this chapter, as well as some others that we have not included.

Corbin, J., & Strauss, A. (2008). *Basics of qualitative research: Techniques and procedures for developing grounded theory* (3rd ed.). Newbury Park, CA: Sage. This is a good overview of how to do qualitative research.

Denzin, N. K., & Lincoln, Y. S. (Eds.). (2011). *The SAGE handbook of qualitative research* (4th ed.). Thousand Oaks, CA: Sage. This book of readings provides a comprehensive overview of all aspects of qualitative research, including the historical development of the field. It is one of the most complete and authoritative statements about this form of research.

Ferrell, J., & Hamm, M. S. (Eds.). (1998). *Ethnography at the edge: Crime, deviance, and field research.* Boston, MA: Northeastern University Press. This remarkable book takes the pioneering—and not necessarily popular—stance that *verstehen* in field research requires that researchers gain experiential immersion in the criminal and deviant activities of those being studied. It is a realistic view of what happens in field research and raises many key methodological and ethical issues.

George, A. L., & Bennett, A. (2005). *Case studies and theory development in the social sciences.* Cambridge, MA: MIT Press. This text presents a comprehensive analysis of research methods using case studies and examines the place of case studies in social science methodology. It argues that case studies, statistical methods, and formal models are complementary rather than competitive.

Hobbs, D., & Wright, R. (2006). *The SAGE handbook of fieldwork.* Thousand Oaks, CA: Sage. The authors present a major overview of this method in all its variety, introducing the reader to the strengths, weaknesses, and "real-world" applications of fieldwork techniques. Each chapter is based on a substantive field of empirical enquiry and written by an expert in the field.

Marshall, C., & Rossman, G. B. (2011). *Designing qualitative research* (5th ed.). Newbury Park, CA: AltaMira Press. The authors of this book provide a good introduction to qualitative research methods in applied research and policy analysis. Although it emphasizes educational research, the book includes vignettes from other social science and human service areas.

Padgett, D. K. (2008). *Qualitative methods in social work research* (2nd ed.). Thousand Oaks, CA: Sage. This book provides a thorough coverage of qualitative methods applied specifically to social work-related topics. It covers six major approaches: ethnography, grounded theory, case study, narrative, phenomenological, and participatory action research.

Silverman, D. (2012). *Interpreting qualitative data* (4th ed.). Newbury Park, CA: Sage. This book discusses the theoretical issues involved in collecting and analyzing data from qualitative research and describes some of the particular data-collection techniques.

REFERENCES

Ababneh, S. (2016). Troubling the political: Women in the Jordanian day-waged labor movement. *International Journal of Middle East Studies, 48*(1), 87–112. doi:10.1017/S0020743815001488

Antonucci, T. (1986). Hierarchical mapping technique. *Generations: The Journal of the Western Gerontological Society, 10,* 10–12.

Armstrong, G. (1994). Like that Desmond Morris? In D. Hobbs & T. May (Eds.), *Interpreting the field* (pp. 3–44). Oxford: Oxford University Press.

Arnault, D. S., & Shimabukuro, S. (2012). The clinical ethnographic interview: A user-friendly guide to the cultural formulation of distress and help seeking. *Transcultural Psychiatry, 49*(2), 302–322. doi:10.1177/1363461511425877

Bailey, K. (1987). *Methods of social research* (3rd ed.). New York, NY: Free Press.

Bales, R. F. (1950). *Interaction process analysis.* Cambridge, MA.: Addison-Wesley,

Benjafield, J. G. (2002). Research methods: A history of some important strands. *Archives of Suicide Research, 6*(1), 5–14. doi:10.1080/13811110213119

Benton, T. (1977). *Philosophical foundations of the three sociologies.* Boston, MA: Routledge & Kegan Paul.

Bernard, H. R. (2006). *Research methods in anthropology: Qualitative and quantitative approaches* (4th ed.). Walnut Creek, CA: AltaMira Press.

Bogdan, R. C., & Biklen, S. K. (1992). *Qualitative research for education: An introduction to theory and methods* (2nd ed.). Boston, MA: Allyn & Bacon.

Bogdan, R. C., & Taylor, S. J. (1975). *Introduction to qualitative research methods.* New York, NY: Wiley.

Bourgois, P. (1995). *In search of respect: Selling crack in El Barrio.* Cambridge, UK: Cambridge University Press.

Brunger, F., & Wall, D. (2016). "What do they really mean by partnerships?" Questioning the unquestionable good in ethics: Guidelines promoting community engagement in indigenous health research. *Qualitative Health Research, 26*(13), 1862–1877. doi:10.1177/1049732316649158

Calvey, D. (2008). The art and politics of covert research: Doing 'Situated Ethics' in the field. *Sociology, 42*(5), 905–918. doi:10.1177/0038038508094569

Cavan, S. (1966). *Liquor license.* Chicago, IL: Aldine.

Charmaz, K. (2006). *Constructing grounded theory: A practical guide through qualitative analysis.* Thousand Oaks, CA: Sage.

Clandinin, D. J., & Connelly, F. M. (2000). *Narrative inquiry: Experience and story in qualitative research.* San Francisco, CA: Jossey-Bass.

Cupchik, G. (2001). Constructivist realism: An ontology that encompasses positivist and constructivist approaches to the social sciences. *Forum: Qualitative Social Research, 2*(1), 29–39.

Denzin, N. (1989). *The research act: A theoretical introduction to sociological methods* (3rd ed.). Englewood Cliffs, NJ: Prentice Hall.

DeWalt, K. M., & DeWalt, B. R. (2011). *Participant observation: A guide for fieldworkers* (2nd ed.). Walnut Creek, CA: AltaMira Press.

Durkheim, E. (1938). *Rules of the sociological method* (trans. S. Solovay & J. Mueller). Chicago, IL: University of Chicago Press.

Estroff, S. E. (1981). *Making it crazy: An ethnography of psychiatric clients in an American Community.* Berkeley: University of California Press.

Feldman, M. S., Bell, J., & Berger, M. T. (2003). *Gaining access: A practical guide for qualitative researchers.* Walnut Creek, CA: AltaMira Press.

Fontana, A., & Frey, J. H. (1994). Interviewing: The art of science. In N. K. Denzin & Y. S. Lincoln (Eds.), *Handbook of qualitative research* (pp. 361–376). Thousand Oaks, CA: Sage.

Fritsche, I., & Linneweber, V. (2006). Nonreactive methods in psychological research. In M. Eid & E. Diener (Eds.), *Handbook of multimethod measurement in psychology* (pp. 189–203). Washington, DC: American Psychological Association. doi:10.1037/11383-014

Gold, R. L. (1958). Roles in sociological field observations. *Social Forces, 36,* 217–223. doi:10.2307/2573808

Graham, K., LaRocque, L., Yetman, R., Ross, T. J., & Guistra, E. (1980). Aggression and barroom environments. *Journal of Studies on Alcohol, 41*, 277–292. doi:10.15288/jsa.1980.41.277

Granot, Y., Balcetis, E., Feigenson, N., & Tyler, T. (2018). In the eyes of the law: Perception versus reality in appraisals of video evidence. *Psychology, Public Policy, and Law, 24*(1), 93–104. doi:10.1037/law0000137

Gubrium, J. F., & Holstein, J. A. (1997). *The new language of qualitative methods*. New York, NY: Oxford University Press.

Halfpenny, P. (1982). *Positivism and sociology: Explaining social life*. London, UK: Allen & Unwin.

Hilton, T., & DeJong, C. (2010). Homeless in God's country: Coping behaviors and felt experiences of the rural homeless. *Journal of Qualitative and Ethnographic Research, 5*, 12–30.

Holstein, J. A., & Gubrium, J. F. (1995). *The active interview*. Thousand Oaks, CA: Sage.

Horowitz, R. (1987). Community tolerance of gang violence. *Social Problems, 34*, 437–450. doi:10.2307/800540

Houston, K. A., Hope, L., Memon, A., & Don Read, J. (2013). Expert testimony on eyewitness evidence: In search of common sense. *Behavioral Sciences & The Law, 31*(5), 637–651. doi:10.1002/bsl.2080

Irwin, D. M., & Bushnell, M. M. (1980). *Observational strategies for child study*. New York, NY: Holt, Rinehart & Winston.

Jorgensen, D. (1989). *Participant observation: A methodology for human studies*. Newbury Park, CA: Sage.

Kirk, J., & Miller, M. L. (1986). *Reliability and validity in qualitative research*. Beverly Hills, CA: Sage.

Klockars, C. B. (1979). Dirty hands and deviant subjects. In C. B. Klockars & F. W. O'Connor (Eds.), *Deviance and decency: The ethics of research with human subjects* (pp. 763–792). Beverly Hills, CA: Sage.

Lane, J. D., & Harris, P. L. (2015). The roles of intuition and informants' expertise in Children's Epistemic Trust. *Child Development, 86*(3), 919–926. doi:10.1111/cdev.12324

Lawless, E. J. (1991). Methodology and research notes: Women's life stories and reciprocal ethnography as feminist and emergent. *Journal of Folklore Research, 28*, 35–60.

Lee, R. M. (2000). *Unobtrusive methods in social research*. Philadelphia, PA: Open University Press.

Leo, R. A. (1996). The ethics of deceptive research roles reconsidered: A response to Kai Erikson. *American Sociologist, 27*, 122–128. doi:10.1007/BF02692002

Lincoln, Y. S., Lynham, S. A., & Guba, E. G. (2011). Paradigmatic controversies, contradictions, and emerging confluences, revisited. In N. K. Denzin & Y. S. Lincoln (Eds.), *Handbook of qualitative research* (4th ed., pp. 97–128). Thousand Oaks, CA: Sage.

Linsk, N., Howe, M. W., & Pinkston, E. M. (1975). Behavioral group work in a home for the aged. *Social Work, 20*(6), 454–463. doi:10.1093/sw/20.6.454

Lofland, J., Snow, D., Anderson, L., & Lofland, L. H. (2006). *Analyzing social settings* (4th ed.). Belmont, CA: Wadsworth/Cengage.

Marquart, J. W. (2001). Doing research in prison: The strengths and weaknesses of full participation as a guard. In J. M. Miller & R. Tewksbury (Eds.), *Extreme methods: Innovative approaches to social science research* (pp. 35–47). Boston, MA: Allyn & Bacon.

Morrow, B. (2010). An overview of case–control study designs and their advantages and disadvantages. *International Journal of Therapy & Rehabilitation, 17*(11), 570–574. doi:10.12968/ijtr.2010.17.11.79537

Mortenson, W. B., Sixsmith, A., & Woolrych, R. (2015). The power(s) of observation: Theoretical perspectives on surveillance technologies and older people. *Ageing & Society, 35*(3), 512–530. doi:10.1017/S0144686X13000846

Noble, H., & Smith, J. (2015). Issues of validity and reliability in qualitative research. *Evidence Based Nursing, 18*(2), 34–35. doi:10.1136/eb-2015-102054

Patton, M. Q. (2002). *Qualitative research and evaluation methods* (3rd ed.). Thousand Oaks, CA: Sage.

Pepler, D. J., & Craig, W. M. (1995). A peek behind the fence: Naturalistic observations of aggressive children with remote audiovisual recording. *Developmental Psychology, 31*, 548–553. doi:10.1037/0012-1649.31.4.548

Powdermaker, H. (1996). *Stranger and friend: The way of an anthropologist*. New York, NY: Norton.

Reynolds, B. M., Robles, T. F., & Repetti, R. L. (2016). Measurement reactivity and fatigue effects in daily diary research with families. *Developmental Psychology, 52*(3), 442–456. doi:10.1037/dev0000081

Roberts, L. D., & Povee, K. (2014). Qualitative research methods. *Australian Journal of Psychology, 66*, 249–256. doi:10.1111/ajpy.12059

Rosenhan, D. L. (1973). On being sane in insane places. *Science, 179,* 250–258. doi:10.1126/science.179.4070.250

Roulet, T. J., Gill, M. J., Stenger, S., & Gill, D. J. (2017). Reconsidering the value of covert research: The role of ambiguous consent in participant observation. *Organizational Research Methods, 20*(3), 487–517. doi:10.1177/1094428117698745

Runcie, J. F. (1980). *Experiencing social research* (rev. ed.). Homewood, IL: Dorsey Press.

Scheper-Hughes, N. (1992). *Death without weeping: The violence of everyday life in Brazil.* Berkeley: University of California Press.

Sheley, J. F. (1976). A study in self-defeat: The public health venereal disease clinic. *Journal of Sociology and Social Welfare, 4,* 114–124.

Shupe, A. D., Jr., & Bromley, D. G. (1980). Walking a tightrope: Dilemmas of participant observation of groups in conflict. *Qualitative Sociology, 2,* 3–21. doi:10.1007/BF02390156

Smith, A. H., Anderson, M. J., & Pawley, M. M. (2017). Could ecologists be more random? Straightforward alternatives to haphazard spatial sampling. *Ecography, 40*(11), 1251–1255. doi:10.1111/ecog.02821

Smith, S. K., Mountain, G. A., & Hawkins, R. J. (2016). A scoping review to identify the techniques frequently used when analysing qualitative visual data. *International Journal of Social Research Methodology, 19*(6), 693–715. doi:10.1080/13645579.2015.1087141

Spano, R. (2006). Observer behavior as a potential source of reactivity: Describing and quantifying observer effects in a large-scale observational study of police. *Sociological Methods & Research, 34*(4), 521–553.

Stadnick, N., Haine-Schlagel, R., & Martinez, J. (2016). Using observational assessment to help identify factors associated with parent participation engagement in community-based child mental health services. *Child & Youth Care Forum, 45*(5), 745–758. doi:10.1007/s10566-016-9356-z

Stott, C., & Reicher, S. (1998). How conflict escalates: The inter-group dynamics of collective football crowd "violence." *Sociology, 32,* 353–377. doi:10.1177/0038038598032002007

Suen, H. K., & Ary, D. (1986). Poisson cumulative probabilities of systematic errors in single-subject and multiple-subject time sampling. *Behavioral Assessment, 8,* 155–169.

Thorne, B. (1993). *Gender play: Girls and boys in school.* New Brunswick, NJ: Rutgers University Press.

Trella, D., & Hilton, T. (2014). They can only do so much: Use of family while coping with rural homelessness. *Contemporary Rural Social Work Journal, 6*(1), 16–39.

Webb, E. J., Campbell, D. T., Schwartz, R. D., Sechrest, L., & Grove, J. B. (1981). *Nonreactive measures in the social sciences.* Boston, MA: Houghton Mifflin.

Weber, M. (1957). *The theory of social and economic organization* (trans. A. M. Henderson & T. Parsons). New York, NY: Free Press (Original work published 1925).

Weinstein, R. M. (1982). The mental hospital from the patient's point of view: The pitfalls of participant-observation research. In W. R. Gove (Ed.), *Deviance and mental illness* (pp. 273–300). Newbury Park, CA: Sage.

Wells, G. L., & Olson, E. A. (2003). Eyewitness testimony. In S. T. Fiske (Ed.), *Annual review of psychology* (Vol. 54, pp. 300–327). Palo Alto, CA: Annual Reviews.

Whyte, W. F. (1955). *Street Corner Society* (2nd ed.). Chicago, IL: University of Chicago Press.

Wilson, T. (1970). Normative and interpretive paradigms in sociology. In J. Douglas (Ed.), *Understanding everyday life: Toward the reconstruction of sociological knowledge.* New York, NY: Aldine.

Yin, R. K. (2009). *Case study research: Design and methods* (4th ed.). Thousand Oaks, CA: Sage.

10

EXPERIMENTAL RESEARCH

INTRODUCTION

Samantha Diggs (age 42) is the executive director at "A New Hope," a domestic violence treatment center in the rural community of Harristown, West Virginia, and works with Sydney Torrie (vignette in Chapter 2). As you will remember from Chapter 2, the center provides Batterer Intervention Programs (BIPs) to approximately 100 offenders a year and treatment delivery is both individual and group therapy. Each treatment group has no more than 12 individuals at a time. These groups consist of all-male or all-female offenders. In Chapter 2, Sydney used the scientific method processes to start exploring how effective the center's BIPs are at reducing violence. In this exploration she discovered that there are two additional types of offender treatment (multi-couple group treatment and circles of peace). Along with the current BIP program, the center would like to evaluate the effectiveness of these programs with their clients.

The BIP "A New Hope" currently uses is an abuser treatment program that is only for offenders of domestic or partner violence; it addresses participants' violent behaviors and provides support for developing new methods of interacting with their intimate partner and family member(s). This treatment is also gender-specific with only all-male or all-female groups. Multi-couple group treatment for interpersonal violence is designed for couples that experience violence in which both members in the relationship have used a form of violence against the other. This treatment is designed to heal the couple and end violence in their relationship. Circles of Peace treat families who have been affected by domestic violence. This approach involves not only the offender and family members, but also members from the community. There are three completely different approaches to treating abusive partners.

Samantha is at the stage in research to conduct an experimental design to look into the effectiveness of these three different programs to end violence in partnerships, families, and communities. She is going to explore their effectiveness with clients in her community of Harristown, West Virginia, to see which treatment model is more effective at reducing violence. As you read this chapter on experimental research, consider the following questions: (a) What different research designs will social workers need to know to obtain effectiveness? (b) Which research design will social workers need to know to provide the most accurate information? (c) How will social workers understanding threats to internal validity potentially impact experimental research? (d) What can social workers do to decrease threats to internal validity? and (e) What additional resources would help social workers to successfully complete experimental research?

When people think of "science" and "research," the word *experiments* often is the first word that comes to mind. All these terms conjure up images of laboratories, white coats, and electronic gear. This points toward a considerable misunderstanding about the nature of experimentation. In fact, we all engage in casual experimenting in the course of our everyday lives. For example, when a mechanical device malfunctions, we probe and test its various components in an effort to discover the elements responsible for the malfunction. In essence, we are experimenting to find the component (or variable) that caused the malfunction.

Human service practitioners also often engage in casual experimentation. For example, when working with clients experiencing specific challenges, human service workers often try new intervention strategies to see if they will prove to be beneficial. For instance, if behavior modification or role rehearsal does not bring about the desired effect, then the human service worker might try a cognitive learning strategy. These are illustrations of casual rather than systematic experiments, but they point toward the essence of an **experiment:** It is a controlled method of observation in which the value of one or more independent variables is changed to assess the causal effect on one or more dependent variables. Practitioner Profile 10.1 illustrates a practical example of how community agencies and researchers can collaborate efforts for effective and meaningful experimental designs.

The word *experimentation* as used in research, then, concerns a logic of analysis rather than a particular location, such as a laboratory, in which observations are made. In fact, experiments can be conducted in many settings. **Laboratory experiments** are conducted in artificial settings that are constructed in such a way that selected elements of the natural environment are simulated and features of the investigation are controlled. **Field experiments,** on the other hand, are conducted in natural settings as people go about their everyday affairs.

The logic of scientific experiments can be illustrated by a more careful look at two elements of the impromptu or casual experimenting that occurs in everyday human service practice. First, many casual experiments fail. In other words, manipulating the variables involved may not produce the desired result. No matter which approach to a client

is used, for example, improvement in functioning may not be forthcoming. In part, failures in casual experiments stem from the fact that they are *casual* and, thus, not carefully planned. For example, the wrong variables may have been selected for manipulation so that no matter how those variables were changed, the desired result could not be obtained. In scientific experimentation, on the other hand, criteria exist to increase the likelihood of success by ensuring that the experiment is soundly planned and that crucial procedures are carried out. It is not that following formalized procedures guarantees success—it does not. Failure in the sense of not achieving the desired results is an unpleasant—but fully expected—outcome of experimenting. Actually, it may be best not to conceive of failure to achieve predicted results as a failure per se. Not achieving predicted results—assuming the results are not caused by poor research techniques—serves to rule out one possible explanation.

The second feature of casual experimenting is a tendency to jump to conclusions that later prove to be incorrect. An effort to improve the performance of a client, for example, may produce temporary changes that later disappear. What went wrong? Maybe the practitioner's change in intervention strategy was not the real source of the change in the client's behavior, and something else actually caused the temporary changes. For example, perhaps the client found a job or his or her mother-in-law recovered from surgery, which led to a temporary improvement in performance. Or, it may be that *any change* from one intervention strategy to another will result in short-term improvements that quickly dissipate. The point is that many things influence people's behavior, and casual experimentation is not organized to sort out these influences. Scientific experimentation is designed to do this and, thus, to reduce the likelihood of reaching false conclusions.

The focus of this chapter is experimental research, but the techniques discussed here can be applied to practice settings. The impromptu experimenting attributed to human service practice certainly has its place. The approach of evidence-based practice, however, stresses the idea that knowledge based on experimentally designed research and practice is the most desirable foundation for practice decisions. A thorough grasp

PRACTITIONER PROFILE 10.1 Kimberly Garner, Reproductive Life Planning Coordinator, Appalachian District Health Department, North Carolina, and Rachel Wright, Assistant Professor, Department of Social Work, Appalachian State University, North Carolina

Research-informed social work practice is vital to help various marginalized populations throughout society. Rural areas are especially in need of informed practice to solve community problems that seem to have no solutions. One area that is gaining popularity is *reproductive justice* or a woman's reproductive autonomy in making decisions about her body and reproductive health. Both Kimberly and Rachel take their research in reproductive justice and translate it to provide education, solutions, and advocacy to better serve, empower, and inform women living in rural communities.

Kimberly Garner currently works in healthcare at *Appalachian District Health Department* and with a grant in northwestern North Carolina to decrease the rate of infant mortality and improve birth outcomes. She also works on a grant that improves the health of children that are 5 years old or younger. Her educational background in both social work and public health give her the appropriate skillset needed to work with communities and conduct research to inform social work practice. Kimberly's interest in translating research into practice began when she had the opportunity to conduct research on the U.S.-Mexican border in El Paso, Texas, while working at a birthing center. After her experience there, she became a strong proponent for translating research into practice to help rural communities improve.

Kimberly's colleague, Rachel, currently conducts research on women's reproductive health experiences while living in rural areas. Her research asks qualitative questions by delving further into women's understanding of their reproductive experiences, autonomy, rights, decisions, care, and where they receive their reproductive information. Her current study measures conflict and control issues within intimate relationships over reproductive autonomy to inquire about how control in intimate relationships affects reproductive matters. Their current work gained much unexpected attention, support, and feedback from community members and service providers. Their project has provided awareness around women's reproductive matters in healthcare. The use of qualitative data is important in healthcare because it informs community healthcare providers about their services and assists them in making appropriate improvements where needed. This is their community and these are the voices of women who live here.

Kimberly and Rachel's relationship in collaborative research is rooted in having mutual support of each other, open communication, and great rapport. Their current work in research informs women's healthcare by creating rural community awareness of reproductive justice, but they want to see their research go further by seeing women being able to have reproductive health discussions with their service providers without feeling shamed. Furthermore, they hope their research paves the way for women to be better informed about their reproductive options, use and choice of contraceptives, reproductive autonomy, access to reproductive counseling, other reproductive choices without bias, and the fostering of a *Reproductive Life Planning Approach,* which is a nonjudgmental approach to women's choices in reproductive health and wellness. They assert that being sensitive yet responsive to communities is necessary when conducting research. Serving the needs of the community and its service providers should be a researcher's intent when informing practice.

of the principles of experimentation can enhance the practitioner's knowledge-building and decision-making efforts.

THE LOGIC OF EXPERIMENTATION

Causation and Control

The strength of experiments as a research technique is that they are designed to enable us to make inferences about causality. The element that makes this possible is *control:* In experiments, the investigator has considerable control over determining who participates in a study, what happens to them, and under what conditions it happens. To appreciate the importance of this, let us look at some of the key terms in experimental research.

At the core of experimental research is the fact that the investigator exposes the people in an experiment, commonly referred to as *experimental subjects,* to some condition or variable, called the *experimental stimulus.* The **experimental stimulus,** or **experimental treatment,** is an independent variable that is directly manipulated by the experimenter to assess its effect on behavior. (Recall from Chapter 2 that independent variables are those variables in a study that are hypothesized to produce change in another variable. The variable affected by the independent variable is called the dependent variable, because its value is dependent on the value of the independent variable.) An **experimental group** is a group of subjects exposed to the experimental stimulus. **Experimental condition** describes the group of people who receive the experimental stimulus.

We can illustrate the logic underlying experimentation by means of a series of symbols. The following symbols are commonly used to describe experimental designs:

O = Observation or measurement of the dependent variable

X = Exposure of people to the experimental stimulus or independent variable

R = Random assignment to conditions

In addition, the symbols constituting a particular experimental design are presented in time sequence, with those to the left occurring earlier in the sequence than those farther to the right. With this in mind, we can describe a very elementary experiment in the following way:

O X O

In this experiment, the researcher first measures the dependent variable (the pretest), then exposes the subjects to the independent variable, and then remeasures the dependent variable (the posttest) to see if there has been a change. One major yardstick for assessing whether the independent variable in an experiment has had an effect is a comparison of the pretest scores or measures with those of the posttest. (Note that this is a slightly different use of the term *pretest* from that in Chapters 1 and 7. In those contexts, the purpose of the pretest was to assess the adequacy of a data-collection instrument before the actual data collection. In this context, the pretest involves the actual data collection, but before the introduction of the experimental stimulus.)

Suppose, for example, that we were interested in the ability of children with developmental disabilities to remain attentive and perform well in classroom settings. We might hypothesize that behavior modification techniques, in the form of reinforcement with praise, would improve the children's performance. To test this hypothesis, we first measure the children's performance so that we have a baseline against which to assess change. Then, we expose the children to rewards for performance—the independent variable. For a specified period, we praise the children each time they show certain specified improvements in performance. Finally, we again measure their performance—the dependent variable—to see if it has changed since the first measurement.

This illustration shows one of the major ways that experiments offer researchers control over what happens: The researcher manipulates the experimental stimulus. In this illustration, the researcher uses praise as reinforcement. The researcher specifies how and under what conditions the reinforcement is delivered, including how much praise is delivered for a given response. The researcher might use one standard level of reinforcement or multiple levels of reinforcement to assess the impact of such variation. The key point here is that the researcher controls the "when" and the "how much" of the experimental stimulus.

The purpose of an experiment, again, is to determine what effects the independent variables produce on the dependent variables. Variation in the dependent variable produced by the independent variable is known as **experimental variability** and is the focus of interest in experiments. Variation in the dependent variable, however, can occur for many reasons other than the impact of the independent variable. For example, measurement error may affect the dependent variable (see Chapter 5), or the people in the experiment may have peculiar characteristics that influence the dependent variable separately from any effect of the experimental stimulus.

It also is possible that chance factors can affect the dependent variable. Variation in the dependent variable from any source other than the experimental stimulus is called **extraneous variability,** and it makes inferences about change in the dependent variable difficult. Every experiment contains some extraneous variability, because chance factors other than the experimental stimulus always exist and influence the dependent variable. Researchers need some way of discovering how much variation is experimental and how much is extraneous; experiments can be designed to provide this information through the use of *control variables* and *control groups.*

Control variables are variables whose value is held constant in all conditions of the experiment. By not allowing these variables to change from one condition to another, any effects they may produce on the dependent variable should be eliminated. In the study of children with developmental disabilities, for example, we might have some reason to believe that, in addition to the presumed impact of the experimental stimulus, the environment in which learning occurs—factors such as the lighting and heating—could affect how well the children perform. To control this, we would conduct all the observations in the same setting with no changes in lighting or heating. With such controls, we have greater confidence that changes in the dependent variable are caused by changes in the independent variable and not by the variables that are controlled.

A **control group** is a group of research subjects who are provided the same experiences as those in the experimental condition with a single exception: The control group receives no exposure to the experimental stimulus. **Control condition** refers to the state of being in a group that receives no experimental stimuli. When we include the control group in the elementary experimental design just described, we end up with the following design:

Experimental group: O X O

Control group: O O

The control group is important in experiments, because it provides the baseline from which to measure the effects of the independent variable. For example, in the study of children with developmental disabilities, the experimental condition involves receiving reinforcement in terms of praise. It might be possible, however, that the children's performance would increase even in the absence of praise, possibly because of the attention they received just by being a part of an experiment. To test for this, it would be desirable to have a control group that receives the same attention as the children in the experimental group but that is not rewarded with praise. Because both experimental and control groups experience the same conditions with the exception of the independent variable, we can more safely conclude that any differences in the posttest value of the dependent variable between the experimental and control groups results from the effect of the independent variable. So, another yardstick in addition to the pretest/posttest comparison for assessing whether an independent variable has an effect is the posttest/posttest comparison between experimental and control groups.

It is important that the ideas of a control variable and a control group be kept distinct, because they serve quite different functions. Researchers use a control variable in an attempt to minimize the impact of a single, known source of extraneous variability on the dependent variable. They use a control group, on the other hand, to assess the impact of extraneous variability from any source—including variables that are not known to the researcher—on the dependent variable.

Matching and Randomization

When making comparisons between the experimental and control groups to determine the effect of the independent variable, it is of crucial importance that the two groups be composed of people who are as much alike as possible. If they are not, then any comparison could be meaningless as far as the effects of the independent variable are concerned. For example, imagine that a teacher decides to experiment with a new teaching technique. As luck would have it, she has two classes on the same subject, one meeting in the morning and one in the afternoon. She uses the new teaching technique in the afternoon (the experimental group) and her conventional teaching methods in the morning section (the control group). At the end of the term, she notes that the afternoon class did substantially better on tests than the morning class. Can she conclude that the new technique is more effective than her old methods? Not with any great certainty. The students in the two classes may have differed from one another in systematic ways, and it may have been these differences between students, rather than the variation in teaching technique, that caused the differences in performance. It may be, for example, that students involved in extracurricular activities took morning classes so that their afternoons were free for those activities. Furthermore, the students involved in extracurricular affairs may have had less time to study or were less academically inclined. Thus, given the kind of students who tended to take morning classes, we would expect the afternoon class to perform better even if there had been no variation in teaching technique.

Two methods avoid the problem that this teacher encountered and ensure that the experimental and control groups are equivalent: *matching* and *random assignment*. The first has a certain intuitive appeal, but on closer inspection, it proves to be the less desirable of the two. As the name implies, **matching** involves matching individuals in the experimental group with similar subjects for a control group. People are matched on the basis of variables that we presume might have an effect on the dependent variable separate from that of the independent variable. By matching, we make

the experimental and control groups equivalent on these variables so that they could not account for any differences between the two groups on the dependent variable. For example, the teacher described earlier might use an IQ test as a matching tool. A high-IQ student in the morning class would be matched with a high-IQ student in the afternoon class. Any students without equivalent matches on IQ in the other class would simply not be used in the data analysis. Other variables in addition to IQ, however, could affect the outcome. Race, sex, socioeconomic status, study habits, reading ability, and math proficiency—the list goes on and on. Though matching on IQ would not be too great a problem, the difficulty of matching would increase geometrically with the addition of more variables. For example, the teacher might need to find a match for an African American female of middle-class background with good study habits and a ninth-grade reading ability who also is in the 95th percentile of math proficiency.

This illustrates one of the problems with matching: So many variables might be needed for matching that it becomes impractical to consider more than a few at a time. A second problem is that the researcher needs to know in advance which factors might affect the dependent variable so that these can be included in the matching process. Often, however, such information is not available. On the positive side, matching is better than no attempt at all to control, and it sometimes may be the only type of control that is available. In our illustration, the teacher may have no control over which students get assigned to which class. Consequently, the best she can do is select subgroup members in one class who have counterparts in the other class in terms of a few key variables.

The second approach to ensuring equivalent groups is random assignment. As the name implies, **random assignment** uses chance to reduce the variation between experimental and control groups. This can be done in many ways. For example, each person in the experiment can be given a random number, and then the numbers arranged in order and every other person on the list is placed in the experimental condition. Or, the names of all the people in the experiment can be listed alphabetically and given a number, and then a computer randomly assigns each number to either the experimental group or the control group. The point is to make sure that each person has an equal chance of being placed into either the experimental group or the control group. Ultimately, this technique offers the greatest probability that the experimental and control groups will have no systematic differences between them, thus allowing differences on the outcome measures to be confidently attributed to the effect of the independent variable. Chance rather than *a priori* knowledge of other variables is the foundation of random assignment.

The problem with relying on chance is that, even though in the long run and over many applications randomization generates equivalent groups, this approach can still yield nonequivalent groups

on occasion, especially when the study sample is small. Table 10.1 illustrates the extreme difference between groups that can occur by chance when using randomization. In these hypothetical data, eight subjects have been identified by sex and height. The subjects are ranked according to their true position on the dependent variable before the experiment, with scores ranging from 2 to 18. The mean score for the entire group is 10. Thus, when divided into an experimental and a control group, the ideal situation (the row labeled "Ideal groups") is for each group to have the same mean score of 10—or at least very close to it—on the dependent variable. Probability theory tells us that, with random assignment, it is most likely that the experimental and control group means will be close to the overall mean. It is possible, however, to obtain groups with very different means, because, by

TABLE 10.1 Randomization and Blocking Illustration

Subject	Sex	Height	True Dependent Variable Score
A	Male	Short	2
B	Male	Tall	4
C	Male	Tall	6
D	Male	Short	8
E	Female	Tall	12
F	Female	Short	14
G	Female	Short	16
H	Female	Tall	18
Total N = 8		Mean = 10	

Possible Groupings

	Group 1	Group 1 mean	Group 2	Group 2 mean
Ideal groups	BCFG	10	ADEH	10
Worst random	ABCD	5	EFGH	15
Worst block on sex	ABEF	8	CDGH	12
Worst block on height	ABCD	5	EFGH	15

chance, any combination of subjects in the two groups is possible. Table 10.1 shows one possible arrangement of subjects into one group with a mean score of 5 and another group with a mean score of 15 (labeled "Worst random").

To reduce the likelihood of such occurrences, researchers often use a combination of matching and randomization known as *blocking*. In **blocking,** the subjects are first matched on one or more key variables to form blocks of similar subjects. Members of each block then are randomly assigned to the experimental and control conditions. Blocking works by reducing the extreme range of groups that are possible. For blocking to be effective, however, the variable on which cases are blocked must be associated with the dependent variable. Notice in Table 10.1 that males have low scores and females have high scores. The variable of sex and the dependent variable are clearly associated, but no such association exists between height and the dependent variable. When blocking on the basis of sex, two males are randomly assigned to each group and two females to each group. The most extreme difference between

groups that is possible in our hypothetical illustration with sex as the blocking variable would be group means of 8 and 12 (labeled "Worst block on sex"). This is a considerable improvement over the extremes of 5 and 15 that are possible with randomization alone. Notice, however, that when the groups are blocked on the basis of height (labeled "Worst block on height"), there is no improvement; the worst possible group difference is still 5 and 15, as it was under randomization. This demonstrates that blocking on an appropriate variable can help reduce differences between groups. Choosing a variable for blocking that is unrelated to the dependent variable does not make matters any worse than random assignment, but neither does it improve the chances of achieving equivalent groups. Whether or not blocking is worthwhile basically comes down to the anticipated improvement in group equivalence versus the cost and complexity of carrying out the blocking procedure. Research in Practice 10.1 describes a field experiment that combined randomization and matching with other procedures to ensure equivalence between experimental and control groups.

RESEARCH IN PRACTICE 10.1 Program Evaluation: Matching and Randomization in a Community-Level Alcohol Prevention Experiment

The evidence–based practice (EBP) approach promotes the idea that knowledge derived from controlled experiments provides the best evidence about which human service practices and policies work. The Communities Mobilizing for Change on Alcohol (CMCA) program is a community-organizing program designed to reduce teens' access to alcohol.

To evaluate the program, the research team used school district criteria to ensure a sample of comparable participants and to minimize influence from other factors besides the independent variable such as impact of other community programs and interaction between intervention and control communities. Because communities and not individual students were the target of this study, the researchers applied randomization at the community level. Twenty-four eligible school districts were identified and 15 agreed to participate. After all baseline data were collected, the 15 participating districts were matched on population size and presence of a college. From within matched sets, seven communities were randomly selected to receive the community organizing intervention and the remaining eight were assigned to the control group.

The intervention itself consisted of a community organizer working with local public officials, enforcement agencies, alcohol merchants and merchant associations, the media, schools, and other community institutions to change community policies to reduce youth access to

(continued)

alcohol. The target of the intervention was the entire community rather than individual young people. The organizing effort resulted in institutional policy changes such as alcohol merchant policies and practices, increases in media coverage of alcohol issues, and changes in practices of law enforcement agencies.

Several outcome measures were employed, including surveys of high school students, surveys of youth aged between 18 and 20, and surveys of alcohol retailers. It is well known that self-reported survey data of sensitive information is subject to bias and underreporting, so even though the data were supportive of the program, what made this field experiment stronger was the fact that the researchers also used direct observation and archival data to measure program impact. Alcohol purchase attempts were conducted at bars, restaurants, liquor stores, and convenience stores. Archival data consisted of drunk driving (DUI) arrest data and traffic crash data for a six-year baseline prior to the program and three years of intervention. The researchers hypothesized that the CMCA intervention would reduce DUI and disorderly conduct arrests and traffic crashes, particularly among 18- to 20-year-olds, since alcohol consumption was reduced among this age group.

The researchers reported that the CMCA organizing process was successful in changing institutional policies to reduce youth access to alcohol and decreased alcohol consumption among 18- to 20-year-olds (Wagenaar et al., 2000). The archival data on arrests and vehicle crashes suggest that this intervention also reduced alcohol-related problems among youth. Reductions were observed in all arrest and traffic crash indicators for both age groups.

Internal Validity

The central issue in experimentation is that it allows us to make statements about causal relationships between phenomena. This is the reason for control variables, control groups, randomization, and matching. In what has come to be considered the definitive work on experiments and experimental designs, Donald Campbell and Julian Stanley (1963) discussed the importance of *internal validity* in experiments. Recall from Chapter 5 that the *validity* of a measure refers to whether it accurately measures what it is intended to measure. Likewise, **internal validity** in experiments refers to whether the independent variable actually produces the effect that it appears to have had on the dependent variable; it is concerned with ruling out extraneous sources of variability to the point where we have confidence that changes in the dependent variable are caused by the independent variable.

In the preceding discussion, we presented the basic logic involved in designing experiments that have internal validity. The problem is much more complex, however, because internal validity can be threatened in many ways. We now turn to the seven most serious threats to internal validity, as identified by Campbell and Stanley.

History. The threat of *history* concerns events other than the experimental stimulus that occur during the course of an experiment and that could affect the dependent variable. History is more of a problem for field experiments than it is for experiments conducted within the confines of a laboratory, because field experiments typically last longer, allowing more time for events that affect the outcome to occur. For example, the homicide rate in the United States declined dramatically between 1980 and 2000—by almost one half—and many commentators attributed this decline to policy changes in the criminal justice system, such as more police officers, better policing, and longer prison sentences for convicted felons. Yet, during the same time period, dramatic improvements occurred in emergency care, including the spread of 911 emergency systems, the development of rapid response emergency teams, and more effective trauma units in hospitals. These developments may well have produced some of the declines in homicide: By 2000, people had a better chance of surviving an assault with a knife or a gun that before 1980, with less effective emergency interventions, would have resulted in death (Harris, Thomas, Fisher, & Hirsch, 2002). The effects of these historical events make it difficult to ascertain what effect the changes in criminal justice policies actually had on homicide rates.

Maturation. *Maturation* refers to changes occurring within experimental subjects as a result of the passage of time. Such things as growing older, hungrier, wiser, more experienced, or more tired are examples of maturational changes. If any of these changes are related to the dependent variable, then their effects can confuse the effect of the independent variable. For example, many believe that people pass through a natural series of stages when grieving over the loss of a loved one: shock, then intense grief and a sense of loss, followed by recovery (Kamerman, 1988). In other words, time brings its own changes, or maturation, to the grieving individual. If we want to assess the effectiveness of some therapeutic intervention in helping people cope with the death of a loved one, then any improvements that people show over time might result from maturation or the natural progression of the grief process rather than from the therapeutic intervention.

Testing. The threat of *testing* may occur whenever subjects are exposed to a measurement device more than once. Because many experiments use paper-and-pencil measures as well as "before" and "after" measurements, testing effects often are of concern. For example, people who are taking achievement or intelligence tests for a second time tend to score better than they did the first time (Frankfort-Nachmias & Nachmias, 2008), even when researchers use alternative forms of the same test. Similar changes occur on personality tests. These built-in shifts in paper-and-pencil measures can lead to changes in the dependent variable that result from testing rather than from the impact of the independent variable.

Instrumentation. The threat of *instrumentation* refers to the fact that the way in which variables are measured may change in systematic ways during the course of an experiment, resulting in observations being measured differently at the end of an experiment than they were at the beginning. In observing and recording verbal behavior, for example, observers may become more adept at recording and do so more quickly. This means that they could record more behaviors at the end of an experiment than at the beginning. If the observers do learn and become more skillful, then changes in the dependent variable may be the result of instrumentation effects rather than the impact of the independent variable.

Statistical Regression. The threat of *statistical regression* arises any time subjects are placed in experimental or control groups on the basis of extremely high or low scores on a measure in comparison to the average score for the whole group. When remeasured, those extreme groups will tend, on the whole, to have scores that are less extreme. In other words, they will *regress toward the overall group average*. For example, suppose the bottom 10% of scorers on a standard achievement test are singled out to participate in a special remedial course. On completing the course, they are measured with the achievement test again and show improvement. Could we conclude that the remedial course was responsible for the higher scores? We would certainly be hesitant to make this inference because of the effects of testing and maturation. In addition, however, there would be a regression effect. Some of those people scoring in the bottom 10% undoubtedly did so for reasons other than their actual level of ability—for example, because they did not get enough sleep the night before, were ill, or were upset over a quarrel. (How many times do students score lower on an exam than they normally do because of factors like these?) When the students take the exam a second time, the conditions mentioned will have changed, and they likely will perform better—even without the special remedial course. Recognize that many—and possibly most—people in the lowest 10% are performing at their normal level. In any such group based on a single test administration, however, a certain number of people probably will score lower than their normal level. If the whole group repeats the exam—even without any intervening experimental manipulation—they can be expected to perform better; thus, the average score of the group will improve.

Selection. *Selection* is a threat to internal validity when the kinds of people who are selected for one experimental condition differ from those who are selected for other conditions. The threat of selection derives from improperly constituted experimental and control groups. Recall the importance of random assignment or matching to equalize these groups. As noted, improper composition of these groups can make findings based on comparisons between them meaningless.

Experimental Attrition. The threat of *experimental attrition* occurs when there is a differential dropout of subjects from the experimental and control groups. Especially in experiments that extend over long periods of time, some people fail to complete the experiment. People die, move away, become incapacitated, or simply quit. If there is a notable difference in attrition rates between the experimental and control groups, then those groups may not be equivalent at the end of the experiment, even though they were at the beginning. An example of the attrition threat can be found in a study concerning the effects of sex composition on the patterns of interaction in consciousness-raising counseling groups (Carlock & Martin, 1977). One group was composed of all female participants, and the other was composed of both males and females. The females were randomly assigned to one group or the other. Originally, the all-female group contained nine members, and the male-and-female group had 16 members. Before the experiment was completed, however, two female members of the male-and-female group dropped out. When the interactional patterns in the groups were compared, substantial differences were found. The authors concluded that these differences resulted from the differing sex compositions of the groups, but, as they noted, confidence in their findings was weakened because of the dropouts from the male-and-female group. With such small groups to begin with, the loss of two members from one group can substantially affect the results.

With this lengthy list of threats to the internal validity of experiments, can we ever be confident that changes in the dependent variable are the result of the independent variable and not some extraneous variability? In fact, such confidence can be established—and threats to internal validity controlled—through the use of good experimental designs.

EXPERIMENTAL DESIGNS

There are three categories of experimental designs. **Preexperimental designs** lack both the random assignment to conditions and the control groups that are such a central part of good experimental designs. Although they sometimes are still useful, they illustrate some inherent weaknesses in terms of establishing internal validity. The better designs are called *true experimental designs* and *quasi-experimental designs*. **True experimental designs** are more complex and use randomization and other techniques to control the threats to internal validity. **Quasi-experimental designs** are special designs that are used to approximate experimental control in nonexperimental settings.

Preexperimental Designs

On the surface, Design P1 in Table 10.2 might appear to be adequate. The subjects are pretested, exposed to the experimental condition, and then tested again. Any differences between the pretest and posttest measures should be the result of the experimental stimulus. As it stands, however, this design has serious weaknesses. With the exceptions of selection and experimental attrition, which are irrelevant because of the lack of a control group, Design P1 is subject to the other five threats to internal validity. If a historical event related to the dependent variable intervenes between the pretest and the posttest, then its effects could be confused with those of the independent variable. Maturational changes in the subjects also could produce differences between pretest and posttest scores. If paper-and-pencil measures are used, then a shift in scores from the pretest to the posttest could occur because of testing effects. Regardless of the measurement process, instrumentation changes could produce variation in the pretest and posttest

TABLE 10.2 **Preexperimental Designs**

P1 The One Group Pretest–Posttest Design:			
	Pretest	**Treatment**	**Posttest**
Experimental Group	O	X	O
P2 The Static Group Comparison:			
	Pretest	**Treatment**	**Posttest**
Experimental Group		X	O
Control Group			O

scores. Finally, if the subjects were selected because they possessed some extreme characteristic, then differences between pretest and posttest scores could be the result of regression toward the mean. In all these cases, variation on the dependent variable produced by one or more of the validity threats could easily be mistaken for variation produced by the independent variable.

The other preexperimental design—the Static Group Comparison, or Design P2 in Table 10.2—involves comparing one group that experiences the experimental stimulus with another group that does not. In considering this design, it is important to recognize that the comparison group that appears to be a control group is not a control group in the true sense. The major threat to validity in this design is selection. Note that no random assignment, which would make the comparison groups comparable, is indicated. In Design P2, the group compared with the experimental group is normally an intact group picked up only for the purpose of comparison. There is no assurance of comparability between it and the experimental group. For example, we might wish to test the impact of a local assistance program by comparing a city that has the program to a city that does not. Any conclusions we might reach about the effects of the program could be inaccurate because of other differences between the two cities.

Despite their weaknesses, preexperimental designs are used when resources do not permit the development of true experimental designs. Human service practitioners especially are likely to be faced

with this dilemma. Conclusions based on such designs should be regarded with utmost caution, however, and the results viewed as being suggestive at best. These designs should be avoided if at all possible. If they are used, however, then efforts should be made to further test the validity of the findings using one of the true experimental designs.

True Experimental Designs

The Classic Experimental Design. Diagrams of true experimental designs are presented in Table 10.3. Probably the most common true experimental design is Design T1 in Table 10.3—the Pretest–Posttest Control Group Design with Randomization. This design is used so often that it frequently is referred to by its popular name: the *classic* experimental design. In all true experimental designs, the proper test of hypotheses is the comparison of posttests between experimental and control groups. This design uses a true control group, including random assignment to equalize the comparison groups, which eliminates all the threats to internal validity except for certain patterns of attrition. Because of this, we can have considerable confidence that any differences between experimental and control groups on the dependent variable result from the effect of the independent variable.

Let us take a closer look at how the classic design avoids the various threats to validity. History is removed as a rival explanation for differences between the groups on the posttest, because both

TABLE 10.3 True Experimental Designs

T1 The Pretest–Posttest Control Group Design With Randomization—The "Classic" Experimental Design:

		Pretest	Treatment	Posttest
Experimental Group	R	O	X	O
Control Group	R	O		O

T2 The Solomon Four-Group Design:

		Pretest	Treatment	Posttest
Experimental Group 1	R	O	X	O
Control Group 1	R	O		O
Experimental Group 2	R		X	O
Control Group 2	R			O

T3 The Posttest-Only Control Group Design:

		Pretest	Treatment	Posttest
Experimental Group	R		X	O
Control Group	R			O

T4 The Multiple Experimental Group With One Control Group Design:

		Pretest	Treatment	Posttest
Experimental Group 1	R	O	X_1	O
Experimental Group 2	R	O	X_2	O
Experimental Group 3	R	O	X_3	O
Control Group	R	O		O
Experimental Group 1	R	O	X_1Y_1	O
Experimental Group 2	R	O	X_1Y_2	O
Experimental Group 3	R	O	X_2Y_1	O
Control Group	R	O	X_2Y_2	O

groups experience the same events except for the experimental stimulus. Because the same amount of time passes for both groups, maturational effects should be equal and, therefore, not account for posttest differences. Similarly, because both groups are pretested, any testing influences on the posttest should be the same for the two groups. Instrumentation effects also are readily controlled with this design, because any unreliability in the measurement process that could cause a shift in scores from pretest to posttest should be the same for both comparison groups.

In situations where regression can occur, the classic experimental design controls it through random assignment of subjects with extreme characteristics. Thus, whatever regression does take place should be the same for both groups. Regression toward the mean, therefore, should not account for any differences between the groups on the posttest. Randomization also controls the validity threat of selection by assuring that the comparison groups are equivalent. Furthermore, the pretest results can be used as a check on precisely how similar the two groups actually are. Because the two groups are similar, attrition rates should be about the same for each group. In a lengthy experiment with a large sample, we would fully expect about the same number of subjects in each group to move away, die, or become incapacitated during the experiment. These can be assumed to be more or less random events. Attrition because of these reasons, therefore, is unlikely to create a validity problem. Attrition because of voluntary quitting, however, is another matter. The experimental stimulus may affect the rate of attrition. That is, subjects might find something about the experimental condition either more or less likeable than the subjects find the control condition, so the dropout rate could differ. If this occurs, it raises the possibility that the groups are no longer equivalent at the time of the posttest. Unfortunately, there really is no effective way of dealing with this problem. About all that researchers can do is to watch for its occurrence and, if attrition bias appears to be a problem, interpret the results cautiously.

The Solomon Design. A second true experimental design—the Solomon Four-Group Design (Design T2 in Table 10.3)—is more sophisticated than Design T1 in that it uses four different comparison groups. In comparing Designs T1 and T2, we see that the first two groups of the Solomon Design constitute Design T1, indicating that it is capable of controlling the same threats to internal validity as that design does. The major advantage of the Solomon Design is that it can tell us whether changes in the dependent variable result from some *interaction effect* between the pretest

and the exposure to the experimental stimulus. Experimental Group 2 is exposed to the experimental stimulus without being pretested. If the posttest of Experimental Group 1 differs from the posttest of Experimental Group 2, this may be the result of an interaction effect of receiving both the pretest and the experimental stimulus—something that we would not find out with the classic design.

Suppose, for example, that we wanted to assess the effect on prejudice toward racial minorities (the dependent variable) of receiving positive information about a racial group (the independent variable). We pretest groups by asking them questions regarding their prejudice toward particular groups. Then, we expose them to the experimental stimulus: newspaper articles reporting on civic deeds and rescue efforts by members of those racial groups. Lower levels of prejudice in Experimental Group 1 than in Control Group 1 might be caused by the independent variable. It also, however, could be that filling out a pretest questionnaire on prejudice sensitized people in the first group to these issues and, thus, that they reacted more strongly to the experimental stimulus than they would have without such pretesting. If this is the case, then Experimental Group 2 should show less change than Experimental Group 1. If the independent variable has an effect that is separate from its interaction with the pretest, then Experimental Group 2 should show more change than Control Group 1. If Control Group 1 and Experimental Group 2 show no change but Experimental Group 1 does show a change, then the change is produced only by the interaction of pretesting and treatment.

Thus, the Solomon Design enables us to make a more complex assessment of the causes of changes in the dependent variable. In addition, the combined effects of maturation and history can be controlled (as with Design T1) and measured. By comparing the posttest of Control Group 2 with the pretests of Experimental Group 1 and Control Group 1, these effects can be assessed. Usually, however, our concern with history and maturation effects is only in controlling their effects, not in measuring them.

Despite the superiority of the Solomon Design, it often is passed over for Design T1, because the

Solomon Design requires twice as many groups, thus substantially increasing the time and cost of conducting the experiment. Not surprisingly, many researchers decide that the advantages are not worth the added cost and complexity. If a researcher desires the strongest design, however, then Design T2 is the one to choose.

The Posttest-Only Control Group Design. Sometimes, pretesting is either impractical or undesirable. For example, pretesting might sensitize subjects to the independent variable. In these cases, we can still use a true experimental design—the Posttest-Only Control Group Design (see Design T3 in Table 10.3). Despite the absence of pretests, Design T3 is an adequate true experimental design that controls threats to validity as well as the designs with pretests do. The Posttest-Only Control Group uses random assignment to conditions, which distinguishes it from the preexperimental Design P2. The only potential question of validity raised in conjunction with Design T3 is selection: The absence of pretests means that random assignment is the only assurance that the comparison groups are equivalent. Campbell and Stanley (1963), however, argued convincingly that pretests are not essential and that randomization reliably produces equivalent groups. Furthermore, they argued that the lack of popularity of Design T3 stems more from the tradition of pretesting in experimentation than from any major contribution to validity from using pretesting.

The Multiple Experimental Group With One Control Group Design. The preceding experimental designs are adequate for testing hypotheses when the independent variable is either present (experimental group) or absent (control group). Yet, many hypotheses involve independent variables that vary in terms of the *degree* or *amount* of something that is present. For example, *how much* treatment of a client (intensity level) is needed to produce some desired behavioral change? In a study of parents who abuse their children, the independent variable was exposure to positive parenting sessions (Burch & Mohr, 1980). Rather than just assess the effect of the presence or absence of such sessions, however, the researchers exposed

some groups to *more* sessions than others. In cases such as this, the Multiple Experimental Group With One Control Group Design (see Design T4 in Table 10.3) can be used. This is an extension of Design T1 with multiple experimental groups and one control group. The symbols X_1, X_2, and X_3 refer to differing amounts or intensities of a single independent variable or treatment. Comparing the posttests of the experimental groups enables us to determine the impact of the differing amounts of the independent variable.

The Factorial Design. The experimental designs considered thus far can assess the impact of only a single independent variable at a time on the dependent variable. We know, however, that variables can *interact* with one another, and the combined effects of two or more variables may be quite different from the effects of each variable operating separately. For example, one experimental study investigated the impact of both social class and race on stereotypes of women (Landrine, 1985). People in that study were asked to describe society's stereotype of four different women: a middle-class Black, a middle-class White, a lower-class Black, and a lower-class White. Landrine found that social class and gender did affect stereotyping: Lower-class people received more negative stereotyping than middle-class people did, and Blacks were viewed less favorably than Whites were viewed. Landrine did not, however, find an interaction effect. In other words, various class/race combinations did not produce more changes in stereotyping than the effects of class and race did separately.

The experimental design used in the Landrine study is called a Factorial Design (see Design T5 in Table 10.3). Design T5 illustrates the simplest Factorial Design, in which two independent variables (X and Y, or race and social class) each have only two values (X_1 or X_2 and Y_1 or Y_2). In Factorial Designs, each possible combination of the two independent variables constitutes one of the experimental conditions. Technically, there may not be a control group, as in the previous example, when there can be no "absence" of the factors involved. After all, one cannot be without race or without social class. If the variables involve the presence or absence of something, however, then a condition that looks like a control group appears in the Factorial Design. Factorial Designs involve enough groups so that all possible combinations of the independent variables can be investigated. Assessment of interaction is accomplished by the comparison of Experimental Group 1, which is exposed to both independent variables, with Experimental Groups 2 and 3. We can see whether the combined effects of the independent variables differ from their separate effects.

Factorial Designs can be expanded beyond this simple example. More than two variables can be investigated, and each variable can have more than two values. As the complexity increases, however, the number of groups required increases rapidly and can become unmanageable. For example, with three independent variables, each with three values, we would need a $3 \times 3 \times 3$ Factorial Design, or 27 different groups. Sometimes, however, field experiments designed to assess the impact of social programs involve such complex designs.

We have covered the major types of true experimental designs in this section. Often, however, circumstances require researchers to use a variant of one of these designs. Research in Practice 10.2

RESEARCH IN PRACTICE 10.2 Program Evaluation: Field Experiments on Police Handling of Domestic Violence Cases

The police telephone operator answered the call from a weeping woman: "Police."
> VOICE: I want a . . . a battered woman.
OPERATOR: What, ma'am?
> VOICE: I am a battered woman.
OPERATOR: Do you want the police to come, ma'am?
> VOICE: (sob) Yes.
OPERATOR: Is he in the house now?
> VOICE: Yes—he's in the house now and I'm scared.

—Sherman (1992, p. 80)

This interchange between a victim of domestic violence and the police was recorded in the course of a landmark experiment on law enforcement intervention in domestic violence conducted in Minneapolis. At first glance, the dialogue appears to stand as eloquent testimony to ethical and logistical barriers that prohibit using true experiments in the real world of human service. No matter how valuable the potential research findings, it is unthinkable to tell a victim, "Sorry, you're in the control group. We can't help you." And how could the researcher get the police officer on the scene to administer treatment A and not treatment B or C on a truly random basis?

On the other hand, the urgency of human need demands that researchers find the best ways of responding to such critical social problems. The most powerful rationale for using experiments in this way is that they deliver a more convincing case for causal relationships between variables than other research methods do because of the control that researchers have over the variables—independent, dependent, and extraneous—in experimental research. If an intervention does prevent future assaults, then a randomized experiment is the best way to find that out. Lawrence Sherman (1992) presents a fascinating account of the Minneapolis study and five replications in Omaha; Charlotte, North .Carolina; Milwaukee; Metro-Dade, Miami; and Colorado Springs. His presentation documents how researchers can overcome the barriers to experimentation in field settings and the lessons learned from the experience. Here, we will

(continued)

highlight three of these studies on responding to domestic assault and focus on how they dealt with three potential barriers to experimentation—namely, the ethics of withholding treatment, randomization, and ensuring that treatments actually are delivered as assigned.

The first of these studies was an investigation by criminologist Lawrence Sherman and sociologist Richard Sherman and Berk (1984). These researchers randomly assigned 314 misdemeanor domestic assault cases to three types of police intervention: advising the couple (including informal mediation), separating the couple by ordering the offender to leave the house for eight hours, and arresting the offender so that he or she spent the night in jail. The independent variable was the mode of police intervention, and the dependent variable was whether or not the perpetrator was involved in another domestic violence incident during the six months following police intervention.

For ethical and practical reasons, the study was restricted to misdemeanor assaults—that is, milder cases lacking severe injury or a life-threatening situation. With such misdemeanor offenses, police *could* make an arrest or could advise or separate, but neither of these responses was *required*. Under normal conditions, police use their own judgment as to which intervention is called for. When participating in the Sherman–Berk study, however, police officers responding to a call first determined if the case fit the study criteria and, if so, then applied one of the three intervention techniques. The ethical concerns raised by withholding treatment and random assignment to treatments thus were addressed by responding to all calls, by providing one of three standard treatments to each case, and by restricting the study to only misdemeanor cases.

Random assignment to experimental conditions was achieved by requiring each police officer to use a pad consisting of color-coded forms corresponding to the three different treatments: arrest, separation, and mediation. The forms were randomly ordered in the pad, and the officers were instructed to select their intervention according to whatever color form came up when they intervened in a case that met the study guidelines. In this study, the officers doing the intervening were responsible for making sure that the randomization was done properly. For the study to work as planned, the officers had to follow the instructions faithfully. In addition, the forms were numbered sequentially so that the researchers could monitor how well the officers followed the assigned interventions. The researchers tried riding patrol with some of the officers to check, but this proved to be impractical because of the sporadic occurrence of assault complaints. Another approach was to have officers complete a brief form after each call that described what happened. Despite these efforts, the study was criticized on the grounds that the treatments might not have been delivered as assigned.

Sherman and Berk concluded that arrest was the most effective of the three options for dealing with a spousal abuser: Those arrested were significantly less likely to be involved in a repeat episode of domestic violence during the following six months. Encouraged by these findings, many communities developed more aggressive arrest policies toward domestic assault. Researchers and policy makers, however, cautioned against placing too much faith in the results of a single study. One criticism was that the study had a small sample size. In addition, a few officers had submitted a disproportionately large number of cases. This may have been because these officers patrolled a more violent section of town and, because of experience, were particularly effective at making arrest an effective deterrent. The officers who did not arrest many offenders may have been more effective at mediation or separation. If so, then the study was really about variations in the skills of police officers rather than about variations in the effectiveness of different treatments. This points toward the importance of assessing *internal validity*: Is it variation in the independent variable that produces changes in the dependent variable, or is it something else that produces these changes?

(continued)

Yet another criticism of Sherman and Berk's study was inadequate control over which treatments actually were delivered and the possibility that surveillance effects from the multiple follow-up interviews distorted the impact of the treatment. Finally, if the sample was biased for any of the foregoing reasons, then the results would not be generalizable to other settings (Hirschel, Hutchison, & Dean, 1992).

A follow-up study in Omaha differed from the Minneapolis project in several key respects (Dunford, Huizinga, & Elliott, 1989). First, in addition to evaluating the three treatments—arrest, mediation, or separation—the research included a unique facet. If the assailant was not present when the officers arrived but the case otherwise met the study criteria, the suspect was randomly assigned to either receive or not receive a warrant for his or her arrest.

To improve generalizability, the researchers wanted to be sure that the project covered all areas of the community, including sections populated by minorities. A competing goal was to maintain control by using those officers who were most likely to encounter assault cases rather than by training and monitoring the entire police force. A review of the 911 dispatch log revealed that about 60% of domestic assault calls occurred during the "C" shift (4 p.m. to midnight). Focusing the project only on this shift kept the project more manageable. As in Minneapolis, the Omaha study was restricted to cases involving probable cause of misdemeanor-level assault.

One criticism of the Minneapolis study had been the reliance on police officers to carry out randomization. The Omaha project addressed this criticism by having random assignment to treatment performed by the Information Unit of the Omaha police force. Upon establishing control at the scene, responding officers determined if the case met the project eligibility requirements, such as being a misdemeanor offense. After information such as time, date, and victim and suspect characteristics had been reported to the Information Unit, the operator assigned an intervention treatment based on a computer-generated randomization procedure. In this way, randomization was centralized, and data about the case and the assigned treatment were immediately stored in the computer file.

For results to be valid, it was crucial that officers actually deliver the assigned treatment. This problem was controlled by three forms of monitoring. First, officers reported dispositions on a Domestic Violence Report form and forwarded it to the project. Second, victims were asked to describe what treatment was delivered. Finally, official records of the police, prosecuting attorneys, and courts were compared with the other forms of monitoring data. Analysis of these various case-monitoring systems indicated that 92% of the treatments were delivered as assigned.

Another replication of the original Minneapolis study, this time in Charlotte, North Carolina, also had unique features (Hirschel et al., 1992): It included only cases involving female victims and male offenders in which both parties were at least 18 years old. The study covered the entire patrol division in around-the-clock, citywide sampling. The interventions also differed somewhat from the other studies. In addition to arrest, the police could issue citations requiring a court appearance by both victim and offender, or they could advise and separate (a combination of the mediation and separation treatments in the other studies). An additional explicit criterion addressed the concern of victim and officer safety: Cases were excluded if the victim insisted on arrest, if the assailant threatened or assaulted the police, or if the officers believed that the offender posed an imminent danger to the victim. After restoring order at the scene, all victims were provided information regarding community resources, including the Victim Assistance Program and the domestic violence shelter.

Choosing the best way to operationalize key variables is an important lesson from these studies. A related issue was whether to rely on official arrest records or interview reports of

(continued)

victims (Maxwell, Garner, & Fagan, 2001). If repeat incidents of domestic assault are measured by rearrest of the perpetrator, then repeat incidents appear to be rather small in number. If the occurrence of repeat events is measured by victims' reports to interviewers, however, then repeat incidents appear to be common, which is another example of the issue of validity discussed in Chapter 5—namely, how accurately does a measurement tool measure some theoretical concept?

The original Minneapolis study, based on 314 cases, concluded that arrest significantly reduced future reports of assaults, and the policy implication appeared to be clear-cut: Implement an aggressive, pro-arrest policy to reduce spousal assault. Based on a total sample of thousands in the six cities included in the various replications, the general conclusions now are less clear-cut and more cautious and complicated (Maxwell et al., 2001; Sherman, 1992):

- Arrest does, in general, reduce future episodes of domestic violence, but the effect is modest.
- Arrest increases domestic violence among people who have less to lose, especially offenders who are unemployed.
- A small but chronic portion of all violent couples produces the majority of reported domestic violence incidents.

The research underscores the point that social problems and societal responses are complex and unlikely to yield singular solutions.

illustrates such a variation that, nonetheless, retains randomization. The designs presented here also form the basis for many other more complex designs that are capable of handling such problems in experimenting as multiple independent variables and order effects.

Quasi-Experimental Designs

Many times, it is impossible, whether for practical or other reasons, to meet the conditions that are necessary to develop true experimental designs. The most common problems include an inability to assign people randomly to conditions and the difficulty of creating a true control group with which to compare the experimental groups. Although these can be problematic for experiments in any context, they are especially acute in field experiments and practice settings. Rather than rule out experimentation in such settings, however, the researcher may be able to use a *quasi-experimental design* that approaches the level of control of true experimental designs in situations where the requirements of the latter cannot be met. Quasi-experimental designs afford considerable control, but they fall short of the true experimental designs and, therefore, should be used only when conditions do not

allow the use of a true experimental design (Achen, 1986). As we will see in Chapter 11, quasi-experimental designs also form the basis of single-system designs used in clinical practice.

The Time-Series Design. One of the simplest—and most useful—of the quasi-experimental designs is the Time-Series Design (see Design Q1 in Table 10.4), which involves a series of repeated measures, followed by the introduction of the experimental condition, and then another series of measures. The number of pretest and posttest measurements can vary, but it is unwise to use fewer than three of each. Time-Series Designs can be analyzed by graphing the repeated measures and inspecting the pattern that is produced. We can conclude whether the independent variable produced an effect by observing when, over the whole series of observations, changes in the dependent variable occur.

Figure 10.1 illustrates some possible outcomes of a time-series experiment. Of major interest is what occurs between O_4 and O_5, because these are the measures that immediately precede and follow the experimental stimulus. The other measures are important, however, because they provide a basis for assessing the change that occurs

TABLE 10.4 **Quasi-Experimental Designs**

Q1 The Time-Series Designs

	Pretests	Treatment	Posttests
Experimental Group	$O_1O_2O_3O_4$	X	$O_5O_6O_7O_8$

Q2 The Different Group Time-Series Design

	Pretests	Treatment	Posttests
R	O_1		
R	O_2		
R	O_3		
R	O_4		
R		X	
R			O_5
R			O_6
R			O_7
R			O_8

Q3 The Multiple Time-Series Design

	Pretests	Treatment	Posttests
Experimental Group	$O_1O_2O_3O_4$	X	$O_5O_6O_7O_8$
Control Group	$O_1O_2O_3O_4$		$O_5O_6O_7O_8$

between O_4 and O_5. As Figure 10.1 shows, some outcomes suggest that the stimulus has had an effect, whereas others do not. In cases A, B, and C, stimulus X appears to produce an effect. In each case, the differences between measures O_4 and O_5 are greater than the differences between any other adjacent measures. Cases E and F illustrate outcomes where we can infer that changes result from something other than the stimulus, because the differences between measures O_4 and O_5 are not substantially different from those between some other adjacent measures. The results of a Time-Series Design are not always clear-cut, as illustrated by case D. The sharp change between measures O_5 and O_6 could be a delayed effect of

X, or it could be an effect of something else. More careful analysis would be required to reach a firm conclusion in that case.

In field studies involving a time-series analysis, the experimental stimulus often is not something that the researcher manipulates; rather, it is something that occurs independently of the research. Thus, any natural event presumed to cause changes in people's behavior can serve as an experimental stimulus. In a study of how the criminal justice system handles violence against women, for example, the experimental stimulus was the passage of the Violence Against Women Act of 1994 (Cho & Wilke, 2005). The VAWA was intended to provide better social service interventions for women

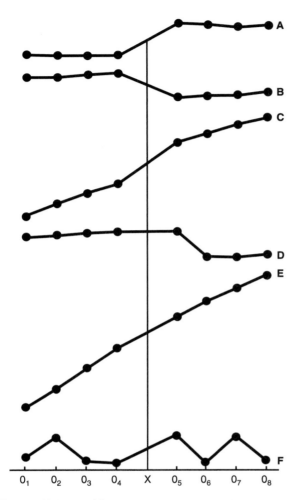

Figure 10.1 Possible outcomes in a Time-Series Quasi-Experimental Design.

who experience intimate partner violence and to improve the law enforcement response in such cases. The dependent variables included such measures of the impact of the VAWA as the incidence of domestic violence, rates of perpetrator arrest, and rates of reporting incidents to the police. The data were provided by the National Crime Victimization Survey of the Bureau of Justice Statistics (see p. 000). These measurements were done for each three-month period from 1992 to 2003. The researchers found a significant decrease in the rate of intimate partner violence and an increase in the arrest of perpetrators. The patterns shown in the

Time-Series Design gave them the confidence to conclude that the passage of the VAWA was at least partly responsible for these changes.

The Time-Series Design fares quite well when evaluated on its ability to control threats to internal validity. With the exception of history, the other threats are controlled by the presence of the series of premeasures. Maturation, testing, instrumentation, statistical regression, and experimental attrition produce gradual changes that operate between all measures. As such, they cannot account for any sharp change occurring between measures O_4 and O_5. Because this design does not use a control group, selection is not a factor. Thus, history is the only potential threat to internal validity. It is always possible that some extraneous event could intervene between measures O_4 and O_5 and produce a change that could be confused with an effect of X. In many cases, there may not be an event that could plausibly produce the noted effect, and we could be quite sure that it was caused by X. Nevertheless, the inability of the Time-Series Design to control the threat of history is considered to be a weakness.

The Different Group Time-Series Design. The Time-Series Design requires that we be able to measure the same group repeatedly over an extended period. Because this requires considerable cooperation from the subjects, there may be cases when the Time-Series Design cannot be used. A design that avoids this problem, yet maintains the other characteristics of the Time-Series Design, is the Different Group Time-Series Design (see Design Q2 in Table 10.4). Rather than make repeated measures on one group, this design substitutes several randomly selected groups, each of which is measured only once but at different times. Design Q2 produces the same type of data as the regular Time-Series Design and can be analyzed using the same graphing procedure. In terms of internal validity, Design Q2 controls the same threats as the Time-Series Design. Random sampling is relied on to equate the several comparison groups. Design Q2 also has the same weakness as the Time-Series Design: Historical events can intervene between measures O_4 and O_5, possibly confusing the results.

Because of the many random samples that this design requires, it is limited to situations in which the cost of those samples is low. For example, if it is possible to draw the samples and collect data by telephone, then the design is ideal. This is essentially the approach that commercial pollsters use to measure public opinion by conducting weekly or monthly telephone surveys of different random samples. Although the pollsters do not conduct experiments, their repeated measures allow the assessment of the impact of events on public opinion. The event in question becomes the X in the design, and the levels of opinion are compared before and after X occurred. For example, the terrorist attacks on New York and Washington in 2001 and the Iraq War in 2003 each caused the popularity of President George W. Bush to climb considerably. His popularity ratings dropped again a short time after each event, but because of the many before and after measurements, we have considerable confidence that it was the terrorist attacks and the war that temporarily increased the president's popularity.

The Multiple Time-Series Design. As noted, both of the preceding designs suffer from the validity threat of history. The addition of a control group to that Time-Series Design controls this last remaining threat. The Multiple Time-Series Design (see Design Q3 in Table 10.4) illustrates this. Design Q3 controls all the threats to internal validity, including history. Events other than X should affect both groups equally, so history is not a rival explanation for differences between the groups after the experimental group has been exposed to X. A design that uses a control group without random assignment might be thought of as being suspect on the threat of selection. This is less of a problem than with preexperimental designs, however, because the series of before measures affords ample opportunity to see how similar the comparison groups are.

Data from Design Q3 are plotted and analyzed the same way as for the two preceding designs. This time, however, the two lines on the graph represent the experimental group and the control group. The patterns of the two groups are compared to see what effect X produced. Figure 10.2

illustrates this by assessing the impact of "stand your ground" laws on justifiable homicide rates. "Stand your ground" laws basically relax the conditions under which a person can legally use lethal force when under a perceived threat. Under such laws, a person is no longer required to try to get away from the threat before using lethal force. Figure 10.2 compares states that passed such laws in 2006 with states that did not have such laws during that period. The data in the figure suggest that rates of justifiable homicide increase when jurisdictions have such laws: In states where these laws became effective in 2006, the rates began to increase right after the laws came into effect and had not increased for some years before that. The control group (states without such laws) shows steady justifiable homicide rates through the whole period under study. The control group protects against the validity threat of history because any events (other than the "stand your ground" laws) that might have affected justifiable homicide rates should have done so in the states without such laws as well.

Quasi-experimental designs have considerable potential for human service research, much of which involves repeated contact with the same clients. Records of clients' situations and progress are routinely kept, so the repeated measures that Time-Series Designs require may be easy to obtain. Various treatments or programs used with clients constitute the experimental condition. Plotting the data as suggested for time-series analysis would reveal whatever impacts those procedures produced. (We will discuss some of these topics and the intricacies of such designs in more detail in Chapter 11.)

Modes of Data Collection in Experiments

A good grasp of experiments in research makes one thing clear: Experiments are defined by a logical and orderly way of collecting data rather than by the form those data take. The research methods discussed in Chapters 7 to 9 are defined by the type of data collected: Surveys collect data in the form of verbal reports, available data uses archival records, and field research uses direct observation.

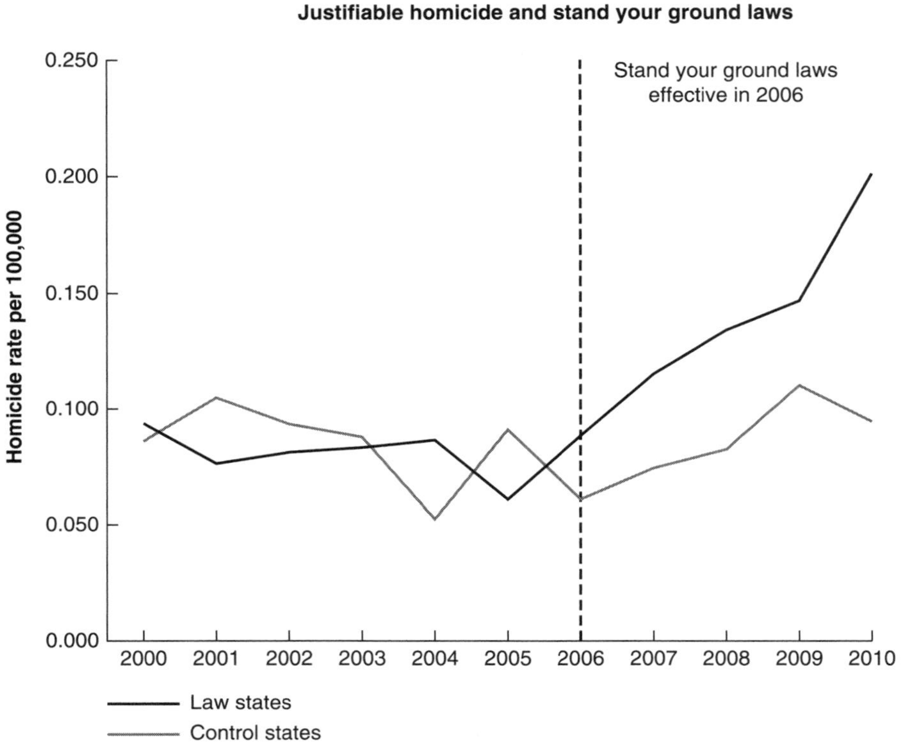

Figure 10.2 Example of multiple time-series data: justifiable homicide rates for states with "stand your ground" laws (law states) and states without such laws (control states), 2000–2010.

Source: Federal Bureau of Investigation, Uniform Crime Reports, various years.

Experiments, on the other hand, can collect data through all three of those sources—surveys, available data, and direct observation. Regardless of the kind of data collected, what makes a research design an experiment is the presence of an experimental group, a control group, random assignment to conditions, and the other factors described in this chapter.

Some experiments, then, measure variables by getting people's responses to survey questions. The study discussed earlier concerning the impact of social class and race on gender stereotypes was of this sort: People were asked to state what society's stereotypes about different types of people were (Landrine, 1985). The Minneapolis study of domestic violence and its replications described in Research in Practice 10.2 relied partially on interviews with victims to measure variables and

also used available data in the form of arrest data (Sherman, 1992).

Direct observation also is a way of collecting data in experiments, as illustrated by a quasi-experimental field study assessing child care program quality (Ridley, McWilliam, & Oates, 2000). In this case, the researchers compared the quality of care delivered by two different licensing levels of child care centers in North Carolina. A key outcome variable was "engagement," which was defined as the amount of time that children spent interacting with the environment in a developmentally and contextually appropriate manner. Observers used a systematic process to code group engagement. They simply counted the number of children who were visible in one pass and then made a second pass, counting the number of children who were nonengaged (e.g., wandering aimlessly, crying, or fighting). The percentage of engaged children was then computed and used as the dependent variable.

Technological advances in recording devices, such as digital cameras and computers, have enhanced the capacity of researchers to collect data by observation.

In designing an experiment, then, a researcher also has to consider the issues involved in the particular kind of data collection being used. If data will be collected for an experiment through a survey, for example, then all the issues of question design, nonresponse, and others discussed in Chapter 7 must be addressed. This chapter focuses on the logic behind experiments, and it leaves the issues related to the various forms of data collection to their respective chapters.

EXTERNAL VALIDITY

In experiments, researchers make something happen that would not have occurred naturally. In laboratory experiments, for example, they construct a social setting that they believe simulates what occurs in the everyday world. In addition to its artificiality, the setting typically is simpler than what occurs naturally, because researchers try to limit the number of social or psychological forces operating so that they can observe more clearly the influence of the independent variables on the dependent variable. Even field experiments, which are considerably more natural than those in the laboratory, involve a manipulation of an independent variable by the researcher—that is, a change in the scene that would not have occurred without the researcher's intervention.

This "unnaturalness" raises a validity problem that differs from internal validity as discussed earlier in this chapter. **External validity** concerns the extent to which causal inferences made in an experiment can be generalized to other times, settings, or groups of people (Shadish, Cook, & Campbell, 2002). The basic issue is whether an experiment is so simple, so contrived, or in some other way so different from the everyday world that what we learn from it does not apply to the natural world. This problem is a part of the

difficulty in generalizing findings from samples to populations (discussed in Chapter 6). With experiments, however, some special problems arise that are not found with sampling in other types of research methods. Indeed, resolving the problem of external validity can be difficult and is less straightforward than is the case with internal validity. Campbell and Stanley (1963, p. 17) succinctly state the problem:

> Whereas the problems of internal validity are solvable within the limits of the logic of probability statistics, the problems of external validity are not logically solvable in any neat, conclusive way. Generalization always turns out to involve extrapolation into a realm not represented in one's sample.

We will review four major threats to external validity as well as ways that these threats can be reduced.

Reactive Effects of Testing

In any design using pretesting, the possibility exists that experiencing the pretest can alter the subjects' reactions to the independent variable. For example, items on a paper-and-pencil pretest measure might make subjects more or less responsive to the independent variable than they would have been without exposure to those items. The problem this raises for generalizability is not difficult to understand: The populations to which we wish to generalize findings are composed of people who have not been pretested. Therefore, if the subjects are affected by the pretest, our findings may not accurately generalize to the unpretested population.

Whether reactive effects of testing are a threat to generalizability depends on the variables that are involved in the experiment and on the nature of the measurement process used. Paper-and-pencil measures may be quite reactive; unobtrusive observation is likely not to be reactive. When a researcher plans an experiment, it is important to consider whether the reactive effects of testing are likely to be a problem. If so, then it is desirable to choose a research design that does not call for pretesting, such as Design T3, or one that includes groups that are not pretested, such as the Solomon Design. With the latter, it is possible to measure the extent of any pretesting effects.

Unrepresentative Samples

As emphasized in Chapter 6, the representativeness of the people who are studied in any form of research is crucial to the issue of generalizability. Unfortunately, it often is difficult to experiment on truly representative samples of any known population. Often, experimental subjects are volunteers, people who are enticed in some way to participate, or people who happen to be available to the researcher. The implications of this for generalizing experimental findings are quite serious. For example, repeated studies over the decades have demonstrated that people who volunteer to participate in experiments often differ in systematic ways from the people in the population from which they are drawn. The exact nature of the differences varies from one study to another: In some cases, volunteers are better educated, from a higher social class, female (or, in other cases, male), have a greater need for social approval, or have a higher achievement motivation (Boynton, 2003; Rosnow, 1993; Zelenski, Rusting, & Larsen, 2003). Some studies show no such differences. Clearly, if these differences exist in a particular study, they could be related to any number of the variables that are likely to be used in human service research. Generalizing findings from such volunteer subjects could be quite hazardous. The best-designed experiments make an effort to measure such differences by comparing the characteristics of the volunteers with those of the population from which they were taken, if such comparative data exist.

Although the use of coerced subjects may reduce the differences between experimental subjects and the general population from which they are drawn, this has problems of its own as far as generalization is concerned. Coerced subjects are likely to have little interest in the experiment and may be resentful about the coercion that was used (Cox & Sipprelle, 1971). This effect has been found even where the nature of the coercion was quite mild, such as gaining extra credit in a college class for agreeing to participate in an experiment.

One can reasonably assume that these effects are amplified where the level of coercion is greater, such as court-ordered participation in a treatment program under threat of incarceration. In fact, a study of a drug treatment program involving court-ordered clients found this anticipated pattern (Peyrot, 1985): The coerced clients were resentful, uncooperative, and unwilling to commit to the therapeutic objectives of the program.

The threat to external validity created by unrepresentative samples is of great importance to human service workers, because we conduct most of our research efforts to evaluate the effectiveness of treatment approaches on volunteers or coerced subjects. Volunteers may make programs look good because they are interested in the treatment and motivated to change in the direction promoted by the treatment. Not surprisingly, however, apparently effective treatment approaches on volunteers often fail when applied to nonvolunteer groups. Alternatively, because of their lack of interest and resentment, coerced subjects tend to make treatments appear to be ineffective when these treatments might be effective on persons who are not coerced.

Reactive Settings

In addition to reactivity produced by testing, the experimental setting itself may lead people to behave in ways that are different from their behavior in the everyday world. One reason for this is that experimental settings contain **demand characteristics**: subtle, unprogrammed cues that communicate to subjects something about how they should behave. For example, people in experiments tend to be highly cooperative and responsive to the experimenter. In fact, the psychologist Martin Orne (1962) deliberately tried to create boring and repetitive tasks for subjects so that they would rebel and refuse to do them. One task was to perform a series of additions of random numbers. Each page required 200 additions, and each person was given 2,000 pages. After giving instructions, the experimenter told them to continue working until he returned; hours later, the subjects were still working—it was Orne who gave up and ended the experiment! On the basis of this and other research, it has become evident that experimental settings can exercise an influence on subjects powerful enough to damage the generalizability of experimental findings. This has been labeled as the problem of the *good subject*—that is, the subject in an experiment who will do whatever the investigator asks, even to the point of confirming the experimenter's hypotheses if they are communicated to the subject (Aronson, Brewer, & Carlsmith, 1985).

Subjects' reactions are not the only way that experimental settings can be reactive. Experimenters themselves can introduce distortion into the results that reduce generalizability. Experimenters, of course, usually have expectations concerning the results of the experiment, wanting it to come out one way or another. These **experimenter's expectations** can be communicated to subjects in such a subtle fashion that neither the experimenter nor the subjects are aware that the communication has taken place (Rosenthal, 1967). A classic illustration of how subtle this can be is recounted by Graham (1977) and involves a horse, not humans. The horse was called Clever Hans because of his seeming ability to solve fairly complex arithmetic problems. Hans and his trainer toured Europe during the early 1900s, amazing audiences and becoming quite famous. Hans would stand on stage pounding out the answers to problems with his hoofs. Amazingly, Hans was hardly ever wrong. Hans would perform his feats even when his trainer was not present. Could the horse really do arithmetic? After very careful observation, it was discovered that Hans was picking up the subtle cues given off by those who asked him questions. As Hans approached the correct number of hoof beats, questioners would move or shift just enough to cue the horse that it was time to stop.

The same phenomenon has been thoroughly investigated in the physician–patient relationship (Kline, 1988). When giving a patient a treatment that is known to be effective, a physician exudes confidence, and the patient picks up on this and expects to get better. The patient's hopeful mood then increases the likelihood that he or she will actually improve. When a physician, however, is giving a patient a placebo—that is, an inert substance the physician doesn't expect to work—then

his or her manner communicates doubt: The patient senses, without being aware of it, what the physician's expectations are and then helps create that reality. People in experiments often do the same thing. Subjects react to subtle cues given off unconsciously by an experimenter that tell them to behave in a way that the researcher wants.

Reactive experimental settings can threaten external validity, because changes in the dependent variable might be caused by demand characteristics or experimenter expectancies rather than by the independent variable. One procedure for reducing reactivity in experimental settings is to conduct the experiment in such a way that subjects are *blind*—that is, unaware of the experimental hypotheses—so that this knowledge will not influence their behavior. In fact, subjects commonly are given a false rationale for what they are to do in an attempt to reduce the reactions of subjects that might interfere with the generalizability of the findings. As an ethical matter, however, subjects should be informed of the experiment's true purpose during the postexperimental debriefing session.

The surest way of controlling reactivity because of the experimenter is to run what is called a *double-blind experiment*. In a **double-blind experiment,** neither the subjects nor the experimenter knows which people are in the experimental condition and which are in the control condition. This makes it impossible for the experimenter to communicate to subjects how they ought to behave, because, for any given subject, the experimenter does not know which responses confirm the experimental hypotheses. Though simple in theory, maintaining a double-blind procedure in practice can be difficult. Another layer of personnel must be added to accomplish the assignment of subjects, sealed instructions issued to the experimenter, and the results tracked. Furthermore, all information relating to these activities must be kept from those who are actually running the experimental groups. It is easy for this structure to break down so that the double-blind feature is lost; however, for true protection against such reactivity, double-blind experiments need to be used. Unfortunately, the nature of the treatment sometimes interferes with use of the double-blind approach. Because of the different activities involved, it may be obvious which condition is experimental and which is control, thus clearly preventing the use of a double-blind experiment.

Multiple-Treatment Interference

In an experiment with more than one independent variable, the particular combination and ordering of experimental treatments may produce change in the dependent variable. If this same combination and this same ordering do not occur outside the experimental setting, however, then the findings from the experiment cannot be generalized. Suppose, for example, that an experiment calls for subjects to experience four independent variables in succession. Furthermore, suppose that the last variable in the series appears to produce an interesting effect. Could the effect of that fourth variable be safely generalized on the basis of the experimental findings? The answer is no. The subjects in the experiment have experienced the three other independent variables first, which might in itself have affected the way that they reacted to the last variable. If people outside the experimental setting do not experience all the variables in sequence, then generalization concerning the fourth variable is risky. The problem of multiple-treatment interference is similar to reactive effects of testing in that the subjects in the experiment experience something that the people in the population at large do not.

The threat of multiple-treatment interference can be effectively eliminated through the use of complex designs in which the different experimental groups experience the independent variables in every possible sequence. If a given variable produces a consistent effect regardless of the ordering of the variables, then multiple-treatment interference is not a threat to the generalizability of the findings. An alternative is to isolate the variable of interest in a multiple-treatment experiment and then conduct a follow-up experiment with that variable as the only treatment. If the follow-up experiment produces an effect similar to that found when it was part of a series of treatments, then multiple-treatment interference can be ruled out.

In designing experiments, especially those to be conducted in laboratory settings, problems of external validity need to be considered. Properly designed experiments can offer researchers substantial confidence in generalizing from an experimental sample to other settings or groups. Efforts to enhance external validity may, however, affect our ability to achieve internal validity, which brings us to the importance of replication for external validity.

Enhancing the External Validity of Experiments

Although both internal and external validity are important to experimental research, a tension exists between the two. On the one hand, internal validity is enhanced through greater control. Consequently, the researcher seeking internal validity is attracted to the laboratory experiment and to precise testing. Yet, we have just seen that the reactive effect of testing is a threat to external validity. Seeking control, the researcher may use a homogeneous sample to avoid the confounding effects of other variables. In the effort to achieve internal validity, the researcher might, for example, use a sample of 18-year-old White males. Although the effects of race, sex, and age are now controlled, the threat to external validity from unrepresentative samples increases. We have suggested the use of complex designs to reduce the threat to external validity of multiple-treatment interference. Complex designs, however, are more difficult to implement in a way that retains the integrity of the research design. Thus, there appears to be a dilemma between seeking internal validity on the one hand and external validity on the other.

Another way to approach the problem of external validity is, when possible, to conduct field experiments rather than laboratory experiments. Although issues of external validity do arise in field experiments, field experiments on the whole have greater external validity, because they are conducted in the real world. This means that the results are more clearly generalizable to some settings in the real world, at least to settings that are similar to the one in which the field study was conducted.

The basic solution to this dilemma, however, is not to seek an answer to both internal validity and external validity in a single study. Ultimately, external validity is established through replication (Shadish et al., 2002). Confidence in generalizing from experimental findings increases as other researchers test and support the same hypotheses in a variety of settings with a variety of designs. Often, this takes the form of initial testing in the laboratory under ideal conditions to see if the hypothesis is supported at all. Then, the same hypothesis can be tested under the less-than-ideal conditions of the field. Through replication, the dual objectives of internal and external validity can be achieved.

Lack of Minority Participation and Analysis

Depending on the setting in which an experiment is conducted, women and minority populations may find themselves underrepresented in laboratory or field experiments—a problem that can affect both external and internal validity. Researchers often choose as subjects for experiments people who are easily accessible to them. For basic research in psychology and sociology, for example, students in introductory psychology or sociology classes often are selected as research subjects. The sex ratio of college students is fairly even: 46% male and 54% female. African Americans constitute about 11% of all college students but account for 13% of the total U.S. population (U.S. Census Bureau, 2011). Thus, experiments using a representative sample of college students will tend to underrepresent African Americans, Hispanics, and some other marginalized populations. In addition, this underrepresentation is more severe at some colleges than at others: Some major research universities, even today, have only 1% or 2% Black enrollment. So, whenever experimental subjects are selected from a setting, care must be taken to ensure representation of minorities in a sample if the minorities are to be included in the generalizations that are made from the data. Otherwise, mention should be made that no special procedures were used in the sampling to enhance minority involvement.

A related problem is what one sociologist calls *gender insensitivity:* "ignoring gender as an important social variable" (Eichler, 1988, p. 66). In experiments, this can happen when no mention is made of the sex ratio of the subjects in the experiment or when data are not analyzed separately by gender. Eichler reports one issue of a psychology journal in which the only article to mention the sex of the subjects was one that used rhesus monkeys; none of those using human subjects did so, despite the fact that practically all those articles focused on variables, such as perception, verbal ability, and learning, on which people's gender might well have an influence.

A final problem relating to minority participation in experiments is failure to consider the gender or minority status of all participants in the experiment. In addition to the researcher and the subject, this might include interviewers, confederates of the experimenter, and any others who interact with the subjects during data collection. We know, for example, that people of the same gender interact differently with people of a different gender. Thus, a male interviewer responds differently when asking questions of a female subject than when interviewing a male subject. In the former case, he might be friendlier, more attentive, or more engaging without even realizing it, and this can influence the subject's response to questions.

These threats to external validity can be reduced by reporting the sex or minority status of the various people who are involved in experiments and by analyzing the data with sex or minority status as an experimental or control variable. There are, of course, reasons for a homogeneous sample in an experiment—namely, to reduce extraneous variation when trying to establish a causal relationship between independent and dependent variables. If the results are to be generalized to all racial and ethnic groups and both sexes, however, then experiments need to be replicated using subjects from these groups.

ASSESSMENT OF EXPERIMENTS

Advantages

Inference of Causality. The major advantage of experimental research is that it places us in the most advantageous position from which to infer causal relationships between variables. (Recall from Chapter 2 that causality can never be directly observed. Rather, we infer that one thing caused another by observing changes in the two things under the appropriate conditions.) A well-designed and well-controlled experiment puts us in the strongest position to make that causal inference, because it enables us to control the effect of other variables, which raises our confidence that the independent variable is, indeed, bringing about changes in the dependent variable. Experiments also permit us to establish the time sequence necessary for inferring causality. We can measure the dependent variable to see if it has changed *since* the experimental manipulation. With other research methods, such as the survey, it often is not possible to directly observe whether the changes in one variable preceded or followed changes in another variable.

Control. Experimenters are not limited by the variables and events that happen to occur naturally in a particular situation. Rather, they can decide what variables to study, what values those variables will take, and what combination of variables to include. In other words, researchers can create precisely what their hypotheses suggest are important. This is in sharp contrast to other research methods, such as the use of available data (see Chapter 8) or observational techniques (see Chapter 9), in which hypotheses need to be reshaped to fit the existing data or observations.

The Study of Change. Many experimental designs are longitudinal, which means that they are conducted over a period of time, with measurements taken at more than one time. This makes it possible to study changes over time. Many other research methods, such as surveys, tend to be cross-sectional—they are like snapshots taken at a given point in time. In cross-sectional studies, we can ask people how things have changed over time, but we cannot *directly observe* that change.

Costs. In some cases, experiments—especially those conducted in laboratory settings—can be considerably cheaper than other research methods. Because of the element of control, the sample size can be smaller, and this saves money. Costly travel expenses and interviewer salaries found in some surveys also are eliminated. Some field experiments, however, can be expensive, because they may require interviewing—possibly more than once—to assess changes in dependent variables.

Disadvantages

Inflexibility. Experimental designs generally require that the treatment (or the independent variable) be well developed and that the same treatment be applied to all cases in the experimental group. If the nature of the independent variable changes as the experiment progresses, then this is extraneous variation, which makes it difficult to say what changed the dependent variable. Because of this inflexibility, experimental designs are not suitable during the early stages of research, when treatments may not be well developed. This requirement for consistently measuring the independent variable is especially true of large-scale, longitudinal experiments, which are best suited for clearly designed treatments (Rossi, Lipsey, & Freeman, 2004).

Randomization Requirement. Human service organizations may be unwilling to accept random assignment to treatment and control conditions, despite the value of this technique for controlling extraneous effects. This is especially so when the design calls for a control group to receive no treatment at all. Organizations may have ethical concerns about randomization, or they may want to be sure that they "get something" for participating in a study and, thus, are reluctant to serve as the control condition. In addition, with field experiments, it sometimes is impossible to find or create a control group that is truly comparable to the experimental groups; thus, the true experimental designs are ruled out. Despite the fact that randomization was achieved, both Research in Practice illustrations in this chapter emphasize the considerable difficulty in carrying out randomization.

Artificiality. The laboratory setting in which some experiments are conducted is an artificial environment created by the investigator, which raises questions of external validity. We often do not know what the relationship is between this artificial setting and the real world in which people live. We cannot be sure that people behave in the same fashion on the street or in the classroom as they do in the laboratory. Even field experiments of human service interventions are, to an extent, vulnerable to this criticism, especially when they create conditions that never exist naturally. For example, the recipients of social services who are the subjects of research may be treated better by the research team than they would be during their everyday contacts with human service agencies. Under the watchful eye of a research team, much greater care may be taken in the form of monitoring and supervision to ensure that the treatment being delivered is true to the theoretical model than might be taken when the same intervention is delivered as a routine part of an agency's service.

Experimenter Effects. As discussed, artificiality of experimental settings in comparison to the real world exists, and there is another side to this coin: The experimental setting itself is a real world—that is, a social occasion in which social norms, roles, and values exist and shape people's behavior. Social processes arising within the experimental setting—and not a part of the experimental variables—may shape the research outcome. Thus, changes in the dependent variable may result from the demand characteristics of experiments, such as repeated measurement, or from the impact of

experimenter expectations, which are factors that obviously do not influence people in the everyday world.

Generalizability. The logistics involved in managing an experiment often necessitate that experimenters use small samples. Furthermore, the goal of holding measurement error to a minimum often compels researchers to make these samples as homogeneous as possible. Despite the advantages of random sampling, experimenters frequently must settle for availability samples to obtain subjects who will participate in the study. The net result is that experiments often are conducted on small, homogeneous, availability samples, and it may be difficult to know to whom such results can be generalized. It often is assumed that representative sampling is not as essential in experiments as in other types of research because of the randomization and control procedures that are used. Although these help, we must still be cautious regarding the population to which we make such generalizations.

Timeliness of Results. Although experiments may produce the strongest evidence of causation, they often are time-consuming to conduct. The urgency of policy decisions may preclude using experimentation simply because it takes too long to generate funding for the project, to design the research, and to carry it out. If the results do not come in quickly enough, they may not be considered in the debate over a rapidly developing policy (Rossi et al., 2004).

REVIEW AND CRITICAL THINKING

Main Points

- Experiments are a controlled method of observation in which the value of one or more independent variables is changed to assess the causal effect on one or more dependent variables.
- Because of the control that experiments afford, they are the surest method of discovering causal relationships among variables.
- Major elements of control in experiments include control variables, control groups, matching, and randomization.
- Internal validity refers to whether the independent variable does, in fact, produce the effect that it appears to produce on the dependent variable.

- Numerous conditions may threaten the internal validity of experiments, but using true experimental designs can control all of them.
- Quasi-experimental designs are useful for bringing much of the control of an experiment to nonexperimental situations.
- External validity is the degree to which experimental results can be generalized beyond the experimental setting.
- Threats to external validity generally are not controllable through design but are more difficult and less straightforward to control than are threats to internal validity.
- Double-blind experiments, in which neither the subjects nor the experimenters know which groups are in the experimental or control condition, are used to control both experimental demand characteristics and experimenter bias.
- To avoid race, ethnicity, or gender insensitivity, the minority composition of experimental groups should be reported, consideration should be given to analyzing the data by controlling for minority impact, and the minority status of all experimental participants should be considered.
- An understanding of experimental procedures can contribute to practice effectiveness as well as research endeavors.

IMPORTANT TERMS FOR REVIEW
. . . .

Blocking	Experimental stimulus	Laboratory experiments
Control condition	Experimental treatment	Matching
Control group	Experimental variability	Preexperimental designs
Control variables	Experimenter's	Quasi-experimental
Demand characteristics	Expectations	designs
Double-blind experiment	External validity	Random assignment
Experiment	Extraneous variability	True experimental designs
Experimental condition	Field experiments	
Experimental group	Internal validity	

CRITICAL THINKING
. . . .

Some people in the field of human service research argue that experiments are the preferred or model research design because they are the best at providing a solid logical foundation from which to infer causality. This also makes experimental designs a laudable model to serve as a guide for critical thinking in the practice and policy realms. People constantly ask questions about causality: Why do people commit crimes? Why did I lose my job? Why did she treat me that way? The following are critical thinking questions raised at the beginning of the chapter and some ideas for how they relate to social work practice. Students are encouraged to develop their own answers to these questions.

Why is it important to understand different research designs? In social work research not all designs are equal and strive to yield conclusive, causal inference between variables. Some are exploratory or descriptive in nature, meaning that they explore or describe a new phenomenon that has yet to have much research. These studies tend to produce a low level of internal validity. For example, social work students may want to explore the impact domestic violence has on transgender populations. But, there might be limited research in this area due to many factors; for example, vulnerable populations may not want to be researched. Therefore, when a study has a low level of internal validity it does not mean that you should disregard the study altogether. Designs that control for more threats to internal validity are quasi-experimental and experimental designs. These studies, due to their design, attempt to control for and maximize threats to internal validity. Results from these studies tend to produce more accurate results.

What is the importance of understanding threats to internal validity? Threats to internal validity are present when anything other than the independent variable can affect the dependent variable. For example, when evaluating the effectiveness of a social work program, the problem of internal validity refers to the possibility that investigations might incorrectly conclude that differences in outcome were caused by the intervention when, in fact, something else really caused the differences. Seven threats to internal validity have been identified in the course textbook, which are history, maturation, testing, instrumentation, statistical regression, selection, and experimental attrition.

Explain how a research design affects the results of a study. This question should be at the front of your mind during and after this week. Specific types of designs have strengths and weaknesses regarding relationships between variables. Due to the type of design we can be confident in results from different studies. A greater understanding of social work experimental research procedures can contribute to practice effectiveness and improving treatment.

EVALUATING COMPETENCY (FROM THE COUNCIL ON SOCIAL WORK EDUCATION [CSWE] 2015 EDUCATIONAL POLICY AND ACCREDITATION STANDARDS [EPAS])

Competency 4: Engage in Practice-Informed Research and Research-Informed Practice

- How does understanding different types of research designs help improve research to practice and practice to research?

Competency 9: Evaluated Practice With Individuals, Families, Groups, Organizations, and Communities

- What challenges may a social researcher face when implementing a research design for a study with community organizations?
- What skills must a social researcher have to conduct effective research with individuals, families, groups, organizations, and communities?

SELF-ASSESSMENT

1. The logic of experimentation consists of:
   a. Causation and randomization.
   b. Validity, randomization, and control.
   c. Causation and control, matching and randomization, and internal validity.
   d. Control, matching, and randomization.

2. Internal validity refers to:
   a. The confidence we have that the results are generalized to all populations.
   b. How confident we are that the results are reliable.
   c. The confidence we have in our statistical analysis.
   d. The confidence we have that the results of a study accurately depict whether one variable is or is not a cause of another.

3. Threats to internal validity consist of:
   a. History, testing, instrumentation, statistical regression, maturation, and selection bias.
   b. Experimental attrition, selection bias, history, instrumentation, testing, maturation, and selection bias.
   c. Maturing, participants' history before the study, selection bias, instrumentation, and testing.
   d. History of the researcher, instrumentation, maturation, and selection bias.

4. External validity refers to:
   a. Internal consistency of the study.
   b. External consistency of the study.
   c. The extent to which causal inferences made in an experiment can be generalized to other times, settings, or groups of people.
   d. Generalizability of your study.

5. Experimental designs consist of:
   a. Preexperimental, quasi-experimental, and true experimental designs.
   b. Postexperimental, quasi-experimental, and control group designs.
   c. Quality, experimental, and quasi-control designs.
   d. Preexperimental, postexperimental, and experimental designs.

6. Quasi-experimental designs consist of:
   a. An experimental design with a control group, but without random assignment into the treatment and control groups.
   b. Randomization into treatment and control groups.
   c. A one-time study.
   d. A design that follows individuals over time, but does not have a control group.

7. Preexperimental designs involve:
   a. Maximum control for threats to internal validity.
   b. Random assignment into both treatment and control groups.
   c. Two-group pretest-posttest design.
   d. Descriptive or exploratory purposes, but lack random assignment and control groups.

8. Experimental designs consist of:
   a. One-group pretest-posttest design.
   b. Maximum control for threats to internal validity by randomly assigning participants to treatment and control groups.
   c. An experimental design with a control group, but without random assignment into the treatment and control groups.
   d. Group comparison design.
9. Assessment of experiments refers to:
   a. Assessing the advantages of an experiment.
   b. Assessing for the disadvantages of an experiment.
   c. Exploring both the advantages and disadvantages of experiments.
   d. Exploring the study of change.
10. A control group consists of:
    a. A group of research subjects who receive the same experiences as those in the experimental condition, but receive no exposure to the experimental stimulus.
    b. A group of research participants who receive the same treatment the experimental group receives.
    c. A group of participants who are isolated from participating in the study.
    d. A group of participants who receive only the treatment effect.

ANSWER KEY FOR SELF-ASSESSMENT QUIZ

1. **c.** Causation and control, matching and randomization, and internal validity.
2. **d.** The confidence we have that the results of a study accurately depict whether one variable is or is not a cause of another.
3. **b.** Experimental attrition, selection bias, history, instrumentation, testing, maturation, and selection bias.
4. **c.** The extent to which causal inferences made in an experiment can be generalized to other times, settings, or groups of people.
5. **a.** Preexperimental, quasi-experimental, and true experimental designs.
6. **a.** An experimental design with a control group, but without random assignment into the treatment and control groups.
7. **d.** Descriptive or exploratory purposes, but lack random assignment and control groups.
8. **b.** Maximum control for threats to internal validity by randomly assigning participants to treatment and control groups.
9. **c.** Exploring both the advantages and disadvantages of experiments.
10. **a.** A group of research subjects who receive the same experiences as those in the experimental condition, but receive no exposure to the experimental stimulus.

FOR FURTHER READING

Campbell, D. T., & Jean Russo, M. (1999). *Social experimentation*. Thousand Oaks, CA: Sage. Donald Campbell was one of the giants in the field of social experimentation. This book presents his views on how social experiments can be used for the betterment of society.

Fairweather, G. W., & Davidson, W. S. (1986). *An introduction to community experimentation: Theory, methods, and practice*. New York, NY: McGraw-Hill. An interesting book ideally suited to those involved in community action programs. It outlines the reasons for experimentation and supplies the designs to evaluate the effectiveness of various intervention programs.

Field, A., & Hole, G. J. (2003). *How to design and report experiments*. Thousand Oaks, CA: Sage. This textbook provides a good overview to experimental design and statistical analysis.

Gabor, P. A., & Grinnell, Jr., R. M. (1994). *Evaluation and quality improvement in the human services*. Boston, MA: Allyn & Bacon. Although this book covers many other research issues, it is especially good at showing the importance of experimental designs in program evaluations. It describes the use of many different kinds of designs used in human service settings.

Gottman, J. M. (1981). *Time-series analysis: A comprehensive introduction for social scientists*. New York, NY: Cambridge University Press. "Comprehensive" is certainly the operative word in describing this book, because it details the mathematical analysis of time-series designs. The author also argues persuasively against the common "eyeballing" approach to time-series analysis.

Kirk, R. E. (1995). *Experimental design: Procedures for the behavioral sciences* (3rd ed.). Belmont, CA: Cengage, Brooks/Cole. This is a thorough overview of how to design both simple and complicated experiments. It goes well beyond the review in this chapter.

Solomon, P., Cavanaugh, M., & Draine, J. (2009). *Designing, developing, and implementing randomized control trials*. New York, NY: Oxford University Press. This "pocket guide" deals specifically with designing and implementing randomized control trials (RCTs), a form of experimental research, in community-based settings. It provides researchers and social service practitioners insight into each step of an RCT.

REFERENCES

Achen, C. H. (1986). *The statistical analysis of quasi-experiments.* Berkeley: University of California Press.

Aronson, E., Brewer, M. B., & Carlsmith, J. (1985). Experimentation in social psychology. In G. Lindzey & E. Aronson (Eds.), *The handbook of social psychology* (3rd ed., pp. 441–486). New York, NY: Random House.

Boynton, P. M. (2003). I'm just a girl who can't say no? Women, consent, and sex research. *Journal of Sex and Marital Therapy, 29*(Suppl. 1), 23–32. doi:10.1080/713847130

Burch, G., & Mohr, V. (1980). Evaluating a child abuse intervention program. *Social Casework, 61,* 90–99. doi:10.1177/104438948006100204

Campbell, D. T., & Stanley, J. C. (1963). *Experimental and quasi-experimental designs for research.* Chicago, IL: Rand McNally.

Carlock, C. J., & Martin, P. Y. (1977). Sex composition and the intensive group experience. *Social Work, 22,* 27–32.

Cho, H., & Wilke, D. J. (2005). How has the violence against women act affected the response of the criminal justice system to domestic violence? *Journal of Sociology and Social Welfare, 32,* 125–139.

Cox, D. E., & Sipprelle, C. N. (1971). Coercion in participation as a research subject. *American Psychologist, 26,* 726–728. doi:10.1037/h0032067

Dunford, F., Huizinga, D., & Elliott, D. (1989). *The Omaha domestic violence police experiment.* Washington, DC: National Institute of Justice.

Eichler, M. (1988). *Nonsexist research methods: A practical guide.* Boston, MA: Allen & Unwin.

Frankfort-Nachmias, C., & Nachmias, D. (2008). *Research methods in the social sciences* (7th ed.). New York, NY: Worth.

Graham, K. R. (1977). *Psychological research: Controlled interpersonal research.* Monterey, CA: Brooks/Cole.

Harris, A. R., Thomas, S. H., Fisher, G. A., & Hirsch, D. J. (2002). Murder and medicine: The lethality of criminal assault 1960–1999. *Homicide Studies Journal, 6,* 128–166. doi:10.1177/108876790200600203

Hirschel, J., Hutchison, III, I., & Dean, C. (1992). The failure of arrest to deter spouse abuse. *Journal of Research in Crime and Delinquency, 29,* 7–33. doi:10.1177/0022427892029001002

Kamerman, J. B. (1988). *Death in the midst of life: Social and cultural influences on death, grief, and mourning.* Englewood Cliffs, NJ: Prentice Hall.

Kline, D. (1988). The power of the placebo. *Hippocrates: The Magazine of Health and Medicine, 2,* 24–26.

Landrine, H. (1985). Race and class stereotypes of women. *Sex Roles, 13,* 65–75. doi:10.1007/BF00287461

Maxwell, C. D., Garner, J. H., & Fagan, J. A. (2001). The effects of arrest on intimate partner violence: New evidence from the spousal assault replication program. *Research in Brief.* Washington, DC: National Institute of Justice, U.S. Department of Justice.

Orne, M. T. (1962). On the social psychology of the psychological experiment: With particular reference to demand characteristics and their implications. *American Psychologist, 17,* 776–783. doi:10.1037/h0043424

Peyrot, M. (1985). Coerced voluntarism: The micropolitics of drug treatment. *Urban Life, 13,* 343–365. doi:10.1177/0098303985013004002

Ridley, S. M., McWilliam, R. A., & Oates, C. S. (2000). Observed engagement as an indicator of child care program quality. *Early Education and Development, 11,* 133–146. doi:10.1207/s15566935eed1102_1

Rosenthal, R. (1967). Covert communication in the psychological experiment. *Psychological Bulletin, 67,* 356–367. doi:10.1037/h0024529

Rosnow, R. L. (1993). The volunteer problem revisited. In P. D. Blanck (Ed.), *Interpersonal expectations: Theory, research, and applications* (pp. 418–436). New York, NY: Cambridge University Press.

Rossi, P. H., Lipsey, M. W., & Freeman, H. E. (2004). *Evaluation: A systematic approach* (7th ed.). Thousand Oaks, CA: Sage.

Shadish, W. R., Cook, T. D., & Campbell, D. T. (2002). *Experimental and quasi-experimental designs for generalized causal inference.* Boston, MA: Houghton Mifflin.

Sherman, L. (1992). *Policing domestic violence: Experiments and dilemmas*. New York, NY: Free Press.

Sherman, L., & Berk, R. A (1984). The specific deterrent effects of arrest for domestic assault. American Sociological Review 49, 261–271.

U.S. Census Bureau. (2011). *Statistical abstract of the United States: 2012* (131st ed.). Washington, DC: U.S. Government Printing Office. Retrieved from https://www2.census.gov/library/publications/2011/compendia/statab/131ed/2012-statab.pdf

Wagenaar, A. C., Murray, D. M., & Toomey, T. L. (2000). Communities mobilizing for change on alcohol (CMCA): Effects of a randomized trial on arrests and traffic crashes. *Addiction, 95*, 209–217. doi:10.1046/j.1360-0443.2000.9522097.x

Zelenski, J. M., Rusting, C. L., & Larsen, R. J. (2003). Consistency in the time of experiment participation and personality correlates: A methodological note. *Personality and Individual Differences, 34*, 547–558. doi:10.1016/S0191-8869(01)00218-5

11
SINGLE-SYSTEM DESIGNS

INTRODUCTION

George Vellner (age 27) is an LCSW who works at "Next Step House" a substance-abuse treatment center in Charleston, South Carolina. The center works with male and female adults who are required by the state to successfully complete treatment. Next Step House works with people who are struggling with substance use and behavioral health disorders and offers a range of services including residential treatment, outpatient treatment, long-term management, case management, and evidence-based treatment. The adults receiving treatment have substance use disorder. George currently has six individual clients out of the 87 adults going through the program that he meets with weekly. The evidence-based treatment the center uses with their clients is motivational interviewing. Motivational interviewing is extremely effective at reducing substance use with people who are dependent. Motivational interviewing emphasizes change talk, rolling with the resistance, and promotes confidence in clients.

George has recently been asked by management to provide evidence regarding his clients' progress at the center. George states, "Providing evidence with numbers can be difficult when you have smaller numbers of clients, but I feel the information is still important and means something." (G. Vellner, personal communication, April 10, 2018). There are many different approaches to monitor clients' progress and he has decided to use single-system design. This type of design is ideal for the current situation, because in single-system design you track an individual's behavior through repeated measures over time. The center currently uses two research measurements to assess client's progress as they go through

treatment, which are the substance abuse severity measurement (SASM), a self-rating five-point Likert scale, and urine analysis (UAs). Prior to each treatment session George will have his clients' rate their attitudes regarding SASM and UAs, which will will be completed at pre-treatment, mid-treatment, and termination. This chapter addresses single-system design. As you read this chapter on single-system design, consider the following questions: (a) Which type of single-subject design would be most appropriate for social workers to use with their clients to assess progress? (b) How will social workers integrate different types of measurements in single-system design? (c) Would it be possible for social workers to have more than one client in a design at a time? If yes, what type of design would that be? and (d) What additional resources will social workers need to help accomplish single-system designs?

The model of evidence-based practice begins with converting the need for information into answerable questions and then systematically seeking, through print and electronic sources, to track down the best evidence for guiding practice decisions. Using the available scientific knowledge base as a guide, however, is only one part of evidence-based practice. Human service professionals also are called upon to evaluate their own effectiveness and seek ways to improve future practice efforts (Sackett, Straus, Richardson, Rosenberg, & Haynes, 2000). Practitioners generally work with one client at a time. Even if the client system is a family or a group or a community, the practitioner does not have randomized control groups, placebo treatments, or other features that make clinical trials such a highly valued form of evidence for advancing practice. So, beyond providing some interesting anecdotal evidence, how can the practitioner–client encounter serve as part of the research process? Seeking to answer this question has led many human service professionals to revise the conception of their roles as clinician–researchers.

The purpose of this chapter is to present a fundamental tool of this role and a central mechanism through which valid research can be conducted in clinical settings: the *single-system design*. **Single-system designs** are quasi-experimental research designs that involve assessing change in a dependent variable on a single research case or subject. In psychology, the term *single case* appears to be replacing *single subject* as the designation of choice (Levin, 1992). We have adopted a term that is more common to social work—single system—to signify the fact that the unit of analysis for this research may not necessarily be an individual person but also a couple, family, group, organization, or other human aggregate. Our own students have designed single-system projects in which the unit of analysis was an individual child with poor study behavior, a pair of squabbling siblings, a nursing home group with poor interaction among participants, and a medication-dispensing program in a mental health setting. In the latter case, the program was the system, and the dependent variable was the proportion of clients who received their weekly dosage of medication on time. So, although the most common application is to focus on the behavior of an individual client, the design is flexible and lends itself to the study of a wide range of practice issues.

The distinguishing feature of the single-system design is that the dependent variable is repeatedly measured, most commonly during a baseline phase and again during one or more intervention phases, when the independent variable is manipulated. Experimental effects are inferred by comparisons of the subject's responses across baseline and intervention phases. We begin by discussing how and why a *clinical research model* has emerged in the human services. Then, we analyze the clinical research process, showing how research can be merged with clinical practice. Next, building on the discussion of experimental designs in Chapter 10, we present the various kinds of single-system designs that are available to clinician–researchers. Finally, we analyze the advantages and disadvantages of single-system designs.

THE CLINICAL RESEARCH MODEL

A fundamental force behind the development of single-system designs is the human service practitioner's professional concern about knowing how a client is responding to intervention. This basic desire has been intensified by the pressure for more accountability in the human services. Funding sources, insurance providers, and regulatory organizations demand documentation that services are being delivered according to standards, and they want to see evidence that clients do, in fact, improve. Unfortunately, traditional research designs have significant limitations for meeting these needs in the practice community (Barlow, Nock, & Hersen, 2009; Gingerich, 1990). A major source of new knowledge for many practitioners has been group experiments. However, group experiments often are impractical—or even impossible—to conduct in practice settings. It may be too time-consuming and costly to assemble clients with similar problems and randomly assign some to treatment groups and others to control groups. A second problem with group experiments in terms of practice implications is that the results often are an average of the whole group's response, obscuring individual reactions. It is, of course, precisely the effects on individuals that are of most interest to clinicians. For example, knowing that a given treatment was effective on 70% of an experimental group may be interesting, but it helps relatively little in predicting the reaction of a particular client in a practitioner's office.

Another problem in some traditional group experimentation is failure of the research design to capture the process by which change was induced. Thus, traditional research sometimes has been referred to as "black box" research, because subjects receive some treatment and are then compared with other subjects who did not receive the treatment. With only a pretest and posttest measure, experimenters may not have information on the process of how the change occurred, only on whether it occurred at all. It is as if the subjects passed through a mysterious black box and came out either improved or not improved. A fourth complaint about traditional group experiments has been that reliance upon statistical procedures for data analysis often requires a high degree of statistical expertise plus access to data-analysis technology; this situation may necessitate that practitioners relinquish control of the study to outside methodologists. Such a reliance on direction from outside of practice may have contributed to the view that these studies are not relevant to practice.

Finally, the use of control groups from which treatment is withheld is a source of ethical concern to human service professionals. Thus, although group experiments are appropriate for some purposes, the deficiencies that are inherent in the method have led both practitioners and researchers to seek alternative approaches for evaluating individual change and refining intervention techniques. Single-system designs, as we shall see, effectively avoid the unattractive features of group experiments.

A second source of clinical knowledge prior to single-system designs was case histories. A case history, of course, is a report from a clinician about a client who has undergone treatment. Although many of these reports are intriguing, they often do not provide a sound basis for the accumulation of knowledge. First, they exhibit to only a limited degree the characteristics that distinguish science from other sources of knowledge (see Chapter 2). For example, vague treatments often are reported to have produced vague improvements. Because of this, other practitioners would have grave difficulty replicating the procedures if they wished. The ability to replicate is, of course, a fundamental characteristic of the scientific method—especially when one is working with a single case at a time. In addition, case histories often are prepared only on successes; information about failures, which may be of equal importance, is not communicated to other practitioners. Another problem with case histories is failure to report valid and reliable data to support conclusions; exaggerated claims of success become common in the absence of hard data (Barlow et al., 2009). Finally, with no controls, these studies fail to consider the possible impact of extraneous variables on the client.

So, it was against this backdrop of unsatisfactory research techniques for clinical settings that the clinical research model emerged. The **clinical**

research model, or the **empirical practice model,** became an effort to merge research and practice, and it includes much more than single-system designs. It involves a stance toward practice that is defined by the following characteristics:

1. Maximum use is made of research findings for understanding human service practice issues.
2. Data are collected systematically to monitor the intervention.
3. Interventions are evaluated empirically to determine their degree of effectiveness.
4. Problems, interventions, and outcomes are specified in terms that are concrete, observable, and measurable.
5. Research ways of thinking and research methods are employed in defining clients' problems, formulating questions for practice, collecting assessment data, evaluating effectiveness of interventions, and using evidence.
6. Research and practice are viewed as part of the same problem-solving process.
7. Research is accepted as a tool to be used in practice.

The systematic evaluation of practice by use of single-system designs is a core component of this model of practice. Through the mechanism of single-system designs, research and practice merge into one enterprise. This approach, however, does not reject traditional large-group research, which is still necessary for testing total programs and for confirming the generalizability of intervention effectiveness.

THE CLINICAL RESEARCH PROCESS

At the outset, we wish to make clear that the clinical research model is not a radically new approach to intervention. In fact, many parallels exist between this model and traditional practice, and many practitioners are likely to do much of what the model calls for anyway. The model does, however, inject greater specificity, objectivity, and empiricism into the clinical process. By following the model, the clinician–researcher is in a position to know precisely what treatment was applied and how much effect was produced—and to have supporting data for proof. The model links research and practice by putting the practitioner in the enviable position not only of bringing about change but also of having valid evidence as to why that change occurred. What follows in this section is an outline of the clinical research process divided into six stages, which are summarized in Figure 11.1.

Identify Problems

Like all practice approaches, the clinical research model begins with an assessment of the client's problem. Typically, the problem involves some aspect of the client's functioning: behaviors, perceptions, attitudes, or feelings. During the initial stage, the practitioner strives to obtain as clear and specific an understanding of the problem as possible through commonly used assessment strategies, such as interviewing or paper-and-pencil assessment tools.

Establish Goals

After the problem is identified, the next step is to determine treatment goals. At this point, we encounter the first real difference between the clinical research model and traditional practice. The clinical research model requires, first, that goals

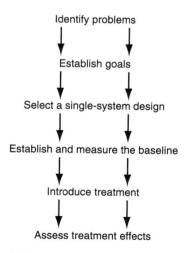

Figure 11.1 Steps in the clinical research process.

be more specific and precisely defined than often is done in conventional practice and, second, that they be measurable in some way (Kazdin, 2010). Although these requirements of specificity and measurability are more rigorous under the clinical research model than in traditional practice, they are best seen as an extension of normal practice procedures rather than as something strangely different. As to the requirement for measurability of outcomes, some practitioners argue that some beneficial outcomes of intervention are so subtle that they are essentially unmeasurable. Countering this attitude in the field of social work is "The First Rule of EPM" (Empirical Practice Model): "There is and can be no such thing as effectiveness until there is measurable positive change in the client's problem" (Nugent, Sieppert, & Hudson, 2001, p. 3). The self-delusion is believing that a real but unmeasurable change has occurred when it actually has not. Effectiveness requires desired, positive change in the level of the client's problem.

One common difficulty in establishing goals is that goals are often long term, making it impractical for the clinician–researcher to monitor progress all the way to achievement of the final goal. In these cases, it may be necessary to identify proximate, intermediate goals whose achievement is evidence of progress toward the final goal. For example, the final goal for an underachiever might be improved academic performance—a long-term goal. Proximate goals that would evidence progress might include improved note taking, longer study hours, and more regular class attendance. Achievement of these proximate goals would be expected to relate to achievement of the final goal. Which measurable, intermediate goals can serve as valid indicators of long-term goals depends, of course, on a theoretical understanding of the long-term changes that are being sought through intervention.

Select a Single-System Design

Once a problem and a corresponding goal for intervention have been identified, the next phase of the clinical research process is to select an appropriate single-system design. Whereas the general principle of single-system research consists of comparing a series of preintervention and postintervention measurements, many variations on this basic scheme exist. Later in the chapter, we will present several common designs and discuss their strengths and limitations. At this point, however, we simply note that we can choose from many design options; we also point out that early in the process, the practitioner should be thinking about the design choices that will best suit the goals and constraints of the particular clinical case. For example, if the primary objective is to provide treatment and simply monitor the client's progress, then a simple design is adequate. For a general behavior deficit, however, where the proposed intervention involves working on increasing the desired behavior in different realms of the client's life, such as at home, in school, and when visiting with friends, more complicated designs take advantage of such an intervention strategy both to monitor client behavior and to maximize validity for research goals. In the "Next Step House" example at the beginning of the chapter George needs to decide on the best type of single-system design to track his client's progress through the program to see if his or her substance use is decreasing based on the treatment. The type of single-subject design he will need to use will be more complicated to monitor client behavior.

The point is that single-system designs are flexible and adaptive to many practice situations. Taking advantage of this flexibility requires the practitioner to have a clear notion of the problem to be addressed, an understanding of how the proposed intervention is supposed to effect change, and an awareness of strengths and limitations of single-system designs. Once a particular design is chosen, the practitioner can address the next step in the clinical research process—namely, establishing and measuring a baseline.

Establish and Measure the Baseline

Single-system designs are based on the quasi-experimental time-series designs discussed in Chapter 10, but they are modified to make them more appropriate for use with a single subject. As such, single-system designs call for repeated measures of the client's condition so that trends and changes can be noted. Typically, the frequency, intensity, or duration of some behavior of the client is measured, such as how many cigarettes are smoked, severity of pain, or how long a depression lasts.

Thus, the fourth step in the clinical research process is to establish a **baseline**: a series of measurements of the client's condition prior to treatment that form the basis with which to compare the client's condition after treatment is implemented. By comparing measurements after treatment with those from the baseline period, the clinician can trace the effect that the treatment is having. Typically, three measurements are needed, as an absolute minimum, to establish a baseline (Barlow & Hersen, 1973). More measurements are better, especially if the variable's condition is unstable. It is important to note that all single-system designs rule out the simple procedure of using only two measurements—one pretest and one posttest—because this results in a preexperimental design that is extremely weak on internal validity (see Design P1 in Chapter 10).

Figure 11.2 illustrates how baseline measurement can serve as a basis for assessing treatment effects. The hypothetical data show a high level of undesirable client behavior before treatment. After treatment is instigated, however, this level drops sharply. Results are not always as clear and dramatic as these, of course, so making interpretations can be more difficult. (We will deal with the issue of assessing treatment effects in more detail later.)

Two major issues in establishing the baseline are (1) what to measure and (2) how to measure it. Typically, the clinical problem itself suggests the appropriate trait to measure. In general, what we seek to change through treatment is what we need to measure. For example, a child whose problem is disruptive behavior in school could be monitored as to the frequency of disruptions that he or she causes each day. On the other hand, treatment philosophy might suggest monitoring the frequency of *appropriate* behavior as a means not only of measuring behavior but also of setting the stage for change. (As emphasized in Chapter 5, measurement and operational definitions should be deduced from theoretical concepts, whether or not those concepts emerge from research or practice theories.)

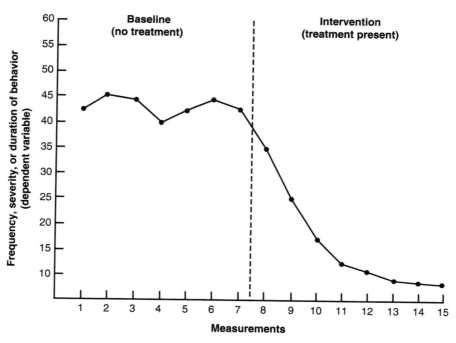

Figure 11.2 Hypothetical baseline followed by successful treatment.

Client problems without specific behavioral outcomes or manifestations are more difficult to measure (Bloom, Fischer, & Orme, 2009). Depression, for example, can be displayed in many different behavioral forms, and in such cases, it is preferable to use several measures. Also, where such an indirect link exists between a concept and behavioral manifestations, multiple indicators help reduce the effects of error in those measures. For depression, we might establish a separate baseline for a behavioral indicator (say, the percentage of the day spent alone), a paper-and-pencil measure of depression, and a self-report from the client for his or her subjective assessment. If the treatment produced positive gains on all measures, then we would have greater evidence for the treatment's effectiveness than if we relied on only one indicator.

Having decided which aspects of the client's condition to measure, we next confront the issue of how to measure them. Basically, the clinician–researcher has four choices: observation, existing records, paper-and-pencil measures, and client self-reports. Of these, observation is of the most general utility and also the most valid and reliable (Weiss & Frohman, 1985).

Unfortunately, many client problems are not directly observable, so there is a limit to the applicability of observation. When it is used, however, there are three important considerations. (These issues regarding observation were discussed in greater detail in Chapter 9.) First, the observations should be unobtrusive. If they are not, then the client may behave differently because of the presence of the observers. This could result in faulty baseline data, which could obscure treatment effects. Practitioner Profile 11.1 illustrates a practical example of how observations can be collected with suicidal ideation measurements. Second, multiple observers should be used where possible to assess the extent of observer reliability. In some cases, videotapes might be substituted for multiple observers, but in natural settings, their use is likely to be difficult. Third, if possible, observers should not be aware of when the treatment actually begins. If they are, their expectations for improvement might affect their objectivity. For example, borderline behaviors that were counted as disruptive during the baseline phase might be ignored during the treatment phase, thus tending to overstate the apparent effectiveness of the treatment to reduce disruptive behavior.

PRACTITIONER PROFILE 11.1 Jessica Krintz, Medical Social Worker, Caldwell County Hospice and Palliative Care in the High Country, North Carolina

Jessica is a medical social worker who works at *Caldwell Hospice Palliative Care* and provides hospice care to those who are terminally ill and who have less than six months to live. Hospice has informal roots but prides itself in keeping the ever-growing costs of healthcare down for patients and their families by keeping patients out of the emergency room and piling up high expenses. She became acquainted with hospice care as an MSW student intern. It was there that she found her passion, and she never looked back.

Jessica's thoughts on research have changed since she was an undergraduate student. Thinking that research classes would never be utilized in practice, she realized that research would become the cornerstone of practice as a medical social worker. She uses the suicide risk assessment, an effective tool, to gauge clients by seeing what level of services and care they need while assessing for risks of suicide. However, assessing suicide can be tricky in hospice care because clients are at the end of their life. Jessica mentions, "You could have a client rate high on the suicide risk assessment, but they are not suicidal because they are dealing with symptoms one has when they know they are going to die" (J. Krintz, personal communication, June 21, 2018). In fact, she states, "A client may say they are ready to die but that does not mean they are going to commit suicide." Jessica makes an excellent point that assessments can only provide so much information. The practitioner needs to take into account not only the assessment, but also the population and client he or she is working with. Beyond assessing for suicide risks, this assessment searches for appropriate resources that best assist patients and their families during their time of need by preserving what's important to them. She also provides spiritual assessments to see their spiritual needs, and financial assessments to see that their financial needs are met.

Jessica mentioned, "Hospice care is continuing to grow and thrive as the costs of end-of-life care continue growing at an *out-of-control* rate." Hospice care's practicality is informed by surveys taken by healthcare providers, members of clergy, and pharmacists who recommend hospice care to those in need. The data collected is instrumental in navigating the direction of care and provides the public with regional rankings of quality. There are growing concerns regarding people whose income is too much to qualify them for Medicaid, yet their age (under 65) disqualifies them from receiving Medicare benefits. The evidence is apparent for this pitfall in the system, and the next step for hospice care research is to slay the gap in society that prohibits those who fall through this gap to qualify for the care they desperately need and deserve.

A second measurement approach is existing records. Some client problems relate to matters on which people other than the clinician or client routinely gather data. For example, existing records, such as grades and school attendance, often are used in assessing a child's school performance. Where existing records are appropriate, they often are a good choice. They also are unobtrusive, because they are collected regardless of whether the client is under treatment. Furthermore, because persons other than the clinician–researcher collected them, time and cost

factors are likely to be favorable. (We reviewed problems associated with using existing records for research purposes in Chapter 8.)

A third common measurement approach is paper-and-pencil measures, which often are useful when the client's problem does not lend itself to direct observation. If the decision is made to use a paper-and-pencil measure, then it is advisable to use an existing one, if available, rather than to devise a new one. In addition to the practical benefits from avoiding the time and trouble of developing a new measure, existing measures usually have established levels of validity and reliability. Furthermore, their use contributes to the accumulation of knowledge, because the standardized measuring devices make for greater comparability across studies. Fortunately, a large number of measures, covering a wide array of client problems, are available. A comprehensive resource for social work researchers seeking screening tools, assessments, and evaluation tools is available online at: https://schoolsocialwork.net/category/interventions. This resource includes a wide variety of tools, many of which have free access. Other sources are available online through Health & Psychosocial Instruments (HaPI) from Ovid Technologies (www.ovid.com). Other compilations of relevant measures include: Fischer and Corcoran (2007), Fredman and Sherman (1987), Groth-Marnat (2009), Miller and Salkind (2002), Spies, Carlson, and Geisinger (2010), and Zalaquett and Wood (1997).

Paper-and-pencil measures have some characteristics, however, that make them less than ideal for use in single-system designs. First, they are obtrusive, because clients obviously know that they are being measured, which can create many problems. For example, completing a questionnaire concerning family relationships might make parents aware that they have been paying less attention to their children than they should, and this awareness could change their behavior. (Recall from Chapter 10 that this is the "testing" threat to internal validity in experiments. Although such change may be desirable, the problem, from a research standpoint, is that it is not possible to determine if the treatment or the measurement process caused the change.)

The second problem with paper-and-pencil measures is that of *demand characteristics* (also discussed in Chapter 10). Clients may deliberately change responses in the direction indicating improvement because of a desire to fulfill the expectations of the clinician. Furthermore, frequent exposure to the measure makes the client familiar with it and raises the specter of multiple-testing effects (see Chapter 10). The same issues appear to apply to computerized administration as well. A study comparing paper-and-pencil testing versus computerized testing found a social desirability effect in web surveys (Morrel-Samuels, 2003), and

that participants are often more honest on computer-based tests, particularly with reporting behaviors which are considered risky (Booth-Kewley, Larson, & Miyoshi, 2007; Locke & Gilbert, 1995) Finally, some paper-and-pencil measures are projective tests, such as the Rorschach Inkblot Test, the Thematic Apperception Test, sentence completion tests, and figure drawings. All these tests rely heavily on the examiner's interpretation of client responses. After reviewing the evidence, Barlow et al. (2009) strongly advise against the use of such measures, because they do not have sufficient validity and reliability to provide a sound basis for single-system experiments.

The last measurement alternative is self-reports by clients who monitor their own behavior or feelings. Although clients' perceptions of their condition are important, many problems are associated with overreliance on self-reports. First, evidence shows that self-reports do not correlate well with objective indicators. For example, studies of assertiveness among female college students have made use of subjects' own reports of how assertive they are as well as trained observers' assessments of how assertively the subjects actually behave. Generally, researchers find that the self-reports do not correlate with the observers' assessments (Frisch & Higgins, 1986).

Second, self-monitoring is reactive, because it sensitizes the client to some aspect of his or her behavior (Hayes, Barlow, & Nelson-Gray, 1999). Research has shown that the mere process of monitoring can change one's behavior. In one study, for example, objective baselines were gathered on how many cigarettes were consumed by a group of smokers (McFall, 1970). Half the subjects were then asked to monitor and record the extent of their smoking; the other half were asked to keep track of the times when they did not smoke. Both groups showed a change from their baseline levels, but in the opposite direction. Those who were monitoring their smoking smoked more, and those who were monitoring their nonsmoking smoked less!

Because of the multitude of problems associated with self-report data, such measurements should be used with caution. Preferably, they should be used as an adjunct to other measures that are less subject to false reports.

Thus, it is evident that some of the measurement options available to clinician–researchers are better than others, so the most objective, valid, and reliable measure available in a given research context should be selected. As noted, direct observation usually is best if the client's problem lends itself to such observation. Otherwise, a more indirect measure is necessary, although these do have limitations. By using multiple measures, however, the weaknesses of the indirect measures can be reduced and the quality of the single-system experiment improved (Gottman, 1985).

Introduce Treatment

Once the baseline is established, the next stage in the clinical research process is to begin treatment. It is important to the clinical research model that only a *single*, coherent treatment be applied (Barlow et al., 2009), because each application of the model is essentially an experiment, with the treatment being the independent variable in that experiment. If more than one treatment is used and the client exhibits a change in behavior compared to the baseline, then we do not know which treatment produced the change and cannot learn anything that might be valuable with similar clients in the future. To assess the effects of the independent variable, we must be able to specify precisely what the treatment consisted of and be consistent in its application during the treatment phase.

The demand for a single, specific treatment is one aspect of the clinical research model that has led to its cold reception in some human service circles, particularly among nonbehaviorists (Nelsen, 1981). Nonbehavioral treatments often lack the specificity that allows practitioners to trace a particular treatment over the period of the treatment phase. In addition, nonbehavioral treatments can be very complex and may even mix a number of treatment modes, making it difficult to identify the precise factors that presumably resulted in change. This is less a criticism of the clinical research model, however, than it is a challenge to those using nonbehavioral treatments: "[Nonbehaviorists] must work hard at choosing interventions that may be effective and

at defining their interventions precisely, preferably by addressing both what they do and how they do it" (Nelsen, 1981, p. 35).

Resistance to the discipline imposed by the clinical research model appears to be greatest among those who are least familiar with it. After some initial frustration with the specificity and single treatment required by the model, practitioners learning to apply the model generally come to accept it (Johnson, 1981). They appreciate that the model increases rationality in the selection of treatments, forces explicit consideration of the assumptions on which treatment is based, and requires specific practice skills rather than reliance solely on intuition or ingenuity. The greatest satisfaction, however, comes from the fact that the model provides solid evidence regarding whether the client benefited from treatment. Although it is rewarding to feel that one has been of assistance, it is even more rewarding to have objective evidence to support those feelings.

During the treatment phase, the measurement of the client's condition, started during the baseline phase, continues to track what changes—if any—the treatment is producing in the client's condition. It is crucial that the conditions under which measurements are made during the treatment phase remain consistent with those under which the baseline measurements were obtained. Any change in such things as observers, settings, examiners, or instructions could confound apparent treatment effects. Remember that a single-system design is an experiment, and only one variable—the treatment—should be allowed to change from one phase to another.

Assess Treatment Effects

When is a treatment judged to be effective? This seemingly simple question, which is addressed in the last stage of the clinical research process, has a surprisingly complex answer. Assessing the effectiveness of a treatment depends, first, on the pattern produced during the baseline measurements: The ease and clarity with which baseline measures can be compared with treatment measures depends, in part, on the *stability* of the baseline measures.

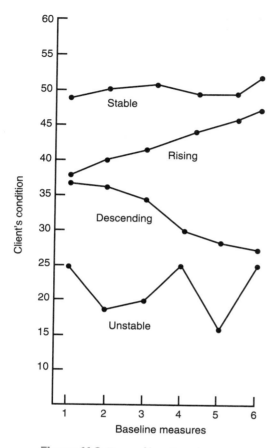

Figure 11.3 Types of baseline patterns.

Figure 11.3 illustrates four possible baseline patterns: (1) stable, (2) rising (client worsening), (3) descending (client improving), and (4) unstable. In this discussion of baseline stability, we will assume that lower measurement scores represent improvement, as in the case of reducing the incidence of some problem behavior. If, however, the goal of treatment is to increase some aspect of client functioning, as it often is, then higher measurement scores indicate improvement. A stable baseline is the ideal, because then, posttreatment comparisons readily reveal treatment effects. If the treatment is helpful, we see a pronounced downward move in measurement levels. A treatment producing negative effects yields an upward move in measurement levels. Little change from baseline levels reveals an ineffective treatment. The value of

a stable baseline is that it allows all three possible treatment outcomes to be readily noted.

Unfortunately, client conditions often are not stable but, instead, worsen, improve, or vary considerably. Assessing treatment effects with baselines like these is more difficult and often puts limits on what we can infer. A baseline with a rising trend (client worsening) is not too problematic, because an effective treatment will produce a reversal of the baseline trend. Such a change provides strong evidence that the treatment was effective. With ineffective or harmful treatments, however, it is difficult to tell if this is just a continuation of the baseline trend (ineffective treatment) or if the continued deterioration is the result of some harmful treatment. A baseline with a descending trend (client improving) has the opposite effect. If the treatment proves to be harmful, then the trend reverses, and the negative effect becomes readily apparent. If the client continues to improve during treatment, however, then it is unclear whether the treatment produced that improvement (effective treatment) or whether it was just a continuation of the baseline trend (ineffective treatment).

The unstable baseline is the most troublesome. With the client's condition changing from one measurement to another, it becomes difficult to identify changes that result from treatment. A couple of strategies do exist, however, for dealing with an unstable baseline (Barlow et al., 2009). One extends the period of baseline measurements with the hope that a stable pattern will emerge—with, of course, no guarantee of stabilization. In addition, we may find practical as well as ethical constraints on how long treatment can be postponed while awaiting baseline stability. A second strategy is the application of statistical techniques that can reveal trends and differences between pretreatment and posttreatment measures that are too subtle to be noted by visual inspection (Achen, 1986; Gottman, 1981). These statistics have limited effectiveness, however, if the pattern is extremely unstable.

The use of statistics to assess treatment effects also raises a problem beyond that of baseline stability—namely, how much change is necessary before we can say that a treatment is effective. From a research perspective, any change from pretest to posttest measures is evidence that the treatment was effective in the sense of bringing about change in the dependent variable. In clinical settings, however, change can take the form of improvement or deterioration in a client's status. Practitioners seek improvement, of course, so treatment effectiveness in single-system designs normally is defined as an improvement in performance after treatment. Yet, assessing whether improvement has occurred is complex, because effectiveness can be based on three different criteria: therapeutic, experimental, or statistical.

A treatment is *therapeutically effective* when it leads clients to fully achieve the goals that have been set for them: The disruptive student is no longer disruptive, the underachiever is now achieving, or the teenage mother can care for her infant independently. When treatment produces these kinds of improvements, its effectiveness is obvious. Visual inspection of the measurements taken during the treatment phase clearly reveals the improvement when compared with the baseline measurements.

A treatment is *experimentally effective* when it produces a pronounced improvement in the client's condition even though the ultimate goals have not been reached. For example, a claustrophobic person may have come to the point where he or she can use an elevator when alone but remains unable to use an elevator that is crowded. As with therapeutic effectiveness, the change in the client's condition from the baseline to the treatment phase is sufficiently dramatic that visual inspection normally reveals it.

Figure 11.4 displays two data plots from single-system designs conducted in a school classroom. In the first case, the teacher monitored disruptive classroom behavior. The second case represents a child in kindergarten who had difficulty adjusting to school; the problem was monitored by counting the number of requests that she made during school to go home. These cases illustrate two criteria for establishing experimental effectiveness (Kazdin, 2010). The first case has nonoverlapping data. All the measurements taken during the treatment phase are higher or lower (whichever direction represents improvement) than those taken during the baseline phase. Stated another way, performance during treatment does not overlap with that of the baseline period. This is a fairly severe guideline—and one that, if met,

is a strong demonstration of experimental effectiveness. The criterion achieved by the second case is somewhat less rigorous: All the measurements taken during the treatment phase are higher or lower than the *average* level of the baseline. This guideline is preferable if the baseline is not especially stable, but it is important to emphasize that these are only guidelines, not rigid rules. Quite possibly, a given single-system experiment could evidence clear experimental effectiveness and achieve neither of these guidelines. Following them, however, does make visual inspection more systematic and less a matter of judgment on the part of the clinician–researcher.

Statistical effectiveness is achieved when the treatment produces statistically significant improvement in the client's condition. In other words, the difference between baseline and treatment levels is sufficiently large that it is not likely to be caused by chance variation. (We will discuss the concept of statistical significance in detail in Chapter 15.) In addition to the magnitude of the difference between baseline and intervention, the number of observations in each phase also determines statistical significance—that is, more is better. So, assuming a relatively large number of observations in each phase—say, 20 or more—statistics may be sufficiently sensitive to detect smaller changes than visual inspection can. With many observations in each phase, statistical effectiveness sometimes requires the least improvement in the client to detect change.

This raises the issue of the difference between statistical significance and therapeutic or experimental significance. A treatment judged to be effective because it produced a statistically significant improvement in the client might be a near failure according to the other criteria. The reason for this is that, in some cases having to do with the peculiarities of statistical analysis, small differences between two measurements can produce a statistically significant result. For example, reducing a juvenile fire-starter's behavior from seven episodes a week to five might be a statistically significant reduction, but we would not likely consider this to be a success from a therapeutic or an experimental perspective. Because statistical significance may be only remotely related to treatment success, statistical analysis is most useful in cases with an unstable baseline, where visual analysis is difficult.

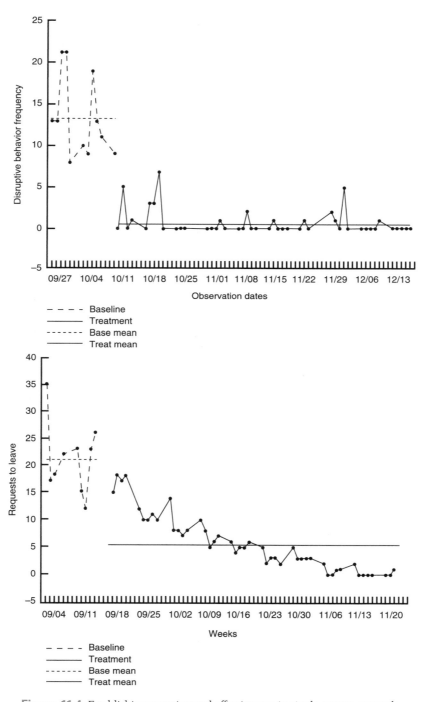

Figure 11.4 Establishing experimental effectiveness in single-system research.

So, the question of treatment effectiveness depends, in part, on the particular criterion of effectiveness that is applied. With the varying criteria, it is important to be aware of their differences and to be precise when discussing what we mean by effectiveness. Furthermore, it is important to recognize that the effect of a treatment may be relatively permanent or may decrease after the treatment is withdrawn. To test for this, the posttreatment measurements become, in effect, a new baseline. Deviation from this baseline as time passes suggests a limit to how long the treatment is effective.

TYPES OF SINGLE-SYSTEM DESIGNS

Although numerous types of single-system designs exist, all involve repeated measurements during the baseline and treatment phases and a comparison across phases as evidence of treatment effects. The designs differ in the number of phases involved, the number of treatments applied, and the number of baselines employed. Perhaps the most important differences, however, are in the internal validity of the designs. Some are more capable of providing evidence for the effect of a treatment when such an effect actually exists. Ideally, of course, clinician–researchers should select the most valid design that fits their particular case (see the discussions of validity in Chapters 5 and 10).

Single-Treatment Designs

The Basic AB Design. It has become customary to present single-system designs by using the first letters of the alphabet to symbolize various phases of the design. The letter *A* signifies a phase in which the client is not receiving treatment. This is the baseline period in all designs, but in some of the more complex designs, it also can refer to a period of treatment withdrawal. The letter *B* indicates a treatment phase during which some specific intervention is in progress. Subsequent letters of the alphabet (*C*, *D*, and so on) symbolize the application of treatments different from *B*.

The *AB design* is the simplest of the single-system designs and forms the basis for the others. It consists of one baseline phase followed by one treatment phase. Treatment effectiveness is determined by comparing the client's condition during treatment with that of the baseline. The basic *AB* design is less than ideal, because its validity is threatened by history: Events other than the

intervention could be responsible for the change in the client. Despite its limitations, however, the *AB* design provides better evidence of treatment effects than nonexperimental case histories do. The *AB* design also has the advantage of applying to most clinical situations, especially cases where more rigorous designs might be precluded.

Reversal and Withdrawal Designs. The *AB* design can be strengthened substantially by moving to a *reversal design* or *withdrawal design*, so called because, after one treatment phase, the treatment is interrupted for a period of time. Some sources distinguish between a withdrawal design (in which the treatment stops entirely after the first intervention phase) and a reversal design (in which the treatment is transferred to a different behavior). For example, a juvenile in a residential facility may participate in a token economy study on completing math homework. After a baseline period, he receives tokens each day for an intervention period based on the number of math problems he completes. In a withdrawal design, giving tokens is terminated (withdrawn) for another baseline. If a reversal design is used, tokens might be made contingent on a different behavior (reversed), such as pages of English read, while the number of math problems completed continues to be monitored for the study. We use the term *reversal design* to apply to both approaches in this discussion. There are basically two versions of the reversal design: *ABA* and *ABAB*. They differ only in that the *ABA* design ends in a no-treatment phase, whereas the *ABAB* design ends with the treatment being reintroduced (see Figure 11.5).

The value of reversal designs stems from their ability to demonstrate more conclusively that the treatment (not some extraneous factor) is producing change in the client's condition. If the client's condition deteriorates when the treatment is withdrawn, then we have evidence that the treatment is the controlling factor. Even more evidence is provided with the *ABAB* design if the reintroduction of the treatment coincides with renewed improvement of the client. Although it is possible for a set of extraneous factors to produce the first client improvement, it is less likely that the same set of factors would recur at precisely the right time to

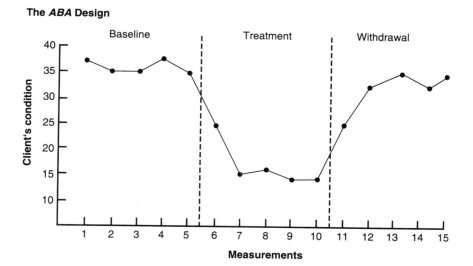

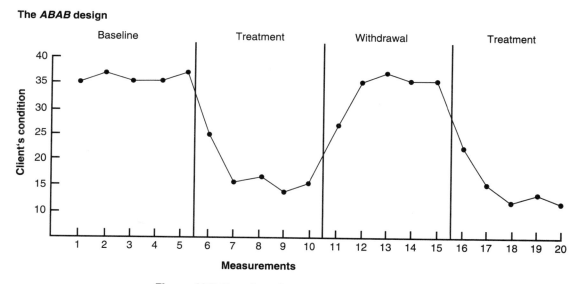

Figure 11.5 Hypothetical examples of reversal designs.

produce the client improvement after reintroduction of the treatment. As Figure 11.5 illustrates, especially with the *ABAB* design, we have great confidence in the efficacy of a treatment that produces similar real-life results. In certain circumstances, the design can be expanded to include even more phases.

Despite their strengths in terms of internal validity, reversal designs often find their use restricted because of practical considerations.

First, treatments that produce permanent changes in clients—often the goal of intervention—are not reversible. For example, if the treatment involves the clients' learning of something, they obviously cannot "unlearn" it at the command of the clinician–researcher. In such cases, reversal designs simply are not applicable. Second, it might be unwise or unethical to attempt to return clients to their pretreatment states; an obvious example would be a case where the suicidal tendencies of a client were alleviated. It is up to the clinician–researcher to decide on a case-by-case basis whether a reversal design is ethically justified.

Multiple-Baseline Designs. The *multiple-baseline design* involves establishing baselines for more than one aspect of a client's condition. Multiple baselines can be established for multiple behaviors, for one behavior in different settings, or for multiple clients who suffer from the same problem. For example, a practitioner working with several alcoholics might establish separate baselines for each, thus applying the multiple-baseline design across individuals. Although it is recommended that a minimum of three baselines be used, clinician–researchers should not be deterred from using only two if conditions do not permit more. The more baselines, however, the stronger the design becomes in terms of internal validity (Barlow et al., 2009).

The multiple-baseline design is essentially a stacked set of *AB* designs, with the same treatment introduced sequentially into each of the baseline conditions:

First client: A_1B
Second client: A_1A_2B
Third client: $A_1A_2A_3B$

In the illustration, the initial baseline measurement (A_1) is made on each client, and then the treatment is introduced to the first client only. A second baseline measurement is taken from the remaining two clients, and then the treatment is introduced to the second client. A third baseline measurement is taken from the third client, who then also receives the treatment. Figure 11.6 illustrates the multiple-baseline design with a successful outcome. In each of the three conditions, the introduction of the treatment is followed by improvement.

The multiple-baseline design is fairly strong on internal validity. The efficacy of the treatment is assessed across three or more behaviors, settings, or individuals. Furthermore, sequential introduction of treatments makes it highly unlikely that extraneous factors could account for apparent treatment effects across the several baseline conditions. Thus, the multiple-baseline design generally is superior to the *AB* design, but the *AB* design with replication also overcomes some of the threats to

internal validity, such as history (Harris & Jenson, 1985). The multiple-baseline design is not as strong on internal validity as reversal designs are, but where reversal designs are inappropriate, the multiple-baseline design is a good alternative.

Multiple-baseline designs can provide strong evidence for the validity of single-system outcomes, as Research in Practice 11.1 and 11.2 illustrates. They do have weaknesses, however. The seepage of treatment effects from one setting to another is a major limitation of the multiple-baseline design. The behaviors, settings, or individuals traced by the several baselines must be relatively independent, or else the treatment effects in one condition can produce changes in other, as-yet-untreated conditions. For example, it would be unwise to attempt a multiple-baseline design with members of the same family. Because of their routine interaction, treatment applied to one family member could affect the others. If the baseline conditions are highly interrelated, then the treatment will show effects after the initial introduction not only in the condition where it is applied but also in one or more of the other conditions. If interrelatedness is sufficiently severe, the power of the multiple-baseline design can be destroyed, rendering it little more than an *AB* design with multiple indicators.

The multiple-baseline design also can reveal *contravariation*: positive changes in one area but negative changes in another (Jayaratne & Levy, 1979). For example, a person with co-occurring substance use disorders might respond to treatment by reducing the intake of one substance but increasing the intake of another. If we traced only one drug, perhaps the most dangerous, then the contravariation would remain undetected. A multiple-baseline design covering all the drugs used, however, would readily reveal such an occurrence.

Specialized Designs

The designs we have just discussed comprise the simplest—and most generally useful—single-system designs, and they have in common the use of only a single treatment (although applied more than once in the *ABAB* design). Some situations, however, call for variations of these simpler designs to handle special problems. So many complex and

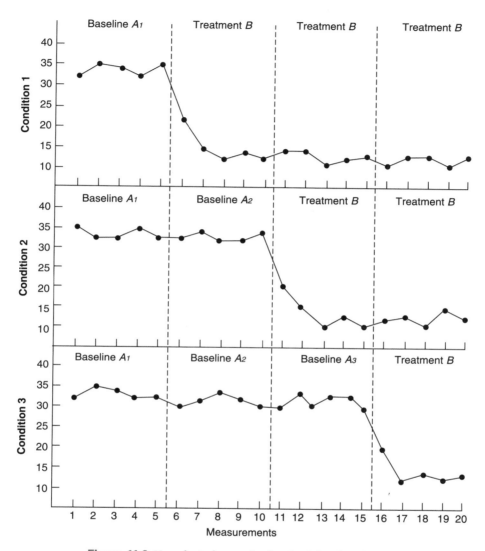

Figure 11.6 Hypothetical example of multiple baseline design.

specialized designs exist that we can touch on only a few of them here.

Multiple-Treatment Designs. In some settings, the practitioner may need to apply several treatments before finding an effective one. By an extension of the reversal designs, *multiple treatments* can be accommodated. A fairly simple extension is the *ABA-C-A* design. It should be apparent that the *ABA* segment comprises a basic reversal design. To that is added a second

treatment phase with treatment *C* instead of treatment *B*, and then another return-to-baseline phase. This design can be extended to include as many treatments as a given case requires. One important limitation of this design is that, if both treatments show some effect, it is not possible to determine which is the most effective (Barlow et al., 2009). The culprit is history, because extraneous variables occurring during the *B* phase cannot be assumed to be the same as those occurring during the *C* phase.

RESEARCH IN PRACTICE 11.1 Practice Effectiveness: Evidence-Based Practice Through Single-System Designs

The evidence-based practice literature emphasizes randomized controlled trials (RCTs) as the "gold standard" for demonstrating program effectiveness (Nezu & Nezu, 2008). However, some human service practice problems do not lend themselves to evaluation by this method. Consider the case of children who are visually impaired and have additional disabilities. Visual impairment is a low-incidence condition and the additional disabilities they have can be highly varied (Ferrell, 2000). Such heterogeneity of disabilities and the geographic dispersion of cases make achieving the sample size necessary for an RCT improbable.

One viable option for practitioners with visually impaired clients would be to rely on single-system designs as a means of building a knowledge base for practice. Parker, Grimmett, and Summers (2008) demonstrated the feasibility of this approach by conducting a literature review similar to what one might find in a Campbell Collaboration review, but focusing specifically on single-system design studies on visually impaired children with additional disabilities. They located 30 studies that matched their search criteria.

They began with three research questions:

1. What studies used single-system research in communication instruction for children with visual impairments, including deaf and blind?
2. What practices and interventions were found to be effective?
3. Are there patterns of replication among the identified studies?

In Research in Practice 12.1, we present a guide, based on the elements of experimental designs, for evaluating the worthiness of evidence from research. Because the research considered here is single-system design and not RCTs, that study assessment guide and others developed by such organizations as the Campbell or Cochrane collaborations cannot be employed to rate the quality of these studies. The researchers turned to an assessment scheme developed specifically for rating single-system designs from the field of special education (Horner, Carr, Halle, Odom, & Wolery, 2005). This guide includes some features that one would use for any effectiveness evaluation, such as:

- Is there sufficient detail in the description of the participants and the setting to permit replication?
- Is the dependent variable operationally well defined?
- Is the independent variable (the program) described sufficiently for replication?
- Is the independent variable manipulated by and under the control of the experimenter?

Other assessment considerations are unique to a single-system design, such as:

- Is the dependent variable measured repeatedly over time?
- Does the design provide at least three demonstrations of experimental effect at three different points in time? For example, is there a change from baseline to treatment, treatment back to a second baseline, and again with another treatment?
- Does the particular design control well the threats to internal validity and does the pattern of results demonstrate experimental control?

(continued)

In order for a practice to have been demonstrated effective, experimental control must be demonstrated across a range of studies, researchers, and participants. The guide developers proposed that a practice could be deemed "evidence based" when it meets three criteria:

1. A minimum of five single-system studies meeting the evaluation criteria had been published in peer-reviewed journals.
2. The studies were conducted by at least three different investigators at three different geographic locations.
3. The five or more studies include a combined total of at least 20 participants.

By employing criteria tailored to the unique features of single-system designs, the authors were able to make a convincing case that visually impaired students with multiple disabilities can develop communication skills and identify promising interventions. They demonstrated that single-system designs can serve as a bridge for bringing scientifically based practices to special populations for which traditional experimentation is not feasible.

RESEARCH IN PRACTICE 11.2 Practice Effectiveness: A Multiple-Baseline Evaluation of Treating Panic Disorder

"It just happened . . . I was walking and all of a sudden my heart started to beat fast and I started to sweat . . . I didn't know what was going on . . . I just felt weird . . . that something bad was happening to me but I didn't know what."
                                   —Quoted in Ollendick (1995, p. 517)

These are the words of a 14-year-old adolescent describing her first panic attack, a condition that is characterized by periods of intense fear or discomfort in which certain somatic and cognitive symptoms develop abruptly. Imagine the concern that such experiences raise for a person, wondering what caused it and when it might happen again, as well as suffering the embarrassment of behaving in such a bizarre manner.

One research project set out to evaluate the effectiveness of cognitive behavioral treatments on panic disorders in adolescents. The researcher chose the multiple-baseline design because it is superior to the *AB* design in reducing the threat of history while still providing a detailed record of individual process through treatment (Ollendick, 1995). The particular research design was a multiple-baseline across subjects. Four adolescents who were being seen at an outpatient clinic specializing in anxiety disorders of children and adolescents participated in the study. The subjects were evaluated on several screening instruments, and each met full criteria for panic disorder with agoraphobia (Ollendick, 1995, p. 517). They reported that "they sometimes felt really scared, for no reason at all, that out of the blue they felt really scared and that they didn't know why," and that there were places that they didn't want to go because they were afraid they "would get scared all of a sudden and couldn't get help or get away" (Ollendick, 1995, p. 517), The researchers hypothesized that the cognitive behavioral treatments found to be effective among adults in treating such conditions also would prove to be effective with adolescents.

(continued)

Multiple measures were used to assess the effectiveness of treatment. One indicator was the frequency of panic attacks. The adolescents were asked to monitor the date, duration, location, circumstance, and symptoms experienced. This provided a weekly measure for the frequency of panic attacks. Another indicator was self-efficacy in coping with three potential agoraphobic situations that were included in one of the screening tests used during assessment. Subjects were asked to rate from 1 to 5 how sure they were that they could cope with situations (1 = not at all sure, 5 = definitely sure). The third indicator was the adolescents' rating of the extent to which they had actually avoided agoraphobic situations, such as going to school, being in an auditorium, or going to restaurants. All indicators were modeled on measures found in the existing literature (Clum, 1990; Rapee, Craske, & Barlow, 1990).

Baseline measures were obtained for one week for subject 1, for two weeks for subject 2, three weeks for subject 3, and four weeks for subject 4. Following baseline, a treatment regimen began that included providing information on the nature of panic attacks and training in progressive muscle relaxation and proper breathing techniques. The adolescents were taught to use positive self-statements and cognitive coping strategies. Later sessions involved *in vivo* exposure to the situations that had aroused panic symptoms. The actual length of treatment varied from one subject to another, based on the termination criterion of two consecutive weeks with an absence of attacks. Brief maintenance sessions were held at two weeks and at one month following treatment, with a systematic follow-up at six months posttreatment.

Each way of assessing the effectiveness of the intervention (frequency of attacks, agoraphobic avoidance, and self-efficacy) was a dependent variable, and each produced a set of data plots that looked like Figure 11.6. If there were three subjects in the design, then Condition 1, 2, and 3 in Figure 11.6 would represent Subject 1, 2, and 3. The resulting data plots provided positive evidence that the treatment was effective in eliminating panic attacks. The project illustrates several points about using single-system designs in support of practice:

- Ollendick relied on the empirical literature to identify promising intervention methods. The literature helped him devise measurement strategies consistent with previous research and likely to be reliable and valid.
- Flexibility of the single-system design permitted this researcher to avoid interference with treatment and permitted documentation of the progress of each case while demonstrating that the intervention was the most likely cause of change.
- By using standardized tests before and after treatment, and at the six-month follow-up, the researcher obtained independent, supporting evidence that corroborated the multiple-baseline data. Alone, such pretest/posttest data are weak, but using them in combination with the multiple-baseline strategy strengthened the project as a whole.

Special designs also can be used when treatments are not applied individually but, rather, in combination to assess the relative effects of the components of the treatment package. The *ABAB-BC-B-BC* design, a complex extension of the reversal designs, accomplishes this. The first part, *ABAB*, is one of the basic reversal designs and provides a strong demonstration of effects of component *B*. The *BC-B-BC* segment indicates the effects of component *C* beyond those of component *B* alone. This design can, of course, be further extended to indicate additional treatments. Because both design extensions are based on reversal designs, however, they cannot be used with treatments that are irreversible or unethical to reverse.

Changing-Criterion Designs. Another specialized design with considerable utility is the *changing-criterion design* (Barlow et al., 2009). With this design, the goal, or criterion, of success changes over time as the client is led to attainment of the final treatment goal in stages—that is, by achieving a series of subgoals.

For example, a smoker can be brought to the final goal of abstinence through phased withdrawal. Figure 11.7 illustrates what a successful application of such treatment with a changing-criterion design might look like. Following the baseline measurement of cigarettes smoked per day, treatment begins. For example, assume the treatment consists of reinforcement. During the first treatment phase, the client is reinforced for achieving the first subgoal—say, a reduction of eight cigarettes per day. In the second treatment phase, reinforcement is received for achieving a reduction of an additional eight cigarettes—the second subgoal. The third treatment phase requires another reduction to receive the reinforcement. The process continues until the client progresses through the subgoals and achieves the final goal of no longer smoking.

The changing-criterion design is related to the multiple-baseline design. In the multiple-baseline design, intervention is independently implemented in relatively distinct areas of the subject's environment. In the changing-criterion design, each time a subgoal is achieved and a new, more stringent subgoal is established, the preceding level essentially becomes a new baseline from which further improvement is measured. Like the multiple-baseline design, the changing criterion design provides greater evidence for treatment effectiveness than the simple *AB* design. Each time the treatment leads to achievement of another subgoal, further evidence of its effectiveness is obtained. The only major limitation associated with the changing-criterion design is that it can be applied only to client problems that can be meaningfully broken up into subgoals.

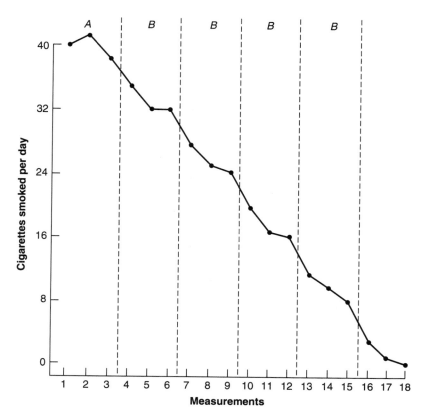

Figure 11.7 Hypothetical example of the changing criterion design applied to phased withdrawal of smoking.

GENERALIZABILITY OF SINGLE-SYSTEM DESIGNS

To build a knowledge base for clinical practice, researchers must have findings that can be generalized to a wide variety of situations and cases. Of course, *one* successful single-system experiment has little generalizability beyond that particular case. Despite success and hard evidence to prove that the treatment produced change, there is no assurance that the same treatment would be effective with other clients, in different settings, or when used by another practitioner. This lack of generalizability, however, does not detract from the value of single-system experiments, because generalizability can be achieved through replication. It requires many replications before we develop a knowledge base concerning which clients can be helped by which treatment, which settings it will work in, and what the clinician must do to apply it successfully. This is a process of slow accretion, because each replication provides a little more knowledge concerning the extent of generalizability of treatment effectiveness.

It is valuable in this context to make a distinction between *direct replication* and *systematic replication*. **Direct replication** involves the repeated application of the same treatment by the same clinician to clients who are suffering from the same basic problem. In direct replication, only the individual clients vary; all other conditions remain constant. Direct replication serves two important functions: First, it increases confidence in the reliability of the findings. For example, a clinician with a series of successes in treating clients with claustrophobia will have far greater confidence in the effectiveness of the treatment than they did after success with the first case. Second, direct replication builds generalizability across clients. As the treatment repeatedly proves effective with additional clients, we discover that the initial success was not a fluke. Direct replication is the beginning of establishing the generalizability of a treatment. It cannot, however, answer questions concerning generalizability across settings, practitioners, or other client problems.

Systematic replication is the attempt to extend a treatment to different settings, practitioners, or client disorders by varying one of these conditions or any combination of them. It normally is conducted after there is evidence from direct replication that the treatment may work. For example, the clinician mentioned earlier with the successful history of intervention with claustrophobics might begin systematic replication by applying the treatment to agoraphobics. If this is successful, it indicates that the treatment is generalizable to a different client disorder from that with which success originally was obtained. Additional replications that vary settings and clinicians would, of course, be required to establish generalizability across these conditions.

A study of using biofeedback to treat depression (Earnest, 1999) provides an example of a successful systematic replication involving different clients. The investigator presented examples of earlier case studies that demonstrated the effectiveness of electroencephalographic (EEG) biofeedback training for treating depression in adults. In this case, the intervention method was successfully extended to an adolescent client. Systematic replication with different clients and different therapists also was illustrated by a study on verbal self-guidance (Martini & Polatajko, 1998). Those authors reported that this intervention had been useful in helping children with developmental coordination disorder. They successfully replicated the intervention using a different therapist and four different children, thus adding further evidence indicating the potential of this intervention for effective treatment. When the same treatment proves to be effective in a replication with so many differences from a previous situation, it suggests that the treatment may have broad generalizability. Many more successful replications, of course, are needed before the parameters of effectiveness for this or any other treatment can be firmly established.

When single-system experiments and their replications are conducted, two practices are crucial. First, substantial information about client characteristics and backgrounds should be collected to serve as *control variables* in assessing the complex effects that treatment can have on dependent variables. The necessity for this arises from the fact that replications often show treatment is not consistently effective or ineffective. The background information may be useful in sorting out the reasons for these mixed results. A simple example would be a treatment that was effective with men but either ineffective or less effective with women.

A second essential practice is that treatments be kept uniform from case to case so that the results of replications are truly comparable. In addition, reports must be clear and include all information relevant to future replication efforts. At the outset, we noted that one source of dissatisfaction with traditional case histories is the tendency of such reports to be too vague to allow replication. The full potential of single-system experiments will not be realized if reports include inadequate information for sound replication.

ASSESSMENT OF THE CLINICAL RESEARCH MODEL

Advantages

Promotes Better Service for Clients. The requisites of the clinical research model—careful assessment of treatment goals, use of specific treatments, and continuous monitoring of client progress—promote more effective treatment for clients and encourage the use of scientifically tested intervention strategies. The model encourages the application of specific practice skills in a systematic and rational fashion rather than a reliance on personal idiosyncrasy, intuition, or vague and shifting treatment efforts. Furthermore, the model promotes consideration of the assumptions underlying various treatment approaches, such as why a given treatment should produce positive results with a particular case. The net result is an increased likelihood that a successful intervention will be selected and that the client will be helped.

Promotes Research Activity. The merger of practice and research in the clinical research model allows practitioners to conduct research when they otherwise might not do so. For obvious and practical reasons, the opportunities for most human service practitioners to be involved in traditional group research are limited. The clinical research model, however, makes each client a possible subject for a single-system experiment. In addition, single-system research is more practical for the typical clinician, because it is research on a small scale,

involving minimal cost and avoiding the complexities of group research. Furthermore, involvement in single-system research can enhance the status of the practitioner, because the results often can be published. On a broader scale, increased research activity can promote the image of the human services as scientifically based professions.

Results Are of Both Immediate and Future Value. The clinical research model provides hard evidence for a client's progress, which is of immediate value to the practitioner. Tracking progress aids in the selection and application of effective treatments. After successful treatment, the data provide a clear demonstration that the client has been helped. In this age of increasing accountability, vague feelings of having helped clients—or even client testimonials—are no longer adequate. To document that intervention does work, critics increasingly demand scientifically based evidence, and single-system experiments hold the promise of providing that evidence.

Disadvantages

Impracticality. Under current practice conditions, application of the clinical research model often may be impractical. Some of the most rigorous of the single-system designs, such as the reversal designs, are especially difficult to apply, because irreversible treatments and ethical considerations may preclude their use. Furthermore, some designs contain many phase segments that may require too much time to complete. Beyond these problems is the fact that some client disorders call for immediate attention, precluding the baseline measurements so crucial to single-system designs.

Limited Generalizability of Results. As noted, results from one single-system experiment have virtually no generalizability beyond that particular case, and they provide less-powerful tests of therapeutic effects than traditional group experiments do. Generalizability is obtained only through successful replication across clients, settings, disorders, and practitioners. This is a slow process, and the potential of single-system research to increase the knowledge base of the profession will not be realized quickly.

REVIEW AND CRITICAL THINKING

Main Points

- Single-system designs are quasi-experimental designs that are used to trace changes induced by treatments to individual clients in a clinical setting.
- Interest in single-system designs developed out of dissatisfaction with group experiments and case histories as sources of knowledge useful in clinical settings.
- The clinical research model using single-system designs is not a radical departure from traditional clinical practice but, rather, an effort to increase the specificity and objectivity of practice and to enhance opportunities for replication and knowledge accumulation.
- Although we have many specific single-system designs from which to choose, all involve a series of pretreatment measures (the baseline) and a series of posttreatment measures that are then compared with the baseline.
- Measurements typically consist of observations, available records, paper-and-pencil measures, or self-reports; observations usually are the most desirable and self-reports the least desirable.
- Effectiveness may be judged against three different standards— therapeutic, experimental, or statistical—with therapeutic effectiveness demanding the greatest client improvement and statistical effectiveness the least.
- The simple *AB* design is highly flexible, but it is not strong on internal validity.
- Reversal designs, such as *ABA* or *ABAB,* are strong on internal validity but often impractical to apply.
- Multiple-baseline designs are quite strong on internal validity and are reasonably flexible, making them a good choice when a reversal design cannot be used.
- In addition to these basic designs, many specialized designs can accommodate such things as changing treatments, combined treatments, or phased achievement of the treatment goal.
- Positive results from one single-system experiment are not generalizable, but generalizability can be built up over time through replication.
- Computer software can simplify and speed both the visual and statistical analyses of data from single-system research.

IMPORTANT TERMS FOR REVIEW

Baseline	Direct replication	Single-system designs
Clinical research model	Empirical practice model	Systematic replication

CRITICAL THINKING

Single-system designs permit the practitioner to more systematically assess the nature of problems presented by clients and to monitor and evaluate the outcome of an intervention with a particular client. The chapter distinguishes between therapeutic, experimental, and statistical significance and also discusses some of the threats to validity posed by single-system designs. The following are critical thinking questions raised at the beginning of the chapter and some ideas for how they relate to social work practice. Students are encouraged to develop their own answers to these questions.

Why is it important to understand how to conduct single-subject designs? For social researchers, single-subject design becomes a great alternative to track clients' behavioral change when they have low numbers of participants. This becomes an excellent tool to evaluate clients and provide evidence to help guide practice decisions.

How can using single-subject design help you understand your clients better? In single-subject design, multiple measures are gathered over a time period looking at a particular target problem. Collecting this information provides practitioners with evidence on how their clients are responding to treatment and helps guide future decisions.

What are different social service settings where single-subject design would be appropriate to utilize? Social researchers work with many different systems from micro to macro. Single-subject design works well with either micro or mezzo systems. Practitioners can implement single-subject design as part of their own clinical practice with individual clients and also within a family system. All participants in single-subject design have their own objectives and target problems.

EVALUATING COMPETENCY (FROM THE COUNCIL ON SOCIAL WORK EDUCATION [CSWE] 2015 EDUCATIONAL POLICY AND ACCREDITATION STANDARDS [EPAS])

Competency 2: Engaging Diversity and Difference in Practice

- How might understanding how to conduct single-subject design help with marginalized and oppressed populations?

Competency 9: Evaluated Practice With Individuals, Families, Groups, Organizations, and Communities

- What challenges might a social researcher face when conducting single -ubject design with individuals?

SELF-ASSESSMENT

1. In single-system design, identifying problems refers to:
   a. An aspect of the client's functioning: behaviors, perceptions, attitudes, or feelings.
   b. What area the client tells you he or she wants to work on.
   c. An ambiguous understanding of the client's problem.
   d. A sensed problem the social researcher has before talking to the client.
2. In single-system design, establishing goals refers to which of the following?
   a. Goals should be loosely defined and flexible.
   b. Goals should be specific, precisely defined, and measurable.
   c. The client and not the social researcher should set goals.
   d. Goals are not important in single-system design.
3. In single-system design, assess treatment effect involves:
   a. Inconsistent assessment of participants through all phases.
   b. Assessment that changes throughout different phases of single-system design.
   c. Assessment that will change based on participant input.
   d. Continuous assessment regarding stability in the baseline phase and how this compares to the treatment phases.
4. What are the different types of single-system designs?
   a. AD, AB, and ABAD designs
   b. ABAB and multiple-ABAB
   c. AB, ABAB, and multiple-baseline designs
   d. ABC, ABAC, and multiple
5. Establishing the baseline refers to:
   a. A series of measurements of the client's behavior prior to treatment, which form the basis for comparison to the treatment.
   b. A series of measurements based on the client's memory recall of events that happened before the treatment.
   c. Multiple measurements, which take place after the treatment is finished.
   d. Multiple measurements based on the client's understanding of a behavior.
6. Generalizability of single-system design:
   a. Is non-existent because of small sample sizes.
   b. Involves direct replication and systematic replication.
   c. Is easy to obtain in single-system designs.
   d. Involves direct generalizability and systematic generalizability.
7. In an ABAB design the withdrawal phase:
   a. Happens after the intervention phase, at which point the treatment is completely taken away.
   b. Is where the client goes through withdrawals.
   c. Is where the client withdraws from the study.
   d. Happens before the baseline phase.

8. In single-system design, introducing treatment refers to:
   a. The phase where multiple behaviors are measured at once.
   b. The phase that follows baseline where treatment is introduced in the design and a single behavior is measured.
   c. The phase where a general treatment is applied.
   d. A phase where the client controls what treatment he or she wants applied.

9. In an ABAB design who acts as the control?
   a. The social researcher
   b. The observer
   c. The client
   d. Participants in the randomly assigned group

10. In single-system design, systematic replication refers to:
   a. The attempt to extend a treatment to different settings, practitioners, or client disorders by varying one of these conditions.
   b. A series of studies that explore the same topic.
   c. A review of the literature in a systematic format.
   d. Repeat application of the same treatment by the same clinician to the same clients.

ANSWER KEY FOR SELF-ASSESSMENT QUIZ

1. **a.** An aspect of the client's functioning: behaviors, perceptions, attitudes, or feelings.
2. **b.** Goals should be specific, precisely defined, and measurable.
3. **d.** Continuous assessment regarding stability in the baseline phase and how this compares to the treatment phases.
4. **c.** AB, ABAB, and multiple-baseline designs
5. **a.** A series of measurements of the client's behavior prior to treatment, which form the basis for comparison to the treatment.
6. **b.** Involves direct replication and systematic replication.
7. **a.** Happens after the intervention phase, at which point the treatment is completely taken away.
8. **b.** The phase that follows baseline where treatment is introduced in the design and a single behavior is measured.
9. **c.** The client
10. **a.** The attempt to extend a treatment to different settings, practitioners, or client disorders by varying one of these conditions.

FOR FURTHER READING

Bloom, M., Fischer, J., & Orme, J. (2009). *Evaluating practice: Guidelines for the accountable professional* (6th ed.). Boston, MA: Pearson. A thorough textbook on all aspects of single-system design for social work and other human services. Includes software for analysis.

Gast, D. L. (2010). *Single subject research methodology in behavioral sciences*. New York, NY: Taylor & Francis. This source provides an overview of single-subject research and includes detailed information on philosophical, ethical, and statistical and visual analysis of data. Although directed at the field of education, it is applicable to all human services.

Haynes, S. N., & O'Brien, W. H. (1999). *Principles and practice of behavioral assessment*. New York, NY: Kluwer Academic/Plenum Publishers. Psychological assessment is the primary focus of this book, which also includes substantial information related to using the single-case approach to assessment.

Hawkins, C. (2001). Single subject research: Applications in educational & clinical settings (Book review). *Journal of Applied Research in Intellectual Disabilities*, 14(2), 155–157. doi:10.1046/j.1468-3148.2001.0044a.x. For the reader seeking a basic, clear, concise coverage of single-system design, this is an excellent source. Very readable and well-illustrated.

Kilgus, S. P., Riley-Tillman, T. C., & Kratochwill, T. R. (2016). Establishing interventions via a theory-driven single case design research cycle. *School Psychology Review*, 45(4), 477–498. doi:10.17105/SPR45-4.477-498. This source expands on the phases of single-case design intervention research, expectations of specific single-case designs, and how to interpret single-case design data once collected. Theoretical implications for current and future mental health interventions are provided.

Morgan, D. L., & Morgan, R. K. (2009). *Single-case research methods for the behavioral and health sciences*. Thousand Oaks, CA: Sage. This guide to single-case design introduces readers to the history, epistemology, and strategies of single-case research design. It offers concrete information on how to observe, measure, and interpret change in relevant outcome variables and how to design strategies that promote causal inferences.

Tate, R., & Perdices, M. (2018). Quantitative data analysis for single-case methods, between-groups designs, and instrument development. *Brain Impairment*, 19(1), 1–3. doi:10.1017/BrImp.2017.34. This source provides a set of articles concerning quantitative data collection on the topic of brain impairment. The three articles act as a guide to researchers or clinicians interested in research, while covering: single-case design, between-group interactions, and psychometrics in instrument development.

REFERENCES
· ·

Achen, C. H. (1986). *The statistical analysis of quasi-experiments*. Berkeley: University of California Press.

Barlow, D., & Hersen, M. (1973). Single-case experimental designs: Uses in applied clinical research. *Archives of General Psychiatry, 29*(3), 319–325. doi:10.1001/archpsyc.1973.04200030017003

Barlow, D., Nock, M., & Hersen, M. (2009). *Single case experimental designs: Strategies for studying behavior change* (3rd ed.). Boston, MA: Pearson.

Bloom, M., Fischer, J., & Orme, J. G. (2009). *Evaluating practice: Guidelines for the accountable professional* (6th ed.). Boston, MA: Pearson.

Booth-Kewley, S., Larson, G. E., & Miyoshi, D. K., (2007). Social desirability effects on computerized and paper-and-pencil questionnaires. *Computers in Human Behavior, 23*, 463–477. doi:10.1016/j.chb.2004.10.020

Clum, G. A. (1990). *Coping with panic: A drug-free approach to dealing with anxiety attacks*. Belmont, CA: Brooks/Cole.

Earnest, C. (1999). Single case study of EEG asymmetry biofeedback for depression: An independent replication in an adolescent. *Journal of Neurotherapy, 3*(2), 28–35. doi:10.1300/j184v03n02_04

Ferrell, K. A. (2000). Growth and development of young children. In M. C. Holbrook & A. J. Koenig (Eds.), *Foundations of education: Volume I. History and theory of teaching children and youths with visual impairments* (2nd ed., pp. 111–134). New York, NY: AFB Press.

Fischer, J., & Corcoran, K. (Eds.). (2007). *Measures for clinical practice and research: A sourcebook* (4th ed.). New York, NY: Oxford University Press.

Fredman, N., & Sherman, R. (1987). *Handbook of measurements for marriage and family therapy*. New York, NY: Brunner/Mazel.

Frisch, M. B., & Higgins, R. L. (1986). Instructional demand effects and the correspondence among role-play, self-report, and naturalistic measures of social skill. *Behavioral Assessment, 8*(3), 221–236.

Gingerich, W. (1990). Rethinking single-case evaluation. In L. Videka-Sherman & W. Reid (Eds.), *Advances in clinical social work research*. Silver Spring, MD: National Association of Social Workers.

Gottman, J. M. (1981). *Time-series analysis: A comprehensive introduction for social scientists*. New York, NY: Cambridge University Press.

Gottman, J. M. (1985). Observational measures of behavior therapy outcome: A reply to Jacobson. *Behavioral Assessment, 7*(4), 317–321.

Groth-Marnat, G. (2009). *Handbook of psychological assessment* (5th ed.). New York, NY: John Wiley & Sons.

Harris, F. N., & Jenson, W. R. (1985). Comparisons of multiple-baseline across persons designs and AB designs with replication: Issues and confusions. *Behavioral Assessment, 7*(2), 121–127.

Hayes, S. C., Barlow, D. H., & Nelson-Gray, R. A. (1999). *The scientist practitioner: Research and accountability in the age of managed care* (2nd ed.). Boston, MA: Pearson.

Horner, R. H., Carr, E. G., Halle, J., Odom, S., & Wolery, M. (2005). The use of single-subject research to identify evidence-based practice in special education. *Exceptional Children, 71*(2), 165–179. doi:10.1177/001440290507100203

Jayaratne, S., & Levy, R. (1979). *Empirical clinical practice*. New York, NY: Columbia University Press.

Johnson, F. C. (1981). Practice versus research: Issues in teaching of single-subject research skills. *Journal of Education for Social Work, 17*(2), 62–68. doi:10.1080/00220612.1981.10778554

Kazdin, A. E. (2010). *Single-case research designs* (2nd ed.). New York, NY: Oxford University Press.

Levin, J. R. (1992). Single-case research design and analysis: Comments and concerns. In T. R. Kratochwill & J. R. Levin (Eds.), *Single-case research design and analysis: New directions for psychology and education* (pp. 187–212). Hillsdale, NJ: Lawrence Erlbaum.

Locke, S. D., & Gilbert, B. O. (1995). Method of psychological assessment, self-disclosure, and experiential differences: A study of computer, questionnaire, and interview assessment formats. *Journal of Social Behavior and Personality, 10*, 255–263.

Martini, R., & Polatajko, H. J. (1998). Verbal self-guidance as a treatment approach for children with developmental coordination disorder: A systematic replication study. *Occupational Therapy Journal of Research, 18*(4), 157–181. doi:10.1177/153944929801800403

McFall, R. M. (1970). Effects of self-monitoring on normal smoking behavior. *Journal of Consulting and Clinical Psychology, 35*(2), 135–142. doi:10.1037/h0030087

Miller, D. C., & Salkind, N. J. (2002). *Handbook of research design and social measurement* (6th ed.). Thousand Oaks, CA: Sage.

Morrel-Samuels, P. (2003). Web surveys' hidden hazards. *Harvard Business Review, 81*, 16–18.

Nelsen, J. C. (1981). Issues in single-subject research for non-behaviorists. *Social Work Research and Abstracts, 17*(2), 31–37. doi:10.1093/swra/17.2.31

Nezu, A. M., & Nezu, C. M. (Eds.). (2008). *Evidence-based outcome research: A practical guide to conducting randomized controlled trials for psychosocial interventions.* New York, NY: Oxford University Press.

Nugent, W. R., Sieppert, J. D., & Hudson, W. (2001). *Practice evaluation for the 21st century.* Belmont, CA: Wadsworth.

Ollendick, T. H. (1995). Cognitive behavioral treatment of panic disorder with agoraphobia in adolescents: A multiple baseline design analysis. *Behavior Therapy, 26*(3), 517–553. doi:10.1016/s0005-7894(05)80098-x

Parker, A. T., Grimmett, E., & Summers, S. (2008). Evidence-based communication practices for children with visual impairments and additional disabilities: An examination of single-subject design studies. *Journal of Visual Impairment & Blindness, 102*(9), 540–552.

Rapee, R. M., Craske, M. G., & Barlow, D. H. (1990). Subject-described features of panic attacks using self-monitoring. *Journal of Anxiety Disorders, 4*(2), 171–181. doi:10.1016/0887-6185(90)90009-x

Sackett, D. L., Straus, S. E., Richardson, W. S., Rosenberg, W., & Haynes, R. B. (2000). *Evidence-based medicine: How to practice and teach EBM* (2nd ed.). Edinburgh, Scotland: Churchill Livingstone.

Spies, R. A., Carlson, J. F., & Geisinger, K. F. (2010). *The eighteenth mental measurements yearbook.* Lincoln: University of Nebraska Press.

Weiss, R. L., & Frohman, P. E. (1985). Behavioral observation as outcome measures: Not through a glass darkly. *Behavioral Assessment, 7*(4), 309–315.

Zalaquett, C. P., & Wood, R. J. (Eds.). (1997). *Evaluating stress: A book of resources.* Lanham, MD: Rowman & Littlefield.

12

EVALUATION RESEARCH

INTRODUCTION

In the summer of 2014, one of the authors of this textbook, Timothy Hilton, and one of his colleagues at Eastern Washington University, Deanna Trella, were asked to conduct an evaluation of a job program serving low-income youth in rural counties within eastern Washington. The program's funder, a foundation serving the area, was interested in determining whether the program model—which included case management, mentoring, on-the-job training and internship opportunities, and permanent job placement services—was a viable model for preventing poverty. The program primarily served youth who had graduated or otherwise left high school but were not attending college. These youth lived in rural communities that tended to have few well-established career paths that offered living wages for people without higher education or job experience.

The researchers met with leaders from the foundation to better understand what they hoped to learn. Their main question to foundation leaders was whether their primary interest was in the agency's performance or in the program model. In other words, did they want the researchers to focus on how well the agency performed the services or the mix of services offered? Foundation leaders explained they were interested in both the agency's performance and the viability of the program model, but that the program model was their main interest. They were particularly interested in the extent to which the mix of services offered was a viable approach for reducing poverty in the region.

The next thing the researchers wanted to determine was how the foundation defined success. While the researchers understood the foundation was most interested in poverty reduction, they also understood that the program had begun less than a year before the start of the evaluation. Most of the program participants were still in the program and many were in its early stages—completing an internship or on-the-job training with an area company. Some had been placed in permanent jobs with local employers, but because they had very limited job experience few were earning enough to live independently from their families. If they were forced to live on their own, most program participants who had been placed in jobs would be considered poor, but they were working and earning more than they had been prior to enrolling in the program. Would earnings gains be considered a positive outcome even if total wages earned were not enough to raise incomes above the poverty line?

After considerable discussion, foundation leaders and the researchers came to a common understanding that the main goal of the evaluation was to assess the viability of the program model (which again included a mix of case management, mentoring, internships and on-the-job training, and permanent job placement) within this rural context (eastern Washington) to increase the long-term employability and earnings potential of youth who have left high school but are not attending college or another technical or trade training program, or enrolled in the military. A secondary goal was to evaluate the performance of the agency in implementing the program model (or the mix of services).

This chapter concerns evaluation research, which refers to the use of scientific research methods to plan intervention programs, to monitor the implementation of new programs and the operation of existing ones, and to determine how effectively programs or clinical practices achieve their goals. We refer back to the youth job program evaluation example discussed earlier to illustrate several evaluation research concepts. As we outline major elements of evaluation research, we ask that you keep the following questions in mind: (a) Why is program evaluation an increasingly critical activity in human services? (b) What factors should be considered in designing an evaluation? and (c) How can leaders of social service systems, human service agency administrators and staff, and individual professionals make better use of evaluations in improving services?

Although evaluation research has been around for many years, it has risen to considerable prominence over the past few decades for a number of reasons. One reason is the advances in theory and policy in the human services, such as evidence-based practice, that call as a matter of principle for greater scientific assessment of practice and policy. The Council on Social Work Education (CSWE) competency standards explicitly refer to social workers' need to understand processes for incorporating research-based evidence into practice (Educational Policy and Accreditation Standards [EPAS], 2015). A second reason is that the amount of public and private funds being channeled into social programs has grown. These changes have led those providing the funds to seek more valid and reliable evidence regarding whether programs achieve their goals, how efficiently they do so, and whether they produce any unintended consequences. Evaluation research is a mechanism for gathering evidence about these issues, and it has become an integral part of most modern social programs.

WHAT IS EVALUATION RESEARCH?

Evaluation research offers a means of supplying valid and reliable evidence about the operation of social programs or clinical practices—how they

are planned, how well they operate, and how effectively they achieve their goals. In the youth job program example described earlier, the foundation was interested in generating and examining valid and reliable evidence about the agency's operation of the program. Their goal was really threefold. First, they wanted to understand if the agency had made good use of funding provided. Second, they wanted to know whether the program worked in terms of reducing poverty or risk of poverty for these youth. Third, they wanted to understand if the mix of services offered was the best mix for achieving antipoverty goals, and related to that, what services and strategies seemed to have the largest impacts on poverty reduction. Similarly, a medical care facility may need to know if a need exists for a day-care program for older adults in a given community. Corrections officials may want to know the size at which a probation officer's caseload becomes too large to provide effective services. Hospital administrators may need to assess the impact on patient care of a 15% reduction in nursing staff.

In these situations, and in others like them, evaluation research uses many of the research techniques that we have discussed in other chapters to provide evidence about the workings of programs and practices in the human services. A typical evaluation effort might involve some combination of interviews, questionnaires, observation, available data, and an experimental design. In fact, we have already discussed evaluation research in many places in this book without calling it by this name.

Why Evaluate?

Evaluation research is conducted for three specific reasons, and each of these reasons can relate to providing support for the evidence-based practice approach in the human services (Rossi, Lipsey, & Freeman, 2004). First, evaluation research may be conducted *to test hypotheses* or *to evaluate practice approaches*. These often amount to the same thing, however, because practice strategies often are based on hypotheses derived from social and psychological theories. Such evaluation not only provides information about a particular practice intervention but also adds to the fund of social scientific evidence about practice, which may be useful in the design of new intervention strategies. In the youth job program, the funders (and the researchers) were interested in evaluating the agency's approaches to connecting youth with training and job opportunities.

A second reason for conducting evaluation research, which can also support evidence-based practice, is *impact assessment*—that is, to see what effects, if any, a program is producing. Typically, impact assessment identifies program goals and measures how well the program achieves those goals. The results provide the evidence to be used in making policy decisions regarding whether to expand, change, or curtail a program. Hilton and Trella's evaluation focused on the impact of the job program in reducing poverty.

Third, evaluation research can be conducted for *administrative purposes,* such as to fulfill an evaluation requirement demanded by a funding source, to improve the service to clients, or to increase the efficiency of program delivery. Evaluations for administrative reasons tend to focus on assessing the daily operations of a program rather than on its overall impact, with the goal of finding the most efficient means to run a program or agency. These administrative evaluations can, nonetheless, provide data, or evidence, to support practice and policy. An unspoken but relevant purpose of the program evaluation was the local foundation's obligation to provide a program evaluation summary and outcome report to the larger national foundation that had provided funding for the rural youth job program. In addition to their desire to learn more about what works and what does not work with respect to reducing poverty in the region, the local foundation believed that providing an in-depth evaluation of the program would enhance their chances of receiving funding in the future.

Evaluation Research and Basic Research

Evaluation research is another form of applied research (see Chapter 1) that involves a special application of the general techniques of basic research. Because of this, there are similarities between the two, but there also are some important differences (DeMartini, 1982; Mertens, 2014; Weiss, 1998). First, the results of evaluation research have immediate practical use in assessing operating programs. Basic research, on the other hand, is oriented toward more general information gathering and hypothesis testing. In the youth job program example, the foundation hoped the evaluation would help them in making decisions about funding decisions related to antipoverty programs in subsequent funding cycles.

Second, in contrast to evaluation research, in which the needs of the decision makers sponsoring the study are paramount in shaping the form and content of the research, the basic researcher has more control over which issues to investigate (Rossi et al., 2004). Some evaluations may allow some latitude to expand beyond the issues of direct interest to the decision makers, but control over the content of the research is shared with them. This can become a source of conflict between researchers and sponsors. In the case of the youth job program evaluation, the sponsor of the research and the researchers worked closely together in designing the parameters of the evaluation. Foundation staff gave the researchers great latitude because both parties had a similar goal—to identify effective strategies for reducing poverty.

A third difference is that evaluation, by its very nature, has a judgmental quality that often is not a part of basic research. The evaluation may deem a program to be a success or a failure based on how well it achieved its purposes; this judgmental quality also can be a source of tension between an evaluator and the sponsors of the evaluation. Understandably, the sponsors are concerned that a negative evaluation could have dire consequences for the existence of the program—and for their own livelihoods and careers. In the youth job program, for example, researchers were to assess whether or not the agency providing services had done a good job implementing the program as designed. Obviously, this can create tension between the researchers and agency staff who may view the results of the evaluation as impacting future agency resources. (In this case, however, agency administrators and staff were very cooperative with the researchers and even excited to receive an outside perspective on their programs and receive recommendations to better serve their clients.)

The fourth difference between basic and evaluation research relates to the issues that are given priority in the research process. In basic research, quite naturally, the requisites for producing a scientifically sound study are given strong weight. Evaluation research, on the other hand, takes place in the context of an ongoing, operating program, and the demands of that program may conflict with the demands of sound scientific practices. When this happens, the program administrators may give higher priority to the program than to the evaluation. The scientific demands of an evaluation, for example, might call for the random assignment of nurses from a home healthcare agency to each new client of the agency. The agency administrator, however, may prefer to assign nurses on the basis of his or her assessment of their competencies and fit with the client. The agency head may be able to override the evaluators' requests and force them to modify their scientific procedures. Similarly in the youth job program example, evaluating the effectiveness of on-the-job training versus internships in terms of increasing clients' long-term employment prospects is best achieved through random assignment into one of these program types. In practice, however, agency staff connected youth with job experiences based on a combination of client preferences and availability of opportunities.

The differences in approach that sometimes are found between practitioners and researchers can, on occasion, aggravate these conflicts. Practitioners tend to emphasize the importance of providing services to people and the role of empathy and concern in the intervention process. Researchers, on the other hand, may give more weight to the understanding provided by rigorous scientific analysis and objectivity. Although these differences should not be overdrawn—researchers do have empathy, and practitioners do recognize the value of scientific analysis—there can be a difference in emphasis between practitioners and researchers, and this can be another source of tension. In fact, one of the beneficial outcomes of developing linkages between practice and research is that the process encourages people to develop ways of combining the two approaches so that advantages accrue to both.

A final difference between basic and evaluation research relates to making the results of the research public. One of the canons of science is that research results be made public for others to see and criticize and thus to reduce the likelihood that errors or personal bias might find their way into the research (see Chapter 2). While evaluation results are often made public by being presented at professional meetings and published in professional journals and books, they are as likely to only be made available to the human service organization or administrator who sponsored the research. One consequence of this lack of public dissemination is that it thwarts the accumulation of information so necessary for scientific progress. A second consequence of no public dissemination centers on ethics oversight requirements. For Institutional Review Board (IRB) oversight purposes, federal regulations define research as "a systematic investigation, including research development, testing and evaluation, designed to develop or contribute to generalizable knowledge" (Protection of Human Subjects, 2018). Because the primary purpose of evaluation is often to simply serve as a management tool for monitoring and improving the program and not to develop or contribute to *generalizable* knowledge, it may be exempt from IRB review. However, clearly not all evaluation research is exempt; this applies especially to any evaluations whose findings will be presented at a conference or submitted for journal publication. Furthermore, universities often will not grant approval retroactively, so it is advisable to err on the side of caution if there is any chance that the results of a study warrant wider dissemination. Of course, even in those cases where IRB approval is not required, evaluators should still follow the basic principles of research ethics presented in Chapter 3.

Despite the differences between evaluation and basic research, there are important similarities. First, both may choose, from the entire array of data-gathering techniques, those that best fit their needs. In fact, as noted, evaluation projects often involve a synthesis of data that are gathered in a variety of ways. Second, both forms of research can focus on determining cause-and-effect relationships. In basic research, researchers seek cause-and-effect relationships between variables of their own choosing, whereas in evaluation research, investigation focuses on variables that are a part of the program being assessed.

The differences between evaluation and basic research are of a practical nature, deriving mainly from the context in which evaluation research is conducted. Although these differences are important—and the potential conflicts alluded to are quite real—the actual process of inquiry is much the same in both types of research. In fact, evaluation research illustrates the dynamic and flexible quality of basic social research methods in that the core methods and techniques can be expanded and changed to confront new problems and issues. Evaluation research is a novel and challenging application of methods that have been used in many other contexts. As such, the distinction between basic and evaluation research is one of degree rather than of kind.

The Politics of Evaluation Research

Decades ago, many evaluation researchers took a fairly straightforward, positivist view of their activities. By this, we mean that they viewed the social programs they were evaluating as interventions attacking clearly identifiable problems in the world. The researchers viewed these problems as obvious social ills that needed rectifying, assumed that almost everyone agreed on what the betterment of those social ills would entail, and saw their own methods as objective and scientific tools to assist in achieving that social betterment. The arguments of nonpositivist paradigms (discussed in Chapter 2), however, have led many evaluation researchers to recognize that reality is not as simple as the straightforward, positivist view would suggest (Bhaskar, 2014; Greene, 1994; Patton, 1987). In particular, these approaches have led to a recognition that evaluation research and the programs they evaluate are inherently political in nature. Politics has to do with power—who has it, who exercises it, and who controls its resources. Social interventions have to do with controlling and distributing resources.

Let us illustrate these issues with an example—namely, programs to reduce teenage pregnancies. The problem of teen pregnancy can be approached in a number of different ways, such as encouraging sexual abstinence, making available safe and reliable contraceptives, or providing abortion services to those who become pregnant. Which of these approaches a particular social program takes is determined by the values of those who fund and control that program and, thus, have the power to see that their values prevail. These people shape what the program is like, which services it provides, and how it provides them. In doing so, policy makers and program managers have great influence on shaping people's definitions of both the problem of teenage pregnancy and the acceptable solutions to that problem. Thus, social programs are the product of political decisions that involve the establishment of priorities and the allocation of resources.

In recent decades, evaluation researchers have come to recognize the importance in social programs of **stakeholders**: all the people who have an interest in whether, or how well, a social program operates. Evaluation researchers also recognize that any program has a large variety of stakeholders, including its funders, administrators, personnel, and clients or beneficiaries. In most cases, these stakeholders have varied and competing interests. The teenagers receiving services from a pregnancy prevention program, for example, may benefit from different kinds of interventions than the bureaucrats who run the program or the policy makers who fund it.

Typically, however, evaluations are sponsored by only one or a few stakeholders, such as the governmental agency that funds the evaluation or the managers who run the program. These sponsors may want to see the evaluation come out a certain way, and they may pay for an evaluation that addresses some questions but not others. If the sponsors want to promote sexual abstinence, for instance, they may include in the evaluation measures that assess how well abstinence works, but they may not ask the teens if they would use contraceptives or abortion referral services if those were available. Thus, it is possible that an evaluation can be directed toward some conclusions and away from others because only some stakeholders in the program are funding—and, in part, directing—the evaluation.

The new approach recognizes that social ills and their betterment are not objective conditions about which a social consensus exists. Rather, social ills and social betterment are political issues based on differing social definitions of reality, about which people disagree and come into conflict. In designing and conducting evaluation research, then, researchers must recognize these competing viewpoints and interests and consider the possibility that some research methodologies may be biased in the direction of certain conclusions and the interests of certain stakeholders.

In the youth job program example the funders (sponsoring the research), the researchers, agency administrators and staff, and even youth program participants all seemed to have very similar ideas regarding the purpose of the evaluation. There were slight disagreements about which types of outcomes to prioritize, however. For example, if the programs are designed to connect youth with jobs, how should the researchers treat other positive outcomes like enrollment in college or technical training? These were issues that the various parties were able to resolve easily through dialogue, but there were certainly different viewpoints from various stakeholders.

Types of Evaluation Research

The term *evaluation research* refers to a diverse collection of strategies that can be used for a broad range of evaluative purposes. One way that evaluation research methods may be classified is in terms of the unit of analysis. (For example, the single-system designs covered in Chapter 11 may be considered to be evaluation methods where the unit of analysis is a single system or an individual. Because of the unique features involved in doing such individual studies, we have chosen to devote a separate chapter to them.) This chapter considers evaluations that focus on programs or organizations as the unit of analysis.

Another useful way to conceptualize the diversity of evaluation research is in terms of the goals of the study. Evaluation research can achieve two basic goals: **Formative evaluation research** focuses on providing information to guide the planning, development, and implementation of a specific program. It is concerned primarily with ensuring a smooth-running, well-integrated program rather than with the ultimate worth or impact of the program. **Summative evaluation research** is concerned with the program's effects. Here, the purpose centers on assessing the effectiveness and efficiency of programs and the extent to which the outcomes of the project are generalizable to other settings and populations. Formative evaluation research has received less attention in the evaluation literature than summative evaluation has. The two forms are closely linked, however, and may be likened to a foundation and a building. The formative component of evaluation may not be especially glamorous or attract much attention, but unless it is carefully prepared and well done, the summative study is difficult to carry out for high-quality results.

FORMATIVE EVALUATION RESEARCH

Formative research poses the questions that arise in the planning, implementation, and operation of social programs. To initiate a program, certain basic information is essential. First, it is necessary to gather data on the target population and their characteristics. The nature of their problems, the number of potential program users, their location in the community, and other demographic information are essential to planning a good program. Second, it is important to be aware of existing services that the program under development might duplicate or on which it may rely for referrals or auxiliary services. Third, program planners need to know about specific intervention strategies that might apply to the problems they uncover. Fourth, program operators must be able to specify the staff skills that are required to deliver the program. Fifth, planners must determine if the program, as conceptualized, is feasible to offer and monitor.

To answer these questions, formative research might take the form of a **needs assessment**: collecting data to determine how many people in a community need particular services and assessing what level of services or personnel already exists to fill a need (Gruber, Wang, Quittner, Salyakina, & McCafferty-Fernandez, 2018; McKillip, 1987). In needs assessments, researchers commonly use a sampling strategy and then survey members of the target population. Thus, survey research methods form the backbone of such needs assessments. We can also rely on direct observation or existing data to gain a profile of the population and to identify its needs. Essentially, any techniques used for descriptive research may be employed to answer this question. We might learn about existing and related services through interviewing potential clients and representatives of existing agencies. Knowledge of possible intervention strategies and program components often results from a thorough literature search, a fundamental step in any research project.

Formative evaluations also sometimes use *focus groups* (a group interview technique discussed at length in Chapter 7). Focus groups are especially useful when the formative evaluation is exploratory in nature or when planners want to learn about people's personal and subjective meanings and experiences. Focus groups are a useful strategy for drawing out such information.

Formative evaluation research can also take the form of a *pretest* or *trial run,* which tests all the procedures to be used in a program before the full program is implemented. For example, the same researchers involved in the evaluation of the youth job program (Hilton and Trella) were also involved in designing a small, pilot program for homeless students and their families. The program included mentorship and tutoring services designed to help homeless students from falling behind and their schoolwork. It also included intensive housing search and placement assistance for these students' families, many of whom were doubled up in crowded homes with extended family members. The purpose of this pilot program was to test the efficacy of a school-based program to address family homelessness. It was initiated at three public elementary schools. The ultimate goal of these pilot projects was to test whether the model was a viable option that could be expanded throughout all schools in the region. Beginning with a small pilot allowed the school system (and program

funders) to test whether or not the program could work before devoting substantial resources to creating a similar program at dozens of schools with thousands of clients.

Because the questions that formative research addresses often are modest in scope, the staff of the agency administering the program frequently conducts the research itself. Such research, however, also may be done on a national scale in conjunction with large programs. Programs such as Temporary Assistance to Needy Families (TANF), food stamps, and vocational rehabilitation involve large sums of money, and initiation of such programs involves estimating the number of potential recipients, which can vary considerably depending on which definition of poverty is applied. Before initiating such programs, formative research based on needs assessment is essential. Although formative evaluation cannot ensure success, it can help reduce instances of unnecessary intervention and increase the potential for success among those programs that are initiated.

Besides serving as a tool for planning an intervention program, formative research may also monitor the implementation of new programs and the ongoing operation of existing ones. Several basic issues in program monitoring are counterparts to program planning. First, is the target population actually being served? It is not uncommon to discover that people do not use programs in spite of obvious need. Even major social welfare programs have been plagued by this problem, which is referred to as the "take-up rate."

Studies have found that less than 50% of eligible recipients participated in the food stamps program. Inadequate information about food stamps and personal attitudes toward the use of food stamps had the greatest impact on the decision to participate (Coe & Hill, 1998). Another study (Kalra, Fieldhouse, & Alam, 2001) reported on the reasons for nonparticipation and avoidance of the New Deal for Young People (NDYP), a public policy program that tries to reduce unemployment among those in the 18–25 age group. Negative experiences at previous youth training programs and the perception that NDYP could not offer desirable jobs were identified as major barriers to involvement. As a means to assess the extent of such problems, a census of program users can compare their characteristics with those of the population for whom the services were intended. Any discrepancy suggests that some members of the target population are not receiving services intended for them. Unless such issues are addressed during the formative evaluation stage, a full-scale program may be destined for failure.

Next, are the services that are supposed to be delivered actually being delivered, and is the quality of the service adequate? Experience with program effectiveness evaluations has shown that a key issue is program fidelity during intervention—that is, operating the program exactly as it was designed to run. Without implementation data, an evaluator might conclude that a program model is ineffective when the real culprit is inadequate implementation that did not permit a valid test of the program (Lynch, Geller, Hunt, Galano, & Dubas, 1998; Slaughter, Hill, & Snelgrove-Clarke, 2015). Service delivery may be assessed in a variety of ways, including questionnaires and direct observation. As in single-system designs, time samples may be used to determine if behaviors associated with service delivery are occurring as planned. Quality-control techniques not unlike those used in industry can monitor the delivery of services in many settings. State departments of social services routinely monitor major financial assistance services, such as TANF. Typically, the process involves selecting a random sample of recipients and examining the most recent action on their files to determine if the action resulted in a correct payment, an overpayment, or an underpayment. States are expected to keep their error rate within certain specific limits. Other settings use follow-up questionnaires to determine if the expected services were delivered.

Finally, agencies commonly use a time-reporting system to make sure that staff members are spending the expected amount of time on specified aspects of the program. When formative evaluation studies use such time-reporting data, they do not address the question of whether the program is actually doing any good; rather, they address the narrower issue of the extent to which the services actually being delivered are true to the intended plan.

While the youth job program example was primarily a summative evaluation, which is discussed in the following text, there were certainly several formative elements to this research. First and most obvious, a major purpose of the evaluation was to create recommendations based on research findings that would be useful in creating future programs, whether within the agency being studied or elsewhere. Second, the research was at least partially focused on program fidelity and the extent to which the program adhered to the program model outlined in the funding agreement with the agency. Third, as was evident at an event where the evaluation findings were released, another purpose of the research was to bring together many community partners to talk openly about past successes and shortcomings, discuss changing contexts and available resources, and plan for next steps to better serve community members struggling to begin careers.

SUMMATIVE EVALUATION RESEARCH

Summative evaluation research involves assessing the impact of a program, and good summative evaluations usually investigate other matters concerning the program's operation as well. The results of summative evaluations are intended for policy-making decisions—whether to continue, expand, or cancel a program, and whether to generalize the findings of a particular project to other settings and populations. Summative evaluations typically are large-scale projects involving considerable time, personnel, and resources. For this reason, as well as to avoid the biasing effect of personal interest, external consultants rather than agency staff often conduct these evaluations.

Although the steps in the research process are much the same for all types of research, including evaluation research, some special planning is called for to take into consideration the unique problems of evaluation research.

Evaluability Assessment and the Logic Model

During the planning of evaluation research, an **evaluability assessment** often is conducted to

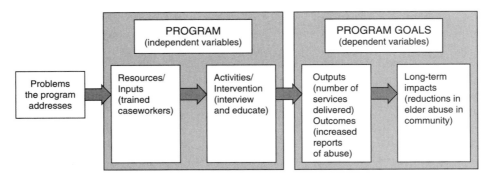

Figure 12.1 An outline of the logic model in program evaluation.

enable investigators to decide whether a program has the necessary elements to be evaluated (Foundation, 2004; Smith, 1989). A good framework for doing this is through the development of a **logic model**, which is basically a visual or verbal description of how you think a program should or does work. It provides a framework for deciding whether a program can be evaluated and how to go about evaluating it. Figure 12.1 presents an outline of such a logic model, with illustrations from a program to detect and reduce elder abuse (Navarro, Wilbur, Yonashiro, & Homeier, 2010).

The logic model begins by identifying the problems that the program is intended to address, including determining the purpose of the evaluation—from the standpoint of the eventual users of the results. This identifies which aspects of the program to assess for impact. The logic model identifies the potential program elements for assessment, such as: program resources or inputs, program activities or interventions, and program goals (outputs, outcomes, and impacts). The resources/inputs and the activities/interventions are the independent variables that are presumed to have some impact on the dependent variables (goals). The resources might include the funding dollars available to the program as well as the training or expertise of agency staff. The interventions might include counseling or educational services that are provided to clients.

Evaluation requires that a program have clearly specified outcomes and goals, because they are the major criteria of the program's success. They are the dependent variables that the input variables

are supposed to affect. Goals can take a number of different forms. For example, *outputs* refer to the things that a program does, such as provide certain numbers and types of counseling or educational services. *Outcomes* refer to the changes in client knowledge, attitudes, or behaviors that the program is presumed to produce. *Impacts* refer to longer term changes in larger social systems, such as communities or society as a whole, because of the program. So, a program evaluation could focus on one or more of these goals (outputs, outcomes, impacts). Unfortunately, the goals of many programs are either so vague or so global—for example, "improve family functioning"—as to be unusable for evaluation purposes. It may be necessary for an evaluator to become actively involved with the staff in developing a set of clear goals before a program can be evaluated. In the youth job program example, the researchers worked closely with the sponsoring foundation and the agency being evaluated to create a desired set of outcomes. While the program was generally aimed at poverty reduction, it was difficult to use poverty, which is based on income, as a measure of success. All or nearly all of the participants were in poverty. Many, however, had some main income gains due to employment and most had been successful in making strides toward creating career paths, including getting new job experiences, completing internships, or enrolling in college or technical trainings. Ultimately the sponsor, researchers, and agency agreed on a set of desirable outcomes based on both income and job skill and experience gains.

So, an important part of an evaluability assessment is to study and gather information about the program design. What are the inputs and the expected results or goals? In addition, a program evaluation should attempt to determine the linkage between the inputs and the outcomes. Essentially, this linkage is the theory on which the program is based. It involves answering the following question: "Why, given these program inputs, should certain outcomes be expected?" This linkage specifies any assumed causal linkages between independent and dependent variables. Any program is likely to have a variety of inputs, activities, and goals. A good evaluability assessment would link specific inputs and activities with specific goals. So, there might be a set of hypotheses stating, for example, that Input A and Activity C are presumed to bring about specified changes such as Output B and Outcome F. Using the elder abuse example, we might hypothesize that increased education on issues of aging and elder abuse for direct caseworkers (the input or intervention) will produce more reports of elder abuse by the caseworkers (the outcome) because the caseworkers with this education will be more knowledgeable of the indicators of abuse. This theoretical linkage may be explicitly recognized as the basis of the program, or it may be implicit in but derivable from the program's rationale or operation. The purpose of identifying this rationale is that it is important in understanding the success or failure of the program. Notice that although the long-term impact of the program might be a reduction in elder abuse, the logic model predicts that the immediate effect of the program will be an *increase* in reports of such abuse. Without a well-specified model, such a finding could be confusing or interpreted as program failure.

The logic model also helps identify program deficiencies. For example, some programs may identify certain outcomes as goals but not direct any effort toward realizing them. (Quite obviously, if evaluated against these goals, the program probably would turn out to be a failure.) If we do not specify the linkage, then the reason for failure may be unclear, and in the case of a success, we would be at a loss to explain why. Knowledge of the linkage reveals the source of the problem as the failure

to direct input resources toward those particular goals. During this step, it is important to monitor the program as implemented, because gaps sometimes develop between the stated program and the program as operated.

The final stage of an evaluability assessment is to review the program model to identify those aspects that are sufficiently unambiguous in terms of inputs, goals, and linkages to make evaluation feasible. The result of the assessment may be that the whole program can be evaluated, none of the program can be evaluated, or, most commonly, only certain parts of the program are amenable to evaluation.

Specification of Variables

As in any research, an important part of evaluation research is the specification of variables and how they will be measured. In some evaluations, the variables of interest take the form of independent and dependent variables. The inputs to a social program, for example, might constitute the independent variables. In some cases, the independent variable takes the form of a dichotomous variable, such as participation or nonparticipation in a program. In other cases, the independent variable is the degree or duration of participation in a program, such as the frequency of contact with a counselor, the level of financial aid received, or the length of time that a service is provided. Commonly, the dependent variables in evaluation research are the goals of a program—precisely what it is supposed to accomplish. Of course, some evaluation research, especially the formative type, does not involve independent and dependent variables. Whatever form the variables take, however, a central issue in evaluation research is that the variables be clearly and properly specified, because numerous problems can arise along these lines. This is especially true when measuring the goals of a program.

A frequent problem is that the goals, as articulated by program administrators, do not easily lend themselves to evaluation. They may be vague, overly broad, or so long term that evaluation is not feasible. For example, the main goal of the youth job program was to help non–college-bound youth escape poverty. Although the success of youth in achieving this goal may be its ultimate test, it would be necessary to wait several years before evaluating the program. Although this goal is a laudable and essential part of the program, funding agencies are understandably reluctant to expend funds for that length of time with no evaluation. Thus, such programs normally include what are called *proximate goals,* or goals that can be realized in the short run and are related to achievement of the long-term goals (Chen, 2015). In the case of the youth job program, successfully securing and completing an internship or on-the-job placement experience, or entering or completing a higher education or training program, is associated with higher future earnings.

For other programs, of course, it is both possible and desirable to assess the long-term impact—for example, a 30-year follow-up of the Cambridge-Somerville Youth Study, a five-year experiment in delinquency prevention begun in Boston in 1939 (McCord, 1978). This field experiment focused on 506 boys, half of whom received counseling and other assistance while the other half served as a control group. The experimental condition consisted of counseling sessions every two weeks, tutoring, medical and psychiatric assistance, summer camps, and organized youth activities. Thirty years later, researchers located 95% of the participants in the experiment. Many of the comparisons showed no differences between the two groups, but the differences that were found suggested that the experimental variables had the *opposite* effect from what was expected! The experimental group committed more crimes as adults, had higher rates of alcoholism, poorer mental and physical health, and less occupational success. The only positive result for the program appeared to be the participants' own subjective evaluations. Two thirds of the experimental group thought that the program had been helpful to them even though their objective situation was worse than that of those in the control group. The program may have produced harmful effects, because it raised participants' expectations to an unrealistically high level. When those expectations were not realized, participants suffered frustration and added stress, which resulted in a greater tendency toward criminality

and alcoholism and deleterious effects on their mental and physical health. Despite the need for early program evaluations, long-term evaluation—accomplished so well in this study—is still essential in assessing many programs.

Vague or overly broad goals must be clarified or reduced in scope so that they are amenable to evaluation. In this regard, it is helpful if program administrators consult with evaluators to develop program goals. During discussions with program administrators, it is important that evaluators not simply accept as all-inclusive the goals the administrators articulate. In fact, one of the major reasons for finding that a program does not have the intended result is that the program goals are too limited (Chen & Rossi, 1980). Too often, administrators state program goals from the standpoint of what they desire, which results in goals that are unattainable given the program inputs. When evaluated against these goals, the program naturally appears to be a failure. If, for example, the foundation and the agency in the youth job program example had determined the youth were earning anything less than about poverty wages through employment, the evaluation would have found that the program was largely a failure. Evaluators should cast a wide net in seeking program effects, including not only those suggested by administrators but also others that could be logically expected given the nature of the program. The model developed during the evaluability assessment and the theoretical basis of the program are productive places to look for possible program effects to include in the evaluation. This approach promises a better chance of finding nonzero program effects and of supplying information on what the program does—and does not—do.

Another problem in specifying the goals and variables for evaluation is that different stakeholders may have different conceptions of what the program should accomplish. All sides may be clear about what the goals should be but disagree with one another on them. This points, again, toward the political dimensions of evaluation research and the possibility that those who control the resources (usually the program funders or administrators) will impose their version of what the program goals should be. The evaluation researcher needs to ensure that other significant stakeholders have input into the process of defining and clarifying the goals.

Measuring Variables

The goals specified for an evaluation program tend to be abstract statements of desired outcomes. Before an actual evaluation can proceed, measurable criteria or operational definitions must specify exactly what observations will be made to determine goal achievement. Evaluators thus distinguish between *goals*, which are the desired end states for a program, and *objectives*, the measurable criteria for success. For example, a goal of a substance abuse prevention program might be to reduce experimentation with alcohol and cigarettes among junior high school students. An objective of the program might be that 85% of program participants be able to correctly list at least five health hazards associated with alcohol use. Some goals can be readily measured because they have clearly quantifiable outcomes. For example, standard achievement tests readily measure the academic effects of compensatory education programs, but measuring such effects of Head Start as improved self-esteem, better adjustment to the classroom environment, or enhanced parent–child relationships requires more inventiveness on the part of the evaluator.

When measures for program effects are considered, alternative indicators of the same program effect may exist. For example, in measuring the effects of a family planning program, we might use as a measure (a) the proportion of participants adopting contraceptive practices, (b) the average number of children desired, (c) the average number of children born, or (d) the attitudes toward large families. All these indicators logically relate to the effects of a family planning program. In the youth job program example, the researchers considered several outcome measures, including: numbers of participants who participated and completed internships, total hours of on-the-job training completed, numbers of participants placed in jobs, job retention (how long participants kept jobs), and income gains.

Multiple indicators—though sometimes prohibited by budget—are more useful than single ones, because they are more sensitive and, therefore, more likely to show an effect if the program produced one (Chen, 2015; Weiss, 1998). If multiple indicators are impractical, then a decision must be made as to which of the alternatives is best. In the case of the four alternatives for the family planning program, the clearest indicator of program success is a low birthrate among participants. Because we have to wait many years before such an evaluation can be completed, however, this indicator might be impractical for some purposes. The two indicators dealing with attitudes are not the best choices, because attitudes can change and, sometimes, only a weak relationship exists between attitudes and behavior. Indeed, attitudinal measures should be avoided whenever a behavioral alternative is available. Of the four possible measures, then, the proportion of participants who adopt contraception probably is the best single indicator for the effectiveness of the family planning program. It is not perfect as a measure, however, because contraceptives must be used conscientiously to be effective, but it is adequate for the short run.

As we have noted, it is preferable to use existing measures where possible. This avoids the work involved in creating new measures, pretesting them, and establishing their validity and reliability. Furthermore, existing measures contribute to the accumulation of knowledge, because they make evaluations of different programs more comparable. The preference for existing measures, however, extends only to the point where good existing measures for the variables of interest can be found. If existing measures are only tangentially related to what we seek to measure, then it is far better to develop new measures. Good measurement is crucial to meaningful evaluation; shortcuts that compromise quality cannot be tolerated.

Assuming that some new measures must be created, it is important to keep in mind the dual criteria for assessing them: *validity* and *reliability*. Measures used in evaluation research must meet the same standards of validity and reliability as those used in basic research, and the methods for assessing those characteristics (considered in Chapter 5) apply here as well.

Designs for Evaluation Research

Summative evaluation research often is concerned with cause-and-effect relationships. For example, the program being evaluated is presumed to bring about changes in such factors as client behavior, so a research design developed for such an evaluation needs to be based on an awareness of this cause-and-effect dimension. In Chapter 10, we noted that true experimental designs involving randomization are the better choice for establishing cause-and-effect relationships, because they best control the threats to validity that can lead to false causal inferences. The ideal approach to determining the effects of a program, therefore, is the randomized experiment. Any of the true experimental designs discussed in Chapter 10 is appropriate for evaluation purposes. Quasi-experimental designs are quite common, however, because these often are far more feasible and expedient than true experimental designs.

Randomized Experimental Designs. As we have noted, the requirements of a true experiment are two randomized equivalent groups, one that experiences the experimental condition and a control group that does not. In summative evaluation research, the experimental condition requires some level of participation in the program under consideration. The crucial feature of the true experiment is that members of the comparison groups are randomly assigned. This is the surest and most reliable way of producing equivalent groups.

Virtually all randomized experiments in evaluation are field experiments, taking place in the setting where the actual program is administered. Because of this, evaluators may encounter a number of impediments to conducting a randomized experiment. The first centers around the control group and the randomization procedure that is used to obtain it. To create a control group, it is necessary to deny some members of the target population access to the program under evaluation, and that denial must be made on a random basis. Evaluators may encounter substantial resistance to such denials. For example, the enabling legislation of some programs mandates that all persons who meet the eligibility requirements have a legal right

to participate in the program. If this is the case, then random denial of service must be ruled out.

In other programs, resistance to random denial of services may spring from the program administrators and staff. Practitioners are accustomed to providing services on the basis of need, and they may be disinclined to use a table of random numbers instead. To them, it seems cold, insensitive, and even immoral to withhold available services from people who need them, especially if intuition leads the practitioner to believe that the provision of services would have beneficial effects. In advocating a randomized experiment, evaluators sometimes find themselves in a no-win situation: If they discover that the program produces harmful effects, then they are blamed for subjecting the experimental group to the harmful program. If the program produces positive results, however, then they are blamed for withholding this valuable service from the control group. Imagine the ethical implications of a randomized experiment for evaluating something like a suicide prevention program, in which life-and-death issues are at stake.

Along these lines, it is important to keep in mind that intuition regarding the impact of programs often is faulty. In fact, the literature on evaluation research strongly suggests that practitioners' assumptions of positive program effects often are wrong. Leonard Gibbs (1991) documented this point with a diverse list of well-intentioned intervention efforts from the annals of medicine and human service—efforts that appeared to be reasonable in their time but later proved to be ineffective. Included were bloodletting, mercuric chloride as a drug, oxygen therapy for premature infants, neuroleptic medication for tardive dyskinesia, a juvenile awareness program known as "Scared Straight," encounter groups, and aggressive relocation of the aged. In the last illustration, a study on providing a full range of human services to older adults who were mentally impaired reported that the death rate for clients receiving the intensive services was 25%, in contrast to only 18% for the controls. Although not statistically significant, the results should make us pause before we assume that good intentions ensure a positive outcome. Because services that our intuition may suggest are effective often turn out not to be, the arguments against withholding services in a randomized experimental design are severely weakened; studies involving true control groups are clearly feasible.

A second impediment to conducting randomized experiments in evaluation research is that they may be more time-consuming and expensive than other designs. Experimental evaluations of programs typically are longitudinal: Sufficient time must pass for programs to have an effect. With many social programs, such as compensatory education or job training, the minimum length of the experiment might be at least one year. Furthermore, a listing of the target population, which is required for randomization, may be difficult or expensive to obtain. These practical considerations mean that randomized experiments are limited to those cases where money and time are available for an elaborate, rigorous evaluation.

Before succumbing to the pressure to settle for a weaker design, however, consider the lesson of the Salk polio vaccine trials. Two experimental methods were used. One was a nonrandomized trial wherein one million volunteer second graders were given the vaccine, and unvaccinated first and third graders served as the control group. The other study was an experiment involving 800,000 volunteers randomly assigned to receive either the vaccine or a placebo without the doctors, parents, or children knowing which group they were in. Although the first study involved a larger sample and may have seemed easier to conduct without complicated randomization, its design proved to be inadequate for estimating the effect of the vaccine. It seems that polio was more prevalent in the middle classes because better hygiene prevented building up the natural immunity that lower class children developed. Second graders who volunteered tended to be middle class and, thus, different from second graders who did not volunteer and from the first and third graders in the control group. Citing this case in his argument for randomized experiments, Lawrence Sherman (1992) concluded, "Only the randomized, fully controlled Salk vaccine experiment provided the clear estimate of the vaccine's benefits which was needed to adopt a national policy of vaccination" (p. 59).

Randomized experiments clearly are the best designs from which to assess causality. The evidence-based approach to human service practice that we have stressed in this book establishes the randomized, controlled experiment as producing the "best" evidence for guiding practice. With some inventiveness on the part of evaluators, much of the resistance to randomized experiments can be overcome. Indeed, there is a growing consensus about the desirability of randomized experiments and an expanding literature documenting their use (Orr, 1998), which should work to reduce the barriers to future randomized experiments in evaluation.

One common situation in particular contributes to the possibility of a randomized experiment. When the target population is larger than the program's capacity to serve it—in short, when the demand for services exceeds the supply—services must be denied to some people. Many programs initially are instituted on a small scale, so excess demand often occurs. Because some members of the target population will not be served anyway, the determination of who will be served might as well be random unless there is some other clear-cut and defensible criterion, such as severity of need. In fact, a reasonable argument can be made that random allocation of services is the fairest method when resources are inadequate to serve everyone and no other criteria seem to be applicable.

If an evaluator is successful in obtaining approval for a randomized experiment, then the random assignment process must be carefully monitored to ensure proper implementation. Lack of such monitoring can destroy the experimental design. For example, an employment and training program with which one of the authors of this book once consulted (DeJong) had agreed to a randomized study. When a large group of eager youths appeared at the agency on the first day, however, the staff was overwhelmed and simply threw the program open to all of them, totally destroying the randomization procedure. When such events go undiscovered, the comparison groups are not equalized, and the eventual results are misleading. A two-step procedure is desirable in which client information is gathered by personnel different from those who do the random assignment. In this way, those personnel handling the assignment do so without knowledge of client identities or characteristics. Insulating the assignment process in this way reduces the opportunity for deviations from randomness to creep in and eases the monitoring task (Cook, Cook, & Mark, 1977).

Alternatives to Randomized Experiments. The barriers to randomized experiments may be sufficiently formidable as to require an alternative design. It is important to remember that anything other than a randomized experiment produces results in which confidence is reduced, because such alternative designs are weaker on internal validity (see Chapter 10). Properly conducted, however, these designs allow evaluation with a reasonable degree of certitude.

One alternative to the randomized experiment is to use a *quasi-experimental design*. When a program is meant to affect behavior about which data are routinely collected, a time-series design may be appropriate. For example, we described a time-series design in Chapter 10 (see Figure 10.2), which looked at whether changes in the laws for justifiable homicide changed the rate of justifiable homicide. The study looked at states that established so-called "stand your ground" laws in 2006, comparing rates of justifiable homicide before and after that date with states that did not have such laws. The comparison showed that states with such laws experienced a considerable rise in justifiable homicide after their passage, whereas states without such laws experienced no such increase. This is a multiple–time-series design that has a control group and thus protects against the validity threat of history. A time-series design without a control group would be subject to the validity threat of history.

A second alternative to randomized experiments is *matching*. If randomization is not feasible, it may be possible to match persons in the experimental group with persons having similar characteristics in a control group. Matching can be unreliable, however, because we can use relatively few variables, which leaves uncontrolled variables that might confound the results.

An example of an evaluation in which a form of matching was used was a study of the effectiveness of a short-term group care program for children in Connecticut (DeSena, 2005). The new program was sequentially introduced into communities in the state until, after a time, it was in operation in all communities. For the evaluation, the experimental group consisted of a sample of children in the new program, whereas the control group consisted of a sample of children receiving traditional foster care in communities in which the program had not yet been implemented at the time of the evaluation. Because the program was implemented in whole communities at a time, it was not possible to randomly assign children to experimental and control groups. To increase the probability that the two groups were comparable, each child selected for the control group was matched on age, gender, and ethnicity with a child in the new program. This provided some assurance that the two groups were comparable (at least on the characteristics used for the matching).

A third alternative to the randomized experiment (really another form of matching) is the use of *cohort groups*. Cohorts are groups of people who move through an organization or a treatment program at about the same time. For example, the following are cohorts: students in the same grade at a school, people receiving public assistance at the same time from a particular agency, and people in a drug rehabilitation program at the same time. Cohorts are valuable alternatives to randomized experiments, because we may be able to assume that each cohort in an organization or a program is similar to the cohort preceding it in terms of the characteristics that might affect a treatment outcome. In other words, each group should be alike in age, sex, socioeconomic status, and other characteristics that may be important. There can be very significant differences, however, and cohorts should always be assessed to detect any possible systematic variation.

An elaborate cohort study evaluating curriculum revision and televised instruction was conducted in El Salvador from 1969 to 1973 (Mayo, Hornick, & McAnany, 1976). Seventh-grade classes in 1969, 1970, and 1971 made up three separate cohorts of students. Within the cohorts, some classes received a new curriculum, some the new curriculum with televised instruction, and some the old curriculum. The cohorts from

1969 and 1970 were followed for three years, and the cohort from 1971 was followed for two years. Comparisons among the groups produced mixed results. The new curriculum was consistently superior to the old one, and televised instruction was superior during its first year. The superiority of televised instruction wore off, however, as the students became accustomed to it.

The major weakness of cohorts is, again, the threat to validity from history. Because the measurements are taken at widely spaced times, extraneous variables may intercede and affect the results. The El Salvador example is instructive on this point. It would be unlikely that a similar cohort study could have been reliably conducted 10 years later, as the country became unstable because of guerrilla warfare. Comparing a cohort from a period of peace with one from a period of near civil war has obvious problems.

A fourth alternative to the randomized experiment is the *regression discontinuity design*: People are selected to receive a treatment based on their score on a test, their eligibility for a program, or some other criterion. The study of recidivism in California discussed in Research in Practice 12.1 was a regression discontinuity design in which prison inmates were eligible for the experimental group if they had worked sufficient hours in prison to be eligible for unemployment benefits when released. Inmates who had worked fewer hours were put in the control group. This design often is implemented for evaluation research field experiments, and it can be useful. Regression discontinuity designs suffer, however, from some of the threats to internal validity, particularly selection and, in some cases, statistical regression. Incidentally, the summative evaluation described in Research in Practice 12.1 was an outgrowth of the formative evaluation project described earlier in this chapter about the provision of financial aid to newly released prisoners.

RESEARCH IN PRACTICE 12.1 Program Evaluation: Evidence-Based Evaluation: The Effectiveness of Programs to Reduce Recidivism

In Chapter 10, we discussed experiments as a research design, and in many ways experimental designs are the most desirable of all research designs because they provide us with the most confidence in making causal statements. Because of this, some proponents of evidence-based practice take the elements of the experimental design as the standard against which to assess the worth of evidence. Therefore, evaluation research often tries to use one of the experimental designs. To provide a more in-depth understanding of what it means to assess evidence, we present a guide, based on the elements of experimental designs, for evaluating the worthiness of evidence from research.

We illustrate how such guides can work by looking at a study designed to assess policies related to the most effective way to release inmates from prison. Policy makers, hoping to reduce recidivism, have promoted programs that provide financial assistance to former prisoners to help them make a successful transition to civilian life. Such programs typically provide a payment, like unemployment insurance, to provide financial support while the ex-inmate gets settled outside prison and searches for a job. Because many crimes are economically motivated, it seems reasonable to hypothesize that such financial assistance would reduce the likelihood that a newly released inmate would turn to crime.

To test this hypothesis, the Baltimore Living Insurance for Ex-Prisoners (or Baltimore LIFE) Project was developed (Lenihan, 1977; Rossi, Berk, & Lenihan, 1980). In this field experiment, high-risk inmates scheduled for release by the Maryland Department of Corrections were given various financial and job-related supports to see if they had an impact on their recidivism. In

(continued)

the following table, we list some of the criteria that the evidence-based practice approach would apply to assess the evidence in this study and then point out how the study meets each criterion.

Criterion	Study
Independent variable (treatment) clearly defined	Two independent variables: (1) receive financial assistance ($60 per week for 13 weeks after release) and (2) receive job placement services. NOTE: One experimental group received both, one received only financial assistance, and one received only job placement services.
Random selection to sample	No sampling—all high-risk inmates being released were included.
Control group	Yes—one group received neither independent variable.
Random assignment to control group	Yes—also random assignment to the three treatment groups.
Validity/reliability checks	Since the variables were well-defined behaviors, face validity was sufficient.
Dependent variable (outcome) clearly defined	Yes—two dependent variables: (1) Did they get a job? and (2) Did they avoid future criminal activity?

Some evidence-based approaches use a longer list of criteria, but this is adequate to illustrate the point that the characteristics of a controlled, randomized experiment can be used as a guide for assessing how good the evidence is in a particular study. Sometimes, the list is used as a checklist, indicating how many of the criteria are met in a particular study. Other approaches assign a numerical value to each criterion (depending on how important it is considered to be), and summing these produces a numerical score for each study that can be compared to other studies. In either case, this approach provides an organized way to assess how much confidence we have in the evidence provided by a study: The more the number of criteria met or the higher the score achieved, the more confidence we have in the evidence.

What did the recidivism study find? The men who received financial aid had an 8% lower rate of arrest for charges of theft. Arrests for other types of crime were not significantly different. Also, those who did not receive financial aid were arrested earlier, were more likely to be convicted, and were more likely to be returned to prison. Job placement services had no apparent impact on recidivism or occupational success.

The Baltimore LIFE Project also served as a model for a legislatively mandated program in California (Berk, Messinger, Berrecochea, & Rauma, 1985). It was designed much like the Baltimore LIFE Project except that the inmates actually applied for unemployment benefits once released from prison and were eligible if they had worked sufficient hours per week in prison. Because of this, however, the random assignment of inmates to experimental and control groups for evaluation purposes was not done; thus, the best research design for assessing program impacts—the randomized experiment—was not used. Instead, investigators used a regression discontinuity design, in which the experimental group consisted of those inmates who had worked enough to be eligible for unemployment benefits and the control group contained those

(continued)

who had not. This did not affect the operation of the program, but it did make the evaluation of it less certain. This would lead evidence-based practitioners and policy makers to give this later study a lower score in terms of the value of its evidence. Nonetheless, a conservative evaluation of its effects concluded that the program saved California $2,000 for each inmate involved. In other words, the costs of the program were far outweighed by the money saved, because some inmates in the program did not commit further crimes and the state saved the cost of incarcerating them.

The last major alternative to randomized experiments is the use of *statistical controls,* which are procedures that allow the effects of one or more variables to be removed or held constant so that the effects of other variables can be observed. These procedures allow comparisons to be made between groups that differ from one another on some characteristics thought to be important. The effects of the variables on which the groups differ are removed through statistical manipulation so that they cannot obscure the results. Statistical controls, however, even in their most elaborate application, can only approximate the level of control that is achievable in randomized experiments. As with matching, only variables that the researcher already knows to be potentially important can be statistically controlled, so there is always the possibility of leaving important extraneous variables uncontrolled. Furthermore, statistical controls tend to underadjust for differences between groups because of the error component in the measurement of the control variables (Berk & Rossi, 1990; Bernerth & Aguinis, 2016). The error allows at least some of the effects of the control variables to remain even after the statistical controls have been applied. Because of these limitations, statistical control alone may not be appropriate, but it is well suited as an adjunct to the physical control obtained through design. For example, in a matched design, we might find out after the fact that an important variable was left unmatched. Assuming that the necessary data were collected, we could make up for this error by applying statistical control to that variable.

The use of both design control and statistical control probably is the best overall approach for evaluation. This is because statistical control can even be useful in randomized experiments.

Nonpositivist Approaches to Evaluation

Nonpositivist approaches make quite different assumptions from positivist approaches about what is going on in a summative evaluation. First, nonpositivists assume that there are multiple stakeholders in—and, thus, multiple perspectives on—social interventions (Greene, 1994). A given research methodology may assess the program in terms of the interests of some, but not other, stakeholders. In fact, some critics of positivist approaches to evaluation argue that, because such evaluations typically are funded and supported by the sponsors and managers of the program, the evaluations tend to address issues of concern to those stakeholders—such as economic efficiency of the program, numbers of people served, or other issues that can be measured in quantitative (often monetary) ways. These approaches tend to focus on the importance of assessing program outcomes, efficiency, and accountability and, in fact, are the issues most readily addressed through the randomized experimental designs that positivists consider to be the ideal evaluation methodology. For evaluators who address different issues or the interests of other stakeholders, the randomized experimental design with control groups may be less important—or, possibly, even irrelevant—as a research design (Cook, 1985).

A second assumption of nonpositivist evaluators, especially those using an interpretive approach, is that interpretation and social meaning are at the core of social interventions (Denzin, 1989; Denzin, 2010; Smith, 1989; Weiss, 1998). In this view, social reality does not just exist "out there" but, rather, is created by people as they interact and exchange meanings. An interpretivist program evaluation focuses attention on how all the stakeholders—the sponsors and managers as well as the recipients of services—experience a social intervention. From some perspectives, such as the perspective of those receiving the services, economic efficiency and other quantitative matters may not be the key elements of the program at all. The point is that nonpositivist evaluators refuse to define issues and solutions solely from the perspective of the more powerful and dominant stakeholders. These concerns lead nonpositivist evaluators to research methodologies that are more useful for discovering the interpretations and perspectives of the various parties to the program: participant observation, in-depth interviewing, case studies, and other, more qualitative, approaches. In these approaches, control groups, random assignment, and random samples are less important than discovering meaning in the social contexts in which people live and allowing participants to frame their own issues and define problems using their own meaningful categories.

A third assumption of nonpositivist evaluators, especially those using a critical approach, is that social interventions typically reflect and reinforce inequitable distributions of power and resources in society. A central goal of the critical program evaluator is to reveal the mechanisms whereby inequities are reinforced and increased and to show how social programs promote the agenda of the powerful while doing relatively little for the less powerful. Critical evaluators might use either quantitative or qualitative approaches, but their approach is more participatory in nature: Less powerful stakeholders participate in designing and carrying out the evaluation, thus increasing the likelihood that the research designed will discover facts and relationships beneficial to them. They are consulted about the research all along the way, and one of the research goals is the empowerment of these groups. A part of this empowerment involves the evaluation serving as a catalyst for social change.

Portions of Hilton and Trella's evaluation of the youth job program reflected a nonpositivist orientation. There were multiple stakeholders in the evaluation, from the sponsoring foundation to the agency operating the program to clients to interesting community members including educators, politicians, and employers. Ultimately, the

researchers viewed their task as providing information to help stakeholders determine whether the program was worthwhile and a good use of scarce resources and the extent to which the program design was optimal to meeting program goals. This approach was complicated, however, by differences in perspectives as to what was "worthwhile" as well as political and economic contexts that made it difficult to reach definitive conclusions. Various stakeholders differed, for example, in the extent to which they viewed youth leaving the area for employment as a positive outcome. There was also some disagreement regarding how to treat enrollment in occupational training versus college enrollment, with some clearly favoring college enrollment as the desired outcome. Further, several youth faced difficult realities whereby they were forced to earn money immediately, making time and financial investments in education extremely challenging if not impossible. In several cases, program staff responded to these situations by helping youth find jobs quickly. Most of these jobs offered low wages, yet they met the needs of youth in difficult circumstances. How were these cases to be treated?

Ultimately Hilton and Trella's evaluation report contained many excerpts from in-depth qualitative interviews with youth participants, agency staff, and partner employees that introduced diverse perspectives toward the program and provided community and other context to understanding youth involvement in the program and various program outcomes. When the report was presented to various stakeholders, all were very pleased that several perspectives and contexts were covered. This led to productive discussion on the nature of these programs and reasonable expected outcomes while planning for future program cycles.

Research in Practice 12.2 provides another illustration of a program evaluation that uses a nonpositivist *approach*. Of course, the distinction between positivist and nonpositivist research does not rigidly follow the separation between quantitative and qualitative research, although there is a relationship. This is also true in the field of evaluation research. Although positivists and nonpositivists do have the methodological inclinations that we describe, the key distinctions between them have to do with assumptions rather than with particular research methodologies. Looking at both the positivist and nonpositivist perspectives achieves a much broader view of what evaluation research can accomplish and of what issues and values can be attended to in such research.

RESEARCH IN PRACTICE 12.2 Program Evaluation: A Nonpositivist Evaluation of a Juvenile Gang Intervention Program

Research in Practice 12.1 presented a program evaluation that was positivist in nature, using quantitative measures of variables and focusing a lot of attention on the economic efficiency of the program. Little consideration, however, was given to treating the released inmates as stakeholders in the program; their views were not solicited. A more nonpositivist approach was used in an evaluation of a juvenile gang intervention program in a rural community (Stum & Chu, 1999). The program evaluated in this study was a school partnership program that followed the philosophy of community policing. The basic idea was to build positive police–citizen partnerships based on trust and mutual respect, accomplished, in part, through daily visits to schools by the police to interact with and get to know the youths. Because there had been little prior research on such programs, especially as they operate in rural communities, the researchers decided that a more nonpositivist, exploratory, qualitative approach was appropriate.

The researchers decided that focus groups (see Chapter 7) and content analysis (see Chapter 8) would be the best methodologies. Earlier in this chapter, we discussed using focus groups as a part of formative evaluations, but this research provides an illustration of the use of focus groups in summative evaluations. The research focused on gang members and at-risk youth, and it explored their perceptions of themselves, their peers, their communities, and the gang prevention and intervention programs operating in their schools. (As discussed in Chapter 9, these qualitative approaches better enable us to understand the subjective experiences of the people being studied, and they better avoid the possibility that a researcher will impose his or her own meanings in a way that misses or distorts what is really going on.)

Recall that focus groups, also called group depth interviews, involve a moderator asking questions of a group and recording people's responses. The questions asked guide the discussion, but the moderator is free to ask additional questions and even to digress into new topics that seem fruitful based on the discussion. In addition, group interaction can stimulate responses that might not have occurred with other methodologies. Overall, focus groups are exploratory and encourage people to respond in their own words and by creating their own meanings. This is based on the assumptions made by nonpositivist program evaluators: The thoughts and perspectives of all stakeholders in a program should be assessed, and powerless or disadvantaged groups should have an opportunity to be heard.

In this study, data collection occurred in three separate focus groups in which each participant was involved. One addressed the school partnership policing program by asking youth about their contacts or relationships with the police. A second focus group addressed the youths' perceptions of themselves, their activities, and the crimes that they committed as well as their perceptions of police, probation officers, judges, and others in positions of authority. The third group had to do with how the youths felt about their peers and their communities.

All focus group discussions were tape-recorded, and a research assistant prepared notes based on his or her observation of the group discussion so that the tapes and notes could be compared as a way of assessing reliability and validity. Then, the tapes and notes were reviewed

(continued)

repeatedly to identify major themes in the data. If researchers disagreed about themes, they went back to the raw data (tapes and notes) to identify what led to the identification of a particular theme.

One of the conclusions the study came to was that, based on the opinions expressed by the youths in the focus groups, the school partnership program had serious weaknesses and might not be an effective intervention program for teens at risk. Most of the youth reported that they did not know—or, at best, hardly knew—the police officers with whom they were supposed to be developing positive relationships. In addition, they expressed concerns that contact with police authorities might bring them difficulties—the police could identify them as potential troublemakers because of their involvement in a program for at-risk teens. With no prior research on these programs, this exploratory, qualitative methodology is more likely to discover attitudes like these.

Cost–Benefit Analysis

One particular type of evaluation research, *cost–benefit analysis*, involves some unique issues and premises and, thus, warrants special attention. In an era of increasing accountability for social programs, this approach often serves as a foundation for social policy decisions, so it is important that it be used properly, with its strengths and limitations being well understood (Boardman, Greenberg, Vining, & Weimer, 2017; Hummel-Rossi & Ashdown, 2002).

On the surface, **cost–benefit analysis** appears to be seductively simple: Add up the costs of a program, subtract them from the dollar value of the benefits, and get the result—either a net gain (benefits exceed costs) or a net loss (costs exceed benefits). Such an approach is appealing to many policy makers, because it seems to clarify complex issues and programs through quantification. They would logically support and, perhaps, expand programs showing a net gain and curtail those showing a net loss. If only it were that simple! As we shall see, quantifying benefits and costs can be extremely difficult and often involves a number of unproved assumptions and estimates.

Cost–benefit analysis can be applied to a program during its planning stages, called *ex ante analysis*, or after the program has been in operation, called *ex post analysis* (Rossi et al., 2004). The major difference is that an ex ante analysis requires more estimates and assumptions than an ex post analysis, because no hard data exist regarding either costs or benefits. An ex post study has records of actual cost outlays and can determine benefits empirically through normal evaluation research procedures. The use of estimates in ex ante analyses means that results are far more tentative, however, and accounts for why ex ante analyses conducted by different parties sometimes come to widely divergent conclusions: They use different estimates and assumptions. Sorting out whose estimates are most valid has produced some lively debates among policy makers. Ex post analyses require fewer estimates, however, and therefore are more reliable.

Estimating Costs. The easy part of cost–benefit analysis—although by no means simple—is determining the **direct costs** of a program. The program has either a record of actual expenditures (in ex post analysis) or a proposed budget (in ex ante analysis). A budget proposal, however, is based on assumptions that may not be accurate. For example, the budget for a supplemental unemployment compensation program must assume a certain unemployment rate. If the actual rate changes, then the cost of the program can skyrocket or fall dramatically.

Considerably more difficult to estimate than direct program costs are what economists call *opportunity costs*. **Opportunity costs** are the value of forgone opportunities.

Human service agencies have limited resources. If they decide to fund a certain program, then the cost of the program includes the opportunity costs of not funding alternative programs. Normally, the estimated value of the benefits of competing programs is used as the basis for computing the opportunity costs of the program being analyzed. Computing the benefits lost by not initiating a program is complex, which makes it difficult to calculate the opportunity costs of the funded program. Such estimates need to be made, however, to provide an accurate picture of the total costs of a program.

Estimating and Monetizing Benefits. The really difficult—and often unreliable—part of cost–benefit analysis comes in determining program benefits and *monetizing*, or attaching a dollar value, to them. This process may be either fairly straightforward or mystical, depending on the program. In general, if a program's benefits are related to some economic activity, then they are easier to monetize—for example, the value of subsidized day care. The market price of private day care plus the added income of the parent who otherwise could not work constitute the major dollar benefits from the program, but what about program benefits less related to economic activity? How can we place a dollar value on such program benefits as improved mental health, improved self-esteem, reduced domestic violence, or other noneconomic outcomes? Cost–benefit analysis attempts, through complex procedures, to place a dollar value on practically anything. Doing so, however, requires many often-controversial assumptions and value judgments. Thus, cost–benefit analysis is of the greatest utility when the relationship between program benefits and a certain dollar value is fairly clear.

Another complicating factor in cost–benefit analysis is that benefits and costs do not accrue at the same time. Costs are incurred immediately upon the program's implementation, whereas benefits may not accrue until some later date, possibly far in the future. In some programs, such as education or job training, at least some of the benefits are long term indeed. This temporal gap is a problem, because the value of both costs and benefits changes with time. A dollar today does not have the same purchasing power that it did 10 years

ago. To make meaningful comparisons over time, we must adjust costs and benefits so that comparisons are made in constant dollars.

This adjustment involves the calculation of what is called the *discount rate*. The discount rate is the amount that future costs and benefits are reduced to make them comparable to the current value of money. Actual calculation of the discount rate involves some accounting procedures. There are also several competing approaches to its calculation (Rossi et al., 2004). As many disheartened investors will attest, predicting the future value of money is a risky business. Furthermore, the discount rate that is used has a marked effect on the outcome of the analysis. For all these reasons, it is common to run several analyses with differing discount rates to see how the program fares under different sets of assumptions.

Whose Costs, Whose Benefits? An important consideration in cost–benefit analysis is that costs and benefits are calculated from particular perspectives. Three different perspectives may be used: program participants, the funding source, or society as a whole. A comprehensive cost–benefit analysis would include all three.

Take the example of early childhood intervention programs, which are efforts by governmental or other agencies outside the family to support and improve the quality of life for youngsters from the prenatal period into the school years. These programs focus on providing health, education, and social service interventions. The theory behind such programs is that they will provide broad benefits to society, because the children they support generally will be healthier, do better in school, and be less likely to create problems of crime or welfare dependence as adults. In Table 12.1, we have listed some of the potential costs and benefits of such early intervention programs, along with an indication of which perspective might see each as a cost or a benefit.

Let us look at some elements in the table. For the mothers (participants) who can work at paying jobs because of the services provided by the programs, their costs are the loss of welfare payments they would receive if they did not work. Their benefits are the income received by working (together

TABLE 12.1 Perspectives on the Costs and Benefits of an Early Childhood Intervention Program

Benefits and Costs	Perspectives		
	Society	Participants	Funding Source
Costs of home visits to children	–	+	–
Reduction in emergency room visits by child	+	+	0
Increase in taxes paid by mother because of her increased employment income	+	–	+
Decrease in cost of government welfare payments to mother	0	–	+
Decrease in mother's arrest and jail costs	+	+	0
Decrease in child's arrest costs as an adolescent	+	+	0
Decrease in child's arrest cost as an adult	+	+	0
Income from mother's increased employment	0	+	0
Decrease in welfare payments to mother	0	–	+
Decrease in losses to crime victims	+	0	0

Note: +, an expected benefit from a given perspective; –, an expected cost from a given perspective; 0, neither a cost nor a benefit.
Source: Adapted from Karoly, L. A., Greenwood, P. W., Everingham, S. S., Hoube, J., Kilburn, M. R., Rydell, C. P., . . . Chiesa, J. (1998). *Investing in our children: What we know and don't know about the costs and benefits of early childhood interventions.* Santa Monica, CA: Rand.

with less tangible benefits, such as enhanced social status, job satisfaction, and freedom from child-care responsibilities). Participants also benefit from any reductions in criminal activity that the mother or child experiences because of participation in the program.

From the perspective of the funding sources—in this case, the federal government—the costs and benefits are quite different. The costs are the direct costs of running the program (e.g., costs of home visits) together with the opportunity costs of not using the money for something else. The benefits are the reduced costs of other public assistance programs and an increase in tax revenues because of the incomes of working mothers.

The societal perspective is the broadest and, frequently, the most difficult to calculate. (If the funding source is the government, then we should not assume that the government's perspective coincides with the societal perspective.

The government represents only those who control a particular government agency.) The costs to society of the early intervention program are the increased taxes or federal borrowing necessary to fund the program, plus the opportunity costs. Benefits are increased productivity of the mothers who are now freer to make economic, social, and cultural contributions to society (although we need to remember that performing as a parent or homemaker also is an essential contribution). Other less direct benefits might accrue if working and the additional income that it provides have positive effects on family relationships, the children's well-being, future aspirations, and the like. Of course, society as a whole benefits when costs associated with crime are reduced.

Early intervention programs involve more elements—and more costs and benefits—than we listed in Table 12.1, but that table helps clarify the idea that program costs and benefits need to be assessed from a variety of perspectives. People might also disagree over whether a particular element in the table is a cost or a benefit from a particular perspective, which only reinforces the point that cost–benefit analysis is difficult, complicated, and, often, contentious. Incidentally, most cost–benefit analyses of these early childhood intervention programs conclude that, if run well, the programs do provide substantially more benefits than costs (Karoly et al., 1998).

Cost-Effective Analysis

Because it is difficult to monetize benefits, interest has developed in an alternative approach that does not require benefits to be ascribed a dollar value. **Cost-effective analysis** compares program costs measured in dollars with program effects measured in whatever units are appropriate, such as achievement test scores, skill performance level, coping abilities, or whatever effect the program is supposed to produce. Such analysis is most useful for choosing among competing programs rather than for evaluating a single program. For example, cost-effective analysis often is used in evaluating HIV prevention programs (Holtgrave, 1998). The challenge to comparing prevention programs is having a meaningful standard of comparison. One approach is to employ cost–benefit analysis by comparing programs based on the benefit of money saved in medical care by preventing an infection. Such cost–benefit analysis, however, is insufficient for policy makers, because medical care dollars saved hardly represent the positive impact of a prevention program.

Evaluators have developed an alternative, nonmonetary measure, called the *QALY*, for cost-effective analysis. The term *QALY* refers to "quality-adjusted life years," or the number of years of additional life that result because infection did not occur, as well as the quality of that life (perfect health vs. some diminished level of capacity). We will not get into the complexity of measuring QALYs except to make the point that a variety of prevention programs can be directly compared in terms of money spent for each additional QALY achieved. Based on experience with the standard of program costs per QALY saved,

policy makers consider a ratio of $50,000 per QALY to be cost-effective.

Such cost-effective analyses of many competing programs make it possible to select the most efficient approach. Interpreting a single cost-effective analysis, however, is less clear-cut than a cost–benefit analysis, because the costs and benefits are not expressed in the same units. For this reason, cost-effective analysis is not an interchangeable substitute for cost–benefit analysis, because they answer different questions.

Like all forms of analysis, cost–benefit analysis is only as good as the data, the estimates, and the assumptions on which it is based. All these complex components should be explicitly discussed in the report and the users encouraged to evaluate their soundness. The real risk associated with cost–benefit analysis comes when bottom-line results are accepted blindly and become the overriding factor in decision making. At its current level of development, cost–benefit analysis is useful, but it must be cautiously interpreted as only one of many factors in the decision-making process concerning social programs.

The youth job program example did not include a cost-effective analysis because this was not a goal of the sponsoring foundation. Job programs like this one are often evaluated for cost-effectiveness, however. These analyses compare overall program costs, including opportunity costs for both the service provider and clients (investing time preparing for a career often means not working another job and earning money for some period of time), to economic impacts of connecting clients with new job opportunities.

IMPROVING UTILIZATION OF EVALUATION RESEARCH

At the beginning of this chapter, we described the purposes of evaluation research as improving service to clients, aiding in the policy-making process, and testing social science theories and practice approaches. In all these areas, the assumption is made that the research results will be used to produce some change in the status quo. In actuality, this often is not the case, because there are many barriers to using the results of evaluation research (MacGregor, 2011).

One barrier is the fault of evaluators. Because of poor design or execution, the evaluation may not produce clear-cut results. It is difficult to overcome resistance to change unless the reasons for change are strong and the direction that change should take is clear. All too often, the basic conclusion of an evaluation is this: "The program as currently operated is not achieving its intended goals." What is one to do with such a conclusion? It offers no indication of why the program is failing or suggestions for improving it. To avoid results like this, evaluation should be broadly conceived so that the findings indicate not only what the program does not do but also what it does do and why.

A second barrier to the use of evaluation research results is poor communication on the part of evaluators (Miller, 1987). Researchers are used to communicating with other researchers who share a common technical language and background. When communicating with one another, they assume those commonalities and write their reports accordingly. If this is done in an evaluation report, the results may be quite unclear to the practitioners, program administrators, and policy makers who are to use those results. Evaluation reports should be written so that they are clear and understandable to the audience who will use them, and evaluators should work through the report with sponsors, explaining it thoroughly and answering all questions.

A third barrier to the use of evaluation research is the failure of the researchers to press for adoption of their research findings. Such an advocacy role is foreign to many researchers, who may feel that their job terminates once the data have been analyzed. Implementation of modifications to a program often is complex, however, and program staff are faced with competing interests. Without active participation by the researcher, adoption of recommendations may not take place at all.

A fourth barrier is the ever-present resistance to change. People become accustomed to established procedures, and vested interests are difficult to overcome. In human service evaluations, it is fairly common for program administrators to ignore results that contradict prevailing attitudes and feelings toward services or that disrupt existing administrative structures. Often this results in administrators and staff creating new rationales for continuing a program and rationalizing negative results.

Back to the youth job program example, the researchers found that the stakeholders—from foundation staff to agency administrators to other community leaders—were eager to discuss the findings and next steps. The researchers sent a full report to the sponsoring agency who shared it with agency leaders and several interested community members. Then the researchers met with all interested stakeholders for an extensive discussion and planning session (where they created plans for a new, revised program). There was little disagreement over the findings or steps needed to improve the program. The discussion focused largely on outcomes and evaluation criteria and whether the program goals should surround long-term goals like permanent job placement in viable careers or shorter term goals like internship completion or enrollment and completion in higher education or skills training. In the end, the group favored a more short-term goal setting. The group also decided that more collaboration was needed with area community colleges and other skill training providers.

Practitioner Profile 12.1 below presents a good example of the complexities of selecting criteria in program evaluations.

PRACTITIONER PROFILE 12.1 Rayan Orbom, Program Manager, Permanent Supportive Housing

Rayan Orbom is program manager for a housing first program in the northwestern United States. Orbom has been working in homeless services within the agency for the past seven years and recently completed a master of social work degree. Orbom's main task at her job is to supervise

(continued)

caseworkers within her agency's housing first program. While she does not maintain a caseload of her own, she works closely with caseworkers, especially those facing challenges engaging clients, and interacts frequently with program participants.

According to Orbom, "We serve clients who meet HUD definitions for chronic homelessness. Our clients go through a coordinated entry system and we take the number one person on that list, the person who ranks as the 'most vulnerable' person in our area" (All quotes are based on personal communication on July 12, 2018.). When asked about how vulnerability is evaluated, she explained that clients undergo a series of evaluations—from what is called the Vulnerability Index-Service Prioritization Decision Assistance Tool (VI-SPDAT; a short version of the Service Prioritization Decision Assistance Tool), which determines if they do a full SPDAT. The full SPDAT ranks people from 0 to 60. When a person scores the highest, then they add his or her months of homelessness—how long someone has been homeless across his or her entire life. That gives them a total score. The person who scores the highest is #1 and the rest are ranked accordingly.

When asked about the SPDAT and what it measures, Orbom explained,

In my opinion what it really measures is their involvement in the community and the overall cost of that involvement to the community. People score high based on how many times they interact with police, how many times they end up in jail, or how many times they use emergency rooms.

According to Orbom, those who score highest are those with substantial substance abuse disorders and those with severe personality disorders. She also explained that since they added months of homelessness to the overall score they are getting more older adults on their caseload. This change, she explains, was a result of a mandate from the Department of Housing and Urban Development (HUD) that local systems needed to prioritize homeless veterans (many of whom are older adults) and people who have been on the streets the longest. Most of her clients had been homeless for more than 10 years.

Orbom explained that her program does not complete initial client assessment (the SPDAT) but that they complete subsequent SPDATs every 30 days for the first three months and every year thereafter. "Initially scores tend to go up," Orbom stated. "After building some rapport with caseworkers the clients tend to be a little more honest about the questions, because some of them are really personal. After that they go down significantly," she explained. When asked whether or not clients might overstate their vulnerabilities to get higher on the list, Orbom explained that the majority do not because they are ashamed to fully disclose the extent of their need. The one group that did tend to overstate their vulnerabilities were those without any substance abuse disorder, particularly the medically fragile homeless. Orbom explained,

These folks tend to have high medical needs, and they may use the emergency room frequently for healthcare. But they don't tend to be disruptive or have police involvement, so they tended not to rise to the top of the list of scores. So some of them maybe stretched the truth a bit about their use of medical services.

Orbom continued, "My campers, those sleeping outside, generally out of sight and out of town, they also don't tend to score as high because they're more self-sufficient, in contrast to the folks who live in the downtown area." Orbom explained that the assessment tool is incredibly important for determining who is served and who is not. Initially, she explained, the goal was to

(continued)

provide permanent housing to anyone who scored an 8 or above of a possible 16 score on the VI-SPDAT. Now she only serves people who score a 16. Orbom's agency serves just under 200 people, but there is a waiting list of more than 900. This makes the assessment tools (the initial VI-SPDAT and the full SPDAT) incredibly political. Orbom explains,

> I have looked closely at these assessment tools and have a good understanding how each question contributes to overall scores. I am not sure it does a really good job of measuring vulnerability. That is why I have said that it really seems to measure costs to communities of homelessness more than personal vulnerabilities of clients. I think that is what researchers said was an issue of measurement validity. To me it is more about who gets services and who does not.

When asked whether or not research and knowledge of research were important to her work, Orbom replied,

> Yes, hands down. That is the only way to show that we're doing good work and if we're off track. It is the only way to get beyond the biases we all have about our own work and what works and what does not. It helps us reach out to new funders and other partners as well.

Orbom explained that having good program data is critical to her work because it helps her in developing housing placements. "Landlord outreach is really important," she explained.

> We recently developed a fact sheet with data from our program that shows our success rates across the entire program. It shows how many clients have entered housing and what percentage have remained, how many have the program to permanent housing. We include demographic data about clients and their disabilities. We let them know that this program can be successful for people with significant challenges. We also include number of violations and damages created. This is much more powerful than just creating one basic and sappy story showing that everything is great once a person is in housing. Landlords feel more secure about our program when they see data. They feel better about leasing units to us.

Orbom also explained that her agency recently received a grant from a local foundation to develop a peer mentoring program whereby formerly homeless adults work with housing first clients to encourage them to engage in healthcare, mental healthcare, and substance abuse treatment services. Orbom and her staff had conducted a series of focus groups with clients to determine whether or not there was interest in this type of program. They found that there was strong support for it and that clients were very excited to work with peers who were not connected to any specific agency or government entity. "We found that people were very interested in the idea of helpers whose only goal was to be supportive but did not have any power over them," she explained.

> Our clients said they really like the idea of working with people who "get it." There is a lot of trauma involved in living in the streets and they don't want to have to explain it over and over to people who do not really understand. When people become housed they tend to lose a lot of friends who were on the streets. And a lot of times that is OK

(continued)

because these people are not healthy friends. But they also want to be around people who "get it." So this is a way for them to meet people who understand but who are healthy.

According to Orbom, the program's success is based largely on their abilities to adapt to better meet clients' needs. Evaluation and research are central to this, she explains. Getting input from clients is critical, but challenging. Orbom has remained focused on creating a welcoming environment in the program, developing rapport with clients, and, most importantly, showing clients that their input matters and can result in real program changes. Orbom noted,

We recognize that it is relatively easy to rely on volunteers to participate in focus groups, but we also know that creates lots of bias in our sample. We're working on creating one-on-one meetings with people more reluctant to participate and those who are not happy with the program to see if they might feel more comfortable in that type of setting. One of the things that really helps is when we're able to show them that their input really does matter and has actually changed the program—like where we've been able to get rules changed about visitors or what is allowed in someone's apartment. That seems to get people more interested in participating.

One change suggested to improve research utilization is increased dissemination of results (Weiss, 1998). Earlier, we expressed concern over the fact that evaluation reports often are not widely circulated. Broader dissemination may bring a report to the attention of someone who is willing to use the results.

Evaluation research reports are published in a number of ways. Sometimes, they are published in social science or human service research journals, such as *Journal of Applied Behavioral Science* or *Journal of Applied Social Science*. Over the past few decades, more outlets for the publication of evaluation research have developed. Evaluation research reports are also published in government documents and reports, especially when the study concerns a government program; these can be accessed like other government documents.

Some evaluation reports are not published, however, and this can make them more difficult—but not impossible—to find. Unpublished results may be presented at meetings of applied research organizations, such as the Association for Applied and Clinical Sociology, the NTL Institute for Applied Behavioral Science, and the National Association of Social Workers. In some cases, unpublished research reports can be obtained from the researchers themselves or from the organizations or agencies for which the research was done. Unpublished reports can be difficult to locate, because they often are not included in the databases that can be accessed online or through libraries to search for published research reports. Some may be found through an Internet search or by participating in networks of professionals doing research in the same area.

Another change that increases the use of the evaluation results is to involve the potential users in the evaluation research itself. Users can help design the research or serve as interviewers. This results in better communication between evaluators and users: The users perceive the evaluation as being more relevant and credible, and they are more committed to the evaluation (Dawson & D'Amico, 1985).

What is really needed to improve research utilization is for policy makers and program administrators to develop an increased willingness to put evaluation results to use. In fact, resistance to research utilization does appear to be declining, and there may be a growing awareness that common sense and conventional wisdom are inadequate bases for designing and operating effective social programs (Rossi et al., 2004). This sentiment is reflected in the CSWE 2015 EPAS, which stresses the importance of evidence-based practice and includes the evaluation of practice as one of nine core social work competencies (EPAS, 2015). Years of experience with ineffective programs have made this conclusion evident.

Such changing perspectives are encouraging for the future of evaluation research and its increased utilization.

REVIEW AND CRITICAL THINKING

Main Points

- Evaluation research is the use of scientific research methods to plan intervention programs, to monitor the implementation of new programs and the operation of existing ones, and to determine how effectively programs or clinical practices achieve their goals.
- Formative evaluation focuses on the planning, development, and implementation of intervention programs.
- Summative evaluation assesses the effectiveness and efficiency of programs and the extent to which program effects may be generalized to other settings and populations.
- Prior to beginning evaluation, an evaluability assessment is conducted to gain knowledge about the program as operated and to identify those aspects of it that can be evaluated.
- Proximate goals are evaluable, short-run goals logically related to the achievement of long-term goals that are impractical to evaluate.
- Despite frequent difficulties associated with their use, randomized experiments constitute the strongest, most desirable designs for assessing program impact.
- Cost–benefit analysis, through the use of complex assumptions and estimates, compares the costs of a program with the dollar value of its benefits.
- Cost–benefit analysis and cost-effective analysis are not interchangeable. Cost–benefit analysis is useful for evaluating a single program, whereas cost-effective analysis is useful for choosing the most efficient program from among competing approaches.
- It is important that bottom-line results from either cost–benefit or cost-effective analyses not be accepted blindly but, rather, that the data, estimates, and assumptions on which the results are based be considered carefully.

IMPORTANT TERMS FOR REVIEW

Cost–benefit analysis
Cost-effective analysis
Direct costs
Evaluability assessment
Evaluation research

Formative evaluation research
Logic model
Needs assessment
Opportunity costs

Stakeholders
Summative evaluation research

CRITICAL THINKING

1. Why is program evaluation an increasingly critical activity in human services? How are programs evaluated in the areas of practice in which you are most interested? Who are the major stakeholders in these evaluations? Who conducts the evaluations? What processes and outcomes are evaluated? How are evaluations reported? How do policy makers and service providers respond to these evaluations?

2. What factors should be considered in designing an evaluation? Imagine you were creating an evaluation for a program with which you are familiar (or in which you have worked). What would you hope to learn from the evaluation? Who would you ask to conduct the evaluation (and what skills would be required)? Would you focus on program processes or outcomes? What outcomes would be evaluated? How would you measure these outcomes?

3. How can leaders of social service systems, human service agency administrators and staff, and individual professionals make better use of evaluations to improve services? Imagine how a large-scale evaluation would be received by various stakeholders of a program that is important to you. Would there be resistance to the evaluation process or findings? Would there be disagreements about what gets measured and how? Would some see the evaluation as a threat? How can stakeholders create evaluation processes and outcomes that are seen as a critical step in creating effective services and not an administrative hurdle?

EVALUATING COMPETENCY (FROM THE COUNCIL ON SOCIAL WORK EDUCATION [CSWE] 2015 EDUCATIONAL POLICY AND ACCREDITATION STANDARDS [EPAS])

Competency 4: Engage in Practice-Informed Research and Research-Informed Practice

- The 2015 EPAS stresses that social workers should know principles of logic and scientific inquiry. Identify a program that is important to you and create a logic model identifying the program's inputs, throughputs, and outputs.
- Now imagine you are creating an evaluation of that program. How would you evaluate each component of that logic model? What data would you collect? What would these data suggest about the program as a whole?

Competency 5: Engage in Policy Practice

- Identify a federal, state, or local policy that shapes a program or service important to you. How is that policy evaluated? Has the policy changed over time based on these evaluations?

- Are the policy evaluations discussed earlier a fair reflection of the effectiveness of that policy? If not, what changes would you suggest for evaluating the policy?

Competency 9: Evaluate Practice With Individuals, Families, Groups, Organizations, and Communities

- Social workers and other human service professionals are often so busy with their clients and other aspects of their jobs that it is difficult to devote enough time to evaluation. How can human service leaders make evaluation a more central component of practice?
- Many human service agencies have specialists within an agency or external consultants who manage the bulk of program evaluation activities within the organization. Why then should social workers and other human service professionals who plan to work directly with clients receive training in evaluation?

SELF-ASSESSMENT

1. Which of these terms refers to the use of scientific research methods to plan intervention programs, to monitor the implementation of new programs and the operation of existing ones, and to determine how effectively programs or clinical practices achieve their goals?
   a. Qualitative research
   b. Policy research
   c. Evaluation research
   d. Field research
2. Which of the following is not a reason that evaluation research has become more important in human services in recent years?
   a. There have been advances in evidence-based practice.
   b. Funders are increasingly interested in program outcomes.
   c. Accreditation agencies like CSWE are increasingly focused on evidence-based practice and evaluation of services.
   d. Students have become more interested in research method courses in recent years.
3. Which of the following statements is accurate?
   a. Basic research generally has immediate application whereas evaluation research is generally only for administrative purposes.
   b. Evaluation research tends to have practical and immediate applications whereas basic research is typically conducted for general information purposes and hypothesis testing.
   c. It is impossible to know the value of any kind of research until long after it has been conducted.
   d. Basic research and evaluation research both tend to have immediate application.

4. Which is more likely to be publicly disseminated?
   a. Basic research.
   b. Evaluation research.
   c. Neither basic nor evaluation research is likely to be disseminated.
   d. They are equally likely to be disseminated.
5. Which of the following focuses on providing information to guide the planning, development, and implementation of a specific program?
   a. Summative evaluation research
   b. Survey research
   c. Focus groups
   d. Formative evaluation research
6. Collecting data to determine how many people in a community need particular services and assessing what level of services or personnel already exists to fill a need is known as a(an):
   a. Community assessment.
   b. Inventory.
   c. Needs assessment.
   d. Factor analysis.
7. Which of the following refers to a process that allows investigators to decide whether a program has the necessary elements to be evaluated?
   a. Evaluability assessment
   b. Needs assessment
   c. Sampling
   d. Summative evaluation
8. In evaluation research, the changes in client knowledge, attitudes, or behaviors that the program is presumed to produce are known as:
   a. Outputs.
   b. Inputs.
   c. Throughputs.
   d. Outcomes.
9. In cost–benefit analyses, opportunity costs refer to:
   a. The value of forgone opportunities.
   b. The costs associated with enrolling a client in a program.
   c. Fixed program costs associated with maintaining buildings and equipment.
   d. Costs associated with following up with clients to measure long-term outcomes.
10. Which of these is not a barrier to utilization of evaluation research findings?
   a. Researchers sometimes fail to produce clear-cut results.
   b. Researchers do not always advocate for the use of findings to shape services.
   c. It is not considered ethical for researchers to help practitioners interpret and make use of evaluation findings.
   d. Agency administrators and staff are sometimes resistant to change.

ANSWER KEY FOR SELF-ASSESSMENT QUIZ

1. **c.** Evaluation research
2. **d.** Students have become more interested in research method courses in recent years.
3. **b.** Evaluation research tends to have practical and immediate applications whereas basic research is typically conducted for general information purposes and hypothesis testing.
4. **a.** Basic research
5. **d.** Formative evaluation research
6. **c.** Needs assessment
7. **a.** Evaluability assessment
8. **d.** Outcomes
9. **a.** The value of forgone opportunities.
10. **c.** It is not considered ethical for researchers to help practitioners interpret and make use of evaluation findings.

FOR FURTHER READING

Boruch, R. F. (1996). *Randomized experiments for planning and evaluation*. Thousand Oaks, CA: Sage. This author stresses the point made in this chapter that good program evaluations should be based on randomized experimental designs. The book is packed with useful examples of how to do this, often in situations where it might seem to be impossible.

Campbell, D. T., & Russo, M. J. (1999). *Social experimentation*. Thousand Oaks, CA: Sage. Donald Campbell was one of the giants in the fields of experimentation and evaluation research. This book presents his approaches to how social experiments should be designed and how they can improve society.

Fitzpatrick, J. L., Sanders, J. R., & Worthen, B. R. (2010). *Program evaluation: Alternative approaches and practical guidelines* (4th ed.). Englewood Cliffs, NJ: Prentice Hall. This text provides an overview of a wide variety of approaches to evaluation and extensive practical guidelines for carrying out evaluation studies.

Ginsberg, L. H. (2001). *Social work evaluation: Principles and methods*. Boston, MA: Allyn & Bacon. In addition to traditional methods of outcome evaluation, this source includes chapters on licensure, accreditation, internal program evaluation, and user satisfaction that make the book relevant to the human service practitioner.

Gupta, K., Sleezer, C. M., & Russ-Eft, D. F. (2007). *A practical guide to needs assessment* (2nd ed.). New York, NY: Wiley/Pfeiffer. This book provides an overview of needs assessment, step-by-step details for several models of needs assessment, and illustrations of various data-collection tools. It is especially useful for staff training program assessment.

Nas, T. F. (1996). *Cost–benefit analysis: Theory and application*. Thousand Oaks, CA: Sage. The author shows, in much more detail than could be included in this chapter, how to conduct good cost–benefit analyses. The book covers all the relevant issues.

Patton, M. Q. (2002). *Qualitative research and evaluation methods* (3rd ed.). Thousand Oaks, CA: Sage. This book considers both theoretical and practical issues in conducting program evaluations. It also emphasizes the use of qualitative research and stresses the perspective that good program evaluations must be designed to be useful to program managers and policy makers.

Shadish, W. R., Jr., Cook, T. D., & Leviton, L. C. (1993). *Foundations of program evaluation*. Newbury Park, CA: Sage. This volume looks at the origins of program evaluation and at the accumulated experiences of veteran program evaluators to provide an insightful discussion regarding both the development of the field and key issues that are relevant today.

REFERENCES

Berk, R. A., Messinger, S. L., Berrecochea, J. E., & Rauma, D. (1985). The foundations of parole in California. *Law and Society Review, 19*(1), 69–106.

Berk, R., & Rossi, P. (1990). *Thinking about program evaluation*. Newbury Park, CA: Sage.

Bernerth, J. B., & Aguinis, H. (2016). A critical review and best-practice recommendations for control variable usage. *Personnel Psychology, 69*, 229–283. doi:10.1111/peps.12103

Bhaskar, R. (2014). *The possibility of naturalism: A philosophical critique of the contemporary human sciences*. London, UK: Routledge.

Boardman, A. E., Greenberg, D. H., Vining, A. R., & Weimer, D. L. (2017). *Cost benefit analysis: Concepts and practice*. Cambridge, UK: Cambridge University Press.

Chen, H. T. (2015). *Practical program evaluation: Theory driven evaluation and the integrated evaluation perspective* (2nd ed.). Thousand Oaks, CA: Sage.

Chen, H., & Rossi, P. H. (1980). The multi-goal, theory-driven approach to evaluation: A model linking basic and applied social science. *Social Forces, 59*(1), 106–122. doi:10.1093/sf/59.1.106

Coe, R. D., & Hill, D. H. (1998). Food stamp participation and reasons for nonparticipation: 1986. *Journal of Family and Economic Issues, 19*(2), 107–130. doi:10.1023/a:1022996506711

Cook, T. D. (1985). Postpositivist critical multiplism. In L. Shotland & M. M. Mark (Eds.), *Social science and social policy* (pp. 21–62). Beverly Hills, CA: Sage.

Cook, T. D., Cook, F. L., & Mark, M. M. (1977). Randomized and quasi-experimental designs in evaluation research: An introduction. In L. Rutman (Ed.), *Evaluation research methods*. Beverly Hills, CA: Sage.

Council on Social Work Education. (2015). *Educational priorities and accreditation standards: For baccalaureate and master's social work programs*. Retrieved from https://cswe.org/getattachment/Accreditation/Standards-and-Policies/2015-EPAS/2015EPASandGlossary.pdf.aspx

Dawson, J. A., & D'Amico, J. J. (1985). Involving program staff in evaluation studies: A strategy for increasing information use and enriching the data base. *Evaluation Review, 9*(2), 173–188. doi:10.1177/0193841x8500900205

DeMartini, J. (1982). Basic and applied sociological work: Divergence, convergence, or peaceful coexistence? *Journal of Applied Behavioral Science, 18*(2), 203–215. doi:10.1177/002188638201800207

Denzin, N. (1989). *The research act: A theoretical introduction to sociological methods* (3rd ed.). Englewood Cliffs, NJ: Prentice Hall.

Denzin, N. K. (2010). Moments, mixed methods, and paradigm dialogs. *Qualitative Inquiry, 16*(6), 419–427. doi:10.1177/1077800410364608

DeSena, A. D. (2005). SAFE homes: Is it worth the costs? An evaluation of a group home permanency planning program for children who first enter out-of-home care. *Child Abuse & Neglect, 29*(6), 627–643. doi:10.1016/j.chiabu.2004.05.007

Foundation, K. (2004). *Logic model development guide: Using logic models to bring together planning, evaluation, and action*. Battle Creek, MI: W. K. Kellogg Foundation.

Gibbs, L. (1991). *Scientific reasoning for social workers: Bridging the gap between research and practice*. New York, NY: Macmillan.

Greene, J. C. (1994). Qualitative program evaluation. In N. K. Denzin & Y. S. Lincoln (Eds.), *Handbook of qualitative research* (pp. 530–544). Thousand Oaks, CA: Sage.

Gruber, J. B., Wang, W., Quittner, A., Salyakina, D., & McCafferty-Fernandez, J. (2018). Utilizing community health needs assessments (CHNAs) in nonprofit hospitals to guide population-centered outcomes research for pediatric patients: Outcomes research for pediatric patients: New recommendations for CHNA reporting. *Population Health Management, 22*(1), 25–31. doi:10.1089/pop.2018.0049

Holtgrave, D. R. (Ed.). (1998). *Handbook of economic evaluation of HIV prevention programs*. New York, NY: Plenum Press.

Hummel-Rossi, B., & Ashdown, J. (2002). The state of cost-benefit and cost-effectiveness analyses in education. *Review of Educational Research, 72*(1), 1–30. doi:10.3102/00346543072001001

Kalra, V. S., Fieldhouse, E. A., & Alam, S. (2001). Avoiding the new deal: A case study of nonparticipation by minority ethnic young people. *Youth & Policy, 72*, 63–79. Retrieved from http://www.youthandpolicy.org/wp-content/uploads/2017/07/y-and-p-72.pdf

Karoly, L. A., Greenwood, P. W., Everingham, S. S., Houbé, J., Kilburn, M. R., Rydell, C. P., . . . Chiesa, J. (1998). *Investing in our children: What we know and don't know about the costs and benefits of early childhood interventions*. Santa Monica, CA: Rand.

Lenihan, K. (1977). Unlocking the second gate. *Department of Labor R&D monograph 45*. Washington, DC: U.S. Government Printing Office.

Lynch, K. B., Geller, S. R., Hunt, D. R., Galano, J., & Dubas, J. S. (1998). Successful program development using implementation evaluation. *Journal of Prevention and Intervention in the Community, 17*(2), 51–64. doi:10.1300/j005v17n02_05

MacGregor, S. (2011). The impact of research on policy in the drugs field. *Methodological Innovations Online, 6*(1), 40–57. doi:10.4256/mio.2010.0027

Mayo, J. K., Hornick, R. C., & McAnany, E. G. (1976). *Educational reform with television: The El Salvador experience*. Palo Alto, CA: Stanford University Press.

McCord, J. A. (1978). Thirty-year follow-up of treatment effects. *American Psychologist, 33*(3), 284–289. doi:10.1037//0003-066x.33.3.284

McKillip, J. (1987). *Need analysis: Tools for human services and education*. Beverly Hills, CA: Sage.

Mertens, D. M. (2014). *Research and evaluation in education and psychology: Integrating diversity with quantitative, qualitative and mixed methods*. Los Angeles, CA: Sage.

Miller, L. P. (1987). The application of research to practice: A critique. *American Behavioral Scientist, 30*(1), 70–80. doi:10.1177/000276486030001008

Navarro, A. E., Wilbur, K. H., Yonashiro, J., & Homeier, D. C. (2010). Do we really need another meeting? Lessons from the Los Angeles county Elder Abuse Forensic Center. *The Gerontologist, 50*(5), 702–711. doi:10.1093/geront/gnq018

Orr, L. L. (1998). *Social experimentation: Evaluating public programs with experimental methods*. Thousand Oaks, CA: Sage.

Patton, M. Q. (1987). Evaluation's political inherency: Practical implications for design and use. In D. J. Palumbo (Ed.), *The politics of program evaluation* (pp. 100–145). Newbury Park, CA: Sage.

Protection of Human Subjects, 45 C.F.R. § 46.102 (2018).

Rossi, P. H., Berk, R. A., & Lenihan, K. J. (1980). *Money, work, and crime: Experimental evidence*. New York, NY: Academic Press.

Rossi, P. H., Lipsey, M. W., & Freeman, H. E. (2004). *Evaluation: A systematic approach* (7th ed.). Thousand Oaks, CA: Sage.

Sherman, L. (1992). *Policing domestic violence: Experiments and dilemmas*. New York, NY: Free Press.

Slaughter, S. E., Hill, J. N., & Snelgrove-Clarke, E. (2015). What is the extent and quality of documentation and reporting of fidelity to implementation strategies: A scoping review. *Implementation Science, 10*, 129. doi:10.1186/s13012-015-0320-3

Smith, M. F. (1989). *Evaluability assessment: A practical approach*. Boston, MA: Kluwer Academic.

Stum, K., & Chu, M. M. (1999). Gang prevention and intervention in a rural town in California: At-risk youth and the community policing school partnership program. *Journal of Gang Research, 7*, 1–12.

Weiss, C. H. (1998). *Evaluation: Method for studying programs and policies* (2nd ed.). Upper Saddle River, NJ: Prentice Hall.

13
SCALING

CHAPTER OUTLINE

Evaluating Competency (From the Council on Social Work Education [CSWE] 2015 Educational Policy and Accreditation Standards [EPAS])

Competency 2: Engage Diversity and Difference in Practice

Competency 4: Engage in Practice-Informed Research and Research-Informed Practice

Competency 7: Assess Individuals, Families, Groups, Organizations, and Communities

Self-Assessment

Answer key for Self-Assessment Quiz

For Further Reading

References

INTRODUCTION

Margaret is a clinical social worker. For the past five years, she has worked in a state prison providing treatment to adult men with a variety of mental health conditions. She recently left this job for a position in a skilled nursing long-time care facility. This is the first time the nursing facility has had a full-time clinical social worker. In the past, mental healthcare was provided by a clinical social worker who came to the facility periodically to meet with the clients. The facility administrators had seen a rise in the number of residents suffering from depression and felt it was important to have a trained mental health professional on-site. Margaret has had lots of experience treating clients for depression, but she is somewhat concerned about working with older adults with depression because the vast majority of her clients in the past have been much younger, most between 20 and 50.

One of Margaret's main concerns is assessing depression in older adults. She is very familiar with the Beck Depression Inventory (BDI), a 21-item questionnaire used to evaluate depression in adults. She found the questionnaire worked well in the prison, and most clients (inmates) could complete it with little difficulty. Both her research on the inventory and her personal experiences showed that it worked. Patients who scored high on the depression scale tended to be those who showed outward signs of depression. Many who scored on the "severe" and "extreme" ends of the scale reported they had been diagnosed as clinically depressed in the past.

Margaret generally felt positive about the BDI. It worked well in her previous job, but she was concerned that it might not work as well with clients in the nursing facility. Her main concerns were the last eight items of the questionnaire that concerned clients' appearance, ability to work, changes in sleep, energy, appetite, weight change, concerns about overall health, and interest in sex. While these items did help her identify potential signs of depression among adults at the prison, she wondered how well they would help her distinguish between people who have depression and people who do not have depression in the nursing facility. While she has not had a lot of experience providing treatment to older adults, she does know that physical changes in older adulthood occur regardless of whether people are suffering from depression or not. Margaret believes her first task at the new job is to do some research and find a depression assessment tool that will work for this population.

We revisit Margaret's dilemma toward the end of this chapter after presenting many types of scales and introducing several factors professionals should consider if choosing scales that meet their needs. Please keep the following questions in mind as we introduce concepts related to scaling: (a) What scales or types of scales are available that pertain to your area of practice? (b) What client-related factors are important to consider when selecting an assessment scale? (c) How can you evaluate the extent to which a given scale will produce valid and reliable measures of a client's situation, condition, or outcome?

We discussed measurement in research at some length in Chapter 5 and explained that some measurement is fairly straightforward and involves the use of only a single *item*, or indicator, of a variable. We can, for example, measure a person's age with one question that asks how old the person is. Likewise, such variables as marital status or number of children in a family normally are measured with a single item. These variables refer to phenomena that are fairly unambiguous and for which a single indicator provides a valid and reliable measure.

Many other variables including depression, however, are much more difficult and complex to measure. In some cases, we may have more than one indicator of a variable. In other cases, the variable may involve a number of dimensions and call for multiple indicators. In still other cases, we may be concerned with the *degree* to which a variable is present. In cases where a single-item measuring instrument is inadequate, we use a **scale**: a number of items that combine to form a composite score on a variable. To measure people's attitudes toward having children, for example, we could ask how much they agree with a series of questions; together, those questions make up the scale that would indicate their overall attitude toward having children.

ADVANTAGES OF SCALING

When the concept to be measured is complex, as in the case of depression, multiple-item scales offer substantial advantages for the researcher—advantages that often outweigh the difficulty of the scale's construction. Scales have four major advantages over single-item measures: improved validity, improved reliability, increased level of measurement, and increased efficiency in data handling.

Improved Validity

When measuring abstract or complex variables, generally a multiple-item measure is more valid than a single-item measure. Consider the variable of depression: It is typically measured by asking people to respond to multiple statements (items) rather than just one or a few because no single question or statement could possibly measure something as complex and multifaceted as depression. There are many multiple-item scales that measure depression. The BDI (see oml.eular.org/sysModules/obxOML/docs/id_170/BDI.pdf) is one example. This 21-item questionnaire includes items from many aspects of a respondent's life, from general feelings about themselves, to suicidality, to social life, to work, to physical symptoms typically associated with depression. Each of the items are to be answered by selecting from a scale of 0 through 3, with 0 indicating the item (such as feeling like a failure or level of interest in other people) does not apply to the respondent and more serious depression being indicated as the numbers increase. The fact that this questionnaire has 21 items is not surprising as no single item could encompass all these aspects of depression. Multiple-item scales such as the BDI provide more valid measures of such complex phenomena.

Improved Reliability

In general (as shown in Chapter 5), the more items a measure contains, the more reliable it is, because the statements making up a scale actually are just a sample of the entire universe of statements that could have been used. A single-item measure is a sample of one, and it is less likely to be *representative* of the universe of statements than more than one item is. Multiple-item scales are larger samples from this universe and are more likely to be representative and, therefore, more reliable than single-item measures.

Increased Level of Measurement

Single-item measures are likely to produce data that are nominal or, at best, *partially ordered data*, a term that refers to data with a few ordered categories but with many cases tied for each category.

Although superior to nominal data, partially ordered data are less desirable than fully ordered data, in which nearly every case has its own rank (see Chapter 14). Multiple-item scales can produce fully ordered and, possibly, interval level data. A higher level of measurement means better measurement in terms of precision and increased flexibility in data analysis.

Increased Efficiency in Data Handling

Because the items in a scale are all related (in that they all measure the same variable), we can summarize the responses to these items into a single number or score for each respondent. This achieves the quantification goal of measurement, and it means that all the separate responses to each of the items do not have to be analyzed individually. Each score summarizes a great deal of information about each respondent and facilitates analysis of the data.

DEVELOPING SCALES

Once a researcher decides to use a scale as a measuring device, he or she needs to find or develop an appropriate scale. In most cases, scales consist of questions to which people respond or statements to which they indicate their level of agreement. (In Chapter 7, we presented guidelines for writing questions to be used in questionnaires or interviews, and those same general rules apply to the development or selection of scale items. Readers should review those guidelines now and consider them in the context of scale construction.)

In many cases, it is possible to use a complete scale already developed by someone else if that scale is a valid and reliable measure of the variables under investigation. A scale can also be made up of statements—or even whole sections—taken from previously developed scales. A major advantage of existing items or scales is that their validity and reliability usually have already been established. A few of the many compilations of measurement scales are listed in the For Further Reading section of this chapter. In addition, scales are reported and described in the many research journals dedicated to the behavioral sciences.

If no existing scale will do the job, then a new scale should be developed (DeVellis, 2012). A certain logic is common to the development of scales, which generally involves the following steps:

1. Develop or locate many potential scale items, far more than will appear in the final scale.
2. Eliminate items that are redundant, ambiguous, or, for some other reason, inappropriate for the scale.
3. Pretest the remaining items for validity, reliability, or other measurement checks to be described shortly.
4. Eliminate items that do not pass the tests of Step 3.
5. Repeat Steps 3 and 4 as often as necessary to reduce the scale to the number of items required.

Sources of Scale Items

One of the most accessible sources of scale items is a researcher's own imagination. Once the researcher has developed and refined a concept, he or she has a pretty good idea of what is to be measured and then can generate a range of statements to satisfy the criteria to be discussed. At this early stage in scale construction, we need not be too concerned with honing and polishing the statements to perfection, because much pretesting remains before an actual respondent ever sees any statement.

A second source of scale items is a group of people, sometimes called *judges*, who are considered to be especially knowledgeable in a particular area. If we are seeking items for a delinquency scale, for instance, it is reasonable to discuss the issue with juvenile probation officers and others who have daily contact with delinquents.

Two social psychologists used this approach to find items for a scale to measure people's tendency to manipulate others for their own personal gain (Christie & Geis, 1970). They turned to the writings of Niccolò Machiavelli, a 16th-century advisor to the prince of Florence in Italy. In his classic book *The Prince,* Machiavelli propounded what is essentially a con artist's view of the world and politics: According to Machiavelli, people are to be manipulated, in a cool and unemotional fashion, for one's own benefit. Lying, cheating, and underhandedness are justified to advance one's own personal position. In the writings of this Florentine four centuries ago, these social psychologists found such statements as "It is safer to be feared than to be loved" and "Humility not only is of no service but is actually harmful." (Christie & Gies, 1970, p. 11). They constructed a scale made up of Machiavelli's statements, somewhat revised, and asked people whether they agreed with each statement. Now known as the Machiavellianism Scale, it has been used widely in scientific research.

A third source of scale items is the people who are the focus of the research project. Claudia Coulton (1979), for example, was interested in person–environment fit among consumers of hospital social services. In developing her scale, she obtained a large number of verbatim statements from hospital patients and then began to form them into a scale. In a similar manner, if we were interested in attitudes among teenagers toward unwanted pregnancies, an excellent beginning would be to discuss the topic with teenagers themselves and gather from them as many statements as possible regarding the issue. When items are garnered from people in this fashion, however, only rarely are their statements usable without editing. Many statements would ultimately be rejected, and most would have to be considerably rewritten. Still, such people are likely to provide a range of statements with meaning from the perspective of the group under investigation.

Characteristics of Scale Items

Once the researcher has amassed a large number of scale items, he or she must select the best ones for the final scale. Good scale items have several characteristics, including validity, range of variation, and unidimensionality.

Validity. A primary concern in item selection is the validity of the statements (see Chapter 5). Each statement considered for inclusion should be assessed for content validity. For example, if we are creating a self-report depression scale, then we assess each statement by how it relates to measuring depression. Statements concerning participation in delinquent acts are reasonable as valid measures of how depressed someone feels or other symptoms of depression. On the other hand, an item relating to whether or not someone feels sad following the loss of a loved one or pet is not a valid indicator of depression.

Range of Variation. Variables that are measured with multiple-item scales normally consist of a number of possible values or positions that a person can take. If we want to measure attitudes toward growing old, for example, then people's positions on that variable could be extremely positive, extremely negative, or anywhere in between. When selecting items for measurement scales, we should ensure that the items cover the actual range of possible variations on the variable being measured. Failure to do so results in a poor scale. When selecting items on the basis of variability, the researcher needs to exercise care to avoid defining the range either too narrowly or too broadly. Failure to include a sufficiently wide range of items results in responses that pile up at one or both ends of the scale's range. If many respondents tie with either the lowest or the highest possible score, then the range in the scale is inadequate. This piling-up effect reduces the precision of the measurement, because we are unable to differentiate among the respondents with tied scores.

Going to extremes with items to define the range is not desirable either. If we include items that are too extreme, then they apply to few—if any—respondents. In the case of a delinquency scale, for example, an item pertaining to engaging in cannibalism would be such an extreme item as to warrant exclusion: The act is so rare in our culture that it is unlikely any juvenile has done it; thus, it contributes nothing of benefit to the scale. The goal is to select items with enough variation to cover the actual range of alternatives that people are likely to choose but without including items so extreme that they do not apply to anyone.

Unidimensionality. In the construction of a multiple-item scale, the goal is to measure one specific variable. We do not want the results confounded by items on the scale that actually measure a different (although possibly related) variable. The items of a **unidimensional scale** measure only one variable. If a scale actually measures more than one variable, then it is called a *multidimensional scale*. In creating a depression scale, for example, we might be tempted to include an item about someone's relationships with close family members on the grounds that depression often negatively impacts relationships with marital partners and children. Although an empirical relationship may exist between depression and family relationships, these are separate variables, and they should be treated and measured as such.

In assessing the unidimensionality of scales, we distinguish between *different variables* and *different aspects of the same variable*. A single variable may have more than one aspect, and we need to be careful to recognize these aspects so that they can be measured appropriately. A concept like delinquency, for example, contains at least two aspects—namely, severity and frequency. In terms of severity, it is reasonable to distinguish between an adolescent who commits petty theft and one who commits aggravated assault. In terms of frequency, an adolescent who regularly commits petty theft might be properly considered to be delinquent—or even more delinquent than one adolescent with a single case of assault.

The different aspects of a variable need to be distinguished and analyzed carefully, because one may correlate with an independent or a dependent variable, whereas another may not. This, again, suggests the complexity of some variables. In a study of person–environment fit, for example, Claudia Coulton (1979) distinguished between the many aspects that might be parts of this variable. "Person–environment fit" refers to the extent to which an individual's needs can be satisfied and his or her aspirations fulfilled in the context of the demands and opportunities available in a particular environment. Coulton distinguished between "fit" in relation to one's economic activities, "fit" in terms of the amount and relevance of available information, "fit" in terms of one's family relations, and the like. In this case, the person–environment fit scale is unidimensional in that it measures one underlying variable, but it also contains a number of distinct aspects that are a part of that variable.

To gain systematic evidence for the unidimensionality of a scale, the researcher can intercorrelate each item on the scale with every other item on the scale, usually during a pretest. If some items do not correlate with the others, then it is possible that they do not measure the same variable or that they are separate aspects of the variable and vary independently of one another. If we suspect that these items measure a different variable, then we should eliminate them from the scale. If we find a few items that have nearly perfect correlations, we only need to use one of them in the scale. Two items to which people respond identically are simply redundant; using both adds nothing to the measurement abilities of the scale. Occasionally, however, highly correlated items should be included to detect response inconsistency or random answering. That exception notwithstanding, the final scale should be composed of statements that correlate fairly highly—but not perfectly—with one another.

A knowledge of the characteristics and sources of scale items provides an important and necessary foundation for the development of scales. By themselves, however, these offer only a general guide to scale development. The more complex intricacies of developing scales are best grasped by looking at specific types of scales and illustrations of how they were developed. Moreover, some types of scales have unique requirements not adequately covered by our previous discussion. We turn, then, to a discussion of the most important types of scales used in human service research.

Research in Practice 13.1 provides an example of the complexities and nuances of scale development in measuring intimate partner violence.

SCALING FORMATS

Scaling can utilize a number of formats, and each format calls for some unique design elements.

Likert Scales

Rensis Likert (1932) developed one of the most popular approaches to scaling. A **Likert scale** consists of a series of statements, with each statement followed by a number of ordered response alternatives. An illustration of a Likert scale is

RESEARCH IN PRACTICE 13.1 Program Evaluation: Developing a Scale to Measure Intimate Partner Violence

Quantifying intimate partner violence has been a challenge for researchers and human service practitioners alike. Instruments such as the Conflict Tactics Scale frame the problem in terms of conflict resolution and ask respondents to estimate the frequency of behaviors such as hits, slaps, and shoves. But experts and those on the receiving end of violence argue that counting events does not capture the emotional pain and underlying meaning of violence for the victim. Family therapist Brian Jory and colleagues made an effort to fill this gap by developing the Intimate Justice Scale (IJS; Jory, 2004). The IJS measures ethical dynamics of couple relationships, which are evident in patterns of action and attitude expressed over the course of the relationship. How this scale was developed illustrates many features of good scale development presented in this chapter.

The scale is based on a human service practice theory, in this case what Jory calls "intimate justice theory," which is about ethical dynamics of close relationships. Intimate justice requires that a relationship be based on:

1. *Equality.* Treating others with respect, making oneself accountable to others, and supporting freedom of others to make choices.
2. *Fairness.* Avoid deception, reciprocity in work and stress of daily living, and accommodation to others and their limitations.
3. *Care.* Empathy for needs of others, nurturing strengths of others, and attachment based on responsibility not exploitation.

Intimate justice concerns how partners use power in relationships—either for beneficent or exploitive motives. Some scale items ask respondents about the ethical beliefs of their partners, regardless of whether the belief is acted upon. For example, one item asks respondents to agree or disagree with "My partner believes he or she has the right to force me to do things." The scale developers argue that believing in force is an effective weapon of domination even if physical force is not used. Other items ask about the impact of a partner's actions regardless of a partner's intentions. For example: "Sometimes my partner physically hurts me." Such items emphasize that unwanted or aggressive physical contact hurts, whether the act was intentional or not.

The development of items for the IJS was a multistage process.

1. Thirty abusive men and their female partners were interviewed individually for about two hours each. The interviews elicited ideas from victims about intimate justice with questions such as: "Do you think that your partner feels accountable to you, and in what ways?" Men were asked: "What if something strange happened and you were suddenly forced to switch places with your partner? Knowing how you treat her, would you still want to be in this relationship?" Analysis of these interviews generated 48 questions. These questions were then presented to members of a therapy group of eight to 10 women who provided feedback on the items.
2. The questions were then presented to 54 marriage and family therapists, all of whom had considerable practice experience with intimate partner violence clients. The therapists rated each item on its perceived predictive value for physical violence and its value as an indicator of psychological abuse. The therapists recommended modifications to existing items and suggested additional items. As a result, 36 original items were retained and four new ones were added.

(continued)

3. Next, with the help of cooperating therapists, the 40 items were administered, along with the Conflict Tactics Scale and the Dyadic Adjustment Scale, to a sample of women who were involved in heterosexual relationships of at least one year's duration and who were receiving mental health treatment for any presenting problem, including but not limited to intimate partner violence. A statistical technique called factor analysis was used to select unidimensional items. Jory and his colleagues then eliminated redundant items and settled on 15 items that appeared relevant to a wide array of potential clients.

4. Finally, the researchers assessed the IJS for internal-consistency reliability and for validity (see Chapter 5). For example, the IJS results were shown to correlate positively with the Conflict Tactics Scale (which measures violence) and negatively with the Dyadic Adjustment Scale (which measures marital happiness). The developers also showed that the IJS differentiated between women who had experienced no violence, minor violence, and severe violence, according to the Conflict Tactics Scale.

The net result of all this scale development is a brief, quickly scored, 15-item instrument that can be used as a screening tool for human service practitioners or by researchers to measure an important but covert aspect of domestic violence—intimate partner justice.

presented in Table 13.1. This table presents items from a self-esteem scale with response alternatives ranging from "strongly agree" at one end of the scale to "strongly disagree" at the other end. Other Likert scales might have different response alternatives (such as "very satisfied" to "very dissatisfied" or "excellent" to "poor") depending on the statement that is used to measure a variable. Five is the most common number of alternatives, because it offers respondents a sufficient range of choices without requiring unnecessarily minute distinctions in attitudes. Sometimes, however, more or fewer than five alternatives are used. Notice in Table 13.1 the numbers ranging from 1 to 4 in brackets next to each response alternative. These numbers are included here for purposes of illustration only. They would not be printed on a scale for actual use, because their presence might influence the respondents' answers. These numbers are used when scoring the scale. The numbers associated with each response are totaled to provide the overall score for each respondent. If our self-esteem scale contained 10 items, then individual scores can range from a low of 10 (if the alternative with the bracketed "1" after it were chosen each time) to a high of 40 (if the alternative with the

TABLE 13.1 Examples of Items (Statements) That Might Appear on a Self-Esteem Scale

	Strongly Agree	Agree	Disagree	Strongly Disagree
(1) On the whole, I feel good about myself.	St.A[4]	A[3]	D[2]	St.D[1]
(2) I more often feel bad about myself than good.	St.A[1]	A[2]	D[3]	St.D[4]
(3) I have a number of good qualities.	St.A[4]	A[3]	D[2]	St.D[1]
(4) I feel that I am not a very good student.	St.A[1]	A[2]	D[3]	St.D[4]
(5) When I am working at my job, I feel that I'm a person of worth.	St.A[4]	A[3]	D[2]	St.D[1]

bracketed "4" after it were chosen every time). The Likert scale is one example of a **summated rating scale**, in which a person's score is determined by summing the number of questions answered in a particular way. Summated rating scales can take a number of different forms, although the Likert format is the most common.

Note that (as discussed in Chapter 5) each item on a Likert scale is an ordinal measure because the response alternatives have a fixed order but not necessarily equal spacing between the alternatives. Because the total score of a Likert scale is the sum of individual, ordinal items, many researchers contend that a Likert scale is ordinal in nature. Technically, one should refrain from using such statistics as the mean and standard deviation with ordinal-level data. However, it is common, especially with well-established Likert scales, to see published studies in which scores are treated as if they were interval level. Whether this application of interval procedures is appropriate is a debated topic among researchers and cannot be resolved here.

Constructing a Likert scale, as with all scales, requires considerable time and effort. The researcher begins by developing a series of statements relating to the variable being measured. The general criteria for such statements, as outlined previously, should be carefully considered during this stage. No matter how diligent we are in following those guidelines, however, some of the statements turn out to be inadequate for a variety of reasons. Because we anticipate having to drop some unacceptable items, we should initially write substantially more statements than we plan to include in the final scale. A common rule of thumb is to start with three times the number of statements desired for the final scale.

A final criterion in deciding which items to ultimately use in a Likert scale is whether the scale items *discriminate* among people. In other words, we want the responses to an item to range over the four or five alternatives rather than to bunch up on one or two choices. Imagine a scale with an item that reads, "People convicted of shoplifting should have their hands amputated." If such an item were submitted to a group of college students in the United States, it is likely that most would

respond with "strongly disagree" and maybe a few with "disagrees." It is highly unlikely that any would agree. So, of what use is this item to us? We cannot *compare* people—that is, assess who is more likely to agree or disagree—because they all disagree. And we cannot correlate responses to this item with the social or psychological characteristics of the students, because there is little or no variation in responses to the item.

We want, then, to eliminate nondiscriminating items from consideration for our scale. *Nondiscriminating items* are those that are responded to in a similar fashion by both people who score high and people who score low on the overall scale. Nondiscriminating items in a scale can be detected on the basis of results from a pretest in which people respond to all the preliminary items of the scale. One way to identify nondiscriminating items is to compute a **discriminatory power score** (or DP score) for each item. The DP score essentially tells us the degree to which each item differentiates between respondents with high scores and respondents with low scores on the overall scale. Although this approach is used less in actual practice today, because of the availability of other, more complex procedures that depend on computer support, it is a straightforward technique that illustrates well the principles of item selection.

The first step in obtaining DP scores is to calculate the total scores of each respondent and then rank those scores from the highest to the lowest. Next, we identify the upper and lower quartiles of the distribution of total scores. The *upper quartile* (Q_3) is the cutoff point in a distribution above which the highest 25% of the scores are located, and the *lower quartile* (Q_1) is the cutoff point below which the lowest 25% of the scores are located. With the quartiles based on total scores identified, we compare the pattern of responses to each scale item for respondents whose scores fall above the upper quartile with the pattern for respondents whose scores fall below the lower quartile. Table 13.2 illustrates the computation of DP scores for one item on a scale to which 40 people responded. Ten respondents are above the upper quartile, and 10 are below the lower quartile. We see that those with high scores tended to agree

TABLE 13.2 Calculation of DP Score for One Item on a Scale

Quartile	N	Response Value 1	2	3	4	5	Weighted Total	Weighted Mean	DP Score
Upper	10	0	1	2	4	3	39	3.90	
Lower	10	2	8	0	0	0	18	1.80	2.10
								2.10	

DP, discriminatory power.

with this item, because most had scores of 4 or 5. Those with low scores tended to disagree, because they are totally concentrated in the 1 and 2 score range. The next step is to compute a weighted total on this item for the two groups, multiplying each score by the number of respondents with that score. For example, for those above the upper quartile, the weighted total is

$$(1 \times 0) + (2 \times 1) + (3 \times 2) + (4 \times 4) + (5 \times 3) =$$
$$0 + 2 + 6 + 16 + 15 = 39.$$

Next, we compute the weighted mean (average) by dividing the weighted total by the number of cases in the quartile. For the upper quartile, we have 39 ÷ 10= 3.9. We then obtain the DP score for this item by subtracting the mean of those below the lower quartile from the mean of those above the upper quartile. In this example, we have 3.9 – 1.8 = 2.1. This process is repeated for every item on the preliminary scale so that each item has a calculated DP score. (Statistical and spreadsheet software can be readily programmed to accomplish this task.)

Once we have DP scores for all the preliminary items, the final selection can begin. The best items are those with the *highest* DP scores, because this shows that people in the upper and lower quartiles responded to the items very differently. As a rule of thumb, as many items as possible should have DP scores of 1.00 or higher, and few—if any—should drop below 0.50. Applying this rule to the item in Table 13.2, we would conclude that it is a very good item, and we would include it in the final scale.

Occasionally, researchers encounter DP scores with negative signs. Under no circumstances should an item with a negative DP score be included, because this means that those with high scores on the overall scale scored lower on this item than those with low scores did. If the size of the negative DP score is small, then it probably is an ambiguous statement that is being variously interpreted by respondents. If the negative DP score is large, however, then it is possible that the item was accidentally scored incorrectly—that is, a negative item was scored as if it were positive, or vice versa.

Many computer software packages have procedures for item analysis that rely on principles other than DP scores but that accomplish largely the same task. For example, the statistical package SPSS includes the procedure Reliability Analysis, which performs an item analysis on the components of additive scales by computing coefficients of reliability. These coefficients show how each item correlates with every other item and with the overall scale. In addition, SPSS provides the reliability coefficient Cronbach's alpha (see Chapter 5) for the proposed scale. Using procedures such as these, the researcher can exclude from the scale those items that detract from or contribute little to the overall reliability of the instrument.

The Likert scale is one of the most popular multiple-item scales because of the many advantages that it possesses. First, it offers respondents a range of choices rather than the limited yes/ no alternatives of other scales. This makes Likert scales valuable if the theoretical assessment of a variable is such that it ranges along a continuum rather than being either present or absent. Second, data produced by Likert scales are considered to be ordinal level, which enables us to use more powerful statistical procedures than we can do with nominal-level data. Third, Likert scales are fairly straightforward to construct.

Although its advantages make the Likert scale one of the most widely used attitude scales, the Likert scale has the same disadvantages as many other scales. In particular, we must be careful in interpreting a single score based on a Likert scale, because it is a summary of so much information (separate responses to a number of items). Whenever we summarize data, we lose some information. (A grade in a college course is a summary measure of a student's performance, and in calculating it, the instructor loses information regarding high—or low—scores on individual exams.) The summary score might hide information about patterns of variation in responses or about possible multidimensionality of the scale.

Thurstone Scales

Thurstone and Chave (1929) developed another approach to scaling. **Thurstone scales** are constructed such that they use *equal-appearing intervals*—that is, it is assumed that the distance between any two adjacent points on the scale is the same. This provides data of interval level quality and enables us to use all the powerful statistical procedures that require interval level data (see Chapter 5).

Construction of a Thurstone scale begins in much the same way as construction of a Likert scale—namely, with the selection of many statements that relate to the variable being measured. Once a sufficient number of statements is at hand, the next step is to provide a value between 1 and 11 for each statement. Figure 13.1 illustrates the

Thurstone scale pattern ranging from 1 (the most favorable statement regarding an object, event, or issue) to 11 (the most unfavorable). Scale items, however, may be arranged positively (high scores represent a favorable attitude) or negatively (high scores indicate an unfavorable attitude). Point 6 on the scale is called "neutral" and is used for statements that are neither favorable nor unfavorable. For example, the statement "teenage girls who get pregnant are immoral" would be considered to be very unfavorable toward teenage pregnancies.

The task of rating each statement as to how favorable or unfavorable it is with regard to the measured variable is, again, assigned to judges. With each of the preliminary statements printed on a separate card, the judges rate the items by placing them in piles corresponding to points on the 11-point scale. The judges place in each pile statements they assess to be roughly equivalent in terms of their favorableness. All the judges will not agree on the exact rating of statements, of course, so the scale value of a particular Thurstone item is determined by using the median of the judges' ratings. The scale values derived by this process are displayed in the first column of Table 13.3.

Once the scale values are computed for all the preliminary items, the next step is to determine the items that are the least ambiguous and, therefore, best for inclusion in the final scale. If the judges differed widely in their ratings on an item, then something likely is unclear about the statement itself, leading to varying interpretations. So, the degree of agreement among judges about the rating of an item is one indicator of ambiguity.

Scales should include the items with the most agreement among judges, and there should be a roughly equal number of items for each of the 11 scale values, ranging from unfavorable to favorable, moving upward in half-point increments. This requires a minimum of 21 items, although some argue that if reliability of .90 or better is desired,

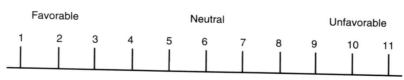

Figure 13.1 Equal-appearing intervals as used in Thurstone scale construction.

TABLE 13.3 Attitude Toward Church Scale

Check (✓) every statement that expresses your sentiment toward the church. Interpret the statements in accordance with your own experience with churches.

(8.3)*	1. I think the teaching of the church is altogether too superficial to have much social significance.
(1.7)	2. I feel the church services give me inspiration and help me to live up to my best during the following week.
(2.6)	3. I think the church keeps business and politics up to a higher standard than they would otherwise tend to maintain.
(2.3)	4. I find the services of the church both restful and inspiring.
(4.0)	5. When I go to church, I enjoy a fine ritual service with good music.
(4.5)	6. I believe in what the church teaches but with mental reservations.
(5.7)	7. I do not receive any benefit from attending church services, but I think it helps some people.
(5.4)	8. I believe in religion, but I seldom go to church.
(4.7)	9. I am careless about religion and church relationships, but I would not like to see my attitude become general.
(10.5)	10. I regard the church as a static, crystallized institution, and as such it is unwholesome and detrimental to society and the individual.
(1.5)	11. I believe church membership is almost essential to living life at its best.
(3.1)	12. I do not understand the dogmas or creeds of the church, but I find that the church helps me to be more honest and credible.
(8.2)	13. The paternal and benevolent attitude of the church is quite distasteful to me.

*Scale value
Source: From Thurstone, L. L., & Chave, E. J. (1929). *The measurement of attitude.* Chicago, IL: University of Chicago Press. Produced by permission of the University of Chicago Press.

then as many as 50 statements may be needed (Seiler & Hough, 1970). Regardless of the number actually used, the last step in the construction of a Thurstone scale is to order the items randomly for presentation to respondents.

Table 13.3 presents the first 13 statements contained in the original 45-item scale developed by Thurstone and Chave (1929), with the scale value of each item indicated in parentheses. This particular scale is designed so that items with high scale values are "unfavorable," and items with low scale values are "favorable," toward the church. The scale values would not, of course, be included on

a working version of the scale and are presented here for purposes of illustration. Note that respondents are required only to check the statements with which they agree, which makes the Thurstone format particularly easy for respondents.

Scoring a Thurstone scale is different from the simple summation procedure used with Likert scales. Because respondents agree to differing numbers of statements with different values, the simple sum of the item values is worthless. Rather, a respondent's score is either the mean or median of the scale values of the items that the person agrees with. For example, if a person agreed with statements 2, 4, 8, and 12 in Table 13.3, that person's Thurstone scale score would be 3.13. Another person choosing 1, 7, 10, and 13 would have a score of 8.18. This scoring procedure distributes respondents along the original 11-point scale.

Thurstone and Likert scaling techniques are essentially interchangeable methods of measuring attitudes. A major advantage of the Thurstone technique is that it provides interval level data. If the interval data properties are not needed, the Likert technique probably is preferable because of its higher reliability with fewer items and its reputed greater ease of construction. A second advantage of Thurstone scales is that people can respond to the items more quickly than with a Likert scale, because they need only indicate whether they agree with an item and need not ponder how much they agree or disagree. Because reliability calls for Thurstone scales to be longer, this advantage may be minimal and, if the longer scale leads people to be overly quick or careless in responding to statements, can even become a disadvantage. Another major disadvantage of Thurstone scales is that they are costly and difficult to construct; however, modern data-processing techniques have substantially reduced the construction time (Seiler & Hough, 1970).

Semantic Differential Scales

Another scaling format that has proved to be quite popular is the *semantic differential* (SD) developed by Osgood, Suci, and Tannenbaum (1957). The **semantic differential** format presents the respondent with a stimulus, such as a person or event, to be rated on a scale between a series of polar opposite adjectives. Normally, the scale has seven points but can have more or fewer if theoretical or methodological considerations call for it.

To illustrate a semantic differential scale, suppose a researcher were investigating how gender affected people's perceptions of police officers. A sample of people could be shown pictures of police officers, in some cases a male officer and in other cases a female officer. Their perceptions of the officers might be measured with a scale including items such as in Table 13.4. They would be told to choose the point between each adjective pair that best represents their assessment of the officer. The adjective pairs are selected based on some theory about which characteristics of officers might be relevant. So, on the first line, circling the "6" means that you view the person as quite unpleasant; circling the "1" is an assessment of quite pleasant. In this example, all the positive adjectives are on the left and all the negative adjectives on the right. Sometimes, however, the positive responses to some adjectives are put on the right to discourage uninterested respondents from placing all their responses in the same column. If we found respondents who had done so, we would probably discard their data, because they obviously had not marked the scale seriously.

Based on their research with the SD, Osgood and colleagues have suggested that, depending on the sets of adjectives used, three different dimensions of a concept can be measured: evaluation, potency, and activity. Semantic differentials can be designed to measure any one—or all three—of

TABLE 13.4 An Example of the Format of a Semantic Differential Scale

Directions: Look at Picture 1 and circle the number at the point between each of the following adjective pairs that best represents your impression of the person in the picture.

Pleasant	1	2	3	4	5	6	7	Unpleasant
Warm	1	2	3	4	5	6	7	Cold
Unselfish	1	2	3	4	5	6	7	Selfish
Calm	1	2	3	4	5	6	7	Aggressive
Genuine	1	2	3	4	5	6	7	False

these dimensions. The measure illustrated in Table 13.4 contains adjectives relating to all these dimensions.

One major problem in constructing an SD is the selection of relevant adjectives for rating a given concept. For example, the adjective pair "alive–dead" is not relevant to an SD rating self-concept. If the researcher is uncertain about the relevance of a set of adjectives, then it is possible to supply the adjectives to a group of subjects and have the subjects rank-order them according to their relevance to the concept being rated. The researcher would then use the pairs of adjectives ranked highest by the subjects (Mitsos, 1961).

A second problem with SDs is determining which of the three dimensions a given pair of adjectives is measuring. Generally, intuition is not reliable for making this determination (Heise, 1970). Accurate identification of the dimension measured by a given adjective pair can be accomplished through the use of a rather complex statistical procedure called *factor analysis,* which correlates each variable with every other variable. Its use in SD construction is to indicate which of the three dimensions correlates most highly with a given set of adjectives and, hence, which dimension is being tapped by those adjectives.

Many SDs are set up like the one in Table 13.4, with only the ends of the scale labeled with the adjectives. Some scales, however, employ such adverbs as "extremely," "quite," and "slightly" at appropriate points between the adjectives. One study found that the use of adverbs improved the quality of responses to SD scales (Wells & Smith, 1960). In light of these findings, it appears advisable to include adverbs when constructing SDs.

Scoring an SD can be done in a variety of ways, depending on the researcher's needs. One way is to treat the response to each adjective pair separately. This procedure is not common, however, because usually we want a summary score for each respondent. To accomplish this, responses on the adjective pairs that constitute each dimension can be summed to provide an overall score on each of the dimensions measured—another variant of the summated rating scale.

Semantic differentials have several advantages in comparison with both the Likert and Thurstone

formats. Unlike the other scaling techniques that require 20 or more items for adequate reliability, SDs require only four to eight adjective pairs for each dimension to reach reliabilities of .80 or better. Approximately 10 adjective pairs often are used to ensure adequate validity. This brevity means that many concepts can be rated by respondents in a reasonable amount of time. In addition, because an SD is fairly easy to respond to, people can be expected to make at least 25 judgments in 15 minutes (Heise, 1970; Miller & Salkind, 2002). Another advantage is that SDs are much easier and less time-consuming to construct than either a Likert or a Thurstone scale. Adjective pairs are easier to develop than unambiguous and unbiased statements about an issue. In addition, adjective pairs from prior studies are more readily adaptable to other studies because of the general and nonspecific nature of the adjectives. This is particularly important if a measuring scale is needed quickly. For example, if we wanted people's reactions to some unanticipated event, time would be of the essence. We would have to get their reactions while the event was still fresh in their minds. Only an SD-type scale could be readied in time.

About the only disadvantage of an SD is that, as with Likert scales, SDs generate ordinal data. If interval data are desired, then a Thurstone scale is preferable.

Guttman Scales

Researchers make efforts to create scales that are unidimensional—that is, scales that measure a single variable or a single aspect of a variable. With a **Guttman scale,** the procedures used in the construction of the scale help ensure that the resulting scale will truly be unidimensional (Guttman, 1944).

Researchers using Guttman scaling achieve unidimensionality by developing the items in such a way that a perfect Guttman scale has only one pattern of response that will yield any given score on the scale. For example, if an individual's score is 5, then we expect that he or she agreed with the first five items on the scale. This contrasts with other scaling techniques that allow obtaining the same score by agreeing or disagreeing with any number of items and having completely different response patterns. Guttman scaling is able to do this because the items on the scale have an inherently progressive order, usually relating to the intensity of the variable being measured. The least intense items are referred to as "easy," because more people are likely to agree with them. The most intense items are referred to as "hard," because fewer people are expected to agree with them. If a person agrees with a certain item, then we also would expect him or her to agree with all the less intense items; conversely, if a person disagrees with a particular item, we also would expect that person to disagree with all the more intense items.

Table 13.5 illustrates a Guttman scale designed to measure attitudes toward gun control. The items are arranged with the "easiest" first and the "hardest" last. Often, only two response categories, either "agree" and "disagree" or "yes" and "no," are provided. Some Guttman scales, however, make use of the Likert-type response categories, as does the scale in Table 13.5. Because these categories are collapsed to a dichotomy at a later point in working with the scale, little is gained by their inclusion other than allowing the respondents greater freedom of expression.

The fact that the items on a Guttman scale are progressive and cumulative leads to the basic means of assessing whether a set of items constitutes a Guttman scale. This criterion is called *reproducibility* or the ability of the total score of all respondents to reproduce the pattern of the responses to the scale items of each individual. For example, all persons with scores of 2 will have agreed with the two "easiest" items and disagreed with the rest, persons with scores of 3 will have agreed with the three "easiest" items and disagreed with the rest, and so on. In a perfect Guttman scale, each respondent's score reproduces one of these patterns, as illustrated in Table 13.5. There is always one more perfect response pattern—namely, zero agreements—in a Guttman scale than there are items on the scale; therefore, the nine-item scale in Table 13.5 would have 10 possible response patterns. In actual practice, perfect Guttman scales are virtually nonexistent; usually, some respondents do deviate from the expected pattern. Nevertheless, Guttman scales with high levels of reproducibility have been developed.

Constructing a Guttman scale is difficult and risky (to a certain extent), because we do not know whether the scale that we have devised has sufficient reproducibility to qualify as a Guttman scale until after we apply it to a sample of respondents. As with the other scaling techniques, to create and select items for inclusion in the scale is a basic first step. In Guttman scaling, this task is further complicated by the need for those items eventually selected to have the characteristic of progression.

The procedure for selecting items for a Guttman scale is known as the *scale discrimination technique* (Edwards & Kilpatrick, 1948). As with both Likert and Thurstone scaling techniques, we begin by writing a large number of statements that relate to the variable to be measured. These statements are then rated by a group of judges along the 11-point Thurstone equal-appearing interval scale. Scale values and interquartile ranges (upper quartile minus lower quartile or $Q_3 - Q_1$) of the judges' ratings are obtained for each item. Half of the items with the lowest interquartile ranges are kept, and the remainder are discarded. The items on which judges were in the greatest agreement are given a Likert-type response format and presented to a pretest group. The pretest results are used to calculate DP scores as described earlier for Likert scaling. Items for inclusion in the final Guttman scale are selected so that they cover the full Thurstone scale range and have the highest DP scores. Despite the effort involved in this approach, all it accomplishes is to increase the likelihood that the selected items will have sufficient reproducibility to constitute a Guttman scale; it does not guarantee reproducibility.

The only way to determine if we have succeeded in developing a true Guttman scale is to administer it to another pretest group and see if it has adequate reproducibility (Dotson & Summers, 1970). Table 13.6 illustrates the most common way of assessing the reproducibility of items. For the sake of simplicity, the illustrated scale contains only four items and data from only 20 subjects. As can be seen from the table, subjects are arrayed according to their total score for the four statements, from the highest (4) to the lowest (0). Subjects' responses to each statement are indicated by an X under either "1" or "0," corresponding to an "agree" or a "disagree" response, respectively. The statements are

TABLE 13.5 A Guttman Scale Measuring Attitudes Toward Handgun Control

Do Not Favor or No Opinion	Strongly Favor or Somewhat Favor	Here Are Some Proposals That Have Been Made for Controlling Handgun Violence. Would You Please Tell Us How You Feel About Each of These Proposals?
0	1	1. Institute a waiting period before a handgun can be purchased, to allow for a criminal record check.
0	1	2. Require all persons to obtain a police permit before being allowed to purchase a handgun.
0	1	3. Require a license for all persons carrying a handgun outside their homes or places of business (except for law enforcement agents).
0	1	4. Require a mandatory fine for all persons carrying a handgun outside their homes or places of business without a license.
0	1	5. Require a mandatory jail term for all persons carrying a handgun outside their homes or places of business without a license.
0	1	6. Ban the future manufacture and sale of nonsporting-type handguns.
0	1	7. Ban the future manufacture and sale of all handguns.
0	1	8. Use public funds to buy back and destroy existing handguns on a voluntary basis.
0	1	9. Use public funds to buy back and destroy existing handguns on a mandatory basis.

Note: The response alternatives in this study were "strongly favor," "somewhat favor," "do not favor," "no opinion," and "no response." They were collapsed into two categories for Guttman analysis: 1 = strongly favor or somewhat favor; 0 = do not favor or no opinion.

				Guttman Scale Pattern							
% Favoring	Item	0	1	2	3	4	5	6	7	8	9
87	1. Waiting period	no	yes	yes	yes	yes	yes	yes	yes	yes	yes
61	2. Permit to purchase	no	no	yes	yes	yes	yes	yes	yes	yes	yes
72	3. License to carry	no	no	no	yes	yes	yes	yes	yes	yes	yes
66	4. Mandatory fine for no license	no	no	no	no	yes	yes	yes	yes	yes	yes
52	5. Mandatory jail term for no license	no	no	no	no	no	yes	yes	yes	yes	yes

(continued)

TABLE 13.5 A Guttman Scale Measuring Attitudes Toward Handgun Control (*continued*)

% Favoring	Item	0	1	2	3	4	5	6	7	8	9
					Guttman Scale Pattern						
40	6. Ban nonsporting manufacture/sale	no	no	no	no	no	no	yes	yes	yes	yes
23	7. Ban all handgun manufacture/sale	no	no	no	no	no	no	no	yes	yes	yes
19	8. Voluntary buy-back	no	no	no	no	no	no	no	no	yes	yes
17	9. Mandatory buy-back	no	no	no	no	no	no	no	no	no	yes
N = 1442	Coefficient of Reproducibility: .915										

Source: Reprinted from Teske, R. H. C., Jr. & Hazlett, M. H. (1985). A scale for the measurement of attitudes toward handgun control. *Journal of Criminal Justice*, 13(4), 373–379. doi:10.1016/0047-2352(85)90007-8. With permission from Elsevier.

arranged from left to right from "hardest" (most disagreements) to "easiest" (most agreements). The lines drawn across each of the statement columns are called *cutting points* and indicate where the pattern of responses tends to shift from agree to disagree. The position of the cutting points must be determined carefully, because these points form the basis from which error responses are counted. Any "1" (agree) responses below the cutting points and any "0" (disagree) responses above the cutting points constitute error responses. Cutting points are drawn at positions that minimize the number of error responses. Inspection of the cutting points in Table 13.6 reveals that locating them in any other position does not reduce the number of error responses.

With the cutting points established, tabulation of error responses is straightforward. In the example under Statement 1 are three "1" responses below the cutting point with no "0" responses above it. Note that in the row marked "Error," these responses are tabulated as 3 and 0, respectively. The same counting procedure was followed for the other statements. As Table 13.6 illustrates,

the error responses for individual statements are summed to indicate the total number of error responses. Tabulating error responses for a longer scale by hand is exceedingly tedious, but computer software, such as the SAS package, can assess the reproducibility of even a long scale quite rapidly.

The total number of errors is used in the following simple formula to calculate the coefficient of reproducibility (R_c):

$$R_c = 1 - \frac{\text{number of errors}}{(\text{number of items}) \times (\text{number of subjects})}$$

Inserting the values from Table 13.6. we have

$$R_c = 1 - \frac{11}{(4)(20)} = 1 - .14 = .86$$

Guttman (1950) suggested that a coefficient of reproducibility of .90 is the minimum acceptable for a scale to qualify as a Guttman scale. According to this criterion, our example does not qualify. Scales with reproducibility coefficients of somewhat less than .90, however, have given satisfactory results. In general, the more the number of items on a Guttman scale, the more difficult it is to

TABLE 13.6 Example of Error Computation for a Guttman Scale

Subjects	\<span\>Statements\</span\>								Scores
	1		**2**		**3**		**4**		
	1	0	1	0	1	0	1	0	
1	x		x		x		x		4
2	x			x	x		x		3
3	x			x	x		x		3
4		x	x		x		x		3
5		x	x		x		x		3
6		x	x		x		x		3
7		x	x		x		x		3
8		x	x		x		x		3
9		x		x	x		x		2
10	x			x		x	x		2
11		x		x	x		x		2
12		x		x	x		x		2
13	x			x		x	x		2
14		x	x			x	x		2
15	x			x		x		x	1
16		x		x		x	x		1
17		x		x	x			x	1
18		x	x			x		x	1
19		x		x		x	x		1
20		x		x		x		x	0
Frequency	6	14	8	12	12	8	16	4	
Error	3	0	2	2	1	1	2	0	$e = 11$

achieve a high level of reproducibility. For a very short scale, .90 would be the minimum acceptable coefficient of reproducibility; with a longer scale, the minimum reproducibility level can be adjusted downward slightly.

Suppose we develop a scale of 11 items, submit it to a pretest group, determine the reproducibility coefficient, and find it to be too low. The game is not over because of this initial failure. It is perfectly legitimate to rearrange the order of the items or drop items to achieve the necessary reproducibility. We might, for example, drop three or four of the items containing the most error responses, leaving a seven- or eight-item scale with adequate reproducibility to qualify as a Guttman scale.

It is important to note that a given Guttman scale may be group specific. This means that if we achieve adequate reproducibility with a given set of items with one sample of respondents, nothing guarantees that the same items will scale when applied to another sample. Only after-the-fact analysis of each sample will reveal if the Guttman scale properties hold for subsequent applications of a scale.

The data generated by Guttman scaling are ordinal level. Given the relatively few items characteristic of these scales and the common "agree–disagree" format, there are few possible scores for respondents to achieve. This means that large numbers of respondents will have tied scores on the scale, so many statisticians believe it is better to consider these numbers as ranks (ordinal) rather than interval level or ratio level data. Guttman scales are unique, however, for the characteristics of unidimensionality and reproducibility. If these attributes are desired, then they are apt to more than outweigh the presence of all the tied scores.

Given the extreme complexity of creating Guttman scales, most human service workers seldom have occasion to develop one. A substantial number of such scales, however, already are in existence, making an understanding of their operating characteristics worthwhile.

Multidimensional Scales

All the scaling techniques presented so far were developed a number of years ago. More recent activity has centered on what is called the **multidimensional scale** for measuring variables composed of more than a single dimension. These scaling techniques are too complex for full presentation here, but we can discuss the basic logic that underlies them.

One purpose of the preceding scaling techniques is to locate respondents' scores along some sort of continuum to determine that various groups or people exhibit more or less of the variable being measured. With these unidimensional techniques, the straight line of a single scale is sufficient to indicate the location of all people on a given variable. When we come to variables of more than one dimension, however, this single line is no longer adequate. Instead, we must think of locating responses somewhere in either two-, three-, or N-dimensional space. A common analogy exists between multidimensional scaling and cartography or mapmaking: Just as the cartographer locates various places along the dimensions of latitude and longitude, multidimensional scaling locates people along the various dimensions of a variable. For example, if we conceive of people's motivation as being composed of the two dimensions of "discomfort" and "hope," then Figure 13.2 illustrates how multidimensional scaling might locate these people with regard to these dimensions (Kogan, 1975). It might be possible to use multidimensional scaling of client motivation to predict the chances of success with clients undergoing various forms of treatment.

Multidimensional scaling can, of course, deal with variables composed of many more than two dimensions.

AVOIDING RESPONSE BIAS

As we saw in Chapter 5, a key issue in measurement is whether people's answers to questions are accurate reflections of their actual feelings, beliefs, or behaviors. In other words, our measure of some phenomenon should be determined by the nature of the phenomenon itself and not by systematic or random errors. One source of such error in responses to questions or statements is called **response bias**: the tendency for answers

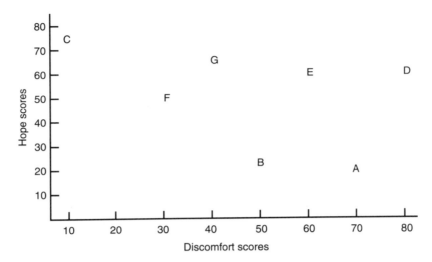

Figure 13.2 Hypothetical two-dimensional space of client motivation.

to questions to be influenced by something other than true feelings, beliefs, and behaviors. Response bias can result in a patterned overestimation or underestimation of variables (Bradburn, 1983).

Sources of Response Bias

One source of response bias is called **response set**: Some people tend to be either yea-sayers or naysayers, tending either to agree or disagree with statements regardless of their content. This sometimes is called the *acquiescence response set,* because it more often takes the form of people being predisposed to agree with statements.

Another source of response bias is **response pattern anxiety:** Some people become anxious if they have to repeat the same response all the time, and they change their responses to avoid doing so. If this occurs, then their reactions to statements do not reflect their actual attitudes but, rather, their reaction to certain response patterns, and the validity of the scale is reduced. (Students sometimes experience this when taking a multiple-choice exam. If several consecutive questions all have the same answer, they become concerned and may doubt answers that they were fairly sure of just because the pattern of responses differs from the more random pattern they expect.)

Another source of response bias is the **social desirability effect**: people's tendency to give socially acceptable, popular answers to present themselves in a good light. For example, the Conflict Tactics Scale is an instrument for measuring modes of conflict resolution and violence between intimate partners (Straus, Hamby, Boney-McCoy, & Sugarman, 1996). It does so by asking (among other questions) whether people have ever used a gun or a knife in resolving a dispute with an intimate partner. Because it is socially unacceptable for most people to admit using a knife or gun on a partner, this may affect how people respond to the Conflict Tactics Scale. People may deny using a knife or gun, even if they have done so, to avoid appearing socially unacceptable to an interviewer.

Reducing Response Bias

Researchers use a number of strategies to reduce response bias. Response set and response pattern anxiety can be avoided by designing statements so that positive statements are not always an expression of the same attitude. Likert scales are routinely designed like this. Mixing the response pattern of items is taken into account when scoring Likert scales. The alternatives that indicate an expression of the same opinion or feeling are given the same numerical score. Another technique for avoiding response bias is to present sensitive issues in a neutral and nonjudgmental context. In the Conflict Tactics Scale, Murray Straus et al. (1996) presented questions about violent acts in the context of disagreements and conflicts, which presumably would appear more socially acceptable to people than abuse and violence.

A third way to reduce response bias has to do with the ordering of questions: Questions can be asked in a hierarchical order, beginning with the less sensitive issues and gradually moving to the more sensitive issues. The Conflict Tactics Scale begins with a few items that reflect positive ways of resolving conflict ("I explained my side of a disagreement to my partner") before moving to questions about psychological and physical abuse. Questions about the use of violence do not appear until well into the instrument. The rationale for this design was that people feel less reticent about divulging acts of violence if they have been given the chance to show that such acts were "the last straw" after attempting other means of conflict resolution.

A fourth strategy for reducing response bias is to use an interspersed pattern for the items, where socially acceptable items are interspersed with the less-acceptable items. So, in the Conflict Tactics Scale, positive items, such as "I said I was sure we could work out a problem," are followed by such items as "My partner needed to see a doctor because of a fight with me." The reason for this pattern is that a straight hierarchical ordering may open the door to a form of response set: A respondent may blindly answer "never" to every item once items begin referring to violent acts. Interspersing sensitive items with positive ones encourages participants to think more carefully about each item. Thus, the Conflict Tactics Scale actually uses a combination of hierarchical and interspersed ordering of sensitive items. For any given scale, whether a hierarchical pattern or an interspersed ordering produces the least bias is an empirical question to be settled through research on the scale itself.

A fifth technique that helps reduce response bias is called *funneling*. A researcher might ask respondents first about conflict in their city, then about conflict in their local community and among neighbors, and finally about conflict in their own family. As another example of this, Moser and Kalton (1972) suggested phrasing questions so that respondents can answer in the third person. For example, "Many men have hit their wives at one time or another. I wonder if you know under what circumstances it happens?" This can be followed with a direct question asking if the respondent has done it.

SCALING IN THE HUMAN SERVICES

Scaling is arguably the best example of a strong linkage between practice and research. Scales developed for research purposes may prove extremely useful in practice, and scales developed for human service practice may be equally useful for research. Practitioners use scales for several purposes. First, scales strengthen the general intake process by providing a systematic means of detecting areas for intervention. For example, the Multi-Problem Screening Inventory (MPSI) scale is a multidimensional self-report measure that helps practitioners assess the magnitude of client problems across a wide array of personal and social functioning areas (Hudson & McMurtry, 1997).

Second, human service practitioners use scales to assess specific problems for intervention. Research in Practice 13.2 describes several scales that are particularly useful for this purpose.

Third, the practitioner uses scales to document the progress of intervention. Although simply administering a scale before and after treatment makes for a weak research design, it still provides more rigorous evidence of improvement than the casual observation that is common in many practice situations. For the practitioner seeking to document case outcomes with stronger evidence, standardized scales may supplement repeated measures in a single-system design. This strategy was illustrated by a report on the treatment of panic disorder. During baseline, treatment, and follow-up, social workers used the client's daily rating of anxiety level for the single-system *AB* design. In addition, the client also completed a standardized instrument, the Clinical Anxiety Scale, before and after treatment. Both the

RESEARCH IN PRACTICE 13.2 Assessment of Client Functioning: Rapid Assessment Instruments

One of the most common applications of scaling in the human services is problem assessment. Protective service workers use scales to systematically assess the risk of child abuse (Children's Research Center [CRC], 1999). At the other end of the age spectrum, gerontology practitioners use instruments such as the NEECHAM Confusion Scale for rapid and unobtrusive assessment of acute confusion in hospitalized older patients (Neelon, Champagne, Carlso, & Funk, 1996) and the FEAR scale to assess generalized anxiety in elderly primary care patients (Krasucki et al., 1999).

Both the confusion scale and the anxiety measure are illustrations of an increasingly popular category of scale known as *rapid assessment instruments* (RAIs), which are distinguished from other measures by several main features. RAIs are short, easy to administer, and easy to complete, and they are written in clear, easy-to-understand language with uncomplicated directions so that disruption of the intervention process is minimized. Scoring normally takes only a few minutes, without the need for special equipment. RAIs have been developed to cover a wide array of settings and common targets of human service intervention and have been applied in family service agencies (Toseland & Reid, 1985) and in agencies serving children and youth (Edlesen, 1985; Nelson-Gardell, 1997). Ogles, Lambert, and Masters (1996) identified instruments for depression, anxiety, and phobias. A number of instruments have been developed in the area of substance abuse, such as the Hudson Index of Alcohol Involvement (Rapp, Dulmus, Wodarski, & Feit, 1999). Probably the best current reference for practitioners seeking measurement instruments to aid in practice evaluation is Fischer and Corcoran (2007).

A good illustration of an RAI is the Michigan Alcoholism Screening Test (MAST), a 25-item questionnaire designed to provide a rapid and effective screening for lifetime alcohol-related problems and alcoholism. The MAST can be completed in less than 10 minutes and scored in less than 5 minutes; it can be used in either paper-and-pencil or interview format or online; it has been productive in a variety of settings with varied populations.

Practitioners may wonder whether it is worth the resources to go beyond a basic interview and use an RAI such as the MAST or to go a step farther and employ a more comprehensive scale. One agency undertook a systematic comparison of the relative benefits of each approach by comparing results obtained with the MAST to those from a screening interview and to information gathered via the Alcohol Use Inventory (AUI), a complex, 147-item, multiscale instrument (Skinner, 1981). The researcher administered the three forms of measurement to a sample of 327 individuals with alcohol problems to assess the relative benefits and liabilities of each approach. In addition, several other instruments were used to assess further the validity of the three procedures, including the Lifetime Drinking History, a detailed, structured interview procedure that yields quantitative indices of drinking patterns. Other measures included several scales to test for understanding of scale items and measures of the tendency to present oneself in a favorable light.

The study found that asking individuals a few simple questions during the intake process was effective in obtaining useful data about alcohol use. However, although the intake interview permitted detection of a potential problem, the MAST procedure was superior, because it produced reliable information on the severity and nature of the alcohol problem. Furthermore, this additional information was gained at only a slight increase in time and money required for the assessment process. In contrast, the AUI procedure required considerably more time to

(continued)

complete the 147-item, multiscale instrument and also required considerable time and skill to score and interpret the results. For the added cost, it did provide detailed information about styles of use, patterns of symptoms, and perceived benefits of use.

The researcher concluded that human service professionals who are in a position to detect alcohol-related problems would definitely benefit from including a procedure such as the MAST in their client-screening routine. The added reliability and validity over and above what can be obtained in a brief screening are achieved for very little additional cost. On the other hand, the added precision and fine distinctions that are possible through use of the AUI cannot be justified for referring agencies. The AUI is better suited for specialized treatment facilities that can set up efficient procedures for scoring and analysis and can make use of the added information in treatment planning for alcoholics. Therefore, the selection of measurement tools and the decision to incorporate scales into practice should be based on the demonstrated capacity of the measurement tools weighed against the added costs in terms of time, money, and skill required for their use.

daily rating and the scale scores indicated client improvement (Alfonso & Dziegielewski, 2001).

Finally, human service organizations rely on scaling as part of their overall program quality and effectiveness-monitoring process. One team of researchers described the use of a comprehensive set of scales both to assess individual clients and to help guide program evaluation in the field of substance abuse treatment (Joe, Broome, Rowan-Szal, & Simpson, 2002). Such use of scales both to inform the practitioner about individual client progress and to provide data for program evaluation is a key element in the evidence-based practice approach that we introduced in Chapter 1. Because the documentation of practice effectiveness is measured using scales that are recognized to be valid and reliable, it can be used in evaluation research as a valuable source of evidence for guiding future practice decisions.

Properly employed, scales can be of immense benefit to practice, but a danger also exists that the uninformed use of scales, or the use of poorly constructed scales, will provide false or misleading information. False data are, in some ways, worse than no data at all, because people believe they have gained some understanding when, in fact, they have not. Social policy or practice techniques based on such erroneous data actually may exacerbate problems rather than alleviate them. For these reasons, we need to be exceedingly cautious about using scales developed without the extensive pretesting and analysis outlined in this chapter. Some

people are under the mistaken impression that one can gather usable data from statements that have been constructed with no pretesting or analysis. It is tempting to believe that a couple of intelligent people can sit down and write unbiased, valid, and reliable statements to measure variables. It is also a dangerously erroneous belief. Great care is always called for in constructing scales. These concerns illustrate the profound responsibility of social researchers and practitioners to take all the steps necessary to ensure that their findings are valid. Any investigator—including a human service practitioner—who casually develops scales without rigorous safeguards and then distributes results based on those scales is, many would argue, engaging in unethical behavior.

The temptation to simply make up a scale rather than seek out a valid and reliable instrument may be especially strong in areas where an understanding of the concepts seems obvious to the practitioner. Terms like *helpful, supportive*, and *sensitive* are commonplace in the human services, so it seems at first glance that a practitioner could quickly make up a good measurement scale by asking a few questions such as "On a scale of 1 to 5, how helpful was the therapist?" What concepts do these terms really represent, however, and how well do the items measure them? What it takes to answer these questions well can be glimpsed in the work of researchers who developed a multidimensional scale on social support (Goldsmith, McDermott, & Alexander, 2000). Their work involved three studies. The first study asked a sample of more than 100 participants to interpret the meaning of the terms *helpful*, *supportive*, and *sensitive*. The second study involved almost 400 participants rating 30 semantic differential items derived from the first study. The third study was conducted to ascertain the scale reliability, validity, and conceptual distinctiveness of the terms. The work on this instrument is typical of the time, resources, and effort needed to design quality scales, and it underscores the value of carefully selecting valid, reliable instruments.

When human service providers select scales for use in practice or research, they need to assess whether the research is methodologically sound. Practitioner Profile 13.1 offers an example of the many factors practitioners consider in selecting and using scales to evaluate client progress. Scale construction requires considering how rigorous

PRACTITIONER PROFILE 13.1 Tea Leonard, Mental Health Counselor/Trauma-Informed Therapist, Washington

Tea Leonard is a mental health counselor providing trauma-informed therapy to both adults and children in Spokane, Washington. She has a bachelor's degree in biology and a master's degree in counseling. The main treatment modality she uses is eye movement desensitization and reprocessing (EMDR), but she also incorporates components of cognitive behavioral treatment and mindfulness-based therapy into her work.

Leonard explained that her counseling training included courses in statistics, psychometrics, and research methodology. When asked about the value of research training to her practice she stated,

> These courses are useful. You want to be evidence-based—not only so your work is reimbursed by insurance companies, but also to make sure you're doing clinically-sound work. It helps to find a modality that is backed by lots of evidence and certainly EMDR is one of those. Using my knowledge of statistics and research methods to review that research has been invaluable to my practice. (Based on personal communication on July 20, 2018.)

According to Leonard,

> Doing evidence-based work is important to me, professionally and ethically. If I'm going to lead a client to believe that I have any business trying to impact their life in a positive way, I want to have some research to show that what I'm doing has worked for other people. This also helps me breathe easier as a professional, knowing that I could be audited, for example, if I'm billing insurance. If I'm not using an evidence-based modality, I could get into some trouble.

When asked about her general approach to evidence-based practice and how she tailors evidence-based models to clients' needs, she explained that understanding clinical perspectives and techniques very well is critical. She explained,

> When I see a client I can't just say "I'll take this evidence-based technique and do it with you." I need to shape it for each individual client. When you really know one or two techniques well, you can use those modalities to paint with a wide range of colors, to apply them to a wide range of clients and issues.

(continued)

Understanding research concepts, Leonard explains, has also been beneficial in the actual treatment she provides clients. She explained,

> I see research skills showing up in a lot of my work. What comes to mind immediately is my use of SRS, Session Rating Scales, and ORS, Outcomes Rating Scales, to evaluate clients' satisfaction with each individual session as well as their feelings about their lives over time. This is important to both attend to clients' needs within sessions—to review ratings and make sure they feel heard and attended to—and to see use outcomes evidence over time. We'll look at how clients have evaluated their lives over time and assess whether or not they feel therapy has worked for them and make any necessary adjustments.

Leonard also explained that providing EMDR treatment requires therapists to be comfortable with assessment scales.

> EMDR protocols are filled with scaled analysis. With respect to a trauma target, we evaluate based on a scale of zero to ten, whereby "0" is no disturbance at all to "10" being the worst trauma you could imagine. We move through EMDR protocols until the disturbance level or impact of the trauma target is as close to zero as possible, based on clients' self-reporting. I also track clients' reports of positive cognition and that scale goes from 1 to 7, whereby "7" would be a complete agreement with positive statements such as "I am powerful." Like with trauma target, we move through EMDR protocols until the report is at a "7" or as close to a "7" as possible. Much of what I do requires tracking clients' self-reports. That impacts my work on a daily basis.

In addition, Leonard sees depression and anxiety scales as critical to her work and uses them to track client progress over time. She also explained that reviewing charts showing movement along these scales over time with her clients is critical to making necessary adjustments to treatment. It also helps with clients' commitment to treatment processes, especially where they are able to better see progress over long periods.

As a trained researcher, Leonard understands the need to critically evaluate the validity of the measures she uses and to ask herself what they are actually evaluating. "I find it necessary to pair my quantitative analysis of clients' self-report measures with something more qualitative," she explains.

> You really want to make sure that your reading of the scales is based on clients' interpretation of that scale and the questions used to measure each concept. So I have to check in periodically to ask things like "What does a '0' mean to you?" or "What does a '10' look like to you?" You really have to check in to understand their subjective understanding of these numbers.

Leonard believes that it is important to evaluate clients and client progress both quantitatively and qualitatively.

> I can't say that either qualitative or quantitative analysis are more important than the other. I think what's important is that they're used in tandem because if a client is telling me that everything feels fine, but they're giving me a "10" on the disturbance scale, that

(continued)

is a clear message to me that something is not adding up. In my opinion you really cannot have real confidence of your assessment until both your quantitative and qualitative assessments line up with one another.

Reflecting on her career and the role of her research training, Leonard explained she was not excited by research as a student, especially quantitative analysis, but sees great value in research skills now. She explained,

If you're going to be an informed practitioner, you need to be able to read and interpret research in a way that it can inform your practice in a positive and meaningful way. You also need to have to be able to track how your clients are doing.

According to Leonard, she engages and sees more value in quantitative analysis than she thought she would have. She explains,

When I was in grad school I was pretty resistant to quantitative analysis. I was very much more aligned with the qualitative experience, the subjective experience. What changed for me is my true desire to do my best possible job, and I knew I could not do my best possible job unless I could read research and apply the findings. Quantitative analysis allows me to set aside my biases that impact my qualitative assessments of my clients.

the investigator was in developing items, whether pretesting was conducted, and whether validity and reliability were tested. In some cases, after reviewing a piece of research, the practitioner may decide that, although the results are tantalizing, the study lacks the methodological rigor necessary to convince him or her to incorporate those results into practice.

Back to Margaret, she used the BDI for many years. This is an example of a self-report scale using a Likert format. There are many studies that confirm the BDI is both reliable and valid. The scale is easy to administer as well. As you can see in this questionnaire, each of the items has a series of potential response statements ranging from a value of "0" to a value of "3" indicating the extent to which the response is an indication of depression. A respondent's total score is calculated by adding the total value of items that he or she selected. A total score of more than 40 indicates the respondent is "Extremely Depressed." A total of 31 to 40 is indication of "Severe Depression," 21 to 30 "Moderate Depression," 17 to 20 "Borderline Clinical Depression," 11 to 16 "Mild Mood Disturbance," and 10 or lower "Normal."

As explained earlier, Margaret's dilemma is that she does not believe the BDI is well suited for her new job at the nursing facility because it includes several items related to physical health that may not help in differentiating people with depression from people without depression among older adults. In her research, she found that several studies have shown the BDI to be valid and reliable with older adult populations. At the same time, however, she also found some studies confirming her belief that this assessment tool is not well suited for older adults with health problems, including those in nursing care. Seeing conflicting evidence on the utility of this assessment tool for her new client group, Margaret was torn as to whether or not this was a suitable assessment tool.

While searching for evidence to see whether the BDI worked well for older adults, however, she also came across references to another scale that may better fit her needs, the Geriatric Depression Scale (GDS; see Exhibit 13.1 for a copy of the GDS). The GDS is a simple scale to administer and consists of 30 questions to which respondents answer with a simple "yes" or "no." Scores range from 0

EXHIBIT 13.1 Geriatric Depression Scale (Long Form)

1. Are you basically satisfied with your life?
2. Have you dropped many of your activities and interests?
3. Do you feel that your life is empty?
4. Do you often get bored?
5. Are you hopeful about the future?
6. Are you bothered by thoughts you can't get out of your head?
7. Are you in good spirits most of the time?
8. Are you afraid that something bad is going to happen to you?
9. Do you feel happy most of the time?
10. Do you often feel helpless?
11. Do you often get restless and fidgety?
12. Do you prefer to stay at home, rather than going out and doing new things?
13. Do you frequently worry about the future?
14. Do you feel you have more problems with memory than most?
15. Do you think it is wonderful to be alive now?
16. Do you often feel downhearted and blue?
17. Do you feel pretty worthless the way you are now?
18. Do you worry a lot about the past?
19. Do you find life very exciting?
20. Is it hard for you to get started on new projects?
21. Do you feel full of energy?
22. Do you feel that your situation is hopeless?
23. Do you think that most people are better off than you are?
24. Do you frequently get upset over little things?
25. Do you frequently feel like crying?
26. Do you have trouble concentrating?
27. Do you enjoy getting up in the morning?
28. Do you prefer to avoid social gatherings?
29. Is it easy for you to make decisions?
30. Is your mind as clear as it used to be?

This is the original scoring for the scale: One point for each of these answers. Cutoff: normal-0–9; mild depressives-10–19; severe depressives-20–30.

1. no	6. yes	11. yes	16. yes	21. no	26. yes
2. yes	7. no	12. yes	17. yes	22. yes	27. no
3. yes	8. yes	13. yes	18. yes	23. yes	28. yes
4. yes	9. no	14. yes	19. no	24. yes	29. no
5. no	10. yes	15. no	20. yes	25. yes	30. no

to 30 based on the number of responses associated with depression selected by the respondent (not all depression-associated responses were "yes," some were "no"). Respondents scoring 23 or higher are considered "Very Depressed" and those scoring a 9 or higher are considered "Mildly Depressed." Unlike the BDI, the GDS does not emphasize health or physical symptoms of depression. Margaret's research also confirms that it has been proven to be both valid and reliable (e.g., Andrews, 2010). After much internal debate and consultation with clinical social workers at other nursing homes, she decided she had found a new depression assessment tool and would use the GDS at the new job.

REVIEW AND CRITICAL THINKING

Main Points

- Multiple-item scales are particularly valuable for measuring complex variables, because they enhance validity and reliability, increase the level of measurement, and improve the efficiency of data handling.
- The five basic steps common to most scaling techniques are as follows: develop many preliminary items, eliminate obviously bad items, pretest the remaining items, eliminate bad items on the basis of pretest results, and select items for the final scale.
- The Likert scale is a popular scale format that involves a series of statements, each followed by a number of ordered response alternatives, ranging from, for example, strongly disagree to strongly agree or from excellent to poor; most Likert scales have four to seven response alternatives.
- An important consideration in selecting items for inclusion in a Likert scale is DP—that is, the ability of each item to differentiate between those who score high and those who score low on the overall measurement scale.
- Thurstone scales use judges to assign a value from 1 to 11 to each item in the scale, which results in a scale capable of producing interval level data.
- Items for inclusion in a Thurstone scale have scale scores that cover the full 1 to 11 range and were most agreed on by the judges.
- The semantic differential (SD) scaling format presents respondents with a concept to be rated and a series of opposite adjective pairs separated by a seven-point scale that is used to evaluate the concept.
- Semantic differentials are a convenient scaling format, because they are considerably easier to construct than the alternatives.
- Guttman scales have the unique characteristic of reproducibility, meaning that a given total score reflects one—and only one—pattern of responses to the items in the scale.
- Multidimensional scaling uses two or more dimensions or components of a complex variable to locate people with regard to the various components of the variable.
- The use of scales or the results of research based on measurement scales should be approached cautiously, with careful consideration given to whether adequate development has gone into the scale, particularly in terms of assessing its validity and reliability.

IMPORTANT TERMS FOR REVIEW

Discriminatory power score	Response bias	Social desirability effect
Guttman scale	Response pattern anxiety	Summated rating scale
Likert scale	Response set	Thurstone scales
Multidimensional scale	Scale	Unidimensional scale
	Semantic differential	

CRITICAL THINKING

1. Identify several scales that pertain to your area of practice. What does each evaluate? For what client groups are they intended?
2. What client-related factors are important to consider when selecting an assessment scale? Think about one or more of the scales identified in question 1. Would these scales work for all clients you might encounter in a given area of practice? If not, are there other scales that can be used to evaluate those clients for whom the scales do not work?
3. How can you evaluate the extent to which a given scale will produce valid and reliable measures of a client's situations, conditions, or outcomes? Is there available research on the reliability and validity of the scales you identified in the preceding questions?

EVALUATING COMPETENCY (FROM THE COUNCIL ON SOCIAL WORK EDUCATION [CSWE] 2015 EDUCATIONAL POLICY AND ACCREDITATION STANDARDS [EPAS])

Competency 2: Engage Diversity and Difference in Practice

- Social workers often use scales to assess clients. Identify a scale that you currently use or may use in the future. To what extent is the scale universal? Does this depend on how it was created?
- One of the reasons social workers use scales is to help them get an objective measure of some phenomenon. At the same time, social workers are often as interested in understanding clients' subjective experiences as they are in evaluating clients from an objective standpoint. How can scales be used in tandem with assessments of clients' subjective experiences?

Competency 4: Engage in Practice-Informed Research and Research-Informed Practice

- Identify and read several articles pertaining to a scale that you currently use or may use in the future to assess clients (whether this be an individual, couple, family, group, or community). Who created this scale and how was it created? What does it evaluate?
- What have researchers suggested about the scale's validity and reliability? For which groups of people is it well suited?

Competency 7: Assess Individuals, Families, Groups, Organizations, and Communities

- Think about a client (or client group) with whom you have worked or a potential client (or client group) with whom you may work. What can a score (or scores) on an assessment scale (or scales) tell you about the client?

- How can this information be used in creating goals and service plans with a client? Do these scores help direct you to appropriate interventions? What other information might be needed?

SELF-ASSESSMENT

1. Which of the following is not an advantage of scaling over single-item measures?
   a. Improved validity and reliability
   b. Increased control over client attitudes toward treatment
   c. Increased level of measurement
   d. Increased efficiency in data handling
2. Which of the following is not a source for scale items?
   a. Researchers' imaginations
   b. Judges
   c. The people who are the subject of research
   d. Random selection of topics
3. The items of a unidimensional scale measure:
   a. Only one variable.
   b. Only one theme but several variables.
   c. Several variables.
   d. As many variables as are needed to fully capture a concept.
4. In which type scale is a person's score determined by summing the number of questions answered in a particular way?
   a. A Likert scale
   b. A summated rating scale
   c. An index
   d. A ratio scale
5. Which type of score essentially tells us the degree to which each item differentiates between respondents with high scores and respondents with low scores on the overall scale?
   a. Discriminatory power
   b. Thurstone scale
   c. Range
   d. Variation
6. Which type of scale is constructed such that they use *equal-appearing intervals*—that is, it is assumed that the distance between any two adjacent points on the scale is the same?
   a. Semantic differential
   b. Thurstone
   c. Likert
   d. Nominal
7. Which type of scale format presents the respondent with a stimulus, such as a person or event, to be rated on a scale between a series of polar opposite adjectives?
   a. Thurstone
   b. Likert
   c. Guttman
   d. Semantic differential

8. The tendency for answers to questions to be influenced by something other than true feelings, beliefs, and behaviors is known as:
   a. Response set
   b. Response format
   c. Response bias
   d. Differential response
9. Response pattern anxiety occurs when:
   a. People become anxious because they do not like tests.
   b. People develop anxieties because surveys are too long.
   c. People become anxious if they have to repeat the same response all the time, and they change their responses to avoid doing so.
   d. People are anxious because they fear a researcher conducting a survey will not believe the results.
10. Which of the following is not a strategy for reducing response bias?
   a. Reordering items
   b. Funneling
   c. Presenting issues in a nonjudgmental way
   d. Introducing humor into response sets

ANSWER KEY FOR SELF-ASSESSMENT QUIZ

1. **b.** Increased control over client attitudes toward treatment.
2. **d.** Random selection of topics
3. **a.** Only one variable.
4. **b.** A summated rating scale
5. **a.** Discriminatory power
6. **b.** Thurstone
7. **d.** Semantic differential
8. **c.** Response bias
9. **c.** People become anxious if they have to repeat the same response all the time, and they change their responses to avoid doing so.
10. **d.** Introducing humor into response sets

FOR FURTHER READING

Albarracin, D., Johnson, B. T., & Zanna, M. P. (Eds.). (2005). *The handbook of attitudes*. Mahwah, NJ: Lawrence Erlbaum Associates. This handbook presents, synthesizes, and integrates the existing knowledge of methods, theories, and data in the study of attitudes. The book is relevant to the topic of measurement in general and attitude scaling in particular.

DeVellis, R. F. (2012). *Scale development: Theory and applications* (3rd ed.). Thousand Oaks, CA: Sage. This is an understandable guide to all the various stages in developing good scales. It includes discussions of how to generate items, how long scales should be, and other useful topics.

Fischer, J., & Corcoran, K. (2007). *Measures for clinical practice and research: A sourcebook* (4th ed.). New York, NY: Oxford University Press. A two-volume set that includes actual scales as well as reliability and validity data. Volume I covers instruments for couples, families, and children. Volume II is devoted to instruments for adults.

McDowell, I. (2006). *Measuring health: A guide to rating scales and questionnaires* (3rd ed.). New York, NY: Oxford University Press. This volume discusses the theoretical and technical aspects of constructing and evaluating scales relating to such health issues as social health, psychological well-being, and depression. It presents and evaluates many actual scales.

Miller, D. C., & Salkind, N. J. (2002). *Handbook of research design and social measurement* (6th ed.). Thousand Oaks, CA: Sage. The latest edition of a classic in the field of measurement. Miller's book provides an overview of the various types of scale construction along with many examples of proven scales.

Netemeyer, R. G., Bearden, W. O., & Sharma, S. (2003). *Scaling procedures: Issues and applications*. Thousand Oaks, CA: Sage. This current resource on scaling examines the issues involved in developing and validating multi-item, self-report scales. The authors present a four-step approach for multi-indicator scale development. The book includes relevant empirical examples and a review of the concepts of dimensionality, reliability, and validity.

Schutte, N. S., & Malouff, J. M. (1995). *Sourcebook of adult assessment strategies* (Applied clinical psychology). New York, NY: Plenum. A text for practitioners, researchers, and instructors in the mental health field. This book presents more than 70 scales on a wide range of adult mental disorders, reviews of their psychometric properties, and user instructions. The scales include self-report, observer-based, and clinician-rating measures.

Streiner, D. L., & Norman, G. R. (2008). *Health measurement scales: A practical guide to their development and use* (4th ed.). Oxford, UK: Oxford University Press. A thorough discussion of issues related to locating and assessing scales for health-related research is the focus of this book.

Touliatos, J., Perlmutter, B. F., Straus, M. A., & Holden, G. W. (Eds.). (2001). *Handbook of family measurement techniques*. Thousand Oaks, CA: Sage. This three-volume set is intended for researchers, clinicians, and students in the family and related fields. It includes abstracts of family measurement instruments published from 1929 to 1996, as well as full versions and scoring instructions for many instruments.

REFERENCES

Alfonso, S. D., & Dziegielewski, S. F. (2001). Self-directed treatment of panic disorder: A holistic approach. *Journal of Social Work Research and Evaluation, 2*, 5–18.

Andrews, L. W. (2010). *Encyclopedia of depression*. ABC-CLIO. ProQuest ebook central. Retrieved from https://ebookcentral.proquest.com/lib/ewu/detail.action?docID=656434

Bradburn, N. M. (1983). Response effects. In P. H. Rossi, J. D. Wright, & A. B. Anderson (Eds.), *Handbook of survey research* (pp. 289–328). New York, NY: Academic Press.

Children's Research Center. (1999). *The improvement of child protective services with structured decision making: The CRC model*. San Francisco, CA: National Council on Crime and Delinquency.

Christie, R., & Geis, F. L. (1970). *Studies in Machiavellianism*. New York, NY: Academic Press.

Coulton, C. J. (1979). Developing an instrument to measure person–environment fit. *Journal of Social Service Research, 3*(2), 159–174. doi:10.1300/j079v03n02_02

DeVellis, R. F. (2012). *Scale development: Theory and applications* (3rd ed.). Thousand Oaks, CA: Sage.

Dotson, L. E., & Summers, G. F. (1970). Elaboration of Guttman scaling techniques. In G. F. Summers (Ed.), *Attitude measurement* (pp. 203–213). Chicago, IL: Rand McNally.

Edlesen, J. L. (1985). Rapid assessment instruments for evaluating practice with children and youth. *Journal of Social Service Research, 8*(3), 17–31. doi:10.1300/j079v08n03_02

Edwards, A. L., & Kilpatrick, F. P. (1948). A technique for the construction of attitude scales. *Journal of Applied Psychology, 32*(4), 374–384. doi: 10.1037/h0057313

Fischer, J., & Corcoran, K. (Eds.). (2007). *Measures for clinical practice and research: A sourcebook* (4th ed.). New York, NY: Oxford University Press.

Goldsmith, D. J., McDermott, V. M., & Alexander, S. C. (2000). Helpful, supportive, and sensitive: Measuring the evaluation of enacted social support in personal relationships. *Journal of Social and Personal Relationships, 17*(3), 369–391. doi:10.1177/0265407500173004

Guttman, L. A. (1944). Basis for scaling qualitative data. *American Sociological Review, 9*(2), 139–150. doi:10.2307/2086306

Guttman, L. (1950). The basis for scalogram analysis. In S. A. Stouffer, L. A. Guttman, & E. A. Schuman (Eds.), *Measurement and prediction* (pp. 60–90). Princeton, NJ: Princeton University Press.

Heise, D. R. (1970). The semantic differential and attitude research. In G. F. Summers (Ed.), *Attitude measurement* (pp. 235–253). Chicago, IL: Rand McNally.

Hudson, W. W., & McMurtry, S. L. (1997). Comprehensive assessment in social work practice: The multi-problem screening inventory. *Research on Social Work Practice, 7*(1), 79–98. doi:10.1177/104973159700700105

Joe, G. W., Broome, K. M., Rowan-Szal, G. A., & Simpson, D. D. (2002). Measuring patient attributes and engagement in treatment. *Journal of Substance Abuse Treatment, 22*(4), 183–196. doi:10.1016/s0740-5472(02)00232-5

Jory, B. (2004). The intimate justice scale: An instrument to screen for psychological abuse and physical violence in clinical practice. *Journal of Marital and Family Therapy, 30*(1), 29–44. doi:10.1111/j.1752-0606.2004.tb01220.x

Kogan, L. S. (1975). Principles of measurement. In N. A. Polansky (Ed.), *Social work research* (pp. 68–92). Chicago, IL: University of Chicago Press.

Krasucki, C., Ryan, P., Ertan, T., Howard, R., Lindesay J., & Mann, A. (1999). The FEAR: A rapid screening instrument for generalized anxiety in elderly primary care attenders. *International Journal of Geriatric Psychiatry, 14*(1), 60–68. doi:10.1002/(sici)1099-1166(199901)14:1<60::aid-gps893>3.0.co;2-g

Likert, R. A. (1932). Technique for the measurement of attitudes. *Archives of Psychology, 21*, 140.

Miller, D. C., & Salkind, N. J. (2002). *Handbook of research design and social measurement* (6th ed.). Thousand Oaks, CA: Sage.

Mitsos, S. B. (1961). Personal constructs and the semantic differential. *Journal of Abnormal and Social Psychology, 62*(2), 433–434. doi:10.1037/h0043406

Moser, C. A., & Kalton, G. (1972). *Survey methods in social investigation* (2nd ed.). New York, NY: Basic Books.

Neelon, V. J., Champagne, M. T., Carlso, J. R., & Funk, S. G. (1996). The NEECHAM confusion scale: Construction, validation, and clinical testing. *Nursing Research, 45*(6), 324–330. doi:10.1097/00006199-199611000-00002

Nelson-Gardell, D. (1997). Child report of treatment issue resolution: Pilot of a rapid assessment instrument. *Child Abuse and Neglect, 21*(3), 309–318. doi:10.1016/s0145-2134(96)00168-8

Ogles, B. M., Lambert, M. J., & Masters, K. S. (1996). *Assessing outcome in clinical practice*. Boston, MA: Allyn & Bacon.

Osgood, C. E., Suci, G. J., & Tannenbaum, P. H. (1957). *The measurement of meaning*. Urbana: University of Illinois Press.

Rapp, L. A., Dulmus, C. N., Wodarski, J. S., & Feit, M. D. (1999). Screening of substance abuse in public welfare and child protective service clients: A comparative study of rapid assessment instruments vs. the SASSI. *Journal of Addictive Diseases, 18*(2), 83–88. doi:10.1300/j069v18n02_08

Seiler, L. H., & Hough, R. L. (1970). Empirical comparisons of the Thurstone and Likert techniques. In G. F. Summers (Ed.), *Attitude measurement* (pp. 159–173). Chicago, IL: Rand McNally.

Skinner, H. A. (1981). Benefits of sequential assessment. *Social Work Research and Abstracts, 17*(1), 21–28. doi:10.1093/swra/17.1.21

Straus, M. A., Hamby, S., Boney-McCoy, S., & Sugarman, D. B. (1996). The revised conflict tactics scales (CTS2): Development and preliminary data. *Journal of Family Issues, 17*(3), 283–316. doi:10.1177/019251396017003001

Teske, R. H. C., Jr., & Hazlett, M. H. (1985). A scale for the measurement of attitudes toward handgun control. *Journal of Criminal Justice, 13*(4), 373–379. doi:10.1016/0047-2352(85)90007-8

Thurstone, L. L., & Chave, E. J. (1929). *The measurement of attitudes*. Chicago, IL: University of Chicago Press.

Toseland, R. W., & Reid, W. J. (1985). Using rapid assessment instruments in a family service agency. *Social Casework, 66*(9), 547–555. doi:10.1177/104438948506600905

Wells, W. D., & Smith, G. (1960). Four semantic rating scales compared. *Journal of Applied Psychology, 44*(6), 393–397. doi:10.1037/h0047419

14

DATA ANALYSIS I: DATA PREPARATION AND PRESENTATION

Important Terms for Review

Critical Thinking

Evaluating Competency (From the Council on Social Work Education [CSWE] 2015 Educational Policy and Accreditation Standards [EPAS])

Competency 9: Evaluate Practice With Individuals, Families, Groups, Organizations, and Communities

Self-Assessment

Answer key for Self-Assessment Quiz

For Further Reading

References

INTRODUCTION

Jennifer Lawler is a recent master of social work graduate. She works at "Rescue House," a homeless shelter in Bangor, Maine. The homeless shelter works at solving homelessness in Maine's communities by using best practices and innovation to safely and efficiently provide shelter to individuals and families in need. The grant writer at "Rescue House" is working on a grant to provide more rooms and hire additional mental health providers for individuals and families at the shelter. Jennifer has worked at the shelter for 18 months and is asked by the grant writer to complete the data-analysis portion for a grant. The shelter has five years of data that have not been properly entered and coded into a data file. In fact, the data are currently in boxes and are in paper form with demographic questions (questions describing the makeup of clients) and two scales that measure mental health (Mental Health Inventory) and physical health (The Health Orientation Scale). Each person and/or family that stayed at the shelter has completed a questionnaire. The shelter houses approximately 100 males, 85 females, and 12 families a year. Jennifer is realizing that she is going to need to start over fresh with entering data since the previous data set has many errors and was not completed. She has three months to get all data properly entered and analyzed for the grant deadline.

Jennifer is feeling optimistic regarding this task, but overwhelmed with the amount of data for this project. She currently is the only staff working on this project, but has help from a social work intern. This chapter addresses data preparation and presentation. All data-analysis projects require data to be properly entered, cleaned, and well structured for data analysis to begin. As you read this chapter, consider the following critical thinking questions: (a) What are the first tasks a social worker needs to accomplish when preparing data? (b) What information does a social worker need to know to successfully build a data set? (c) How will a social worker make sure that no mistakes have occurred when entering data before analysis begins, and what different types of data distribution do social workers need to know when analysis begins? (d) What additional resources would help a social worker successfully complete a data set and start analysis?

All research involves some form of **data analysis**, which refers to deriving some meaning from the observations made during a research project. Data analysis can take many forms. In some cases, it is qualitative, such as a summary description of an investigator's field notes from a participant-observation study. The focus of this chapter, however, is on quantitative data analysis, in which observations are put into numerical form and manipulated in some way based on their arithmetic properties. Practitioner Profile 14.1 illustrates a practical

PRACTITIONER PROFILE 14.1 Jennifer Oxborrow, Licensed Clinical Social Worker (LCSW) and Executive Director of the Utah Domestic Violence Coalition (UDVC)

Jennifer is the executive director of the Utah Domestic Violence Coalition (UDVC). The UDVC is the direct result of an important federal policy, the Violence Against Women Act, which was enacted in the mid-1990s. This law created state coalitions that serve women and families affected by domestic violence and sexual assault by raising community awareness, helping victims find appropriate housing, and by bipartisan assurance of funding and programs to help and assist survivors.

The importance of using research to inform policy and legislation is essential in macro social work practice, because it strengthens communities, advocacy, and partnerships with legislators. A major improvement in victim services as the result of research was the creation of the Lethality Assessment Protocol (LAP). This assessment tool was created to help both law enforcement and victim advocates develop professional cohesion when they serve domestic violence victim populations. Jennifer mentions, "Using this assessment tool to determine risk factors of lethality in intimate partner relationships has saved countless lives by educating victims on the risks they face in their abusive relationships." This trauma-informed tool creates awareness and promotes safety by letting law enforcement know the possible danger they face when responding to domestic violence calls in addition to keeping victim advocates and victims of domestic violence safe.

Jennifer has recently started using the LAP risk assessment tool across the state of Utah. Under Jennifer's leadership, UDVC and law enforcement seek to utilize more evidence-based practice to treat offenders. A partnership between victim services and law enforcement has brought about effective change for survivors of domestic violence. Jennifer explains, "Bringing victim services and law enforcement together was essential to reduce violence and this started with something as simple as everyone speaking the same language around assault" (J. Oxborrow, personal communication, June 1, 2018). She further explains how empirical research has helped her as a professional in several ways and has made her more effective at her job as a social work practitioner because understanding data and how to apply it to practice has proven vital for perceiving what the state faces. Research helps her find the most effective approaches, treatments, and programs for her clients and populations she serves. Research raises public awareness while making issues relevant by generating questions and their solutions.

example of how data can be used at the state level to create change. The analysis of quantitative data typically involves the use of **statistics**, which are procedures for assembling, classifying, tabulating, and summarizing numerical data to obtain some meaning or information.

This chapter begins our coverage of common methods of data analysis, which we continue in Chapter 15. Primarily designed for those who have not taken a course in statistics, these chapters also may serve as a refresher for those who have. To learn to do statistical analysis requires at least a full course devoted solely to that topic, but our goals here are more basic: to introduce the issues of preparing a data set for analysis, to guide selection of the most appropriate statistics

to accomplish a particular task, and to provide guidance in the interpretation of statistical results. This knowledge prepares us to better understand various statistics when we encounter them in research reports and the popular media and to assess whether the statistics are being used properly. This chapter explores some of the fundamentals of preparing and managing data—an often overlooked portion of the research process that falls between the generation of observations by the research design on the one hand and the production of statistical results on the other. Although it may not seem to be as challenging or intellectually demanding as developing the design or analyzing the data, it is still a critical step that can determine the success of the overall project.

PREPARATION FOR DATA ANALYSIS

In this chapter, we generally assume that the data have already been collected and that the task now is to enter the data into a computer file and begin the data analysis. Recall from Chapter 1 that data analysis is part of the overall research process and that many questions regarding data analysis should be resolved before any data are collected. As emphasized in Chapters 2, 4, and 5, theoretical and conceptual considerations are important in determining the nature of the data to be collected, and the nature of the data determines the kinds of statistics that can be applied. Furthermore, as we discussed in Chapter 7 in relation to survey data collection, procedures such as computer-assisted telephone interviewing (CATI) essentially merge the steps of data collection, data coding, and data set creation into one process, because responses of participants are entered directly into a computer file data set. So, even though the actual data analysis occurs toward the end of a research project, many of the issues discussed in this chapter will have been settled—or at least envisioned—*before* any data are collected.

Imagine that a researcher has completed a survey with a sample size of 400. The completed questionnaires are neatly stacked on the desk. Presumably, these questionnaires contain much information and the data for assessing the hypotheses that the researcher set out to test. But as long as the data are on the questionnaires—or in any other raw form, for that matter—they are useless. The raw data are in a highly inconvenient form from the standpoint of deriving usable meaning from them. Indeed, even if we tediously read through the 400 questionnaires, we would have little idea about the overall contents. The collected data must be reorganized before we can go on and apply the necessary statistics for their analysis.

Coding Schemes

In the current context, *coding* refers to the process by which a researcher transforms raw data into a machine-readable format suitable for data analysis, which requires that each observation be translated into a numerical value or set of letters. The numbers or letters assigned to an observation of a variable are called a *code*. The raw data set may have resulted from an observational study, a survey, an experiment, or an analysis of existing data; and it can be in one of several forms, including completed written questionnaires, survey interview schedules, observation notes, or agency records. In the following discussion, we use survey data to illustrate the coding process, but the basic principles apply to other research methods as well.

Coding data requires adapting the data as collected to the constraints of the program used for statistical analysis. On the one hand, the researcher must consider the data source, such as a completed questionnaire, and determine how to translate the data into coded form. On the other hand, the researcher must also be cognizant of the capabilities and restrictions of the computer program that will analyze the data. Although we present these perspectives somewhat independently, in practice the researcher must give simultaneous attention to both. The plan by which the researcher organizes responses to a variable or an item, together with how the variable is defined for computerization, constitutes the **coding scheme** for a variable. The initial purpose of the coding scheme is to provide the rules and directions for converting the observations into code. Referring to our example of the 400 completed questionnaires, the researcher's first task is to convert the responses into numbers and letters for computer entry.

As explained in Chapters 8 and 9, coding refers to categorizing a variable into a limited number of categories. Sometimes, this coding is built into the way that a question is asked and answered (see Chapter 7). This is the case with the following question format:

Which of the following best describes where you live? (Circle the number of your choice.)

1. Large city
2. Suburb of a large city
3. City of 50,000 or less
4. Rural but nonfarm
5. Rural farm

In this case, the circled number is the code for how a particular respondent answered a question.

This example also illustrates one reason why issues of coding and data analysis need to be considered before data collection is initiated. The number of options in the question predetermines the maximum number of response categories that can be used later to look at possible relationships between "residential area" and other variables. Because we did not provide a separate option for "City of 50,000 to 300,000," however, we could not use this as a category in our data analysis.

With some variables, the actual value of the response is a number and can be used to code the data. Family size, income, and number of arrests are variables of this type. When the data take the form of responses to open-ended survey questions, field notes, or other non-numerical entities, however, the data must be translated into numbers for quantitative analysis. This process is essential for most data analysis, because the substitution of numbers for observations greatly reduces the volume of data that must be stored and facilitates its analysis, especially by computer. (As we noted in Chapter 9, qualitative analysis often does not involve the substitution of numbers for the actual observations.) Many computer programs permit the use of words or letters to stand for categories, but these generally are more cumbersome and, thus, are used only infrequently. (Recall from Chapter 5, however, that assigning a number to coding categories does not necessarily mean that we can perform the various mathematical functions, such as addition and subtraction, on them. Whether we can do this depends on the level of measurement.)

When establishing coding categories, the researcher should follow two general rules. First, the categories should be *mutually exclusive*—that is, a given observation is coded into one, and only one, category for each variable. The universal practice of categorizing people by sex as either male or female exemplifies mutually exclusive categories. Second, the coding categories should be *exhaustive,* which means that a coding category exists for every possible observation that was made. For example, it might be tempting not to bother to code the "no opinion" response with Likert-type questions, on the grounds that those responses probably will not be included in the data analysis. A researcher

might well decide not to analyze those responses in the end, but the coding stage is not the time to make such decisions. If the researcher fails to code a response and later decides to include it in the analysis, then it becomes necessary to develop a new coding scheme and to reenter the data into the computer. A good rule of thumb when coding is to do it in such a way that *all* information is coded.

Today, virtually all quantitative—and much qualitative—data analysis is done with computers. In its most basic form, a computerized data set can be conceptualized as a rectangular table of cells where the columns represent variables and the rows designate individual cases.

For variable names, computer program data entry screens typically use a default designation, such as C1, C2, and C3 (in the case of Minitab) or var001, var002, and var003 (in SPSS), to identify variables. Spreadsheet programs, such as Lotus, Excel, and Quattro, label them a, b, c, . . ., aa, ab, and so on. Obviously, such designations convey little information about the meaning of a particular variable. With even a few variables, relying on such default designations for variable names quickly becomes confusing, so the researcher needs to provide more recognizable variable names. A variable name should be an indicator of the content of that variable. A common practice is to use a mnemonic device when naming variables. Thus, "lname" and "fname" clue the user that the variable names stand for last name and first name, respectively.

Variable names also may be selected to help group variables together. For example, a data set on domestic violence may include similar variables on both the suspect and the victim, such as date of birth, age, and alcohol use. Beginning each variable related to victims with the letter "v" and each suspect-related variable with an "s" helps the researcher quickly distinguish to which party a given variable refers. Another benefit of this approach is that data-analysis programs commonly display variable lists alphabetically. Beginning all victim-related variables with the letter "v" causes them to be grouped together whenever the computer displays a variable list. This reduces the need to scroll through a long list of variables when selecting variables for inclusion in a data-analysis procedure. When a variable is measured by combining responses to a number of separate items, it often is useful to use a number as part of the name to identify the variable's position in the set. Variables representing individual items of a 10-item self-esteem scale, for example, might be designated as se1, se2, se3, and so on, through se10. Such a designation can reduce the amount of work involved when combining the items into a single score. Thus, a total score on self-esteem can be generated by a computer command like "Sum se1 to se10" instead of requiring a listing of all 10 individual items.

In addition to the variable name, a coding scheme specifies the *variable format,* which determines how many characters a coded entry may have, whether it is non-numeric or some form of numeric variable, and where identifiers, such as decimals, commas, or dollar signs, should be placed.

Data-analysis programs vary in terms of the kinds of variables that they accept, but the two major types are *numeric* and *alphanumeric.* **Numeric variables** sometimes are called "values" because they have the property of a quantitative value. **Alphanumeric variables**, on the other hand, consist simply of type characters; they sometimes also are referred to as "string" variables or labels. An alphanumeric variable has no quantitative meaning and cannot be used in mathematical computations. Thus, the variable "lname" is clearly an alphanumeric variable, because its field (column) consists of text, such as "Smith" and "Hernandez." What makes a variable alphanumeric, however, is determined by how the variable is defined in the coding scheme, not simply by what characters are displayed on the computer monitor. For example, we could enter Social Security numbers in a data set and designate these as alphanumerical values. Even though the entire column consists of numerical characters, such as 375426174, a statistical program would not compute the mean, standard deviation, or other statistics on this variable because it is designated as an alphanumeric or string variable. Data-analysis programs commonly accept almost any keyboard character in a variable designated as alphanumeric. Although one can enter numeric characters in an alphanumeric variable, statistical packages such as

SPSS and Minitab only accept numerical symbols in a variable designated as numeric.

In addition to string and numeric variables, many programs also permit the specification of other types of variables, such as currency and date or time. Although the format code is not visible on the screen, it is stored with the data file and tells the program how much space to reserve for a given variable in the data set as well as how to display it. In the case of the variable LNAME, when defining it as an alphanumeric variable, you have to specify the maximum number of characters possible (specified as 12 characters in Table 14.1). Similarly, the date-of-birth variable would have to be identified as a date with 11 characters in it. When defining a numeric variable, such as PRIORS, you have to specify the number of decimal places, if any, permitted. With currency variables, you can specify a range of display options, such as $9 (one character, no decimals, maximum value of nine dollars) to $99,999,999.99 (ten characters, two decimal places, maximum value ninety-nine million and change)—all depending on how precisely you are measuring the variable. In Table 14.1, the variables DOB and CRDATE are defined as date variables. If we want to determine how old each suspect was at the time of the offense, we can enter a computer command that will subtract DOB from CRDATE and then display the result in years. Although different computer programs use their own conventions of designating variable types, the important point is that how the variable is defined before data entry determines its type, and the researcher must plan how variables will need to be used in the analysis and define them accordingly.

Additional elements may be added to a coding scheme to enhance its usefulness. Besides a brief variable name, the researcher may specify a variable label, which is an extended description of a variable that the data-analysis program will display in addition to the variable name whenever output is generated for that variable. Thus, in a table using the variable CRDATE, the designation "crime date" can be printed to make the table more understandable. Similarly, the coding scheme may include "value labels," which designate in words what a given value represents. For example, in Table 14.1, numbers are used to designate the following

TABLE 14.1 Domestic Violence Study Codebook

Item	Variable Name	Variable Label	Variable Type and Value Labels	Number of Characters	Number of Decimals	Missing Values	Level of Measurement
1. List offender last name	LNAME	last name	Alphanumeric	12	0	999	Nominal
2. List offender first name	FNAME	first name	Alphanumeric	10	0	999	Nominal
3. Enter date of birth	DOB	date of birth	Date	11	0	999	Ordinal
4. How many prior arrests for domestic violence?	PRIORS	number of prior arrests	Numeric	8	0	999	Ratio
5. What was the date of offense?	CRDATE	crime date	Date	11	0	999	Ordinal
6. What was offender's relationship with victim?	RELATION	relation to victim	Numeric	8	0	999	Nominal
			Value Label:				
			1 = married				
			2 = cohabiting				
			3 = separated				
			4 = divorced				
			5 = dating				
			6 = other				
7. What was offender's adjusted gross income reported to IRS for 2010?	INCOME	2010 income	Dollars	7	0	999	Ratio

IRS, Internal Revenue Service.

relationship possibilities between offender and victim: 1 = married, 2 = cohabitating, 3 = separated, 4 = divorced, 5 = dating, and 6 = other. Because this is a nominal variable and, thus, without an inherent quantitative meaning to the numbers, the value labels are displayed on outputs to help make clear what quality each number represents.

Finally, the coding scheme also should show how to interpret special codes, such as *missing values.* Missing values arise when no response is recorded for a particular item. Depending on why the item is a nonresponse, the researcher may either leave the variable blank in the data set or enter a value that signifies why the item was missing. For example, an item might be coded "–1" if the respondent refused to answer the question or "99" if the item does not apply to a particular respondent. This could be an important distinction for some types of analysis, so the coding scheme must specify how these various entries should be handled in computations.

Preparing and Using a Codebook

The coding scheme results in a specification of the variable name, variable format, range of permissible response codes, location of the variable in the data set, and optional features, such as variable labels, value labels, and missing value codes. Researchers commonly develop a *codebook* for the data set, which is an inventory of all the individual items in the data-collection instrument together with the coding schemes (see Table 14.1). The codebook provides lasting documentation on how the data set is constructed. Whenever a question exists about how a variable is constructed or can be used in analysis, the researcher can turn to the codebook for help. Not only does the researcher who collected the data need the codebook, it would be impossible to conduct a replication study on a previously collected data set or to explore new hypotheses with existing data without such documentation. Finally, the codebook is invaluable for data file management. A data set may consist of hundreds of variables; so, to make the analysis more efficient, researchers commonly create subfiles containing only the variables needed for a particular analysis. The codebook plays an essential role in selecting the variables and creating new files.

The preliminary codebook normally is prepared before data are entered into the computer and then used as a guide for data entry; however, the codebook is not a static document. Researchers often recode original variables and compute new ones. It is critical that these manipulations of the original data also be documented in the codebook so that any researcher can determine how these new variables were derived, what they mean, and where they are located in the data set.

DATA ENTRY

The goal of the data entry process is to produce a complete data set, free from errors, that the data-analysis applications can access and process. Today researchers benefit from the significant strides that have been made in minimizing data entry error and increasing the speed of transforming raw data into a data set that is ready for analysis.

Raw Data Entry

When the raw data must be extracted from existing documents, such as court records, or from printed questionnaires or survey schedules, the data must be entered manually into the computer. Several options exist for this process. Sometimes, the questionnaire data are coded onto pages known as "transfer sheets," which consist of numbered rows and columns that look much like the computer screen in Figure 14.1. In other cases, questionnaires have space along the border for writing the code, referred to as "edge coding." Whether one uses a transfer sheet, edge coding, or simply the raw questionnaires themselves, the next step is to enter the data using the data entry facility of the statistical application that will eventually analyze the data.

Conventions and individual features vary from one statistical application to another, but the basic process of data entry is similar in all of them. The data entry screen is laid out in columns and rows (see Figure 14.1). Each column represents one variable (field), and each row represents one case (record). Assuming that the variable names, labels, and other specifications have already been entered during the preparation of the codebook, the value for each variable is simply typed into the respective cell in the row corresponding to the individual case. Errors can be corrected by reentering the correct code in a cell. If the coding scheme's data definition for the computer has not already been entered into the computer file, then this step can be completed as data are entered into each variable.

Often the data a researcher is interested in are already in an electronic form: a human service agency has already computerized the data into a spreadsheet or database program as part of its administrative or management functions, or the data was collected via an online survey. In these cases, the data can usually be imported directly into a statistical application, such as SPSS or Minitab, often with the variable definition information included.

Another innovation in data entry is the use of optical scanning technology. A data-collection instrument is designed using a special program. Respondents either mark a circle corresponding to their choice or, in more sophisticated programs, write a response. Then, the questionnaire is read by a scanner or via fax, and the coded values are entered directly into the database for analysis. Whether one uses specialized data entry like this or relies on manual entry into the data-analysis program depends on several factors. The specialized equipment is cost-effective for large projects, where a staff of data entry personnel would otherwise be needed. For a small data set, however, designing, setting up, and testing an automated data entry program may be prohibitively expensive. Researchers today have many options to choose from. The most important issue is to select the process that yields the most accurate, usable data set.

Data Cleaning

No matter how much care one takes during the data entry process, errors can be expected, such as skipping variables for certain cases, entering the wrong value, or entering the value in the wrong location. If uncorrected, some errors can cause the analysis program to abort a statistical procedure or, at least, seriously distort the findings of the analysis. Thus, before the analysis begins, the researcher should examine the data set carefully and make any corrections that are needed. Although no system is foolproof, researchers have developed a variety of techniques for locating errors.

If the data set is small, the researcher may be able to detect some errors simply by scanning the data with the data editor screen. Scrolling through the rows and columns of data on the screen can turn up obvious errors, such as blank cells, unusually large numbers, or stray alphanumeric characters. It is best, however, to rely on a more systematic approach. One simple technique with a statistical package, spreadsheet, or database is to use a sort procedure. Sorting rearranges the order of all cases in the data set on the basis of the values of the variable selected as the sort key. Alphanumeric variables are sorted alphabetically, and numerical variables are sorted in numerical order. Scanning the sorted data on the monitor, the researcher can detect misspellings and missing or out-of-range values. For example, if the variable used in the sort procedure is a scale item where expected values are integers from 1 to 5, blank entries and entries of "0" would be at the top of the list, decimals such as 1.5 would show up between "1" and "2," and values of 6 or more would be at the end of the list. This can be a cumbersome process with large data sets, but for only 50 or so variables, sorting the data works well.

With a statistical package such as SPSS, another option is to generate a frequency distribution on all variables. This produces a list of every value that actually occurs in the data set for each variable in ascending order and the number of cases for each respective value. This helps detect variables with out-of-range values or values that should not be present. Of course, knowing that some cases exist somewhere with the wrong entries for a variable and finding those cases are very different things, especially when the data set may contain a thousand or more cases. Having identified a variable with one or more suspect cases, the researcher can use a conditional selection process. The exact command differs from program to program, but basically, the researcher enters a command to select those cases for which the value for the variable in question meets a certain condition. For example, if no one in the data set should have an age greater than 18, execute a command to select all cases where AGE > 18; then include a second command to list the case numbers or the last and first names of all cases meeting that condition. Armed with this information, scroll through the data set to the identified cases and correct them. The researcher may edit the entry by replacing it with the correct value, enter a missing value code if the correct value is not available, or in cases where the correct data cannot be determined, eliminate the case entirely.

These techniques help find data entries that are too large or too small; sometimes, however, the data are within the acceptable range but simply wrong for that case. Some of these errors can be detected by looking for logical inconsistencies. For example, if the value in a month variable is April, June, September, or November, then the value in a day variable associated with that month should not be greater than 30. If the variable entry for the number of adults in the household is 2 and the number of children is 4, then the entry for total household size should be 6. Depending on the software program, it is possible to build queries that detect cases in which such inconsistencies are present. Large-scale professional surveys have the benefit of specialized software to help detect errors and employ supervisory personnel who review data entry to detect problems, but most human service practitioners are unlikely to have access to such services. Rigorous application of these procedures, however, can locate many errors. Finally, error detection underscores the importance of numbering the questionnaires or other raw data sources and keeping the raw data in a safe, accessible location so that you can compare the original data to the computer file when needed.

Creating New Variables

At this point, the data have all been entered and checked for error, but one task remains before proceeding to the data analysis: The variables as recorded may not be in the final form for the desired analysis procedures. If this is the case, the researcher needs to modify the variables—or to generate usable new ones. Such data manipulation may sound unusual, but it is a legitimate and necessary part of the research process.

Here is one example of how and why this is done. Recall from Chapter 13 that some scale items are stated in positive terms and other items in negative terms to avoid problems such as response set. With a 10-item Likert scale for depression, for instance, having choices ranging from 1 to 5, half the items would be stated such that a positive response, such as "strongly agree" or "1," would indicate low depression. The other items would be stated such that a negative response, such as "strongly disagree" or "5," would indicate low depression. To conduct statistical analysis, some items need to be reverse-scored so that a score of 1 on all items signifies a low value on the concept being measured and a 5 signifies a high value. This can be accomplished by the use of a *recode* procedure in statistical programs. A recode statement specifies the existing values in a given variable and what the new values should be. In our example, for the five items in which a negative response (a "5") indicated low depression, we would change the values as follows:

Old Item Value		Revised Item Value
1	□	5
2	□	4
3	□	3
4	□	2
5	□	1

Having recoded the negative items, we now have 10 consistent items where low values indicate low levels of depression and high values indicate high levels of depression. What we really need, however, is a total scale score on depression. This can be obtained by using a *compute* procedure in the data-analysis program. A compute procedure creates a new variable by performing mathematical computations using one or more existing variables. Depending on the conventions of the particular software, we enter a formula like this:

DEPSCORE = sum (DEP1 to DEP10).

With this formula, a new variable called DEPSCORE is created. Its value is computed for each case by summing all 10 individual items that make up the depression scale (DEP1 through DEP10). The new variable—the total depression scale score—is added to the data file. As with the existing variables, the researcher can attach a variable label and value labels to such newly created variables. Whenever the researcher modifies the data set, whether by recoding or by computing new variables, the steps used in the data manipulation must be recorded and added to the codebook. Fortunately, this is easy to do, because statistical programs typically record all executed data transformations in a special file. Documenting these transformations ensures that any researcher using the data file will be able to confirm how the new variables were generated. Recoding and computing new variables is an essential step in the process of unlocking the findings contained in the data set.

DATA DISTRIBUTIONS

Once the data have been stored as a computer file, systematically inspected for error, cleaned, and possibly revised through recoding and variable creation, we are ready to begin actual data analysis. Data analysis is the process of seeking out patterns within individual variables or the patterns in relationships between variables. The term *univariate analysis* refers to the process of describing individual variables. Even when our ultimate goal in a research project is to determine how two or more variables are related, the process of describing the data by specifying the characteristics of individual variables is critical to a research project. Learning how individual variables are distributed can help determine which variables to use in studying relationships and which data-analysis procedures we should use.

Types of Data Distributions

One of the first steps usually taken with a data set is to look at the range of values for each variable. To accomplish this, a *frequency distribution*

TABLE 14.2 Hypothetical Grade Distribution for a Social Science Research Class

Grade	Frequency
A	4
B	7
C	10
D	5
F	3
	N = 29

is constructed. In Table 14.2, the variable is the grade for a college class, with the traditional five categories. The frequency column shows the number of class members who received each grade. Of particular interest is the *shape* of a frequency distribution. A distribution's shape derives from the pattern that the frequencies produce among the various categories of the variable. A number of labels are used to describe the shapes of distributions. First, distributions may be symmetrical or asymmetrical (see Figure 14.1). *Symmetrical distributions* are balanced, with one half of the distribution being a mirror image of the other half. In reality, most distributions only approach perfect symmetry. *Asymmetrical distributions* have cases bunched toward one end of the scale, with a long "tail" caused by a small number of extreme cases trailing off in the other direction. Asymmetrical distributions are said to be *skewed,* with positively skewed distributions having long tails extending in the direction of the higher values and negatively skewed distributions having tails going in the direction of the lower values. (Note that the concepts of positive and negative skewness apply only to distributions involving data of the ordinal level of measurement or higher. Because the categories of nominal data have no inherent order, the shape of a distribution of nominal data is purely an arbitrary matter of how we choose to arrange the categories.) Determining the amount of skewness is an important preliminary step for later

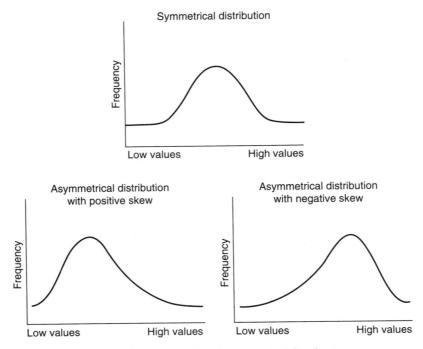

Figure 14.1 Symmetrical and asymmetrical distributions.

analysis. Certain inferential statistics, for example, are based on the assumption that the variables are normally distributed. One of the basic properties of a normal distribution is that of being symmetrical. Therefore, our analysis at this stage may be critical for helping decide later which inferential procedures are appropriate.

Constructing Frequency Distributions

Simple Frequency Distributions. When data are collected, they are in the form of a *raw data distribution*, which means that the distribution contains all the different values that were observed on a variable. Table 14.3 displays a raw data distribution of the ages of a sample of 71 residents in a veterans' facility. A first step in data analysis might be to construct a *simple frequency distribution*, in which each value of a variable is listed only once, along with the number of cases that have that value. Table 14.3 includes a simple frequency distribution of the ages of the people in the facility. The X column refers to the values

or categories of the variable, while the *f* column indicates the frequency, or the number of cases, that have each value.

Simple frequency distributions can be constructed on variables at any level of measurement. In Table 14.3, it is much easier to gain some sense of the age distribution of the residents from the simple frequency distribution in comparison to the raw data distribution. Sometimes, however, simple frequency distributions are too cumbersome. Table 14.3 shows a lot of categories to look at, and many categories have either no or only a few cases. In these situations, it often is preferable to collapse a distribution further by creating a grouped frequency distribution.

Grouped Frequency Distributions. At its core, data analysis is basically a search for patterns in data. Sometimes, however, searching for patterns in raw data is akin to the old adage of not being able to see the forest for the trees. Even if we order the observations with a simple frequency distribution, the large number of observations, the small

TABLE 14.3 Two Types of Data Distributions of Patients' Ages

A. Raw Data Distribution

98	82	78	70	68	60
96	81	76	70	68	60
95	80	76	70	68	59
92	80	75	70	68	59
91	79	74	70	68	59
89	79	73	70	67	58
87	79	72	70	66	56
85	79	72	70	66	54
85	79	71	70	66	52
84	79	71	69	64	51
82	79	71	69	63	50
82	79	71	69	63	

Total $N = 71$

B. Sample Frequency Distribution

X	F	X	f	X	f
98	1	76	2	59	3
96	1	75	1	58	1
95	1	74	1	56	1
92	1	73	1	54	1
91	1	72	2	52	1
89	1	71	4	51	1
87	1	70	9	50	1
85	2	69	3		
84	1	68	5		
82	3	67	1		
81	1	66	3		
80	2	64	1		
79	8	63	2		
78	1	60	2		

variations between some observations, and large gaps between others combine to hide the pattern inherent in the data.

Grouping is the process of combining a large number of individual variable categories into a smaller number of larger categories. It permits us to step back from the data and see the big picture by ignoring minor variations between cases and focusing our attention on larger patterns. One reason for grouping is to summarize the data into a manageable number of categories; a table or graph may be unreadable if it has too many categories. Another purpose is to eliminate categories with either no or few cases in them. In addition to making it easier to see patterns in the data, grouping often is necessary for certain data-analysis procedures. For example, a statistical computation may require enough cases so that each cell in a table could, theoretically, have at least five cases in it. Grouping helps meet this requirement, because reducing the number of categories increases the number of cases falling into the newer, larger categories.

The manner in which grouping is done depends, in large part, on the level of measurement of the data. Table 14.4 shows the hypothetical results of a small survey that includes the variable "religious affiliation." This frequency distribution clearly is in need of grouping: Some categories have no cases at all; others have few cases. The coding scheme also has a large number of categories. When grouping nominal data like these, we rely on logic and common sense to group categories that, in some way, fit with each other. For example, it is logical to group all Protestant denominations into a new category called "Protestant," because they all share some core beliefs and practices. On the other hand, those categories with few or no frequencies could reasonably be grouped into a category called "other," simply because none of them contain a sufficient number of cases. The difference in reasoning behind each group is important to note, because it may be significant for later analysis. For example, if we are evaluating how religious or nonreligious affiliation relates to attitudes toward volunteering for community service, then "Catholic," "Jewish," "Protestant," and "Atheist/Agnostic" are meaningful categories, whereas "other" is a hodgepodge

TABLE 14.4 Illustration of Grouping a Nominal Variable

Value	Original Code Scheme RELIGION religious affiliation Label	Frequency	Value	Recoding Scheme RELIG2 religious affiliation groups Label	Frequency
1	Roman Catholic	10	1	Roman Catholic	10
2	Methodist	3	2	Protestant	20
3	Presbyterian	2	3	Jewish	10
4	Lutheran	5	4	Other	5
5	Baptist	4			
6	Unitarian	3			
7	Episcopalian	3			
8	Jewish	10			
9	Moslem	1			
10	Eastern Orthodox	0			
11	Hindu	1			
12	Buddhist	1			
13	Shintoist	0			
14	Atheist	2			
15	Other	0			
Total $N = 45$					

of cases that we really cannot describe in terms of common theology. For purposes of analysis, we may want to classify these latter cases as "missing" and exclude them from analysis.

Grouping ordinal data can be a very straightforward process of merging adjacent categories. For example, if we decide that the nine social-class categories in Table 14.5 are too many, it is easy to collapse them down to the conventional three shown in the table. In this illustration, going from nine to three categories makes logical sense, because the nine small categories are gradations of the three larger groupings.

This is not always the case, however. A survey may include an item that asks for years of education but not have a variable for the highest degree attained. In this case, the desired variable could be approximated by grouping the existing variable. Although years of education could, conceivably, be construed of as a ratio level variable, if it is applied as an indicator of preparation for employment, then it might better be treated as an ordinal. In terms of getting a job, having a high school diploma, an associate degree, or a bachelor's degree may be the critical determinants. People who dropped out without completing the 12th grade are all coded in the dropouts category, whether they completed 9, 10, or 11 years. People who have 13 to 15 years of education probably have some college but not a bachelor's degree. Rather than using equal multiples, as in the social-class example, a researcher might approximate employment preparation by

TABLE 14.5 **Grouping Ordinal Data**

Social Class	f	Social Class	f
Upper upper	8		
Middle upper	14	Upper	57
Lower upper	35		
Upper middle	56		
Middle middle	92	Middle	212
Lower middle	64		
Upper lower	44		
Middle lower	32	Lower	87
Lower lower	11		
Total (*N*) = 356		Total (*N*) = 356	

grouping years of education into the following categories:

1 = <9 years (no high school)
2 = 9–11 years (some high school)
3 = 12 years (high school graduate)
4 = 13–15 years (some college)
5 = 16+ years (college graduate)

This scheme would not be perfect, of course, because not everyone with 12 years of schooling graduated, but it would approximate the desired variable. As this example illustrates, the fact that the original categories are ordered is a starting point for grouping a variable, but the researcher must still rely on logic and knowledge of the application to which the grouped variable will be put to decide on the boundaries of the intervals.

Grouping interval level data is a fairly direct process. Unlike ordinal data, the distance between units of interval level data are, by definition, equal, so one general principle is to use equal-width intervals when grouping data. Nevertheless, common sense and knowledge of the use to which the grouped data will be put are essential to planning the group intervals. Intervals of $10 might make perfect sense if grouping data on the weekly earnings of high school students, but these intervals are completely inappropriate if the data concern

the annual income of single-parent households. All raw frequency distributions of interval data have units of 1, such as length of jail sentence in days, earnings in dollars, or live births per year. In grouping, we merely increase the number of units in each new interval from 1 to 3, 10, 1,000, or whatever amount both makes logical sense given the data and provides the desired number of intervals for describing that data and doing data analysis. The size of the grouped intervals is called the *interval width*. Consider the distribution of ungrouped ages for the residents of the veterans' residential facility in Table 14.3. Clearly, these scores are in need of grouping, because they are so spread out that any pattern is difficult to see.

To illustrate grouping interval data, we will group the scores in Table 14.3 into 10 new intervals. We want enough intervals so that we do not obscure significant variation in the data, but we also want to reduce the clutter of too many categories. Once the decision regarding the number of intervals is made, we must determine the number of measurement units that will go into each new interval—that is, the interval width. In this example, with a range of 48 years in the age variable and the number of grouped intervals set at 10, it is quite obvious that the interval width should be 5. In other situations, however, the interval width may not be so easy to determine, so there is a formula that one can apply to find the interval width:

$$\text{Interval width} = \frac{H_s - L_s}{N_i},$$

where H_s is the highest actual score in the distribution, L_s is the lowest actual score in the distribution, and N_i is the number of desired intervals. Now, if we applied this equation to the data in Table 14.3, we would have

$$\text{Interval width} = \frac{98 - 50}{10} = \frac{48}{10} = 4.8.$$

In many cases, the result of this formula is a decimal of some sort that one merely adjusts upward or downward to the nearest convenient interval width. In our case, we would adjust upward for an interval width of 5. The resulting frequency distribution is displayed in Table 14.6.

TABLE 14.6 Patient Age Data Grouped by Intervals of Five Years

Interval Width	Value	Frequency	Percentage	Valid Percentage	Cumulative Percentage
50–54	52	4	5.6	5.6	5.6
55–59	57	5	7.0	7.0	12.7
60–64	62	5	7.0	7.0	19.7
65–69	67	12	16.9	16.9	36.6
70–74	72	17	23.9	23.9	60.6
75–79	77	12	16.9	16.9	77.5
80–84	82	7	9.9	9.9	87.3
85–89	87	4	5.6	5.6	93.0
90–94	92	2	2.8	2.8	95.8
95–99	97	3	4.2	4.2	100.0
	Total	71	100.0	100.0	
Valid cases 71	Missing cases 0				

When selecting interval widths, we suggest that the width be an odd number, such as 3, 5, or 7, because intervals with an odd-numbered width have a whole number for their *midpoints*. For example, with an interval of size 5, 50–54 has a midpoint of 52, but with an interval of size 4, 46–49 has a midpoint of 47.5. When working with grouped interval data, the midpoints have a number of uses, such as they could be used as category labels in Table 14.6, and it is far more convenient to work with midpoints that do not have decimals.

Compare the grouped data in Table 14.6 with the ungrouped and simple frequency distributions in Table 14.3. Do you notice anything in the grouped distribution that you did not see when you first looked at those distributions, especially the ungrouped distribution? The grouped distribution clearly shows the characteristic accumulation of people in the middle of a distribution with the frequencies tapering off toward both tails of the distribution. Such a distribution is commonly

referred to as a "normal curve" and is an important characteristic of data distributions that will be used in choosing some statistics in Chapter 15.

GRAPHICAL DISPLAY OF DATA DISTRIBUTIONS

In addition to describing variables by means of a frequency distribution, another common procedure is to use a graph. The visual impact of a graph can help identify and summarize patterns in data that might not be detected as readily by perusing frequency distribution tables. Today, statistical software can produce a diverse array of graphs that can be enhanced with color and editing capabilities. Used correctly, graphs are a powerful tool for communicating information about data; used incorrectly, they can confuse and even mislead viewers about the meaning of a distribution. One situation in which graphs are popular occurs when the results of a frequency distribution must be presented to an audience that is unfamiliar with reading such tables.

Here, we present a few of the more common ways to graph individual variables. Basically, these graphs are visual representations of a frequency distribution. Earlier, we discussed ways of grouping data for presentation in a frequency distribution table. Many of these same issues apply to graphing data. For example, a graph is more effective if there are a manageable number of categories. If several categories have a very low frequency, they will be hard to see on a graph. An effective graph, then, begins with organizing the data appropriately, just as one would for a frequency distribution table.

Bar Graphs

One of the most commonly used types of graphs is the **bar graph.** A distinguishing feature of the bar graph is the space between the bars. These spaces illustrate that the categories of the variable being represented are separate, or *discrete*. In Chapter 5, we pointed out that only certain categories are theoretically possible in a discrete variable, such

as sex, religious affiliation, and household size. Nominal and ordinal variables are, by definition, discrete variables, so bar graphs are especially useful for these levels of data. Figure 14.2 illustrates a typical bar graph, with the height of the bars representing the frequencies in each category of the variable. As can be seen from the figure, a bar graph makes it easy to note trends, such as the upward one in Figure 14.2.

When constructing a bar graph—and most other types of graphs, for that matter—care should be taken when establishing the dimensions of the graph. The vertical axis, which represents the frequencies, and the horizontal axis, which represents the categories of the variable, should be about equal, with reasonably equal spacing of the categories on both axes. Again, Figure 14.2 illustrates this. The concern for roughly equal dimensions is important, because it is possible to accidentally—or purposely—construct a graph that gives a false impression. For example, by expanding the dimensions of the vertical axis, a graph can be constructed that makes small differences among categories appear to be large, at least to the casual observer. On

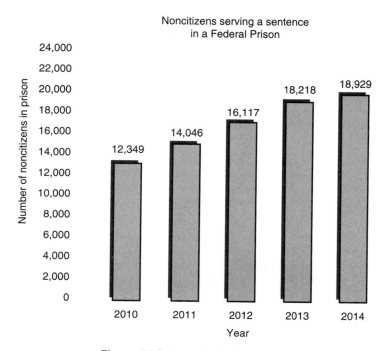

Figure 14.2 Example of a bar graph.

the other hand, expanding the horizontal dimension has the opposite effect; a graph can be constructed that appears to minimize differences among the categories. Purposeful manipulation of graph dimensions in an attempt to deceive viewers is considered to be unethical. It should be noted, however, that misleading graphs are produced all the time, so anyone reading a research report should always carefully inspect any graph to be sure that viewers are not being misled by its initial appearance.

Histograms and Frequency Polygons

Although some variables, such as household size or a frequency count of a behavior, are discrete variables, the variables at the interval or ratio level of measurement are conceived of as *continuous,* meaning that, unlike the discrete variables, there are no gaps or spaces between the categories. Thus, age is a continuous variable. This continuous nature of interval and ratio data should be reflected in graphs used to present them. The researcher wishing to graph interval or ratio data has a choice of two popular methods.

The **histogram** bears a considerable resemblance to the preceding bar graph. Once again, as we see in Figure 14.3, bars of various lengths represent the magnitude of the frequencies from a frequency distribution. The only difference between a bar graph and a histogram is that the bars in a histogram touch, signifying the continuous nature of the data.

Figure 14.3 also illustrates the alternative technique of graphing interval or ratio data, the **frequency polygon**, which is simply a line graph that connects the midpoints of each category of the variable. The choice of either a histogram or a frequency polygon is purely a matter of personal preference, because they are interchangeable.

Pie Charts

The **pie chart** is another type of commonly used graph that is particularly good for showing how some whole amount is divided. As such, pie charts often are used to illustrate how budgets are distributed for varying functions. Anyone who has occasion to prepare a grant proposal will most likely have to create one or more pie charts indicating how the money would be spent. Figure 14.4 is a pie chart based on projected revenue to the federal government for the 1997 fiscal year.

A pie chart gets its name from its resemblance to the slices of a pie. The size of each slice visually depicts the percentage of the whole that each category represents. Preparing a pie chart via a computer program now involves simply choosing a variable and the pie chart option from the

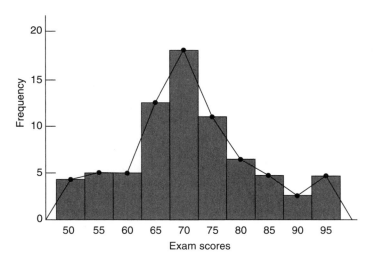

Figure 14.3 Histogram and frequency polygon of hypothetical exam scores.

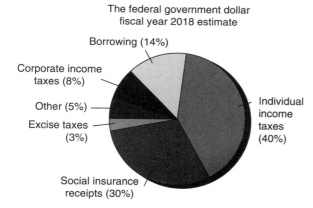

Figure 14.4 Example of a pie chart.

graphing menu. However, the process that the graphing program uses involves determining how many of the 360 degrees of an entire circle are to be allocated to each of the categories. For example, Figure 14.4 indicates that 11% of revenues are expected to come from corporate income taxes. To determine how large a slice to allocate to corporate income taxes, the data-analysis software multiplies 360 by 11%, obtaining a value of 39.6 degrees. So, the slice devoted to corporate income taxes is drawn such that it occupies 39.6 degrees of the 360 degrees of the circle.

CONTINGENCY TABLES

Thus far, we have discussed ways of describing the distribution of cases on a single variable and of presenting single variable data in the form of frequency distributions and graphs. Now, we turn our attention to ways of describing and exploring how two or more variables are distributed together. That is, given the values in a data set on one variable, how are values distributed on one or more other variables? Classifying or organizing the data on one variable according to values on a second variable is the basis for contingency table analysis.

Bivariate Relationships

The statistics that we have considered so far describe the distribution of a single variable and,

therefore, are called **univariate statistics**. Most data analysis in research involves dealing with two or more variables simultaneously. Statistical procedures that describe the relationship between two variables are called **bivariate statistics**, and **multivariate statistics** deal with three or more variables. When two or more variables are analyzed with descriptive statistics, the major feature of interest is the relationship between the variables, especially the extent to which they covary, or vary together. If two variables are related, then a change in one of the variables is associated with a change in the other.

A convenient way of investigating bivariate relationships is to cross-tabulate the data in the form of a table. A *contingency table* contains raw frequencies, percentages, or both. Here, we discuss the construction of such tables for only two variables; however, contingency table analysis can be applied to three or more variables.

Table 14.7 illustrates the general form of a contingency table. We use two conventions to standardize the construction of contingency tables. First, when we have an independent variable and a dependent variable, the vertical *columns* represent categories of the independent variable, and the horizontal *rows* represent categories of the dependent variable. In Table 14.7, the variable *Income* is the independent variable, and *Number of Hours of Television Watched* is the dependent variable. Second, when ordinal-level or higher level data are cross-tabulated, the categories should be ordered as illustrated in Table 14.7, with columns running from lowest on the left to highest on the right and rows from lowest at the bottom to highest at the top. These conventions are not universally applied, however. Some tables are constructed differently, but following the conventions does contribute to consistency and ease of interpretation. Furthermore, the computational routines for some statistics assume that tables are constructed according to this convention and, therefore, must be modified to produce correct results with differently structured tables.

Several labels refer to the various parts of tables. The squares of the table are called *cells*, and the frequencies within the cells are labeled *cell frequencies*. Values in the "Totals" column or row are called

TABLE 14.7 A Contingency Table With Frequencies and Percentages

		INCOME		
		Low	Medium	High
Number of Hours of Television Watched	High	49 (19.2%)	19 (8.6%)	10 (6.7)%
	Medium	164 (64.3%)	136 (61.5%)	86 (57.5%)
	Low	42 (16.5%)	66 (29.9%)	53 (35.6%)
	Totals	255 (100%)	221 (100%)	149 (100%)

Dependent Variable — *Independent Variable*

Cell frequency — *Cell percentage* — *Column marginals*

Source: From Davis, J. A., & Smith, T. W. (1994). *General social surveys 1972–1994: Cumulative codebook*. Chicago, IL: National Opinion Research Center.

marginals (only the column marginal is shown in Table 14.7). Tables often are identified according to the number of rows and columns they contain. A table with two rows and two columns becomes a 2 × 2 (read "2 by 2") table. A table such as Table 14.7 is a 3 × 3 table. In addition, because the number of rows is always designated first, a 2 × 3 table is not the same as a 3 × 2 table.

Contingency tables almost always include *cell percentages*, because by themselves, cell frequencies are difficult to interpret if the number of cases varies in each column and row. Converting frequencies to percentages makes interpretation much easier and can be done by dividing each cell frequency by the appropriate marginal total and then multiplying the result by 100. We would use column marginals if we wanted to see how the dependent variable was distributed across categories of the independent variable. Percentages in the first column of Table 14.7 were obtained by dividing the cell frequencies 49, 164, and 42 by the column marginal 255, with the result multiplied by 100. Below each column, the percentages are totaled and indicated as equaling 100%. This informs the reader that the column marginals were used to compute the percentages. Sometimes, the cells in a contingency table contain only percentages and no frequencies. In this case, the marginal frequencies should always be included, because they supply valuable information regarding the number of cases on which the percentages are based and enable the reader to compute the cell frequencies if needed.

Reading percentage tables is a straightforward process similar to constructing them. Whereas we computed the percentages down the columns, we read percentage tables by comparing percentages along the rows. Of particular interest is the *percentage difference* (% d) between any two categories within a given row. For example, in Table 14.7, the difference between the low-income column and the high-income column in the top row is 12.5%, meaning that substantially more low-income people watch high levels of television. The % d suggests that high levels of television watching are less common among high-income groups. Note that, with a 2 × 2 table, a single % d summarizes the complete table. As the number of rows and columns in a table increases, the number of % d's that can be calculated increases rapidly.

The magnitude of % d's is a crude indicator of the strength of the relationship between two variables: Small differences of 1% or 2% indicate weak and, possibly, meaningless relationships, while % d's of 15% or more usually indicate substantial relationships. Unfortunately, no hard-and-fast rules concerning evaluation of the magnitude of % d's can be offered because of the complicating factor of sample size. For example, if we are dealing with employment data for the entire nation, a difference of 1% or less could represent a million more workers with or without jobs. With large samples, smaller % d's are more important. Alternatively, with small samples, % d's must be large before they indicate a substantial relationship. (We discuss other statistics for assessing the strength of relationships in contingency tables in Chapter 15.)

Multivariate Analysis

As noted in Chapter 2, analyzing an independent and a dependent variable and finding a bivariate relationship between them does not prove that the independent variable *causes* variation in the dependent variable. To infer causality, the possible effects of extraneous variables must be investigated. Although research projects may focus primary attention on two variables, they typically consider others to assess the full complexity of social phenomena. A set of procedures for conducting this kind of multivariate analysis is called either **table elaboration** or **contingency control**. Contingency control involves examining a relationship between an independent and a dependent variable while holding a third variable (also called a *test factor*) constant. Three variable tables are constructed such that the relationship between the independent and dependent variable can be examined within each category of that third variable. The general format of contingency control is illustrated in Figure 14.5.

The original table that the researcher begins the analysis with is called the *zero-order table*, and the relationship contained within it is known as a *zero-order relationship*. The *zero* in these labels indicates that no control or test variables are being

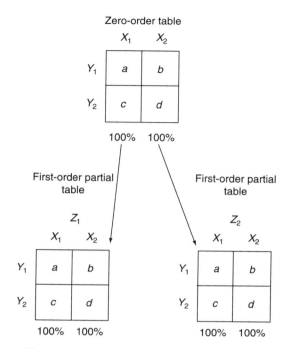

Figure 14.5 General format for partialing tables.

used. As we introduce test variables, the tables produced are called *partial tables*, and the relationships within them are known as *partial relationships*. A partial relationship is a relationship between an independent and a dependent variable within one category of the test or control variable.

Partial tables are referred to by the number of test variables being controlled at one time. If we are controlling one test variable in our partial tables, then these tables are referred to as *first-order partials*, indicating that the number of variables being controlled is one. If more variables than one are being simultaneously controlled, then the tables are called *second-order partials*, *third-order partials*, and so on. Often, research does not go beyond the first order with contingency control. One reason is that as we add more test variables, the number of partial tables that are generated increases rapidly, and interpreting all these tables becomes difficult. The other reason that table elaboration often is not taken beyond the first order is that the sample gets divided quickly, to the point that individual cell frequencies may become too small and reduce our confidence in the results. In other words, we literally run out of cases. This effect can be seen in Figure 14.5, where in the zero-order case, the sample is divided among the four cells of the zero-order table; but when we move to the partials, the same number of cases is spread among the eight cells of the two tables, thus reducing the magnitude of the cell frequencies. For analyzing multivariate relationships beyond the first order, we normally use techniques other than table elaboration.

A number of outcomes can occur when a test variable is introduced and partial tables are created. Describing some of these outcomes offers an idea of the basic logic behind multivariate analysis. First, the partial tables may show *no effect*. This is also called *replication*, because the results in the partial tables replicate, or repeat, the results in the zero-order table: The relationship in the partial tables is approximately the same in terms of strength and direction as it was in the zero-order table. In this case, we have tested a variable that is unrelated to either the independent or the dependent variable; therefore, it could not affect the relationship between those variables. We have illustrated this in Figure 14.6, where the zero-order table shows the relationship between *gender*

and *whether people believe life to be exciting, routine, or dull*. You can see in the zero-order table that about 10% more of the men believe that life is exciting. It is possible, however, that *marital status* might influence whether men and women perceive life to be exciting. So, in the partial tables, we look at the relationship between the two variables separately for married and single people (to simplify the example, we have left out the other possible marital statuses). You can see that this third variable has almost no effect on the original relationship. In each of the categories of marital status, about 7% to 8% more men than women see life as exciting.

A second possibility when doing table elaboration is that the strength of the relationship found in the zero-order table may be substantially reduced—or even disappear entirely—in the partials. We described this kind of situation in the discussion of causality in Chapter 2, but without calling it by these names. We have reproduced that data in Figure 14.7. The zero-order table shows how reading reports about the health consequences of smoking impacted on whether people quit smoking. The table shows that people who

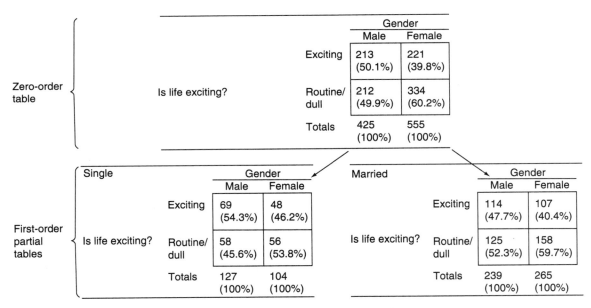

Figure 14.6 Table elaboration showing "no effect" of the test variable (replication).

Source: From Davis, J. A., & Smith, T. W. (1994). *General social surveys 1972–1994: Cumulative codebook*. Chicago, IL: National Opinion Research Center.

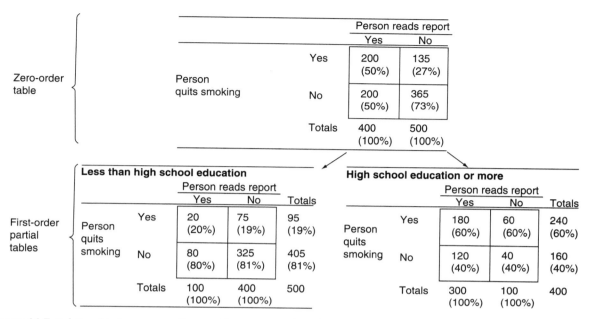

Figure 14.7 Relationship between reading smoking reports and smoking cessation, with level of education as a control variable.

read such reports are substantially more likely to quit smoking (% d = 23%). When we control for education, however, the original relationship disappears. In each educational grouping, quitting smoking is as common among those who have not read the report as it is among those who have.

This result can be difficult to interpret, because there are two possibilities and we need more information, which may or may not be available, to choose between the two. One possibility is that in terms of temporal order, the test variable intervenes between the independent and the dependent variables (see Figure 14.8). When such an intervening variable is controlled, it is called *interpretation*. The independent variable is changing the test variable, which in turn is changing the dependent variable; in other words, a causal sequencing is being specified. When there is such a causal chain, the relationship between the independent variable and the dependent variable is effectively blocked in the partial tables. In our example, an intervening variable relationship means that reading of the report is what produces their level of education and that level of education, in turn, causes them to quit smoking. This probably is not an appropriate assessment of these

variables, however, because there is no logical or theoretical reason to assume that reading a health report would change people's level of education. So, interpretation probably is not what is going on in this table.

This brings us to the other possibility—namely, that the zero-order relationship is either all or partly *spurious*. In this case, which is called *explanation*, the test variable is temporally located before either the independent or the dependent variable and is related directly to both. This is called an *antecedent variable relationship*. When the effects of the test variable are controlled, the apparent relationship between the independent variable and the dependent variable is reduced or eliminated, because the operation of the test variable was to inflate the actual relationship between the other two variables in the zero-order table. In other words, the relationship shown in the zero-order table was a false reading. In Figure 14.7, we know that people's educational levels are antecedent: Their educational levels were established before they had a chance to read the report or quit smoking. In addition, theoretical reasons allow us to conclude that level of education can influence both whether people read the report and whether they quit smoking.

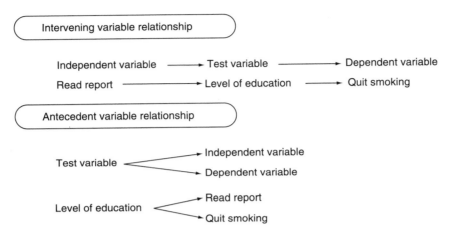

Figure 14.8 Comparison of intervening and antecedent variable relationships.

This tells us that the relationship in the zero-order table is spurious.

So, when a relationship disappears in a partial table, we need to establish the appropriate temporal location of the test variable or use some theoretical or logical considerations to determine whether interpretation or explanation is the proper assessment of what is going on. If that cannot be done, as might occur with survey data, then we cannot be sure whether the partials are indicating the presence of an intervening variable or a spurious relationship. (As noted in Chapter 2, determining temporal order is crucial in sorting out causal relationships among variables.)

Yet another possibility can be discovered in table elaboration. *Specification* refers to a situation where the relationship between the independent and dependent variables is found in the zero-order table but the partial tables show different relationships from one table to another. One partial table may show no relationship or only a weak relationship, while the other shows a strong relationship. In other words, the table elaboration specifies the categories of the test variable in which the relationship occurs or does not occur.

We want to mention one final possibility that can be found in table elaboration: The partial tables may show an even stronger relationship between the independent and dependent variables than was indicated by the zero-order table. This outcome occurs because the action of the uncontrolled test variable in the zero-order table is to suppress the relationship between the independent and the dependent variables. In fact, variables that produce this result are called *suppressor variables*, and the result itself is known as *suppression*. This occurs when the test variable and the independent variable are exerting forces on the dependent variable that are at least partly offsetting. In other words, as values of the independent variable increase, they influence the dependent variable to increase, but as the test variable increases, it influences the dependent variable to decrease, thus masking part of the relationship between the independent and the dependent variables. When the influence of the test variable is controlled, this masking effect is removed, and the relationship between the independent variable and the dependent variable is revealed to be stronger than in the zero-order table.

A number of other possibilities can occur in table elaboration, but these examples illustrate the importance and difficulty of this kind of multivariate analysis. It is important because it enables us to discover the complexity of social reality where dependent variables are influenced by a number of factors at the same time. It is difficult because it requires time, patience, and creativity to tease out what can sometimes be hard-to-discover relationships.

REVIEW AND CRITICAL THINKING

Main Points

- Data analysis refers to deriving some meaning from the observations that have been made as part of a research project. Quantitative data analysis involves putting observations into numerical form and manipulating them based on their arithmetical properties.
- Data preparation and organization is an essential part of the research process, including knowing the best way to enter data into an electronic file and manipulate that data.
- Data analysis begins by developing a coding scheme and a codebook, which is a set of mutually exclusive and exhaustive numerical codes into which the raw data are categorized.
- After the data have been entered into a computer file, they must be carefully checked for coding or input errors.
- New or revised variables may be created by recoding existing variables or by computing new variables based on existing variables.
- Frequency distributions may be effectively communicated with bar graphs, histograms, frequency polygons, and pie charts.
- Frequency distributions reveal the pattern that the frequencies produce among the various categories of the variable and may be symmetrical or asymmetrical.
- Contingency tables and percentage tables are particularly useful for analyzing bivariate and multivariate relationships with categorical or partially ordered data.

IMPORTANT TERMS FOR REVIEW

Alphanumeric variables	Data analysis	Pie charts
Bar graph	Frequency polygon	Statistics
Bivariate statistics	Histogram	Table elaboration
Coding scheme	Multivariate statistics	Univariate statistics
Contingency control	Numeric variables	

CRITICAL THINKING

Today we are confronted with massive amounts of numerical information in our daily lives, due in part to modern communications technologies. This makes it especially important to develop some critical thinking skills that will enable you to evaluate this deluge of information and to separate what is legitimate and useful from what is meaningless or deceptive. The material presented in this chapter can serve as a guideline for this critical thinking. The following are critical thinking questions raised at the beginning of the chapter and some ideas for how they relate to social work practice. Students are encouraged to develop their own answers to these questions.

Why is it important to understand how to build a data set? Data analysis is a process for transforming data, usually from numbers, into information that can be useful for describing and making inferences on a sample. The starting point for data analysis is how to properly build a data set that can yield data analysis.

Why is it important for people working in the social services to understand data analysis? Social workers are not always known for their data-analysis skills or for their love of math. If you were to ask social workers why they chose social work as their profession, they would probably not say, "Because I love data analysis." However, understanding data analysis will help you become a more well-rounded and skilled social worker.

Can understanding data analysis improve your skills in social services and help you to improve systems of change? Understanding quantitative analysis may help you improve lives and change systems that oppress individuals in society.

EVALUATING COMPETENCY (FROM THE COUNCIL ON SOCIAL WORK EDUCATION [CSWE] 2015 EDUCATIONAL POLICY AND ACCREDITATION STANDARDS [EPAS])

Competency 9: Evaluate Practice With Individuals, Families, Groups, Organizations, and Communities

- What challenges might a social researcher face when developing a data set for different organizations?
- What knowledge does a social researcher need to understand how to build a data set for agencies in the community?

SELF-ASSESSMENT

1. Preparation for data analysis involves:
   a. An answerable research question.
   b. Literature review search.
   c. Coding scheme, numeric variables, and preparing and using a codebook.
   d. Measurement validity.
2. Data cleaning refers to:
   a. Making sure data is clean from dirt or debris.
   b. A process there is no need for if you took much care during data entry.
   c. Checking measurement reliability.
   d. A process of checking errors that may have occurred during data entry.

3. Raw data entry consists of:
   a. A process where data are extracted from existing documents and entered into a statistical application that will be used for analysis.
   b. Data that are not yet collected.
   c. Data that have not received permission to be analyzed.
   d. A process of gaining permission to analyze data.
4. Data distribution involves:
   a. Statistical frequencies.
   b. The process of distributing the findings of the data.
   c. Dissemination of the data.
   d. Types of data distribution and constructing frequency distributions.
5. Creating new variables consists of:
   a. Conducting a new survey.
   b. Changing participants' data.
   c. Modifying variables or generating usable new ones.
   d. Changing variables that were not consistent with your research question(s).
6. Bar graphs refer to:
   a. Bars that blend together in the graph.
   b. A chart that resembles a pie.
   c. Showing how a whole amount is divided into separate parts.
   d. A commonly used graph with a distinguishing feature of space between the bars.
7. Histograms and frequency polygons consist of:
   a. A line graph that connects at the midpoint.
   b. A graph that displays something significant in history.
   c. Something resembling a bar graph, but the bars touch to signify the continuous nature of the data.
   d. A circular shaped graph.
8. Preparing and using a codebook involves:
   a. An inventory of all the individual items in the data-collection instrument together with the coding schemes.
   b. A book that is used by social researchers to code data.
   c. Creating variable codes for items that were not found in the data.
   d. A book that provides information on what analysis to run for your data.
9. Bivariate relationships refer to:
   a. The description of a single variable.
   b. The relationships between four or more variables.
   c. The relationships between three or more variables.
   d. The description of the relationship between two variables.
10. Multivariate analysis refers to:
    a. The relationship between three or more variables.
    b. The relationship between multiple variables.
    c. The relationship between two or more variables.
    d. The relationship between one or more variables.

ANSWER KEY FOR SELF-ASSESSMENT QUIZ

1. **c.** Coding scheme, numeric variables, and preparing and using a code-book.
2. **d.** A process of checking errors that may have occurred during data entry
3. **a.** A process where data are extracted from existing documents and entered into a statistical application that will be used for analysis
4. **d.** Types of data distribution and constructing frequency distributions
5. **c.** Modifying variables or generating usable new ones
6. **d.** A commonly used graph with a distinguishing feature of space between the bars
7. **c.** Something resembling a bar graph, but the bars touch to signify the continuous nature of the data
8. **a.** An inventory of all the individual items in the data-collection instrument together with the coding schemes
9. **d.** The description of the relationship between two variables
10. **a.** The relationship between three or more variables

FOR FURTHER READING

Blevins, M., Wehbe, F. H., Rebeiro, P. F., Caro-Vega, Y., McGowan, C. C., Shepherd, B. E., & Caribbean, Central, South America Network for HIV Epidemiology. (2016). Interactive data visualization for HIV cohorts: Leveraging data exchange standards to share and reuse research tools. *PLOS ONE*, *11*(3), e0151201. doi:10.1371/journal.pone.0151201. This article provides tools and download codes for data visualization graphics that were created for disseminating results from public health studies on HIV. Further information is provided specific to presenting longitudinal data, bubble plots, and heat maps.

Gravetter, F., & Wallnau, L. B. (2013). *Statistics for the behavioral sciences* (9th ed.). Belmont, CA: Cengage/Wadsworth. This is a standard but well-written introductory textbook in statistics. It covers all the topics discussed in this and the next chapter, going into more detail and including additional topics.

Green, S. B., & Salkind, N. J. (2011). *Using SPSS for Windows and Macintosh: Analyzing and understanding data* (6th ed.). Upper Saddle River, NJ: Pearson. This book provides an introduction to use the most widely used statistical package today, SPSS. This handbook will show you how to do all the things that are discussed in this and the next chapter.

Healey, J. F. (2012). *Statistics: A tool for social research* (9th ed.). Belmont, CA: Cengage/Wadsworth. This is another standard but well-written introductory textbook in statistics. Along with the Gravetter and Wallnau book, it can help you understand all the material in this and the next chapter.

In, J., & Lee, S. (2017). Statistical data presentation. *Korean Journal of Anesthesiology*, *70*(3), 267–276. doi:10.4097/kjae.2017.70.3.267. This article provides suggestions for presenting data, via text, tables, graphs, and so on, and walks the reader through strategizing effective communication for presenting data.

Jones, G. E. (2006). *How to lie with charts* (2nd ed.). Santa Monica, CA: LaPuerta. An ideal guide for all who want to understand how presenters can use charts to deceive an audience. Readers will learn how to make their presentations more effective.

Journal of Technology in Human Services. New York, NY: Haworth, quarterly. This journal began publication in 1984, focusing on the potential of computer technology to assist with human challenges such as mental health and developmental disabilities. It provides a timely contribution to this area.

Padgett, D. K. (2016). *Qualitative methods in social work research* (3rd ed.). Thousand Oaks, CA: Sage. A textbook that offers in-depth skills for completing qualitative research with a social work perspective.

Wallgren, A., Wallgren, B., Persson, R., Jorner, U., & Haaland, J.-A. (1996). *Graphing statistics and data: Creating better charts.* Thousand Oaks, CA: Sage. This book suggests how to create graphs and charts that make viewers aware of the qualities of data. It introduces the elements of charts, such as axes, scales, and patterns; describes steps to make charts clearer, using real data for examples; and walks the reader through the entire process from data to a finished chart.

REFERENCES

Davis, J. A., & Smith, T. W. (1994). *General social surveys 1972–1994: Cumulative codebook.* Chicago, IL: National Opinion Research Center.

Rosenberg, M. (1965). *Society and the adolescent self-image.* Princeton, NJ: Princeton University Press.

15

DATA ANALYSIS II: DESCRIPTIVE AND INFERENTIAL STATISTICS

INTRODUCTION

We introduced you to Jennifer Lawler in the beginning of Chapter 14. Jennifer works at "Rescue House," a homeless shelter in Bangor, Maine. This shelter serves approximately 100 males, 85 females, and 12 families a year. Jennifer was asked by the grant writer to complete the data analysis portion for a grant. The shelter has five years of data that needed to be entered into a data set before analysis could begin. The "Rescue House" questionnaire consists of demographic questions (questions describing the makeup of clients) and two scales that measure both mental (Mental Health Inventory) and physical health (The Health Orientation Scale). Jennifer has successfully built a data set and finished entering all data in the homeless shelter's statistical software.

Jennifer has properly cleaned all data and now is ready to begin statistical analysis. There is a total of 881 complete surveys (455 individual males, 375 individual females, and 51 families) over the past five years at the shelter. Jennifer needs to conduct data analysis using both descriptive and inferential statistics for the analysis. For the grant, she will need to report characteristics of the people who stayed at the homeless shelter and make generalizations of the sample to the overall population of homeless shelters.

Jennifer is excited to start exploring the data using data analysis. She does understand that she must run the appropriate statistics for the population she has. This chapter addresses descriptive and inferential data analysis; as you read this chapter, think of the following critical thinking questions: (a) What statistics does a social worker need to run to provide information on the makeup of people in their sample? And why? (b) What statistics does a social worker need to run to provide generalizations on those in their sample? And why? (c) Why is it important for social workers to understand and properly run data for their clients? and (d) What additional resources would help a social worker successfully complete data analysis?

This chapter is a continuation of the introduction to data analysis that began in Chapter 14. Recall that data analysis is the process of deriving some meaning from the observations that are made during the research process. Thus far, the focus has been on describing data using relatively simple procedures such as frequency distributions, data plots, and contingency tables. Although these means of summarizing and displaying data are useful, researchers often rely on more sophisticated statistics to describe data precisely and to examine relationships between variables.

Statistics have become common to the lexicon of modern living. We often hear people casually referring to something being "above the norm," "below average," or "correlated" with something else. Tune into the evening news and you might assume that death from cancer is imminent, because research has shown a "statistically significant correlation" between your favorite food and the dreaded disease. Or, you might hear a report stating that the relationship between underage drinking and traffic-related injuries to adolescents is "statistically significant." Because statistics are ubiquitous in our modern world, people often use statistical terms, such as *correlation* or *statistical significance*, without fully comprehending what they mean. It is imperative to have a basic understanding of statistical concepts to be an informed consumer of both the popular media and the professional literature in the social sciences and human services.

It is also very likely that, as a human service professional, you will need to compile data, analyze it, and present the findings as part of a needs assessment, funding proposal, or documentation of program outcome. This requires knowing not only how to interpret a statistic but also which statistics to use and how to compute them. Practitioner Profile 15.1 illustrates a practical example of how a human service professional can analyze assessments to improve service delivery. We believe that it is especially important to emphasize choosing the correct statistic. Computer technology has made statistical computation relatively easy, but the proper selection of statistical procedures and interpretation of statistical results cannot be done by the computer—it requires an intellect informed about statistical analysis.

This chapter is not intended as a thorough coverage of statistical procedures; to provide such coverage requires a book devoted solely to the subject. We do, however, provide a basic introduction to the fundamentals of statistical analysis in order to draw conclusions from the data and to understand their broader implications.

PRACTITIONER PROFILE 15.1 Kristin Harmon, Lecture, Department of Social Work, Appalachian State University, North Carolina

One of the most important practices a social worker can engage in is that of knowing his or her client better. Getting to know a client better can better assist a social worker in his or her practice, but most importantly, it helps the social worker better meet the *specific* needs of clients. So how can a social worker learn more about his or her clients?

Kristin Harmon, an LCSW, who is part of the faculty at Appalachian State University's social work department, has been practicing social work for 25 years. She first began using research as a medical social worker after obtaining her BSW. Initially, to her, research was all about numbers, or about the *quantitative* approach. She thought she would never use research in social work practice until she began inquiring about how she could better serve her clients and meet their needs. She would use the information from her client assessment notes to look for themes, watch for nonverbal cues, and look for cultural trends to have a better understanding of where clients are by observing them holistically. She then realized that research is *all* she did, and it impacted her and how she approached clients and their various needs.

Assessing clients is where it all begins. Collecting information from clients while interviewing them is the best way to learn about their unique *lived experiences* while connecting the dots between specific needs and the best resources available unique to *that* client. Kristin asserts that "you can discover a lot about clients, their families, essential needs, what their support system is like, and what the availability of community resources is like within the county" (K. Harmon, personal communication May 12, 2018). The use of qualitative research helps her see where the gaps in client needs and services are and how she can better assist those in need. Because no

(continued)

assessment is the same, the use of investigative research by using a qualitative approach gives her a genuine understanding of her clients' needs and experiences and allows her to use the most optimal and effective treatments specific to client needs.

She explains her approach to developing relationships. "The best way to meet a client's needs is to build a good working relationship with them by getting to know them better," she explained. Her past experience working in crisis settings where clients are quickly assessed and connected to appropriate resources showed her that a better understanding of clients lacked in that setting. Her experience working in hospice settings was a different experience because she had to build rapport with clients and get to know them and their families to best serve them by meeting their needs. Research is about exploration, but qualitative research takes it further by humanizing research. Using qualitative research throughout her career as a social worker and later as a clinician has helped develop her own unique approach to research in helping her clients by meeting them where they are and helping them with the best treatments uniquely fit to them and their specific needs.

CONSIDERATIONS IN CHOOSING STATISTICS

Once the data are coded and in a computer file, the researcher is ready to begin the data analysis that will unlock the information that the data contain. One of the major errors that can occur in data analysis is selecting a statistic that is inappropriate for the kind of data gathered in a research project. Although many factors need to be taken into account in choosing statistics appropriately, five major considerations are especially important.

Level of Measurement

One consideration is the level of measurement of the data collected. Chapter 5 addressed the four levels of measurement: nominal, ordinal, interval, and ratio. Each level of measurement involves different rules of permissible mathematical operations that can be performed on the numbers produced while measuring variables at that level. The nominal level involves merely classifying observations into categories. The categories have no order, and the numbers associated with a category only serve as a label for the category. In other words, the numbers have no mathematical value, and performing any arithmetic operation on them is inappropriate. On the other hand, a ratio level of measurement has

a true zero point, making all mathematical operations permissible.

Each statistical procedure involves mathematical operations that are appropriate at one of the levels of measurement. For example, a nominal statistic assumes that the data have only mutually exclusive and exhaustive categories and none of the mathematical properties of the other levels of measurement. Likewise, a ratio statistic assumes that the data have a true zero point and requires mathematical operations appropriate to that.

The basic rule is that variables measured at a given level can be analyzed either with a statistic designed for that level of measurement or with a statistic designed for a lower level of measurement. As Table 15.1 illustrates, nominal, ordinal, interval, or ratio data can be treated as nominal and used with a statistical procedure designed for nominal data. For example, a frequency distribution (as described in Chapter 14) can be used with a nominal-level variable such as religious affiliation; however, a frequency distribution also can be used to classify data at higher levels of measurement, such as levels of agreement to Likert scale items (ordinal level) or annual income in dollars (ratio level). Because it can handle data at all levels of measurement, a frequency distribution is a good statistical procedure with which to begin data analysis.

Even though data measured at higher levels can be analyzed with lower-level statistics, a trade-off

TABLE 15.1 Relationship Between Statistics and Level of Measurement

Level of measurement statistic is designed for	Level of Measurement of the Data			
	Nominal	**Ordinal**	**Interval**	**Ratio**
Ratio	No	No	No	Yes
Interval	No	No	Yes	Yes
Ordinal	No	Yes	Yes	Yes
Nominal	Yes	Yes	Yes	Yes

No = Inappropriate to use the statistic with this data.
Yes = Appropriate to use the statistic with this data.

results in terms of the kind of information and relationships that we can discover about the data based on the statistics. With annual income, for example, it is much more informative to be able to say that the people in the upper 10% of the income distribution range earn eight times more money than people in the bottom 50% than to simply report the number or percentage of people who are in a particular income category. Therefore, researchers generally prefer to use the highest level of statistic that is appropriate for a particular variable. In addition, it is definitely inappropriate to use a statistic designed for a level of measurement higher than the level of measurement of the data being analyzed.

Thus far, we have discussed the role of levels of measurement in selecting a statistic on the basis of individual variables. Many research questions, however, involve examining relationships between two or more variables simultaneously, and these may involve different levels of measurement. For example, we might study whether substance abusers abstain or use drugs (nominal) after attending one of several treatment programs (nominal) while also taking into account religious affiliation (nominal), age (interval), and severity of addiction (ordinal). One reason why so many different statistical procedures exist is that they address different possible combinations of levels of measurement among variables. For any data-analysis problem, then, the researcher must be able to classify each variable in terms of its level of measurement.

Goals of the Data Analysis

The second consideration in assessing the appropriateness of statistics is to determine what goals the statistic is meant to accomplish. Each statistical technique performs a particular function, revealing certain information about the data. A clear conception of the analytical goals of the data analysis is a prerequisite for selecting the best statistics for achieving those goals. Statistical techniques have one of two goals: *description* or *inference*. **Descriptive statistics** assist in organizing, summarizing, and interpreting data. The data might be from a sample or from a whole population (see Chapter 6); in either case, descriptive statistics organize and summarize the body of data. **Inferential statistics** allow us to make generalizations from sample data to the populations from which the samples were drawn. Recall from Chapter 6 that the ultimate reason for making observations on samples is to draw conclusions regarding the populations from which those samples were drawn. We make observations on a sample of clients in an agency because it is too expensive, time-consuming, or impractical to observe all the clients, yet we want to draw conclusions about all the clients. Inferential statistics are based on probability theory, and they basically tell us the probability of being wrong if we extend the results found in a sample to the population from which the sample was taken.

Statistics must be chosen that are appropriate to the goals of the data analysis. In some cases, we use both descriptive and inferential statistics, because the analysis intends to accomplish both goals. If, however, a population were small enough that the data could be collected from every element in the population, inferential statistics would not be necessary and would be inappropriate. In addition, inferential statistics should not be used if the goals of the analysis are descriptive, and descriptive statistics should not be used if the goal of the analysis is inference.

Number of Variables

A third consideration in choosing an appropriate statistic is the number of variables to be analyzed: **Univariate statistics** are those that analyze only one variable, **bivariate statistics** analyze two variables, and **multivariate statistics** analyze three or more variables. An example of a univariate statistical problem would be an investigation of the average income paid to correctional officers in a particular correctional facility. The only variable in this problem is "amount of income." The correctional facility is not a variable but, rather, is a constant—that is, it has only one value or category. This problem could be changed into a bivariate problem by introducing a second variable: How does gender affect the average income paid to the correctional officers in the facility? Now, the problem has two variables—namely, gender and amount of income. A multivariate problem could be hypothesized by adding additional variables: How do gender, race, and seniority influence levels of income in the facility?

Each statistic is designed to be used on either a univariate, bivariate, or multivariate problem. A point of clarification, however, is warranted: Some univariate statistics also are calculated as *part* of some bivariate or multivariate statistics. For example, among the statistics to be discussed in this chapter, the mean is a univariate statistic, but it is also calculated as a part of some bivariate statistics, such as Student's *t,* and some multivariate statistics, such as multivariate analysis of variance (MANOVA). In these cases, however, the univariate statistic is only one step in the more complex and lengthy calculation of the bivariate and multivariate statistics.

Properties of the Data

To be properly used, some statistics require that the data to be analyzed have certain mathematical or other properties. We have already discussed an example of this as levels of measurement, which involves the mathematical properties required for particular statistical tests. This is discussed separately, because it is of paramount importance and relates to every statistical procedure. Other assumptions about the properties of the data, however, also need to be considered.

One important assumption of many statistical procedures is that the observations on the dependent variable are independent of one another. For example, if we are evaluating the effectiveness of a counseling program for men who abuse their partners, then we might randomly assign 20 men to receive treatment and 20 men to the control group. Upon completion of the program, each man participates in a video recorded simulation exercise where an observer rates the subject's use of controlling tactics with his partner. The 20 control recordings are graded first, and then the 20 treatment recordings are graded. The grading process is a complex task, and the observer becomes more skilled in grading as he or she gains practice and counts more controlling behaviors as a consequence. In this situation, subjects who are scored later are likely to have higher scores than those who are rated first, so the scores are correlated with—that is, are "dependent" on—rating order. This condition is referred to as *serial dependence,* because the scores are dependent on their position in the series of measurements. Serial dependence often is hard to detect. It can be a serious problem, however, because one may reach erroneous conclusions when comparing the average rating for the treatment group with the average rating of the control group. (Statistical procedures exist to detect such a correlation with serial position and to estimate how much of the difference between groups results from it.)

In other situations, it is more obvious that observations are not independent; in fact, some research problems call for designs that include related observations. This is particularly the case when we want to study change over time. For example, perhaps we classified homeless shelters by funding source in 1986 and again by funding source in 1996 to determine if there was a trend. A similar situation occurs when the same group of people is given a pretest and a posttest or, possibly, several tests over the course of an intervention. Single-system designs (discussed in Chapter 11) are another example of a research design that often fails to satisfy the assumption of independence. In these three examples, because the same organizations or individuals are being observed at different points in time, the observations are not independent, and we would consider this fact when selecting statistical procedures.

Another important assumption for some statistics concerns the shape of the distribution of observations on a variable. Some statistics require that this distribution be normal or symmetrical. If the distribution is not normal, then the statistic that is calculated on the data may be misleading.

As part of the process of selecting an appropriate statistic, researchers review these various assumptions about the nature of the data they are analyzing and assess the risk of using a statistic that requires assumptions not met (or not fully met) by the data. The more the data violate these assumptions, the greater the risk of producing a misleading result.

Audience

If all the preceding considerations are weighed and more than one statistic can appropriately be used, we next consider the audience for whom the data analysis is intended. If that audience has limited statistical expertise, then a relatively simple, easily understood statistic is preferred over a more complex, possibly confusing statistic. Among the simpler statistics are the visual forms of presenting data (discussed in Chapter 14) and univariate statistics. Some bivariate statistics—and, especially, the multivariate statistics—may be beyond the comprehension of most audiences without at least an elementary introduction to statistics.

With these considerations in mind, we now turn to the descriptive statistics that are most commonly used in the social sciences and human services.

DESCRIPTIVE STATISTICS

Imagine that we are selected to spend a year studying abroad. We say good-bye to our friends and family and board a plane for Europe, Asia, or another far-off locale. During the course of our stay, we will likely be asked by our hosts to describe what Americans are like. For example, we might be asked to describe American college students. We might talk about what is typical or common among American college students: American college students are middle-class kids who like to attend sporting events such as football, basketball, and hockey. They eat junk food, head south during Spring Break to party, and pay for school by relying on their parents and taking out loans. They love to use social media to communicate, and they watch a lot of television.

That is not a complete description, however, and hardly a fair one. Many students do not attend athletic events at all, nor do they get to sport a tan after Spring Break. Some do not get any financial aid, and although a majority of freshmen may be age 18, some are in their 50s! So, in trying to describe what American college students are like, we really need to talk about the diversity among students, not just what is most common. Beyond describing similarities and differences, we also might discuss the characteristics of particular groups. So, we might say, for example, that women at our school are more likely to major in social work and men in criminal justice. As we engage in this process of describing what students are like, we would be using, albeit casually, the basic principles of descriptive statistics. Descriptive statistics provide quantitative indicators of what is common or typical about a variable, how much diversity or difference there is in the variable, and how values on one variable are associated with values on one or more other variables.

Measures of Central Tendency

Although valuable for revealing patterns within the data and the shape of the distribution, frequency distributions (discussed in Chapter 14) can be cumbersome. In fact, with variables that can take on many values, such as age or income, a frequency distribution can become so massive that it is difficult to detect patterns in it. **Measures of central tendency,** more commonly known as *averages,* summarize distributions by identifying the "typical," or "average," value and are one of the most commonly used statistics. The three most widely used measures of central tendency are the *mode, median,* and *mean,* each of which has unique qualities and is designed for use with a particular level of measurement.

The *mode* is the category in a frequency distribution that contains the largest number of cases. The mode for the grade distribution in Table 14.2 on page 443 is C, because more people received that grade than any other. Although the mode can be determined for data of any level of measurement, such as the grade distribution, which is ordinal, the mode usually is used with data of the nominal level for two reasons. First, the mode is the least stable of the three measures—that is, its value can be changed substantially by rather minor additions, deletions, or changes in the values that make up the distribution. With the other measures of central tendency, adding more cases produces less dramatic shifts in their values. Second, if two or more categories are tied with the largest number of cases, we could have two, three, or more modes, none of which would necessarily be very typical of the distribution. The presence of several modes also undermines its utility as a summary statistic to describe the average case.

With ordinal data, the *median* is the appropriate measure of central tendency. The median is the point in a distribution below which 50% of the observations occur. For example, a distribution of six scores—10, 14, 15, 17, 18, 25—results in a median of 16. Note that when the distribution contains an even number of values, an observed score may not fall on the median; then, the median is the value halfway between the two central scores. If we add another score greater than 16 to the preceding distribution so that it contains seven cases, the median is 17, an observed score. Because the median does not take into account the actual value of the scores but only the number of observations, whether the score we add is 17, 100, or 1,000 makes no difference—the median is still 17. This makes the median very stable, because

the presence of extremely high or low scores in a distribution has little effect on the value of the median.

The *mean* is the measure of central tendency that most people think of when they hear the word *average*, and it is calculated by summing all the values in a distribution and then dividing by the number of cases. The mean, however, is only suitable for interval- or ratio-level data, where there is equal spacing along a scale and various mathematical functions can be performed (see Chapter 5). There is one exception to this—namely, dichotomous nominal- or ordinal-level variables that have only two values. Many interval-level statistics, such as the mean, can be meaningfully computed on such variables. This is called *dummy variable analysis* and is beyond the scope of this chapter.

Because the mean takes into account the actual value of all the scores in a distribution, it is less stable than the median. The presence of a few extreme scores will pull the mean in that direction. Because of this, the median often is the preferred average when summarizing skewed distributions, even with interval-level data, because it more accurately reflects the central value. For example, although the mean could be used to summarize income data, the U.S. Census Bureau typically reports median income, because the relatively few wealthy people tend to pull the mean to such a high level that it overstates typical family income. Because it is less affected by extreme scores, the median also often is preferred in clinical practice research, where treatment and control groups usually are small and violate the assumptions required for statistics based on the mean.

Selecting the most appropriate measure of central tendency for a given set of data is not difficult. Level of measurement and skewness are the primary considerations. With relatively symmetrical distributions, the only factor is level of measurement.

Measures of Dispersion

Like measures of central tendency, measures of dispersion describe and summarize distributions. Whereas central tendency indicators describe the middle or average of the distribution, **measures of**

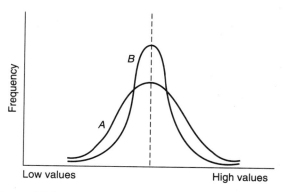

Figure 15.1 Two distributions with the same average but different dispersions.

dispersion indicate how dispersed or spread out the values are in a distribution. Measures of dispersion add valuable information about distributions. On the basis of central tendency measures alone, we might assume that two distributions with similar averages are basically alike. Such an assumption would be erroneous, however, if the spread of the distributions were different. As illustrated in Figure 15.1, distribution A is more dispersed, with values deviating widely from the central value; the values in distribution B are more tightly clustered near the average. To avoid possible erroneous assumptions about the spread of distributions, researchers report a measure of dispersion along with a measure of central tendency.

The three commonly used measures of dispersion are *range, semi-interquartile range,* and *standard deviation*. The *range* is the simplest of these, referring merely to the difference between the highest and lowest scores in the distribution. As such, the range indicates the total spread of a distribution. Knowing the end points of a distribution, however, tells us nothing about how the remaining values are dispersed within the distribution. Furthermore, because the range is based on only two values, it is unstable. Adding or deleting extreme scores causes the range to vary widely, whereas the bulk of the distribution may change little. Moreover, despite its simplicity, the range is suitable only for interval data. The operation of subtraction used to obtain the range assumes that the values of the scores in a distribution have meaning; however, this is true only for interval- and ratio-level data. Because of these limitations, the range usually is used as an adjunct to other measures of dispersion and is not reported alone.

The *semi-interquartile range* (sometimes called the *quartile deviation*) is symbolized by the letter Q; it is closely related to the median and is the measure of dispersion usually reported with it. The semi-interquartile range is obtained by first dividing a frequency distribution into fourths or *quartiles*. The first quartile (Q_1) is the score below which 25% of the scores occur, and the third quartile (Q_3) is the score below which 75% of the scores occur. (The median is the second quartile [Q_2] and is the point below which 50% of the scores occur.) The semi-interquartile range is equal to half the difference between the third quartile and the first quartile. The larger the value of the semi-interquartile range, the more dispersed the scores are from the median. The value of Q is calculated as

$$Q = \frac{Q_3 - Q_1}{2}$$

The *standard deviation,* symbolized by the letter *s,* indicates the average (or mean) spread of the scores from the mean and, therefore, is the measure of dispersion usually reported along with the mean. The larger the value of the standard deviation, the more dispersed the scores are from the mean. Actual calculation of the standard deviation is relatively complex and beyond the scope of this chapter. In addition to its use as a descriptive statistic, the standard deviation has important applications in inferential statistics.

One final note on measures of dispersion: Although their overall purpose is to assist in the description of distributions, a single dispersion value from a single distribution is not particularly revealing. The major utility of dispersion indicators is in comparing several distributions, because they enable us to tell at a glance which has more or less spread.

Measures of Association

Measures of association describe the nature of relationships between variables, particularly the *strength* of the relationship or how closely the variables are related. The strongest relationship is a *perfect* one, in which a given change in one variable is *always* associated with a given change in the other variable. Rarely, however, are perfect relationships found in human service research. A less-than-perfect relationship indicates only a tendency for the variables to vary together. With ordinal- or higher-level data, relationships between variables also can be positive, negative, or curvilinear. Recall from Chapter 2 (p. 36) that a positive relationship is one in which the change in value of the variables is in the same direction—that is, both increase or both decrease. A negative relationship is one in which one variable increases while the other decreases, and a curvilinear relationship is one in which the direction of change in one variable is not consistent with changes in the other. For example, in a U-shaped curvilinear relationship, both low and high values of the independent variable may be associated with high values of the dependent variable. In this case, a negative relationship exists between the two variables for low values on the independent variable and a positive relationship with high values on the independent variable. Most measures of association indicate a perfect positive relationship by +1.00 and a perfect negative one by −1.00. The closer the value of the measure is to −1.00 or +1.00, the stronger the relationship is. Likewise, the closer the value is to 0, the weaker the relationship is.

The overriding determinant in selecting a measure of association is the level of measurement of the data at hand. Therefore, we will consider measures of association according to the level of measurement for which each was designed.

Nominal Data. Some data are dichotomous in form—that is, the variables have only two values, such as yes/no or male/female. A useful measure of association for two dichotomous variables is the *phi* (pronounced *phee*) coefficient (φ). The data are cast into a 2 × 2 table, as illustrated in Table 15.2. The value of phi indicates the strength of the relationship between variables by yielding a value between −1.00 and 1.00. Although phi may yield negative values, the negative sign is simply ignored, because it has no meaning in the case of nominal data.

TABLE 15.2 Nominal Data Suitable for Phi

Is Life Exciting?	Sex	
	Male	Female
Exciting	213 (50.1%)	221 (39.8%)
Routine/Dull	212 (49.9%)	334 (60.2%)
Totals	425	555
	(100%)	(100%)
	Phi = 0.11	

Source: From Davis, J. A., & Smith, T. W. (1972–1994). *General social survey*. Chicago, IL: National Opinion Research Center; Storrs, CT: The Roper Center for Public Opinion Research, University of Connecticut.

The value of phi is considered to be a good measure of association for three reasons. First, it is quite easy to compute. Second, it is mathematically related to measures of association that are suitable for other levels of measurement, which makes comparing the strength of different relationships possible. Measures of association that are not mathematically related have different operating characteristics and produce values that are not comparable, precluding meaningful comparisons. Third, phi is a member of a group of measures of association that can be given what is called a **proportional reduction in error** (PRE) interpretation. The PRE interpretation means that the measure shows how much the independent variable helps reduce error in predicting values of the dependent variable. To interpret phi in this way, it is first necessary to square it (φ^2). For example, $\varphi = 0.11$ is squared to become $\varphi^2 = 0.01$. This latter value is treated as a percentage and is interpreted to mean that the independent variable reduced the error in predicting values of the dependent variable by 1%. All PRE statistics are interpreted in this way.

Because phi is suitable only for two dichotomous variables, a different measure of association

TABLE 15.3 Nominal Data Suitable for Lambda and Goodman and Kruskal's Tau

| | | Region | | | |
		Northeast	Midwest	South	West
Religious Preference	Protestant	54 (41.2%)	140 (64.5%)	206 (84.8%)	80 (53.3%)
	Catholic	55 (42.0%)	56 (25.8%)	28 (11.5%)	43 (28.7%)
	Jewish	10 (7.6%)	1 (0.5%)	1 (0.4%)	3 (2.0%)
	None	12 (9.2%)	20 (9.2%)	8 (3.3%)	24 (16.0%)
	Totals	131 (100%)	217 (100%)	243 (100%)	150 (100%)

Lambda = 0.07

Goodman and Kruskal's tau = 0.07

Source: From Davis, J. A., & Smith, T. W. (1972–1994). *General social survey.* Chicago, IL: National Opinion Research Center; Storrs, CT: The Roper Center for Public Opinion Research, University of Connecticut.

must be used for nominal data with more categories. The most generally useful measure for data of this type is *lambda* (l). As with phi, the data are cast into a tabular form, as given in Table 15.3.

Lambda is a bit different from most measures of association in that its value can range only from 0 to 1.00. Lambda is never negative, but this is not a disadvantage since the negative sign is meaningless with nominal data anyway. Lambda is always positive because it is a direct-reading PRE statistic. In other words, lambda indicates the proportional reduction in error as calculated and need not be squared (as with phi). This is an important point to remember, because the values that lambda produces usually look rather small. The reason is not that lambda understates relationships but, rather, that the lambda values are "presquared," which makes them appear to be small.

Although phi and lambda are the most common nominal measures of association, several others are available. For two dichotomous variables,

an alternative to phi is Yule's Q. However, Q cannot be given the PRE interpretation and tends to make relationships appear to be stronger than they actually are. For nominal data with more categories, Goodman and Kruskal's *tau* (t) is often used. Sometimes, tau is preferred to lambda, because the former uses data from all cells in the table while the latter only includes data from some of the cells. The value of tau, however, does not always vary from 0 to 1.00, especially when the dependent variable has more categories than the independent variable.

Ordinal Data. Many commonly used measures of association exist for ordinal data. A major consideration in selecting one has to do with whether the data are *fully ordered*. In situations where every—or nearly every—case has its own unique rank and there are no or few ties, the data are said to be fully ordered. Table 15.4 illustrates fully ordered data. The most popular measure of association

TABLE 15.4 Ordinal Data Suitable for Spearman's Rho

Independent Variable	Dependent Variable
Ranks	*Ranks*
10	9
8	10
1	1
3	5
2	2
9	6
4	7
6	3
5	4
7	8
	$r_s = 0.77$

for fully ordered data is Spearman's rho (r_s). Like phi, Spearman's rho is mathematically related to other measures and, thus, facilitates comparisons of relationships. It also has the desirable characteristic of varying between +1.00 and –1.00. Note that now, with ordinal data, the negative sign has meaning and indicates a negative relationship. Also, rho may be squared (r_s^2) and given the PRE interpretation.

When we have only a few ordered categories and many cases to place into them, the data will contain many ties—far too many for Spearman's rho to be usable. Data of this type are called *partially ordered* and are handled in tabular form, as illustrated in Table 15.5. Several alternative measures of association are available for data of this type; for example, gamma (γ), Somer's *D*, and Kendall's tau (τ) are all suitable and vary between –1.00 and +1.00. Some subtle differences among them, however, make one or another most appropriate in a given situation.

The value of gamma is the easiest of the three to compute, but unfortunately, it does not take

TABLE 15.5 Ordinal Data Suitable for Gamma, Somer's D, or Kendall's Tau

		Income		
		Low	**Medium**	**High**
Number of Hours Television Is Watched	High	49 (19.2%)	19 (8.6%)	10 (6.7%)
	Medium	164 (64.3)	136 (61.5)	86 (57.5)
	Low	42 (16.5)	66 (29.9%)	53 (35.6)
	Totals	255 100%	221 100%	149 100%
		Gamma = 0.33		
		Somer's *D* = 0.18		
		Kendall's tau = 0.20		

Source: From Davis, J. A., & Smith, T. W. (1972–1994). *General social survey*. Chicago, IL: National Opinion Research Center; Storrs, CT: The Roper Center for Public Opinion Research, University of Connecticut.

into account any of the tied scores and tends to overstate the strength of the relationship. Indeed, on the basis of a positive gamma alone, we cannot safely assume that as X increases, Y also increases, which is a normal assumption of a positive relationship. Because of its failure to consider ties, all that a positive gamma allows us to conclude is that as X increases, Y does not decrease, which is a much weaker conclusion.

Somer's D is used when we are only interested in our ability to predict a dependent variable from an independent variable. When predicting Y from X, Somer's D takes into account ties on the dependent variable. This has the effect of reducing the value of D in comparison with gamma when the two are computed on the same data. Somer's D, however, gives a more accurate indication of how much the independent variable reduces error in predicting the dependent variable.

Finally, Kendall's tau takes into account all the tied scores. It indicates the degree to which the independent variable reduces error in predicting the dependent variable and also how much the latter reduces error in predicting the former. Because it considers the relationship both ways, Kendall's tau is particularly appropriate when we do not have a clearly identifiable independent and dependent variable and merely wish to determine if two variables are related. By including all the ties, a positive tau allows us to conclude—correctly— that as X increases, Y also increases. This is the type of statement that we expect to make on the basis of a positive result, so Kendall's tau is more generally useful than gamma is.

Interval Data. The most used measure of association for interval data is the *correlation coefficient* or *Pearson's γ*. The correlation coefficient is mathematically related to both phi and Spearman's rho, making comparisons among them possible. As with the other two, Pearson's γ varies between −1.00 and +1.00 and may be squared (r^2) and given the PRE interpretation. When squared, this value is called the *coefficient of determination.*

The correlation coefficient has a unique characteristic that is important to remember when applying or interpreting it. Pearson's r indicates the degree to which the relationship between

two interval-level variables can be described by a straight line when plotted on a scattergram, as in Figure 15.2. The formula for r mathematically determines the best-fitting line and then considers the amount by which the scores deviate from perfect linearity. This feature of Pearson's r means that, if the relationship between the two variables is curvilinear, r will understate the actual strength of the relationship, producing a coefficient that is smaller than it should be. Therefore, it is advisable to plot a *scattergram* or a table with the scores of both variables plotted on it. The scattergram provides a visual indication of the relationship between the two variables and is useful for uncovering curvilinearity. Figure 15.2 illustrates three typical scattergrams. For those instances in which curvilinearity is discovered, a measure of association other than Pearson's r should be selected. Curvilinear measures of association do exist, but these are beyond the scope of this discussion.

Before we leave measures of association, one important matter requires emphasis: Association or correlation does not imply causality! Just because one variable is labeled independent and another dependent and a relationship is found between them does not prove that changes in one variable cause changes in the other. Correlation is only one step toward inferring causality. In addition, it is necessary to affirm the appropriate temporal sequence and rule out rival causal variables.

The Normal Distribution

Chapter 14 discussed frequency distributions as descriptive statistical procedures that transform a raw data distribution into a form that is more meaningful. There is another way to transform raw data to derive additional meaning from it, and this transformation also will serve as our transition from descriptive to inferential statistics. A transformation is a set of arithmetical operations that are executed on a variable to obtain a new variable. One common transformation is known as *standardizing.* Raw scores are transformed into *standard scores,* also known as *z-scores.* Symbolically, a standardized score, z, is given by

$$z = \frac{x - \bar{x}}{s}$$

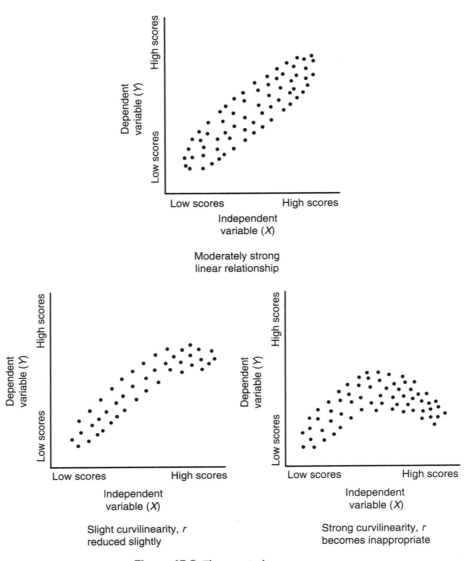

Figure 15.2 Three typical scattergrams.

Standard scores are obtained by following these two steps:

1. Subtract the mean, x, from each raw score, x.
2. Divide the $x - \bar{x}$ difference by the standard deviation, s, of the distribution.

If all the raw scores in a distribution are transformed to z-scores, then a new distribution is obtained that will always have $x = 0$ and $s = 1$. This

is called a *standard normal distribution,* and as it turns out, this distribution has some quite convenient properties.

One way to think about the z-transformation is that it expresses raw scores in a distribution in units of standard deviation rather than the original unit of measurement. A z-score of 1.5 indicates a score point that is 1.5 standard deviations greater than the mean, whereas a z-score of -1.5 indicates a score point 1.5 standard deviations below the mean. In other words, a standard score, z, is a number indicating the distance that a raw score deviates from the mean as measured in standard deviation units. Furthermore, the sign of a z-score indicates whether the score point is above (+) or below (–) the mean of the distribution.

On first encounter, it may seem strange to express raw scores in terms of standard deviation units, but doing so allows us to make comparisons between distributions that otherwise would be difficult to make because their original units of measurement differ. Standardizing equalizes the units so that a meaningful comparison can be made. For example, the comparison of a person's raw scores on two different IQ tests would not be legitimate unless the IQ tests have a common unit of measurement and operate on the same scale. Therefore, mental testers commonly employ the z-transformation as a way of making different IQ tests comparable.

Consider the data in Table 15.6. In both tests, someone received a score of 99, but are both scores really equal? In terms of raw scores, they certainly appear to be, but in relative terms—that is, compared to the other scores in the distribution—the 99 on Test 2 is far more remarkable, and a z-score transformation will reveal this. On Test 1, with a relatively high mean and small standard deviation, the 99 transforms to a z-score of 1.46,

which means it is 1.46 standard deviations above the mean of 94.6. The 99 on Test 2, with a low mean and high standard deviation, transforms to a z-score of 2.47, which means it is 2.47 standard deviations above the mean of 49.6. The comparison of z-scores shows that the two scores of 99 are, in fact, far from equal compared to the other scores in their respective distributions. Allowing these types of comparisons to be made is one important use of z-scores.

Another important use of z-scores has to do with what is called the normal distribution. The normal distribution is a continuous, bell-shaped distribution, as shown in Figure 15.3. The **normal distribution** is a symmetrical, unimodal distribution in which the mode, median, and mean are identical. Actually, there is not just a single normal distribution; there are many. Normal distributions may, for example, have different means and different standard deviations. What makes them all normal is that they all are symmetrical and unimodal and have the three measures of central tendency at the same point. In addition, all normal distributions have the same proportion of cases between the same two ordinates. This statement means that between, say, –1 and +1 standard deviations from the mean for any normal distribution, the proportion of the total cases bounded by those points is the same for all those normal distributions.

In Figure 15.3, the shaded area is the proportion of the total area under the curve bounded by points that are 1 standard deviation on either side of the mean. For any normal distribution, no matter what the mean and standard deviation happen to be, the area bounded by $\bar{x} - s$ and $\bar{x} + s$ is always equal to 68.26% of the total area under the curve, whereas 95.46% of the total area is between $\bar{x} - 2s$ and $\bar{x} + 2s$. In place of $\bar{x} - s$ and $\bar{x} + s$, one may substitute any two points that one wishes and carves out a proportion of the total area that will be the same for all normal distributions. Figure 15.3 shows selected points and the proportions of the total area that fall between them for any and all normal distributions.

This indicates another use of z-transformations, namely to assess the relative position of a score in a distribution of scores. For example, suppose a female student took a national merit exam and

TABLE 15.6 Two Sets of Hypothetical Test Scores

	Test 1	Test 2	
	99	99	
	98	45	
$\bar{X} = 94.6$	96	44	$\bar{X} = 49.6$
	95	44	
$s = 3$	95	43	$s = 20$
	93	41	
	91	41	
	90	40	

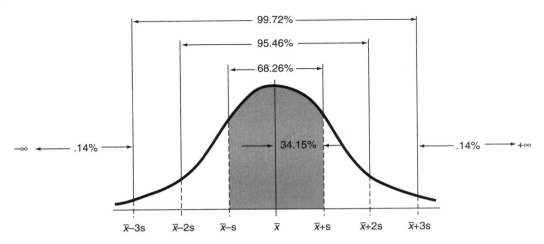

Figure 15.3 Proportions of the area under the normal curve between selected points.

received a score of 580. How well did she do compared with the others who took it? If she knows that the scores on this exam are normally distributed and if she knows the values of the mean score and the standard deviation, then she can calculate her position relative to the others who took the exam. Suppose that the mean was 490 and the standard deviation 72. She could then use the z-formula to transform her exam score of 580 into a z-score as follows:

$$z = \frac{x - \bar{x}}{s} = \frac{580 - 490}{72} = +1.25$$

So, her score is +1.25 standard deviations above the mean for all the students who took the test. By looking at Figure 15.3, she can determine that she scored better than at least 84% of the students who took the exam. She can figure this out because 50% of the students scored below the mean and another 34.15% scored between the mean and +1.00 standard deviation above the mean. To figure out what additional percentage is included

between +1.00 and +1.25 standard deviations, she can refer to tables that tell what proportion of cases fall between any two points in a normal distribution. (These tables can be found in any introductory statistics text.) From those tables, she can determine that 89.44% of all cases in a normal distribution fall below +1.25 standard deviations above the mean. So, she did better than more than 89% of all the people who took that examination! Transforming her test score into a z-score enabled her to make a precise statement about her place in the distribution relative to others in the distribution.

The standard normal distribution is useful for comparing distributions with different means and standard deviations, and it helps us make precise statements about relative position in a distribution. A third important use of this distribution is that it serves as the foundation for inferential statistics.

Research in Practice 15.1 addresses some important ethical issues relating to statistical analysis in research.

RESEARCH IN PRACTICE 15.1 Thou Shalt Not Lie (or Even Mislead) With Statistics!

Many people mistrust statistics. Mark Twain is alleged to have said: "There are three kinds of lies: lies, damned lies, and statistics." Another sentiment regarding statistics was expressed by Mrs. Robert A. Taft:

(continued)

I always find that statistics are hard to swallow and impossible to digest. The only one I can remember is that if all the people who go to sleep in church were laid end to end they would be a lot more comfortable. (Patton, 1982, p. 243)

Such sentiments suggest that statistics can be manipulated to reach any conclusion you want. And it is possible to manipulate statistics to support misleading or inaccurate conclusions. That, however, is not the fault of statistics but rather of the person who uses them unethically. The ethical researcher follows the fundamental principle that one must always give a thoroughly accurate representation of research and statistical data.

Researchers rarely present all of the data they have; usually, they report some sort of summary or distillation that purports to be an accurate characterization of the data. While many ways exist to misrepresent data, one example will illustrate how this can be done with graphical representations. Figure 15.4 presents data on the infant mortality rate in the United States for each year from 1990 to 2000. The data are presented in two separate graphs, although the data

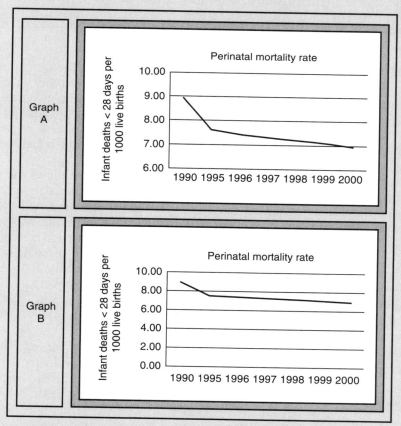

Figure 15.4 Two graphs showing the rate of infant mortality, 1990–2000.

Source: Data adapted from U.S. Census Bureau. (2008). *Statistical abstract of the United States: 2009* (128th ed., Table 109). Retrieved from https://www2.census.gov/library/publications/2008/compendia/statab/128ed/tables/vitstat.pdf

(continued)

are exactly the same. The actual data on infant mortality for that period suggest a modest decline over that period: 22% fewer infant deaths in 2000 than in 1990. Now if we look at the visual impression given by the two figures, Graph A seems to imply a much more sizable decline than Graph B, with far less infant mortality at the end of the period. The reason is that the vertical axis in Graph A is designed so that each measurement unit (each additional infant death) takes up a lot of space on the axis. The vertical axis also does not show the whole range of measurement units. When we lengthen that axis and add in all the measurement values, as in Graph B, the visual impression given by the graph is of a much more modest decline, which is a more-accurate representation of what the data actually say.

Now, a number of good reasons can be found to shorten one or another axis on a graph, such as saving space, but it must not be done in a way that produces a misleading visual impression of the patterns actually found in the data. And certainly it must never be done to deliberately distort the data. What is said regarding this illustration is true of all statistical analysis in the social sciences: Data analysis can distort results, but social science researchers consider it highly unethical to do so. The prime responsibility of the researcher is to give a complete and accurate representation of the data and conclusions.

INFERENTIAL STATISTICS

As noted in Chapter 6, most social research is conducted on relatively small samples that are drawn from much larger populations, and all the statistical procedures discussed so far are designed to assist in describing, summarizing, and interpreting data from samples. Findings from sample data, however, are of little scientific value if they cannot be generalized beyond the members of the sample to the larger population from which the samples were drawn. For example, it would do other practitioners little good to learn that a researcher had successfully raised the school performance of 50 underachievers unless they could reasonably expect the new approach to work on children who were not in the researcher's sample. In other words, for the new technique to be worthwhile, it must be generalizable to members of the population of underachievers.

Probability Theory

How do we know when research findings are generalizable? Generalization is always an uncertain business, but inferential statistics can reduce the uncertainty to the point where reasonably safe generalizations can be made and the probability of a given amount of error can be estimated.

Inferential statistics are based on probability theory—the same probability theory that works to make probability samples representative. Because of this, inferential statistics can be meaningfully applied only to data based on probability samples or experiments in which random assignment has been implemented.

Probability theory allows the mathematical calculation of the likelihood, or probability, that random events or outcomes will occur. For example, if 10,000 raffle tickets are issued and the winning ticket is chosen in such a way that each ticket has an equal chance of being selected, then each person who purchases one ticket has 1 in 10,000 chances of winning. If you buy 10 tickets, then you have 10 in 10,000 (or 1 in 1,000) chances of winning. You have increased the probability of your winning even though the mechanism for selecting the winner is unchanged. This does not mean, of course, that you *will* win. Less likely events do occur, although with less frequency than more likely ones, and a person who purchased only one ticket could certainly win the raffle. In other words, probability theory tells us the *likelihood* of something occurring, but it does not tell us what *will* occur. For this reason, inferential statistics can tell us whether the odds are on our side that a particular generalization is accurate, but they do not make it a sure bet.

As noted in Chapter 6, probability samples are supposed to represent the populations from which they are drawn, but we can expect differences between a sample and its population because of chance alone. Because these differences are the result of the random process used in the selection of samples, their probability can be readily calculated. For example, suppose that a researcher draws a probability sample of 50 boys with delinquent behavior and applies a special intervention that is designed to reduce future involvement in delinquency. At the end of one year, the success rate of the sample is 75%, whereas for the population of untreated delinquents, the rate is 60%. Can we conclude that the experimental intervention was a success? At the level of the sample alone, it is clear that the treated boys had a better rate, but the differences could have resulted, either in part or completely, from sampling error. Even with random sampling, the researcher might have obtained a sample of boys who were better risks, on average, than those in the general population of boys with delinquent behavior. The question that inferential statistics answers is whether the difference between the sample results and the population results is too great to be likely on the basis of chance alone. In the example, running the appropriate inferential statistic would tell us what the chances are of obtaining, through random error, a 15% difference between a population and a probability sample drawn from that population. If such a difference were highly probable, then we would conclude that the seeming effect of the experimental treatment was the result of chance differences between the sample and the population. On the other hand, if the result indicated only a small likelihood that a 15% differential resulted from chance, then we would reject chance variation as the explanation and conclude that there is a generalizable effect associated with the treatment group.

Sampling Distributions

Our ability to determine the likelihood that a sample difference is the result of chance derives from the properties of the normal distribution, discussed earlier in this chapter, and what are called *sampling distributions*. To explain sampling distributions,

let us return to the example of the 50 delinquents with the 75% success rate. If we had selected 10 samples of size 50 and computed a success rate on each sample, then we would have found that the success rate differed somewhat from sample to sample, because each sample would have consisted of a different set of 50 boys. For the 10 samples, we might have found the following success rates: 72%, 71%, 73%, 69%, 66%, 70%, 73%, 69%, 71%, and 67%. The success rate for these 10 samples is distributed over the range of possible sample results. If we took many more samples of size 50, then we would see a pattern emerge as the number of samples approached infinity. We would find the occasional extremely high or low value, but most frequently, the samples would lie in the middle of this range. A **sampling distribution** is a theoretical distribution of a statistic from all possible samples of a certain size drawn from a population; the distribution shows the probability of occurrence of each value of the statistic. If we actually knew the success rate among all boys with delinquent behavior in the population from which these samples were taken, this would be referred to as the *population parameter,* and it is this population parameter around which all the sample success rates are distributed in a statistically predictable pattern.

This sampling distribution has certain properties that are very important in inferential statistics. In particular, the **central limit theorem** from mathematics tells us that when a large number of large, random samples are selected from a population, the resulting distribution of sample statistics has two key properties: First, the sampling distribution approximates a normal distribution, and second, the population parameter is equal to the mean of the sampling distribution. In our example, the distribution of all sample success rates is normal, and the success rate in the population is equal to the average of all those sample success rates. This means that we can determine the probability that a sample result will fall between any two points in the sampling distribution, just as we did with z-scores and the normal distribution. It also means that we can determine the probability that a sample result will fall far away from the population parameter. Recall from the earlier discussion that approximately 68% of all cases in a normal distribution fall within 1 standard deviation above and below the mean of the distribution and that approximately 95% of cases fall within 2 standard deviations. Likewise, in a distribution of samples, 95% of the sample results will fall within 2 standard deviations of the mean of the sampling distribution, which also is the population parameter. Only 5% of samples will fall more than 2 standard deviations away from the population parameter.

Going back to our example, we can choose one of two alternatives: First, the treatment did not work, and we have selected a sample of boys that, by chance, is very different from the boys in the population (sampling error). Second, the treatment worked, and this is what makes the treatment boys different from the nontreated boys in the population. If, however, the success rate in the population is 60% and the sample success rate of 75% is more than 2 standard deviations away from 60%, then the z-transformation tells us that 75% is way out in one of the tails of the normal distribution, and the probability of obtaining such a sample by chance would be highly unusual. Therefore, we are on safer grounds, just in terms of probabilities, to conclude that the sample success rate of 75%, probably, is not the result of sampling error but, rather, is showing that the treatment had an effect on this group of boys.

Although many different kinds of inferential statistics are used, they all follow the basic logic involving sampling distributions and normal distributions. The formal process by which researchers decide whether the results of data analysis could be caused by chance or are better explained by relationships between variables is called *statistical hypothesis testing.*

Statistical Hypothesis Testing

When we use inferential statistics, we are engaging in a special form of hypothesis testing in which we develop two hypotheses that are precisely the opposite of each other. Then, the outcome of a statistical test is used to determine which hypothesis most likely is correct. The first hypothesis, called the **null hypothesis,** states that no relationship exists between two variables in the population or

that there is no difference between a sample statistic and a population parameter. "There is *no* relationship between variable *X* and variable *Y* in the population" or "There is *no* difference between the success rate of the sample and the success rate of the population" are two examples of null hypotheses. Alternatives to null hypotheses are called **research hypotheses.** Suitable research hypotheses to go with the two preceding null hypotheses are: "There *is* a relationship between variable *X* and variable *Y* at the level of the population" and "There *is* a difference between the sample success rate and the population success rate." In each application of a statistical test, we assess the research hypothesis by determining whether the opposite null hypothesis is probable or improbable.

On first exposure to statistical hypothesis testing, it is not uncommon to question the utility of null hypotheses. If we believe that the research hypothesis is true, why not just test that hypothesis? The need for null hypotheses stems from the fact that it is not possible with inferential statistics to prove research hypotheses directly; however, by determining the likelihood that the null hypotheses are false, we indirectly provide evidence that their opposites, the research hypotheses, probably are true. To illustrate this point, we will use an example with a clear criterion to use in testing a hypothesis.

Imagine attempting to determine whether a die is unbiased. If it is, then each side should appear an approximately equal number of times—that is, about one sixth of the times that the die is thrown. If the die is biased, however, then one or more outcomes will occur a disproportionate number of times—that is, one or more numbers occurring substantially more than one sixth of the time. Suppose the die is tossed 12 times, with each outcome occurring twice, or one sixth of the time. Would this prove the die is unbiased? The answer is no. The bias, if it exists, might be too slight to appear after only 12 trials. What if the die is tossed 144 times and each outcome occurs one sixth of the time? Such a result would still not make it certain that the die is unbiased, because a slight bias might be revealed by even more trials. Indeed, no number of trials would provide absolute assurance that the die is unbiased; however, a large number of trials with no evidence of bias would make the hypothesis of a biased die so unlikely that it is reasonable to reject it. By finding no evidence of support for one hypothesis, we indirectly obtain support for its alternative. In all applications of statistical hypothesis testing, if the evidence fails to support the null hypothesis, then the opposing research hypothesis is accepted as probably true.

Although their computational routines vary, all inferential statistical tests use the properties of sampling distributions and normal curves to yield a result indicating the probability that the null hypothesis is true. In choosing between the competing hypotheses, we ask, "How unlikely must it be for the null hypothesis to be true before we are willing to reject it as false and accept the research hypothesis?" This is determined by the **alpha level**: the probability at which the null hypothesis will be rejected (see Table 15.7). Researchers have some discretion in setting alpha levels, but they must guard against the two types of inferential errors that can be made. **Type I error,** or **alpha error,** is the probability of rejecting a null hypothesis that is actually true. The alpha level selected determines the amount of alpha error that we are willing to tolerate, so the researcher directly controls Type I error by setting the alpha level. Usually, alpha levels are written as "$p < 0.20$" and are read as "a probability of less than 20%."

Alpha levels can be understood in the following way: Suppose the null hypothesis is that "no relationship exists between variable X and variable Y in the population." We draw a sample from that population to test the hypothesis and, indeed, find a relationship in the sample data. An alpha level of 0.20 means that we would find a relationship as large as we did in 20% of the samples we draw, even though the null hypothesis actually is true and there is no relationship between the variables in the population. We are now faced with a difficult dilemma: "Is the null hypothesis true and our sample an unusual one, or is the null hypothesis false?" Inferential statistics cannot answer that question for us. It can, however, tell us that, in the long run and by testing many hypotheses, we would be correct 80% of the time in rejecting null hypotheses when differences of a given size have an alpha level of 0.20.

Setting an alpha level as low as 0.20 makes it easy to reject the null hypothesis, but we are also assured of frequently rejecting a true null hypothesis. To avoid so much Type I error, we might establish a very stringent alpha, such as 0.001, meaning that we would reject the null hypothesis only if its odds of being true were less than 1 in 1,000. If the null hypothesis can be rejected at such an alpha level, we would be quite confident that it was false and that we were not committing a Type I error.

Setting extremely rigorous alpha levels, however, raises the probability of making the other possible inferential error. **Type II error,** or **beta error,** is the probability of failing to reject null hypotheses that actually are false. Alpha levels such as 0.001 make it so difficult to reject null hypotheses that many false ones that should be rejected are not. Thus, in selecting suitable alpha levels, we face a dilemma: Guarding against one type of error increases the chances of making the other type.

TABLE 15.7 Illustration of Type I and Type II Errors

Decision	Condition in Population	
	Null Hypothesis Is True	**Null Hypothesis Is False**
Reject null hypothesis	Type I (alpha) error prob. = alpha	Correct decision (power of test) prob. = 1 – beta
Fail to reject null hypothesis	Correct decision prob. = 1 – alpha	Type II (beta) error prob. = beta

Fortunately, conventions regarding appropriate alpha levels have been developed. In general, social researchers operate with alpha levels of 0.05, 0.01, or 0.001. Although these levels are the most common ones in research reports, there is nothing sacred about them. The researcher must consider the purpose of the research and the alternative risks in selecting a given level. For example, medical research into the safety and effectiveness of new drugs or treatments typically operates with very stringent alpha levels, because life-and-death issues are at stake. If the null hypothesis in a research project is "Drug X is not safe," then we want to reject it only if we are very sure that it is false. If it is wrongly rejected, people will be exposed to an unsafe product. On the other hand, a practitioner with a null hypothesis of "Reminder phone calls do not reduce the number of no-shows for clinic appointments" might select an alpha level as low as 0.10. If the procedure shows any chance of working, the clinic may want to try it. In this case, the consequences of rejecting a true null hypothesis are not severe. Some additional issues related to hypothesis testing as well as alpha and beta errors are discussed in Research in Practice 15.2.

RESEARCH IN PRACTICE 15.2 Program Evaluation: Designed for Failure: Statistical Power in Human Service Research

Although much attention is given to the issue of statistical significance or alpha levels in evaluation research, a related and equally important issue—statistical power—often is overlooked. *Statistical power* refers to the probability of *correctly* rejecting a null hypothesis in a research study (see Table 15.7). Another way of looking at statistical power is to conceptualize a study designed with low power as being a study with a high probability of failure, because it cannot detect an intervention that works. If the number of cases in the treatment and control groups is small and the variation within each group is large, then there may be insufficient difference between the groups to generate a statistically significant result.

In technical terms, the problem is that the study has insufficient effect size. The concept of effect size has been receiving increasing attention among researchers (Bloom, Fischer, & Orme, 2009; Prentice & Miller, 1998; Schmidt, 1998). Although various ways exist to measure effect size, for illustration purposes, we will use a simplified version:

$$ES = \frac{\bar{X}t - \bar{X}c}{S}$$

where

ES = Effect size
X_t = Treatment mean
X_c = Control mean
S = Standard deviation of both groups combined

The effect size coefficient is basically a standardized indicator of how big a difference exists between the treatment and control groups. Compare this formula to the one for standardized scores, or z-scores, on page 474; they are almost identical—both are formulas to transform raw scores into standardized scores. Basically, the formula shows that the larger the standardized difference between groups, the larger the effect size. Other things being equal, a larger effect size is more likely to generate a significant statistic. For example, assume that we conduct a test of a

(continued)

family intervention program using a treatment group of 15 families that receive the intervention and a control group of another 15 families that do not. Assume also that the intervention program does work, although the effect is modest. If we perform a statistical test on the difference between the two groups, the results may not be statistically significant, despite the fact that the intervention works.

This is a quite real problem, as evidenced by examinations of published human service research indicating that almost half the studies reviewed could not detect even a medium-sized effect (Orme & Combs-Orme, 1986; West, Biesanz, & Pitts, 2000). A consequence of this shortcoming is that policy decisions may be made to curtail or not implement potentially useful innovations. Another important consideration is that a research effort is wasted if it is unable to detect a program effect when one is present.

In the typical evaluation of a human service program, the investigator formulates a null hypothesis such as "There is no difference between the treatment group and the control group," expecting to reject it at the specified level of statistical significance or alpha level. The sample data are analyzed, and the null hypothesis is rejected if the difference between the experimental group and the control group is sufficiently large to be considered an improbable event at the preselected alpha level such as 0.05, 0.01, or 0.001. An unfortunate error of interpretation is to assume that failure to reject the null hypothesis is equivalent to proving that the treatment had no effect. A more correct assessment is that the data generated from this study, *as designed*, failed to detect a difference between the treatment and the control conditions. Unless care is taken in the design of the study, that study might not be able to detect an effect even if one is present.

Statistical power is determined quantitatively as

1 – beta

or

1 – (the probability of a Type II error)

The beta level is complex to calculate and beyond the scope of this book. For a particular research problem, beta can be looked up in a reference work, such as Cohen (1988), or calculated by appropriate computer software. Once this is done, the adequacy of beta can be assessed by the following rule of thumb: The minimum acceptable ratio of Type II errors to Type I errors should be about 4 to 1. Thus, if alpha is set at 0.05, beta should be 4 × 0.05 or 0.20. Because power equals 1 beta, power equals 1 – 0.20 or 0.80. (This means we have an 80% chance to correctly reject the null hypothesis.) Similarly, if alpha is 0.01, power should be a minimum of 0.96, and if alpha is 0.001, power should be a minimum of 0.996. The 4-to-1 rule is only a general guideline, however. The power level that is acceptable in a particular research project should be determined by the nature of the research project and its implications.

Reviews of published research studies in the human services and other fields have consistently reported that the actual power of a large proportion of studies is well below these standards of 0.80, 0.96, and 0.996 (Orme & Tolman, 1986). What can be done to improve the power of a research project? Although the concept of power is complex, it has three major determinants: sample size, alpha level, and effect size. By manipulating them, one can improve statistical power.

The larger the sample, the greater the statistical power of a research project. Using the rule of thumb described previously with an alpha level of 0.05 and power equal to 0.80, it can be shown that (with participants evenly divided between treatment and control groups) a total of

(continued)

52 participants are needed to detect a large effect, 126 participants to detect a moderate effect, and 786 to detect a small effect (West et al., 2000). Therefore, a straightforward solution to increase power may be to increase sample size. Going back to our illustration of the family intervention program, it would obviously make sense to increase the size of our groups from 15 each to 30 each. It is also apparent, however, that going to about 800 participants to detect a small effect could greatly complicate a research project and make it prohibitively expensive. Another option is to consider reducing the alpha level. Because Type I and Type II errors are related, it may be an acceptable trade-off to set alpha at 0.1 with beta at 0.40, according to the rule of thumb of 4 times alpha. Under this scenario, power is equal to $1 - .40 = 0.60$. This would make it easier to detect an effect, but it does increase the risk of a Type I error.

Of course, neither of these solutions is without drawbacks. Fortunately, a researcher may use additional steps in an effort to increase statistical power (Lipsey, 1997). The best approach may be to increase the effect size of the independent variable in the sample (or increase the difference between X_t and X_c in the ES formula). Other things being equal, the larger the effect of the independent variable relative to other factors, the more likely the null hypothesis will be rejected. One way to increase effect size is to select samples that minimize measurement error and ensure that a high proportion of the difference between treatment and control groups is the result of the independent variable (see Chapters 6 and 10). Another solution lies in taking steps to eliminate as much extraneous variation as possible. Thorough training of service providers, careful rehearsal of procedures, and attention to program detail can all serve to eliminate variation caused by factors other than the program effect (or reduce the size of the denominator, or variation, in the ES formula).

We do not often think of social interventions in terms of dosage, but the evaluation researcher should make sure that the participants receive a sufficient dose of the independent variable to make a difference. If the program is financial aid, then it might be better to give a small sample large amounts of aid instead of a little aid to many. If the program is counseling, then the program should provide an intensive counseling experience. Using the most valid and reliable measurement tools can help detect a difference that exists between groups.

A common way of expressing that the null hypothesis was rejected is to indicate that a given result is "statistically significant" at some specified alpha level. Unfortunately, the use of the word *significant* can cause some confusion. In popular usage, "significant" means important or notable. Its meaning in statistics, however, does not have the same connotation. Whether a set of research findings is important or notable depends far more on the topic, theory, sample, and quality of measurement than it does on statistically rejecting null hypotheses. Research on trivial matters or that is procedurally flawed cannot produce important results no matter how many "statistically significant" findings it might contain. Be sure to remember that the meaning of "significant" in statistics is simply that a null hypothesis has been successfully rejected.

Statistical Procedures

Some of the basic considerations for selecting inferential statistical procedures are much like those for selecting descriptive statistics. One important consideration is the nature of the dependent variable. For nominal dependent variables, the commonly used procedures, such as chi-square, are discussed later. Many additional procedures, such as log-linear analysis, go beyond the scope of this book but are prominent in the research literature. With ordinal dependent variables, many procedures are, in addition to being applicable to ordered data, compatible with small clinical samples. Furthermore, many procedures that are technically appropriate for interval-level data also are used with ordinal variables, because they are "robust"—that is, not readily affected by violation of their theoretical assumptions. Finally, many procedures have been developed to handle interval-level data, such as Student's *t*, analysis of variance (ANOVA), and regression.

Beyond the level of measurement in the dependent variable, another consideration is the character of the independent variable. Some procedures are designed for single independent variables with only two levels. Other procedures handle two or more independent variables simultaneously and estimate combined effects.

Finally, another issue concerns how the data were generated. Some procedures, such as ANOVA, are intended for data generated by an experiment, in which one or more control groups are compared with one or more treatment groups. Other procedures, such as regression analysis, are well suited for analyzing large samples, such as surveys, to estimate effects. Still other procedures, such as MANOVA, are suitable for both statistical control of nonexperimental variables and analysis of experimentally generated variables at the same time. Many of these procedures are highly complex and beyond the scope of this text. The point is that specific factors favor the use of some statistical procedures over others, so it is important to select the appropriate procedures. Through other courses, you may learn to use and select the procedures yourself, or as a human service professional, you may rely on outside consultants to assist you with this aspect of your research.

In experimentation, researchers often make comparisons between a control group and a treatment group. If these two groups are comparable in all respects except for the treatment received, a commonly used statistic is Student's *t*. This statistic compares the mean of one group against the mean of the other. Recall from Chapter 6 that the groups may have different means by chance alone. Large differences, however, suggest a treatment effect, but what is a large difference? The answer depends on the scale of the variable being measured and on the size of the samples. The Student's *t* test results in a statistical value that is referred to a table for samples of different sizes. This table indicates the probability of obtaining a value that is as large or larger by chance. If the table value is less probable than the alpha level, one rejects the null hypothesis and concludes that the difference is significant. Tables indicating the value of *t* and other inferential statistics necessary for rejecting null hypotheses at various alpha levels may be found in any introductory statistics textbook. Computer packages, such as SPSS, provide the significant value.

In many experimental situations, the research involves more than two groups. The researcher also may want to measure the difference between groups. For example, if four treatment groups each receive different amounts of tutorial help, then the researcher might be interested in the effect that each level of help has on the number of problems the members of the different groups can solve. For this situation, which involves an experimental design and an interval-level dependent variable (number of problems solved), a commonly applied statistical procedure is *analysis of variance,* or *ANOVA,* which compares the variability in the scores of members within each group (within-group variance) with the variability between treatment groups. We do not expect all members of a treatment group to do equally well. In fact, even if one level of treatment works better than another, some members of a group receiving a lower-level tutorial program might do better than some members receiving a better tutorial program. Use of ANOVA permits the researcher to estimate how much of the variance in performance between groups results from the treatment.

Another commonly used statistical procedure is *multiple-regression analysis.* Multiple regression is used for a variety of purposes, but a typical application involves estimating the effect of multiple independent variables. For example, we might be interested in determining if a person's income is influenced by gender, race, and age—plus *how much* each of these variables affects income. As discussed earlier, correlation indicates whether two variables are associated, but regression permits the researcher to estimate how much change in the dependent variable is produced by a given change in an independent variable. Multiple regression is especially useful in that it can handle a large number of independent variables simultaneously, permitting researchers to estimate the effects of one variable while controlling for others. We know, for example, that income is correlated with race, education, age, and occupation—among many other variables. If we collect these data from a number of respondents, regression permits us to estimate the contribution of each independent variable to income. Multiple regression produces coefficients that indicate the direction and amount of change in the dependent variable to be expected from a unit change in the independent variables. Thus, if the dependent variable is dollars of income, a regression coefficient of $580 for the variable "years of education" indicates that one more year of education is worth an additional $580 per year in income, assuming that the other independent variables are held constant. In our illustration, regression would produce an equation as follows:

$$Y'(\text{income}) = a + b_1(\text{race}) + b_2(\text{education}) + b_3(\text{age}) + b_4(\text{gender})$$

where a is the value of Y before other factors' effects are considered, b_1 is an estimate of the effect of race on income, b_2 is the estimated effect of education,

b_3 is the estimated effect of age, and b_4 is the estimated effect of gender. Y' is the estimated change in income produced by the combination of all these factors.

A widely used inferential statistic suitable for nominal data is chi-square (X^2), which is applied to data in tabular form. The several versions of chi-square allow its application to data of different types. All versions, however, operate by comparing the number of cases that are actually found in the cross-classification of two or more variables with the number of cases that would be expected by chance. For example, Table 15.8 shows the relationship between region and religious preference in a sample of 741 people in the United States. The null hypothesis for this table would be that there is no relationship between the two variables. Chi-square compares the actual values in a table like this with what would be expected if the variables were unrelated. Table 15.8 also contains these expected values (given within parentheses in each cell). Expected values can be calculated from

TABLE 15.8 Nominal Data From Table 15.3. Suitable for Chi-Square, Showing Observed and Expected Values

		Region				
		Northeast	Midwest	South	West	Totals
Religious Preference	Protestant	54	140	206	80	480
		(exp = 85)	(exp = 141)	(exp = 157)	(exp = 97)	
	Catholic	55	56	28	43	182
		(exp = 32)	(exp = 53)	(exp = 60)	(exp = 37)	
	Jewish	10	1	1	3	15
		(exp = 3)	(exp = 4)	(exp = 5)	(exp = 3)	
	None	12	20	8	24	64
		(exp = 11)	(exp = 19)	(exp = 21)	(exp = 13)	
	Totals	131	217	243	150	N = 741

Chi-Square = 107, $p < 0.001$

Source: From Davis, J. A., & Smith, T. W. (1994). *General social survey 1972–1994: Cumulative codebook.* Chicago, IL: National Opinion Research Center.

the marginals in the table. The expected proportion of cases in each cell is what would be found in the population if there were no relationship between the two variables. For example, because people in the Northeast make up 17.7% of the whole sample, we expect 17.7% of all Protestants in the sample, or 85 out of 480, to be from the Northeast if the variables of religious preference and region are unrelated. Because of random variation, we would expect that the actual values in the sample will not be exactly the same as the expected values in the population even when there is no relationship. The more the actual cell frequencies in a sample diverge from the expected frequencies, however, the more likely it is that the null hypothesis is false and that an association does exist between the two variables in the population. In Table 15.8, "Chi-Square = 107" shows the actual chi-square coefficient calculated for the table, and "$p < 0.001$" means that the likelihood of having differences between expected and observed values as large as we found in this table when the null hypothesis actually is true in the population (meaning that there are no differences between

expected and observed values in the population) is 1 out of 1,000.

Small values of chi-square indicate little or no association, whereas large values indicate that an association is likely. With chi-square, the value of the statistic is influenced by the sample size and by the number of categories on each variable. Computer data-analysis packages automatically take this into account in reporting significance level; however, when doing hand calculations, researchers must refer the statistical value to a special table that states the probability of obtaining a chi-square value of that magnitude by chance, given the sample size and number of variable categories. Chi-square does not indicate the strength of the association but, rather, whether one exists at the level of the population.

For the consumer of research, this introduction provides some basic guidelines for interpreting statistical analyses encountered in reading research. Those who will conduct research and engage in statistical analysis themselves need to go beyond the materials presented here and to books such as those mentioned later in *For Further Reading*.

REVIEW AND CRITICAL THINKING

Main Points

- The major considerations in choosing statistics properly are level of measurement of the variables, goals of the research, number of variables involved, properties of the data, and audience.
- Descriptive statistics are procedures that assist in organizing, summarizing, and interpreting sample data.
- Measures of central tendency, or averages, summarize distributions by locating the central value of frequency distributions.
- Measures of dispersion indicate how dispersed or spread out the values are in a distribution, with most indicators revealing the average spread of the scores around the central value.
- Measures of association indicate the strength of relationships and, with ordinal- or higher-level data, the direction of relationships.
- Sometimes data are transformed into z-scores or standard normal distributions. These distributions enable us to compare distributions with one another, to assess the relative position of cases in a distribution, and to conduct inferential statistics. The properties of the normal distribution are important in this regard.

- Inferential statistics allow generalizations to be made from sample data to the populations from which those samples were drawn. Inferential statistics derive from the properties of the normal distribution, sampling distributions, and central limit theorem.
- In inferential statistics, a research hypothesis is paired with an opposite null hypothesis, and the results of a statistical test are used to decide which is most likely to be correct.
- Particular inferential statistics are linked to the level of measurement. Among the inferential statistics are Student's *t*, analysis of variance, regression, and chi-square.

IMPORTANT TERMS FOR REVIEW

Alpha error
Alpha level
Beta error
Bivariate statistics
Central limit theorem
Descriptive statistics
Inferential statistics

Measures of association
Measures of central
Tendency
Measures of dispersion
Multivariate statistics
Normal distribution
Null hypothesis

Proportional reduction in
  error (PRE)
Research hypothesis
Sampling distribution
Type I error
Type II error
Univariate statistics

CRITICAL THINKING

Information in professional journals will use much of the technical jargon used in this chapter, such as alpha levels, statistical significance, or chi-square. Information from other sources, however, such as in a newspaper or magazine or on a website, may not discuss these matters even though the conclusions they arrive at relate to them. The following are critical thinking questions raised at the beginning of the chapter and some ideas for how they relate to social work practice. Students are encouraged to develop their own answers to these questions.

Why is data analysis important for social work students? Some reasons include: you will be better prepared for advanced courses in social work and the social sciences, understanding statistics will help set you apart from your peers who have not worked with statistics, and you will be able to apply data to improve your practice.

What are the different measures of central tendency and how will knowing this information help you as a social worker? A measure of *central tendency* is a single value that attempts to describe a set of data by identifying the central position within that set of data. These measurements are used to identify an average score, a range, or a central location. The *mean* (known as the average) may be the measure of central tendency you are most familiar with, although there are others.

What is the difference between statistical significance and meaningfulness? And explain how understanding statistical significance will enhance your social work practice.

Understanding probability and statistical significance is the basis for comprehending statistics. Testing for statistical significance means calculating the probability, or odds, of findings due to chance alone. The concept of statistical significance is that any difference between different groups is due to a systematic influence rather than chance. For this reason, statistical significant levels are set at 95% (0.05), 99% (0.01), or 99.9% (0.001) out of 100.

A study can be statistically significant but not very meaningful. This usually comes from statistical significance being overused and conclusions drawn without meaning. For example, imagine that a study finds that people with long hair do well on course exams. Despite the statistical significance of the results, it is not useful information because nothing can be done with it.

EVALUATING COMPETENCY (FROM THE COUNCIL ON SOCIAL WORK EDUCATION [CSWE] 2015 EDUCATIONAL POLICY AND ACCREDITATION STANDARDS [EPAS])

Competency 9: Evaluated Practice With Individuals, Families, Groups, Organizations, and Communities

* What challenges might a social researcher face when evaluating different aspects of his or her practice? And with different groups and organizations?
* What knowledge does a social researcher need to understand how to conduct data analysis?

SELF-ASSESSMENT

1. Levels of measurement consist of:
   a. Normal, ordinal, and interval.
   b. Ordinal and ratio.
   c. Nominal, ordinal, interval, and ratio.
   d. Ordinal, ratio, internal, and nominal.
2. Measures of central tendency refer to:
   a. Models and medians.
   b. Most common and most frequent.
   c. Median, mean, and measurement.
   d. Mode, mean, and median.
3. Probability theory involves:
   a. The likelihood of something occurring, but not what will occur.
   b. Predicting what will occur with more than one variable.
   c. Providing facts of what will happen.
   d. Knowing what will happen in a specific situation.

4. Statistical hypothesis testing refers to:
   a. Developing a hypothesis based on a hunch.
   b. Developing two hypotheses that are opposite of each other where a statistical test will determine which one is most likely to be correct.
   c. Developing multiple hypotheses to prove your project is effective.
   d. Developing a hypothesis based on hearsay.

5. The normal distribution consists of:
   a. A distribution that represents 20% of the population.
   b. A distribution in which only the mode is represented.
   c. A symmetrical distribution in which the mode, median, and mean are identical and has a shape that represents a bell.
   d. A distribution where there are no outliers.

6. Descriptive statistics involve:
   a. Statistics that compare variables.
   b. Statistics that provide statistical significance in your sample.
   c. Statistics where there is a null hypothesis.
   d. Statistics that are reported to describe the characteristics of a sample or to describe the relationships among variables in a sample.

7. Inferential statistics involve:
   a. Statistical measures used to make inferences to the overall population.
   b. Statistics that describe characteristics of a sample.
   c. Statistics that provide frequencies of a sample.
   d. Statistics that can only be interpreted by statisticians.

8. Number of variables to be analyzed refer to:
   a. Bivariate and multivariate analysis.
   b. Univariate, bivariate, and multivariate analysis.
   c. Univariate and bivariate analysis.
   d. Systematic analysis.

9. Sampling distribution consists of:
   a. A symmetrical distribution of a sample.
   b. A distribution of a sample that is conducted at a certain time and place.
   c. A distribution of a sample that starts with word of mouth.
   d. A theoretical distribution of a statistic from all possible samples of a certain size drawn from a population.

10. Statistical procedures refer to:
    a. Understanding the nature of the dependent variable and the characteristics of the independent variables that are being analyzed.
    b. Using any variable in a sample for statistical analysis.
    c. Understanding statistical significance.
    d. Understanding different types of statistical analysis.

ANSWER KEY FOR SELF-ASSESSMENT QUIZ

1. **c.** Nominal, ordinal, interval, and ratio
2. **d.** Mode, mean, and median
3. **a.** The likelihood of something occurring, but not what will occur
4. **b.** Developing two hypotheses that are opposite of each other where a statistical test will determine which one is most likely to be correct
5. **c.** A symmetrical distribution in which the mode, median, and mean are identical and has a shape that represents a bell
6. **d.** Statistics that are reported to describe the characteristics of a sample or to describe the relationships among variables in a sample
7. **a.** Statistical measures used to make inferences to the overall population
8. **b.** Univariate, bivariate, and multivariate analysis
9. **d.** A theoretical distribution of a statistic from all possible samples of a certain size drawn from a population
10. **a.** Understanding the nature of the dependent variable and the characteristics of the independent variables that are being analyzed

FOR FURTHER READING

Aron, A., Coups, E., & Aron, E. N. (2011). *Statistics for the behavioral and social sciences* (5th ed.). Upper Saddle River, NJ: Pearson. This readable introduction to statistics explains the issues clearly and minimizes the use of formulas.

Frankfort-Nachmias, C., & Leon-Guerrero, A. (2011). *Social statistics for a diverse society* (6th ed.). Thousand Oaks, CA: Pine Forge Press. This book provides a comprehensive overview of descriptive and inferential statistics and the applications of statistics by using them to elaborate on issues of race, class, and gender diversity.

King, B. M., Rosopa, P. J., & Minium, E. W. (2011). *Statistical reasoning in the behavioral sciences* (6th ed.). Hoboken, NJ: Wiley. This book is a good resource for introductory material on understanding statistics and statistical logic in the behavioral science. It includes a multidisciplinary framework of social sciences, as well as information relevant to using SPSS.

See also the books listed in *For Further Reading* in Chapter 14.

REFERENCES

Bloom, M., Fischer, J., & Orme, J. G. (2009). *Evaluating practice: Guidelines for the accountable professional* (6th ed.). Boston, MA: Pearson.

Cohen, J. (1988). *Statistical power analysis for behavioral sciences* (2nd ed.). Hillsdale, NJ: Lawrence Erlbaum Associates.

Davis, J. A., & Smith, T. W. (1994). *General social survey 1972–1994: Cumulative codebook.* Chicago, IL: National Opinion Research Center; Storrs, CT: The Roper Center for Public Opinion Research, University of Connecticut.

Lipsey, M. W. (1997). Design sensitivity: Statistical power for applied experimental research. In L. Bickman & D. Rog (Eds.), *Handbook of applied social research methods* (pp. 39–68). Thousand Oaks, CA: Sage.

Orme, J. G., & Combs-Orme, T. D. (1986). Statistical power and Type II errors in social work research. *Social Work Research and Abstracts, 22*(3), 3–10. doi:10.1093/swra/22.3.3

Orme, J. G., & Tolman, R. M. (1986). The statistical power of a decade of social work education research. *Social Service Review, 60*(4), 619–632. doi:10.1086/644403

Patton, M. Q. (1982). *Practical evaluation.* Beverly Hills, CA: Sage.

Prentice, D. A., & Miller, D. T. (1998). When small effects are impressive. In A. E. Kazdin (Ed.), *Methodological issues and strategies in clinical research* (2nd ed., pp. 127–137). Washington, DC: American Psychological Association.

Schmidt, F. L. (1998). Statistical significance testing and cumulative knowledge in psychology: Implications for training researchers. In A. E. Kazdin (Ed.), *Methodological issues and strategies in clinical research* (2nd ed., pp. 437–460). Washington, DC: American Psychological Association.

U.S. Census Bureau. (2008). *Statistical abstract of the United States: 2009* (128th ed., Table 109). Retrieved from https://www2.census.gov/library/publications/2008/compendia/statab/128ed/tables/vitstat.pdf

West, S. G., Biesanz, J. C., & Pitts, S. C. (2000). Causal inference and generalization in field settings: Experimental and quasi-experimental designs. In H. T. Reis & C. M. Judd (Eds.), *Handbook of research methods in social and personality psychology* (pp. 40–84). Cambridge, UK: Cambridge University Press.

16

ANALYSIS OF QUALITATIVE DATA

INTRODUCTION

In the fall of 2011, one of the authors of this textbook (Hilton) was sitting at his desk at Northern Michigan University when he was visited by one of his students, Joseph Masters. Masters was a bachelor of social work student and had just applied for the McNair Scholars program, a scholarship program that supports first generation college students who are interested in pursuing graduate school after graduation. The program supports scholarship recipients' engagement in research with a faculty mentor. Masters was looking for a research opportunity and a mentor. At the time, Hilton was in the process of completing publications based on previously collected data and did not feel the work would provide a meaningful research experience to a student.

Masters and Hilton talked at length about the student's interests and long-term goals. Masters was a member of the Keweenaw Bay Indian Community, a Native American tribe in Michigan's Upper Peninsula. His tribal affiliation, Masters explained, was very important to him as were the spiritual and cultural aspects of his tribal associations. He credited his tribe with much of his success, including his going back to college after having had some difficulties in his youth, including legal troubles. As they talked about the meaning of Masters' culture, heritage, and tribal membership they also began to speak about the importance of culture and community to people experiencing major life changes, including transitions from prison or jail back to their home communities.

By the end of the discussion, Masters had outlined a new research project and Hilton had agreed to serve as his faculty mentor and research partner. The two had decided to examine Native Americans' transitions from prison back to their home communities, including tribal reservations. The goal of the research was to understand the subjective experiences of people making this transition and the roles that communities play in helping them become reintegrated into the community. They also wanted to better understand how various services and policies impacted this transition and reintegration experience.

This meeting led to a research partnership that lasted more than a year and resulted in a publication entitled "Return to the Rez: Native American Parolees' Transitions to Community Life" (Masters & Hilton, 2014). The research process and even the main questions evolved over time. While the researchers knew they were interested in Native Americans' transitions from prison to civilian life, they were less certain what factors would be important to understanding parolees' experiences returning home and reintegrating into the community. They were not even fully certain what they meant by "reintegration" because this would likely mean something different for different people and there was little existing research on Native

American parolees. Given these uncertainties and their goal of understanding subjective experiences, they decided on a grounded theory, qualitative study design.

Masters and Hilton created a research design that included semi-structured, in-depth qualitative interviews with parolees from each of the five major tribes in the Upper Peninsula. The interviews would cover several areas related to reintegration, including housing, employment, family, human services, and community involvement. They also decided to interview tribal leaders and human services agency staff to learn more about policies and programs pertaining to community reintegration. All interviews would be audio-taped with a digital recorder.

The Institutional Review Board (IRB) process went smoothly and the two were able to conduct their interviews over the course of six months. They had dozens of hours of audiotape. Now they had to determine what to do with them. How could they begin the process of analyzing these audio files to learn about and report on the participants' experiences?

This chapter focuses on the analysis of qualitative data, like the audio recordings of Native American parolees. Throughout the chapter we will refer back to Masters' and Hilton's analysis of these recordings as an example of the qualitative analysis process. As you read this chapter please keep the following questions in mind: (a) How can researchers and practitioners conduct qualitative analysis in a way that helps ensure findings are both valid and reliable? (b) What parallels exist between qualitative analysis and professional human services practice? and (c) What unique insights can be obtained through qualitative analysis that may be difficult to obtain through quantitative analysis?

In Chapter 9 we argued that there were parallels and linkages between practice and qualitative research. In fact, it has been argued that many traditional social work methods for evaluating and assessing practice also are traditional qualitative methods for collecting and analyzing data (Smith, 1998). So, as we present the ways by which qualitative researchers make sense of their data, it should help the student of human services to see that the techniques used for drawing meaning from

qualitative research data lend themselves equally well to making sense of practice information. For example, process recording, a technique long used in social work for training students in clinical methods and for documenting case progress, is closely related to the case study method used by qualitative researchers. Social workers commonly are required to write case summaries, and these reports closely parallel a qualitative researcher's report that analyzes, interprets, and integrates data from a qualitative study. Human service students in internships or field placements often are required to maintain a log or journal of their experiences. Again, the student's task of synthesizing and summarizing the content of such a journal is similar to the qualitative researcher's task of analyzing field notes. Students who have covered the use of such techniques as genograms, sociograms, and timelines to graphically represent practice phenomena will find themselves on familiar ground as we present some of the same approaches here (although sometimes with different labels). What differentiates these approaches in research and in practice is the greater emphasis on systematic and rigorous application found in research.

The raw material for qualitative data analysis often is in the form of field notes and in-depth interviews (discussed in Chapter 9). Qualitative data, however, also may come in the form of diaries, narratives, video recordings, and other sorts of texts that are nonquantitative. In the previous example, the primary data were in the form of audio recordings of in-depth interviews. In qualitative data analysis, the researcher attempts to transform these raw data and extract some meaning from it, mostly without quantifying the data. (We pointed out in Chapter 9 that field research can produce some quantitative data; when it does, these data are analyzed using the procedures discussed in Chapters 14 and 15.)

GOALS OF QUALITATIVE DATA ANALYSIS

The goals of qualitative data analysis are both similar to and different from the goals of quantitative data analysis. The specific strategies used in qualitative data analysis are different from those used in quantitative data analysis, but nonetheless, it is still data analysis—that is, extracting meaning from observations. The goals of a qualitative research project might be the same as those discussed in Chapter 1, especially description, explanation, and evaluation. In addition, qualitative research often strives for understanding by generalizing beyond the data to more abstract and general concepts or theories. The ultimate end may, in some cases, be to generalize the results to people, groups, or organizations beyond those observed. Thus, qualitative data analysis creates meaning, in part, by using raw data to learn something more abstract and general. In this respect, qualitative and quantitative data analyses are similar.

In the previous example, Masters' and Hilton's main goal was to describe the unique experiences, including subjective experiences, of parolees' transitions back to their communities. They also hoped that they could identify factors that are important to understanding these experiences. Where possible, they aimed to reveal patterns in parolees' experiences and explain how various factors contribute to these patterns. Thus, their aims were to both describe unique experiences and create more general explanations of Native American parolees' experiences as a whole.

Qualitative and quantitative approaches have obvious differences. First, qualitative research recognizes that abstraction and generalization are matters of degree and that they may be of less importance in some studies. Masters and Hilton, for example, aimed to understand more about this very unique population (Native American parolees in Michigan's Upper Peninsula), not to make generalizations about community reintegration overall.

Second, qualitative research lays more emphasis on the effort to contextualize—to understand people, groups, and organizations within the full context or situation in which they act. In fact, some qualitative data-analysis strategies devote more effort to contextualizing than to abstracting or generalizing. This is based on the position that scientific knowledge is found not only in abstracting and generalizing but also can derive from a deep and full description of a context. In other words, some qualitative research focus on idiographic explanations rather than nomothetic ones

(see Chapter 2). In their study, Masters and Hilton spent considerable time and effort understanding the unique context of each reservation and Native American community and how these contexts shaped each research participant's experiences.

Third, qualitative research tends to place more emphasis on inductive reasoning than on deductive reasoning. Qualitative researchers stress the value of letting concepts and abstract ideas emerge from the data rather than using the data to provide evidence for preexisting concepts and theories. In their study of Native American parolees, Masters and Hilton did not begin with any hypotheses other than the general idea that community, family, human services, and policy contexts may play some role in understanding research participants' experiences. They did not aim to test any specific hypotheses or theory. Rather, their primary aim was to develop new hypotheses and identify perspectives or theories that help make sense of their data.

As a part of the goal of stressing the contextual, qualitative research maintains a close, interactive link between data collection and data analysis. In Chapter 1, we presented the stages in the research process as a sequence in which one stage is mostly completed before the next stage is begun. In particular, we suggested that the data-collection stage be completed before the data-analysis stage begins and that data analysis be largely finished before conclusions are drawn (see Figure 1.1). This is the way many quantitative and positivist researchers describe the process. One major reason for this sequencing is to ensure that the data-collection procedures used are the same over time; if the measurement procedures change from the beginning to the end of the data-collection phase, then researchers may be measuring different variables (see Chapters 5 and 13). This is an important consideration in research, where there are clearly stated and quantifiable variables and hypotheses and where quantitative measurement procedures are used.

For many qualitative researchers, on the other hand, the process looks more like Figure 16.1: The stages of data collection, data analysis, and drawing conclusions are more simultaneous and interactive (Maxwell, 2012; Seidman, 2006). The researcher begins to analyze and draw conclusions almost as

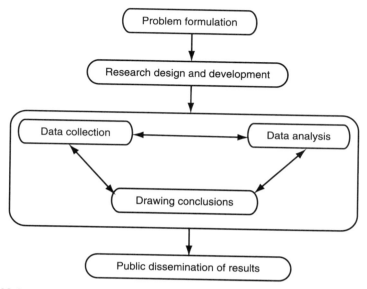

Figure 16.1 The stages of social research as conceptualized by some qualitative researchers.

soon as data collection begins, and these analyses and conclusions provide direction for whatever additional data collection needs to occur. Unlike the positivists, for whom comparability over time is essential, many qualitative researchers see that aspect of data collection as being problematic, in the sense that it is a decision to be weighed given the particulars of a research project. In many cases, the advantages gained by adjusting and refocusing the data-collection efforts as they proceed outweigh the disadvantages of changing the manner in which the data are collected. One of the advantages gained when data collection and analysis overlap is **theoretical sensitivity:** having data collection and analysis closely guided by emerging theoretical issues (Glaser, 1978; Strauss, 1987). Now, data collection and analysis are guided by theoretical issues in all research but in a different way. In most research, theoretical issues are used to create measuring devices before collecting the data, and what occurs during the process of data collection does not lead to changes in the measuring devices. Because many qualitative researchers do not see a rigid separation between data collection and data analysis, however, their stance opens the door for the possibility of theoretical issues, arising *during* data collection, to change what kind of data are collected or from whom. So, theoretical sensitivity

involves a constant interaction between theory and data collection. Data collected in one interview, for example, may raise some theoretical issues for the researcher such that later interviews are modified to collect data addressing those issues.

Following Miles and Huberman (1994), we find it helpful to organize qualitative data analysis into three categories: data reduction and analysis, data displays, and drawing conclusions and verifying theories. Keep in mind that these are not sequential steps but, rather, overlapping activities that mutually support one another. As Miles and Huberman (1994) state, "The three types of analysis activity [data reduction, data displays, and conclusion drawing] and the activity of data collection itself form an interactive, cyclical process" (p. 12). All three activities occur, at least in part, during the process of data collection and may influence and change that process.

In the Native American parolees' example, the timing of data collection and analysis overlapped. They developed their coding scheme after listening to audio recordings based on themes and categories that emerged during the interviews. As they conducted more interviews and continued with their data analysis they refined their coding scheme to incorporate new variations related to existing categories and allowed for new themes and categories to be created. In some cases this required them to recode and re-summarize interviews they had already analyzed. Using NVivo software to directly code audio interviews made this relatively easy as the software allows for easy reconfigurations of existing coding schemes, electronic or automated re-coding of previously analyzed material, and quick creations of new codes and themes.

DATA REDUCTION AND ANALYSIS

As we describe different kinds of qualitative data analysis, it may seem at times as if we are talking again about the process of data collection in the field (the topic of Chapter 9). That confusion can arise because in qualitative research, data collection and data analysis often occur simultaneously. In qualitative field research, for example, the data-collection phase involves collecting field notes and other materials. *Data analysis* refers to the application of coding schemes and other procedures to those field notes that are described in this section. So, the analysis is sometimes occurring as the data are being collected.

The data-analysis strategies discussed in this section tend to be of two types. **Categorizing strategies** attempt to generalize and abstract by generating concepts and even theories from the raw data. **Contextualizing strategies** attempt to treat the data as a coherent whole and to retain as much of the raw data as possible to capture the whole context (Maxwell, 2012). Actually, however, many specific qualitative data analyses can involve elements of both.

We will first review categorizing strategies in the form of coding, reflective remarks, and memos. Then, we will discuss the contextualizing strategies.

Codes and Coding

We have talked about the process of *coding* at a number of points in this textbook—as a part of doing content analysis of available data in Chapter 8, of making structured field observations in Chapter 9, and of quantitative data analysis in

Chapter 14. Coding is also a form of data analysis with qualitative data, and it has some similarities to coding done in other contexts.

Coding refers to the categorizing of observations into a limited number of categories. In most qualitative data analyses, however, coding is distinct from other forms of coding in at least three important ways. First, it is not an effort to quantify the data or to create a set of numerical categories, as often is the case with other types of coding. Coding in qualitative analysis reduces and simplifies the data, but it does so by retaining words and their essential meanings. Second, in qualitative analysis, codes and coding schemes are created, at least in part, from the data themselves during the process of data collection; in other words, the data create the codes. Quantitative coding schemes are more typically derived from some preexisting theoretical stance, and then an effort is made to see if the data fit the coding scheme. Third, the purpose of coding in qualitative analysis is different. In quantitative research, coding usually is a part of the process of measurement: The coding categories constitute the operational definition of the underlying variable. Although this principle applies, to an extent, in coding for qualitative research, qualitative coding goes beyond measurement: It is also an integral part of conceptual development and theory building. So, the process of coding in qualitative research spans the realms of both measurement and the more abstract process of developing concepts and theories.

In qualitative research, then, the data are in the form of field notes, narratives produced by respondents, or, possibly, written documents or archival material. As with the case of the Native American parolees study, data can also come in the form of audio or video recordings of meetings, focus groups, or interviews. Coding is the process of categorizing sections of that data—a phrase, a sentence, a paragraph. Coding is a way to see which parts of the data are connected to one another in terms of some issue, concept, theme, or hypothesis. Some researchers use different terms, such as *thematic analysis,* for strategies of data analysis that basically involve categorizing the data (Braun & Clark, 2012; Seidman, 2006).

In the Masters and Hilton example, the researchers' codes pertained to several general themes related to reintegration experiences of parolees, including relationships with family members, use of human services, employment, involvement in community activities, relationships with friends, and housing. At times some interview segments pertained to multiple themes. For example, an interviewee describing a situation where he lived with a friend as opposed to his family (his parents and siblings) because his friend lived closer to his place of employment than his family members and because he had a strained relationship with one of his siblings who also lived at his parents' house may be coded under multiple themes (relationships with family, employment, housing, and relationships with friends).

Approaches to Coding. Three approaches exist to developing the coding schemes used by qualitative researchers. One is to create a fairly complete coding scheme before going out into the field to collect observations (Miles & Huberman, 1994). This would be based on theoretical considerations regarding what will be observed in the field and what the important variables, social mechanisms, and causal processes are. This approach might rely on prior research or on preexisting coding schemes developed by others and used in research on similar topics. For example, a qualitative evaluation of a high-school mental health program involved coding focus-group responses according to four topics: (1) positive aspects of the program, (2) suggestions for improving services, (3) how to reach youth in need of mental health services, and (4) ideas for measuring treatment outcomes (Nabors, Reynolds, & Weist, 2000). Examples of coding categories included therapist behaviors and academic, personal, and neighborhood changes.

This coding scheme can be readily adapted to studies of similar programs. When using this approach, the list of coding categories should be fairly complete in terms of what the observer expects to see in the field and may be quite detailed and lengthy. One thing that distinguishes this approach to coding, however, from what most quantitative researchers do is that the qualitative researcher still expects to change and adapt the coding scheme

as observations are made in the field. With almost any coding scheme, some categories prove to be more useful and others less so. Some categories might not be used at all, whereas others get used too much—that is, so many observations fall into the category that it needs to be divided into subcategories based on differences among the various observations. Thus, the coding scheme continues to develop as the data are collected.

The second approach to developing coding schemes is the reverse of the first: Observers enter the field with no preestablished coding scheme (Strauss, 1987). Coding categories are developed as observations are made in the field context. One example of this is the grounded theory approach (described in Chapter 9), a data-driven, contextualized approach to data analysis. Without the restrictions of a preexisting coding scheme, the observer describes what happens, tries to identify relevant variables, and searches for explanations of what is observed. Beginning with these concrete observations, the researcher then develops a coding scheme that points toward more abstract concepts, propositions, and theoretical explanations that would be plausible given those observations. In this way, preexisting theory does not limit the kind of data collection that occurs.

This is the approach that Masters and Hilton used. As previously explained, their data collection included semi-structured interviews. While they anticipated they would hear things about the role of family, friends, and the community as interviewees described their reintegration experiences, they did not have any preconceived coding scheme for categorizing or classifying data. Their interviews with parolees did not involve any interview script and each interview began with a general question about what the person has done since leaving prison and general impressions of the reintegration experience. From there the interviews followed up with probing questions based on topics raised by the interviewee. While these tended to concern family, friends, housing, and jobs, other themes emerged within some interviews, including spirituality, tribal affiliations, and culture. In these cases, new themes and coding schemes were created for analysis and in some cases were applied to previously analyzed interviews (that were re-analyzed and re-coded).

Even this open approach to coding is given some structure, however, by some proponents of grounded theory, such as Anselm Strauss. These proponents argue that coding should address four general categories of phenomena:

- Conditions or causes
- Interaction among people
- Strategies and tactics
- Consequences

A third approach to developing coding schemes falls in between the first two: A general coding scheme is developed that identifies domains of observation rather than referring to specific content within those domains. Then, coding schemes are inductively developed within those domains (Bogdan & Biklen, 1992; Lofland, Snow, Anderson, & Lofland, 2006). These domains are more specific and detailed than the four general categories just mentioned that are used by some grounded theory researchers. A possible list of such domains might include the following:

- Actions/events
- Activities (actions of some duration)
- Meaning (what people say and do to define a situation)
- Perspectives (ways of thinking or orientations)
- Relationships
- Setting/context
- Social structure (status, roles, and their relationships)

Most—or all—of these domains are likely to be relevant in a field setting, yet the categories are so general that context still plays a strong part in shaping the observations made and the specific coding scheme that emerges.

To show more concretely how coding is done, we can look to a research example described in Chapter 3, Hilton and DeJong's study of rural homelessness. This was qualitative research that used ethnographic interviews as a source of data (Hilton & DeJong, 2010). The study focuses on coping behaviors and felt experiences of homeless adults in a rural area while identifying behavioral patterns and strategies for meeting basic necessities. Relying on audio recordings of interviews, the researchers identified major concepts and themes related to coping behaviors and dilemmas faced by those struggling to survive while homeless. The researchers identified areas in the interviews where these concepts and themes were prominent by listening for certain phrases and words indicative of these concepts and themes. Table 16.1 presents some excerpts from interviews, with the key words highlighted that indicate a particular abstract coding category. The homeless adults interviewed were asked about their possessions and how they managed them without a permanent home. Issues related to storing and transporting items were common so the researchers created codes for these concepts. The researchers used these codes to assess hypotheses related to difficulties associated with managing possessions.

Notice a couple of characteristics in the coding in Table 16.1. First, the coding does not focus on counts of how often things happen but, rather, on descriptions of what is applicable to a particular person or context. The data analysis produces words, phrases, and descriptions as meaning rather than as numbers to extract meaning. Second, there is a close link between the codes and the data: When a code is applied, it is linked to a particular section (word, phrase, sentence, or paragraph) of the raw data. This is important in terms of assessing validity.

Descriptive Versus Abstract Coding. Coding schemes vary in terms of how general or abstract the coding categories are. Different qualitative researchers have developed different descriptions of this. Miles and Huberman (1994), for example, suggest three different types of coding.

Descriptive codes are coding categories that involve fairly directly observed behaviors or events; the coder need not do a great deal of interpretation to place a statement in the field notes into these categories. So, field notes that say "Jane left the room" or "Jim shook hands with the nurse" can be fairly directly coded as "departure" and "greeting," respectively.

Interpretive codes are coding categories that require field researchers to use some of their deep understanding of the social context to place a section of the field notes into a category; in other words, they must interpret the meaning of

TABLE 16.1 A Section of Transcribed In-Depth Interview, With Codes

Codes	Interview Statements
Self-perception Awareness of difference Identifying self through ill health Comparing health to others'	A 29-year-old man with renal failure was discussing his high school years and events that occurred long before he was diagnosed.
	. . . I knew I was different. I caught colds very easily and my resistance was very low, and so I knew that, generally speaking, my health wasn't as good as everybody else's, but I tried to do all the things that everybody else was doing.

Normalizing the context of illness
Self-esteem:
    feelings of failure
    failure of self
Reality contradicts idealized experience
	A 29-year-old woman with colitis was recounting her first episode of illness.

	. . . I was under a great deal of stress as a result of all this bouncing around and trying to get a job and trying not to have to go home to my parents and admit that I had failed. [I] failed at life. I had left college, and left there saying, "Gee, I can do it on my own," so I was trying this exciting existence I read about and there was something wrong; I had all this pain. I didn't know what to do about it.
Self in retrospect Self-esteem Outcome of timed struggle Improving self-esteem as treatment goal	A 54-year-old woman who had had cancer and currently had a crippling collagen disease was explaining her view on why she had had a recurrence of cancer.
	. . . When I look back on my second bout of cancer, I was not feeling good about myself and the whole struggle of the last three years put me into X (a cancer institute) to try and get me to feel better about myself.

Source: Reprinted by permission of Kathy Charmaz, from Charmaz, K. (1988). The grounded theory method: An explication and interpretation. In R. M. Emerson (Ed.), *Contemporary field research: A collection of readings*. Prospect Heights, IL: Waveland Press. (Original work published 1983).

a particular entry in the field notes. Interpretive codes might involve assessing people's motivations or moods or the meanings that people attach to things. So, if the field notes say that "Jane left the room angrily" or "Jim gave the nurse a cool greeting," the words *angry* and *cool* are interpretive in nature—that is, they involve a judgment or interpretation by the researcher. Thus, placing these parts of the field notes into categories of "angry" and "distant" is more interpretive and subjective than the descriptive codes are.

The third type of coding involves *pattern codes,* which are "explanatory or inferential codes, ones that identify an emergent theme, configuration, or explanation. They pull together a lot of material into more meaningful and parsimonious units of analysis" (Miles & Huberman, 1994, p. 69).

Pattern codes reduce the amount of data into more manageable amounts and help focus later data collection on data that assist in better understanding the patterns or themes. A section of field notes is identified as representing some abstract or theoretical theme or pattern in the events that are occurring. An explanatory code may refer to an abstract social process. So, "Jane left the room angrily" might be coded as exemplifying the social process of "rejection of deviant," whereas "Jim gave the nurse a cool greeting" might be coded as the social process of "role distance."

Pattern codes usually focus on one of four general categories of phenomenon: themes, causes or explanations, relationships among people, and theoretical constructs. The danger with pattern coding is that the researcher might prematurely impose a certain meaning on the data and then try to fit everything else into that pattern. To prevent this, Miles and Huberman recommend that the researcher remain tentative and flexible:

> The trick here is to work with loosely held chunks of meaning, to be ready to unfreeze and reconfigure them as the data shape up otherwise, to subject the most compelling themes to merciless cross-checking, and to lay aside the more tenuous ones until other informants and observations give them better empirical grounding. (Miles & Huberman, 1994, p. 70)

Keep in mind that a single section of a text or field notes can be given more than one type of code; in fact, it might be given a descriptive, an interpretive, and a pattern code.

Going back to Table 16.2, notice that it is fairly straightforward to give a descriptive code to some segments, such as "stored things with friends";

however, it is more difficult—requires more interpretation and judgment—to give interpretive codes. For example, it requires some judgment to say that "worry about your stuff" is an instance of the code "storage issues." It is even more inferential to assign a pattern code, such as "worry about your stuff as a possessions dilemma." Such abstract coding might be based on things said in other parts of the interview or on the researchers' deep knowledge of the field setting in which the interviewees live and the interviews occurred. This is why Miles and Huberman caution against settling on pattern codes too quickly.

Open Versus Focused Coding. Another approach to coding is to begin by looking for any types of codes that might emerge from the data and then focus on a limited number of codes to see how well they fit various parts of the data (Charmaz, 2006; Glaser, 1978). The initial coding of field notes, interviews, or other documents is called *open coding,* and it involves unrestricted coding to produce concepts and dimensions that seem to fit the data

TABLE 16.2 Excepts From Ethnographic Interviews With Homeless Adults, With Suggested Coding

Abstract Concept	More Specific Behaviors	Excerpts From Ethnographic Interview
Possessions Dilemma	Storage Issues	"I have **stored things with friends**, but I learned that friends can't be responsible for your things, ya know. Friends move and you can't keep track of them all the time, so you're like 'Well, I lost this or that.' Over time I learned that I got what I got."
		"If you're sleeping in the woods you have to **worry about your stuff**—because someone could come by and steal things."
	Transporting Issues	When you need to go in town, you **don't want to carry everything**, but if you leave it someone could take your things, or an animal could get at it too."
		"I **carry 75 to 80 pounds of stuff in a backpack on wheels**. I load it on and off the bus. I carry it across town so a day really wears on you. I tried **storing some things in a friend's car** and going with the bare minimum, but I ended up in the rain, soaking wet and cold."

Source: From Hilton, T., & DeJong, C. (2010). Homeless in God's country: Coping behaviors and felt experiences of the rural homeless. *Journal of Qualitative and Ethnographic Research, 5*(1), 12–30.

fairly well. These codes can be linked to the various dimensions mentioned previously (conditions, causes, etc.), and the coding categories are provisional and tentative. The point of open coding is to open up the data—to open up possibilities—rather than to finalize anything. Anything that is wrong or unclear at this stage will be rectified and clarified at later stages of coding. As Strauss (1987) puts it, at this stage of coding, researchers "play the game of believing everything and believing nothing" (p. 29). Whereas in quantitative research the goal of coding is to produce counts (how many cases fall into each category), the point of open coding, according to Strauss (1987), is to "fracture, break the data apart analytically" (p. 29)—in other words, to create new categories and to split apart and rearrange existing categories. There is nothing fixed about the category system, at least, at this stage; it is emerging out of the data and, therefore, is in flux. Especially early in the process, open coding is likely to be more of the descriptive variety, but it also may include some interpretive and pattern codes.

Masters and Hilton learned the importance of open coding while coding an interpretative code related to research participants' perceived reception by their tribes. The researchers had noticed early on that several interviewees had described their tribes' reception to them following their return from prison. In most cases interviewees described their tribes as warmly receiving them back into the community. In a few cases interviewees described a mixed reception, partially related to their past crimes that may have victimized other tribal members. A new interpretative code emerged based on these initial interviews that categorized perceived receptions by the tribe as welcoming and friendly or mixed. In subsequent interviews, however, discussions about parolees' relationships within the tribe took on new meaning. Some did not see their tribes' treatment toward them as different than it was before they went to prison. They explained that tribal membership was a birthright and that acceptance of tribal members was absolute and did not change based on criminal record or time away from the community. Others explained that the process of reintegration in the community was not a function of a tribe's acceptance but a willingness of the parolee to enter back into the fold of the community. Obviously Masters and Hilton had to be willing to modify their coding scheme related to parolees' perceived reception by tribes. Luckily, their analysis software, NVivo, allowed them to quickly identify relevant interview segments and apply a modified coding scheme.

After open coding has proceeded for a while, the field researcher can turn to *focused coding* or what Strauss calls *axial coding:* intense analysis around one or a few of the coding categories. (Each of the general coding categories is called an "axis," hence the name "axial coding.") Focused coding is more selective and conceptual; it involves applying a limited set of codes to a large amount of data. Focused coding enables the researcher to assess how extensively a set of codes applies and to discover the various forms in which the categories appear. This enables the researcher to explore one of these dimensions of social reality throughout the field notes and, thus, to expose relationships that may not have been obvious with open coding. Focused coding cannot be done until open coding has already provided a plethora of potential concepts, but after a period of open coding, focused coding can be done periodically. In open coding, the center of attention is the raw data; in focused coding, the focus of attention is the emerging coding categories. Focused coding begins to expose the core concepts and categories as well as the relationships among them that emerge from the data. Focused coding, however, is still strongly linked to the data, because the researcher must constantly go back to the original texts to validate decisions about what the core concepts are and what the relationships appear to be among them. Furthermore, focused coding may lead to revisions in the coding that are done during open coding, as new concepts emerge from the data. What occurs at this stage is essentially conceptual development (discussed in Chapter 4), but here, conceptual development grows out of the process of data analysis rather than occurring before research design development.

Hilton and DeJong's study of rural homelessness (2010) and Hilton and Trella's follow-up study of parenting while homeless (Trella & Hilton, 2014) offer a good example of focused or axial coding. Hilton and DeJong's study focused on homeless adults' experiences, including their felt experiences—including their emotional states, attitudes, and outlook on the future. One of the themes emerged related to felt experiences was the sense of urgency, near panic, and crisis management orientation shown by homeless parents with respect to caring for their children. Hilton and Trella built on this theme raised in the Hilton and DeJong study and completed a new round of interviews with homeless adults, but this time only with homeless parents. Relying on those interviews from the first round (Hilton and DeJong) that addressed parenting while homeless and their new interviews, Hilton and Trella zeroed in on the theme of felt experiences of homeless parents (pertaining to parenting). Their analysis, which included a closer examination of themes identified in the previous analysis, resulted in the development of a new concept they called "survival parenting," which they defined as the homeless parents' survival-related efforts, associated stress, and methods of coping with this stress.

Selective coding is a term used by Strauss (1987) to describe coding that focuses on the core concepts and categories that emerged during focused coding. It is, in a sense, a more-intense form of focused coding. All elements of the text are coded in terms of how they relate—or do not relate—to the core concepts and theories that are emerging from the data. This is similar to Miles and Huberman's pattern coding. Selective coding builds on open and focused coding and can begin only after some of those forms of coding have been accomplished. As data analysis proceeds, selective coding comes to predominate in the process. In addition, as core concepts and theories emerge from selective coding, they can point toward what additional data need to be collected to provide further tests and comparisons for the theory.

Operational Definitions and Reliability. As a coding scheme is developed, each category within it must have a good operational definition to ensure that all observers use the coding scheme both properly and consistently. The *operational definition* is a verbal statement of the kind of observations that should be placed in a particular category. The definition might emerge from an existing theoretical framework, or it might emerge out of the observations, as in grounded theory. Nevertheless, it is critical that the definition be clearly specified and understood by all observers. Otherwise, observations that are placed in one category by one observer might be placed in another category by another observer—or even ignored altogether. One way to clarify these operational definitions is through *double coding:* Two observers code the same set of field notes, and then cases where these observers disagree on the coding can be evaluated. Discussion about their disagreements usually produces a sharper, clearer operational definition or a revision in the coding scheme that takes the difficulty into account.

Reliability of coding schemes can be assessed in a number of different ways. As discussed in Chapter 8, one way is double coding, and then the degree of agreement between the two coders can be assessed. One simple way to do this is to calculate the percentage of judgments on which coders agree out of the total number of judgments that they must make:

$$\text{percentage of agreement} = \frac{2 \times (\text{number of agreements})}{\text{total number of observations recorded by both observers}}$$

Some disagreement exists about what level of agreement is acceptable, but many researchers argue that, after revisions and adjustments, the final coding scheme should achieve at least 85% to 90% agreement. Another way to check the reliability of a coding scheme is to have each observer code the same set of field notes twice, separated by a period of at least a few days. Again, the ultimate code–recode reliability should achieve at least 85% to 90%.

Reflective Remarks and Memos

In performing qualitative data analysis, researchers need some mechanisms for moving away from the immediate, raw data toward the general and abstract. Pattern coding and selective coding are two ways to achieve this, but field researchers have identified other methods as well. One is **reflective remarks** on field notes: reflections, interpretations, connections, or other thoughts that occur to the researcher while transcribing the field notes or coding the data. This can take many different forms: questioning the original interpretation of some events in the field notes, a recollection of something about the relationship between two people that was not put into the field notes, an elaboration on something that was only sketchily described in the field notes, or a new hypothesis to explain something that happened in the field. All these might be useful in understanding and coding the field notes, and they should be committed to writing.

Writing reflective remarks helps while analyzing and reviewing coded interviews. Coding was done directly from the audio recordings using NVivo software. Basically coders highlight sections of an audio file (seen as an audio timeline) and then assign codes to each section. Coders are also able to create "Notes" alongside these codes where they can summarize emerging ideas and hypotheses related to various sections of the interview or entire interviews.

If the field notes are being transcribed when the reflective thoughts occur, such thoughts can be incorporated directly into the field notes. It is a good idea, however, to keep the data recorded in the field separate from the reflective remarks, because the latter could be influenced by selective recall or retrospective interpretation. One way to keep the field notes separate from the reflective remarks is to set the remarks apart from the notes with some device—a different font, double parentheses, brackets, or any other device not used anywhere else in the field notes—that clearly identifies these remarks. If the reflective thoughts occur during coding, they can be written into a margin of the field notes but not in the margin where the codes are placed. NVivo allows researchers to either view or not view these notes when viewing how various sections of interviews are coded.

Another significant step away from the raw data are what are variously called *memos, analytical memos,* or *theoretical memos.* **Memos** refer to attempts at theorizing: The researcher writes down ideas about the meanings of the codes that are emerging from the data and the relationships between the various codes (Glaser, 1978; Strauss,

1987). Memos do not just describe the data, however; they are more conceptual and abstract in nature, showing that a particular part of the data is an instance of a particular concept or social process. Or, a memo might link various pieces of data together as sharing some abstract property in common. Whatever form they take, memos represent a move beyond the raw data toward more-abstract theorizing. Memoing can be done as the data collection and data analysis proceed. In fact, memoing can begin as soon as abstract ideas begin to occur to the researcher, which may be fairly early in the data-collection process. This is quite different from quantitative research, in which data collection and analysis must be pretty much complete before the theoretical implications begin to emerge.

Memos can be short or long, anywhere from a few sentences to a few pages. Most researchers identify on the memo exactly what parts of the field notes are referred to by the memo. This is theoretically important for such approaches as grounded theory because of their stance about the close link between raw data and abstract theory: All abstract ideas should be tied to specific parts of the data. In these approaches to qualitative data analysis, it is not adequate for researchers to report on general impressions from the data; this has low validity. Instead, memos should identify the lines in the field notes or other memos to which they relate so that there is a clear link between bits of data and abstract conclusions. The memos also should identify what codes or concepts they refer to and be dated so that it is clear when the thoughts occurred during the research process. Some of the memos, or at least parts of them, may later be incorporated into the final research report.

Beyond saying that memos are abstract and general, it is difficult to specify their content, because it is so highly variable. A memo might clarify an idea or an existing coding category, suggest some new coding categories or subcategories, or link data from different parts of the field notes or, possibly, even from other research projects. A memo might propose a hypothesis or a new pattern code, or it might identify something puzzling that does not fit in with the conceptual framework emerging in other memos. As the memoing process continues, what begins to emerge is a more formalized, coherent set of propositions or explanations of what is found in the data. (We discussed the development of propositions and theories at length in Chapter 2.) The propositions in qualitative data analysis emerge out of the data in an inductive process. In fact, some qualitative researchers eventually force themselves to state some tentative propositions that they can then review in light of all the memos, codes, and data to see if the propositions have any validity. In some cases, propositions may emerge early in the process of data analysis. Some propositions will eventually be discarded as they are shown to be inconsistent with much of the data, but at some point, a set of propositions emerges that seems to be consistent with all or most of the observations. Propositions can take a number of different forms such as:

When *A* happens, *B* is also found.
A causes *B* to occur.
A is found when *B*, *C*, and *D* exist.
A is found when *B* and *C* but not *D* occur.

In whatever form they take, however, the propositions are abstract explanations of phenomena. In qualitative research, these explanations are viewed as tentative; another sweep through the data by the same or different researchers could produce different coding, memoing, and proposition development. In addition, field observations of different groups or different locations could produce different outcomes. Figure 16.2 diagrams these categorizing strategies; the double arrows illustrate, once again, how interactive this process is. As the analysis proceeds, the researcher constantly goes back and forth among the memos, reflective remarks, and coding; in addition, he or she goes back and forth between these three elements and the data and conclusions.

As with notes, NVivo and other qualitative software programs allow researchers to insert memos within text, as well as audio or video documents. This feature is similar to the notes feature, but gives researchers more space to write. In the Native American parolee study, the researchers wrote several memos to summarize their emerging ideas pertaining to connections between participants' experiences. Ultimately, these memos served as a basis for developing new frameworks for understanding ex-offenders' reintegration experiences that built on social ecological theory.

Contextualizing Strategies

Qualitative researchers, in general, stress the importance of context and of viewing and analyzing data with an appreciation for the complete context in which the data were produced. The categorizing strategies that we have just discussed, however, tend, to a greater or a lesser degree, to move the researcher and the analysis away from the concrete data and toward more abstract categories and propositions. Some qualitative researchers argue that something is lost using this strategy (Maxwell, 2012; Phillipi & Lauderdale, 2018; Seidman, 2006). They argue for *contextualizing strategies:* approaches to data analysis that treat the data as a coherent whole and retain as much of the raw data as possible to capture the whole context. Contextualizing strategies are less concerned with abstracting from one set of data to generalize to other people or circumstances and are more interested in a deep, rich appreciation of the individuals from whom, or situations from which, the data were collected. In other words, these contextualizing strategies focus more on idiographic than on nomothetic explanations (see Chapter 2).

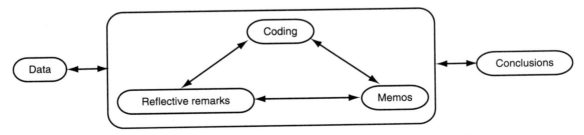

Figure 16.2 The data analysis process in some types of qualitative research.

One type of contextualizing strategy is the use of *profiles,* as promoted by Irving Seidman (2006). **Profiles** refer to vignettes of a person's experience, usually taken from in-depth interviews, that are stated largely in the person's own words, with relatively little interpretation or analysis by the researcher. Profiles are, fundamentally, narratives that tell a story. Telling stories is a key way for people to make sense of themselves and their world, and hearing others' stories is a valuable way to learn about those people's lives. Profiles are constructed by transcribing in-depth interviews and then identifying parts of the interviews that seem, to the researcher, to be especially important in telling the person's story. Then, the parts of the interview are put together into a preliminary profile. This profile is then reviewed with a critical eye to see if any passages are redundant or irrelevant and whether the passages are sequenced properly to tell the most-effective story. This review process continues until the researcher is satisfied with the profile. The final profile is mostly in the person's own words, although the researcher might include some comments to clarify or provide transitions. Any comments of the researcher should be clearly identified as such.

The researcher has to exercise considerable judgment about what to include in the story and how to sequence passages, and the possibility exists that some bias might enter into this selection process. Yet, Seidman (2006) argues that the researcher is in the best position to make these judgments. It is, after all, the researcher more than anyone who is most intimately familiar with the interviewee, the transcripts of the interview, and the literature on the topic. Certainly, the researcher might consult with those interviewed to see if they concur with the researcher's judgment, but ultimately, the researcher needs to be confident that his or her intuitive and professional judgments about how to shape the best profile are the right ones. The final step in developing a profile is analogous to the conceptualizing or theorizing of other researchers: The researcher spells out what he or she has learned from the whole process of collecting data, reviewing data, and developing the profile. Undoubtedly, some abstracting and conceptualizing are part of this conclusion, but it is probably grandiose to call it theory building.

As previously stated, Masters and Hilton used NVivo software to analyze audio recordings in their study of Native American parolees. One of the features of NVivo they found helpful was the ability to group and retrieve data in several different ways, including by cases. This software allows researchers to label various materials—from entire interview recordings, to interview segments, to notes and memos and any number of other documents—as belonging to a particular case. In this research, a case referred to an interview participant. Masters and Hilton were able to look at each case and the collection of materials assigned to that case when creating profiles for each participant. These profiles summarized demographic information and highlights from the interview, as well as notes and memos related to emerging ideas and themes.

An approach similar to profiling is **narrative analysis,** in which interviews, autobiographies, life histories, letters, and other personal materials are used to form a descriptive narrative of a person's life or circumstances (Clandinin & Connelly, 2000; Fina, Alexandra, & Gary, 2015; Merriam, 1998). As with the profile, this narrative tells a story and relies heavily on the person's own words as taken from their letters, autobiography, or other sources. Narrative analysis does not rely so heavily on interviews, however; it uses a broader range of data sources than profiles do.

A similar contextualizing strategy, but one that does not rely so heavily on the subject's own words, is the **case study:** a detailed, descriptive account of one individual, situation, organization, group, or other entity (Merriam, 1998; Patton, 2002). As with profiles, data analysis in case studies focuses on description and narrative rather than on categorizing strategies. Furthermore, the description in case studies is detailed and what sometimes is called "thick"—that is, a complete and literal accounting of the person or setting under study. Some quantitative data might be presented as part of a case study, but the emphasis is on telling a story in prose or narrative, although not completely in the words of the people being studied, as in the profile or narrative. The idea, however, is the same: The researcher describes people's lives and experiences in great detail.

In addition to the researcher's description, the case study might use quotations from those being studied, along with photos, videos, artifacts, and any other materials that help provide an in-depth description of the subject of the case study. Social work students who have to complete a process recording as part of their practice methods training find the case study method to be familiar, because the two methods have many features in common. By way of illustration, Katherine Tyson (1999) essentially used process recording from therapy with a 3-year-old boy in presenting a qualitative study demonstrating the effectiveness of an empowering approach to crisis intervention. Her presentation of the research interspersed quotations of interchanges between the therapist and child with analysis and discussion of the principles of the therapeutic approach.

Case studies can be based on direct observation, interviews, document analysis, organizational records, or some combination of these—basically, any data that would contribute to a description of the case under study. Historical research often focuses on a case study and might use a wide variety of materials as data, such as historical accounts, published newspapers and magazines, biographies, letters, government statistics, official records, and so on.

The primary goal of the case study and the other contextualizing strategies is an idiographic explanation that focuses on an in-depth understanding of this particular case. Such an understanding might enhance one's comprehension of other cases and situations, but the primary focus is description, not generalization. The advantage of profiles, narratives, and case studies is the rich and detailed descriptions they provide of people's lives, experiences, and circumstances. A disadvantage of these contextualizing strategies is that they depend heavily on the subjective and intuitive judgments of the researchers who are closest to the data. Another researcher producing a case study or profile of the same person or situation might come up with quite a different story. Yet another disadvantage is the limited ability to generalize beyond the individual case.

DISPLAYING DATA

A **data display** is an organized presentation of data that enables researchers and their audiences to draw some conclusions from that data and to move on to the next stage of the research (Miles & Huberman, 1994; Strauss, 1987; Verdinelli & Scagnoli, 2013). In any data analysis, the researcher must display the data so that a convincing argument can be made to support the conclusions drawn in the research. In science, we do not take the researcher's word in regard to conclusions; we need to be convinced by a display of the data. In quantitative data analysis, an important part of the display of data is the numbers, in the form of contingency tables, charts, or descriptive and inferential statistics (see Chapters 14 and 15). Some narrative is required to explain how the numbers were arrived at and to explain clearly their interpretation, but the core of the argument is the display of the numbers. In qualitative data analysis, however, the core of the argument is not numbers. Although the qualitative researcher may have some numbers to show, he or she uses different kinds of data displays. Creating data displays is very much a part of data analysis; creating the displays assists the researcher in identifying and clarifying the concepts and categories that are emerging from the coding and other strategies being used on the data.

Narrative Text

One key type of data display in qualitative research is the description, narrative, or verbal argument that is made by the researcher. In the contextualizing strategies, the narrative provides as full a description as possible to give an in-depth picture of the field, interview, or person that is the center of attention. The narrative attempts to be true to the meaning of the original experience—as interpreted by the researcher. The anthropologist Philippe Bourgois (1995), in his study of street drug dealers, points out "the impossibility of rendering into print the performance dimension of street speech. Without the complex, stylized punctuation provided by body language, facial expression, and intonation, many of the transcribed narratives of crack dealers appear flat, and sometimes even inarticulate" (p. 341). The challenge for Bourgois was to produce a narrative that conveyed the rich, detailed meanings that he perceived in the field setting based on all the linguistic and nonlinguistic cues available to him.

In the categorizing strategies, the researcher's narrative describes the concepts and propositions that emerged from the research, along with excerpts from the field notes or other data sources that illustrate these concepts and propositions and that corroborate the conclusions drawn (see Tables 16.1 and 16.2). In neither quantitative nor qualitative research do researchers report *all* the data, which would mean the raw data. A research report is always a summarization of the data, and it is ethically incumbent on the researcher to give an accurate summarization. For the qualitative researcher, this means that the illustrations presented to corroborate the conclusions are representative illustrations and not selective or distorted.

Visual Displays

Qualitative researchers also use a variety of visual formats to display data, just as quantitative researchers use contingency tables, graphs, and charts in their data analysis (Miles & Huberman, 1994; Patton, 2002; Strauss, 1987; Verdinelli & Scagnoli, 2013). These visual data displays are considered to be part of the data analysis, because the process of their development serves as an assist in conceptualization and theory development. By summarizing what is found in the data, these displays help clarify conceptual categories and give further insight concerning relationships between categories. They also enable the researcher to see weaknesses in the analysis and, thus, to suggest areas where additional data analysis is needed. Of course, visual data displays also are an effective adjunct to the narrative text in communicating results to a variety of audiences. Although these visual displays can take a variety of formats, there generally are two types. One is a figure that serves as a visual mapping of some physical or conceptual terrain. The second is a table, chart, or matrix into which some text, phrases, or other materials

are placed. Although the specific form that these visual displays can take is highly variable and dependent on the specific data and concepts, we can provide a few illustrations to offer a sense of their nature, function, and development.

One type of visual display is a **context map,** which describes in graphic form the physical or social setting that is the context of the observations. Qualitative researchers stress the centrality of the context in understanding people's behavior; they are fond of pointing out that everything must be contextualized or situated. Positivist, quantitative research, however, often collects and analyzes data without regard to the context. A survey researcher, for example, will collect data on a questionnaire without regard to whether those attitudes might be important, different, or possibly irrelevant *depending on the context in which the person is behaving.* Many nonpositivists refer to this as "decontextualized" data collection and analysis, and they argue that those attitudes only take on a life—that is, become important—in a particular context. Just as a percentage table informs the audience about some of the meaning in the data, a context map provides meaning to the data by describing the context in which the behaviors occurred.

In some cases, the context map is a drawing of the physical or geographic setting in which the observations are made. In Chapter 9, we suggested that each session of field observation might begin by drawing a map of the setting. This map might be a drawing of a room, building, street, or neighborhood, and it might include physical objects, entrances and exits, the locations of people or groups, and whatever else is relevant to understanding the social interaction described in the narrative. In other cases, the context map describes the social setting: the individuals, statuses, roles, groups, or organizations that are relevant to the observations; it would also show connections and relationships between these elements using lines and arrows. Some forms of this are called **sociograms** or **network analysis.** Figure 16.3 gives an example of what this might look like by showing the friendship choices made among a group of people. Network analysis may be the primary analytical approach used in a study, as was the case in a research project on the role that social networks

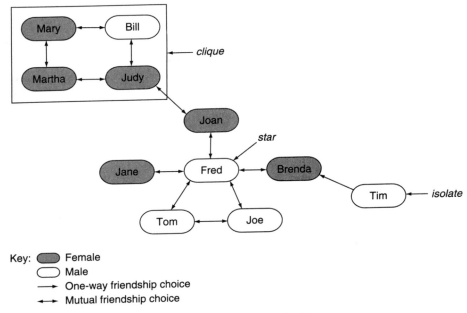

Figure 16.3 A sociogram as an example of a context map.

play in the daily survival of homeless Latino and African American men (Molina, 2000).

A common strategy for developing a sociogram is to conduct a sociometric interview with each member of a group. Each member is asked questions such as these:

- Whom of your group would you like to always be beside you during classes (or work or other relevant activity)?
- Whom do you think can get the group organized best of all?
- Whom of your group would you invite to a party at your home?
- Whom would you not invite?
- Whom do you work with if you have to but really do not like very much?

The visual representation that results helps us better see certain social phenomena such as particular patterns of relationships. Figure 16.3 provides evidence for certain social phenomena such as the clique (a group of people who all make mutual friendship choices) or the star (a person who is selected as a friend by a large number of people). Figure 16.3 is based on friendship or attraction

choices, but it could map other aspects of relationships, such as deference, submission, dominance, or giving and receiving help. As with other context maps, the specifics depend on the particular observational setting and the concepts that emerge from it.

Another type of visual display in qualitative research is called a **matrix display,** which looks very much like a contingency table with rows and columns. The difference is that, whereas the cells of a contingency table contain numbers or percentages, the cells of a matrix contain text, quotations, phrases, or symbols from the field notes or other sources of qualitative data. The rows in the matrix may represent the categories of a variable (as in contingency tables) or different concepts that emerged from the field notes or different points in time. The columns may also represent such a range of possibilities. Table 16.3 is a matrix used to analyze data in a study of homelessness in rural communities. The rows represent different strategies to secure shelter utilized by the homeless, whereas the columns represent different kinds of family circumstances of the homeless. Notice that the material in the cells is not an attempt to quantify how many people felt or acted a certain way but,

TABLE 16.3 Example of a Matrix Display: The Housing Strategies Utilized by Homeless People and Their Family Circumstances

Housing Strategy	Homeless Person's Family Circumstances	
	Unattached Adults	**Attached Adults w/ Children**
Camping	Freedom—"I can come and go as I please." Outdoor life—"August is the best month up here cause there's no bugs." Avoid societal sanctions—"I got a record, so this way I don't have to deal with them."	Fear of Child Protection Services—"The worker said, 'If you can't provide for your son, CPS will take him' So I was afraid to ask for help." Survival Parenting—"All we do is walk. A child needs a schedule, but we never know from one day to the next."
Shelter Living	Rigidity—"I'm a sex offender, so I can't stay anywhere near kids." Homeless label—"Nobody will hire you when they see you're living at the shelter." Occupying time—"They kick you out at 7:00 a.m. and don't let you in until 4:00 p.m. All I do is walk."	Stability—"At least we know where we're staying but my partner can't be here because we're not married." Homeless label helps—"When you have kids, they try to help you more. They put us at the top of the list to get a place." Safety—"Sometimes I'm more afraid of the other residents than being out in the woods."
Couch Hopping	Independence—"I'll stay with one friend for a while and any time I want I can just take off." Excitement—"We party a lot." Minimal space needs—"I just crash. I keep most of my stuff at a friend's place, so I don't need much." Network Rationing—"I share my food stamps, and I don't stay too long; don't want to wear out my welcome."	Dependence—"It makes you feel obligated, because it's a real burden on my mom. They don't have much themselves." Lack own space—"We had to sleep in the laundry room. Anytime she wanted to do wash, we had to be out of there." Network exhaustion—"My mom has a boyfriend and they have a life of their own. He doesn't want the little kids around."

Source: Constructed from the field notes of DeJong, C. R., & Hilton, T. P., from the research project "Homeless in God's Country."

rather, to give an overall assessment or judgment of each group's housing strategies and then some quotes from the field notes to support that judgment. In this study, for example, the matrix display suggests the very different considerations made by the attached adults with children when assessing housing strategies as compared with the unattached adults. Sometimes in matrix analysis, the rows might be each individual who was observed and the columns different categories from the data.

Thus, matrix displays are a good way to summarize data from the field notes. It is possible to summarize as many as 20 pages of field notes into one matrix, which makes this a much easier and more-effective way to communicate the results to an audience. Matrix displays also are used as an assist in the data analysis, because the researcher can review the matrix in an effort to detect patterns, themes, or trends, which may be difficult or impossible to detect by reading and rereading the field notes or other texts. This is analogous to what a quantitative data analyst would do in looking at a contingency table rather than the raw numerical data.

Beyond what we have said here, there are few fixed rules about creating matrices. It is a creative process, and the exact nature of the matrix is very much driven by the data. If, however, we begin qualitative data analysis thinking in terms of matrices, then it may be easier to discover in the data how possible matrices can be created.

CONCLUSIONS AND VERIFICATION

Data analysis involves discovering meaning in the data. In qualitative research, this means identifying themes, patterns, and regularities and, in some cases, stating propositions, causal connections, and developing theories. In this regard, qualitative research is identical to quantitative research; however, the differences between the two are important to emphasize. One difference is that drawing conclusions in qualitative research occurs, at least in part, during the process of data collection and analysis, whereas in quantitative research, this stage usually occurs after the data have been collected and analyzed (compare Figure 1.1 on page 12 and Figure 16.1). Second, most qualitative researchers hold their conclusions more tentatively, or "lightly," especially during early stages of the analysis, because they recognize that additional analysis could lead to reinterpretations or reconceptualizations of the data. As the analysis proceeds, however, conclusions become more complete and certain. Third, the conclusions in qualitative research are more grounded in the data, which means that the conclusions are more clearly allowed to flow out of the data rather than being imposed on that data by measurement devices created before the data were collected. In a grounded approach, the data analysis and conclusions are allowed to adapt to what is discovered in the data. Finally, in qualitative research, more than in quantitative research, the primary data-gathering instrument is the researcher herself or himself and that raises concerns about the many ways in which the instrument/observer may bias the observations. This also is a problem in quantitative research; we have discussed ways in which a researcher might build a bias into, for example, a question or a multiple-item scale used during survey research. When the observer is the data-gathering instrument, however, then his or her own personal values or biases can seriously compromise the collection of data and must be taken into account when assessing conclusions.

Qualitative researchers not only draw conclusions but also make efforts to verify those conclusions by finding evidence of their truth and validity. Are the conclusions reasonable and plausible? Without verification, one researcher's conclusions are simply his or her own account of what is going on. This verification is part of the overall argument that a researcher makes to convince himself or herself, along with any relevant audiences, that the conclusions are both reasonable and justified. In Chapter 5, we discussed some of the procedures used to assess validity in quantitative research, such as criterion and construct validity. In Chapter 9, we discussed ways to assess the validity of observations made in qualitative research. Here, we are discussing the validity of the data analysis and conclusions, but some of the points made about the observations also apply to the conclusions. Some additional points also can be made:

1. *Assess whether the conclusions are based on a thorough description and interpretation of the situation, including competing interpretations and explanations.* As soon as something resembling a pattern, generalization, or conclusion seems to be emerging from the data, researchers need to ask what rival explanations or conclusions are possible. This serves as a check against bias, misinterpretation, or laziness, and it will likely require additional passes through the data to see what evidence supports the rival explanations. It can be helpful to enlist other researchers in this process, because the researcher's own bias may prevent him or her from recognizing and clearly evaluating alternatives. If the conclusions are justifiable, then the rival explanations will find considerably less support in the data, thus providing more verification for the conclusions.

In the Native American parolee study, for example, one of the emerging findings was how eager most of the research participants were to get back to their reservations after prison. At first the researchers believed this was largely a function of their longing for home and cultural connection. One of the rival explanations they entertained, however, was that many parolees had nowhere else to go after leaving prison and believed they would be welcome to stay with friends, relatives and fellow tribal members on the reservation. In time the researchers found that both explanations had merit and applied to each case to varying degree.

2. *Consider negative evidence and deviant cases.* Although much data analysis is a search for evidence to support a theme or a conclusion, it is also important to search for evidence that does not support it. Especially in qualitative research, it can be easy to miss negative evidence because the researcher is so focused on developing evidence to support a conclusion. If possible, have other researchers go back to the raw data—namely, the field notes—to see if they can find any negative evidence. If they do not, then the researcher has fairly powerful support for the conclusions. A part of this is to search for *deviant cases* or *outliers*—that is, cases that do not follow the themes or patterns that are being discovered in the data. Deviant cases may be difficult to find, but the search for them is important and can be assisted by some of the data displays discussed in this chapter. It is important not only to discover the deviant cases but also to explain them. Can their deviation be understood within the context of the overall themes and propositions of the research? Explaining deviant cases may call for modification in the concepts and propositions or, in extreme cases, a total revamp of the theoretical approach.

One advantage that Masters and Hilton had was the ability to check one another's work with respect to coding and emerging findings. They spent a great deal of time on negative cases, situations that were outside of the normal pattern found in the data. In several cases, negative and deviant cases provided opportunities to look deeper into factors that help explain differences in cases. For example, there were a few cases where families were not as welcoming as most other families were of parolees. Looking deeply in these cases we saw

the nature of crimes for which parolees were sentenced and their connection to other family members can help explain this variation.

3. *Carefully assess the desires, values, and expectations of the person analyzing the data to see if these might bias the conclusions drawn.* People's perceptions are drastically shaped by their expectations—or lack of them. If we expect something to occur, then we are much more likely to observe it—whether it actually occurs or not. If we expect welfare recipients to be lazy, then we become acutely aware of all those entries in field notes that might be interpreted as laziness. Thus, the validity of conclusions is reduced to the extent that expectations—whether recognized or unrecognized—mold interpretations of data. On the other side of the coin, a lack of expectations may lead us to miss entirely something of importance in the data.

As previously explained, Masters was a member of one of the tribes that was being studied. He was also strongly connected to the tribe in many ways. At times he was concerned this may impact his ability to be objective when considering the importance of tribal communities to reentry. Having a research partner, Masters believed, forced him to strive for objectivity. Far from being a problem, Hilton believed the advantages of Masters' tribal affiliation in terms of accessing participants and understanding community contexts far outweighed any lost objectivity.

4. *Have other researchers analyze the data to see if they come to the same conclusion.* There are problems with this method, because these other researchers probably were not involved in collecting the data in the field. That experience of being in the field provides all kinds of information and insights, which may not appear in the raw data (the field notes). Nonetheless, if these other researchers do come to the same conclusions, then they provide validation that the conclusions are valid. Masters and Hilton each independently analyzed more than half the interviews and then compared their coding, notes, and memos pertaining to each case. After each case was compared for consistency across raters, they met to discuss differences, which were very minor overall. These meetings

resulted in discussions about codes and emerging themes that led to modifications to ensure greater consistencies.

5. *Compare the conclusions reached through field observations with the conclusions being reached through other research methodologies.* These other research methodologies include observational research in other settings or survey data, available data, or experimental research. This is a variation on criterion validity (discussed in Chapter 5). Sometimes, it is also called *triangulation,* that is, approaching the problem from a number of different directions. If various methodologies yield the same conclusions, then we have greater confidence that the field observations have validity. Field research whose conclusions are at wide variance with the results of other research should be accepted with caution, especially if none of the other checks on validity are available.

6. *Consider how the condition of the observer might influence both observations and conclusions.* Hunger, fatigue, stress, or personal problems can lead to distorted perceptions and interpretations. Likewise, physical characteristics, such as the lighting in an establishment, may lead to invalid observations. (This is another good reason for keeping complete field notes—field conditions affecting validity can be assessed at a later point.) If a number of these conditions exist, it may be judicious to terminate observation and then resume when conditions are more favorable.

7. *Look for behavior that is illegal, stigmatizing, or potentially embarrassing or that risks punishment.* If people engage in these kinds of behaviors when they know they are being observed, then they probably are acting naturally and not putting on a performance for the benefit of the observer.

Masters and Hilton believed it was very important for them to look for illegal or stigmatizing behavior in their research because that is a sign that the interviewee is being truthful and communicating his or her experiences openly. They found that for the most part participants were very forthright in sharing their experiences. Some admitted to staying with relatives and even tribal leaders,

even when this was not allowable because federal policy restricts who is allowed to stay in federally subsidized housing and excludes many ex-felons. One man described sex crimes they had committed prior to going to prison and the process of asking for forgiveness from victims. With Masters being a member of a tribe, the researchers believed that was likely a major factor in their candor during interviews.

8. *If possible, make a video or audio recording of the scene.* Although such recordings have their weaknesses as records of what occurred, they do provide another way for observers to check and validate their observations and conclusions. These recordings can also be reviewed by others, which offers further checks on possible bias or misinterpretation.

As stated earlier, Masters and Hilton made audio recordings of all interviews they conducted with research participants. This was important because it helped them avoid missing details or nuances of participants' descriptions and explanations.

9. *Assess the representativeness of the individuals, groups, informants, and observational sites.* Qualitative researchers do not typically use probability samples, but this does not absolve them from addressing the issue of how representative their observations are and how valid their generalizations are. (We already addressed this issue in Chapter 6 when talking about some types of nonprobability samples.) To generalize beyond the individuals, groups, or sites observed, we need to make a case that those individuals, groups, or sites are representative of other individuals, groups, or sites. We do this by showing that the characteristics of those observed are similar to the characteristics of other individuals, groups, or sites that were not observed. If we cannot make claims of representativeness, this does not completely invalidate the research, but it does throw into question any conclusion that we claim to be generalizable. Of course, with some qualitative methodologies, especially the contextualizing strategies, generalization may be of secondary importance in the research.

Masters and Hilton's research included just a small number of research participants, 15. They purposely included at least one member of five different tribes from the region. Given their topic, it was not possible for them to get a sampling frame and thus it is not possible to estimate with any certainty how representative this sample was of the larger population of Native American parolees who have reintegrated with tribal communities in Michigan's Upper Peninsula. Their main goal was not to make generalizations about this population as a whole. Rather, they were interested in developing an understanding of how families, services, and communities impact reintegration experiences. This sample was adequate for this purpose and allowed them to see several patterns with respect to the roles of families, human services, and communities.

10. *Evaluate whether the subjects of the research agree with or support the conclusions.* Who knows the field better than those whose field it is? Masters and Hilton were able to share the initial results of their research with members of Native American communities, including several research participants, in the region prior to publishing their research. This allowed Masters to assess the extent to which research participants and the community at large agreed with and supported the study conclusions. They were overwhelmingly supportive.

An important clarifying and validating step in qualitative research is to assess the reactions of those being observed to the conclusions. Do they agree with the themes, patterns, and propositions that form the conclusions? Depending on who is being observed, they may or may not understand the more abstract and theoretical parts of the conclusions, but many of the patterns and themes will be comprehensible to them, or possibly require only a little explanation. If they generally agree with the conclusions, then this provides additional evidence for the validity of those conclusions. If they disagree with some or all of the conclusions, then this can have two positive effects. One effect is to stimulate the researcher to consider changing or clarifying the conclusions to take into account the objections. Of course, it is possible that the researcher will conclude that no change or clarification is necessary. This can lead to the second positive effect—namely, explaining why the people disagree with the conclusions. In other words, their objections become further observations to be described and explained by the research. This may, in fact, provide more support for the conclusions.

As many of these guidelines as possible should be followed in verifying the conclusions that are drawn in qualitative data analysis. No single guideline, of course, is the key to having confidence in the conclusions; the key is that the more that are incorporated, the more confidence we can have.

Practitioner Profile 16.1 offers an example where human service professionals use a combination of qualitative and quantitative data to better understand service needs of homeless youth.

USING COMPUTERS IN QUALITATIVE RESEARCH

Most people are at least somewhat familiar with what computers do with quantitative data: They "crunch the numbers" by performing various statistical procedures on the numerical data. When the data take a more qualitative form, however, such as field notes, audio and video recordings, or the text of a magazine article, the manner in which computers analyze the data is less widely understood. As early as the 1960s, computer programs could perform some content analysis tasks, at least on text files. Since then, advances in computer hardware and software, artificial intelligence, and optical scanning technologies have expanded dramatically the kinds of tasks that computers can do in qualitative research (Bazeley, 2013; Fielding, 2002; Flick, 2009; Silver & Lewins, 2014). We have already touched on using qualitative software for analysis in discussing Masters' and Hilton's use of NVivo. We will not discuss specific software programs here but, rather, the general capabilities of what is now called **computer-assisted qualitative data analysis** (CAQDA).

There is no substitute for the creative insight of the researcher, but CAQDA software provides a wide array of tools to help the researcher organize the data, sift through it, identify concepts, and communicate the findings. Consider a qualitative study of eating disorders among people referred to an addiction treatment center. The data in this study might consist of open-ended interviews with the clients, client social histories and treatment plans, and chart logs taken from client records. There also might be videotapes of meetings where the staff discusses cases. Many of these "documents" would be in narrative form, but others could be photographs of the clients or video and audio recordings of interviews. CAQDA software permits the researcher to organize these diverse data sources into one project. Although it is common to convert most data into text files, some CAQDA programs enable the researcher to

---

PRACTITIONER PROFILE 16.1 Homeless Youth Bridge Program (Bridget Cannon— Director of Youth Services, Volunteers of America. Shawna Sampson—Homeless Services Operations Coordinator, Spokane Neighborhood Action Partners. Matt Davis, City of Spokane)

Bridget Cannon, director of youth services at Volunteers of America in Spokane, Washington, is not a researcher. In fact, she has little interest in research and has a distaste for evaluating data. Still, she sees research as critically important to her work with homeless youth. She explained,

> It can shine a light on what we do. For the past three to four years we have been tracking ACEs [Adverse Childhood Experience Study] scores amongst the youth we serve. Their scores are very high, in the 4.5 range on average [ACE scores are on 5-point scale with 5 being the most severe scores for exposure to childhood trauma.], and that is based on low self-reports. The youth are scared to tell us everything because they fear we'll call Child Protection Services and they don't want to get involved with them. But when we get to know them better we learn things about them, so we know they're underreporting. This data tracking helps drive us. It really points out that we all need to be trained in trauma-informed care because these kids have been through a lot. (Based on personal communication on May 7, 2018.)

It was Bridget's concern with homeless youth that led her to begin working with two other professionals in Spokane, Shawna Sampson, an MSW and homeless services operations coordinator at Spokane Neighborhood Action Partners, and Matt Davis, a homeless program specialist with the City of Spokane's Community, Housing and Human Services Department who has a background in data collection and analysis. As Sampson explained, "In this community, you work together. You really have to work together if you're going to get something done."

Cannon, Sampson, and Davis explained they came together to address an important unmet need in the community, temporary housing for homeless youth age 18 to 24. As Sampson stated,

> We've used data, both quantitative and qualitative, to identify gaps in our community. The City does a great job looking at data to see holes in our services and then we all work together to understand them and then fill them.

Cannon provides important context for the unique needs of these youth.

> These youth may age out of the under 18 shelters, but they're not then going to go to the adult shelters, at least most of them. For 18-year-olds these places are scary. They just don't want to be there. They don't see their peers there.

(continued)

Davis explains the situation with quantitative data.

> They are not utilizing adult shelters at the rate you would expect given their numbers. They are just not going to shelters for adults. We see this data and it is pretty obvious to us that they don't wake up on their eighteenth birthdays and suddenly have different needs. So they're not going to go get services at a place that does not do a lot to address those needs. We also know they continue to access some services from the youth agencies and continue to speak with their staff about their needs and where they're staying

Cannon stated, "Many of them feel safer under the bridge or camping in a group."
All three explained that attending to the unique needs of young adults is a new idea in human services and funders are just catching on to the need for separate sets of services for this group.

> We are lucky that in Washington we have some fairly new funding set aside to serve this population and I think we're going to see more and more services for this group. This is about preventing the new homeless from becoming the chronically homeless

Sampson explained,

> The group worked together and submitted a proposal for a transitional housing program for young adults. When they received funding they found there were not sufficient housing units available among the human services agencies in the area to meet the needs of homeless youth. They then designed a housing placement and rental assistance program, but were faced with two challenges. One, it was difficult finding rental units available for young adults with poor credit. Two, many youth were dropping out of the program before securing permanent housing.

Reflecting on their experiences and program data and looking at the available resources, the group decided to try something new. As Sampson explained,

> Our ideas evolved over time, but ultimately our data pointed to the need for more flexible housing, where youth can come and stay for short periods of time, but are not necessarily required to have a long-term lease. We were considering a 'bridge housing' model that was really a combination of housing placement services and rental assistance mixed with a transitional shelter.

A new rule pertaining to use of housing services funding, Davis explained, had given service systems new flexibility in creating hybrid programs like the "bridge model" Sampson had described.
Currently, Cannon explained, Volunteers of America is working to identify apartment units to serve as bridge housing units. The very tight housing market in Spokane is a challenge, but the group has found some units they believe may work. The group has high hopes the current model will work well. Cannon explained,

> It has taken some time to get to this point and it is constantly evolving because there are many moving parts, but we're feeling good about it and continuing to talk with each other and examine data to see what's working.

work directly with image and audio files. This has the advantage of saving time in comparison to conversion to text; but in addition, working directly with the audio or video recordings preserves the richness of the data, including such things as voice inflection and facial expression that might be lost in the transcription process.

Coding and Retrieving Data

At a very elementary level, computer software can provide counts of how often particular words or phrases appear in a text or in field notes as well as indicate which words and phrases tend to appear together or near one another in the text. Most qualitative data analyses, however, go far beyond this. A more important use for CAQDA software is to assist the researcher in creating and using a coding scheme and in coding the qualitative data. When working with data as text files, the researcher displays the text on the screen and selects a portion of interest. In some software, this is done by blocking the section of text on the screen in much the same way that you block a section of text in a word processor to copy or cut it. Other software automatically divides the text into sections based on lines, sentences, or paragraphs, and the researcher then places a marker at the beginning or end of the section to code. For example, a section of text describing the way in which a mother disapproved of her daughter's behavior could be selected and marked with a code for "Mother disapproval of daughter behavior." Then, the CAQDA software could search through the text, identifying and counting the number of times that various codes appear in the field notes. Advanced software also can analyze whether certain words, phrases, or codes tend to be used together, how far apart from one another they tend to be, whether words or codes in a text tend to be positively or negatively evaluated, and whether certain words or codes tend to be associated with certain other words or codes (Kelle, 2004; Seale, 2010; Silver & Lewins, 2014). Audio or video data coding follows a similar pattern. The recording may be displayed as a line across the screen. As the researcher listens to or watches the video, key sections of the recording are identified, and the researcher designates one or more codes for that segment of the recording. The researcher can also append notes or memos linked to the recording segment. As the researcher progresses through the various data sources, new code designations may be created and organized.

One of the advantages of this computerized system is that the researcher can quickly locate and pull together all the data elements, whether official records, interview notes, or audio recordings where a particular code was applied. In this hypothetical study, we begin by locating all cases that contain the codes "Mother pressured" or "Father pressured." This process is similar to conducting a computerized literature search by entering combinations of key words. Using these codes joined by the key term "OR," we can identify a subset of all cases where parental pressure was indicated and then save that group of files for further analysis. Having selected a subset of cases based on one or more codes, the program can produce a report with whatever information the researcher wishes: the individual's name, the name given to various codes, the frequency of use of various codes, and which source material the data were taken from. Conversely, for the coding category "Mother pressured," the researcher can quickly review all locations in the data where that code was applied. This aids the researcher in honing and revising the concepts as they emerge from the data.

Most CAQDA software programs store the codes for a given case in a special file, sometimes called an "index card." After coding the material for one case, the index card file contains all the codes that the researcher used for all the materials pertaining to that individual. Thus, the computer program follows a logical procedure much like the traditional practice of manually preparing note cards for cross-referencing cases. To help with coding, the program provides a code list containing all the codes used thus far for all the cases in the study. Some programs also can "autocode," which means to give the same code to all identical words or phrases in a document. For example, if one data source for the eating disorder study were case intake forms that are stored as text files, the researcher can import these files into the CAQDA software program, which can then automatically apply the heading sections of the form as coding categories. In addition, we can store information about each case or individual in the study, such as age, gender, or whatever else is available in the data, and the software allows us to give more than one code to a given segment of text. We can revise the coding scheme in a variety of ways as well. For example, we can create different levels of codes. If a number of codes all share something in common, then we can group them under a higher-level or more-abstract code. The program retains all levels of coding, and the data can be retrieved using any level of code. Or, we can go the opposite way: A single coding category can be elaborated into a series of more-specific or concrete categories.

Data Analysis and Hypothesis Testing

Some content analysis software can test hypotheses by performing searches for all cases containing particular combinations of codes. Suppose our hypothesis is that "mothers who are critical of their daughter's body image have a negative effect on their daughter's self-image." The software could search for all cases that include the codes "Mother critical of daughter's body image," "Mother–daughter relationship strained," and "Daughter experiencing weight loss." To each of those cases, it then adds the code "Mother negative influence on daughter self-image," indicating that these cases confirm the hypothesis. Only cases meeting all three conditions have the new code added to their files. In a similar way, we can construct codes for other combinations of interest.

Some content analysis software can perform statistical analyses regarding the frequency of occurrence of various codes and display the data using some of the graphs and matrices discussed in this chapter. Some software also can import data from and export data to statistical programs and spreadsheets. In addition, beyond merely automating content analysis procedures, some programs provide important advances in the validation, reliability, and generalizability of qualitative data analysis. For example, an independent researcher can code the same data with the codes already developed and stored and, thus, determine inter-rater reliability. To assess validity, an independent researcher might code the same material blindly—that is, without benefit of the existing coding scheme—to determine if the second coder develops the same or similar meanings as the first coder.

Conceptualization and Theory Building

Some CAQDA software is designed to assist in the tasks of conceptualization and theory building (Cope, 2014; Fielding, 2002). Of course, the software does not actually create coding schemes or build theories, but it can provide the researcher with some assistance in these tasks by showing links in the data between concepts, coding categories, and observations that he or she might not have observed without such assistance. In fact, this type of CAQDA software has been used heavily by some proponents of grounded theory methodology, because the software assists in going back and forth from data to concepts, a key feature of grounded theory.

One way the software supports theory building is by providing opportunities for the process of memoing (discussed earlier in this chapter): Researchers can write their own comments, and the software will link those comments/memos to sections of identified text. The memos can be stored separately from the field notes or inserted as annotations directly into the field notes or other text. Annotations to field notes are identified as such by the software, and the annotations themselves can be coded. As explained earlier in this chapter, these memos and annotations are expressions of conceptual and theoretical ideas, and the software assists in this process by enabling the researcher to build a conceptual scheme and theory that gradually provides a more-abstract understanding of the data while still remaining closely linked to the data. Also, by being able to code these memos, the researcher is helped with noticing linkages that might have escaped his or her attention otherwise. Some software also provides maps that provide a visual representation of links between concepts and other concepts and between concepts and data. This visual picture can be of substantial assistance in theory building:

> Maps may help the analyst picture the project's theoretical shape, the concepts in use, the relationships between those concepts, and the ethnographic data that have been collected regarding each of those concepts and links. Theory-building software facilitates experiments with different concepts and links within the research process (Dohan & Sánchez-Jankowski, 1998, p. 490).

REVIEW AND CRITICALTHINKING

Main Points

- Qualitative data analysis focuses on extracting meaning from nonnumerical data without transforming those data into numbers. Though nonpositivist paradigms have been receptive to qualitative approaches, a one-to-one link does not exist between a particular paradigm and a tendency to use qualitative rather than quantitative research.
- In qualitative research, the stages of data collection, data analysis, and drawing conclusions tend to overlap. One of the advantages of this overlap is greater theoretical sensitivity. Qualitative research pursues goals of description, explanation, and evaluation as well as attempts to abstract and generalize; it also seeks to contextualize the analysis.
- Qualitative data analysis can pursue a categorizing strategy or a contextualizing strategy. One approach to the former is to code the data. One approach to coding is to create a fairly complete and detailed coding scheme before gathering data; other approaches let the coding scheme emerge as the data are collected and analyzed.
- Specific types of coding can focus on the concrete versus the abstract or on open versus more-focused coding. Coding schemes should have clear operational definitions and should be tested for reliability.
- Reflective remarks and memos can assist in coding, conceptualization, and theory building. Contextualizing strategies include profiles, narrative analysis, and case studies. Their primary goal is idiographic—that is, to understand a particular case rather than to generalize from other cases.
- Data displays are important in helping the researcher in developing coding schemes and conceptual categories as well as in communicating his or her conclusions to audiences. Data displays come in the form of narrative texts and visual displays, such as context maps and matrix displays.
- Qualitative data analysis produces conclusions that must be verified. A variety of guidelines are applied to assess the validity of conclusions, and confidence in the conclusions increases as more of the guidelines are satisfied.
- Qualitative data analysis often is accomplished with computers, which can assist in coding and retrieving data, analyzing data, testing hypotheses, and engaging in memoing and other strategies that help in conceptualization and theory building.

IMPORTANT TERMS FOR REVIEW

Case study	Contextualizing strategies	Profiles
Categorizing strategies	Data display	Reflective remarks
Coding	Matrix display	Sociograms
Computer-assisted qualitative data analysis	Memos	Theoretical sensitivity
	Narrative analysis	
Context map	Network analysis	

CRITICAL THINKING

1. How can researchers and practitioners conduct qualitative analysis in a way that helps ensure findings are both valid and reliable? Think about a practice situation that involves qualitative assessment. What can professionals do to help ensure their qualitative assessments are consistent and accurately reflect clients and their environments?
2. What parallels exist between qualitative analysis and professional human services practice? In what ways is qualitative data analysis similar to client assessments and in what ways is it different? What can practitioners learn from qualitative researchers that they might apply in practice?
3. What unique insights can be obtained through qualitative analysis that may be difficult to obtain through quantitative analysis? Think about a situation where a practitioner is assessing a client? What can the practitioner learn from quantitative assessments (e.g., using an assessment scale) that might be difficult to evaluate qualitatively? What can the practitioner learn from qualitative assessments that would be challenging to learn from a quantitative assessment?

EVALUATING COMPETENCY (FROM THE COUNCIL ON SOCIAL WORK EDUCATION [CSWE] 2015 EDUCATIONAL POLICY AND ACCREDITATION STANDARDS [EPAS])

Competency 1: Demonstrate Professional and Ethical Behavior

• Both qualitative research and qualitative assessment require professionals to make judgments about the quality or nature of a person, context, or other phenomena. Describe a situation where you may be required to make such a judgment. Do you believe there would ever be pressures or incentives to make an inaccurate judgment? If so, how might you avoid this temptation?
• What ethical principles are relevant in this situation? Is there an ethical dilemma? If so, describe the ethical decision-making process you would use in resolving this dilemma. What principles would you consider? What outcomes would you anticipate are associated with the various choices? With whom would you consult in making this decision?

Competency 2: Engage Diversity and Difference in Practice

• Qualitative research is particularly useful when researchers and practitioners do not begin with hypotheses of what they expect to find and when their goals are to understand how others view and experience a situation. How might this approach be applicable when working with diverse populations?

- Both researchers and human services professionals see themselves as lifelong learners. How can qualitative analysis contribute to new learning?

Competency 4: Engage in Practice-Informed Research and Research-Informed Practice

- Social workers are called on to use critical thinking when interpreting research findings, whether quantitative or qualitative. What critical questions should social workers ask when interpreting qualitative research studies (with respect to study design, data collection, measurement, and analysis)?
- There is often a preference for quantitative as opposed to qualitative evidence when designing new programs or services. How might qualitative research be helpful when designing new programs or services?

Competency 7: Assess Individuals, Families, Groups, Organizations, and Communities

- Given the number of valid and reliable quantitative assessments tools, why is qualitative assessment still important to social work practice?
- Imagine you met a client within a mental health clinic for the first time and had to describe her qualitatively. She came to the clinic because she says she feels extremely anxious meeting new people. What approach would you take to your assessment? What types of questions would you ask? What other information would you gather and how would you record it?
- Do you believe that another social worker meeting this client would have a similar assessment? How might you go about ensuring your assessment was reliable?

SELF-ASSESSMENT
· ·

1. Which of these strategies refers to attempts to generalize and abstract by generating concepts and theories from raw data?
   a. Contextualizing strategies
   b. Grounded strategies
   c. Categorizing strategies
   d. Rationalizing strategies
2. Coding refers to:
   a. Categorizing observations into a limited number of categories.
   b. Categorizing observations into an infinite number of categories.
   c. Categorizing observations into a Likert scale format.
   d. Describing but not categorizing observations.
3. Which of the following statements is true?
   a. Descriptive codes involve directly observed behaviors or events and interpretative codes require deep understanding of context for categorization.

    b. Descriptive codes require deep understanding of context for categorization and interpretative codes involve directly observed behaviors or events.

    c. Descriptive and interpretative codes both require researchers to have a deep understanding of social context to interpret meaning and categorize events.

    d. Neither descriptive nor interpretative coding allow researchers to categorize events or situations that involve human behavior.

4. Which of these terms refers to the initial coding of qualitative data that involves unrestricted coding to produce concepts and dimensions that seem to fit the data well?

    a. Focused coding

    b. Latent coding

    c. Manifest coding

    d. Open coding

5. Reflections, interpretations, connections, or other thoughts that occur to the researcher while transcribing field notes or coding the data are known as:

    a. Reflexology.

    b. Inductive remarks.

    c. Memos.

    d. Reflective remarks.

6. In qualitative research, memos are:

    a. Researchers' initial drafts of research articles.

    b. Researchers' initial coding schemes.

    c. Notes between researchers about disagreements in coding.

    d. Researchers' attempt at theorizing and writing down ideas about the meanings of codes and the relationships between various codes.

7. Approaches to data analysis that treat the data as a coherent whole and retain as much of the raw data as possible are known as:

    a. Case studies.

    b. Coding strategies.

    c. Narrative strategies.

    d. Contextualizing strategies.

8. A case study is:

    a. A detailed, descriptive account of one individual, situation, organization, group, or other entity.

    b. A particularly unique person that raises questions about the validity of existing coding schemes.

    c. A group of cases that seem to be associated with one another.

    d. A finding that is of unique theoretical value.

9. An organized presentation of data that enables researchers and their audiences to draw some conclusions from that data and move on to the next stage of research is known as:

    a. A context map.

    b. A sociogram.

    c. A data display.

    d. A qualitative table.

10. Which of the following statements is true about computer-assisted qualitative data analysis (CAQDA)?
   a. CAQDA is useful because it replaces the need for creative insight on the part of researchers.
   b. CAQDA is helpful for coding, but cannot be used for data analysis or hypothesis testing.
   c. CAQDA is a tool used by researchers in coding, data analysis, hypothesis testing, and theory building stages of research.
   d. CAQDA is used by some researchers but makes data coding and analysis longer and less intuitive.

ANSWER KEY FOR SELF-ASSESSMENT QUIZ

1. **c.** Categorizing strategies
2. **a.** Categorizing observations into a limited number of categories
3. **a.** Descriptive codes involve directly observed behaviors or events and interpretative codes require deep understanding of context for categorization.
4. **d.** Open coding
5. **d.** Reflective remarks
6. **d.** Researchers' attempt at theorizing and writing down ideas about the meanings of codes and the relationships between various codes.
7. **d.** Contextualizing strategies.
8. **a.** A detailed, descriptive account of one individual, situation, organization, group or other entity.
9. **c.** A data display
10. **c.** CAQDA is tool used by researchers in coding, data analysis, hypothesis testing, and theory building stages of research.

FOR FURTHER READING

Bazeley, P. (2013). *Qualitative data analysis with NVivo* (2nd ed.). Thousand Oaks, CA: Sage. This book provides a good overview of how CAQDA is done and focuses on how to use one fairly popular CAQDA software package.

Corbin, J., & Strauss, A. (2008). *Basics of qualitative research: Techniques and procedures for developing grounded theory* (3rd ed.). Thousand Oaks, CA: Sage. This book offers a complete introduction to the data-analysis techniques developed to support the grounded theory approach. It is both readable and practical.

Fielding, N. G., & Lee, R. M. (1998). *Computer analysis and qualitative research.* Thousand Oaks, CA: Sage. This book focuses on the ways that computers can be used in qualitative data collection and analysis, including discussions of available software and how qualitative research might change to adapt to computer capabilities.

Flick, U. (2009). *An introduction to qualitative research* (4th ed.). Thousand Oaks, CA: Sage. This book covers all aspects of qualitative research, including how to analyze data and how to present the data visually.

Merriam, S. B. (Ed.). (2002). *Qualitative research in practice: Examples for discussion and analysis.* San Francisco, CA: Jossey-Bass. Qualitative research has been popular in human service fields, such as education, for decades, and this book gives a good introduction on how to collect and analyze qualitative data in such practice settings.

Richards, L., & Morse, J. M. (2012). *README FIRST for a user's guide to qualitative methods* (3rd ed.). Thousand Oaks, CA: Sage. This provides a general overview of qualitative methods, but it also focuses on issues of data analysis.

Rossman, G. B., & Rallis, S. F. (2012). *Learning in the field: An introduction to qualitative research* (3rd ed.). Thousand Oaks, CA: Sage. These authors describe the complexity of doing field research while still making the basic data-analysis tools accessible to the student.

Sandelowski, M., & Barroso, J. (2007). *Handbook for synthesizing qualitative research.* New York, NY: Springer Publishing. Evidence-based practice often relies on synthesizing data from randomized controlled trials, but these authors argue that such synthesis can also be done with qualitative studies. The authors identify ways to optimize the validity of qualitative research synthesis studies and ways to present the results of qualitative research synthesis studies in effective, audience-appropriate ways.

REFERENCES

Bazeley, P. (2013). *Qualitative data analysis with NVivo* (2nd ed.). Thousand Oaks, CA: Sage.

Bogdan, R. C., & Biklen, S. K. (1992). *Qualitative research for education: An introduction to theory and methods* (2nd ed.). Boston, MA: Allyn & Bacon.

Bourgois, P. (1995). *In search of respect: Selling crack in El Barrio.* Cambridge, UK: Cambridge University Press.

Braun, V., & Clarke, V. (2012). Thematic analysis. In H. Cooper, P. M. Camic, D. L. Long, A. T. Panter, D. Rindskopf, & K. J. Sher (Eds.), *APA handbook of research methods in psychology, Vol. 2. Research designs: Quantitative, qualitative, neuropsychological, and biological* (pp. 57–71). Washington, DC: American Psychological Association.

Charmaz, K. (1988). The grounded theory method: An explication and interpretation. In R. M. Emerson (Ed.), *Contemporary field research: A collection of readings* (pp. 109–126). Prospect Heights, IL: Waveland Press. (Original work published 1983).

Charmaz, K. (2006). *Constructing grounded theory: A practical guide through qualitative analysis.* Thousand Oaks, CA: Sage.

Clandinin, D. J., & Connelly, F. M. (2000). *Narrative inquiry: Experience and story in qualitative research.* San Francisco, CA: Jossey-Bass.

Cope, D. (2014). Computer-assisted qualitative data analysis software. *Oncology Nursing Forum, 41*(3), 322–323. doi:10.1188/14.onf.322-323

Dohan, D., & Sánchez-Jankowski, M. (1998). Using computers to analyze ethnographic field data: Theoretical and practical considerations. *Annual Review of Sociology, 24*(1), 477–516. doi:10.1146/annurev.soc.24.1.477

Fielding, N. G. (2002). Automating the ineffable: Qualitative software and the meaning of qualitative research. In T. May (Ed.), *Qualitative research in action* (pp. 161–178). Thousand Oaks, CA: Sage.

Fina, A., Alexandra, G., & Gary, B. (2015). *The handbook of narrative analysis (Blackwell handbooks in linguistics).* Malden, MA: Wiley Blackwell.

Flick, U. (2009). *An introduction to qualitative research* (4th ed.). Thousand Oaks, CA: Sage.

Glaser, B. (1978). *Theoretical sensitivity.* Mill Valley, CA: Sociology Press.

Hilton, T., & DeJong, C. (2010). Homeless in God's country: Coping behaviors and felt experiences of the rural homeless. *Journal of Qualitative and Ethnographic Research, 5*(1), 12–30.

Kelle, U. (2004). Computer-assisted analysis of qualitative data. In U. Flick, E. von Kardorff, & I. Steinke (Eds.), *A companion to qualitative research* (B. Jenner, Trans., pp. 276–283). Thousand Oaks, CA: Sage.

Lofland, J., Snow, D., Anderson, L., & Lofland, L. H. (2006). *Analyzing social settings* (4th ed.). Belmont, CA: Wadsworth/Cengage.

Masters, J., & Hilton, T. (2014). Return to the rez: Native American parolees' transitions to community life. In S. Bowan (Ed.), *Critical perspectives on race, ethnicity and the prison system* (pp. 451–478). Santa Barbara, CA: ABC Clio.

Maxwell, J. A. (2012). *Qualitative research design: An interactive approach* (3rd ed.). Thousand Oaks, CA: Sage.

Merriam, S. B. (1998). *Qualitative research and case study applications in education.* San Francisco, CA: Jossey-Bass.

Miles, M. B., & Huberman, A. M. (1994). *Qualitative data analysis: An expanded sourcebook* (2nd ed.). Thousand Oaks, CA: Sage.

Molina, E. (2000). Informal non-kin networks among homeless Latino and African-American men: Form and functions. *American Behavioral Scientist, 43*(4), 663–685. doi:10.1177/00027640021955487

Nabors, L. A., Reynolds, M. W., & Weist, M. D. (2000). Qualitative evaluation of a high school mental health program. *Journal of Youth and Adolescence, 29*(1), 1–13. doi:10.1023/a:1005129403974

Patton, M. Q. (2002). *Qualitative research and evaluation methods* (3rd ed.). Thousand Oaks, CA: Sage.

Phillipi, J., & Lauderdale, J. (2018). A guide to field notes for qualitative research: Context and conversation. *Qualitative Health Research, 28*(3), 381–388. doi:10.1177/1049732317697102

Seale, C. (2010). Using computers to analyze qualitative data. In D. Silverman (Ed.), *Doing qualitative research* (3rd ed.). Thousand Oaks, CA: Sage.

Seidman, I. E. (2006). *Interviewing as qualitative research* (3rd ed.). New York, NY: Teachers College Press.

Silver, C., & Lewins, A. (2014). *Using software in qualitative research: A step-by-step guide* (2nd ed.). Los Angeles, CA: Sage.

Smith, P. R. (1998). How do we understand practice? A qualitative approach. *Families in Society: The Journal of Contemporary Human Services, 79*(5), 543–550. doi:10.1606/1044-3894.720

Strauss, A. L. (1987). *Qualitative analysis for social scientists.* Cambridge, UK: Cambridge University Press.

Trella, D., & Hilton, T. (2014). They can only do so much: Use of family while coping with rural homelessness. *Contemporary Rural Social Work Journal, 6*(1), 16–39.

Tyson, K. (1999). An empowering approach to crisis intervention and brief treatment for preschool children. *Families in Society, 80*(1), 64–77. doi:10.1606/1044-3894.640

Verdinelli, S., & Scagnoli, N. I. (2013). Data display in qualitative research. *International Journal of Qualitative Methods, 12*(1), 359–381. doi:10.1177/160940691301200117

17

WRITING FOR RESEARCH: GRANT PROPOSALS AND REPORT WRITING

INTRODUCTION

Richard is a social worker at a community-based organization in a medium-sized city in the Midwest. He has been at the organization for many years. Richard started as a Master of Social Work intern and was then hired as a caseworker within the agency's adult basic education (ABE) program after graduation. Three years ago he was promoted to director of the program. Recently, the ABE program has been under scrutiny by a very vocal member of the agency's board of directors. Richard was surprised to hear that the program was "in the cross hairs" of some of the board members. The program, Richard believes, is well-regarded by clients and the community at large. It is also financially sound because of state, federal, and local foundation funding that has been relatively stable in recent years.

The executive director of the agency met with Richard to explain the board members' concerns. "Some of the people on the board want the agency to fade out direct services for adults to focus more on children." One of the board members even suggested that adult education and training programs are a waste of money because many of the adults in the community are "too far gone" and a "bad investment." Focusing on the children, he believes, is a "better bet" and more likely to produce a "high return on investment," she stated. The executive director explained that she did not share the board members' sentiments, but worries that others may have found his argument persuasive. She suggested that it may be beneficial to do some research to examine the value of the program to clients, families, and the community-at-large. She also suggested partnering with faculty researchers from a nearby university because of their ability to provide an objective perspective. "Having good data is pretty powerful," she suggested.

While Richard was very discouraged by the summary of the recent board meeting, he was happy to hear his boss supported his program and somewhat encouraged by her advice to have a study conducted on the value of the program. Now he wondered how to get it done? He does not have money in his program budget to support such a study and does not expect faculty at the university would conduct the research without at least some financial support. Is there anyone who would support such a study? Would he need to write a proposal to request money? This chapter focuses on two important elements of applied research that often are neglected in introductory texts on research methods—namely, the role of grants in research and human service practice and the importance of good writing. Throughout the chapter we will revisit Richard's situation and discuss his work creating a research grant proposal and eventually writing a research report. As you read, please consider the following critical thinking questions: (a) When might a human services agency (or staff within a human services agency) become involved in a grant-funded research project? and (b) What roles could (and should) human services professionals who are not research specialists take in creating, submitting, and completing a funded research project?.

The term **grant** refers to the provision of money or other resources to be used for research or service delivery. Grants are an important funding source for social research and the provision of human services. In fact, the amount of grant monies awarded each year is truly staggering. Among the agencies of the federal government that dispense funds, the Department of Education awarded approximately $8.9 billion in 2017 and the U.S. Department of Health and Human Services' research, demonstration, and evaluation budget (RD&E) for 2017 totaled almost $2.3 billion (Yamaner, 2017). The National Institute of Justice awarded approximately $45 million for research (Congressional Research Service, 2017). Private foundations give out grants worth well over $1 billion each year for projects in the social sciences and human services (U.S. Census Bureau, 2011). Given the large role that grants play in funding research, demonstration projects, and some activities of nonprofit human service organizations, it is highly likely that most future human service practitioners will be directly involved in grant-funded projects during their careers.

Despite the pervasiveness of grants, preparing a grant proposal without previous experience can feel overwhelming. Grant writing sometimes is perceived as a mystical process, with strange jargons and convoluted procedures through which only seasoned professionals having the right connections succeed in receiving funds. Grants, however, range from complex, multimillion-dollar undertakings to fairly modest projects for small agencies. Some universities offer small research grants specifically for undergraduate student research. So, preparing a successful funding proposal is an attainable goal even for the beginning human service professional. A neophyte understandably has many questions: What do I do first? Whom do I contact? What do they want to know? Although the prospect of writing the first grant proposal can be daunting, preparing a fundable proposal involves many of the principles of sound practice and research that are part of professional education. If approached systematically, writing grant proposals can be an interesting challenge rather than something to be feared.

In this chapter, we can neither explore all aspects of grantsmanship nor go into much detail. Instead, we will focus on obtaining grants for agency functions, including both service delivery and research purposes. In fact, grants for service delivery typically include a call for needs assessment data and an evaluation of the service delivery; therefore, many grants combine practice and research activities. Depending on the demands of the funding source, minor differences may arise between preparing a proposal for a research project, service delivery, or a combination of the two. Those who are serious about seeking grants should consult the listings in *For Further Reading* at the end of this chapter.

THE GRANT-FUNDING PROCESS

Sources of grant money fall into three general categories: governmental agencies, private foundations, and corporations (Bauer, 2011; Gitlin & Lyons, 2014). Of these, government agencies are by far the largest source of grant monies; they also are about the only sources of grants for more than a few thousand dollars. Even in the case of smaller grants, it often pays to start first with governmental sources, because many of the private foundations refuse funding automatically unless the researcher can prove that efforts to obtain governmental funding have failed. Among governmental agencies, branches of the federal government are the largest source for grant money.

Federal Government Funding Sources

The federal government maintains a website called Assistance Listings, which recently replaced the *Catalog of Federal Domestic Assistance*. The website (https://beta.sam.gov) identifies several types of financial assistance provided by the federal government. One of the most important types of federal support is the *project grant* or *categorical grant* (the terms are synonymous). **Project grants** or **categorical grants** provide funding, for fixed or known periods of time, to specific projects, including research grants, training grants, experimental and demonstration grants, evaluation grants, and planning grants, among others. Grant seekers design approaches, within specified guidelines provided by the governmental agency, to meet the need or ameliorate the problem specified by the government agency. The agencies make their requests for programs or research opportunities known through what is called a **Request for Proposals** (RFPs): a formal request for people or agencies to submit proposals on how they would conduct some research or establish and run some program. Agencies or researchers then submit proposals in a competition to obtain the grant money. Because these grants are awarded selectively, on a competitive basis, to those submitting the best proposals within the guidelines established by the granting agency, they also are known as **discretionary grants.**

Another type of grant generally is dispensed to all eligible units. A **formula grant** is an allocation of federal money to states or their subdivisions, in accordance with distribution formulas prescribed by law or administrative regulations, for activities of a continuing nature not confined to a specific project. For example, at times of high unemployment, the federal government commonly sponsors various job-creating activities through formula grants. Because various places in the country experience unemployment in varying levels of severity, the money is allocated by a "formula" (hence the name) that provides most of the funds to those areas hardest hit and prorates the remaining funds to other areas as needed. Normally, formula grants are channeled through state and local governments until they reach the agency level. This allows each state and locality to tailor its approach to the problems of its particular situation. For example, unemployment may be concentrated among displaced factory workers in one locale and among minority teenagers in another. The most effective approach in the first locale may be retraining programs, but the second locale may benefit more from providing adult basic education to young adults.

The term *block grant* sometimes is used interchangeably with *formula grant,* but it generally refers to a package of funding that is created by consolidating several existing programs into one. **Block grants** are awards that are allocated to states by formula and are funded by annual congressional appropriations. A block grant often is a fixed or capped alternative to more open-ended funding approaches. The state government does the final allocating to state agencies and nonprofit service providers. Block grants are special in that they cover broad areas, such as maternal and child health or elementary and secondary education, and they are ongoing, year after year. For example, the Community Mental Health Services Block Grant is authorized by the Public Health Service Act for the purpose of improving mental health service systems across the country. A stated goal of the program is to promote cost-effective systems of community-based care for people with serious mental disorders (Substance Abuse and Methal Health Services Administration, 2017). Although individual human service agencies do not receive federal block grants directly, this type of grant is still important to human service providers, because they may be able to access the funds by submitting proposals to the state or local government office that does receive them.

Though not strictly grants, **federal government contracts** also can be an important source of funds. With contracts, the government decides precisely what it wants and how it wants it done, leaving little flexibility to the researcher or the service provider. The government then looks for agencies that can perform the desired tasks at the lowest price. Sources of information about contracts and the rules under which they are awarded are different from grants. Also, the number and variety of contracts is vast, so considerable research may be needed to get involved with the contract side of the federal government. Despite the obstacles, however, nonprofit agencies regularly pursue contracts to fund both research and services.

State Government Grants

Although states have always dispersed some of their own tax revenue through the granting process, the rise of federal block grants and the occasional formula grant have greatly expanded the dispersal of funds at the state level. Because each state disperses these monies differently, we cannot make any blanket statements about how to bid successfully for such funds. Regarding block grants, however, something consistent across all states is a federally mandated series of open meetings to discuss how the grant money should be used. The Community Mental Health Services Block Grant follows this procedure. Although showing up and speaking at these meetings will not ensure that a practitioner or an agency will get a grant, it will help ensure that some money is allocated for the area of greatest concern to that practitioner or agency. Another way to increase the chances of getting state grant monies is to keep in contact with the state departments and agencies that oversee and fund research and services related to the human services, such as the Department of Corrections, the Department of Mental Health, and the Department of Social Services. These state agencies may also publish RFPs to solicit grant proposals.

While Richard is enticed by the amount of federal and state funding available for human services research, he does not believe pursuing federal or state grants is his best strategy. He does not believe

federal nor state agencies will have much incentive to fund a research project focusing on his program alone. He also does not believe he will have the time to apply for and receive a federal or state grant to conduct this research before his board makes a decision regarding the future of his program.

Private Funding Sources

A **foundation** is a nonprofit, legally incorporated entity that is organized for the purpose of dispersing funds to projects that meet the guidelines of its charter. The number of private foundations is staggering—upwards of 86,000. In 2012 these foundations made more than $22 billion in grants, however, only roughly $4 billion was to support research (Foundation Center, 2014). Not all foundations, however, are created equal. The largest 20% of foundations control 97% of all foundation assets, so this narrows the number of likely prospects considerably. Most foundations also award only small grants; only about 500 foundations typically give grants in excess of $5,000 each.

Submitting a proposal—no matter how noble the purpose or how well prepared the paperwork—that calls for a grant of $20,000 to a foundation that has never awarded more than $5,000 in any one grant is a waste of time. The person looking for a small grant must begin looking at some of the other characteristics of foundations to sort through the possibilities and find those few that are most likely to fund the proposal. In general, private funding sources are good places to seek grants for agency activities or applied research, because they prefer to fund action programs that produce immediate results rather than research projects that, at best, have some long-term payoff. Also, the complexity of proposal preparation and submission is much less than that encountered with federal agencies.

There are five distinct types of foundations. These are community foundations, general-purpose foundations, special-purpose foundations, family foundations, and corporate foundations.

Community foundations exist to serve their immediate local area. Therefore, if a project is modest in scale and serves some local need, a community foundation may be a good choice.

General-purpose foundations often are large, such as the Ford Foundation, and operate nationwide. If a project is large in scope, with the potential for having an impact broader than just the local community, these large foundations may be ideal. These foundations particularly like innovative demonstration projects that show the way for other communities to solve various problems.

Special-purpose foundations carve out a particular area of interest and award grants only to projects that deal directly with that area of specialization. Successful funding from these sources requires some research into which foundations fund what kinds of projects. Fortunately, large foundations usually publish annual reports, much as corporations do, outlining recently funded projects (Gitlin & Lyons, 2014); from these, we can tell what issues and projects various foundations are interested in and willing to support.

Family foundations are the most difficult to categorize, both because there are so many—more than 42,000, according to the Foundation Center (data.foundationcenter.org/#/foundations/family/nationwide/total/list/2014)—and because they are so different. Some are large and have the resources to award fairly substantial grants, whereas others have a cap on grant size of a few thousand dollars. Some are quite general in the projects that they fund, whereas others have very narrow interests. For example, some only fund projects that benefit a particular religious or ethnic group, whereas others only fund projects that address a particular problem, such as alcoholism or child abuse.

Corporate foundations are used by some corporations as the conduit for corporate philanthropy. Other corporations engage in philanthropy but do not use the foundation mechanism. In either case, nonprofit agencies are common recipients of corporate giving. To maximize the chances for sharing some of this corporate wealth, grant seekers must understand a few things about corporate giving, as investor-owned, profit-making enterprises and corporations are giving away stockholders' money. As such, the directors who make the philanthropic decisions are careful to fund only those activities that they can justify to their stockholders. This tends to mean that the corporation or its employees must stand to benefit in some way from the projects that are funded. For example, a nonprofit child care facility used by many corporate employees might receive a corporate grant or other corporate support. Also, because of this need to benefit, corporate giving is concentrated largely in areas where the corporations have their offices, headquarters, or manufacturing facilities.

Richard spent some time reviewing types of foundations and believes that a community foundation may be his best bet. There are two community foundations that serve his area. The first is the Lincoln Park Community Foundation, which has a long history of supporting a range of nonprofit activities through grants of $5,000 to $50,000, including human services, education, and community-based research. The second is the Paragon Community Foundation. It also has a long history of supporting human services through relatively small grants, especially in the creation of new programs. Paragon very rarely supports research activities, however. Richard decides to focus his efforts on the Lincoln Park Community Foundation.

Learning About Funding Opportunities

Given all the separate agencies and organizations that disperse grants, how do we find specific funding opportunities? Publications and computer databases can help. The *Catalog of Federal Domestic Assistance* (CFDA), for example, is available on the Web (beta.sam.gov) and it describes all federal government programs. Detailed information is provided for a vast array of programs. The CFDA explains the objectives of each program, eligibility requirements, steps in the application process, examples of funded projects, and criteria for selecting proposals. The USAspending.gov website can help search the CFDA by providing information on people and organizations that have successfully applied for grants from programs listed in the CFDA (information about older grants is made available by the National Archives and Records Administration, www.archives.gov). Grant seekers can also search for federal funding opportunities at www.grants.gov/web/grants/home.html.

Another useful publication is the *Federal Register*. This daily, magazine-sized volume reports on the activities of the federal government and also is available online (www.federalregister .gov). Although the *Federal Register* includes a lot of information of little use to grant seekers, new programs are announced first in it, so this is a good resource for the ever-changing opportunities to obtain federal funding. Guidelines for obtaining funds under the new programs also are first provided in the *Federal Register*. Eventually, this information gets into the Assistance Listings, but because that is only published annually, many months can pass before a new program gets listed there.

Grant opportunities from private foundations can be found at the Foundation Center's website (foundationcenter.org). The Foundation Center supplies a considerable amount of information about each foundation or organization it includes—information that is useful in sorting out to whom to make a grant request. For example, financial information about each organization gives some idea about the size of grants that a foundation typically makes. It also provides information on a foundation's purpose and activities, types of support, and limitations to further screen potential funders. In these sections, you can learn whether a particular foundation provides grants for research purposes (some do not). Also, procedures for making applications are described and memberships of the boards of directors are provided. Many funding agencies publish periodic newsletters or bulletins describing their latest activities and programs. It is easy to get on these mailing lists, which often contain RFPs that may unveil a funding opportunity.

The Annual Register of Grant Support: A Directory of Funding Sources, like *The Foundation Directory,* is an excellent source of information on grant sources. Of particular interest to human service professionals is that funding sources are organized according to funding purposes. One category is "Special Populations," which includes subcategories for African Americans, Native Americans, Spanish-speaking people, and women. Additional listings for children and youth, community development, crime prevention, and public health and social welfare are covered under "Urban and Regional Affairs." Another good source is *The Grants Register* (Springer).

GRANT PROPOSAL PLANNING

The grant-funding process involves two players: the funding sources, who sift through proposals seeking worthy projects in which to invest, and the agencies with project ideas that deserve funding. Getting the two together is the heart of the granting enterprise. Having described the funding sources, we now turn to the second process—namely, the development of a fundable proposal (Locke, Spirduso, & Silverman, 2013; Miner & Miner, 2013).

Proposal Development as a Process

Let us explode one myth about obtaining grants: Successful proposals are not started and finished in short order. Rather, they are developed in detail and carefully honed over time. The preparation of grant proposals should be considered an ongoing, continuing function within an agency rather than a sporadic event. All too often, grants are begun in haste and rushed to partial completion to meet some fast-approaching deadline. The result, frequently, is rejection.

When conceptualized as a process instead of as a single event, grant development has many principles in common with the research process introduced in Chapter 1. When the grant is for the purpose of conducting a research project, the connection with the research process is obvious, but a sound understanding of research principles also is directly applicable to grants for service delivery. In seeking funds, the prospective grantee must identify a problem, hone it into a well-defined and manageable topic, develop objectives for the project, search the literature to devise a method of intervention, and plan an evaluation strategy. Furthermore, just as one research study leads to new questions for study, the lessons learned in one grant-funded project lead to new ideas for further projects.

In this section, we describe a number of key elements of the grant-funding process. These are not a series of sequential steps but, rather, are a number of separate and interconnected elements that can be accomplished in different orders at different times. Some are ongoing agency activities; others are specific things that must be done at a particular point. Together, they culminate in and make possible the actual writing of the grant proposal.

To promote the concept of the generation of grant proposals as an ongoing part of agency activities, the use of a *proposal development workbook* (PDW) is recommended (Bauer, 2011). This loose-leaf binder becomes the mortar that holds the building blocks of a proposal together. As the proposal develops from a vague idea to a full-blown project—complete with a demonstration of need, evidence of community support, funding source possibilities, and much more—the PDW organizes everything that goes into a successful proposal as the various components are obtained or completed. Agency staff should be encouraged to watch for items to contribute. For example, favorable news stories about the proposed project are effective demonstrations of community support that help influence funding decision makers. Some of the materials in the PDW for one project also might be useful for a later project.

Identifying the Topic

Before we can begin filling our PDW, of course, we need an idea that can be developed into a fundable proposal. Problems that need to be solved exist in abundance, and many sources of research problems are discussed in Chapter 4. What tends to be in short supply, however, are innovative ways of attacking them. One approach is to organize brainstorming sessions (Bauer, 2011), where members of the staff divide into small groups and develop as many possible solutions or approaches to the selected problem as they can. All the proposed solutions are recorded for further consideration. The goal is to generate ideas, not to reach a consensus regarding which solution is best. In fact, it is desirable to maintain alternative approaches to the problem. One or another of these alternatives may be more palatable politically to a particular funding source, and the chances of obtaining a grant can be significantly enhanced by choosing a solution favored by a funding source.

Back to our vignette, Richard has a general idea that the research project he is interested in creating will evaluate benefits of the ABE program for clients, families, and the community at large. He does not have a clear idea of what outcomes should be evaluated specifically nor how to go about measuring these. He decided to invite several people to meet at his agency to discuss options. He invites several staff from his agency, other human services professionals doing similar work in educating and training adults, business leaders from the community that hire program graduates, and several current and former program participants and their family members.

After brainstorming, the next step is evaluation. Thanks to group dynamics, wildly impractical or just plain stupid ideas usually never make it out of the group. Realistically, however, some ideas will be better than others. We want to sort the best few ideas to save for building into a proposal. One important part of this evaluation is to work out cost–benefit or cost-effectiveness analyses (see Chapter 12). The cost–benefit analyses reveal whether the suggested solutions are economically viable. With any luck, one or more of the considered approaches will show benefits outweighing costs. The cost–benefit analyses of the chosen approach also will be important later, when they become one of the arguments for funding the proposal. Cost-effectiveness analyses, of course, allow selecting the approaches that produce the greatest effect for the least cost. Being able to argue that the project for which an applicant is seeking funds is the most cost-effective of the several projects being considered can only be looked on favorably by decision makers at the funding source.

Several ideas are generated during their brainstorming session. After evaluating these ideas, a smaller group from the brainstorming sessions reaches some consensus about the goals of the research being proposed. They decide to focus on program enrollment (numbers of students served), grade advancement (grade levels students advance in various subject areas), program completion (students completing a GED or high school degree program), current student and graduates' employment, and graduates' earnings. The group also decides the research should include multiple focus groups with current students, graduates, family members of students and graduates, and employers who have hired students and graduates to identify their perceptions of program benefits and limitations. The groups also want to conduct additional focus groups with leaders from education, human services, and government in the area as well as additional members of the business community to identify unmet needs with respect to adult education and training.

Needs Assessment

One of the most important components of a successful grant application is establishing the existence of some problem or need that requires amelioration. All funding sources must operate within their annual budgets, so the competition for available funds is fierce. If an agency can make the case that the problem or need that it wishes to address is the most pressing, then that agency greatly increases its chances of being funded.

There are a variety of ways to make a case for your proposal, and those who are successful include information from more than one source. The core of the evidence supporting the existence of need will likely come from a *needs assessment survey*. With a properly drawn sample, it is possible to make quite accurate estimates concerning the extent of some need within a given population. Additional supporting evidence can come from *key informants,* or people who are particularly close to and knowledgeable about the problem at issue. *Community forums* can gather testimony about the problem, and examples of individuals suffering from the problem can be used as *case studies*, which illustrate the problem in more human terms than abstract statistics can. Finally, data from *public records* may be used as additional evidence of need. Bauer (2011) makes the useful analogy between the grant seeker and a lawyer preparing a case for trial. Each wishes to prepare as persuasive a case as possible to influence a set of decision makers (a jury or review panel) to reach the desired conclusion. In the case of obtaining grants, documenting need is a crucial part of the process. Just as it is not enough for a defendant who is innocent of the crime to be found not guilty by a jury, it is not enough for a need to actually exist to convince a funding source to approve a relevant proposal. In both situations, evidence must be gathered and the case presented to the decision makers with great care to generate a favorable verdict.

In some cases, it may be possible to obtain a grant to conduct needs assessment research. Especially with problems about which we know little, funding agencies sometimes are willing to fund a survey to obtain more information. In other cases, a funding agency may require that a needs assessment survey be included as part of a larger funding proposal, which may include a service delivery program that affects the problem. In any event, needs assessment often plays an important part in the grant-funding process.

Richard and his emerging working group found that in addition to identifying research goals the brainstorming group also created several ideas to support the need for this research—pointing toward low high school completion rates and low skills levels among adults living in the area as well as employers' inability to hire many local residents because they lack basic reading and math skills. Richard is working closely with education and business leaders in the area to collect data pertaining to the need for ABE programs. He is also collecting data from his and other agencies on numbers of people who have sought ABE services compared with their capacities to serve clients and their current waiting lists.

Specifying the Organization's Mission

Not only must the need for services or research be documented, the funding source must be convinced that a particular organization is the proper site for a program to address that problem. This entails demonstrating to the funding source that the problem described in the needs assessment is within the applicant's domain or mission. Many organizations, such as universities, have formal mission statements that appear in official publications. Often, however, such statements are global in nature and may not be adequate for such a purpose. At a minimum, the mission statement should include both how and why the organization was started and detail its primary goals. Generally, funding sources look more favorably on organizations with a history and a track record of accomplishment related to the project to be funded;

a new organization might have to work hard to prove its viability. The mission statement also should address the current activities of the agency, because organizations change with the changing needs of society—an organization that originated for one purpose may be doing something else today. Finally, the mission statement should include the organization's future plans. Funding sources like organizations that appear to be serious and well managed. One way of demonstrating this is by showing careful plans for the future.

Another way to convince a funding source that an applicant is best suited for a particular project is to focus on the uniqueness of that agency. The goal here is to stand apart from other agencies. There is a tendency to think that agencies providing similar services are not very different, but with some thought—and, perhaps, another brainstorming session—the staff should be able to come up with some characteristics that make it special. Perhaps it is the geographical location, such as a particularly remote area or proximity to a large minority population. Possibly something is unusual about the clientele or staff. Or, maybe, the problem-solving approach is different and uniquely successful. With a little careful consideration, the grant seeker should be able to develop unique qualifications to address the documented need.

Richard's agency, the Lincoln Park Community Action Agency, will very likely be the lead agency on this grant; however, Richard has also approached researchers from the nearby regional state university's social work program for assistance. Faculty within the social work department are very interested in the research, especially two researchers who have a strong interest and background in education and training programs for adults. Richard has identified both his agency's mission statement, which emphasizes providing human services to meet community residents' economic, educational, and developmental needs, and the stated goals of the ABE program, emphasizing the extension of basic education and skills development services to adults in the community. Richard has also collected information from the social work department about their newly created Community Action Research Institute, which provides research and technical assistance to community-based organizations that serve disadvantaged populations.

Developing a Program

The most crucial component of any proposal is the research or service project itself. Having established a need, it is necessary to translate that need into specific outcomes for the project and to develop a plan by which those objectives can be achieved. In the case of a research grant, such as Richard's proposal to evaluate the need for and impact of an ABE program, the task is fundamentally one of preparing a detailed blueprint of the stages of the research process (presented in Chapter 1). Hypotheses must be developed and a method of testing these hypotheses devised. Issues of subject selection, study design, and data collection and analysis must be taken into account. A service delivery grant requires specification of exactly what will be done to address the need. Direct connections between the goals of the project and the content of the program must be explicated. Even though service delivery may be the primary emphasis of the proposal, most grants require an evaluation component, so a strategy for monitoring the program and securing data for evaluation purposes must be included.

An important consideration is the time sequencing of the project. Before subjects can be interviewed, interviewers must be trained, and instruments need to be selected or developed. Richard will have to work closely with the research faculty from the university to develop a timeline for the research. He will have to determine how long each of these steps will take. He will also have to specify which people on the project will perform each task. Accounting for all these details requires developing a work plan that shows the flow of procedures from the beginning to the end of the project and that identifies how the various activities coordinate. Although a simple time schedule with beginning and ending dates for various phases may suffice for some projects, the use of graphics, such as a flow chart, often is convincing—and may even be preferred. Such charts can clearly portray the relationships among elements of the project, when each element begins and ends, and which elements overlap. Planning the steps of the project and determining the amount of time for each require a great deal of effort, but this effort is well spent. For one, it forces the agency to analyze how the various parts of the program fit and function together. It also serves to uncover difficulties before the proposal is written and approved, avoiding, for example, the discovery midway through the project that some significant and expensive component was overlooked. Finally, when the time comes to develop the budget and ask for dollars, the plan serves as a justification for the resources.

A number of tools have been created to aid in developing the work plan. Two of the most common are PERT (Program Evaluation Review Technique) and CPM (Critical Path Method). With these techniques, a collection of tasks is specified that results in a final outcome, which in this case is the completed project. Circles, rectangles, and arrows graphically illustrate the progression of events. The technical details of PERT and CPM are beyond the scope of this text, but a variety of computer applications are available that employ these program-planning principles. A major advantage of these applications is that we can readily see the budgetary impact of changing situations by manipulating the variables that affect the budget when we play "what if." For example, we can determine additional costs associated with bringing on another researcher from the university by inputting a single number. Likewise, all other costs can be easily evaluated and a final, accurate budget prepared.

Targeting a Funding Source

By this point, the raw material of a proposal—including a clear idea of the problem, data regarding the need, the preferred program alternative, and cost estimates for the components of that alternative—have been amassed. Before organizing the final proposal, however, consideration must be given to potential funding sources. As a first step, the most appropriate organizations should be identified from among the myriad governmental agencies and private foundations. Sending numerous duplicate proposals to whichever funding sources appear to be most receptive, however, probably will

not work. Each proposal must be fine-tuned specifically for each funding source, because each has different rules and needs. This requires research into the various funding sources—their rules of submission, project areas they have funded in the past, and their particular political viewpoints. Having created a list of possible funding agencies, the grant seeker then begins to narrow the list. One consideration is whether the organization has any advocates who are associated with the funding agency or can make contact with it.

As stated earlier, Richard has already decided to apply for research support from the Lincoln Park Community Foundation. He has contacted staff from the foundation to inquire about funding cycles and processes. Luckily the foundation has a strong relationship and long history with his agency.

By *advocates,* we refer to individuals who will not only speak on the agency's behalf to funding sources but also offer guidance and advice throughout the funding process. Previously, we described the grant seeker preparing a proposal as being analogous to a lawyer preparing a case for trial. This analogy applies once again in the area of advocates to help make the case for the grant. The lawyer uses witnesses to help convince a jury, and advocates are the grant seeker's witnesses, supplying favorable testimony about the proposal to funding sources. Like an attorney, grant seekers need to envision how advocates might be viewed and select those who can make the most favorable impression, because advocates can play a key role in the final outcome.

The best advocates are people who are favorably disposed toward the agency and the proposed project and who have some influence on the funding source. In this respect, securing grant funding is a political process, requiring strategies similar to those used by practitioners in community practice. The range of people who can help influence a funding source is vast and difficult to discuss in general terms, but some possibilities include people with membership on both the agency's and the funding source's governing boards, members of the agency's staff (do not forget their spouses) with special contacts at funding sources, politicians at all levels who support the agency's efforts, and agency volunteers who may have useful contacts.

Once the advocates are identified, along with the funding sources that they can help with, it is time to put them to use. Advocates can be helpful in a variety of ways. At the initial stage, they can help contact representatives of the funding sources to establish a working relationship. They can set up appointments with funding sources. They may even accompany grant seekers when visiting a funding source, and they may know someone at the funding source who can help ensure that the proposal receives a fair and complete review. When the proposal has actually been written, advocates also can provide letters of support. All these efforts are intended to increase the likelihood that a proposal will receive attention. Funding agencies have limited resources, and they receive many more proposals than they can possibly fund. No matter how numerous or powerful, no collection of advocates can substitute for a worthy project and a well-prepared proposal, so in all of this, we are assuming that those two conditions are met. Advocates are important because a meritorious proposal is in competition with others that are also deserving. It is when decision makers are forced to choose from among numerous worthy proposals that advocates come into play.

Richard's agency has strong advocates in the community, starting with local government officials who believe the agency's ABE program is a major community asset. One state representative who has been a strong advocate for the program in the past also has strong ties to the foundation as her family is a major donor. In addition, the agency's executive director and chief financial officer (CFO) both have strong relationships with administrators at the foundation. Richard contacts these potential advocates and asks to meet with them about his proposal. When they meet they each agree to contact foundation leaders to voice support for the agency and the ABE program.

Contacting and Visiting Funding Sources

Having identified a few agencies or foundations as likely funding sources, contacting them may be the next step. Doing so can sometimes substantially increase the chances of funding (Miner & Miner, 2013). Today, most agencies and organizations maintain a website, and visiting it is a good start to gathering information—sometimes even including funding guidelines and applications. If the research organization has advocates who are associated with the funding agency or can make contact with it, then they could make the first contact. Otherwise, contact the funding source by letter. Such a contact letter has a number of purposes: to inform the granting organization of your agency's intent to apply for a grant and to obtain some much-needed forms and other information. Assuming that the agency's initial response is not negative, such as "no funds available," it may be worthwhile to arrange for a personal or telephone contact to explore research plans and gather more information about the source. Some funding agencies also will review drafts of a grant proposal and make suggestions for revision and improvement.

In some cases, it may be possible to make an actual visit to the funding agency. This is especially feasible with local agencies, such as a county social service department or school district office, and can accomplish three general purposes. First, it will confirm or reject the selection of this organization as a likely source of funding. With large federal agencies that offer funding under numerous special programs, information gained during this visit ensures that the grant seeker is applying to the agency that is most appropriate for the project. For example, a research proposal submitted to a program designed to fund action-oriented projects probably would be rejected, even though it might have been funded under some other program controlled by the same agency. Second, the visit supplies additional information on how best to tailor the proposal to the funder's special needs, thus increasing the chances for funding. Third, the visit provides a personal touch for the proposal when it is submitted. Instead of representing a faceless organization, the proposal will be from people who are known personally and who made an impressive presentation about a serious need and their plans to fill it. Whether the grant seeker calls, writes, or visits the organization, he or she should check Box 17.1 for suggestions about what to learn about an agency.

BOX 17.1 What to Learn About a Granting Agency

- Does the funding agency have a real commitment to funding in the area of the proposed project, as evidenced by previous grants funded?
- Does the amount of funds requested in the proposed grant fit within the granting agency's typical range of funding?
- What proportion of agency grants go to new projects, as opposed to the continuation of currently running projects? Will this proportion change in the coming year?
- Does a new grant from an agency like ours have a chance for funding, especially when competing against those requesting a continuation of funding?
- To see what has worked in the past, can we review grant proposals that have received funding from this agency in the past?
- What are the most common reasons for rejecting a grant proposal submitted to this agency?
- What is the most common mistake that people make when submitting a grant request to this agency?
- Can we submit a draft of our grant proposal to this agency and receive feedback before submitting the final proposal?
- Are there any packaging guidelines that must be followed or the proposal will not be seriously considered (e.g., length, number of copies, binding, format, etc.)?
- What is the deadline for submitting a grant proposal?

Note that one thing that should be acquired, whether through letter contact or personal visit, is a list of last year's grant recipients. Before finalizing the grant proposal, the grant seeker should contact one or more of these successful organizations, because the range of useful information that they can supply is vast. They have experience with the agency, and there is no substitute for that in learning the ins and outs of successful grantsmanship with that particular agency. Each agency develops its own particular style of operating as well as its own perspective on problems and ways to solve them. It is important to learn about these bureaucratic idiosyncrasies from past grant recipients to tailor the proposal to match the agency's expectations.

In addition to asking advocates to speak with foundation leaders on behalf of his program, Richard also contacts the foundation to set up an information meeting to learn more about the foundation's expectations for proposals. He asks the CFO from the agency to accompany him as she helps guide agency staff on various grant applications. Foundation staff agree to meet and give Richard and the CFO a guide and tips for completing the grant application.

WRITING THE GRANT PROPOSAL

Having identified a topic, collected supporting documentation that confirms the need for action or research, formulated a method for addressing the problem, and targeted a funding source, you have completed the groundwork. Actually writing the proposal, with the information gleaned from these earlier steps, should be a relatively straightforward endeavor—but it still requires a great deal of care (Miner & Miner, 2013). In a number of places in this book, we emphasize that a very important part of both research and practice is to communicate to others about both plans and accomplishments. Such communication can occur at a number of different points in the research process, of which we emphasize two in this chapter—namely, preparing a grant proposal and writing a research report. Anyone who cannot prepare a comprehensible and convincing grant proposal will not gain the financial support that is needed to complete a research project. In turn, the research findings of anyone who cannot write a clear and thorough research report—no matter how important—cannot be translated into policies and practices by practitioners. We do not pretend that we can create accomplished writers here, but we do hope to offer some useful suggestions and resources.

Appearance and Writing Style

The old adage that you cannot judge a book by its cover may be true, but people routinely make such superficial judgments. Because of this, both outward appearance and style of presentation in a grant proposal are crucial to success. Demand for grant monies is great, so funding agencies may look for any excuse to reject proposals to reduce the number that have to be given a full review. Failure to follow any guideline may be seized on as a reason not to consider a proposal further. So, to begin with, follow the guidelines to the letter—even if they appear senseless. In particular, be careful about length restrictions. Submitting an overly long proposal, no matter how worthy, may result in rejection.

Reviewers have a limited amount of time to review many proposals, so a proposal should be attractive and capable of being skimmed easily. Uncomplicated sentences and short paragraphs work toward this end. Emphasizing key phrases or the use of bullets (solid dots or other symbols used to set off a series of points in a text) for highlighting purposes helps, too. Different type styles, boldface headings, and variable margins and spacing further contribute to overall appearance and readability. Include charts and graphs to enhance visual impact and convey information in a small space. For example, use of a graph depicting the increasing incidence of some problem is often far more effective at making the point than use of a simple reference to that fact in the text. The graph also is less likely to be unintentionally passed over by busy reviewers.

Not long ago, great effort and a professional printing company were required to produce a proposal with these desirable features. The advent of word processing and computerized desktop publishing systems, however, has placed the ability to produce high-quality documents within easy reach of most agencies and many individuals. Such systems are strongly recommended for producing grant proposals—the competing grant

applicants will likely produce a slick and attractive grant request using such technology. Beyond appearance, the style of the text is important. A dull, lifeless proposal, regardless of its merit, has less chance of being funded than one that exudes interest and excitement. Use action words, and express emotions wherever appropriate. Interest the reviewers in the problem and in the proposed innovative approach to it by reaching them at an emotional level. Citing dialogue is one effective approach: Presenting possible future clients describing their problems in their *own words* is better received than a third-party description is. As a general rule, try to maintain a fairly light, readable style.

As in all writing, a sense of one's audience is crucial to preparing a successful grant proposal. Of particular importance is the fact that review panels for both federal agencies and private foundations may contain at least some nonspecialists (Krathwohl, 1988). This means that grant seekers must be careful to communicate their intentions in language that is clear to someone who is not a professional in the field. More specifically, jargon should be avoided or, if unavoidable, should be explained. Beyond that, no assumptions can be made regarding prior knowledge of the problem, its importance, previous approaches, measurement devices, or analytical techniques. Explain everything in detail—and in terms that a layperson can understand. Doing so and, at the same time, not boring the specialists requires a difficult balancing act in writing.

Writing a proposal requires such extreme care because the proposal represents the agency to the funding source and is an indicator of the quality of the agency's personnel and their work. A great idea presented in a sloppy proposal will not get the funding it deserves. A worthy idea deserves proper presentation so that funding can be obtained to implement it. The ultimate goal, after all, is not just to get grant money but, rather, to finance programs that accomplish some good.

After a draft of the proposal is completed and before the proposal is submitted, it is a good idea to have several members of the agency who were not directly involved in its production proofread it. This step is important because people who are unfamiliar with the proposal will approach it more like a reviewer will—that is, with no prior knowledge of its content. The proposal will have to stand on its own, just as it will during the review by the funding source. In addition to looking for the usual typographical and grammatical errors, proofreaders should assess the total package for content and presentation. Is all the needed information included? Is the problem adequately documented by the needs assessment? Does the proposed project logically address the problem identified in the needs assessment? Is the budget adequately detailed to justify the requested funds? These and many other questions regarding the content of the proposal should be addressed during this final proofreading stage.

All these suggestions regarding the appearance, style, and presentation of a proposal should not distract from the central importance of the proposed project itself. No amount of fancy wrappings will make up for an ill-conceived idea. The importance of these matters is to separate one agency's deserving proposal from all the other deserving proposals to the point that yours gets funding.

Luckily Richard is a skilled writer, but he has very limited experience with research grant proposals. He decides to meet with research faculty from the university for assistance with the proposal. They agree to help by providing some background information on ABE programs and collecting demographic and economic data on the community. They also agree to review Richard's application for language, grammar, and consistency with foundation expectations and guidelines. Several community members and agency leaders have also agreed to review the proposal before it is submitted and make suggested edits.

Components of the Proposal

A typical proposal to a government agency or major foundation will contain most or all of the components shown in Box 17.2, probably in the order listed. The precise components depend on the requirements of the specific agency or organization and on whether the proposal is to fund research, service delivery, or both. Notice that the order in Box 17.2 is quite different from the grant development sequence, because the proposal is organized according to the needs of the reader and not necessarily according to the order in which one prepares the parts.

The Cover Letter. The cover letter probably is the last item to be completed, but because it is the first thing read by those who will evaluate your proposal, it is crucial. One important function of the cover letter is to remind the agency personnel of who the grant seeker is and that he or she bothered to visit the funder and take into account their suggestions when designing the proposal. The idea is to show that everything has been done right (according to the funder's views) so that, now, the proposal deserves careful consideration.

Title Page. The title page often is a standard form supplied by the granting organization. Box 17.3 illustrates the common elements of a title page. A good title is one that describes the project and communicates the anticipated results. Thus, the title "Reducing Homicide in Family Disputes" is preferable to "Applying Mental Health Crisis Intervention Techniques to Family Violence": The first title indicates what the project plans to achieve with the funds, whereas the second title

---

BOX 17.2 Typical Proposal Contents and Sequence

1. Cover letter
2. Title page
3. Summary
4. Problem/Need
5. Objectives
6. Methods
7. Evaluation
8. Future funding
9. Dissemination
10. Budget
11. Attachments

merely describes a service. Beyond serving as a label for the proposal, the title page will route the application to the various officials who must process it. The page should clearly identify the applicant's name and address as well as the specific program being applied for and the granting organization contact person. Richard decides on the title, "Improving Basic Skills in the Lincoln Park Community: A Needs Assessment and Program Evaluation."

Summary. Most granting agencies request a brief summary of the proposal so that agency administrators can quickly assess who should receive a copy. This should be no more than a paragraph, and it should briefly mention all elements of the proposal: research problem or service to be delivered, methods used, and anticipated results.

Problem or Needs Statement. This is where the applicant really begins to make the case. What should go here has already been discussed in the previous section while analyzing the needs assessment and mission of the organization. What must be done is put clearly and coherently into prose, describing what the problem is and why this agency can help solve it. After much debate, Richard and his team of helpers decide on the following problem statement:

> Lincoln Park Community Action Agency's Adult Basic Education has served thousands of adult students, but there has not been a comprehensive evaluation of its function and impact in the community. This research will evaluate the value of this program to students and their families, employers, and

the community, assess the need for ABE programs in the community, and identify best practices to create more effective ABE opportunities for Lincoln Park residents.

Objectives. Objectives state very clearly and precisely what the proposal will achieve—that is, exactly what research will be done or what service will be delivered in concrete and achievable terms. No funding agency will be impressed if the objective is "to discover the real truth about spousal abuse." A more concrete objective would be to learn about the role of economic independence in the ability of women to avoid such abuse. List all the objectives with no more than a sentence or two devoted to each, and present them in the order of their potential importance and contribution, with the most important first. In a research proposal, this section should contain theoretical considerations and the development of hypotheses.

Richard and his helpers create a short list of objectives stemming from the problem statement. These include the needs assessment, program evaluation, and identification of best practices that can be applied to improving ABE services in the community. The best practices section, the team decides, will include a focus on connections between basic skills education programs and employers.

Methods. The proposal should include a complete description of how the applicant plans to conduct research or provide a service. In a research proposal, this section should contain all the mechanics of carrying out the research: sample size, sampling technique, research design, and statistical procedures to be used in analyzing the data. Richard's associates from the university agree to complete the methods section of the proposal, which will highlight: their quantitative analysis of program data; focus groups to assess students', family members', and employers' perceptions of the program's value; analysis of demographic, employment, and other economic data from the community to help determine the need for ABE programs; and analyses of existing research on ABE programs to create recommendations for improving program outcomes.

Evaluation. Federal funding sources place particular emphasis on evaluation. It is politically (as well as practically) important to gather evidence that shows the funded activities are achieving the objectives claimed for them. Therefore, virtually all proposals must contain adequate methods for assessing both whether and how well the program is achieving its goals. In a service delivery grant, this typically involves conducting research to assess whether the program resulted in the improvements or changes intended. (A review of Chapter 12, along with some of the suggested readings, should be helpful in preparing this part of the proposal.)

Because this is an application to conduct research as opposed to delivering services, evaluation will entail a review of the study design and methodology. Richard summarizes the team's plan to have outside researchers conduct peer-reviews of their study design, analysis, findings, and program recommendations throughout the research process.

Future Funding. A grant, by its very nature, is a one-time dispersal of funds. Human service organizations, on the other hand, typically support ongoing programs that require continuous funding. The disjunction between the one-time grant and the ongoing needs of the program should be addressed in the proposal. What happens when the grant money ends? The agency will want to see that this problem has been thought through and that plans have been made to deal with it. Plans for local funding, other grants, fund-raisers, telethons, and so on, should be included.

Agencies like to see lasting and successful programs develop out of their seed money. Inclusion of money in the budget for future fund-raising efforts is perfectly appropriate.

In the proposal Richard emphasizes that because one of the goals of this research is the creation of program recommendations based on needs assessment, program evaluation, and best practices evidence, the agency will also seek additional funding to develop the ABE program based on these recommendations. In the proposal he also identifies several potential funding sources for future program development.

Dissemination. Dissemination refers to spreading the word about the research, service delivery program, grant, funding source, and, we hope, successes. Inclusion of comments regarding dissemination of results is looked on as an indicator of confidence. Agencies like positive publicity about the good that they do and tend to look favorably on opportunities to obtain it. This is a small item. Alone it will not secure funding, but successful grantsmanship ultimately is a result of doing a lot of little things right—and better than the competition.

In the proposal, Richard outlines his plan for disseminating research findings, which include: posting research findings on the agency's website, printing full research reports and summaries and disseminating them at various community meetings, and sharing reports with other organizations in the community. Richard also writes that he and his partners from the university will hold a community forum where they will present their findings and answer questions from the audience.

Budget. A carefully detailed budget is an important part of any grant proposal, because granting agencies are punctilious in their accounting demands of grant recipients. Table 4.3 on page 105 provides an example of a research budget for a survey interview, showing the major elements that would be included in a budget. Essentially, every dollar requested must be accounted for. The methods section of the proposal, which spells out precisely what the program will do, provides the guide for developing the budget. All costs that will be incurred must be identified and included. Novice grant seekers often underestimate costs or leave out expenses. Because the developers of the project usually are researchers or practitioners and not financial officers, it is important to seek consultation in determining costs. The grant seeker's agency may have standard formulas for fixing fringe benefit costs, travel, and overhead, and it may require bidding procedures for purchasing equipment. The budget, however, must be realistic. Promising the moon on a shoestring budget will not endear the proposal to a funding source. It will merely be seen as the amateurish effort that it is. If costs are reasonable and well justified, however, it may be possible to negotiate reductions if the total amount is too high.

Richard and his team develop a budget that includes research-related travel and other data collection expenses, printing, and time allotments (salary for both university faculty and Richard's own time). The total request is relatively modest, $7,500, but it includes most of the major expenses the team will incur beyond those that can be covered by their organizations.

Attachments. The attachments section provides important supporting evidence for claims made elsewhere in the proposal. Bauer (2011) suggests the following as appropriate for inclusion in the attachments section: needs assessment and supporting research, résumés of key personnel, minutes of advisory committee meetings, names of board members, auditor's financial statement, letters of support from advocates, evidence of tax-exempt status from the Internal Revenue Service, any pictures or diagrams, and copies of any organization publications.

Documentation of community support also is important. Some funding sources demand a demonstration that the community is behind a project, but this should be provided even for those who do not. Evidence of community support generally comes from two sources—namely, advisory board minutes and newspaper articles. Many agencies of the type that we are discussing here have advisory boards that oversee their operations. These boards, which are comprised primarily of other professional service providers, former consumers of the agency's services, and people whose expertise lies in the area of fund-raising, hold regular meetings to discuss the activities of the agencies they oversee. Minutes from meetings when the project for which funding is being sought was discussed can be used as evidence of community support. Newspaper articles that reflect positively on the project form the other major source of evidence for community support. Grant seekers can actively seek publicity for the agency and the project they are trying to get funded.

Several attachments are included in Richard's proposal, including: résumés from all people involved in the research, letters of support from supporters throughout the community, and letters of support from both agency and university leaders (explaining that they support the research and staff's involvement in it).

Submitting the Proposal

Public funding sources have quite rigid guidelines—not to mention firm deadlines—that govern the submission process. Applicants, of course, have to obtain these along with all other relevant information from the funding agency. Because deadlines are involved, the proposal should be submitted either in person or by registered mail. In either case, it is a good idea to telephone the funding source to verify receipt.

With many of the private foundations, generalizing about submission procedures is difficult, because each foundation has its own unique way of doing business. This places an added burden on the grant seeker. In some cases, private foundations do not require the lengthy and detailed proposals that we have described. They do not have the resources, in the form of reviewers, to evaluate such complex documents. Instead, they rely on what is called the *letter proposal* (Miner & Miner, 2013). As the name suggests, the letter proposal outlines the need, the plans to meet that need, and the grant request, all in a fairly brief letter of no more than a few pages in length. Even something as important as the budget is abbreviated. Usually, the estimated total cost is all that is required. Rather than the voluminous detail characteristic of a federal proposal, each important issue in the letter proposal must fit into a paragraph. Brevity and clarity are the watchwords.

Because the applicant has done the homework, chances are good that the grant will be approved, but what if it is not? Understandable disappointment aside, rejection is an opportunity to learn. The applicant may contact the funding source and inquire about what was wrong (and right) about the proposal. He or she can learn from them how to do a better job the next time. The only grant seekers who are never turned down are those who never submit a proposal. It is the nature of the game.

Grantsmanship is an exciting and increasingly essential element of human service research and practice. We hope that this chapter has made the prospect of preparing a grant proposal less daunting. Remember, however, that we have been able to present only a limited amount of material on obtaining grants. We strongly recommend that you read carefully a complete book devoted to grantsmanship.

Richard is new to writing a research grant, so he is especially attentive that the proposal meets the expectations of the foundation. He checks and double checks the proposal with the guidelines given to him by foundation staff. He makes sure the writing is reviewed several times and that edits have been made appropriately. While the foundation accepts proposals continuously he also makes sure that the proposal arrives by the date by which he told foundation staff it would arrive. He is also attentive that he submit both hard and electronic copies of the proposal as requested.

Practitioner Profile 17.1 offers another example of the importance of grant writing in practice while presenting some of the important skills involved.

WRITING A RESEARCH REPORT

One of the strengths of the scientific method is the public character of scientific results. Publicizing scientific findings accomplishes several important functions. First, unless research findings are made public, they accomplish little social good.

How can others learn from the findings of research if those findings are withheld? Clearly, publication of research findings is necessary to be able to apply those findings in developing programs and policies.

Second, publication allows the process of replication to ferret out the errors, frauds, and falsehoods that inevitably creep into the products of human endeavor. This self-correcting nature of science, which has contributed so much to its success, depends on the wide dissemination of research results.

Third, publication of research findings makes attempted suppression of those findings more difficult. In Chapter 12, we noted that, historically, this had been a problem for evaluation research reports. A few copies were supplied to a sponsor, who then had complete control over what was—or was not— done with the results. Broader publicity concerning research findings makes it more likely that such findings will come to the attention of someone who will use them.

Finally, the publication of research findings, like any written publication, is an effort at persuasion, an attempt to influence the readers to accept specific ideas or conclusions. Chapter 3 discussed the idea of advocacy in research and showed that human service researchers are especially likely to advocate some particular use for their research findings. To be effective, advocates must communicate positions to others, and one major mode of communication is through the written word. An interesting, well-written, and smooth presentation is more likely to be persuasive.

Given the central role that communication of research results plays in the entire scientific enterprise, proper preparation of the research report is vital. In this section, we assume knowledge of appropriate English grammar and usage. The complexity of the English language being what it is, however, we strongly recommend consulting one or more of the style manuals listed in *For Further Reading*. No matter how well we think we write, our writing always benefits from regular application of a style manual. Practitioner Profile 17.1 explores some of the ethical considerations in the publishing of research.

PRACTITIONER PROFILE 17.1 Jack Cameron, Community Relations Director

Jack Cameron is community relations and development director for a large nonprofit agency providing homeless and other emergency assistance services in a large city in the northwestern United States. According to Jack,

> I never imagined I would become a grant writer or fundraiser, but that's now the bulk of my job. I meet people, convince them that the services we provide are important, and then I ask them for money. When they give me money, I wait a while and then ask them for more. (Based on personal communication on June 2, 2018.)

Cameron explained that he began his career after completing an MSW program in homeless services. "I loved working with the homeless and I thought it was important work," he explained. "But then I would get frustrated with the system that limited what I could do for folks, so I began to do some community organizing." Jack described his efforts to seek donations from area businesses so he could provide basic necessities for clients like clothing, shampoo, razors and tampons. "Over time I realized I was really good at asking for things and making arguments about why helping the homeless was so important," he explained.

Cameron described his relatively recent move to his current position.

> In my organizing work I began to get involved in fundraising. I was also talking to politicians and other policy folks a lot too. Then the executive director of my agency asked if I would consider a community relations and fundraising position. At first I thought "Hell no" because I knew I would miss the contact with clients, other staff and people around the community. Then it occurred to me that I would still be serving the homeless and interacting with lots of people in the community. Maybe this is a good path for me. At least I could give it a try.

According to Cameron, he has found a new home in grant-writing and community relations. He explained,

> I was never a data-guy. I didn't love research or statistics in school. I also didn't like writing. But now . . . I see how important these tools are to garnering resources for our staff so they can provide services for our clients. And I'm realizing I'm O.K. at research, at least reading it and seeing how it relates to our programs and clients. Plus I am really good at making connections with researchers in the area who can help me make sense of data and how it relates to our work. I have also learned I'm a good writer. I see grants as a conversation where my job is to convince a funder that what I want to do is important and worth supporting. Beyond that it is just about following instructions and paying attention to details

He continued,

> The community relations and development director job is really a development position at the agency, but it also requires me to understand what is happening in the area with respect to policy and larger services systems. It helps to be on boards and committees,

(continued)

but it is also important to have strong personal relationships with lots of people, and I like that. Personal relationships are also important in grant-writing. It helps me in getting help from other people, including researchers, who can help me find and include data in my application. It also helps to have relationships with funders—whether that is the city, state or federal government or foundations. They say we're judged based on the merits of the application, but it also helps to have connections with the people who evaluate your grant. If they know me and know what I'm trying to do for my agency and that I am serious about putting funds to good use, then you know they are more likely to score your application favorably.

Reflecting back on his move from direct services to program development and community relations, Cameron has no regrets. He explained,

I still get out to the programs, see staff and clients too. I need to really understand their challenges and needs so I can ask for [the] right things. If I don't understand what they're doing, there will be a problem. I have seen it before where agencies have gone after funding that really doesn't enhance what they already do well. They end up doing a million things and none of them well. I don't want that to happen to us, so I stay connected to programs, staff and clients. Besides, I really like talking with them.

Consideration of the Audience

An important consideration before beginning any writing assignment is the intended audience. For the writing to be most effective, it must be tailored to its specific audience. Although it is possible to identify several distinct audiences for research reports, the most significant distinction is between a *professional audience* and a *lay audience*. Of course, within these two broad categories are several more specific audiences that may require special consideration. Not all professionals are created equal. Even in the social sciences and human services, those pursuing research careers develop a different expertise and professional jargon than those following a more practice-oriented career. Likewise, those concentrating on clinical practice gain different expertise from those dealing with administration or community practice. They may all be professionals within the same discipline, but they do not share the same knowledge. It is important to keep these distinctions in mind when writing reports.

When a report is aimed at an audience of other professionals, we can make certain assumptions, such as familiarity with basic concepts of the discipline and knowledge of common statistical terms. Although these assumptions make writing for other professionals easier, such an audience is likely to be more critical of such things as following proper format, elements of style, and substantive content.

If the intended audience is the lay public or others who are less familiar with research and the human services, then we cannot make those assumptions. Instead, we must minimize the use of professional jargon, which is likely to be meaningless or, possibly, misleading to such an audience. Occasionally, jargon cannot be avoided. Social science disciplines do not make up jargon for its own sake but, rather, to enhance precision or to describe phenomena that everyday language does not have words for. When used, professional jargon should be carefully explained to lay readers. Presentation of data to a lay audience also must be simplified. They probably will not know what a probability coefficient is, and they may even have difficulty grasping the importance of a percentage table. Instead, the visual impact of graphs and charts helps get the message across. Also, explain fully what each statistic used accomplishes and what the result means. Professionals who do not routinely work with statistics and data analysis also may need some assistance of this sort. If we believe in the importance of our research and want it to be useful, careful attention to our audience will further that goal immensely.

Because different journals are read by different audiences, requirements of professional periodicals vary from one publication to another. If a research report is being prepared for possible publication, care must be taken to follow the specifications of the particular journal to which the manuscript will be submitted. A helpful resource toward this end is *An Author's Guide to Social Work Journals* (NASW Press Staff, 2009). Published by the National Association of Social Workers, the guide includes more than 130 social work, social welfare, and human service journals. Readers will find information on the journal's review process, editorial focus, format, and suggested style guide. In addition, the guide indicates where each journal is abstracted and indexed.

Richard knows the audience for his report is fairly diverse and includes both people who are research savvy and likely to critically evaluate the study design and findings and others who may lack research knowledge and experience but are nonetheless interested in ABE programs and the community in general. Because of this, he is careful that the report is clearly written, direct, and relatively easy to read, but contains enough description of research processes to suit the needs of research-savvy critics. As explained earlier, Richard also views his agency's board members as a very critical target audience. He knows that they may be very interested in the nature of the research and findings and that some may closely scrutinize the study design and findings. Thus, he errs on the side of providing more rather than less detail on study design, data collection, analysis, and findings. One way Richard accomplished both goals—aiming for detail and simplicity—was to create both an executive summary that clearly and briefly summarizes major findings and a full report that also offers details of research methods and specific findings and recommendations.

Organization of the Report

Despite the variation depending on the audience, research reports usually include most or all of the following elements: title, abstract, introduction and problem statement, methods, results, discussion, and references.

Title. The title is an important part of a report and the first element a reader sees. The major function of the title is to give prospective readers an idea of what the study is about so that they can decide whether they are interested in reading more. Therefore, a good title informs the reader about the major independent and dependent variables and, possibly, the major findings. A second reason to develop a good title is that online library searches use key words in titles as one means of selecting articles.

Abstract. Most scientific journals and reports contain an abstract, which is a brief summary of the study that allows the reader to learn enough to decide whether to read the whole report. (Some examples of this type of abstract are presented in Chapter 4.) Abstracts also often are published in reference volumes or online in searchable databases. In these collections, the abstracts allow the reader to decide whether to locate the complete articles. Because of their importance and brevity (125–175 words), abstracts must be carefully written. The first sentence should be a clear statement of the problem investigated by the study. The research methodology and sampling techniques are then indicated. Finally, a brief summary of the findings and conclusions completes the abstract. Exhibit 17.1 shows an abstract with its component parts identified.

Introduction and Problem Statement. The first part of the body of the report states the research problem and its importance, including a literature review of the history of the problem in previous research and theory. This material indicates how the current study flows from what has gone before. Presentation of the theoretical material sets the stage for presenting the hypotheses that were tested in the study. Of necessity, this section must

EXHIBIT 17.1   Example of an Abstract, With Its Component Parts Identified: 1 = Statement of Problem, 2 = Sample Selection, 3 = Method of Study, 4 = Results

1	This research examines homelessness in Michigan's Upper Peninsula, a remote area in the northern Midwest, while comparing coping tactics, felt experiences, and unmet needs of homeless single adults and families. A major goal of the study was to understand how the homeless use family, friends, and services to secure food, shelter, and other basic necessities.
2	The authors recruited 116 homeless persons (58 single adults and 58 adults with children) throughout the Upper Peninsula for the study. Participants were recruited through social service agencies, flyers, and snowball sampling.
3	Data include audio recordings of in-depth, semi-structured interviews focused on: methods of securing basic necessities; relationships with family, friends, and human service organizations; and the felt experiences of homelessness, including the social and psychological impacts of homelessness. Directly coding audio recordings using NVivo software, the authors employed a grounded theory approach to reveal coping patterns; identify relationships between personal, family, and community factors and help-seeking behaviors; and create hypotheses related to differential homeless experiences.
4	Adults with children tended to have greater access to social services than single adults and reported that providers were more willing to accommodate them. Some avoided social services, however, because they feared being reported to child protection services. Services for singles were very limited, especially in smaller communities, and many homeless individuals were reluctant to use available services, especially shelters, as these were associated with decreased freedom. Assistance from non-homeless family members was often limited to a portion of the homeless family, and in many cases there were social, psychological, and financial costs associated with help from non-homeless family members. These costs often limited homeless families' seeking help within the extended family. Singles were more likely to report receiving assistance from non-homeless family members, although help received was often limited, especially for those with substance abuse histories. Help from friends was limited for many homeless families due to space and financial constraints (it is more costly to house an entire family than a single person). Almost all homeless individuals received help from friends and many maintained an extensive and diverse network of friends. Overall data suggests that while there are more services available for homeless families than singles, the psychological toll of homelessness is far worse for those with children. Available help from family and friends (and costs associated with receiving this help) and the fear of losing children to child protection services helps explain differences between homeless singles' and families' felt experiences.

Source: From Hilton, T., DeJong, C., & Trella, D. (2012). *Experiences of homelessness among singles and families in a rural area: Comparing coping, felt experiences and unmet needs.* Unpublished paper.

be kept relatively brief. For example, the literature review typically consists of numerous citations of previous work in the topic area, with comments on only the most relevant aspects of each study. This emphasis on brevity, however, should not be overdone. Clarity of presentation in this section is a must—without it, the remainder of the report loses its meaning.

Methods. The methods section describes the sample that was studied and the research techniques employed. It also shows how concepts were operationalized and what measurement devices, such as scales, were used. This section is important because it provides the basis on which the validity and generalizability of the conclusions will be judged. It also is the basis for any future replication efforts.

As such, this section must be written with sufficient detail so that it can perform both of these functions. Readers must be able to tell precisely what was done in the study and who participated.

Results. This section is a straightforward presentation of the findings of the study, devoid of any editorializing or comment as to the meaning of the results—that comes later. Typically, the presentation of results involves the use of tables, graphs, and statistics. The one exception to this is the results section from a participant observation study, which is likely to have little quantitative data. As noted previously, consider your audience, and fashion your presentation so that the data can be readily understood.

Discussion. In this section, conclusions are drawn regarding the implications of the data that are presented in the results section. Each tested hypothesis should be related to relevant data and a conclusion stated about the degree of support (or nonsupport) that the data provide for it. Beyond that, any broader implications of the findings for research, practice, or social policy should be noted. Any limitations or weaknesses of any of the results should be noted honestly as well. Often, research results raise new questions as they answer others. Therefore, it is common practice to identify opportunities for future research.

References. A list of all works cited in the report usually is presented as the last element of the report. A variety of formats can be used, but the one known as the *Harvard method* is common in the social sciences. As sources are cited in the body of the text, the author's last name and date of publication are placed in parentheses at the end of the sentence. The references are then listed in alphabetical order by the first author's last name at the end of the report. An alternative format is called the *serial method,* in which the citations are indicated numerically in the body of the text. The references are then presented in the reference section, with each reference identified by the number associated with it in the text.

Preparing a list of references or a bibliography for a grant or research report generally is a difficult and not a very pleasant task. All the names of the authors must be spelled correctly, and the page numbers and dates must be correct. In addition, the punctuation is not like that used anywhere else. Computer software, however, can take some of the drudgery out of preparing bibliographies. Bibliography-formatting software creates a file of references with all the required information for each reference (still a lot of work). Once the file is complete, the program reformats and prints the information in a variety of popular bibliographic styles. In addition, some programs interface with word-processing programs, search documents for citations, and make up a correct bibliography from the file of references. It also flags any citations not in the file and any references in the file that are not cited. When revising a long document, such as a book or a grant proposal, this feature can save a lot of work and reduce errors. Bibliographic software does not do all the busywork, but it can reduce the drudgery considerably and greatly enhance the accuracy of the finished product.

The Process of Writing

It is not possible, of course, to cover in a brief chapter all the elements involved in writing. This is done in writing courses and through practice at writing. A few points, however, are of special importance.

First, writing is a process rather than a product. We never finish writing, although we may finish a paper or a report because it has to be submitted by a deadline. This, however, does not mean that we could not write and revise further. Writing aims at the expression and communication of clear thought. It is difficult to write because, in some respects, language is a poor mechanism for communicating the subjective reality of our thoughts. If we hear that someone was almost hit by a car on the way to school this morning, words like *car* and *hit* seem to be straightforward and comprehensible, but do those words actually encompass the experienced reality? It was a bright red car, and it was speeding, and the driver seemed not to notice, and. . . . How much detail communicates an experience? We say that we were frightened by the close call and then realize that we cannot make clear the wrenching terror, so we repeat that we were "really" frightened, using qualifiers, emphasis, and inflection to make our point. The words seem to be inadequate to communicate the experience, but this is precisely the challenge that any writer confronts: using words to describe a very complex and confusing reality. Researchers face the challenge of using words to describe a very complex theoretical and methodological reality to various audiences.

A second point, which really flows from the first, is that rewriting and revision are an inherent part of the writing process. Few writers are capable of making the first draft the final draft. Most writers, especially professional writers, must rewrite their material several times before they consider it to be clear, comprehensible, and smooth. (The term *smooth* in this context simply means the writing contains few errors or awkward constructions that distract the reader from the content.) One of the keys to revision is to be able to read the prose through the eyes of the intended audience. Would they understand a particular word, phrase, or sentence? Can they follow the sequential organization in the report? Do they grasp the transitions that move the reader from one sentence to another, from one paragraph to another? What is perfectly clear from the writer's perspective may be muddled and unclear from the reader's. The writer's talent is to perceive his or her writing from that other perspective.

Rewriting is an essential—if sometimes tedious—task, but it also is creative. As with other creative efforts, the energy and attention needed to create is greater at some times than at others. This means that the best writing usually is not produced in one sitting. Most writers find it useful to approach revisions after they have been away from a paper for some time. This enables them to work on it with fresh insight and attention. For this reason, words written at the last minute, with a deadline rapidly approaching, may not be the best words after all.

Richard is careful to follow the previously described report writing format. (This was also the foundation required for research grants.) He is also very attentive to writing mechanics and style as he writes his final report. As with the proposal, he drafts with his research partners and other critical readers to solicit feedback and editorial suggestions. He asks both savvy researchers and other community members to read his drafts to ensure it is both sufficiently detailed and easy to follow. In the end he has created a very solid research study and report that will raise awareness about ABE services in the community, draw attention to needs to develop ABE programs, and offer critical insights to important constituents, including board members at his agency, about the value of his program.

REVIEW AND CRITICAL THINKING

Main Points

- Grants have become a very important source of funding for both social research and human services. To gain funding successfully, grant proposals must be written well.
- Sources of grant money fall into three categories: governmental agencies, private foundations, and corporations. Governmental agencies are the largest source.
- Government funds come in a number of different forms: project (categorical or discretionary) grants, formula grants, block grants, federal contracts, and state government grants.
- Although many foundations fund grants, most fund only small projects, and some fund research only on limited subject areas. Corporations tend to fund grants that can be justified to the stockholders, such as for services or improvements from which the corporation or its employees will benefit.

- Many funding sources can be located through online computerized search services.
- The preparation of grant proposals should be considered to be an ongoing, continuing function of a human service agency. The steps in the grant development process are analogous to the steps in the research process.
- The first step in grant development is to identify a fundable topic. Conducting a needs assessment can assist with this task.
- Once the project has been identified, the next step is to target a funding source that will be interested in the project. This might call for visits to potential funding sources to assess their interest.
- To be successful, grant proposals must be written well, and this requires paying attention to the appearance and to the writing style. Proposals must be neat, interesting to read, and addressed to the audience that will read them.
- A grant proposal should contain all the components necessary to provide a funding source with adequate information to assess it.
- Research reports also should be well written, because the communication and publication of scientific results accomplish important functions for science.
- A research report should be written at the level of the audience for whom it is intended. These might be researchers who are conversant with the jargon of research and statistics, practitioners who are unfamiliar with such jargon, or the lay public.
- Most research reports include the following elements: title, abstract, introduction and statement of the problem, description of the methods and results, discussion of the implications of the findings, and a list of references.

IMPORTANT TERMS FOR REVIEW

Block grants	Federal government contracts	Grant
Categorical grants	Formula grant	Project grants
Discretionary grants	Foundation	Request for proposals

CRITICAL THINKING

1. When might a human services agency (or staff within a human services agency) become involved in a grant-funded research project? Identify a scenario pertaining to your human services area of interest where you may play a role in the research grant process. Describe the goals of the research and the roles you would likely play. Which agencies (state or federal) or foundations might support this research?
2. Relatively few human services professionals are research specialists, yet many play roles in research at least occasionally. Why should human services professionals who work primarily with clients get involved in creating, submitting, and completing a funded research project?

EVALUATING COMPETENCY (FROM THE COUNCIL ON SOCIAL WORK EDUCATION [CSWE] 2015 EDUCATIONAL POLICY AND ACCREDITATION STANDARDS [EPAS])

Competency 1: Demonstrate Ethical and Professional Behavior

- In the vignette for this chapter, Richard had a vested interest in the results of the research—to show the value of his program to board members and other potential supporters. At the same time, he was in a better position than anyone else in the community to create research to evaluate the need for and impacts of adult basic education services. Can Richard have a lead role in objective research while also having a vested interest in its outcome?
- What steps might he take to help ensure the research is both valid and reliable?

Competency 3: Advance Human Rights, and Social, Economic, and Environmental Justice

- Social workers and other human services professionals are committed to human rights and social, economic, and environmental justice. Should these commitments impact their research activities?
- Can social workers and other human services professionals engage in research-informed practice and practice-informed research while also actively promoting an agenda characterized by human rights and social, economic, and environmental justice?

Competency 4: Engage in Practice-Informed Research and Research-Informed Practice

- While social workers and other human services professionals are called to use practice experiences to inform their research, research activities are rarely well-supported by human services organizations. What strategies should social workers and other professionals use to conduct research related to their practice?
- How might social workers and other human services professionals develop partnerships with researcher specialists in evaluating services and conducting other practice-related research?

SELF-ASSESSMENT

1. Fixed grants or categorical grants provide:
   a. Ongoing funding for research without set time frames.
   b. Funding for specific projects for known periods of times.
   c. General research support for think tanks and research institutes to cover fixed costs associated with maintaining research centers.
   d. Research to study minority populations.

2. Allocations of federal money to states or their subdivisions in accordance with the distribution formulas prescribed by law or administrative regulations, for activities of a continuing nature not confined to a specific project, are known as:
a. Request for proposals.
b. State's rights.
c. Formula grants.
d. Discretionary grants.

3. Formal requests for people or agencies to submit proposals on how they would conduct some research or establish and run some program are known as:
a. Request for proposals (RFPs).
b. Abstracts.
c. Research prospectus.
d. Research theses.

4. Which of these is a nonprofit entity organized for the purpose of dispersing funds to projects that meet the guidelines of its charter?
a. Think tanks
b. Research institutes
c. Charity organization societies
d. Foundations

5. Foundations that exist to serve their immediate local areas are known as:
a. Area foundations.
b. Community action agencies.
c. Community foundations.
d. Family foundations.

6. When applying for a research grant, an advocate refers to:
a. Somebody who will write segments of the application.
b. Someone who agrees to analyze research results.
c. Someone who helps disperse research findings to advocacy groups.
d. Someone who will speak on the agency's behalf to funding sources and offer guidance and advice throughout the funding process.

7. Which of the following is not a reason to visit with leaders or staff from a funding organization prior to submitting a grant application?
a. It can help confirm or reject the selection of the organization as a likely source of funding.
b. The visit may help you collect information to better tailor your proposal to the funder's needs and expectations.
c. You may convince the funder to give you tips of inside information that will move your proposal ahead of others being considered for funding.
d. The visit may provide a personal touch for the proposal when it is submitted (as the proposal will represent people known personally to those making funding decisions).

8. Which of the following is not a typical section of a research grant proposal?
   a. Title page
   b. Problem/needs statement
   c. Dissemination plan
   d. Research findings
9. When the intended audience of a research report is the lay public (who are not research specialists):
   a. It is important to include jargon and complex research language to make a favorable impression regarding your research expertise.
   b. It is important to present data simply and explain findings carefully.
   c. It is important to avoid discussing research processes and stick to findings and implications.
   d. Explain that research findings should only be interpreted and used by professional researchers.
10. When writing a research report it is important to remember:
   a. That first drafts are usually the right drafts so it is best to avoid rewriting or editing your first draft.
   b. That writing is a process best left to professional writers and avoided by human services professionals.
   c. That rewriting is essential and can also enhance creativity.
   d. That writing takes prolonged focus and is best completed in extended writing sessions.

ANSWER KEY FOR SELF-ASSESSMENT QUIZ

1. **b.** Funding for specific projects for known periods of times.
2. **c.** Formula grants
3. **a.** Request for proposals (RFPs)
4. **d.** Foundations
5. **c.** Community foundations
6. **d.** Someone who will speak on the agency's behalf to funding sources and offer guidance and advice throughout the funding process.
7. **c.** You may convince the funder to give you tips of inside information that will move your proposal ahead of others being considered for funding.
8. **d.** Research findings
9. **b.** It is important to present data simply and explain findings carefully.
10. **c.** That rewriting is essential and can also enhance creativity.

FOR FURTHER READING

Brown, L. G., & Brown, M. J. (2001). *Demystifying grant seeking: What you really need to do to get grants*. San Francisco, CA: Jossey-Bass. This book takes the reader through the steps of setting up a usable office, making matches between agencies and foundations, writing grant applications, and evaluating the process. The authors use one agency as an example, taking the reader through the entire process.

Chicago Manual of Style. (2017). Chicago, IL: University of Chicago Press. Retrieved from https://www.chicagomanualofstyle.org/home.html. Prepared by the editorial staff of the University of Chicago Press, the *Chicago Manual* has long been considered to be the definitive writing reference work. If you take your writing seriously, you should have a copy.

Cuba, L. (2002). *A short guide to writing about social science* (4th ed.). New York, NY: Longman. This book is a good review of what you need to know about writing research papers and preparing presentations on topics in the social sciences.

Hall, D., & Birkerts, S. (2006). *Writing well* (9th ed.). Reading, MA: Longman. Hall, the author of dozens of books, brings his experience and expertise to a book that can help anyone improve his or her writing. Unlike many such books that present the rules in a rather stiff and direct fashion, Hall makes learning to write interesting.

Henson, K. T. (2004). *Grant writing in higher education: A step-by-step guide*. Boston, MA: Allyn & Bacon. This is a practical resource for developing effective grant proposals. Specific strengths of this resource are sections on preparing budgets and locating funding sources.

Miner, J. T., & Miner, L. E. (2005). *Models of proposal planning and writing*. Westport, CT: Praeger. This is another excellent guide to developing grant proposals for research or other types of grants.

Ogden, T. E., & Goldberg, I. A. (2002). *Research proposals: A guide to success* (3rd ed.). San Diego, CA: Academic Press. This book focuses on research grants and includes topics not found in more general works. It covers the National Institutes of Health and other sources of research support. The book addresses the various components of a research proposal, such as preliminary studies, research design and methods, and human subjects.

Thyer, B. A. (2008). *Preparing research articles*. New York, NY: Oxford University Press. Aimed at the profession of social work, this book is written by an experienced author and journal editor. Its topics include selecting an appropriate journal, handling rejections and revisions, understanding confusing concepts like impact factors and electronic publishing, and avoiding common methodological and formatting pitfalls.

Yuen, F. K. O., & Terao, K. L. (2003). *Practical grant writing and program evaluation*. Belmont, CA: Wadsworth. This brief and practical text covers program planning, grant writing, and program evaluation, with emphasis on the interrelationship between these components. Readers will learn both the development and the implementation of grant proposals, program evaluation plans, data collection and analysis, and report writing.

REFERENCES

Bauer, D. G. (2011). *The "How To" grants manual: Successful grantseeking techniques for obtaining public and private grants* (7th ed.). Lanham, MD: Rowman & Littlefield.

Congressional Research Service. (2017). *FY 2018 appropriations for Department of Justice Grant Programs*. Retrieved from www.crs.gov

Foundation Center. (2014). Foundation stats. Retrieved from http://data.foundationcenter.org/#/foundations/family/nationwide/total/list/2014

Gitlin, L., & Lyons, K. J. (2014). *Successful grant writing: Strategies for health and human service professionals* (4th ed.). New York, NY: Springer Publishing Company.

Hilton, T., DeJong, C., & Trella, D. (2012). *Experiences of homelessness among singles and families in a rural area: Comparing coping, felt experiences and unmet needs*. Unpublished paper.

Krathwohl, D. R. (1988). *How to prepare a research proposal: Guidelines for funding and dissertations in the social and behavioral sciences* (3rd ed.). New York, NY: Syracuse University Press.

Locke, L. F., Spirduso, W. W., & Silverman, S. J. (2013). *Proposals that work*. Los Angeles, CA: Sage.

Miner, J. T., & Miner, L. E. (2013). *Proposal planning and writing* (5th ed.). Santa Barbara, CA: Greenwood.

National Association of Social Workers Press. (2009). *An author's guide to social work journals* (5th ed.). Washington, DC: Author.

Substance Abuse and Methal Health Services Administration. (2017). Community mental health services block grant. Retrieved from https://www.samhsa.gov/grants/block-grants/mhbg

U.S. Census Bureau. (2011). *Statistical abstract of the United States: 2012* (131st ed.). Washington, DC: U.S. Government Printing Office. Retrieved from https://www2.census.gov/library/publications/2011/compendia/statab/131ed/2012-statab.pdf

Yamaner, M. (2017). Total federal research and development funding down 1% in FY 2015, but funding for research up 1%. Retrieved from https://www.nsf.gov/statistics/2017/nsf17316

INDEX